CYBERSECURITY FOUNDATIONS

AN INTERDISCIPLINARY INTRODUCTION

FIRST EDITION

LEE M. ZEICHNER

© 2014 by Lee Mark Zeichner

All rights reserved. No part of this book may be reproduced or transmitted in any form or by any means, electronic or mechanical, including photocopying, recording, or by any information storage and retrieval system without the written permission of the author, except where permitted by law.

Although every precaution has been taken to verify the accuracy of the information contained herein, the author and publisher assume no responsibility for any errors or omissions. No liability is assumed for damages that may result from the use of the information contained within.

Published by:
Zeichner Risk Analytics, LLC
4601 North Fairfax Drive, Suite 1130
Arlington, VA 22203
www.ZRA.com

Zeichner Risk Analytics also publishes this textbook for eBook readers. Some content that appears in the print edition may not be available in the eBook editions, and vice versa. For more information about this textbook, please contact us at www.cybersecurityfoundations.com.

Library of Congress Control Number: 2014902942

ISBN-13: 978-1-939798-09-1
ISBN-10: 1-939798-09-4

10 9 8 7 6 5 4 3 2 1

Acknowledgements

The author would like to thank those who contributed to the publication of this book:

Morgan Allen, Joseph Chen, Vince Crisler, Jack Dafoe, Kamolika Das, Lindsay Dorland, Matt Fiedelholtz, Jeanne Geers, Meghan Green, Sam Kane, Alexis Lavi, John Mier, Alejandra O'Leary, Alexis Ovitt, Matt Piscitello, Lauren Waldron, Jan Wright, Patricia Yacob, and Kent Zwikl.

Credits:
Graphics by Joseph Chen, Kamolika Das, Sam Kane, Alexis Lavi, Alexis Ovitt, and Kent Zwikl
Videos by Alexis Ovitt
Covers by Washington Graphic Services

CYBERSECURITY FOUNDATIONS
AN INTERDISCIPLINARY INTRODUCTION

ACADEMIC PACKAGE

Pedagogy
Lesson Plan
Syllabus
Case Studies
Worksheets
Reading List

Available for free download at
www.cybersecurityfoundations.com

Table of Contents

Preface IX
Pedagogy X
Key abbreviations XVI

Introduction 2

Sputnik and ARPANET 2

The 1980s: PCs, Floppy Disks, and Spies 3

Hackers: Kevin Mitnick and the 414s 3

Poindexter's Bold Move 4

The Morris Worm 5

Cybersecurity Fundamentals 7

Chapter 1: Risk management for cybersecurity 12

Overview of Risk Management 12

Introduction 13

Risk Management Frameworks 14

The Process of Risk Management 14

Risk Framing 15

Risk Assessment and the Risk Formula 19

Threat Assessment 20

Vulnerability Assessment 22

Consequence Assessment 24

Risk Determination 26

Risk Response 45

Table of Contents

Risk Monitoring 46

Conclusion 47

Key Questions 48

CHAPTER 2: CYBERSECURITY LAW AND POLICY 52

Overview of Cybersecurity Law and Policy 52

Introduction 53

The Genesis of Cybersecurity Law and Policy (1945-1984) 56

The Cybersecurity Control Conflict (1984-1995) 58

The Development of Cybersecurity Law and Policy (1995-2001) 60

Cybersecurity and Homeland Security (2001-2008) 66

CNCI and the Age of Cyber Warfare (2008 – Present) 72

Recent Developments in Cybersecurity Law and Policy 74

Conclusion 76

Key Questions 76

CHAPTER 3: FUNDAMENTALS OF MANAGEMENT FOR CYBERSECURITY 80

Introduction: Organizations, Missions, Managers, and Capabilities 80

Managerial Fundamentals 83

Managerial Challenges for Cybersecurity: Introduction and Case Study ... 89

The Cybersecurity Management Framework 92

Management and Acquisition 104

Measuring Progress Against Projections: Earned Value Management ... 108

Compliance and Reporting 121

Conclusion 127

Key Questions 128

CHAPTER 4: COMPUTER SCIENCE FUNDAMENTALS AND

Table of Contents

CYBERSECURITY OPERATIONS... **130**

Overview of Computer Science Fundamentals
and Cybersecurity Operations... 130

Technical Fundamentals... 130

An Introduction to the Internet... 134

Cryptologic Methods for Internet Security... 139

Attacks, Exploits, and Vulnerabilities.. 141

Cybersecurity Operations... 145

Conclusion... 149

Key Questions... 150

CHAPTER 5: CYBERSECURITY FOR THE PRIVATE SECTOR.. 152

Overview of Cybersecurity in the Private Sector... 152

Introduction... 153

The Structure and Legal Obligations of Private-Sector Companies................ 154

Cybersecurity Law and the Private Sector... 159

The Model Corporate Cybersecurity Program.. 165

Internal Controls and Audits... 171

Conclusion... 172

Key Questions... 173

CHAPTER 6: ADVANCED CYBERSECURITY STUDIES:

RESEARCH METHODS AND SOURCES 176

Overview of Advanced Cybersecurity Studies.. 176

Introduction to Research Methods... 177

The U.S. Constitution and the Three Branches of Government........................ 179

Table of Contents

The Role of the Executive Branch 180

The Role of the Legislature 186

Federal Regulations 190

The Role of the Judiciary... 192

Cybersecurity: A Global Perspective.. 196

Conclusion... 203

Key Questions 204

Appendices 205

Appendix A: More on Survey Design and Statistical Modeling 205

Appendix B: EVM Indexes and EVM Forecasting 213

Appendix C: Types of Policy Documents.. 217

Appendix D: Case Study - Convenience Versus Security 219

Appendix E: Case Study - It's Not A Cyber Problem; It's a Management Problem.... 227

Appendix F: Case Study - The Human Element of Risk Management 239

Appendix G: Case Study - Technology Needs Management............. 249

Glossary... 261

Notes 281

References 287

Extended Reading 291

Syllabus 295

Lesson Plan 307

index 343

afterword 373

about the author 376

Preface

The existing literature on cybersecurity has yet to fully capture and emphasize the interdisciplinary nature of the field. Cybersecurity is a dynamic and growing industry that develops in unexpected ways, and the lack of continuity among cybersecurity disciplines presents a serious challenge for the academics and professionals of those disciplines. Appreciating and understanding the scope of cybersecurity therefore requires an interdisciplinary approach. By first exploring the depth of each discipline before identifying the ways they are connected, this book will allow you to develop the skills needed to face the infinite number of ever-changing challenges in cybersecurity.

Cybersecurity is a highly complex discipline because the Internet is a highly complex asset. At one point, computers were exclusively owned and operated by the Federal government. Today, computers are integrated into everything we own, and the data they collect and store has reshaped the U.S. economy. Consequently, all of these devices and the networks on which they run are prime targets for cybercriminal activity across the world, from any country, with any organization. If the Internet is to remain a free environment of connectivity and information, cybersecurity professionals must connect with one another and apply their knowledge and expertise to secure this critical asset.

A true understanding of cybersecurity requires a firm grasp on everything from computer science to public policy, from risk analysis to management. Information Technology professionals and cybersecurity experts are challenged with identifying and reconciling malicious code and network vulnerabilities that cybercriminals exploit in order to disrupt and compromise the security of computer systems. Executives and managers of businesses are challenged with creating and developing industry standards and best-practices for cybersecurity and risk management. Policymakers must develop legislation that balances consumer protection with business liability, while also giving law enforcement the means to prosecute threat actors across and within borders. But in order to take on cyberthreat, the world's leaders, policymakers, business managers, and security experts will need to find workable solutions with a broader vision, and Cybersecurity Foundations is meant to reflect this reality.

Each discipline is applied in different ways and for different reasons, ultimately working together on one of the most pressing challenges of the modern age. Just as the Internet is a series of interconnected machines and devices, cybersecurity must also be a confluence of professional backgrounds. Consider the topics of computer science, public policy, risk analysis, as the elements of the formula for professional cybersecurity. For this reason, we must cultivate a new generation of individuals with the knowledge and skills required to take on this highly advanced challenge.

Cybersecurity is a remarkably complex field, and the ambitious student could read every text on the subject and still lack critical information needed to capture the bigger picture. However, Cybersecurity Foundations can serve as a starting point of sorts by providing you with the educational tools you need to grasp and understand the cybersecurity challenge.

Pedagogy

The modern world is characterized by increasing levels of technological sophistication, and cybersecurity has emerged as a defining challenge for the global community. In order to confront threats from cyberspace, the world will need leaders and policymakers who possess a proficiency in cybersecurity fundamentals and an understanding of the challenges facing the field.

If these individuals are to craft effective solutions to cybersecurity challenges, they will need more than just an understanding of computer science and engineering. Certainly, a grasp of these topics is important – however, cybersecurity is a truly interdisciplinary field, drawing upon subject areas ranging from risk management to US law and policy.

Our textbook is designed with cybersecurity's interdisciplinary nature in mind. Over the course of seven chapters, students will become familiar with the numerous threads that complete the cybersecurity tapestry. This interdisciplinary approach will encourage students to make connections between seemingly-disparate academic disciplines, and to appreciate the "big picture" of cybersecurity, rather than solely focusing on a narrow aspect of the field. By the end of this course, each student will understand how his or her unique skill set can be applied to cybersecurity, as well as how students with other interests can contribute.

This pedagogy includes a suggested class structure for instructors to follow in teaching this course. This structure is based on a combination of traditional lectures and interactive discussion. The former is useful for teaching such "hard" subjects as quantitative risk assessment or earned value management, while the latter is better suited for instruction on "soft" subjects, such as how different components of the US government interact in the development of cyber-legislation. Regardless of which method teachers choose to utilize, however, they should bear in mind that this course aims to impart two kinds of knowledge to students– "Textbook Fundamentals" and "Cybersecurity Applications." "Textbook Fundamentals" refer to concepts and lessons explicitly explained in the textbook, such as the various steps of the risk management process. "Cybersecurity Applications," on the other hand, may be mentioned or alluded to in the textbook, but require further explanation from the instructor. In so elaborating, we recommend that the instructor draw from this textbook's Academic Package, which includes supplemental readings and case studies that instructors can use to illuminate topics that the textbook does not fully explain.

Ultimately, however, it is important to bear in mind that this pedagogy is not a concrete blueprint – different classes will have different needs, and so it is up to individual instructors to determine the needs of their class, and construct lessons that will serve their students most effectively.

The interdisciplinary approach is not without its challenges – these issues range from a perceived lack of continuity between the different disciplines explored in the class, to difficulties in crafting effective modes of assessments for students with diverse academic backgrounds. Nonetheless, we believe that achieving an understanding of the cybersecurity field demands an interdisciplinary approach. Only by developing an in-depth grasp of cybersecurity's many component parts can the world's future leaders develop the skills needed to craft effective solutions to the most pressing cybersecurity challenges.

As an academic field, cybersecurity is ripe for development and new contributions, having evolved from a relatively obscure concentration into a highly complex and interdisciplinary subject of research, study, and practice.

Pedagogy

Cybersecurity's growth as an academic field corresponds with its emergence as a dynamic and growing industry. The United States has long served as a central hub of this industry, producing reams of policy documents, laws, and regulations on cybersecurity-related matters. Scholars trace the root of all cybersecurity theory and practice to the U.S. government's interest in securing critical information and infrastructure at the dawn of the Cold War. At that time, nearly all of the computers in the United States were located in the offices of the federal government, whose primary concern was to protect these newly developed mainframe computers, as well as the limited but sensitive data stored on them.

The world's cyber capabilities have come a long way since the days of mainframes. Today, digital data is stored and transferred far beyond the walls of government offices, and has become the foundation of business and personal transactions around the modern world. Indeed, the basic security of our society depends on the security of digital information, as all businesses, from grocery stores to investment banks, have developed a strong reliance upon IT tools. The public benefit of these new cyber tools has been incalculable, but they are not without their vulnerabilities – vulnerabilities that have, in turn, led to the emergence of revolutionary new threats.

In the cyber age, governments and other institutions confront a threat environment that is markedly different from that of decades past. Equipped with modern technologies, one person with limited resources can damage a huge organization on the other side of the world easily, cheaply, and quickly. For hundreds of years, large superpowers could easily handle small attackers by way of force. This is no longer true in the modern world, where threats can strike over long distances with unprecedented speed and impact.

As businesses and individuals have deepened their dependence upon information technology systems, the U.S. federal government has continued to increase its role in establishing cyber policies, laws, and regulations. While proactive, this approach has raised significant concerns about the appropriate balance between national security and privacy in the cyber realm.

To address this multitude of complex problems, the world will need a cadre of professionals from a wide range of academic and professional backgrounds. Recognizing this need, we believe it is important to begin teaching the fundamentals of cybersecurity as an introductory course to college students. Not every student who takes this course will ultimately concentrate in computer science or other "traditional" cybersecurity-related fields, but we feel that the nature of the modern world demands that every citizen understand the global significance and interdisciplinary application of cybersecurity.

Students might assume that a course titled "Cybersecurity Foundations" is only for engineering and computer science majors. In reality, most cybersecurity problems require solutions that draw from a range of academic disciplines. Many of the issues involved in achieving cybersecurity goals have nothing to do with computer science or engineering, but require skill sets developed in the humanities, in business classes, in political science studies, and in a variety of other academic fields.

Even those who enjoy the computer science and engineering-based approaches to solving cyber problems will need to understand these other aspects of cybersecurity in order to fully appreciate and comprehend the field. Our interdisciplinary cybersecurity course will allow all students to consider perspectives on the topic from multiple vantage points, and to recognize the fundamental importance of the following areas:

A. *Risk Management*

Risk management is the foundation of all cybersecurity theory and practice. It is critical for future cybersecurity professionals to understand both the qualitative and quantitative aspects of managing risk. Our course walks students through the formalized process of risk management for organizations and introduces newcomers to the complexity of managing both cyber and physical risk.

Pedagogy

B. Computer Science and Engineering

Computer science and engineering jargon constitutes a significant portion of industry language in cybersecurity, and computer science and engineering specialists create the technical tools to protect critical information and infrastructure. In order for anyone to truly comprehend the cybersecurity field, they must have a basic understanding of the technical language and skills that engineers and computer scientists use.

C. Law and Policy

The U.S. federal government is the world's leading actor in the field of cybersecurity. It is critical for future cyber professionals to recognize the broad influence of U.S. federal cybersecurity policy and the ways in which the U.S. federal government involves the private sector in its cybersecurity policymaking process.

D. The Private Sector

The private sector plays an increasingly active role in U.S. national cybersecurity law and policy. Moreover, all organizations, even those with no intention of working in coordination with the federal government, must have an understanding of the cybersecurity systems needed to protect their most critical assets and insulate them from legal action in the event of a cyber attack.

E. Management

It is essential for students to understand that management, not technology, dictates the success or failure of most cybersecurity programs and operations. Only with the guidance of skilled managers can organizations carry out effective programs to secure critical information, networks, and systems. Managers play a crucial role in coordinating cybersecurity professionals across disciplines and overseeing the "big picture" in organizations and government.

F. Research and Methods

Many of cybersecurity's most important documents and informational sources are not easily accessible through popular Internet search engines. Therefore, cybersecurity professionals must possess the ability to conduct more advanced and in-depth research, which will, in turn, allow them to access documentation and legislation on cybersecurity topics from each of the three branches of the US government, as well as from other external sources.

The Benefits of Teaching Cybersecurity as an Interdisciplinary Topic

Interdisciplinary courses approach a general topic by drawing upon a variety of disciplines and perspectives. We recommend this approach to instructors teaching the fundamentals of cybersecurity. Achieving a true grasp of cybersecurity issues requires one to draw upon knowledge and skills rooted in a range of academic fields. Our course is designed with this reality in mind, as we firmly believe that future cyber professionals must have an understanding of each of the disciplines discussed above in order to create and apply solutions to cybersecurity problems.

Pedagogy

Interdisciplinary courses challenge students to actively draw connections between seemingly-disparate course materials, and to understand the "big picture" rather than to specialize immediately in one aspect of the field. Moreover, interdisciplinary courses encourage students to appreciate how their particular skill sets and interests apply to a broader issue. At the end of this class, each student will recognize how their interests and areas of expertise apply to cybersecurity: business majors will learn how cybersecurity policy affects large corporations; history majors will be able to use their skills in analyzing historical documents and trends to examine important cybersecurity statements and policies, and engineers will be able to apply their math and science backgrounds to cybersecurity and risk management tools. At the end of this course, students will also be able to appreciate the skill sets of others and to understand how these myriad skill sets can be combined to create interdisciplinary solutions to cybersecurity problems.

Teaching cybersecurity in an interdisciplinary manner will give students an accurate introduction to the complexities of the cybersecurity field and provide an opportunity for those with a range of backgrounds, skills, and interests to come together in one classroom to explore this revolutionary topic.

Suggested Cybersecurity Class Structure

Almost all interdisciplinary courses include a mixture of traditional lectures and interactive discussion. Each class will involve a range of students with different skill levels and different levels of both intrinsic and extrinsic motivation. Accordingly, instructors must recognize the diverse academic backgrounds of their students and structure class time in a manner geared towards meeting the specific needs of each class. Some classes will need more time dedicated to covering technical material, while others may need more time to discuss policy-related content. Some classes will need more grounding in the structure of the U.S. federal government, while others may require more of a focus on management strategies. It is advised that all instructors use the class schedule on the syllabus only as a guide, and adjust their own course according to the needs of the students.

This course requires a fair amount of "hard-learning" when approaching subjects such as quantitative risk assessment or earned value management. These kinds of subjects require that a portion of class time be devoted to traditional lecturing. However, "softer" subjects, such as the influence of government in creating cybersecurity legislation, or the extent to which private sector companies must leverage resources to protect customer information, requires more discussion-based learning. How professors choose to structure their class time will depend on their professional judgment, as well as consideration of their students' needs and the relative difficulty of the day's course content.

Regardless of whether class time is structured as a discussion, a lecture, or a mix of both styles, each string of classes devoted to a particular chapter should always teach two types of information – "Textbook Fundamentals" and "Cybersecurity Applications".

"Textbook Fundamentals" consist of the lessons and objectives explained in the textbook, such as the risk management process or the federal government's use of the program management framework.

"Cybersecurity Applications" are the topics that may be mentioned in the book, but require further elaboration from the instructor. The instructor may make use of supplemental readings and case studies as a trajectory for Cybersecurity Applications. Examples and suggestions can be found in the Lesson Plan portion of the academic package.

Pedagogy

Common Issues Unique to Interdisciplinary and Cybersecurity Courses

Although interdisciplinary courses provide a range of benefits to students, covering every topic in equal depth may prove challenging to instructors. Another problem to overcome may be a lack of continuity and connectivity between the disciplines explored in the class. An interdisciplinary cybersecurity course is even more susceptible to this problem because of the wide range of academic fields that it draws upon. In order to prevent this cybersecurity course from appearing to be a randomly configured assortment of lessons, we advise instructors to follow a few recommended processes.

First, all instructors should develop a logical order to the course. This will ensure that students understand the course's progression from lesson to lesson and the reason why certain topics must be covered before others. The course syllabus lists a logical schedule of lessons from the beginning to the end of the course. Instructors may adjust the schedule in consideration of their specific audience.

In addition to developing a logical order for the course, the instructor should always stress the interdisciplinary nature of both the course and cybersecurity as a field. Always consider questions from an interdisciplinary perspective. Instructors should encourage students to explicitly draw connections between the topics covered in the course, and each lesson should relate back to earlier material in discussions, lectures, and assessments. Instructors should also encourage students to relate the content of each individual lesson to the broader topic of cybersecurity as much as possible. In this way, the "big picture" will illuminate more specialized topics at each step in the course, and vice-versa.

Another concern frequently raised by instructors of interdisciplinary courses is that their students will suffer from "disciplinary egocentrism." This is the idea that students will only concentrate on the course content that connects to their respective academic concentrations. Within our cybersecurity course, this means that computer science students will only focus on the computer science section, or that political science majors will focus solely on the law and policy content.

To ensure that students recognize the significance of every topic covered in this interdisciplinary course, it is important for instructors to give assessments and assignments that encourage students to be proficient in all facets of the cybersecurity field. This approach requires that instructors give equal weight to all subjects – a difficult task for educators with deep connections to one discipline.

Assessments can also be a challenge for instructors of interdisciplinary courses. Students from different academic backgrounds will be accustomed to different assessment methods. While many humanities majors may feel more comfortable writing papers, most math students will be used to taking calculation-based exams and completing problem sets. Providing a variety of assessment opportunities and encouraging students to stretch beyond their comfort zones will benefit all involved. In group projects, students from diverse academic backgrounds can work together to share their knowledge and learn from each other's unique problem-solving approaches.

Additionally, educators should promote in-class discussions that draw from a variety of disciplines. For instance, when discussing the role of government in implementing cybersecurity mandates, make sure to consider business perspectives and the technological and management constraints associated with various policies. Promoting interdisciplinary discussions will help students develop their critical reasoning skills and give them a realistic picture the variety of challenges associated with most cybersecurity issues.

Pedagogy

The guides and assessments found in the syllabus and in the academic package address some of these pedagogic challenges. And yet, while it is important to ensure that students understand all of the disciplines that comprise cybersecurity, this does not mean that students shouldn't be able to look deeply into the subjects that they enjoy. Students should be challenged to apply what they know to projects and discussions, and to explore areas of particular interest.

Conclusion

Now, more than ever, as threats from cyberspace continue to grow in quantity and sophistication, it is crucial that students possess a basic understanding of cybersecurity issues. It is our hope that this teaching note provides a set of guidelines for those with experience in cybersecurity to teach an introductory cybersecurity course to college-aged students.

---

1. *"Disciplinary egocentrism,"* http://scholar.lib.vt.edu/theses/available/etd-05092008-110413/unrestricted/Richter_Thesis.pdf

Key Abbreviations

AC: actual cost

ACWP: actual cost of work performed

ANPR: advance notice of proposed rulemaking

APA: Administrative Procedure Act

APB: acquisition program baseline

APT: advanced persistent threat

AQL: acceptable quality levels

ARPA: Advanced Research Projects Agency

ARPANET: Advanced Research Projects Agency Network

BAC: budget at completion

BCWP: budgeted cost of work performed

BCWS: budgeted cost of work scheduled

BGP: Border Gateway Protocol

BJR: business judgment rule

BUR: Bottom-Up Review

CEO: chief executive officer

CFAA: Computer Fraud and Abuse Act

CFR: Code of Federal Regulations

CIA: Central Intelligence Agency

CIAO: Chief Infrastructure Assurance Office

CICG: Critical Infrastructure Coordination Group

CIKR: critical infrastructure and key resources

CIO: chief information officer

CISO: chief information security officer

CIWG: Critical Infrastructure Working Group

Key Abbreviations

CMS: continuous monitoring system

CNCI: Comprehensive National Cybersecurity Initiative

CONOPS: concept of operations

CPI: Cost Performance Index

CPU: central processing unit

CRS: Congressional Research Service

CS&C: Office of Cybersecurity and Communications

CSA: Computer Security Act

CV: cost variance

DDoS: distributed denial of service

DHS: Department of Homeland Security

DIA: Defense Intelligence Agency

DNS: Domain Name System

DNSSEC: Domain Name System Security Extensions

DOD: Department of Defense

DoS: denial of service

EA: enterprise architecture

EAC: estimate at completion

ECPA: Electronic Communications Privacy Act

EDGAR: Electronic Data Gathering, Analysis, and Retrieval (system)

EO: executive order

EOP: Executive Office of the President

ERM: enterprise risk management

ES ISAC: Electricity Sector Information Sharing and Analysis Center

ETC: estimate to complete

EV: earned value

EVM: earned value management

FASA V: Federal Acquisition Streamlining Act of 1994, Title V

Key Abbreviations

FBI: Federal Bureau of Investigation

FDA: Food and Drug Administration

FedCIRC: Federal Computer Incident Response Center

FISMA: Federal Information Security Management Act

FTC: Federal Trade Commission

FTCA: Federal Trade Commission Act

FTE: full-time equivalent

FTP: File Transfer Protocol

GAO: Government Accountability Office

GLB Act: Gramm-Leach-Bliley Financial Modernization Act

GSA: General Services Administration

GUI: graphical user interface

HHS: Department of Health and Human Services

HIPAA: Health Insurance Portability and Accountability Act

HITECH Act: Health Information Technology for Economic and Clinical Health Act

HLR: high-level requirement

HRA: human reliability analysis

HSA: Homeland Security Act

HSPD: Homeland Security Policy Directive

HTTP: Hypertext Transfer Protocol

HTTPS: Hypertext Transfer Protocol Secure

IANA: Internet Assigned Numbers Authority

IC: intelligence community

ICANN: Internet Corporation for Assigned Names and Numbers

ICT: information and communications technology

IDS: intrusion detection system

IETF: Internet Engineering Task Force

IGCE: independent government cost estimate

Key Abbreviations

IMP: integrated master plan

IMS: integrated master schedule

IP: Internet Protocol

IP: Office of Infrastructure Protection

IPS: intrusion prevention system

IPSec: Internet Protocol Security

IPV4: Internet Protocol Version 4

IPV6: Internet Protocol Version 6

ISAC: Information Sharing and Analysis Center

ISP: Internet service providers

IT: information technology

LAN: local-area network

MD: message-digest (algorithm)

MILNET: Military Network

MNS: mission needs statement

NATO: North Atlantic Treaty Organization

NERC: North American Electric Reliability Corporation

NIPC: National Infrastructure Protection Center

NIPP: National Infrastructure Protection Plan

NIST: National Institute for Standards and Technology

NNSA: National Nuclear Safety Administration

NPPD: National Protection and Programs Directorate

NSA: National Security Agency

NSC: National Security Council

NSDD: National Security Decision Directive

NSFNET: National Science Foundation Network

NSPD: National Security Presidential Directive

NVD: National Vulnerability Database

Key Abbreviations

OCIA: Office of Cyber and Infrastructure Analysis

OHS: Office of Homeland Security

OIRA: Office of Information and Regulatory Affairs

OMB: Office of Management and Budget

ORD: operational requirements document

OSTP: Office of Science and Technology Policy

PC: personal computer

PCCIP: President's Commission on Critical Infrastructure Protection

PCIPB: President's Critical Infrastructure Protection Board

PDD: Presidential Decision Directives

PHI: protected health information

POA&M: plan of action and milestones

POP: period of performance

PPBE: planning, programming, budgeting, and execution (model)

PPD: Presidential Policy Directive

PRA: Paperwork Reduction Act

PRA: probabilistic risk assessment

PSD: Presidential Study Directive

PV: planned value

PWS: performance work statement

QHSR: Quadrennial Homeland Security Review

RAM: random-access memory

RFC: Request for Comments

RFI: request for information

RFP: request for proposal

RIR: Regional Internet Registry

SBU IT: sensitive-but-unclassified information technology

SEC: Security and Exchange Commission

Key Abbreviations

SHA: Secure Hash Algorithm

SME: subject matter expert

SOO: statement of objectives

SOW: statement of work

SOX: Sarbanes-Oxley Act (of 2002)

SPI: Schedule Performance Index

SSA: sector-specific agency

SV: schedule variance

TCP: Transmission Control Protocol

TIC: Trusted Internet Connection

TJX: parent company of TJ Maxx

TLD: top-level domain

UN: United Nations

US-CERT: United States Computer Emergency Readiness Team

USSC: United States Sentencing Commission

WAN: wide-area network

WBS: work breakdown structure

INTRODUCTION:
From ARPANET to Stuxnet

CHAPTER OUTLINE

- **Sputnik and ARPANET**
- **The 1980s: PCs, Floppy Disks, and Spies**
- **Hackers: Kevin Mitnick and the 414s**
- **Poindexter's Bold Move**
- **The Morris Worm**
- **Cyber Weapons**
- **Cybersecurity Fundamentals**

Introduction

Chapter In Focus

- The origins and growth of the Internet.
- The interplay between technological advances and public policy decisions.
- The interdisciplinary nature of cybersecurity.

Sputnik and ARPANET

On October 4, 1957, a Soviet R-7 missile was launched from the Baikonur Cosmodrome, the hub of the Soviet Union's space program, in the desert of Kazakhstan. The Soviet Union had launched missiles before, but this one was flying toward space carrying *Sputnik 1*, the world's first artificial satellite. *Sputnik* was launched into low-earth orbit where, for three months, it sent radio signals back to Earth.

Although *Sputnik* posed no real threat to the safety of the United States, the American public nevertheless perceived it to be a direct threat from its Cold War enemy. The public and government demanded to know how the Soviets had succeeded where they had not and what the consequences of that success would mean for American society and national security. This uproar sparked the Space Race, in which the United States government intensified its efforts to achieve scientific and technological superiority over the Soviet Union.

The uncertain climate of the Cold War, coupled with the unprecedented success of the *Sputnik* program, created a sense of urgency in the halls of U.S. power. Not long after *Sputnik* fell back to Earth, the United States began redoubling its efforts to surpass the Soviet Union in science, technology, military power, and security. After several failed attempts at launching its own artificial satellites, the U.S. launched *Explorer 1* into orbit on January 31, 1958. With the first American success of the Space Race, President Eisenhower initiated a series of policy decisions that would soon lead to some of the most influential technological breakthroughs in modern history, including the invention of the Internet.

In 1958, Eisenhower oversaw the establishment of the Advanced Research Projects Agency (ARPA). At the time of its creation, the mission of ARPA was to "to prevent technological surprise like the launch of *Sputnik*."[1] Soon, ARPA's computer scientists were pursuing a system of interconnected research computers. On October 29, 1969, just 11 years after the *Sputnik* crisis, the first message was sent over the **Advanced Research Projects Agency Network (ARPANET)**, launched from a computer at the University of California, Los Angeles (UCLA) and received on a computer at Stanford University.

From its humble beginnings, ARPANET continued to grow at a rapid pace. In December of 1969, ARPANET consisted of four linked computers located at UCLA, Stanford, the University of California, Santa Barbara (UCSB), and the University of Utah. In 1973, Norway connected to ARPANET via satellite. By 1975, there were 57 computers connected, and the network began to grow every month. It was in this same year that the Department of Defense (DOD) gave the responsibility for operating and managing ARPANET to the Defense

A replica of *Sputnik 1* at the National Museum of the United States Air Force in Dayton, Ohio.

2

Introduction

Communications Agency (DCA) (now known as the Defense Information Systems Agency). The DCA managed the military's use of the computer network, while the National Science Foundation was given the opportunity to continue developing the network for civilian uses.

The 1980s: PCs, Floppy Disks, and Spies

In 1985, the **National Science Foundation Network (NSFNET)** was created. The NSFNET was a three-tiered network consisting of a "backbone" (a large system of smaller computers), three regional networks, and five supercomputing centers located in universities across the country. This network formed the basis for the Internet that we use today. As the NSFNET developed and spread, new threats to the network began to emerge.

Throughout the Cold War, networks of spies from around the globe collected intelligence and implemented sophisticated counterintelligence measures. Soviet spies obtained American secrets and sensitive government and military documents. The ability of spies to cause harm by passing stolen documents from person to person was a defining concern of national security experts and policymakers for decades after World War II. And at the tail end of the Cold War, the United States government faced an entirely new information security problem: the personal computer (PC).

In the years between the creation of ARPANET and the growth of the NSFNET, the first personal computers were being developed. The IBM 5150, more familiarly known as the IBM Personal Computer, was introduced on August 12, 1981. The IBM PC was not the first personal computer (Apple and others arrived in the late 1970s), but it was the first to achieve widespread acceptance and respectability beyond the hobbyist market.

With the entry of IBM into the marketplace, more and more employees in both the private and public sectors embraced PCs, and the implications of this revolution began to worry members of the U.S. national security community.

Hackers: Kevin Mitnick and the 414s

The development of personal computers and the means to link them over great distances through network connections during the 1980s had both positive and negative implications for the United States government. On the one hand, PCs could store and share more information than mini- and mainframe computers, creating convenience and efficiency for the government. On the other hand, the interconnectedness of these personal systems made the possibility of undetected intrusion into government networks easier than it had ever been before.

Moreover, PCs were introduced into the federal government at a time of heightened Cold War tensions. Spying was still a major national security concern. PC technology made it possible for a single computer or floppy disk to store huge numbers of documents, thus intensifying the potential extent of damage from espionage. PCs gave rise to a new and more sophisticated means of espionage, and along with it, a new breed of intruders known as "hackers."

Kevin Mitnick was considered one of the first "boy-genius hackers." In 1979, at age 16, Mitnick penetrated the computer system of Digital Equipment Corporation, a major American computer company. After gaining access to this network, Mitnick copied the company's software, a crime for which he was later convicted. In 1988, he was sentenced to one year in prison and three years of supervision. During his period of supervision, Mitnick violated his probation by hacking into the voicemail computers of Pacific Bell. Rather than go back to prison, Mitnick disappeared and became a fugitive from the law for the next two and a half years.

Throughout this time, as the Federal Bureau of Investigation (FBI) pursued him, Mitnick continued to hack and commit computer crimes. In 1995, the FBI eventually found Mitnick in an apartment in Raleigh, North Carolina. The state of California sentenced Mitnick to 68 months in prison and gave Mitnick extensive probation terms for years after his release. Mitnick was not allowed to use a computer for three years after the attack, and he was not allowed to profit from his story until seven years after his release.

Mitnick was certainly not the only child prodigy hacker operating in the United States. In 1983, **the 414s**, a group of six teenage hackers based in Milwaukee, Wisconsin, created great concern in the federal government.

Using personal computers and basic hacking techniques, the 414s infiltrated several high-profile computer systems. Among the systems they hacked was the Los Alamos National Laboratory, a research facility in which nuclear weapons are designed, and the origin of the famous Manhattan Project. Their intrusion into Los Alamos gave rise to an FBI manhunt, and the boys were later apprehended. None of them received jail time, and those who went on the record claimed not to have any malicious intentions. The well-publicized case of the 414s gave rise to public fears about the power of hackers, and in Congress, several bills were introduced that dealt with the issue of computer crimes and safety.

The apprehension of the 414s took place in the same year as the release of the American movie *War Games*. The 1983 computer espionage film—about the exploits of a teenage hacker—was advertised with the tagline, "Is it a game, or is it real?" The similarities between the film and the real life activities of the 414s highlighted the new possibilities of the cyber realm. Government authorities took the actions of the young hackers as a warning sign about potential dangers to critical computer systems. If teenagers could use personal computers to hack into a nuclear weapons facility, what could a foreign adversary accomplish?

Kevin Mitnick and the 414s are also significant because their computer crimes demonstrated the concept of asymmetrical warfare. In cyber attacks, the side with the most money and might (e.g., the Digital Equipment Corporation or the Los Alamos National Laboratory) was no longer guaranteed to prevail. Now anyone with a computer, the knowledge, and the intention could enter a network and wreak havoc. State-sponsored hackers hired by foreign adversaries could work day and night to gain access to U.S. military computer networks. Cyber spies could steal massive amounts of sensitive information and then vanish without a trace. On the emerging cyber battlefield, individual hackers could take down well-funded organizations, including the federal government.

Poindexter's Bold Move

Throughout the 1980s, many more hackers would emerge to exhibit the evolving skills of computer criminals. Without a robust policy for how to deal with these emerging threats, U.S. critical infrastructure stakeholders were vulnerable to attack. Those in power knew that key telecommunications systems had to be secured. In 1984, **Admiral John Poindexter**, who managed the National Security Council staff from 1983 to 1985 and acted as President Ronald Reagan's National Security Advisor from 1985 to 1986, crafted a new federal policy to do just that.

By the early 1980s, the nuclear arms race between the U.S. and its enemies made the protection of classified information a critical objective of the United States national security community. The emergence of hackers using PCs demonstrated the need to immediately and comprehensively secure U.S. telecommunications systems. ARPANET had expanded and had given rise to a separate Defense Department application, MILNET, short for Military Network. MILNET was the branch of ARPANET used for unclas-

Admiral John Poindexter.

Introduction

sified Department of Defense communications.

During this era, the use of PCs was growing, in both the public and private sectors. The U.S. government hoped to harness the computing and storage capabilities of PCs to make its large bureaucracy run more efficiently. However, while affording government workers a new way of storing and organizing information, this new means of telecommunication came with many security concerns. How would the government protect its computers and networks from hostile intrusions?

Securing computers became a priority within the security community. Admiral Poindexter took a particular interest in the potential consequences of a failure to secure the nation's computers. In 1984, Poindexter was the principal architect of **National Security Decision Directive 145 (NSDD-145)**, the "National Policy on Telecommunications and Automated Information Systems Security." The directive outlined the security concerns of the Reagan administration.

NSDD-145 recognized that the cyber realm was on the fast track to becoming a battlefield on which foreign governments and spies would be able to attack the United States. Unable to ignore the growth of PCs in particular, Poindexter had to confront the inherent trade-offs involved in the government's use of these new and powerful machines. He knew that PC enthusiasts would have to be checked by the realism of those like him who foresaw a new threat environment. And to Poindexter this understanding meant that the defense community, not the civilian government, was best equipped to take control over computer security.

NSDD-145 stated that, "information, even if unclassified in isolation, often can reveal highly classified and other sensitive information when taken in aggregate." Even if a malicious cyber intruder was only able to access bits and pieces of a document or other information from a government computer, classified or not, the fear was that those pieces could be cobbled together to reveal a more substantive clue. For Poindexter, this reality meant that the computers at risk were not only those owned and operated by the federal government. Rather, within every private-sector PC was the potential for a knowledgeable user to create a back door into the cyber vaults that housed the most important secrets in America.

In response to Poindexter's legitimate fear, NSDD-145 stated: "Systems handling other sensitive, but unclassified, government or government-derived information, the loss of which could adversely affect the national security interest, shall be protected in proportion to the threat of exploitation and the associated potential damage to the national security." Poindexter meant that this information would now be protected by the Department of Defense. In essence, NSDD-145 gave the defense and national security communities control over securing private sector computers. This was a novel and controversial concept, which sparked a long political battle between the defense community and the civilian government about which arm of government should be in charge of cybersecurity. As the policy debate began its slow and arduous journey through the halls of power in Washington, D.C., the urgent need for this discussion was clear.

The security concerns of NSDD-145 were reignited by the highly publicized launch of one of the first Internet worms.

The Morris Worm

On November 2, 1988, a computer worm was launched from the Massachusetts Institute of Technology and began making its way through the fledgling Internet. The worm was designed and deployed by a student at Cornell University named Robert Tappan Morris, who claimed that the purpose of his worm was to measure the size of the Internet. By moving from computer to computer, the worm would be used to count the number of computers it infected.

Cyber Weapons

Of course, this concept would only work if the worm actually got into every computer without being rejected. Therefore, in order to ensure that a given host computer did not reject it, Morris programmed the worm to override any user command that acknowledged the worm was in fact already running on its system. In this way, the worm was sure to infect every computer it encountered. Furthermore, because of this override mechanism, the worm could enter a computer and then copy itself over and over until the computer was no longer able to function properly. And that is exactly what happened in Internet-connected computers across the country.

When Morris realized the damage that his worm was causing, he reached out to a colleague at Harvard University. For several days, the worm caused chaos in computers everywhere as groups of computer experts tried to fix the situation. Computers in both the private and public sectors were damaged by **the Morris worm**. Sources speculate that the worm may have caused up to $100 million in total damages.[2] While substantial, however, the financial damage it caused is not what made the Morris worm such a major event in cybersecurity history. Rather, the launch of what was referred to as the "Great Worm," and the damage that ensued, was significant because it underscored the urgent need for public and private cybersecurity measures. Using his knowledge of programming code, Morris had been able to cripple computers across the country. If a student could wreak such havoc with an experiment run amok, what might happen if an enemy of the state launched a full-scale malicious cyber attack on United States computer networks? The power of expert keystrokes to topple a complex system served as a wake-up call for those in the cyber community, leading to intensified efforts to define and contain cyber crime.

In part because of the efforts of Admiral Poindexter and the policies introduced in NSDD-145, the U.S. Congress already had in place a structure for punishing cyber criminals: **the Computer Fraud and Abuse Act (CFAA) of 1986**. Robert Morris became the first person to be tried and convicted of violating this law. Morris's case was significant because the arguments given by both the prosecution and the defense during the trial helped to define "unauthorized access," a term that was—and remains—at the very foundation of U.S. cybersecurity law. The precedent established in the case would prove important in the decades to come: in the 1990s and early 2000s, hackers launched many more worms and viruses across the Internet, often making use of a revolutionary new Internet application called the World Wide Web, which was introduced in 1991. Today, daily cyber attacks on the Internet using worms and viruses are innumerable.

Cyber Weapons: Stuxnet

In 2012, the New York Times reported on a joint U.S.-Israel cyber attack known as Operation *Olympic Games*.[3] The New York Times concluded, based on a number of unofficial statements given by U.S. government officials, that after years of preparation and technical work, the U.S. and Israel had released a powerful worm called **Stuxnet** into the computer networks at an Iranian uranium enrichment facility. Public testimony before the Senate Committee on Homeland Security indicates that, through a series of cyber attacks likely spread over several years, Stuxnet had succeeded in infecting and shutting down centrifuges at the Natanz nuclear facility.[4]

A refined and enhanced version of the worm attack that Robert Morris first accidentally created in the 1980s, Stuxnet was able to target specific information, rather than just running wild across connected computers.[5] A cybersecurity advisory issued by ICS-CERT observes that Stuxnet created distributed denial-of-service attacks—a process that essentially overloads targeted computers until they cannot perform their intended tasks—and had the ability to reprogram various processes within the networks it infiltrated.[6]

In addition to the computers at Natanz, Congressional research reports indicate that Stuxnet infected at least 30,000 other Iranian computers, as well as thousands of computers in other countries.[7] The attack proved to be highly effective and was difficult and expensive to clean up. Congressional research further shows that

Introduction

Stuxnet was the first known attack against an industrial control system, thus establishing a revolutionary platform for the future of international cyber warfare.[8]

The implication that the United States was able to partner with an ally in order to create and successfully deploy such a powerful cyber weapon further implies that other nations would be able to do the same. Is the United States ready to sustain a cyber attack like Stuxnet?[9] What can be done to protect America's critical infrastructure—both cyber and physical—from such an attack, and who will be in charge of planning and overseeing that protection?

Cybersecurity Fundamentals

The need for cybersecurity is clear, constant, and urgent. Computers remain at the center of government and private sector operations, and cyber criminals are more numerous, sophisticated, and well-funded than they have ever been. The United Stated must train an army of cybersecurity managers, risk analysts, computer scientists, and policy analysts to keep ahead of continuous and emerging threats.

In this textbook, you will find all of the information you need to become a contributing member of the cybersecurity community. Upon completion of this text, you will possess foundational knowledge of the six essential areas of cybersecurity: Risk Management, Law and Policy, Management for Cybersecurity, Computer Science Fundamentals and Cybersecurity Operations, Cybersecurity for the Private Sector, and Cybersecurity Theory and Research Methods. In this book, each of these fundamental disciplines has a dedicated chapter that focuses on both theory and practice.

Chapter 1: Risk Management for Cybersecurity

Risk management, the process by which risk specialists develop and implement a continuous and systematic plan for containing risk, is the practice at the heart of cybersecurity.

A hybrid of the physical and borderless worlds, cyberspace is a risk-laden virtual environment. The possibilities for disaster and data theft are infinite in cyberspace: systems fail, hackers are omnipresent and always developing new methods of attack, and physical damage can destroy servers and databases. Each time you use a device with an Internet connection, you are putting your personal information at risk. Therefore, to secure operations in cyberspace, risk managers and organizations must think through, select, and implement a customized risk management plan and continuously monitor the plan's successes and failures.

Chapter 2: Cybersecurity Law and Policy

This chapter covers cybersecurity law, the government-made rules governing the protection of computer systems, and cybersecurity policy, the principles behind these rules. We'll consider how presidents, Congresses, and federal agencies and departments have stated principles and created programs to protect the nation's critical infrastructure from cyber threats and to ensure the security of the information resources maintained by the federal government.

The history of cybersecurity law and policy in the United States has been shaped by the interplay between the legislative and executive branches of the federal government. For the past half century, presidents and Congresses have disagreed over fundamental questions of cybersecurity policy. This chapter focuses on the key documents that illuminate this tug-of-war and the key governmental entities that Congress and the president have tasked with protecting the nation's computer systems.

Chapter 3: Fundamentals of Management for Cybersecurity

Like the management process in other private and public fields, management for cybersecurity is a process of translating a broad, high-level organizational vision into the planning and execution of a successful real-world project. For this reason, the simplest way to explain the cybersecurity management process is perhaps the most illuminating: senior managers and other high-level leaders offer a statement of broad goals, after which cybersecurity program managers craft meticulously detailed strategies and plans that chart out exactly how these goals will be fulfilled. Finally, they execute and evaluate the plan at each stage in its execution.

In both the public and private sectors, cybersecurity program managers must balance their programs' goals against time and resource constraints. These initial constraints, as well as new obstacles, could turn into serious problems and undermine the program's success if not effectively planned for, managed, and proactively monitored by a skilled and coordinated program staff. Ultimately, the success or failure of any cybersecurity program hinges on managerial issues, including long-term planning, budgeting and measurement skills, human resource management, and how well managers are able to gather, process, interpret, and synthesize the input of essential stakeholders.

Chapter 4: Computer Science Fundamentals and Cybersecurity Operations

The Internet began as a U.S. military project during the Cold War to safeguard communication in the event of a nuclear attack. The U.S. government expanded the scope and use of the Internet by connecting universities to share information. Because of the very limited initial use of the Internet, the concept of an adversary exploiting this network for malicious purposes was not considered at this early stage. As a result, as this incredibly powerful tool has grown in capability and complexity, it has remained fundamentally insecure. This insecurity makes the Internet a threat-laden environment in which attackers and defenders must work constantly to outsmart each other.

Computer engineers and cybersecurity professionals think about computers and the Internet in highly specific ways that may be different from the way the general public understands these modern phenomena. Computer science and engineering terminology also comprises a significant portion of industry language in cybersecurity. In order for anyone to understand cyber legislation or achieve cyber-related initiatives, they must have a basic understanding of the technical language and skills that engineers and computer scientists use and the problems they address. This chapter will ground you in computer science terms of art and demonstrate how engineers and other professionals who work on cybersecurity problems think about computers, cyber attacks, and cybersecurity operations.

Chapter 5: Cybersecurity for the Private Sector

More than ever before, private-sector companies need to understand the unique threats, vulnerabilities, and criticalities they face in the cyber realm. They also need to understand their unique legal standing and legal obligations to their shareholders, customers, and the U.S. government.

Across every industry sector, corporations are increasingly storing their customers' information in digital

Introduction

form. As dependence on digital technologies to conduct operations increases, so do the risks to that information. Corporations are responsible for taking steps to safeguard customer data because of its potential sensitivity. It may contain personally identifying information (e.g., names, addresses, or email addresses) or other confidential information (e.g., Social Security numbers, financial records, or health records). Because sensitive customer information is routinely stored and transmitted online, cybersecurity must be a major priority in any corporate risk-management strategy.

This chapter will focus on the legal duties of corporations, the development process for a corporate cybersecurity program, and the purpose of an audit. We'll also examine the unique cybersecurity issues that arise in the private-sector context.

Chapter 6: Advanced Cybersecurity Studies: Research and Methods

Original research is also fundamental to the development of cybersecurity as a technical and academic discipline. For students contemplating careers in cybersecurity, the challenge is how and what to study within a vast and growing field. The U.S. government is a leading institution in the development of cybersecurity law, policy, technology, and research. However, access to databases and documents is not enough to generate original research. Rather, researchers must begin their investigation by understanding the processes and problems that inform these research sources. Understanding the origin and authorities behind cybersecurity policy and legal documents equips the cybersecurity student to contribute to the field, in the form of original scholarship or otherwise.

CHAPTER 1:
Risk Management for Cybersecurity

CHAPTER OUTLINE

- **Overview of Risk Management**
- **Introduction**
- **Risk Management Frameworks**
- **The Process of Risk Management**
- **Risk Framing**
- **Risk Assessment and the Risk Formula**
- **Threat Assessment**
- **Vulnerability Assessment**
- **Consequence Assessment**
- **Risk Determination**
- **Risk Response**
- **Risk Monitoring**
- **Conclusion**
- **Key Questions**

1 Risk Management for Cybersecurity

Chapter In Focus

- The theory, process, and practice of risk management for organizations and individuals.
- The assumptions, constraints, tolerance level, priorities, and trade-offs involved in risk framing.
- The three assessments—threat assessment, vulnerability assessment, and consequence assessment—that inform the process of assessing overall levels of risk.
- Qualitative and quantitative approaches to risk determination, including the probabilistic risk assessment (PRA).
- The possible variations of risk response: risk acceptance, risk avoidance, risk mitigation, and risk transfer.
- The steps of the ongoing risk monitoring process: compliance, effectiveness, and identification of changes.

Overview of Risk Management

Risk management, the process by which risk specialists develop and implement a continuous and systematic plan for containing risk, is the practice at the heart of cybersecurity. Risk managers use words like "manage" and "contain" to describe their work because in the cyber realm, as in the physical world, risk can be managed but never completely eliminated.

Cyberspace is a risk-laden virtual environment. The possibilities for disaster and data theft are infinite in cyberspace: systems fail, hackers are omnipresent and always developing new methods of attack, and physical damage can destroy servers and databases. Each time you use a device with an Internet connection, you are putting your personal information at risk. Therefore, to secure operations in cyberspace, risk managers and organizations must think through, select, and implement a customized risk management plan and continuously monitor the plan's successes and failures.

Risk management strategies for the physical world, including plans for national security emergencies, have influenced risk management strategies for cyberspace operations. Before the terrorist attacks of September 11, 2001, national security experts had not considered the possibility that terrorists might fly planes into skyscrapers. Because this kind of attack was so improbable as to be inconceivable, national security risk managers never developed a comprehensive risk management strategy to prepare emergency responders, civilians, and national leadership for the possibility of an airplane attack on civilians. But 9/11 revealed to the United States and the world the dangers of disregarding the risk of improbable events. In the post-9/11 world, both private and public

Chapter 1: Risk Management for Cybersecurity

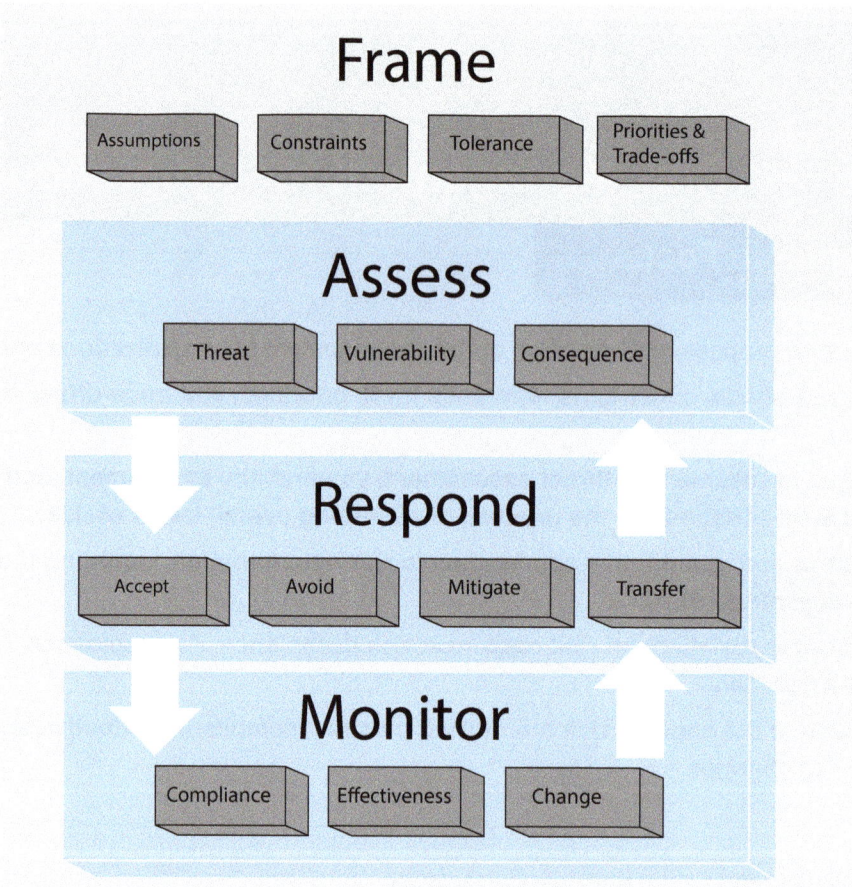

Figure 1-1: Risk framing process.[1]

sector risk management strategists now include calculations for highly improbable events into their planning and strategies. Moreover, the devastation of 9/11 has impressed upon the cybersecurity community the need to prevent a "cyber 9/11."

Because risk can never be eliminated, risk management is a field in which innovations and adjustments are always possible and often necessary. Each recent national catastrophe the U.S. has faced, from Hurricane Katrina to the financial meltdown of 2008, has influenced risk management models at the highest levels of both the federal government and the private sector. Cyber risk management models now frequently incorporate elements from both government and private sector strategies. Nevertheless, because of the complexities and unique challenges facing individuals, organizations, businesses, and governments operating in cyberspace, risk managers for cyber operations must develop highly specific plans to contain cyber risk.

Introduction

Risk management is a process that formalizes the steps of identifying the most critical assets to an individual, organization, or company; assessing the risk; and determining the best method to prevent harm to these assets. Risk is the likelihood that a given threat will exploit a particular vulnerability and the resulting

Introduction

consequence of that negative incident occurring. Risk management permits cybersecurity specialists to weigh technical and financial costs of security measures that support the organization's function.

Some kinds of risk management are intuitive: when you approach a street crossing, you know that you face the risk of being hit by a car. You protect yourself by looking both ways and assessing the situation before deciding how to proceed. Similarly, if you're deciding whether to come down from a tree by jumping or using a ladder, you consider the potential consequences of each choice and minimize the possibility of bodily harm by opting for the ladder.

In neither of these intuitive examples is the process formalized. Both examples lack (and do not require) a thoughtful and systematic approach to the process of protecting the most critical asset at stake, your physical health.

In contrast, risk management as a professional practice follows a codified process. A schematic representation of this process is shown in Figure 1-1. Note that the process is not strictly linear. Each of the four major elements—"Frame," "Assess," "Respond," and "Monitor"—is interlinked with the others, and the process is continuously changing and reacting to circumstances in real time.

Risk Management Frameworks

The **National Institute for Standards and Technology (NIST)** has developed various risk management frameworks based on the intended system or organization. NIST is a federal agency that works with technology companies to create standards and procedures. These standards and procedures establish baselines for the deployment of products or services across an industry. All industries work with NIST to develop industry-wide standards for the products and services they deliver.

Cyber Fact

NIST Special Publication 800-30 defines an "IT system" as a "general support system (e.g., mainframe computer, mid-range computer, local area network, agencywide backbone) or a major application that can run on a general support system and whose use of information resources satisfies a specific set of user requirements."

Although this chapter loosely follows the NIST model for risk management, it is important to note that alternative frameworks exist. Within the federal government, in fact, each department and agency has its own methodology, whether formalized or not. One important alternative to NIST is the National Infrastructure Protection Plan (NIPP), established by the Department of Homeland Security (DHS). DHS has also adopted a **Risk Lexicon** that we will refer to frequently in the course of this chapter.[2]

The Process of Risk Management

This chapter will explain the four major steps of the risk management process: framing, assessing (including determining), responding, and monitoring risk. We will dissect each step using two non-cyber examples—a group of friends driving to a party or nightclub on New Year's Eve and a homeowner dealing with the possibility of burglary—as well as a cybersecurity example—an organized crime group that targets e-commerce sites, predominately commercial retail-

Chapter 1: Risk Management for Cybersecurity

> **Cyber Fact**
>
> An **organized crime group** is a domestic or international non-state actor with a political, social, or economic ideology. The group impresses its ideology on its targets through illegal activities and/or violence. Lulz Security (LulzSec) and its affiliate, Anonymous, are infamous organized crime groups that have been implicated in major cyber crimes in recent years. Other organized crime groups are purely interested in financial gains or other types of resources.

ers, with the intent of disrupting commerce and stealing customer information. The friends on New Year's Eve face the risks associated with drunk and reckless drivers, in addition to the everyday risks of traffic accidents and automotive malfunction; these risks represent unintentional threats, because drivers do not ordinarily intend to harm one another. The family intent on securing its house and property against burglars, in contrast, faces intentional threats, because burglars don't burgle by accident.

As we'll see, cyber risk managers must consider both intentional and unintentional threats at each step in their work process. Based on our hypothetical organized crime group's sophisticated hacking tools and vast financial resources, the group is able to conduct a large-scale and devastating attack against an online retailer. For the purposes of our discussion, this cyber example temporarily suspends the concept of regulations or legal requirements with which the company must comply (to learn more about these requirements, see Chapter 5).

Figure 1-2 shows a systematic breakdown of the cyber example with specific examples of activities at each phase. We suggest that you consider Figure 1-2 now and then return to it after you have worked through the chapter.

Risk Framing

The first step in the cyber risk management process is **risk framing**. Risk framing is the process of examining and evaluating the "big picture" risk environment in which a company or organization operates. Risk framing establishes the context for making **risk-based decisions**. Risk-based decisions, according to the DHS Risk Lexicon, are "determination[s] of a course of action predicated primarily on the assessment of risk and the expected impact of that course of action on that risk." Organizations and individuals routinely make risk-based decisions that affect investments and operations. For example, when a company allocates resources to managing risk, this decision means that resources are taken away from other program areas. Risk framing establishes the context in which the risk must be managed and establishes the risk-based restrictions around organizational decisions. The purpose of risk framing is to produce a risk management strategy.

Risk framing examines the assumptions, constraints, tolerance level, and priorities and trade-offs associated with risk. Figure 1-3 considers these elements of risk framing as they pertain to our example of an organized crime group that sends malicious code to a large company in an attempt to disrupt commerce and obtain personal customer information.

Assumptions

Assumptions are the reasonable expectations of actions, tools, and policies that may already be in place to protect critical assets, or reasonable expectations of the risk faced. The friends on New Year's Eve make the assumption that it is riskier to drive on New Year's Eve than on other nights. The homeowner and his family

Risk Framing

The Scenario:	An organized crime group sends malicious code in an email to a popular U.S. company known for the high volume of traffic on its website. The organized crime group wants to crash the company's website, which will disrupt commerce.

1. Frame Risk

Assumptions	Anti-virus software has been updated and installed on all company computers. This software will prevent malicious intrusions.
Constraints	Not all of the company's financial resources and personnel can be devoted to securing the website.
Tolerance	A major U.S. company that relies on web sales has a low tolerance for disruption to its website.
Priorities & Trade-offs	Protecting the website from being disrupted is a high priority for the company. Therefore, the company must take action to avoid the disruption of online business. As a result of the funds dedicated to website security, another office within the company will face budget cuts.

2. Assess Risk

Threat	An organized crime group emailing malicious code that could seriously disrupt the company's web functioning and sales.
Vulnerability	An individual within the company, unaware of the repercussions, opens an email containing malicious code.
Consequence	Financial loss, disruption of service, and harm to the company's reputation.

3. Risk Response

Accept	Receive emails from unknown users.
Avoid	Stop using the company's computers.
Mitigate	Protect the server with a firewall.
Transfer	Purchase cyber insurance.

4. Monitor Risk

Compliance	Verify the implementation of a company-wide firewall.
Effectiveness	Continually test and ensure that the firewall is working.
Identify Changes	Identify new threats and vulnerabilities, critical assets, and consequences as the risk environment changes and evolves.

Figure 1-2: Risk management outline and examples.

Chapter 1: Risk Management for Cybersecurity

1.

Frame Risk	
Assumptions	Anti-virus software has been updated and installed on all company computers. This software will prevent malicious intrusions.
Constraints	Not all of the company's financial resources and personnel can be devoted to securing the website.
Tolerance	A major U.S. company that relies on web sales has a low tolerance for disruption to its website.
Priorities & Trade-offs	Protecting the website from being disrupted is a high priority for the company. Therefore, the company must take action to avoid the disruption of online business. As a result of the funds dedicated to website security, another office within the company will face budget cuts.

Figure 1-3: Risk framing elements and examples.

assume that their home is a target for burglars. In our cyber example, there may be an assumption that antivirus software is installed and working correctly. For government employees, another assumption might be the presence of a **Trusted Internet Connection (TIC)** (see "Cyber Fact" on the following page). However reasonable these security assumptions may seem, they still must be checked, tested, and confirmed before an organization (including, in this case, a group of friends, a family, or a company) can develop and formalize its strongest possible risk management plan.

Constraints

Risk constraints are the factors that inhibit the execution of a 100-percent secure risk management plan. The most common risk constraint in many scenarios is the finite nature of financial resources. Organizations and individuals operate on restricted budgets, and they can't afford to spend all of their resources to protect a critical asset. For this reason, organizations and individuals must distribute resources strategically and intelligently to ensure that all of their critical assets have some measure of appropriate protection from harm.

Cyber Fact

The Office of Management and Budget mandated the use of the **TIC** in order to decrease Internet access points on government networks and to verify that all access to these networks is routed though designated TIC Access Providers. The TIC initiative is intended to "optimize and standardize individual external network connections currently in use by federal agencies, including connections to the Internet."[3]

In the New Year's Eve example, a constraint may be that the group of friends cannot drive an indestructible tank through a modern city in order to reach its destination. One of the family's constraints is that it only has a certain amount of money to spend on a home security system. In the cyber example, the company cannot shift its entire budget to reduce the threat of an organized cyber attack; the company, like the family, is financially constrained. Another possible constraint for the company is the need to maintain a user-friendly website. Online retailers must strike a balance between website security and website accessibility; customers may eschew a website that has too many security protocols in place because additional security measures may feel cumbersome and delay transaction time.

Risk Framing

Tolerance

Risk tolerance is the degree to which an organization can handle or incur a specific harm. A car has a lower harm tolerance in the event of a collision than a tank does. A home without an alert system has a lower risk tolerance than a home with an alert system. The risk tolerance level of a situation or organization depends upon both the situation's total vulnerability and the threat's potential to inflict harm. We will discuss the critical risk management concepts of threat and vulnerability later in this chapter.

A measurement of risk tolerance offers information about whether or not a potential risk is acceptable to an individual, organization, or entity. A low risk tolerance level indicates an unacceptable risk. According to the DHS Risk Lexicon, unacceptable risk is the "level of risk at which, given costs and benefits associated with further risk reduction measures, action is deemed to be warranted at a given point in time." Unacceptable risks must be addressed with action and resources. In our cyber example, the company's tolerance for the risk of receiving a malicious code embedded in an email is greater when the code comes from a lone hacker rather than when it comes from an organized crime group. The company can tolerate the risk posed by a lone hacker, because this hacker probably does not possess the capability to crash the company's website singlehandedly; the lone hacker probably also has fewer resources than the organized crime group. The company cannot tolerate a sophisticated hacking ring, but it can probably tolerate the activities of a lone hacker. Therefore, if the company has reason to believe that its network is the target of a cyber attack by an organized crime group, it must take action and commit resources to contain this unacceptable risk.

Priorities and Trade-offs

As the final step in a comprehensive risk framing process, an organization or individual identifies **priorities and trade-offs** that must be negotiated between all stakeholders in the scenario. For the individuals in our New Year's Eve example, priorities include safe and timely arrival at their destination as well as minimization of transportation costs. If the group designates a non-drinking driver, a trade-off is that the driver must remain sober and alert throughout the evening. The family decides that a priority is to secure its house from a burglar; as a result, they might have to make the trade-off between devoting money toward a new alert system and spending it on a vacation.

The company in our cyber example must make a similar financial trade-off if it hopes to contain the major risk represented by the organized crime group's potential to launch a cyber attack.

Indeed, the company facing the threat of malicious code crashing its website must prioritize the containment of this specific risk. Understandably, the company ranks these kinds of massively disruptive cyber threats as a primary concern, so it dedicates extra funds to staff, programs, and technology to protect its network. The trade-off for the company is that prioritizing these cybersecurity concerns reduces the funds available to other activities, such as employee training, marketing, or business development. Prioritizing security concerns against other business or management issues can be a difficult decision for executives to make. Ultimately, managers must make trade-offs based on the assumptions, constraints, level of tolerance, and priorities identified during the risk framing process.

Risk framing is the first step in creating a strategy to reduce risk. Thorough risk framing also provides a long-term strategic view of an organization's decision-making process. The strategy that an organization generates from the risk framing discussion outlines the challenges and mechanisms involved in protecting its most critical assets from harm.

Chapter 1: Risk Management for Cybersecurity

Risk Assessment and the Risk Formula

The second phase in the cyber risk management process is **risk assessment**. The DHS Risk Lexicon defines risk assessment as a "product or process which collects information and assigns values to risks for the purpose of informing priorities, developing or comparing courses of action, and informing decision making." The purpose of a risk assessment is to reveal the factors that, taken together, constitute a full picture of the risk that an organization faces. The full risk assessment consists of three distinct elements: threat, vulnerability, and consequence assessment. If a threat and/or vulnerability exists, then risk exists.

It is often easier to consider the three assessments together as one risk assessment. In many risk assessments, the three components are virtually inseparable from each other. Threat assessments and vulnerability assessments, in particular, can be difficult to separate. Nevertheless, a careful consideration of threat, vulnerability, and consequence as individual components of a risk assessment will yield a stronger, more nuanced assessment.

The Risk Equation

The generic formula for the summation of risk is shown in Figure 1-4. This equation cannot be used to calculate the likelihood of a specific harm occurring. Later in this chapter, we will consider equations that can be employed to produce hard calculations of specific risks.

Risk = Threat × Vulnerability × Consequence

Figure 1-4: The risk equation.

To understand the risk that a company or an individual faces in any given situation, we must identify and measure threats, vulnerabilities, and consequences inherent in the situation. None of these three aspects of the risk assessment can be fully effective without the other two. All three of these words – threat, vulnerability, and consequence – have casual meanings for everyday use that are related to, but not exactly the same as, their technical meaning for the process of assessing risk. For risk assessment purposes, *threats* are the agents that cause harm to an individual or organization. *Vulnerabilities* are identifiable weaknesses in processes, personnel, networks, or other technologies. The *consequence* is the specific result that occurs if a threat exploits a vulnerability and causes damage or harm to an individual or organization. Consider the following:

- The threat of a drunk driver on New Year's Eve; the threat of a burglar invading a home; the threat of an organized crime group bringing down a company's website.

- The vulnerability inherent in driving a car; the vulnerability of living in a particular home; the vulnerability of the IT network architecture at an online company.

- The consequence of a car accident on New Year's Eve; the consequence of a burglar entering a family's home; the consequence for the online company of an attack on its computer network and company website.

Once we conduct separate threat, vulnerability, and consequence assessments for these situations, we will possess a unified and comprehensive view of the risk facing the group of friends driving on New Year's Eve, the family trying to protect its home from a burglar, and the online company facing cyber threats from an organized crime group. After conducting a risk assessment, we will have the indicators necessary to determine the severity and magnitude of a risk, as well as the general (non-specific) likelihood of a risk occurring.

Threat Assessment

The DHS Risk Lexicon defines a **threat** as a "natural or man-made occurrence, individual, entity, or action that has or indicates the potential to harm life, information, operations, the environment, and/or property." In other words, threats are the agents that cause harm to an organization's processes, systems, personnel, hardware, software, or physical location. Threats cause harm by exploiting vulnerabilities.

According to DHS, a **threat assessment** is a "product or process of identifying or evaluating entities, actions, or occurrences...that have or indicate the potential to harm life, information, operations, and/or property." The purpose of the threat assessment is to identify the intention (target or goal), capability (power to commit harm), and lethality (level of harm) of a threat.

As we discussed earlier, a threat may or may not be intentional. Risk managers must consider both *intentional* and *unintentional* threats at this stage in the risk assessment. Types of intentional threats include physical or cyber attacks. The burglar entering the family's home is an intentional threat. In our cyber example, the crime group's intention may be to gain access to customer information. The group could use this information to open new credit card or bank accounts, or sell the information to third parties. Other cyber crime groups simply want to embarrass a company or organization, or make an ideological point by disrupting a business or government's ability to function.

2. Assess Risk	
Threat	An organized crime group emailing malicious code that could seriously disrupt a company's web functioning and sales.
Vulnerability	An individual within the company, unaware of the repercussions, opens an email containing malicious code.
Consequence	Financial loss, disruption of service, and harm to the company's reputation.

Figure 1-5: Risk assessment elements and examples.

Unintentional threats include human errors of omission or commission and natural or man-made disasters. A drunk driver on New Year's Eve may not intend to cause a fatal accident, but this lack of intention does not make his presence on the road any less dangerous. The individuals in the New Year's Eve scenario face many unintentional threats: the specific elevated threat of a drunk driver on New Year's Eve, in addition to the threats inherently associated with driving a car at any time (malfunctioning parts, distracted drivers, animals in the road, etc.).

Professional risk managers are charged with breaking down and analyzing threats, vulnerabilities, and consequences as separate factors in a risk assessment. In the case of national security questions, this task involves sophisticated algorithms and may take months or years to complete to a satisfactory level. Even at a basic level, threats and vulnerabilities may be difficult to distinguish from one another. The driver of the group of friends on New Year's Eve may lose concentration at the wheel. While this may at first seem to create a new vulnerability, the driver has also become an unintentional threat to himself, to the car, to the other passengers in the car, and to other cars, passengers, and drivers on the road.

In the case of the organized crime group, the threat has a capability level (power to commit harm) that is determined by the hacker's level of skill and sophistication, expertise, resources, and quality of tools for access-

Chapter 1: Risk Management for Cybersecurity

ing secured systems. The lethality (level of harm) to the company could take the form of immediate financial loss, short-term and long-term loss of customers, damage to the company's reputation, and the need to allocate additional resources for security and public relations. In this specific case, the lethality of both financial and non-financial losses would be highly detrimental to this company's business if its website were temporarily rendered inoperable, or hacked into in order to extract customer information. The exact figure of financial loss or non-financial consequence is calculated in the consequence assessment and risk determination step of the risk management process. We will discuss both processes later in the chapter.

In our cyber example, it is not difficult to identify many ongoing threats inherent when using a computer for critical company operations. To offer just one of the many possible examples, there is always the threat of a pipe breaking and water harming the company's server. Another unintentional threat might be that a programmer makes an error that introduces a new vulnerability into the system. A strong cyber threat assessment identifies these kinds of internal threats in addition to external threats such as the organized crime group. Figure 1-6 provides a breakdown of different types of threats and the possible consequences that they may result in.

Finally, a threat assessment may reveal threat shifting. **Threat shifting**, according to DHS, is the "response of adversaries to perceived countermeasures or obstructions, in which the adversaries change some characteristic of their intent to do harm in order to avoid or overcome the countermeasure or obstacle." In other words, threat shifting occurs when an intentional threat actor becomes aware that mitigations or controls are in place to thwart its activities, prompting the threat actor to alter its strategy to achieve its purpose. Cyber attacks are constantly evolving in new ways to exploit computer systems and gain access to sensitive information in storage and transmission (see Chapter 4 for more on common cyber attacks and exploits). Threat shifting is a major reason why risk management is a non-linear, ongoing process demanding constant monitoring, evaluation, and starting over.

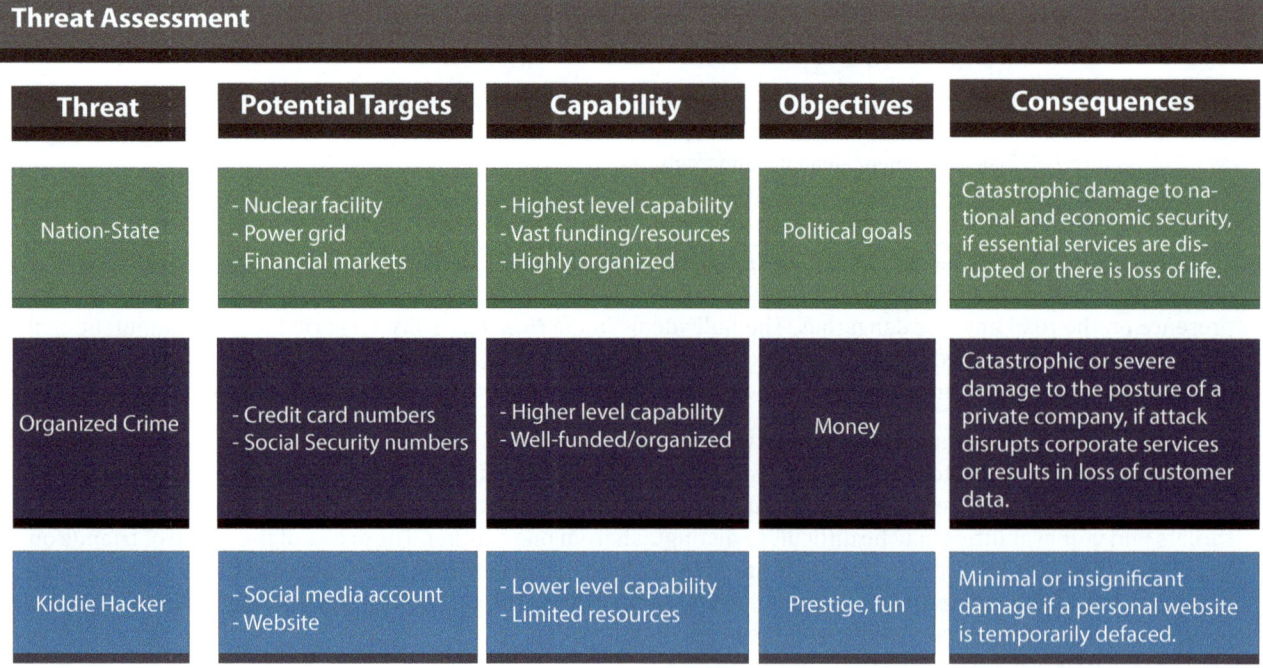

Figure 1-6: Threat assessment chart.

Vulnerability Assessment

National Security Threats	Information Warrior	Reduce US decision space or strategic advantage, chaos, target damage
	National Intelligence	Information to gain political, military, or economic advantage
Shared Threats	Terrorist	Visibility, publicity, chaos, political change
	Industrial Espionage	Comparative advantage
	Organized Crime	Retribution, financial gain, institutional change
Local Threats	Institutional Hacker	Monetary gain, thrill, challenge, prestige
	Recreational Hacker	Thrill, challenge

Figure 1-7: The threat spectrum.[1]

Vulnerability Assessment

The purpose of the **vulnerability assessment** is to reveal weaknesses in facilities, personnel, systems, networks, technology, or processes. The vulnerability assessment specifically looks for particular weaknesses that correspond to specific threats.

According to DHS's Risk Lexicon, a **vulnerability** is a cyber or "physical feature or operational attribute that renders an entity, asset, system, network, or geographic area open to exploitation or susceptible to a given hazard."

Just as threats are omnipresent and inevitable in nearly every kind of scenario, vulnerability is also a universal condition. For instance, all devices connected to the Internet are vulnerable to some form of cyber intrusion, just as all buildings are vulnerable to physical intrusion or damage. Therefore, the vulnerability assessment goes hand-in-hand with the threat assessment.

Cyber Fact

DHS defines a **vulnerability assessment** as a "product or process of identifying physical features or operational attributes that render an entity, asset, system, network, or geographic area susceptible or exposed to hazards."

Chapter 1: Risk Management for Cybersecurity

2.

Assess Risk	
Threat	An organized crime group emailing malicious code that could seriously disrupt a company's web functioning and sales.
Vulnerability	An individual within the company, unaware of the repercussions, opens an email containing malicious code.
Consequence	Financial loss, disruption of service, and harm to the company's reputation.

Figure 1-8: Vulnerability assessment example.

In our New Year's Eve example, the car's crushable exterior or lack of airbags may represent a vulnerability to the passengers. If the family's house lacks an alarm system, this lack may represent a crucial vulnerability in the event of a break-in. In our cyber example, a vulnerability may be a direct result of human error. Even though employees in the company may have received cybersecurity training and education, human susceptibility to error can never be completely eliminated. For example, an employee might open an email from an unknown source that runs a malicious code on his or her computer.

Additional vulnerabilities in the network architecture of a company may be the lack of an intrusion detection system or firewalls that are not strategically located to protect the organization's most critical assets. NIST has compiled a national database of information technology (IT) vulnerabilities that is helpful for all cybersecurity students and professionals to review.[5] Still, some IT vulnerabilities are more complicated than others, so NIST's list is not exhaustive.

In the event a vulnerability is exploited by a threat, the confidentiality, integrity, availability, or functions of critical assets may be compromised. Compared to the process of identifying threats, the process of identifying vulnerabilities may seem more challenging. Nevertheless, in many cases the threat's capability, lethality, and target or intention is specific enough to help narrow down the relevant vulnerabilities. Combined, the threat assessment and vulnerability assessment should yield a picture of the degree of potential harm to critical assets in the event that a vulnerability is exploited by a threat.

Vulnerability Assessment

The purpose of a vulnerability assessment is to reveal weaknesses in personnel, facilities, technology, and processes vis-à-vis a threat. Below is a vulnerability assessment of the personnel, facilities, information technology, and processes of a company against the threat of a global organized crime group seeking to obtain customer personal information from the company's popular online store.

Organized Crime Group	Personnel	Facilities	Technology	Processes
The organized crime group is well-funded. If their attack on the online store results in the theft of customer information, they could cause severe damage to the company. The company could lose money and consumer confidence, and could also be subjected to lawsuits.	There are weaknesses in the company's personnel, because it has been determined that not all personnel have had appropriate information and computer security training. In this scenario, the personnel are not the most critical assets, but they should still be treated with importance.	There are zero weaknesses identified in the company's facilities, because the threat is not targeting a physical asset. In this scenario, the facilities are not critical.	There are weaknesses in the company's computer networks and systems, creating potential vulnerabilities to be exploited. For example, in the vulnerability assessment, it was determined that the company's anti-virus software was not updated. Information technology is a critical asset to the company.	There are zero weaknesses identified in the company's processes, because the threat is targeting customer information stored digitally. In this scenario, the processes are not critical.

Figure 1-9: Vulnerability assessment diagram.

Cyber Fact

An **intrusion detection system (IDS)** is a monitoring device that identifies malicious activity in a network. A firewall protects a network by observing and detecting data, and then determining whether or not the data can pass through the network's firewall.

Consequence Assessment

The **consequence assessment** evaluates the potential impact on an organization in the event that a critical asset is exploited by a threat. **Consequence** is defined by DHS as the "effect of an event, incident, or occurrence." Consequence in risk assessment is determined by many factors, including the purpose and function of critical assets, the interdependencies between each critical asset and other assets, and how easy or difficult it would be to replace or repair each asset in the event of a breakdown or a lethal attack.

Both indirect consequences and direct consequences may ensue if a threat exploits a vulnerability. According to the DHS Risk Lexicon, an *indirect consequence* is an "effect that is not a direct consequence of an event, incident, or occurrence, but is caused by a direct consequence, subsequent cascading effects, and/or related decisions"; while a *direct or primary consequence* is an "effect that is an immediate result of an event, incident, or occurrence." For example, an indirect consequence to an online company attacked by an organized crime group is a damaged reputation; a direct consequence is a loss of money due to theft or lost sales during the time the website was down. The difference between the types of consequence may not always be this clear. Still, based on the scenario, the risk analyst will be able to define and separate the two types of consequence.

Before conducting the consequence assessment, we must answer the following question: "The threat will cause harm to which asset?" Determining and prioritizing an organization's critical assets is a key consideration for security policymakers and executives when they decide how to allocate limited resources in the face of conceivably unlimited threats. The value of each critical asset and the potential fall-out if any asset were to be harmed are the most crucial pieces of information that inform any consequence assessment.

Consequence is defined as the product of **criticality** and **impact**. *Criticality* refers to the importance of the critical asset and *impact* is the result of damage to the asset. A formula for the summation of consequence appears in Figure 1-10.

Consequence = Criticality × Impact

Figure 1-10: The consequence equation.

Let us examine ways of thinking about an asset's criticality or importance. One such method, highlighted by an official from the Government Accountability Office in an October 2001 statement before the House Subcommittee on National Security, Veterans Affairs, and International Relations, assigns the following labels to categories of criticality (in descending order of criticality): "catastrophic," "critical," "marginal," or "negligible."[6] These labels can then help decision-makers rank the potential criticality of the loss of or harm to any given asset.

Let us return to our two non-cyber examples to illustrate a consequence assessment. The harm to the individuals driving on New Year's Eve if a vulnerability (e.g., the car) is exploited by a threat (e.g., an intoxicated driver) is bodily damage to the passengers and damage to the car. The harm may be "marginal" if only the car is damaged, but the harm would be "catastrophic" if an individual is injured or killed in such a collision. If a burglar invades a family's home, the consequence may be defined as the value of the goods stolen. The harm is "marginal" if the items are replaceable within the family's budget, but it would be "catastrophic" if a family member is injured or killed in a fight with the burglar.

Chapter 1: Risk Management for Cybersecurity

2. Assess Risk

Threat	An organized crime group emailing malicious code that could seriously disrupt a company's web functioning and sales.
Vulnerability	An individual within the company, unaware of the repercussions, opens an email containing malicious code.
Consequence	Financial loss, disruption of service, and harm to the company's reputation.

Figure 1-11: Consequence assessment example.

In our cyber example, the consequence of an employee opening malicious code that leads to the leak of customer information may be only "marginal" if fewer than ten customers are affected. The consequence may be "catastrophic" if thousands of customers have their information stolen and exploited; the indirect consequence of this scenario might be that the online retailer must pay damages to their customers and incur negative media attention.

Let us consider one more example: The economic and national security consequence and impact of a hacker causing catastrophic damage to New York City's power grid is greater than the consequence of the same hacker disrupting the power grid of a small town in North Dakota. In North Dakota, the consequence of such a disruption would be "marginal," whereas in New York City the consequence would be "catastrophic." The reason for these different levels of severity is that both the impact (more people affected) and the criticality (more important centers of industry) in New York City are greater than in any town in North Dakota. Because the consequence formula is criticality multiplied by impact, the consequence of an attack that damages or disrupts New York City's power grid will almost always be greater than the consequence of an attack on any other power grid in the United States.

These labels of criticality are subject to the particularities of each risk scenario, because each risk scenario redefines the consequence metric. For example, consequence may be expressed in terms of the hours a business's website is down, the legislation enacted as a result of a data breach, the financial loss to individuals after a hacking incident, or the number of people harmed in the event.

The combined threat, vulnerability, and consequence assessment is a valuable tool for identifying the nuances and complexities of the risk facing an individual, organization, government, or nation. We next turn to the step of risk determination, in which the specific risk that the organization faces is identified and analyzed.

Cyber Fact

According to its official website, **the Government Accountability Office (GAO)** "investigates how the federal government spends taxpayer dollars" and "advise[s] Congress and the heads of executive agencies about ways to make government more efficient, ethical, equitable, and responsive."

Risk Determination

Risk determination is the step in the risk management process that follows the risk assessment. It is often the most in-depth and technical step in the entire risk management process. Many risk methodologies include risk determination as part of the risk assessment, but it can be beneficial to consider it as a separate process that focuses on the risk in greater depth than the assessment.

Nevertheless, a focused and effective risk determination is contingent upon a solid and thorough risk assessment. For example, by first determining the various threats and vulnerabilities an organization faces, as well as the intention, capability, and lethality of the threats, a risk management team can decide which threats and vulnerabilities to focus on, thereby devoting its energies to containing the most significant risks. A comprehensive risk assessment may alter the initial risk management strategy by tweaking the risk manager's original assumptions, constraints, priorities, and trade-offs from the risk framing process, or by drawing attention to the organization's tolerance for a specific kind of harm. After a threat assessment and a fresh understanding of the capabilities of a threat, an organization's first assumptions about the kind of risk it faces will likely change. The risk determination must acknowledge and build on the results of the risk assessment.

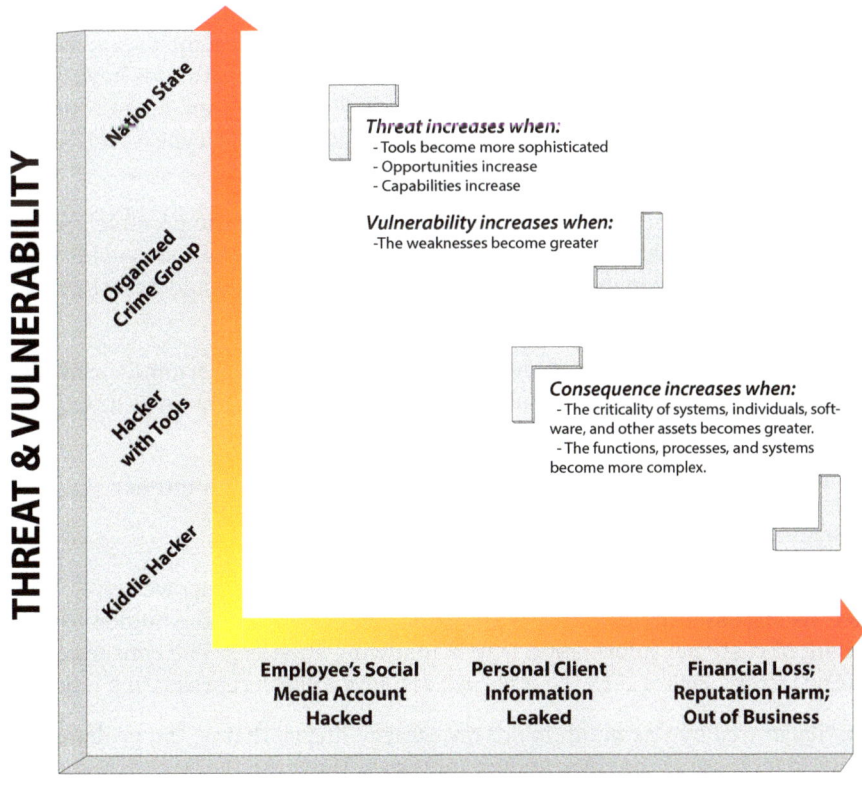

Figure 1-12: Consequence versus threat and vulnerability.

Chapter 1: Risk Management for Cybersecurity

A risk analyst's first major insight into the level of risk an organization faces comes from examining threat and vulnerability versus consequence. Figure 1-14 illustrates different levels of risk. From a risk analyst's standpoint, the ideal quadrant for risk is Quadrant I; the most severe and undesirable level is Quadrant IV. The chart in Figure 1-14 will help guide our understanding of risk determination.

Because threat and vulnerability go hand in hand, when a risk analyst evaluates the level of risk an organization faces, threat and vulnerability are considered together. In Quadrant I, the combined threat and vulnerability level is low; therefore, the consequence level is also low. In Quadrant IV, the threat and vulnerability level is high; therefore, the consequence level is also high. If an organization's risk level is determined to be in Quadrant IV, then the risk is severe and the organization must address it immediately. When an organization's risk level falls in Quadrant II or Quadrant III, risk analysts and risk managers must decide how best to approach the risk. Risk analysts will evaluate the options for controls and mitigations available as part of a customized security program to address the specific risk.

Figure 1-12 provides insight into the progression of the level of risk. The horizontal axis describes the increase in consequence to the most critical assets. The vertical axis describes the increase to both the level of threat and the level of vulnerability. As a risk analyst thinks through this chart, he must consider what is happening along both axes simultaneously. The graph in Figure 1-12 is the visual representation of the equation we saw in Figure 1-4: *Risk = Threat x Vulnerability x Consequence*.

As you consider this graph, keep in mind that the terms of the vertical axis (threat and vulnerability) are not fixed. Nation states all possess different capabilities from one another, and some organized crime groups may have greater capabilities than some nation states. However, in general, nation states have the greatest capabilities (resources, people, and skills) to devote to a cyber attack. For this reason, many countries have recently devoted defense and civilian resources to educating their populations about cybersecurity issues, such as the issue of preventing cyber attacks on national networks, in particular.

Thus, the risk determination process provides a complete overview of the possible levels of risk and provides a guide to the appropriate risk response at each particular level. If the risk level is low and appears in Quadrant I, then the risk response plan does not need to be as robust as it would be if the risk level appears in Quadrants III or IV.

However, the likelihood of a specific risk occurring is still unknown. To determine the likelihood of a risk occurring, we rely on the total risk equation: the probability of an event occurring times its expected consequence value. A formula for the calculation of total risk appears in Figure 1-13.

Total Risk = Probability of an Incident Occurring × Expected Consequence

Figure 1-13: The total risk equation.

In order to calculate the precise mathematical likelihood of risk occurring, we require a numerical value for the consequence. As discussed, consequence is assigned a value, such as the number of hours a website is defaced or the amount of customer information leaked following an attack. The consequence value may be a combination of several factors. Figure 1-15 (on page 46) displays a graph representing risk likelihood.

The relationship illustrated by this graph is not necessarily linear; that is, the probability of an event occurring does not have to increase as the consequence increases. However, the level of risk does increase as the consequence increases.

According to this graph, if the probability of an incident occurring is low and the consequence is low, then the overall risk to the organization will also be low. The company's risk response, therefore, may be minimal.

Risk Determination

Determining Levels of Risk

Quadrant	Threat and Vulnerability	Consequence	Level of Risk	Cyber Example
Quadrant I	Low	Low	Ideal level	Individual employee's social media account hacked.
Quadrant II	High	Low	Acceptable	An organized crime group with money, many tools, and high capability accesses the company's private customer database. However, the database is encrypted, and the crime group cannot exploit the information.
Quadrant III	Low	High	Needs mitigation	An organized crime group with simple tools gains access to the company's private client database, which is not encrypted.
Quadrant IV	High	High	Must mitigate	An organized crime group with the intention, opportunity, capability, money, and tools is able to crash the company's entire website.

Figure 1-14: Risk determination quadrants.

However, if the probability of risk occurring is high, and the consequence of risk is also high, then the total level of risk is high and a comprehensive response plan must be implemented immediately. Figure 1-15 complements Figure 1-12, which explored the relationship between threat and consequence. Magnitude and severity is represented by Figure 1-12. The likelihood of risk is determined using a probability model represented by Figure 1-15. The graphs do not mirror each other, but when viewed and analyzed in conjunction, they reveal an in-depth and near-complete picture of risk.

Qualitative and Quantitative Risk Determination Methodologies

Determining the magnitude and the likelihood of risk is a process that can be conducted qualitatively, quantitatively, or using a combination of qualitative and quantitative methods.

Cyber Fact

Iran, China, the U.S., and Israel all have capabilities to launch offensive cyber attacks against other nations or groups. Both Iran and China are widely suspected of utilizing cyberwarfare tactics, while, according to public testimony before the Senate, the U.S. and Israel organized and deployed Stuxnet in 2010, which successfully neutralized Iranian centrifuges at an Iranian nuclear plant.[7] Many countries have created national strategies for the prevention of cyber attacks, including the UK, with its 2011 Cyber Security Strategy. As part of the European Network and Information Agency, Germany, France, and the Netherlands have all implemented civilian cyber defense strategies.

Chapter 1: Risk Management for Cybersecurity

> **Cyber Fact**
>
> **Likelihood** is the "chance of something happening, whether defined, measured or estimated objectively or subjectively, or in terms of general descriptors (such as rare, unlikely, likely, almost certain), frequencies, or probabilities," according to DHS's Risk Lexicon.

A **qualitative risk determination** approaches risk using non-numerical data. In a qualitative assessment, past records and data, patterns of data, behavior of technology, behavior of personnel, and interviews with personnel may all be sources that play into the determination of a risk's level and/or likelihood. A **quantitative risk determination** assigns numerical values to qualitative statements. In some cases, it is necessary to combine both qualitative and quantitative methodologies to best determine the level and likelihood of risk occurring.

All risk determination processes, whether surveys or statistical models, must begin with specific definitions of threat, vulnerability, and consequence that can form a risk research question. A **research question** or set of questions will guide the risk determination process. All research questions should be clear and concise and should accurately test the research subject. Though often extremely hard to do well, creating a research question or set of questions will provide a framework for the entire risk determination process; therefore, crafting research questions requires a fair amount of effort and thought.

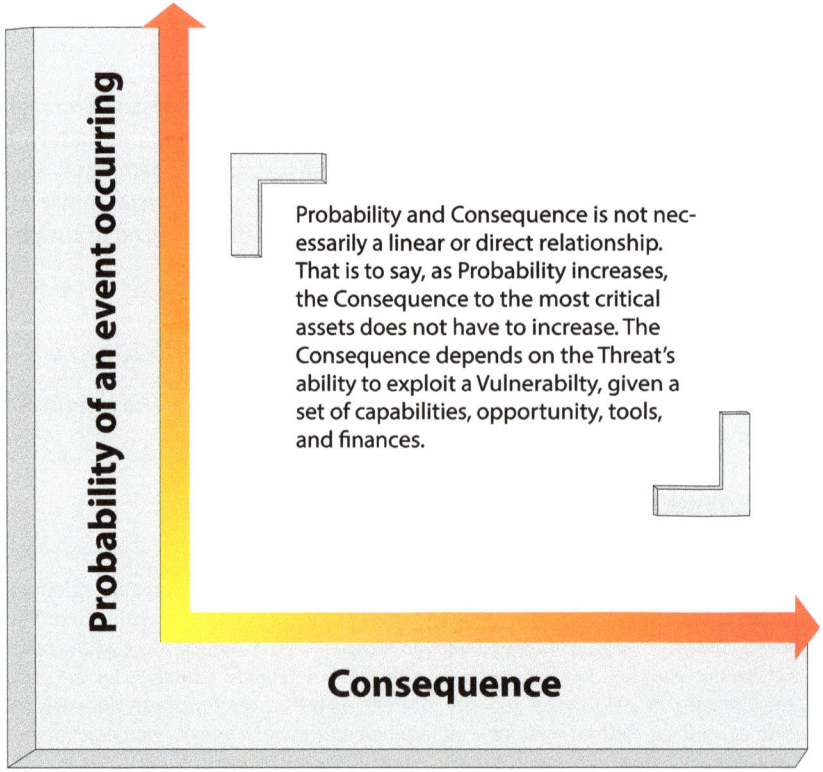

Figure 1-15: The likelihood of risk.

Risk Determination

All cyber risk determination research questions should be valid and reliable to help standardize the process and to report the results of the risk determination. A valid design means you are measuring and/or testing exactly what you are interested in studying. Reliability indicates that if others were to conduct the same test through the same process, they would reach the same conclusion. In other words, **validity** indicates that the research answers the initial question, while **reliability** indicates the consistency of the research design. We will further discuss elements of research methodology in Chapter 6.

Qualitative and quantitative risk determination processes should follow the scientific method. The first step in the scientific method is to propose a hypothesis. The purpose of a hypothesis is to make a prediction or establish a relationship between two or more variables. It does not prove causality between one event and another; it simply states that a relationship exists between two variables. Hypotheses typically follow the model of an "if-then" statement, either explicitly or implicitly. Many researchers will begin by determining a **null hypothesis**, denoted H_0, which describes no relationship between variables. An **alternative hypothesis**, H_A, represents the relationship between the variables being tested. The goal of the research is to reject the null hypothesis in favor of the alternative hypothesis and prove a relationship between variables.

An example of a hypothesis is, "If one drives on New Year's Eve then there is an expectation of a car accident." Without an "if-then" statement, the hypothesis reads, "There is an expectation of a car accident when driving on New Year's Eve." Here is a null-hypothesis paired with an alternative hypothesis:

H_0: An individual's IT security training has no influence in deterring an email spear phishing attack.

H_A: An individual's IT security training is significant in deterring an email spear phishing attack.

Qualitative Risk Determination

Before jumping into the case study established by the hypotheses above, we will review the basics of qualitative research, particularly survey design. We will use the process of survey design to illustrate fundamental elements of qualitative risk determination.

Basics of Qualitative Design

Qualitative research is easy to do but hard to do well. The purpose of qualitative research is to define or explain descriptive events, personal views and understandings, or other kinds of ideological trends. Unfortunately, the flexibility of qualitative risk assessments often limits its precision. Unlike quantitative assessments, qualitative assessments may not be able to identify an exact risk measurement. Rather, they provide a more nuanced and holistic understanding of a particular issue.

Acquiring relevant qualitative data depends on the researcher's skills, available resources, and the research question. Data in qualitative designs can take the form of visuals, verbal discussions, and recorded observations. Interviews, focus groups, and surveys are popular methods of qualitative research, and all of these methods can be applied to the risk determination process.

Survey Design

A **survey** consists of a series of questions created in order to gather information about a particular research question. Although surveys are not always the most useful tools for determining exact relationships, they can provide descriptive or explanatory information about a large population that can later inform hypotheses about relationships between variables. The danger inherent in interpreting survey results is *extrapolation*—inferring a conclusion beyond the data.

Chapter 1: Risk Management for Cybersecurity

Therefore, while quantitative research is generally better for generating precise numerical values related to risk, surveys allow management to gain insight into the level of risk that might exist within an organization. Surveys allow managers to understand a risk from the top to the bottom of their value chains because surveys are effective tools for gathering information across a population, particularly about human behavior, opinions, and preferences.

Surveys may take the form of personal interviews, self-administered surveys, or phone surveys. Each type of survey has its own benefits, drawbacks, and specific uses. For instance, personal interviews generally have high response rates and generate large amounts of detail from the respondents, but they are also the least efficient kind of survey to conduct in terms of time and money. Self-administered surveys are generally cost effective, but they have lower response rates. Lastly, phone surveys are cost effective, but may not generate the same depth of detailed information as a personal interview.

For more fundamentals of survey design for risk determination, see Appendix A.

Qualitative Example of Risk Determination

The National Nuclear Security Agency (NNSA) is a federal government agency that works to maintain the security and safety of the United States' nuclear weapons. This government agency is a likely target for a cyber attack because of the highly sensitive information about nuclear weapons that it is charged with protecting.

Let's look at a scenario in which there have been rumors that a foreign country with sophisticated hacking abilities and vast resources is attempting a spear phishing attack against the NNSA. The spear phishing attack will send an email from a seemingly known and friendly email address and will invite the recipient to click on a link in order to RSVP for a conference on radiation protection. When the recipient clicks, the hackers get control of the recipient's computer, thereby gaining access to the NNSA network and highly sensitive NNSA information.

Based on these rumors, the NNSA wants to test for its level of risk, specifically focusing on human vulnerability to a spear phishing attack. To determine its level of risk, the NNSA has decided to use a qualitative risk determination. The NNSA believes that this qualitative design will allow the agency to understand the human behavior that will determine the level of risk. Since the potential attack may come in the form of a spear phishing attempt, human error is one of the largest vulnerabilities to test for and work into the risk determination. Of all of the qualitative risk determination possibilities available, the NNSA has decided to design a survey to determine the level of vulnerability to such attacks within the organization.

The research question for the survey is:

"What is the level of risk within the NNSA to spear phishing email attacks targeting NNSA personnel?"

Cyber Fact

Phishing attacks are a popular form of cyber attack. These attacks "fish" for a user's personal information by trying to deceive the user into voluntarily entering personal information, or taking action that would provide the attacker with access to their system (e.g., "click this link" or "open this site"). **Spear phishing** is a targeted form of phishing—in order to carry out a spear phishing attack, the attacker must know something specific about the person being attacked. The spear phisher finds ways around common cybersecurity precautions by learning important facts about the person who is the target of their attack. They may learn what projects the person is involved with, or the people they communicate with most often. Spear phishing attacks are difficult to recognize because they are customized for the target and often look like they are coming from sources that the target knows and trusts.

Risk Determination

The information security officer for the NNSA has decided that, for the sake of efficiency, she will conduct a self-assessment survey across a randomized sample of 150 NNSA employees. The NNSA employs approximately 3,000 people, so the sample will be roughly 5% of the total population. Using this model, the team of statisticians place each person's identification number into a random digit generator, thereby producing a sample group of 150 subjects to take the survey.

The information security officer has decided to distribute the survey via email. She chose this distribution method for two reasons. First, by having the participants fill out the survey on their computers, the data from their results will automatically be stored in a statistics software package. Second, in order to combat the low response rates that can accompany a computer-based survey, the security information officer requires that selected members print out a certificate designating that they have completed the survey. They are instructed to turn the certificate in to the Human Resources Department. Fortunately, this method is successful and results in a 100% response rate. Figure 1-16 displays the example survey. The purpose of this exercise is to illustrate the types of questions that the information security team would ask the personnel at the NNSA in order to evaluate the level of risk of a phishing attack. Before reviewing the survey, note the following six assumptions:

- All federal government employees have annual IT training.
- All federal IT training includes a module on phishing attacks.
- The NNSA conducts regular patching and vulnerability scans.
- Spam filtering is in place.
- .exe attachments are blocked in e-mail.
- Virus scanning is installed and kept up to date.

Based on these assumptions, the NNSA also assumes that cyber attacks against the organization will be highly sophisticated.

Survey for NNSA Personnel

Directions: Please fill out all questions to the best of your knowledge, using the following scale:

1= Poor

2= Fair

3 = Good

4= Excellent

5= Not applicable

Following completion of the survey, print out the certificate and return it to the HR Department.

Chapter 1: Risk Management for Cybersecurity

Questions:

Training:

1. How informative was your most recent IT training?
   a. 1
   b. 2
   c. 3
   d. 4
   e. 5

2. How well do you recall the information for your annual training?
   a. 1
   b. 2
   c. 3
   d. 4
   e. 5

3. How well do you remember the phishing module from the annual training?
   a. 1
   b. 2
   c. 3
   d. 4
   e. 5

Delivery:

4. How often do you receive emails from unknown sources?
   a. Daily
   b. Weekly
   c. Monthly
   d. Every few months
   e. Never

Risk Determination

5. Do you knowingly open emails that are delivered to your spam folder?
   a. Yes
   b. No

6. Do you pay attention to the addressee list of the email to verify the validity of content and/or sender of the email? In other words, do you pay attention to whether the addressee list makes sense given the nature of the email?
   a. Yes
   b. No

Payload:

7. How often do you open email attachments from unknown sources without verifying the email is valid?
   a. Never
   b. Sometimes
   c. Often
   d. Very Often
   e. Not applicable/not sure

8. How suspicious are you of attachments in general?
   a. Not at all
   b. Somewhat
   c. Suspicious
   d. Very suspicious
   e. Not applicable/not sure

9. If an error or malfunction occurs when you open an attachment (e.g., Adobe Acrobat crashes), do you ignore the error or check with the sender to receive a working version?
   a. Ignore the malfunction
   b. Check with the sender, and not inform the IT Department of the event
   c. Check with the sender, and inform the IT Department of the event

Chapter 1: Risk Management for Cybersecurity

Execution:

10. In general, do you report suspicious activity on your system to the IT Department?

   a.   Never

   b.   Sometimes

   c.   Often

   d.   Very Often

   e.   Not applicable/not sure

11.   If your computer seems to be working harder than normal, do you report the abnormal behavior to the IT Department?

   a.   Never

   b.   Sometimes

   c.   Often

   d.   Very Often

12.   If someone asks if you sent an email with an attachment but you did not, how likely are you to report this case to the IT Department?

   a.   Never

   b.   Sometimes

   c.   Often

   d.   Very Often

   e.   Not applicable/not sure

Other:

13. If you would like to elaborate on any of the questions or responses covered in this survey, please comment in the space below:

Figure 1-16: An example survey.

The NNSA will be able to analyze the results of this survey to determine the level of risk from a spear phishing attack that the agency faces. The NNSA has decided to aggregate the responses and generate the percentage for each response. The percentage for each response will inform the level of risk determined and therefore the risk response plan.

Risk Determination

Quantitative Risk Determination

Now let's consider the quantitative process in risk determination. Quantitative analysis uses numerical values to test one variable, such as harm, against another variable, such as a threat's capability or lethality. There are many types of quantitative analysis methods that governments and organizations use in high-level risk determination processes. The following section assumes that the reader has a basic knowledge of statistics and logical reasoning. Statistics is a crucial element of quantitative risk determination and is therefore a foundation of the entire risk management process.

Probabilistic Risk Assessment (PRA)

The U.S. Nuclear Regulatory Commission (NRC), the Environmental Protection Agency (EPA), and the National Aeronautics and Space Administration (NASA) all use **probabilistic risk assessment (PRA)**[7] in their risk management strategies. PRA is specifically concerned with:

- the magnitude or severity of the consequence, and
- the probability of an event occurring.

A PRA model generates a value or range of values for the probability of risk occurring. The probability is based on a set of variables. **Variables**, also known as *indicators*, are the various factors that influence the likelihood of risk occurring. For example, in the New Year's Eve scenario, the variables can include: the safety features of the car, the time of night at which the friends are on the road, the number of people in the car, and the alertness level of the driver. All of these factors influence the likelihood of getting in an accident or not getting in an accident on New Year's Eve. Indicators of a burglar invading a family's home include whether or not the front door was locked, whether or not a fence surrounds the perimeter of the home, whether or not an alert system is installed, and whether or not there are any witnesses present when the burglar attempts the invasion.

In a PRA model, consequences are expressed numerically. In the New Year's Eve example, we will need to consider the number of people potentially injured. In the cyber example, we will need to consider the number of hours that the website is defaced and the number of customers affected. Our goal is to graphically represent the probability of an event occurring; this probability is the unknown value. Event trees, multivariable statistical analysis, and other PRA models generate equations or processes to determine a value for the probability of a risk occurring. We will return to specific PRA models and a statistical model later in this chapter. First, we need to have an understanding of the quantitative process and probability.

Basics of Probability

Probability can be as simple as flipping a coin or as complex as calculating the probability of catastrophic damage to New York City's electrical grid. When studying probability, the following questions arise: Will an event occur? How certain can I be that an event will occur?

Probability (P) is defined as a value between 0 and 1, representing 0% and 100% probabilities that an event will occur. You cannot have a 150% chance of an event occurring, just as you cannot have a -50% chance of an event occurring. Therefore, probability distributions are between 0 and 1. The sum of all of the probabilities for a given scenario must equal 1, or 100%. Figure 1-17 illustrates probability distribution.

$0 \leq P(event) \leq 1$

Figure 1-17: Probability distribution.

Flipping a coin has two possibilities, heads or tails, so you have a one out of two probability (50%) of landing heads. You also have a 50% probability of landing tails. In a deck of cards, there are a total of 52 cards, of which exactly four are queens, so the probability of randomly picking a queen from a deck of cards is 4/52 (roughly 8%).

Chapter 1: Risk Management for Cybersecurity

Type of Probability	Example
Independent	Flipping a coin
Mutually Exclusive	Rolling a dice
Not Mutually Exclusive	Drawing a card out of a normal deck of cards
Conditional	Event A depends on Event B (expressed as "the probability of A given B")

Figure 1-18: Definitions and examples of probability.

The terms **independent** and **exclusive** do not have the same meaning in probability as they might in everyday language. The term *independent* suggests that the knowledge of one event occurring does not affect the probability of the other, or next, event occurring. Rolling a seven on one throw of the dice, for example, does not diminish or increase the probability that the next throw will also be a seven. *Exclusive*, also referred to as disjoint, indicates that two events can never occur at the same time. **Conditional probability** is defined as the probability of one event occurring with the knowledge of the outcome(s) of the other event(s).

Our study of cyber risk management is going to focus on conditional probability, because the likelihood of harm is contingent upon multiple events either occurring or not occurring. Once we understand the basics of probability, we can use this knowledge to perform research using PRA models or statistical models.

As discussed earlier, we need to set up a null and alternative hypothesis to help us solve for risk. A null hypothesis, denoted H_0, describes no relationship between variables. An alternative hypothesis, H_A, represents the relationship between the variables in research based on the scientific method. The goal is to reject the null hypothesis. In an "if-then" statement, the H_A asserts: "If malicious code is sent to a company, then the network will be harmed." To be clear, this statement does not indicate causality between events. For example, malicious code alone does not cause information to be leaked.

We will test the following hypotheses using different quantitative models.

H_0: There is no association between malicious code and harm to a company's website.

H_A: There is an association between malicious code and harm to a company's website.

The Four PRA Models

Four different PRA models can reveal a level and likelihood of risk. The following section provides examples for event tree analysis and fault tree analysis.

Event Tree Analysis

Event tree analysis traces the probability of a response to an incident. This response is usually expressed as a binary—yes or no.

Event trees create great visuals for tracing a sequence of events and the probability of each event. Event tree analyses begin with an initiating event. In our New Year's Eve example, the initiating event is the drive to the nightclub

Risk Determination

or party. In the cyber example, the initiating event is malicious code being sent to an online company. An event tree then traces the possible outcomes after the initiating event occurs and indicates the probability of subsequent events.

In an event tree analysis, an outcome is the probability of a combination of events occurring. If we were to make a chart for the possibility that a car speeds in the New Year's Eve example, we might also take into account some other potential outcomes, such as skidding on ice and brakes failing. We would then continue to trace outcomes back to the initiating event. "What will happen if the car speeds, skids on ice, and brakes fail?" is one sequence of events that will produce a unique outcome. After the event tree is complete, each sequence will be quantified and the outcome of each event happening will be calculated, thereby quantifying the potential risk of any given incident on the event tree.

Figures 1-19 and 1-20 show event trees for two scenarios, the New Year's Eve drivers and the malicious code sent to an online company. The "Risk Level" boxes at the rightmost end of each tree refer to the four risk quadrants that were depicted in Figure 1-14.

In each case, the risk level is based on the severity of the sequence of events. In the New Year's Eve scenario, for instance, speeding, skidding, and brake failure constitute a more serious and dangerous sequence of events than not speeding, not skidding, and normal brake function; hence, the first sequence results in a Quadrant 3 (Q3) assessment, while the second generates a Q2. Similarly, in our cyber example, if an intrusion detection system is not in place, if a firewall is not protecting a server, and if there is no policy to discourage employees from opening suspicious emails, then the risk level is greater than it would be in a scenario in which all of these elements had been implemented. Based on the definition of conditional probability, the final outcome in each case is calculated by multiplying the probabilities of each incident.

Fault Tree Analysis

Fault tree analysis examines an entire organization or enterprise from a top-down perspective and identifies the combination of failures that may contribute to the system's malfunctioning; it is a deductive methodology, because it derives possible conclusions from a given set of premises.

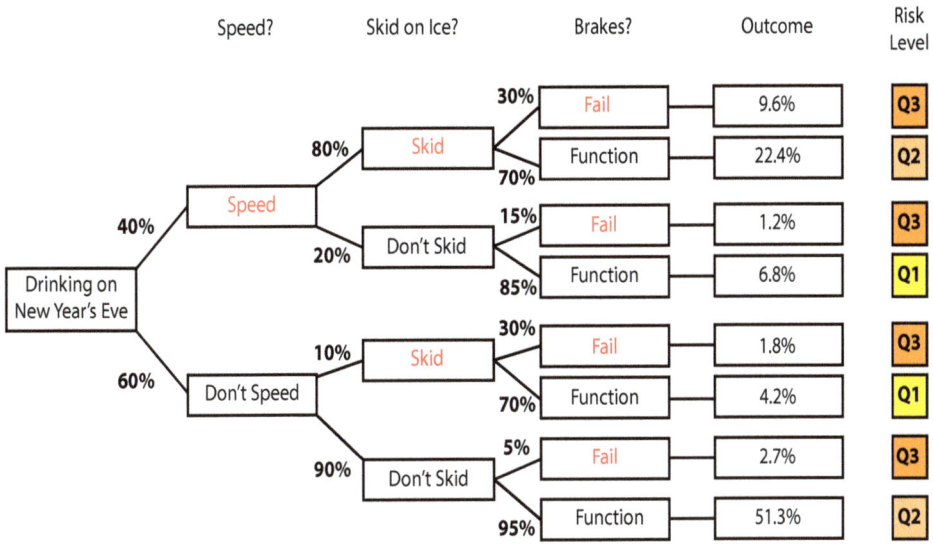

Figure 1-19: Event tree for the New Year's Eve scenario.

Chapter 1: Risk Management for Cybersecurity

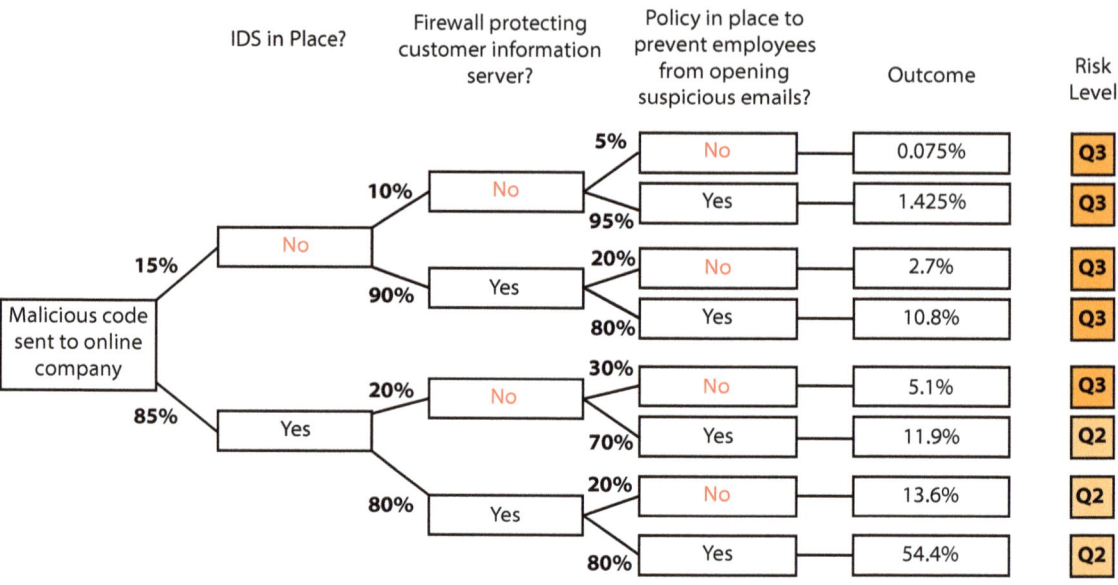

Figure 1-20: Event tree for the cyber scenario.

Risk analysts and risk managers use fault tree analysis to analyze the probability of an undesired final event. Using this type of analysis, an upper level manager begins by designing the top of a fault tree diagram—beginning with the undesired event. This is where a fault tree analysis would place an event such as a car crash in the New Year's Eve scenario, a burglar intruding into a family's home, or a malicious code taking down a website. In fault tree analysis, the top events are always the final events.

From a final event, the risk analyst or risk manager will trace possible causes of that event using a series of coordinated symbols. These possible causes could be traced from one particular event that begins the line of action until reaching the final event at the top of the fault tree diagram. The symbols and their meanings are shown in Figure 1-21, while Figures 1-22 and 1-23 show fault tree diagrams for the New Year's Eve and cyber scenarios.

Human Reliability Analysis (HRA)

Human reliability analysis (HRA) calculates the human errors that may affect a risk-induced incident. The probability of a risk occurring is determined using indicators that can influence the likelihood of the risk occurring. Examples of indicators are the sophistication of training for personnel and the implementation of policy procedures for an individual or an organization. In the New Year's Eve case, the possibility for human error is particularly important because, more than on any other night of the year, a large number of intoxicated drivers are likely to be on the road. The more intoxicated a driver is, the more likely it is that a human error will occur. Therefore, to calculate the risk of driving to and from the nightclub or party, it would be helpful to use an HRA analysis to quantify the amount of human error that factors into the risk of driving on New Year's Eve.

In the cyber realm, spear phishing techniques explicitly aim to exploit an individual. In this way, spear phishing capitalizes on human vulnerabilities.

Risk Determination

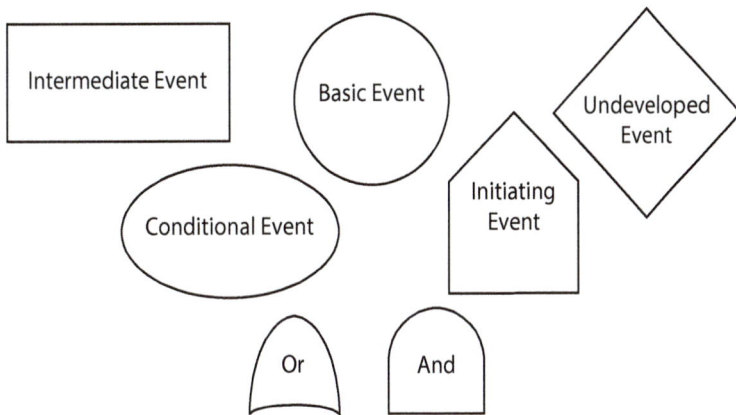

Figure 1-21: Fault tree symbols.

Monte Carlo Analysis

A **Monte Carlo model** is a multivariate statistical analysis for computing mathematical risk. A Monte Carlo analysis considers possible variations in each individual factor of the analysis and examines the many possible ways in which the factors may interact. For example, one set of factors may influence the likelihood of risk occurring to a greater or smaller degree than another set of factors. A Monte Carlo method will test thousands of iterations of ways that situational factors may combine to create a simulation of a scenario with a large enough sample size of possible outcomes to calculate probability statistics for each outcome.

For the cyber risk determination, a Monte Carlo model would take into account factors such as the implementation of a firewall, updates to anti-virus software, encrypted hard drives, properly secured computers, and threat

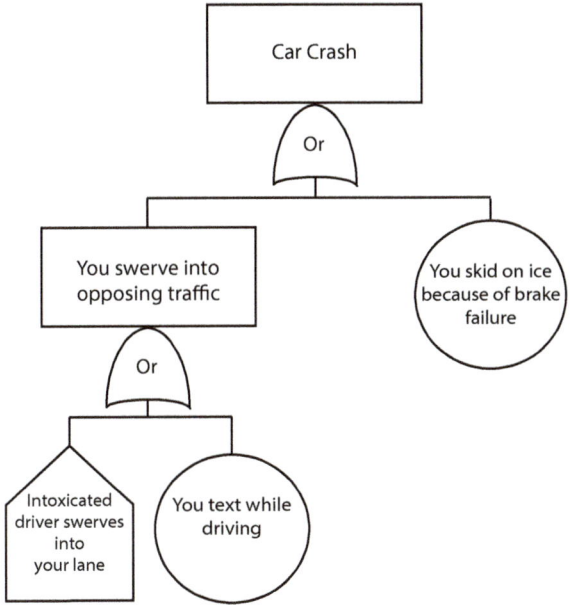

Figure 1-22: Fault tree for the New Year's Eve scenario.

Chapter 1: Risk Management for Cybersecurity

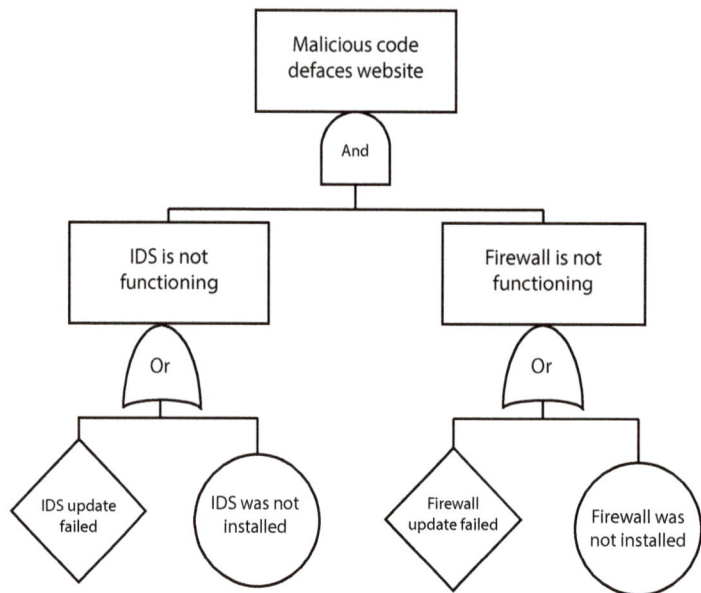

Figure 1-23: Fault tree for the cyber scenario.

levels to determine the risk to an organization's computer network. The model would then run simulations varying those factors and calculate the overall risk, as well as the variations to the risk that each factor presents.

The Monte Carlo model generates a probability value that a risk will occur. This model will inform the organization about the factors that contribute most to the risk of harm to their network, so that they can take steps to reduce these contributing risk factors as much as possible. The Monte Carlo method is not the only statistical model used to identify the probability of an event occurring, but it is one of the most popular models that professional risk managers use.

These PRA models represent only a few of the quantitative methods available to risk managers to conduct in-depth risk determination processes. Risk managers, like many other social scientists, have started to use a wide variety of mathematical models to quantify their reasoning and to provide evidence for their hypotheses. These models include game theory, logic decision processes, and multivariable statistical analysis, which we will discuss later in this chapter. The appropriate model to use in any given risk management situation depends on the kind of answer a risk manager is seeking and the type and amount of data available.

Statistical Modeling

An online retailer wants to reduce the risk of customer information being leaked; the retailer, therefore, is interested in which security controls are the best at preventing information from being leaked. The mathematical concepts and statistical background helpful to understanding risk are available in Appendix A.

A Quantitative Risk Determination Example: Determining the Likelihood of Harm Occurring to an Online Retailer

The following probability model is for illustrative and educational purposes only. The dataset was randomized using Microsoft Excel in order to illustrate how risk can be quantified using statistical inference. All statistical results were produced using Stata 11.

Risk Determination

Let's imagine that the risk management team at a popular online retailer wants to know what kind of risk they face with regard to critical customer information being leaked. They want to answer the following question:

"Which security controls are the best at protecting customer information from being leaked?"

To evaluate this question, we will use a statistical regression model. A **regression model** uses multiple independent (x) variables to predict or estimate a dependent (y) variable. Presumably, a change to any of the independent variables will affect the outcome(s) of the model. In other words, the y value is dependent on the x value(s). In the case of multivariable analysis, each x value must be mutually exclusive; the x values cannot be affected by, nor dependent upon, each other.

Cyber Fact

Game theory is a strategic decision making process between rational actors. The "prisoner's dilemma" is an example of a game theory model. DHS's Risk Lexicon defines game theory as a "branch of applied mathematics that models interactions among agents where an agent's choice and subsequent success depend on the choices of other agents that are simultaneously acting to maximize their own results or minimize their losses."

In order to determine which security controls are the best at securing information, 200 (n=200) online retailers will be examined. They will answer the question of whether or not, yes or no, customer information was leaked on one random day (24 hours) in 2011.

Because we have a binary (yes or no) question, we will use a **logistic (logit) regression model** to evaluate risk. Logit models are used when the dependent variable is a binary response. The model generates a probability value. A logit model reveals the most statistically significant indicators and the type of association the indicators form with the dependent variable, the latter expressed as *positive* (direct) or *negative* (indirect). A positive relationship indicates that if the independent variable increases, the dependent variable increases; a negative relationship means that if the independent variable increases, the dependent variable decreases (or vice versa).

Analysis of the Most Significant Factors Influencing Customer Information Leaked

Based on the most complete model generated using the logit equation (Model 3), *Strength of Password* and a *2-Factor Authentication* are the two most significant security controls.

An example of a strong password would be one that includes capitalization, a number, a symbol, and at least eight characters unrelated to any personal information; for example, "rh7TL!9" would be a strong password. A particularly weak password might be a word that is found in a dictionary, such as the word "password."

A 2-factor authentication is a security control that requires the user to enter two pieces of data from the following three: "something the user possesses" (such as a member number); "something the user is" (such as an item of biometric data); and "something the user knows" (such as a password).

According to the logit analyses (see Appendix A for the logit analyses of Models 1, 2, and 3), the independent variable *Password* is significant in determining the probability of a risk, defined as customer information being leaked, and as the password becomes stronger by gaining in complexity, the likelihood decreases that customer critical information will be leaked.

Chapter 1: Risk Management for Cybersecurity

Analysis, however, shows that a 2-factor authentication is the most significant variable, based on its low p-values in all three models.[8] Therefore, if a 2-factor authentication is present as a security control on a company's website, the likelihood of customer information being leaked decreases. According to this analysis, and based on its statistical significance in each model, 2-factor authentication is the most significant form of security control that the online retailer can use.

Interestingly, in Model 3, *Number of Users* was another statistically significant variable.[9] This result indicates that as the number of users increases, the likelihood of customer information being leaked decreases. Risk analysts may draw many different conclusions from this outcome. When we consider this statistically significant variable, it is important to remember that correlation does not equal causation; the number of users does not cause a website to be defaced or not be defaced. Rather, and most likely, the most popular online stores, measured by number of users, must have the greatest security controls in place for their consumers. Therefore, these stores also have a lower probability of customer information being leaked.

The *Strength of Hacker* variable was only significant in Model 3. Therefore, common knowledge prevails: as the strength of the hacker increases, the likelihood of customer information being released increases.

To sum up the findings from this study: When an online retailer considers which security controls to employ in order to protect customer information from being leaked, requiring a strong password of its consumers and consideration of a 2-factor authentication should be at the top of the list.

Based on these models, risk managers may suggest to the chief information officer (CIO) or chief information security officer (CISO) of an online retailer that the website require a strong password and a 2-factor authentication in order to secure customer information. Decisions made in these areas should be based on an effective risk management program. However, the CIO and/or CISO have limited resources for the deployment of security controls, so they must choose a combination of controls that securely safeguards customer information, avoids customer inconvenience, and works for the company's budget. At this point, a cost-benefit analysis is necessary to determine which controls should be in place.

Predicting the Probability of Customer Information Leaked

The strength of multivariate statistical analysis lies in its predictive capabilities. A thorough, valid, and reliable design will allow a risk manager to extrapolate future trends that will help the company to protect its critical assets. A CIO or CISO's job is to present the company's board of directors with the best set of security controls, given limited resources and other constraints, such as the constraint of maintaining a user-friendly website. The specific mathematical forecasting techniques used to predict the probabilities of customer information leaked based on this scenario are available in Appendix A.

The graph in Figure 1-24 expresses the probability of customer information leaked as the "Probability of Risk Occurring." One can see how the probability of customer information leaked changes as the degree of security controls differs in each model.

Cyber Fact

The **CIO** is in charge of an organization's IT planning, budgeting, and performance, including its information security components.

Risk Determination

Recall that the best security controls for protecting customer information are a strong password and a 2-factor authentication. However, the risk analysis team wants to know the combination of security controls that will best protect customer information from malicious code, based on the resources allocated and constraints placed on the online retailer.

Model A is the riskiest scenario: There is a 93.136% likelihood of customer information being leaked under the set of conditions in Figure 1-24. Model D is the safest and most realistic option, which even takes into consideration a hacker with strength level 7 out of 10, 10 being the strongest.

Model D is the only model that has a 2-factor authentication, and it has the strongest password. While Model D does contain multiple security controls, it is a realistic option. Consumers may not enjoy having a 2-factor authentication; however, on a popular website that is a target for strong and capable hackers, consumers should feel confident that there is only a 0.641% likelihood that their critical information may be leaked. There are additional models to reduce the probability of risk occurring, but incorporating additional levels of security may become too burdensome for the consumer and deter them from using the site. The store must strike a balance between a high level of security and consumer convenience.

The likelihood of a risk occurring and the level of risk are two of the most crucial pieces of information that go into the risk management process. Determining the likelihood of a harm (in our example, customer information leaked) occurring is a critical calculation for risk managers. Following our risk determination process in this example, the CIO or CISO now has four different models to present to the board of directors as reasons to promote the security controls of Model D versus Model A. They will emphasize the need for 2-factor authentication and a strong password for consumer login. At the same time, a good risk analyst, CIO, or CISO will account for the possible variations in a potential hacker's level of sophistication, as well as other external factors that play a role in the outcome of the probability model. Variation in the independent factors will prepare the company for a variety of situations. For these reasons, the risk determination process is one of the most important phases in the formation of an effective risk response. By quantifying and identifying various and varying risks, a manager will be well prepared to respond to a dynamic risk environment.

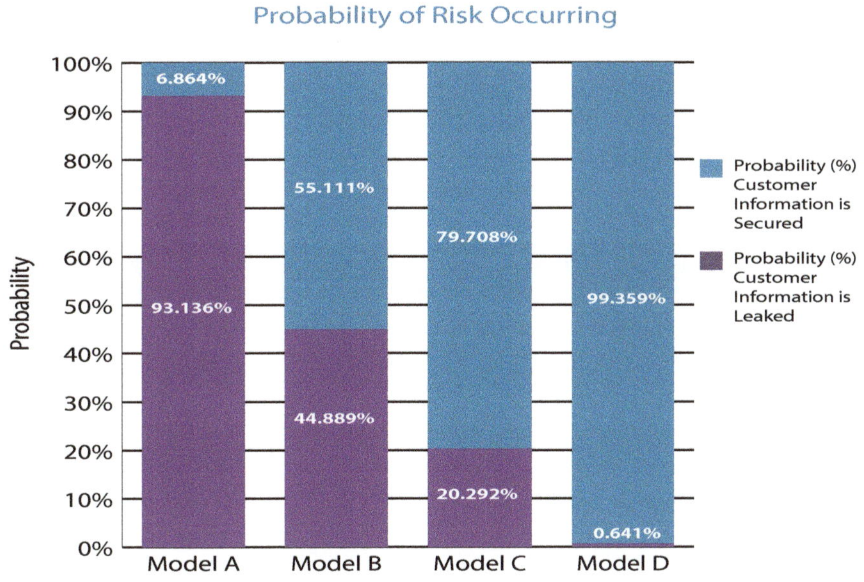

Figure 1-24: Graph of Probability of Risk Occurring.

Chapter 1: Risk Management for Cybersecurity

Risk Response

A **risk response** is the most appropriate response to the determined risk. After a thorough evaluation of many possible responses, the response that the risk managers choose prevents harm to an individual, organization, or enterprise, while also staying within budget. Potential responses depend upon the threat's capability and the criticality of the assets. Risk managers evaluate these potential courses of action against the calculated risk, and then choose the most appropriate course of action. A risk response plan may incorporate various mechanisms, decisions, or policies to construct the best response to protect against risk.

The response plan must fit the determined level of risk; the course of action for a high-risk situation is not appropriate for a low-risk situation. For example, installing a firewall at the FBI against the threat of a foreign adversary hacking into the computer system is not the appropriate course of action to protect this high-risk and nationally critical asset.

In a low-risk cybersecurity situation, a risk response plan may be as simple as encrypting a hard drive. However, if the cyber risk is determined to be high, then the risk response plan may be more complex and include buying additional monitoring technicians, purchasing cyber insurance, replacing virus software, and creating stronger passwords for employee computers. Regardless, the risk response plan will be constrained by the available resources.

In short, the purpose of the risk response is to evaluate, determine, and implement the best course of action to contain and manage the determined risk. A risk response plan *accepts*, *avoids*, *mitigates*, or *transfers* risk. Figure 1-25 outlines these four different types of risk response plans and applies them to our cyber example.

Risk acceptance does not mean that one allows a threat to cause damage. Rather, it means that one accepts that a certain degree of risk is unavoidable. An example of accepting risk is allowing one's email system to permit any user to send an email. When one accepts this scenario, one accepts the ever-present risk that an email may contain malicious code that will infect a computer—and perhaps a computer network; however, email correspondence is essential for conducting business, so it makes sense for a company to accept this risk. To refer back to our New Year's Eve example, the group of friends accepts risk by riding in a car at all, and accepts even more risk by riding in a car on New Year's Eve.

Risk avoidance is perhaps the most obvious way of reducing the possibility of harm. Risk avoidance means that one evades or circumvents a threat by removing a critical asset from potential harm. However, avoiding risk does not mean eliminating risk, and risk avoidance is rarely a practical strategy for conducting business or living

3.

Risk Response	
Accept	Receive emails from unknown users.
Avoid	Stop using the company's computers.
Mitigate	Protect the server with a firewall.
Transfer	Purchase cyber insurance.

Figure 1-25: Risk response elements and examples for an online retailer.

one's life in a risk-filled world. In the New Year's Eve scenario, avoiding risk would mean staying at home and not traveling anywhere. In our cyber example, avoiding risk could mean not using computers at all to conduct company business. Of course, both of these risk-avoidance measures are highly inconvenient to people who want to celebrate a holiday or conduct business in the modern world.

Risk mitigation is a strategy to contain an imminent or current incident. In the cyber example, risk mitigation includes taking steps to manage the protection of network operations and recover damages when vulnerabilities are exposed or cyber incidents occur. An example of a company's mitigation device might be placing a firewall on a network when a threat is identified. The New Year's Eve partiers may mitigate the possibility of a potential crash by assigning a designated driver. The family can mitigate risk by installing an alarm system.

Risk transfer is a strategy that rests on the assumption that although risk can never be eliminated, it can be displaced or shifted. The DHS Risk Lexicon defines risk transfer as an "action taken to manage risk that shifts some or all of the risk to another entity, asset, system, network, or geographic area." An example of risk transfer is the purchase of insurance.

Cybersecurity insurance works the same way that automobile or home insurance does: it transfers some of the risk of operating in cyberspace. For example, cybersecurity insurance protects a company against some of the fallout in case the company suffers a data breach. Insurance may cover the fees associated with notifying customers of a breach, including consulting costs and credit and fraud monitoring services. Other cybersecurity insurance policies may also cover legal expenses. Insurance does not eliminate the risk of doing business in cyberspace, nor does it cover all of the direct and indirect consequences that may stem from a cyber emergency, but it does make cyberspace a more friendly and attractive place to do business, in spite of the risks.

Risk Monitoring

The final stage in the cyber risk management process is **risk monitoring**. Risk monitoring is an ongoing process that takes place after the response plan has been implemented. The risk monitoring stage involves developing a strategy for constantly monitoring changes in threats, vulnerabilities, and criticalities. There are three main elements in the risk monitoring phase: compliance, effectiveness, and identifying changes (see Figure 1-26).

Compliance measures how well an implemented policy has been followed. If a policy has been issued, then it is the duty of the monitoring team to guarantee that the policy is followed. For example, in the cyber-related scenario, compliance means verifying that the prescribed firewall has actually been installed. The next step is to guarantee that the firewall is working—in other words, to check and ensure its effectiveness. If it is not working, then it must be replaced, or an alternative protection mechanism must take its place. The risk monitoring process also takes note of changes to the system or the risk environment. This process of identifying changes may alter the way the risk is framed and therefore start the risk management process all over again. This step in the risk monitoring process incorporates all of the information within the risk determination and response sections.

A company may identify changes based on an intelligence report. For example, the company may learn from the U.S. government that a foreign adversary has invested additional money in its cyber warfare capabilities. This foreign adversary now represents a threat to the company. Since the threat has grown in strength, the company will have to reevaluate its risk management strategy to account for the new level of threat.

Figure 1-27 provides a breakdown of each aspect of risk monitoring with an application for our cyber example.

Chapter 1: Risk Management for Cybersecurity

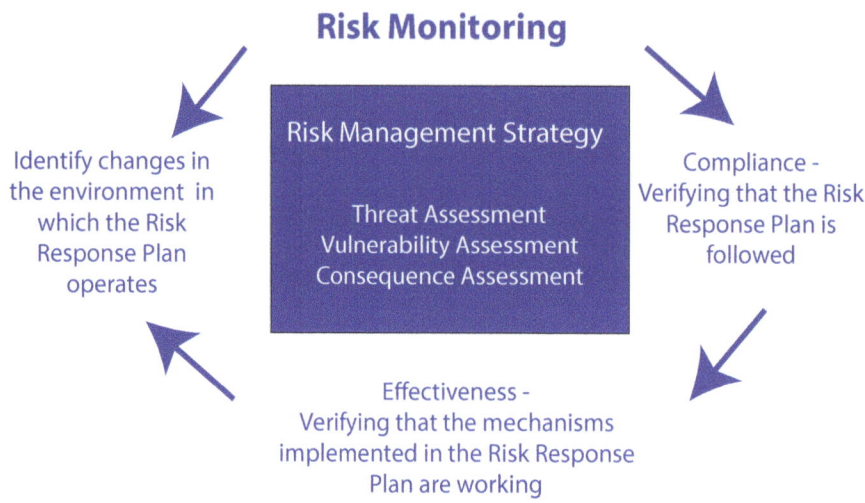

Figure 1-26: Risk monitoring cycle.[10]

Monitoring risk is an ongoing process of reevaluating and refocusing upon the threats, vulnerabilities, and potential harm to critical assets. The monitoring process should methodically identify risks, manage the response plan, and collect data and information for future assessments. The risk monitoring process will also shed light on the best allocation of resources, and whether or not a redistribution or reprioritization of resources should take place.

Conclusion

Risk management is a fundamental process safeguarding the critical assets of both individuals and industries. The formalized structure of the risk management process provides the regimented focus required for generating the most comprehensive risk assessment and therefore the most appropriate risk response.

There are multiple methods for performing the risk determination. This chapter highlights only a few ways of determining risk: event and fault trees, qualitative surveys, and statistical multivariable analysis. The rigid scientific method of calculating risk can be applied to the risk determination process no matter what method is used to quantify the risk.

In some cases, taking on risk can be good for businesses and individuals. Taking on risk may allow individuals and/or organizations to advance their positions competitively, and taking on risk may be the only way to try something new. However, this chapter focuses on how the negative repercussions of an unintended risk can cause significant harm or damage.

Because of the cyber realm's many nuances, challenges, emerging developments, and inherent complexities, it is helpful to approach the protection of cyber assets through a risk management lens. By applying the risk management process identified in this chapter to cybersecurity, individuals, companies, governments, and other enterprises will have: (1) identified their most important assets; (2) evaluated the threats to the assets, the vulnerabilities that a threat could exploit, and the consequences if these vulnerabilities were succesfully exploited; (3) determined the level of risk and the likelihood of risk occurring, using either qualitative or quantitative reasoning; and (4) generated a risk response to counter the threat.

Key Questions

4. Monitor Risk	
Compliance	Verify the implementation of a company-wide firewall.
Effectiveness	Continually test and ensure that the firewall is working.
Identify Changes	Identify new threats and vulnerabilities, critical assets, and consequences as the risk environment changes and evolves.

Figure 1-27: Risk monitoring elements.

Risk management is a circular process; it never stops. All cybersecurity professionals must approach risk management as a key aspect of their job. Risk management is not merely a compliance issue to be considered once a year. Rather, every organization's cyber risk management plan must also be refocused and adjusted constantly to protect against the latest threats in cyberspace.

Key Questions:

1. Chart the steps of the risk management process for two scenarios:
   (a) The scenario of protecting the most critical asset in your home.
   (b) The scenario of protecting the most critical asset, sensitive documents, on a government computer.

2. How might the private sector and public sector approach risk management differently? How might their approaches be the same?

3. Which of the following is NOT an element of risk framing?
   (a) Tolerance
   (b) Trade-offs
   (c) Threat assessment
   (d) Constraints

4. Which of the following is NOT an element of risk response?
   (a) Avoid
   (b) Mitigate
   (c) Manage
   (d) Transfer

5. What does the PRA model focus on?
   (a) Magnitude and severity of risk
   (b) The consequence assessment
   (c) The probability of risk occurring
   (d) Risk response

Chapter 1: Risk Management for Cybersecurity

6. Which is an effective method of determining the level and likelihood of risk?

    (a) Human reliability analysis

    (b) Statistical modeling

    (c) Event tree analysis

    (d) Survey design

    (e) None of the above

    (f) All of the above

Cyber Connections

Some individuals, companies, and organizations view risk management as a burden or a checklist merely to comply with standards and regulations. This approach fails to consider that a clear and robust risk management strategy is essential to any successful program, endeavor, business, or institution. See Chapter 3 for more on program management. See Chapter 5 for more on the legal obligations of corporations with regard to risk management.

A robust risk management strategy means a strategy in which all elements of the specific risks an organization faces, as well as the organization's most critical assets, are explicitly understood by all stakeholders. The strategy should not be a checklist of standards to be checked off in order to meet the demands of an outside regulator. Rather, the organization's risk management strategy must combat identified risks with a specific plan that will be continually monitored and reassessed.

CHAPTER 2:
Cybersecurity Law and Policy

CHAPTER OUTLINE

- **Overview of Cybersecurity Law and Policy**
- **Introduction**
- **The Genesis of Cybersecurity Law and Policy (1945-1984)**
- **The Cybersecurity Control Conflict (1984-1995)**
- **The Development of Cybersecurity Law and Policy (1995-2001)**
- **Cybersecurity and Homeland Security (2001-2008)**
- **CNCI and the Age of Cyber Warfare (2008 – Present)**
- **Recent Developments in Cybersecurity Law and Policy**
- **Conclusion**
- **Key Questions**

2 Cybersecurity Law and Policy

Chapter In Focus

- The social and governmental historical trends, as well as technological factors, that drive the creation of new federal cybersecurity laws and policies.
- The ongoing struggle between the civilian and military sectors of the federal government for control over the protection of information systems, and the evolving responsibilities granted to each of these sectors by the president and Congress.
- The historical events and technological developments that gave rise to the significant cybersecurity law and policy documents of the 20th and 21st centuries.
- The relationship between cybersecurity law and policy and the federal government's evolving strategy to protect national critical infrastructure.
- The ways in which cybersecurity laws and policies build on and respond to each other.
- The evolving role of the private sector in federal cybersecurity strategy.

Overview of Cybersecurity Law and Policy

In this chapter, we'll look at cybersecurity law and cybersecurity policy. By *law*, we mean the government-made rules governing the protection of computer systems; by *policy*, we mean the principles behind these rules, from the perspective of the United States federal government. Specifically, this chapter considers how presidents, Congresses, and federal agencies and departments have stated principles and created programs to protect the nation's critical infrastructure from cyber threats and ensure the security of the information resources maintained by the federal government.

The history of cybersecurity law and policy in the United States has been shaped by the interplay between the legislative and executive branches of the federal government. For the past half century, presidents and Congresses have disagreed over fundamental questions of cybersecurity policy, such as the question of which entities in the executive branch should be in control of which aspects of national cybersecurity. Most important, the power of protecting information networks and systems has shifted back and forth between the military and the civilian departments and agencies of the federal government. This chapter focuses on the key documents that illuminate that tug-of-war and the key governmental entities that Congress and the president have tasked with protecting the nation's computer systems.

Tension between the civilian and military sectors of the government is a function of cybersecurity's importance to national security. The military sector of government has traditionally been responsible for defending the country from threats, but the practice of cybersecurity at the federal level involves control of civilian government information systems and the personal information of U.S. citizens. The involvement of the military in the protection of civilian information systems may make privacy advocates and others uneasy. On the other hand, civilian agencies may want to protect their own systems, but they need the technology and intelligence capabilities of the military sector to keep up with increasingly sophisticated threats. From the development of

Chapter 2: Cybersecurity Law and Policy

mainframe computers to the evolution of the personal computer, from the growth of the Internet as a popular communication tool and a site of control for critical infrastructure to the emergence of cyber weapons as legitimate military threats, technological advancements have raised questions of who should control cybersecurity at the highest levels of the U.S. federal government.

In attempting to craft laws and policies to protect the nation's cyber assets, Congresses and presidents have often struggled to find solutions and compromises between the civilian and military sides of government. A compromise that completely satisfies both sectors has never been reached; only partial compromises have been achieved. In addition, since the 1990s, the private sector has emerged as yet another major player in these debates, as private-public partnerships have become one of the federal government's main strategies for protecting critical infrastructure from both cyber and physical attacks.

Cybersecurity law and policy will continue to evolve. The roles and responsibilities of government agencies will shift. New programs and initiatives will come and go. This chapter aims to outline themes and patterns so that the student of history can understand where cybersecurity law and policy may be headed in the years to come.

Introduction

The history of the federal government's cybersecurity laws and policies is a history of information resource management—the way that a large, bureaucratic organization, such as the U.S. government, manages, shares, processes, catalogs, classifies, protects, and disseminates information. Just like a private company or a family, the government must manage its information and prevent this information from being compromised. Because the government manages such vital information, ranging from the nation's nuclear launch codes to the personal identification information of each citizen, secure information resource management is especially crucial. Due to the size and scope of the federal government, creating robust risk management policies is often a complex and contentious matter, with different departments and agencies vying to control their own information assets, or oversee the assets of other departments and agencies.

For the past 50 years, Congresses and presidents have struggled with the fundamental question of whether the military or civilian spheres of government should have ultimate control over protecting federal information systems. The military sphere has the intelligence and technological capabilities to confront computer-based attacks on the government's information systems, whether the attacks are launched by lone hackers or hostile foreign nations. However, policymakers may have libertarian or privacy concerns about the idea of essentially granting the military access to civilian data, such as the personal financial records maintained by the Internal Revenue Service. Since the 1980s, Congresses and presidents have usually divided control over national information systems security between departments and agencies, with both the military and civilian spheres retaining control over particular aspects of information security.

However, in recent years, policymakers have increasingly characterized the protection of information systems as a core issue of national security. With the federal government facing a growing barrage of sophisticated cyber attacks, the military and intelligence sectors of the federal government may come to play an increasingly central role in information security. In order to understand this dynamic, it is important to understand the different roles played by the departments and agencies of both the civilian sphere and the military and intelligence sphere.

The Military, Intelligence, and Civilian Spheres of the Federal Government

Military and intelligence agencies are responsible for the activities of the U.S. armed services, either directly or indirectly, and are housed, for the most part, in the **Department of Defense (DOD)**. The DOD is responsible

Introduction

> **Cyber Fact**
>
> The **National Security Agency (NSA)** was created in 1952 to serve as the nation's cryptologic (code making and code breaking) service. In addition to signals intelligence—intercepting and translating foreign signals for counterintelligence and military uses—one of the NSA's primary missions is "information assurance." Information sssurance means preventing unauthorized persons from tampering with or compromising information systems. Therefore, a major aspect of the NSA's responsibilities within the Department of Defense is preventing foreign adversaries from gaining access to sensitive or classified national security information.

for the activities of the Army, Navy, Air Force, and Marine Corps. However, the U.S. Coast Guard is part of the Department of Homeland Security (DHS), a civilian agency. Each branch of the armed services also has its own intelligence branch. For example, the Army has the Intelligence and Security Command, while the Navy has the Office of Naval Intelligence.

In addition to each armed service's intelligence office, the Department of Defense houses the Defense Intelligence Agency (DIA) and the National Security Agency. Along with these intelligence offices, DHS, the Department of Justice, Department of State, Department of the Treasury, Department of Energy, and the Coast Guard each has its own intelligence components. Beyond these, there are additional intelligence components in the Office of the Director of National Intelligence (ODNI), established in 2005, such as the Office of the National Counterintelligence Executive (ONCIX). In total, there are 16 intelligence agencies; they are depicted in Figure 2-1.

In the landscape of information security, the NSA is a powerful actor. The NSA is a cryptological intelligence body responsible for the U.S. government's signals intelligence. The NSA is charged with intercepting and breaking encrypted foreign communications, as well as securing the communications of the United States. In addition, the NSA is also in charge of the U.S. Cyber Command, which oversees the DOD's cyber operations.

Members of the Intelligence Community (IC)
• Air Force Intelligence
• Army Intelligence
• Central Intelligence Agency
• Federal Bureau of Investigation
• Coast Guard Intelligence
• Defense Intelligence Agency
• Department of Energy
• Drug Enforcement Administration
• Department of Homeland Security
• Department of State
• Department of the Treasury
• Marine Corps Intelligence
• National Geospatial Intelligence Agency
• National Reconnaissance Office
• National Security Agency
• Naval Intelligence

Figure 2-1: Members of the intelligence community.

Chapter 2: Cybersecurity Law and Policy

Cyber Fact

The Office of Management and Budget (OMB) is the largest office within the Executive Office of the President, which houses the president's closest support staff and advisors. OMB is responsible for implementing and enforcing presidential policy across the federal government through budget development and execution; oversight of federal agencies; review of all significant federal regulations; coordination of legislative agendas with presidential policy; and communication of executive orders and presidential memoranda to agencies.[1]

The General Services Administration (GSA) was established in 1949 to improve the efficiency of the federal government's administrative work. The GSA's largest offices are the Public Buildings Service, responsible for maintaining existing and constructing new federal buildings, and the Federal Acquisition Service, responsible for procuring goods (e.g., computers) and services (e.g., information management training) for the federal government.

The National Institute of Standards and Technology (NIST), a non-regulatory agency within the U.S. Department of Commerce, was created in 1901, but known until 1988 as the National Bureau of Standards. NIST's mission is to "promote U.S. innovation and industrial competitiveness by advancing measurement science, standards, and technology in ways that enhance economic security and improve our quality of life."[2]

Thus, the military and intelligence sphere of the federal government comprises the intelligence bodies listed in Figure 2-1, along with the armed services component of the DOD.

The civilian sphere of the federal government comprises all other federal government entities that are not part of the military or intelligence communities. The civilian agencies' roles and responsibilities range from law enforcement to regulating the financial sector to directing relief efforts during natural disasters. Some agencies, such as the Central Intelligence Agency (CIA), are considered to be part of the civilian sphere even though their functions include intelligence gathering. The civilian agencies that play key roles in federal information security include the **Office of Management and Budget**, the **General Services Administration**, the National Institute of Standards and Technology, and DHS.

The Making of Law and Policy

Each federal government agency, whether military or civilian, is subject to control by both Congress and the president. Congress, pursuant to its powers under Article I of the United States Constitution, can pass a law that directs an agency to meet certain goals or create regulations in a given area. Congress also can control agencies through either its budgetary powers (by putting conditions on agency funding) or its oversight powers (by requiring agency reporting and holding oversight hearings).

The president, as head of the executive branch of the federal government, can control agencies by issuing **presidential directives**, documents that set policy or require an agency to take a certain action. The history of cybersecurity law and policy for the U.S. federal government has been shaped by congressional legislation and presidential directives. In particular, presidents have used **executive orders (EOs)** and **national security instruments** to set cybersecurity policy.[3]

Executive orders, which direct federal agencies to take specific actions, carry the full force of law. National security instruments are similar to executive orders, but concern national security; they are issued by the president after consultation with the **National Security Council (NSC)**. Each president has given his national security instruments a different name. For example, President Reagan titled them National Security Decision Directives (NSDDs), while President Clinton titled them Presidential Decision Directives (PDDs). Regardless of the name, these documents have been the major vehicles for articulating presidential cybersecurity policy and for assigning responsibility for various aspects of information security to different agencies.

Presidents and Congresses have been the major voices in the formation of cybersecurity policy at the federal level. However, other parties have played a role in policy debates. Public advocates may argue that one group of agencies should control protection of the nation's information systems, as opposed to another group of agencies. For example, privacy advocates tend to favor having civilian agencies manage national information systems, while staunch security advocates tend to favor giving the military and intelligence agencies more control. In recent decades, as policymakers have increasingly focused on protecting information systems for national critical infrastructure, from power plants to phone lines, private sector owners of this infrastructure have become a part of the policy discussion. Indeed, because the private sector controls approximately 80% of U.S. critical infrastructure,[4] the federal government's emphasis over the past 15 years has been to build and sustain private-public partnerships to defend critical infrastructure. This new emphasis marks the first time in U.S. history in which the government has explicitly included private sector companies in its national defense planning.

The Genesis of Cybersecurity Law and Policy (1945-1984)

The federal government's need to systematically manage vast amounts of information began well before the Internet. Political and demographic developments in the 1930s and 1940s drove an unprecedented expansion in the size of the federal government. With the New Deal, President Franklin Delano Roosevelt created a host of new government agencies and programs, many of which still exist today.

> **Cyber Fact**
>
> **The New Deal** is the catch-all name for a series of economic reform programs implemented between 1933-1936 under President Franklin Delano Roosevelt. The New Deal addressed the economic and social problems of the Great Depression, and created new federal laws, agencies, and programs, including Social Security.

In the mid-1940s, demographic changes drove a further expansion in the size of the federal government. Between 1940 and 1950, the U.S. population increased from 130 million to 150 million people, boosted by the return of American troops from the battlefields of World War II and the "baby boom" that followed. The expansion of the federal government meant an expansion in the amount of information that the federal government had to manage and protect. Systems were needed to handle interagency requests for information, so that various agencies could coordinate their activities. Systems were also needed to manage information flow between government agencies and the public, especially for those agencies created to provide social services, such as the office that would become the Social Security Administration.

Dealing with this vast amount of new information would be difficult. However, the federal government had a new technology at its disposal—the mainframe computer. First appearing in federal government agencies in the late 1940s, mainframe computers were enormous, cabinet-sized devices that could process immense quantities of data and perform mathematical tasks. In the 1940s and 1950s, they were so expensive that government agencies were virtually the only place in the country where they could be found. Although they were extremely

Chapter 2: Cybersecurity Law and Policy

limited in their functions compared to today's computers, mainframes made government information processing and management more efficient, and reduced labor costs.

The major drawback to mainframe computers was that the information a mainframe contained could be accessed by anyone with physical access to the computer itself. During the 1950s and 1960s, federal government agencies feared that the country's Cold War adversaries (particularly the Soviet Union, through its espionage programs) would compromise the information systems responsible for storing and processing both national security information and sensitive civilian data. The government needed to develop security and reliability standards for its computers.

At this point, policymakers faced difficult questions: Who should be in charge of developing security standards for the government's mainframes? And, most important, which department or agency should be responsible for implementing and enforcing new computer security standards across the entire federal government?

The Brooks Act of 1965

Modern cybersecurity law began with Congressman Jack Brooks. A Texas Democrat who served in the U.S. House of Representatives from 1953 until 1995, Congressman Brooks recognized two problems in the federal government's early procurement of mainframe computers. First, the mainframes that government agencies purchased during the 1940s and 1950s often malfunctioned and were extremely vulnerable to security breaches. Second, each government agency purchased computers on its own, without consulting other agencies. With no interagency coordination or federal guidelines, there was little oversight of these purchases and no government-wide information security standard.

In 1965, Brooks sponsored and Congress passed the **Automatic Data Processing Act**. It has been known as the **"Brooks Act"** ever since. The Brooks Act attempted to make computer procurement by federal agencies a more coordinated effort. It also promoted an approach to federal computer procurement that took into account innovations in secure technology.

The Brooks Act delegated responsibility for acquiring computer systems to the GSA, meaning that individual departments and agencies would no longer be purchasing or leasing computers for themselves. The only major exceptions to this new system would be computer purchases by the DOD and the CIA. The Brooks Act also gave the GSA broad responsibility for overseeing how computer equipment would be used by federal departments and agencies, including the authority to transfer equipment between agencies and set up programs to coordinate the use of equipment between multiple agencies. Finally, the Brooks Act charged the Department of Commerce with creating security standards for computer systems. After the Brooks Act, basic security standards would now automatically be included in government contracts for the purchase of mainframe computers across all federal government departments and agencies. Any computers purchased by federal agencies had to be manufactured according to standards at least as stringent as those created by the Department of Commerce.

A computer from the 1950s

The Cybersecurity Control Conflict

The Brooks Act had a profound effect on the development of computer technology and the evolution of cybersecurity law and policy. With regard to computer technology, the act spurred technological innovations in computer design throughout the 1960s and 1970s. During this period, the federal government was the major purchaser of computers. The stringent standards created by the Department of Commerce pursuant to the Brooks Act therefore defined the market and pushed computer manufacturers to innovate in the area of computer security.

Concerning policy, the Brooks Act embodied several key principles. First, by mandating the creation of security standards for federal computer procurement, it implied that the federal computer procurement process was a national security issue. Second, by giving the GSA centralized responsibility for all federal computer procurement, the Act implied that protecting federal information could not be done piecemeal, on an agency by agency basis. Third, by giving a civilian agency, the GSA, major control over national computer security, the Brooks Act implied that computer security could be handled by civilian agencies. In this regard, the Brooks Act was the first round in what would soon become a battle between the civilian and military spheres of the federal government for control of the nation's computer security.

The Cybersecurity Control Conflict (1984-1995)

In the 1980s, advances in computer technology allowed even greater amounts of information to move from paper filing cabinets to electronic databases in the departments and agencies of the federal government. The most significant innovation in computing was represented by PCs – machines much smaller than mainframes that could perform much more advanced and diverse tasks, and store more information, than their predecessors could. When PCs entered the federal government, even more potentially sensitive government information began to be stored and transferred by the government's information technology systems.

Early IBM personal computer.

In the 1980s, PCs provoked security concerns similar to those engendered by mainframes in the 1950s, but of a different order of magnitude. Policymakers still feared that Soviet spies could infiltrate government information systems and compromise both classified and "sensitive but unclassified" information. In particular, policymakers were concerned that spies could steal information about American technology, including information that could give the Soviet Union an advantage in its ongoing nuclear arms race with the United States. PCs presented fewer glaring security vulnerabilities than mainframes had, but they were still potentially insecure, and there were many more of them in the federal government than there had ever been mainframes.

National Security Decision Directive 145

In 1984, responding to both technological change (PCs) and ongoing threats (Soviet spies), President Ronald Reagan issued **National Security Decision Directive 145** ("National Policy on Telecommunications and Automated Information Systems Security," or NSDD-145). As described in this book's introduction, NSDD-145 was written by Admiral John Poindexter, then the deputy national security advisor for the NSA, on President Reagan's behalf. This directive expressed a cybersecurity vision different from that expressed in the Brooks Act of 1965.

58

Chapter 2: Cybersecurity Law and Policy

Poindexter, whom President Reagan would promote to director of the NSA in 1985, wanted the NSA to be in charge of protecting U.S. federal computer networks from foreign espionage. Like Congressman Brooks, Poindexter recognized the need for a coordinated approach to cybersecurity across the federal government. However, unlike Brooks and the system put in the place by the Brooks Act, Poindexter did not believe that a civilian agency like the GSA should play a central role in protecting government information from external threats like Soviet espionage. Poindexter believed that this power would be better assigned to military and intelligence agencies.

Admiral John Poindexter

Poindexter wrote NSDD-145 in a world that had changed since the passage of the Brooks Act in 1965. The widespread use of PCs in both the federal government and the private sector meant that national cybersecurity policy was more crucial than ever before. Poindexter recognized the security challenges inherent in these new information systems. PCs were "highly susceptible to interception, unauthorized electronic access, and related forms of technical exploitation," he wrote. Poindexter believed that the vulnerability of classified and "sensitive but unclassified" information-processing systems, combined with the government and public's reliance on these systems to communicate and store sensitive information, made these computer systems an urgent matter of national security. Only a sophisticated military agency could be trusted to protect them. Thus, NSDD-145 gave the NSA full responsibility for developing and implementing standards and guidelines to protect classified and "sensitive but unclassified" information. The GSA was stripped of the oversight power it had been delegated by the Brooks Act, and the military and intelligence sectors seized control of federal information systems.

NSDD-145 was immediately controversial. Poindexter's document never clearly defined the term "sensitive, but unclassified, government or government-derived information"—the type of information that the NSA would be called on to protect. Many citizen groups raised concerns about the military having too much control over, and access to, the personal information of civilians. Experts called on the Reagan administration to clearly

Cyber Fact

Defining the Scope of "Sensitive But Unclassified" Information

Policymakers have struggled with precisely defining what types of unclassified information should be awarded special protections because of their "sensitive" nature. Creating a definition is of interest to policymakers because limiting access to information may be costly, may impede the efficient operation of the government, and may restrict the public from accessing information they would otherwise have a right to see. The Computer Security Act of 1987 defined "sensitive" information as "any information, the loss, misuse, or unauthorized access to or modification of which could adversely affect the national interest or the conduct of Federal programs, or the privacy to which individuals are entitled...but which has not been specifically authorized under criteria established by an executive order or an act of Congress to be kept secret in the interest of national defense or foreign policy." Other statutes, like the Freedom of Information Act (FOIA) have also provided broad definitions for "sensitive but unclassified" information. However, despite guidance from entities like NIST, there is no uniform standard across the federal government for designating information as "sensitive." For example, agencies have applied over 50 different "protective markings" (e.g., "Sensitive But Unclassified," "Limited Official Use," or "For Official Use Only") to restrict access to certain information.

define what information was covered by NSDD-145. Furthermore, in 1984, many civilians and members of Congress did not agree with the NSA's identification of federal computer security as a national security issue. Even those who did agree that federal computer security was an issue of national concern did not agree with NSDD-145's decision to grant vast oversight powers to the NSA. The predominant concern among critics of NSDD-145, however, was that it conflicted with the responsibilities of civilian agencies—the GSA, the Department of Commerce, and the OMB—that had been established by the Brooks Act.

A majority of Congress was opposed to the new power structure that NSDD-145 put into place. Many in Congress and across the federal government feared that President Reagan, Admiral Poindexter, and the NSA were seeking not simply to protect classified information and other sensitive information concerning national security, but also to control access to information and information systems housed in civilian agencies.

The Computer Security Act of 1987

As a clear response and rebuke to Poindexter, Congress superseded NSDD-145 with the **Computer Security Act (CSA) of 1987**. The CSA gave power to NIST, an agency within the Department of Commerce, to create minimum acceptable information security practices for all federal departments and agencies. The NSA retained responsibility for setting standards for classified computer systems, but in all other computer security matters, it would be limited to providing technical assistance to NIST. The CSA, then, reestablished the balance of power between the civilian and military sectors of government that had been originally created by the Brooks Act and subsequently rejected by NSDD-145. A civilian agency once again would play the lead role in overseeing computer security for the federal government, at least when it came to unclassified systems.

Many legislators, however, wanted to split the difference between Poindexter's view of cybersecurity and the repudiation of this view represented by the CSA. In 1988, Congress passed **the Warner Amendment to the Brooks Act**, which effectively gave the NSA a limited sphere of control over specific types of "sensitive-but-unclassified information technology" (SBU IT), and allowed these systems to be treated as "classified technology." The Warner Amendment also gave the NSA some degree of control (particularly procurement control) over IT that is critical to military or intelligence missions—for example, cryptographic (code breaking) equipment, IT equipment related to national security, equipment related to the direct command and control of military forces, and equipment that is an integral part of a weapon or weapon system. Subsequent debates in Congress led to the passage of new laws that explicitly excluded civilian agencies from creating and overseeing standards for these types of computer systems.

Thus, the Warner Amendment, along with subsequent laws, restored some important powers to the military and intelligence sectors that the CSA had taken away. The restoration of these powers also foreshadowed the coming age of cyber warfare, in which computer systems would play a key role in military activities.

After the back-and-forth between Congress and the military and intelligence sectors over the control of computer security for the federal government, cybersecurity law and policy remained fairly stable until the mid-1990s. However, a series of developments—the growth of the economy and the size of government, the phenomenal growth of the Internet as a popular communication and business tool, and a series of terrorist attacks on U.S. soil—forced policymakers to take a fresh look at the central issues of cybersecurity law and policy.

The Development of Cybersecurity Law and Policy (1995-2001)

The 1990s in the United States were years of economic prosperity and rapid technological advancement. As the economy grew, tax dollars poured into Washington, D.C., and the information technology budgets of federal

Chapter 2: Cybersecurity Law and Policy

agencies ballooned. During the 1990s, because of its massive size, the federal government became the single largest producer, collector, consumer, and disseminator of information in the entire country.

Managing this quantity of information involved planning and budgeting on a massive scale. Few agencies had the resources or manpower to handle this task, so Congress turned to the **Executive Office of the President (EOP)**. Within the EOP, Congress singled out the OMB as the control center for the nation's information security programs in two monumental pieces of legislation—the Paperwork Reduction Act and the Clinger-Cohen Act.

The Paperwork Reduction Act

During the late 1970s, Congress had become increasingly concerned that the absence of a coordinated information strategy for the federal government was placing an information management burden on the government and a paperwork burden on entities interacting with the government. A coordinated federal information resources management strategy would reduce the collection of unnecessary or duplicative information. Thus, the primary goal of the **Paperwork Reduction Act (PRA) of 1980** was to improve the "productivity, efficiency, and effectiveness of Government programs" through the creation of government-wide information resources management policies that would minimize information-related costs. To this end, the PRA charged OMB with overseeing the improvement of information management systems across the federal government.

The PRA created the **Office of Information and Regulatory Affairs (OIRA)** within OMB to take the lead on administering the act's provisions. Through the OMB, OIRA would be responsible for developing and overseeing the implementation of government-wide information resource management policies, principles, standards, and guidelines. For example, OMB would manage the acquisition, maintenance, and use of every federal agency's information and computer systems.

Although the focus of the PRA was reducing the amount of information the federal government collected, Congress was also concerned with keeping this information secure. The 1995 amendments to the PRA charged OMB with overseeing the development and implementation of computer security policies for each federal agency.

With the PRA and its 1995 amendments, Congress centralized control of information resources management with the Office of Management and Budget. But Congress wasn't finished overhauling the federal government's information resources management systems.

The Clinger-Cohen Act of 1996

The PRA gave OMB a centralized role in creating and implementing the federal government's information resource management policy. However, through the Brooks Act of 1965, the GSA retained a statutorily defined lead role in managing the acquisition of computer systems by most federal agencies. With the **Clinger-Cohen Act of 1996**, formerly known as the Information Technology Management Reform Act, Congress replaced the Brooks Act and stripped the GSA of its former role. After Clinger-Cohen, each federal agency became responsible for purchasing its own information technology systems, subject to OMB policies and oversight. In this way, Clinger-Cohen supported the information resource management policy of the PRA. Since the OMB was now the lead civilian agency for U.S. government information resources management, it made sense that the OMB, rather than the GSA, would take the lead in overseeing the acquisition, use, and disposal of federal government information systems.

The Clinger-Cohen Act did more than consolidate the OMB's role, however. Implementing Clinger-Cohen transformed the federal government's procurement processes by requiring the OMB, as part of the overall budgeting process, to evaluate the costs, benefits, and risks associated with major investments in information technology.

The Development of Cybersecurity Law and Policy

> **Cyber Fact**
>
> **OMB Circular A-130**
>
> OMB's guidance document **Circular A-130**, "Management of Information Resources," is a key document for understanding how agencies and departments implement requirements created by complex pieces of legislation. In Circular A-130, OMB provides guidance to the heads of executive departments and agencies on how to implement the information resource management requirements contained in legislation like the PRA and Clinger-Cohen.

In October 1996, as directed by Clinger-Cohen, the OMB released "decision criteria" to guide agency procurement that would be enforced through the budget process. OMB's **Memorandum 97-02 (M-97-02)**, "Funding Information Systems Investments," explains that agency procurement of computer systems must be guided by multiyear strategic plans and take risk management principles into account. The CIO of each agency is responsible for the strategic planning, but the OMB will not recommend new or continued funding for purchases that do not meet the decision criteria that it articulates.

CIOs within each agency were a key part of implementing the comprehensive federal information resources strategy envisioned by the PRA and Clinger-Cohen. Agency CIOs were responsible for mitigating risks associated with the purchase and use of new technologies, managing information technology spending, and ensuring compliance with OMB directions and standards. Essentially, the CIOs were asked to establish and maintain a capital planning and investment control process, similar to that of a for-profit business enterprise. The OMB would have oversight responsibilities, including participating in the investment review process for information systems, monitoring and evaluating the performance of those information systems on the basis of applicable performance measures, and, as necessary, advising the agency director to modify or terminate those systems. However, the OMB's ultimate enforcement power lay in its ability to dictate budgets for the civilian departments and agencies.

The PRA and Clinger-Cohen responded to challenges presented by the growth of the federal government and the resulting increase in the amount of information managed by the federal government. These pieces of legislation, and the executive documents implementing them, gave the OMB within the EOP, a centralized role in creating standards for the acquisition and use of information technology systems, as well as the ability to enforce these standards through the budgeting process. In other words, the OMB would not approve agency expenditures on computer technology that did not meet applicable security standards. At the same time, policymakers in the 1990s were increasingly aware that ensuring the reliability and security of the government's own computer systems was only one part of a robust national cybersecurity policy.

> **Cyber Fact**
>
> **The CIO Council**
>
> In July 1996, President Clinton's Executive Order 13011 established the **Chief Information Officers Council (CIO Council)**, the principal interagency body devoted to improving agency practices related to information resources. The council is composed of CIOs from numerous federal agencies and serves as a forum for developing recommendations on information resource management and for sharing information, experiences, and ideas among the agency CIOs.

Chapter 2: Cybersecurity Law and Policy

Cybersecurity Policy and the Response to Terrorism

The U.S. government's modern homeland security agenda emerged in response to two terrorist attacks launched on U.S. soil during the presidency of Bill Clinton. On February 26, 1993, foreign terrorists detonated a truck bomb under the World Trade Center's North Tower in New York City. The attack was intended to collapse the North Tower into the South Tower, bringing down both towers in the process. This large-scale plan failed, but six people were killed and over 1,000 people were injured in the attack.

Two years later, on April 19, 1995, Timothy McVeigh, with planning assistance from Terry Nichols, detonated a truckful of powerful explosives in front of the Alfred P. Murrah Federal Building in Oklahoma City, Oklahoma. The blast killed 168 people, including more than a dozen children in the building's day care center. At the time, it was the most deadly and physically destructive terrorist attack ever perpetrated on American soil.

Both of these deadly attacks were committed with explosives, but they triggered a broader discussion among policymakers about the nation's susceptibility to terrorism. The same revolution in computing that expanded PC use and introduced private users to the Internet had deeply affected the United States' energy, transportation, telecommunications, and banking and finance sectors, among others. The systems that Americans depended on in their daily lives were increasingly managed by, and reliant upon, computers and cyber communications. This meant that a terrorist could wreak havoc simply by launching a cyber attack on a computer system. This reality of terrorism suggested that America needed a national security strategy to protect its critical infrastructure from both physical and cyber threats.

Following the Oklahoma City bombing, President Clinton's attorney general, Janet Reno, formed the **Critical Infrastructure Working Group (CIWG)**. The CIWG's task was to review new federal laws covering information resources management and to review laws and policies covering terrorism, law enforcement, and national security. In addition, the CIWG studied threats to the nation's critical infrastructure from the perspective of the federal government, private sector owners, and state and local partners, including first responders in emergencies. This review was groundbreaking because it explicitly recognized the need for the federal government to work with the private sector to protect national critical infrastructure.

Cyber Fact

Critical Infrastructure

Since the early 1990s, the federal government has increasingly focused its cybersecurity strategy on protecting national **critical infrastructure**, the United States' most important public and private assets. Critical infrastructure includes the transportation, communications, and energy delivery systems that allow commercial and government activities to function smoothly on a daily basis. Train networks, cell phone towers, and power plants are all examples of a nation's modern critical infrastructure.

Approximately 80 percent of the United States' critical infrastructure is owned by businesses in the private sector. However, any large-scale attack on critical infrastructure—whether with explosives or with computers—may result in enormous costs to state and local governments, the national economy, national security, and the general public. Private sector owners have a stake in protecting their own assets. Yet these owners may not have the incentive or resources to protect against threats that are unlikely, but potentially extremely destructive. For this reason, policymakers have encouraged public-private partnerships between the federal government and the private sector to protect critical infrastructure against attacks that could have a major impact on national security and the national economy.

The Development of Cybersecurity Law and Policy

Based on the CIWG's recommendation, President Clinton issued an executive order creating the **President's Commission on Critical Infrastructure Protection (PCCIP)**. This commission's report, *Critical Foundations: Protecting America's Infrastructures*, issued in October 1997, was an important document that described the cyber threat to critical infrastructure and stated the policy that would underline much of cybersecurity law and regulation for years to come.

President Bill Clinton

The PCCIP's report focused on cyber threats, "because cyber issues are new and not well understood." It explained that "threats to computer systems cover a broad spectrum that ranges from prankish hacking at the low end to organized, synchronized attacks at the high end." Whether undertaken by a prankster or a hostile foreign government, "the tools and know-how required to do harm are inexpensive, readily available, and easy to use." A computer could be used to make illegal financial transfers, introduce a virus into a program that remotely controls a vital system, or shut down email service. According to the PCCIP's report, these are "shared threats" because both the government and the private sector are vulnerable to cyber attacks. And because of the technological similarity between potential attacks on the government and on the private sector, there is a "shared responsibility" to create a "shared response, built from increased partnership between government and the owners and operators of our infrastructures."

The PCCIP's core finding, then, was that a national cybersecurity policy should be developed collaboratively between the federal government and other stakeholders on the "front line" of the cyber threat, from private sector owners of electric utilities and banks, to municipal water companies and local government emergency response agencies. The commission also expressed the view that the best way to get results would be to increase information sharing between different private sector industries and the government, have the government assist the private sector in identifying vulnerabilities, and support research and development of new technologies to prevent cyber attacks. The PCCIP's report included a host of recommendations for how the public and private sectors could collaboratively develop a National Policy for Infrastructure Protection, including creating an Office of National Infrastructure Assurance under the NSC. This office would have responsibility for overseeing coordination between federal agencies, as well as between agencies, state and local governments, and the private sector.

Presidential Decision Directive 63

Presidential Decision Directive 63 (PDD-63), a national security instrument issued by President Clinton in May 1998, incorporated many of the PCCIP's recommendations and was a landmark statement of modern U.S. critical infrastructure protection policy. PDD-63 first recognized that the U.S. military and economy had become "increasingly reliant upon certain critical infrastructures and upon cyber-based information systems." It defined critical infrastructures as "those physical and cyber-based systems essential to the minimum operations of the economy and government," including "telecommunications, energy, banking and finance, transportation, water systems, and emergency services, both governmental and private." The directive notes that "[a]s a result of advances in information technology and the necessity of improved efficiency...these infrastructures

Chapter 2: Cybersecurity Law and Policy

have become increasingly automated and interlinked...creat[ing] new vulnerabilities to equipment failure, human error, weather and other natural causes, and physical and cyber attacks."

Thus, the foundation of PDD-63 is the "shared threats-shared responsibilities" perspective outlined in the PCCIP's report—an emphasis on the development of public-private partnerships between the federal government and other stakeholders.

PDD-63 set a national goal of developing the ability to protect the nation's critical infrastructure from significant cyber attacks by 2003. To achieve this goal, the directive created several new structures within the executive branch. To develop collaborative public-private partnerships between government and private sector owners of critical infrastructure, PDD-63 designated a different agency to coordinate government and private sector activities for each critical infrastructure sector. For example, the Department of Energy was designated the lead agency to coordinate with a private sector representative from the electric power and oil and gas production companies. Each public-private partnership would work to identify vulnerabilities across the sector and help create a sector-based National Infrastructure Assurance Plan to mitigate these vulnerabilities and protect against physical and cyber attacks.

PDD-63 emphasized that, in these new partnerships, the cooperation of the private sector would be voluntary. Rather than proposing new government regulations and reporting requirements, PDD-63 favored encouraging private sector cooperation by providing economic incentives to create voluntary risk assessment programs and sharing valuable information with private sector owners, including information about the latest technologies for preventing cyber attacks.

At the same time as it outlined a system of public-private partnerships, PDD-63 also created new structures within the federal government. Among other changes, the directive created a Critical Infrastructure Coordination Group (CICG), made up of officials from various agencies and departments and chaired by a national

Cyber Fact

Preparing for Y2K

At the close of the 20th century, computer experts warned of a potential catastrophe. Older computer systems, which used only two digits to express the date (e.g., 99) instead of four (e.g., 1999), were programmed to assume that "99" meant "1999" and that "00" meant "1900." Computer experts hypothesized that vital computer systems, including those used to regulate nuclear power plants, might crash and wreak havoc on global communications and other critical infrastructure systems on the first day of the year 2000, at the moment ascending number assumptions in software suddenly became invalidated.

To oversee the effort to update the nation's computer systems and to prepare for any potential system breakdowns, President Clinton formed the President's Council on Year 2000 Conversion. National governments around the world spent over 300 billion dollars to avert a potential disaster.

On January 1, 2000, system disruptions were minimal and there were few reports of computer failures. Some experts believe that, although the government's emergency preparations for Y2K may have been excessive at the time, infrastructure protection measures implemented in anticipation of Y2K may have helped to avert or mitigate other potential emergencies. For example, after the terrorist attacks of September 11, 2001, New York City's public transit and telecommunications systems were quickly restored. Experts believe that without the critical infrastructure backup systems developed in preparation for Y2K, such a quick recovery of vital systems in the wake of a major catastrophe wouldn't have been possible. In addition, in preparing for Y2K, managers and policymakers began to fully understand the way in which cyber failures could have dramatic ramifications for physical infrastructure. This awareness influences cybersecurity law and policy to this day.

coordinator for security, infrastructure protection and counter-terrorism. This coordinator would be appointed by the president and would report to him through the assistant to the president for national security affairs. The coordinator would oversee interagency coordination, as well as the creation of the sector-based National Infrastructure Assurance Plan. The directive also created a National Infrastructure Assurance Council, to be composed of "major infrastructure providers and state and local government officials," to advise the president on improving the public-private partnerships. Moreover, PDD-63 directed each federal government department and agency to appoint a chief infrastructure assurance officer to oversee the creation of agency-specific plans for protecting agency critical infrastructure, including "cyber-based systems." The efforts of these officers would be coordinated by a Critical Infrastructure Assurance Office (CIAO) within the Department of Commerce.

Finally, PDD-63 authorized the creation of a National Infrastructure Protection Center (NIPC) and an Information Sharing and Analysis Center (ISAC). NIPC would be a "national critical infrastructure threat assessment, warning, vulnerability, and law enforcement investigation and response entity," led by security and law enforcement agencies, including the FBI, the Secret Service, the DOD, the Department of Justice, the CIA, and the intelligence agencies. The ISAC would gather information about vulnerabilities, threats, and new technology and share this information with the private sector and the NIPC, or share information from the NIPC with the private sector.

PDD-63 was the definitive statement of cybersecurity policy in the late 1990s. However, just as the attacks on the World Trade Center and the Oklahoma City bombing prompted a new focus on cyber threats, the terrorist attacks of September 11, 2001, would prompt a fundamental change in the federal government's organizational approach to national security and critical infrastructure protection.

Cybersecurity and Homeland Security (2001-2008)

On the morning of September 11, 2001, 19 members of a radical Islamist group hijacked four commercial airplanes. The hijackers drove two of the planes into the twin towers of the World Trade Center in New York City, causing both towers to collapse. A third plane was crashed into the Pentagon building in Washington, D.C. The fourth plane crashed in rural Pennsylvania after passengers fought with the hijackers. All told, these terrorist attacks claimed the lives of 2,977 people, making these attacks the most deadly ever committed on U.S. soil.

The "9/11" terrorist attacks dramatically revealed the nation's continuing vulnerability to large-scale, coordinated attacks. In response, President George W. Bush began a dramatic reorganization of the governmental structures responsible for domestic security.

Executive Order 13228

Before the attacks, dozens of departments and agencies in the federal government were collectively responsible for domestic security, with no one federal agency in charge. On October 8, 2001, less than one month after 9/11, President Bush issued **Executive Order 13228**. This EO created a new federal office and federal council, and effectively split national security issues between the civilian and the military and intelligence sectors of government.

The Office of Homeland Security (OHS) was created within the EOP to oversee and coordinate a national homeland security strategy. Under the direction of former Pennsylvania Governor Tom Ridge, OHS (which later became DHS) would be responsible for coordinating the 46 federal government departments and agencies with jurisdiction over domestic security. OHS would also be responsible for coordinating efforts to protect critical

Chapter 2: Cybersecurity Law and Policy

President George W. Bush

infrastructure with the private sector and state and local governments. The creation of OHS marked the first time a sole government office would be responsible for coordinating the executive branch's efforts to detect, prepare for, prevent, protect against, respond to, and recover from terrorist attacks.

In contrast to OHS's coordination mission, the Homeland Security Council was created to advise and assist the president on issues of domestic security. The council's core membership would include the secretary of defense, the director of the FBI, and the director of central intelligence. The structure of the Homeland Security Council was similar to that of the NSC, and many Homeland Security Council members were also members of the NSC. In this way, the creation of the Homeland Security Council ensured that the military and intelligence sectors would have a central oversight role in matters of national security, including cybersecurity.

Executive Order 13231

On October 16, 2001, President Bush issued Executive Order 13231, which specifically addressed cybersecurity policy in the post-9/11 world. This executive order demonstrated that the foundational principles of cybersecurity policy had not changed dramatically. Like PDD-63, EO 13231 recognized that an "information technology revolution has changed the way business is transacted, government operates, and national defense is conducted." Because critical infrastructure systems, including emergency preparedness systems, rely on secure information systems, EO 13231 stated that "[i]t is the policy of the United States to protect against disruption of the operation of information systems for critical infrastructure…and to ensure that any disruptions that occur are infrequent, of

Cyber Fact

When Critical Infrastructure Fails: The Northeast Blackout of 2003

On August 14, 2003, an outage of energy generation and transmission facilities triggered a catastrophic blackout throughout most of New York (including all of New York City) and large parts of Pennsylvania, Ohio, Michigan, and Ontario. Over 500 electricity-generating units failed, leaving almost 50 million people in the United States without power. It was the second-largest power outage in world history, and the most severe outage in North American history. Telephone networks (both cellular and landlines) became overloaded, and in some cases failed. Some TV and radio stations went out. Municipal water supplies lost pressure. Airports closed. Gas stations could not pump gas. Traffic lights didn't work. Transportation slowed to a halt in many places, and industries temporarily shut down across large regions of the northeastern U.S. and eastern Canada.

The outage was likely triggered by accident rather than by an attack. In most places, electricity service was restored within 24 hours. However, the incident serves as a stark reminder of the nation's vulnerability to failures of a critical infrastructure system, like the electricity delivery system.

---

minimal duration, and manageable, and cause the least damage possible." And like PDD-63, EO 13231 emphasized the importance of building voluntary public-private partnerships for the implementation of this policy.

To this end, EO 13231 created the President's Critical Infrastructure Protection Board (PCIPB), with members drawn from a wide array of executive branch departments, agencies, and offices. The PCIPB's role would include coordinating outreach and consultation with private sector and state and local government owners of critical infrastructure, with the goal of developing voluntary standards and best practices and increasing information sharing. The board would also coordinate critical infrastructure protection efforts with the recently-created Office of Homeland Security. The board would be chaired by a special advisor to the president for cyberspace security, who would report directly to the both the assistant to the president for national security affairs and the assistant to the president for homeland security, ensuring coordination between the PCIPB, the NSC, and the OHS, respectively. Demonstrating the importance of public-private partnerships, EO 13231 also created a National Infrastructure Advisory Council, with members chosen from the private sector, academia, and state and local governments, to advise the president on improving the security of information systems for critical infrastructure.

Executive Order 13231 did not dramatically change the existing roles of the federal departments and agencies in relation to cybersecurity. The OMB would continue to "develop and oversee the implementation of government-wide policies, principles, standards, and guidelines for the security of information systems that support the executive branch departments and agencies," while the secretary of defense and the director of central intelligence would still be responsible for overseeing the security of computer systems under their control. Nevertheless, because of the creation of the Homeland Security Council and its close connection to the NSC, the military and intelligence sectors would be able to play a more central advisory role in relation to cybersecurity for critical infrastructure.

The Homeland Security Act and the Department of Homeland Security

Unprecedented change in the federal government's organization around national security arrived one year after 9/11. In November 2002, Congress passed the **Homeland Security Act (HSA) of 2002**, and President Bush signed it into law. This act consolidated many government agencies, including the Federal Emergency Management Agency (FEMA) and the Secret Service, under the newly formed, civilian DHS. which would bear ultimate responsibility for national security risk management, including cyber risk management.

Chapter 2: Cybersecurity Law and Policy

The HSA transferred many existing cybersecurity programs and functions from other departments and agencies to the newly-created DHS. For example, the HSA transferred the functions, assets, and personnel of the NIPC, the CIAO, the Federal Computer Incident Response Center (FedCIRC), and the National Communications System to the new department.

Both the NIPC and the CIAO had been created by President Clinton's PDD-63. The former had been housed within the FBI and tasked with analyzing and preventing cyber attacks on critical infrastructure, while the latter had been housed within the Department of Commerce and tasked with helping to integrate the various sector-based critical infrastructure protection plans into a national plan. The FedCIRC was established in 1996 by NIST, administered by the GSA, and tasked with encouraging information sharing and coordination between federal agencies to prevent and respond to cyber attacks. The National Communications System was established by President Kennedy in 1963 within the DOD to ensure the integrity of federal government communications systems during national emergencies. After the HSA, all of these programs would be housed within DHS.

> **Cyber Fact**
>
> **The Department of Homeland Security's Cybersecurity Structure**
>
> Today, DHS's cybersecurity programs are housed within its **National Protection and Programs Directorate (NPPD)**, which is tasked with the protection the nation's physical and cyber infrastructure. Within the directorate, three offices deal directly with cybersecurity issues: the Office of Cyber and Infrastructure Analysis, the Office of Cybersecurity and Communications, and the Office of Infrastructure Protection
>
> The **Office of Cyber and Infrastructure Analysis (OCIA)** provides analysis of various threats to cyber and physical infrastructure, and of the potential consequences of disruptions to this infrastructure.
>
> The **Office of Cybersecurity and Communications (CS&C)** seeks to protect the nation's cyber and communications infrastructure. CS&C, in turn, houses five divisions: (1) the Office of Emergency Communications (OEC); (2) the National Cybersecurity and Communications Integration Center (NCCIC); (3) the Stakeholder Engagement and Cyber Infrastructure Resilience division (SECIR); (4) the Federal Network Resilience division (FNR); (5) Network Security Deployment division (NSD).
>
> Finally, the **Office of Infrastructure Protection (IP)** oversees the nation's critical infrastructure protection programs, including the programs outlined in the National Infrastructure Protection Plan, such as the public-private partnerships across critical infrastructure sectors.

Many experts saw the creation of DHS as the most significant restructuring of government since the Cold War. The reassignment of cybersecurity programs, however, fundamentally continued existing trends in cybersecurity law and policy. For example, the transfer of cybersecurity programs from various agencies and departments to the civilian DHS consolidated the civilian side of government's control over cybersecurity operations, although military and intelligence agencies maintained oversight over some classified and military-specific areas of cybersecurity. Recall that civilian departments had gained increasing control of cybersecurity since the Brooks Act gave oversight power to the GSA. In addition, DHS would continue to build public-private partnerships to protect critical infrastructure, a strategy first laid out in PDD-63.

The new department would come to play a central role in not just executing, but also formulating, cybersecurity policy. In February 2003, for example, DHS published the landmark **"National Strategy to Secure Cyberspace,"** a component of the broader "National Strategy for Homeland Security." The report outlined a framework for prioritizing and implementing cybersecurity programs, with the goal of meeting three strategic objectives: (1) preventing cyber attacks against America's critical infrastructure; (2) reducing national vulnerability to cyber attacks; and (3) minimizing damage and recovery time from cyber attacks that do occur. Underlying the entire strategy was a focus on coordinating efforts between the federal government, state and local governments, the private sector, and the public, in order to "engage and empower Americans to secure portions of cyberspace that they own, operate, control, or with which they interact." Prioritized programs included crisis management in response to attacks on critical infrastructure; technical assistance to the private sector to develop recovery plans for failures of critical information systems; coordination with other agencies in the federal government to provide warning information to local governments, private industry, and the public; and research and development to create new homeland security technologies.

Homeland Security Presidential Directive 7

DHS's central role in protecting critical infrastructure was cemented by President Bush's **Homeland Security Presidential Directive 7 (HSPD-7)** of 2003, "Critical Infrastructure Identification, Prioritization, and Protection." HSPD-7 technically superseded President Clinton's PDD-63, but it reiterated and expanded upon the infrastructure protection procedures outlined in the earlier presidential document. HSPD-7's purpose was to "establish a national policy for Federal departments and agencies to identify and prioritize United States critical infrastructure and key resources and to protect them from terrorist attacks." HSPD-7 stated that it was the policy of the United States to prevent and minimize damage from terrorist attacks on critical infrastructure. To this end, the secretary of DHS would "serve as the principal Federal official to lead, integrate, and coordinate implementation of efforts among Federal departments and agencies, State and local governments, and the private sector to protect critical infrastructure and key resources."

HSPD-7 continued a focus on sector-based partnerships between the federal government and private sector owners, as well as on partnerships between federal agencies and state and local governments.[4] However, whereas PDD-63 had given the OMB a centralized role, HSPD-7 confirmed that DHS would now be the lead agency for coordinating the nation's overall critical infrastructure protection efforts, with responsibility for collecting and disseminating threat information, assessing vulnerabilities, and developing contingency plans. Specific agencies would continue to conduct vulnerability assessments and develop risk management strategies for critical infrastructure within their control. These agencies would also continue to collaborate with private sector and local government owners of similar infrastructure. However, these agencies would now be required to report annually on their efforts to DHS.

Cyber Fact

The National Infrastructure Protection Plan

First released in 2006 and updated in 2009, the **National Infrastructure Protection Plan (NIPP)** is the Department of Homeland Security's plan for implementing the policies of HSPD-7 and coordinating programs to protect the nation's critical infrastructure.

One of the key aspects of the NIPP is the assignment of federal agencies, known as **sector-specific agencies (SSAs)**, to work with private sector and state and local government owners and operators in specific sectors to develop and coordinate infrastructure protection plans. The NIPP defines 18 critical infrastructure sectors, from agriculture and food to banking and finance, and assigns specific federal agencies and departments to work with each sector. For example, the SSA for the energy sector is the Department of Energy. DHS is itself the SSA for several important sectors, including the information technology sector and the emergency services sector. Of course, this sector-based, public-private approach to protecting critical infrastructure is an extension and refinement of the sectoral approach outlined in PDD-63.

Chapter 2: Cybersecurity Law and Policy

After HSPD-7, DHS would begin to craft cybersecurity policy in its own right. For example, HSPD-7 tasks the secretary of DHS with producing "a comprehensive, integrated National Plan for Critical Infrastructure and Key Resources Protection to outline national goals, objectives, milestones, and key initiatives." This assignment would eventually become DHS's **National Infrastructure Protection Plan (NIPP)** for protecting the nation's critical infrastructure and key resources (CIKR), or those "physical or virtual assets, systems, and networks so vital to the United States that the incapacity or destruction of such assets, systems, or networks would have a debilitating impact on security, national economic security, public health or safety, or any combination of those matters." In the NIPP, DHS sets out goals and objectives, and assigns governmental roles and responsibilities, for a national CIKR strategy.

The Federal Information Security Management Act of 2002

Following the passage of the HSA, Congress passed another landmark piece of legislation, the **Federal Information Security Management Act (FISMA)** as Title III of the E-Government Act of 2002. FISMA was prompted by the 9/11 attacks and the gaps in security procedures that the attacks revealed. But unlike Executive Orders 13228 and 13231, the HSA, and HSPD-7, FISMA focused on protecting the integrity of the federal government's own information systems, rather than on broader protection of information systems for critical infrastructure. FISMA's stated purpose was to "provide a comprehensive framework for ensuring the effectiveness of information security controls over information resources that support Federal operations and assets."

FISMA defines information security as "protecting information and information systems from unauthorized access, use, disclosure, disruption, modification, or destruction" in order to ensure the integrity, confidentiality, and availability of the information the government collects. For example, the Social Security Administration collects personal identification information for every American. Information security would mean ensuring that the government has ready access to this information, but also that the information is not corrupted, erroneously released, hacked, or seen by unauthorized personnel.

To close information security gaps, FISMA requires every federal agency to develop and implement an agency-wide information security program that includes periodic risk assessments by the agency, the implementation of policies that cost-effectively reduce information security risks to appropriate levels, security awareness training to inform agency personnel and government contractors about information security risks, and periodic testing and evaluation of information security policies. These information security programs would be risk-based, meaning that the agencies would implement "protections commensurate with the risk and magnitude of the harm resulting from the unauthorized access, use, disclosure, disruption, modification, or destruction" of information collected or used by an agency or its contractors. Under FISMA, each agency must submit its information security program to the director of the OMB for approval and must report annually to both the OMB and Congress. In addition, each agency must undergo an annual evaluation of its information security procedures by an independent auditor.

To assist the OMB, FISMA tasked NIST to develop "standards and guidelines, including minimum requirements, for information systems used or operated by an agency or by a contractor of an agency or other organization on behalf of an agency...." NIST would eventually develop a risk-based framework that was made binding for all federal agencies and departments by the secretary of commerce, pursuant to FISMA.

FISMA was a new stage in the evolution of cybersecurity legislation because it borrowed from traditionally contrasting perspectives on how the government should protect its information systems. FISMA took the perspective of Admiral Poindexter by implicitly recognizing that security gaps in federal information systems are an issue of national security, even if the information in question is not classified, or otherwise directly a part of the national security system.

At the same time, while recognizing the need for the "coordination of information security efforts throughout the civilian, national security, and law enforcement communities," FISMA consolidated the oversight role of the civilian OMB, continuing the move toward civilian control of information security begun by the Brooks Act, the CSA and the Clinger-Cohen Act. The military and intelligence sectors of the federal government did retain an important role, however. As in the Warner Amendment to the CSA, the military and intelligence sectors were essentially exempt from FISMA's requirements in that they would continue to set their own security standards and would not be subject to OMB oversight. Thus, through FISMA, the OMB was once again "crowned" as the chief agency for cybersecurity, while a niche was carved out for the military and intelligence sectors of the federal government.

CNCI and the Age of Cyber Warfare (2008-Present)

Even after the passage of major legislation to help prevent cyber attacks, the volume of cyber attacks on government and private networks continued to increase, from 4,095 attacks in 2005 to 72,065 attacks in 2008. As the technical capabilities of cyber attackers increased, it became clear that the federal government had to ramp up its cyber defense efforts.

The Comprehensive National Cybersecurity Initiative (CNCI)

In January 2008, President Bush issued **National Security Policy Directive 54 (NSPD-54)/Homeland Security Policy Directive 23 (HSPD-23)**, which shifted cyber policy once again toward the military and intelligence sectors of the federal government. NSPD-54/HSPD-23 was classified, but some details of its contents have been released. The directive launched the **Comprehensive National Cybersecurity Initiative (CNCI)**, a highly complex and ambitious multibillion-dollar program. CNCI focuses on establishing a frontline defense

President Barack Obama

Chapter 2: Cybersecurity Law and Policy

to reduce current vulnerabilities and prevent cyber intrusions into federal networks. The initiative also encompasses increasing U.S. counterintelligence efforts, protecting the supply chain for key information technologies, and increasing research and development efforts for new technologies to prevent cyber attacks.

In general, however, CNCI's defining aspect is its central embrace of military and intelligence community technologies and capabilities as a central part of reinvigorating the nation's cybersecurity efforts. Like Admiral Poindexter's NSDD-145, CNCI aimed to expand the cybersecurity roles of the military and intelligence sectors.

One example of CNCI's approach to cybersecurity is its "Initiative #3". This initiative's purpose is to "[p]ursue deployment of intrusion prevention systems" across the federal government. **Intrusion prevention systems (IPS)** automate inspection of Internet traffic entering or leaving government networks in order to allow a response to malicious software threats before government networks are harmed.

The federal government's IPS program is called **Einstein 3**.[5] This program was developed from NSA threat signature technology. Threat signature technology enables an intrusion detection system to recognize a threat by comparing an intrusion with known attack patterns, or signatures. For example, the Einstein 3 program compares a suspected attack against computer codes that the NSA has compiled by studying hackers' previous attempts to compromise military systems.[6] If the Einstein 3 system generates an alert, it may automatically send NSA the suspicious information packet for further examination.[7]

Because Einstein 3 covers all government networks, the NSA may monitor data traffic on civilian government networks.[8] Concerns about the intelligence community monitoring civilian information are, in part, what motivated congressional legislation that gave cybersecurity oversight powers to civilian agencies like the GSA and OMB. Thus, CNCI reflects a transition in the federal government's cybersecurity policy—a shift back to Admiral Poindexter's view of cybersecurity as a national security priority that military and intelligence experts should play a key role in managing.

The administration of President Barack Obama retained many of the Bush administration's cybersecurity policies, including the basic power structure established by CNCI. Nevertheless, upon entering office in January 2009, President Obama directed the assistant to the president for homeland security and counterterrorism "to

Cyber Fact

Case Study: Estonia

Despite its small size, Estonia is a country with strong ties to the Internet. It was home to the first supercomputer in the Soviet Union; the communications program Skype was invented in the capital, Tallinn; and one-quarter of all votes in national elections are now submitted via the Internet. Estonia also played an important role in drawing the attention of world leaders to the threat of foreign cyber attacks on critical infrastructure.

Following the Estonian relocation of a Soviet war monument in 2007, pro-Russian hackers supplemented rioting on the streets by attacking Estonian government, media, and banking for three weeks. The attacks cut online communications to Estonia's banks for two hours, which is significant in a country in which nearly 100% of banking is conducted online.[9]

The attack on Estonia was an important turning point in the history of cybersecurity, not because the attacks were particularly large or sophisticated, but because they offered a vivid example of how damaging a cyber attack on national critical infrastructure can be. For example, Suleyman Anil, head of cyber defense in the North Atlantic Treaty Organization's (NATO) Emerging Security Challenges Division, stated that "Estonia was the first time ... [we saw] that the cyber attack can bring down a complete national service, banking, media..."[10] The U.S. government would incorporate its knowledge of the Estonia attacks into subsequent cybersecurity policy documents involving the private sector.

lead an interagency review of ways to reform the White House organization for counter-terrorism and homeland security...." In addition, Obama ordered a 60-Day Cyberspace Policy Review to assess policies and organizational structures for cybersecurity. The review recommended appointing a cybersecurity policy official to anchor leadership in the White House, a recommendation President Obama followed in 2009 with the appointment of Howard A. Schmidt, a former Bush administration cybersecurity expert and the chief architect of CNCI, as "cybersecurity coordinator."

In 2010, President Obama partially declassified CNCI and offered some information about the program beyond general summaries of its initiatives.[11] For example, it is now publicly known that President Obama has continued the Einstein 3 program. In addition to continuing the Bush administration's defensive risk management policies for federal cybersecurity, President Obama also adopted Bush-era offensive cyber-weapons and cyber warfare programs. Until recently, large-scale cyber attacks launched by one nation against another were assumed to play only an auxiliary role in military operations. However, this perception has changed as cyber attacks have become legitimate weapons in a modern military arsenal.

CNCI and Cyber Warfare

One cyber warfare program that provides ample evidence for the importance of cyber weapons, according to the *New York Times*, is a U.S. program—begun under President Bush and continued under President Obama—code-named **"Olympic Games."** In June 2012, The *New York Times* concluded that *Olympic Games* gave birth to the **Flame** and **Stuxnet** worms that the U.S. military used to target Iran's nuclear program in 2010. The *New York Times* drew other conclusions about Flame and Stuxnet that can be found below.

The military first laid the groundwork for a cyber attack on Iran's nuclear facilities using the Flame worm. Flame took control of the central computers of Iran's nuclear facilities, instructing the computers to turn on cameras and microphones inside so that U.S intelligence analysts could observe personnel and listen to conversations. According to some reports, Flame also mapped out the computer infrastructure of the Iranian nuclear facilities to determine the best place to insert Stuxnet. The military then infected the facilities' computers with the Stuxnet worm. Stuxnet instructed electric motors within the facilities to speed up to unsustainable velocities and then slow down, causing the motors to break apart.

The Flame and Stuxnet attacks on Iran proved that a computer code alone can cause significant physical damage to a nation's industrial infrastructure. In fact, some analysts argue that the attack was more successful than a conventional military attack could have been and that it played a significant role in protecting the region from nuclear war. The *New York Times* reported that Stuxnet was part of a joint U.S.-Israeli covert operation, and that the U.S. has continued to use cyber attacks to wage a silent war on Iran's nuclear program.[12]

Recent Developments in Cybersecurity Law and Policy

Recent years have witnessed a continuing development of cybersecurity policies and programs by both the legislative and executive branches of the federal government.

Congressional Action: The Cybersecurity Act of 2012

In 2012, Congress considered several major pieces of cybersecurity legislation. Among these was the **Cybersecurity Act of 2012**, introduced by Senator Joseph Lieberman (I-CT). The Cybersecurity Act would have had two major effects on the cybersecurity landscape. First, it would have "reformed" FISMA by shifting the

Chapter 2: Cybersecurity Law and Policy

OMB's oversight role in ensuring "information security" to the DHS. Whereas, under FISMA, the OMB was responsible for approving agency information security plans and overseeing the implementation of information security policies, under the Cybersecurity Act, DHS would have played that role.

However, this shift would not have been as large as might be expected, because the OMB had already begun to surrender some of its cybersecurity responsibilities to DHS. In 2010, the OMB issued **Memorandum M-10-28**, which sought to "outlin[e] and clarif[y] the respective responsibilities and activities of [the OMB], the Cybersecurity Coordinator, and DHS, in particular with respect to the Federal Government's implementation of [FISMA]." The memo stated that the OMB would continue to be responsible for the submission of the annual FISMA report to Congress, and for budgetary and fiscal oversight of agency action, but that DHS would be responsible for overseeing agencies' cybersecurity activities, pursuant to FISMA. The FISMA "reform" provisions of the Cybersecurity Act, then, would mainly have formalized the existing trend towards consolidating power over cybersecurity programs in DHS.

The second major aspect of the Cybersecurity Act was more controversial, however. The act would have directed the president to establish a National Cybersecurity Council, chaired by the secretary of DHS, which would perform sector-by-sector risk assessment of critical infrastructure and develop cybersecurity best practices for each sector. Private-sector owners of critical infrastructure would be required to report cyber incidents to the council. In addition, the act would have created a voluntary, incentives-based program to encourage infrastructure owners to adopt designated best practices. The program would have rewarded private-sector owners with prioritized technical assistance, threat information, and potential federal procurement preference if they agreed to implement the best practices identified by the council.

This aspect of the Cybersecurity Act was controversial because it could have laid the groundwork for regulatory requirements on the private sector, and may have restricted information sharing between the private sector and the federal government. Critics of the act thus breathed a sigh of relief when it was defeated by a 52-46 Senate vote in August 2012.

Despite, its defeat in the Senate, the Cybersecurity Act made it clear that coordination between the government and private sector owners of critical infrastructure would continue to be a major part of national cybersecurity. With the legislative route stymied by the Senate's rejection of the Cybersecurity Act, the Obama administration turned to executive action in order to strengthen the cybersecurity of the nation's critical infrastructure.

Presidential Action: A New Directive on Cybersecurity

In February 2013, President Obama released **Executive Order 13636** ("Improving Critical Infrastructure Cybersecurity") and **Presidential Policy Directive 21** ("Critical Infrastructure Security and Resilience"). Together, these two documents focused on fostering increased cooperation and information-sharing between the public and private sectors, as well as streamlining the federal government's various infrastructure-protection initiatives.

Though EO 13636 and PPD-21 shared similar themes, they differed slightly in their specific recommendations. Specifically, EO 13636 centered on improving information sharing between the federal government and critical infrastructure owners; creating a framework of cybersecurity standards and minimum security requirements applicable across all critical infrastructure; and initiating a regulatory review process that would allow regulatory agencies to compare their existing cybersecurity requirements with the aforementioned framework and determine if new regulations are necessary.

Meanwhile, PPD-21 focused primarily on the federal government's broad approach to critical infrastructure protection. A key component of this approach, as articulated by PPD-21, is the need to approach infrastructure protection in an "integrated, holistic manner," by merging physical and cybersecurity efforts. In order to achieve this vision, PPD-21 identified DHS as the primary coordinating agency for national infrastructure protection, marking a clear shift in responsibility from the intelligence community to the federal civilian government.

Conclusion

The history of cybersecurity law and policy has been shaped by the battle for control over cybersecurity strategy between the military and civilian sectors of the federal government. The Brooks Act of 1965 centered control of federal information security in the GSA, a civilian agency. In 1984, President Reagan issued NSDD-145, which shifted control of federal information systems to the NSA, a military and intelligence agency. This change was short-lived, however, as Congress gave power back to the civilian sector (specifically, the OMB), in the CSA of 1987.

At the dawn of the 21st century, Presidents Bush and Obama gave significant control over the nation's cyber operations back to the military and intelligence sectors, recognizing the emergence of cyber-weapons as a significant national threat. This new focus is embodied in the CNCI.

Presently, the civilian sector, specifically DHS, is responsible for managing overall protection of critical infrastructure, while the NSA and the military maintain control over federal intrusion prevention systems and cyber weapons. It also seems likely that the military and intelligence sectors will retain their control over securing federal civilian networks and launching cyber attacks against foreign adversaries.

Against the backdrop of the military-civilian struggle, the private sector has come to play an increasing role as the federal government commits itself to public-private partnerships to protect national critical infrastructure. PDD-63 was the first major policy document to recognize cyber threats to critical infrastructure networks and the need for public-private partnerships to combat these threats. This emphasis on public-private partnership has been further reiterated by President Obama's EO 13636 and PPD-21, suggesting that the prominence of the private sector in shaping and implementing national cybersecurity policies will only continue to grow.

Understanding cybersecurity law and policy is not easy. It involves understanding not only the conflict between the civilian sector and the military and intelligence sector, but also the executive and legislative branches' patterns of assigning, then reassigning, control of federal cybersecurity leadership. As long as technology, the size and structure of the federal government, and the cyber threat landscape evolve, cybersecurity law and policy will evolve, as well. The history of cybersecurity law and policy provides strong indications, however, of what the future of cybersecurity law and policy will be.

Key Questions

1. What piece of legislation granted the General Services Administration responsibility for all government computers at the point of procurement?

    a) The Computer Security Act

    b) The Warner Amendment

    c) The Brooks Act

Chapter 2: Cybersecurity Law and Policy

    d) PDD-63

2. Who wrote NSDD-145?
    a) Bill Clinton
    b) Janet Reno
    c) Jack Brooks
    d) John Poindexter

3. In 2007, what country faced major cyber attacks?
    a) Russia
    b) Iran
    c) Estonia
    d) Lithuania

4. Einstein 3 is an intrusion prevention system based on software developed by what agency?
    a) NSA
    b) OMB
    c) NIST
    d) DHS

5. The civilian OMB was significantly empowered by what piece of cybersecurity legislation?
    a) The Clinger-Cohen Act
    b) The Brooks Act
    c) The Warner Amendment
    d) The Homeland Security Act

6. What document emphasized the importance of public-private partnerships for critical infrastructure protection?
    a) PDD-63
    b) NSDD-145
    c) CNCI
    d) a) & c)

Cybersecurity and Homeland Security

Cyber Connections

The federal government hires highly-trained risk managers to help protect its computer networks according to the laws and policies discussed in this chapter. Chapter 1 discusses the technical aspects and challenges of risk management. This chapter discussed DHS's central role in cybersecurity. Chapter 3 looks more closely at how DHS initiates and manages its cybersecurity programs based on the guidance set out in the presidential documents analyzed in this chapter. This chapter focused on cybersecurity laws and policies directly affecting the federal government. Chapter 5 focuses on rules and regulations that specifically affect the private sector. This chapter introduced the types of documents that shape cybersecurity at the federal level. Chapter 6 explains in depth how a researcher can use congressional and presidential documents to conduct original research in cybersecurity.

7. What piece of cybersecurity legislation did Congress pass after 9/11?

    a) FISMA

    b) The Brooks Act

    c) The Clinger-Cohen Act

    d) The Computer Security Act

CHAPTER 3:
Fundamentals of Management for Cybersecurity

CHAPTER OUTLINE

- **Introduction: Organizations, Missions, Managers, and Capabilities**
- **Managerial Fundamentals**
- **Managerial Challenges for Cybersecurity: Introduction and Case Study (US-CERT)**
- **The Cybersecurity Management Framework: From Day Zero to Execution**
- **Management and Acquisition**
- **Measuring Progress Against Projections: Earned Value Management (EVM)**
- **Compliance and Reporting**
- **Conclusion**
- **Key Questions**

3 Fundamentals of Management for Cybersecurity

Chapter In Focus

- Learn the key concepts of management and the role that managers play in cybersecurity operations.
- Understand the cybersecurity management framework used by the Department of Homeland Security to protect the networks and information of the United States federal civilian government.
- Understand that the goal of a cybersecurity program is to build capabilities – specific powers or abilities – in response to the needs of a broad, high-level mission.
- Understand how cybersecurity programs are developed, funded, and implemented to build specific capabilities over the long-term.
- Learn the steps that program managers in the public and private sectors use to develop a concept of operations (CONOPS) and an operating model (op model)— detailed plans of action outlining each step in the program's long-term timeline.
- Learn how managers are able to monitor and measure the performance of their projects at any given point in their execution.

Introduction: Organizations, Missions, Managers, and Capabilities

The Task of Managers: Realizing Organizational Missions Through Programs and Projects

An *organization* is a stable institution that aligns people (labor) and money (capital) in order to produce products or services. The U.S. federal government, the U.S. military, a small business, and an international corporation are all examples of organizations. A *mission* is a broad goal that senior managers want their organization to achieve. These missions are pursued by the organization's programs or projects, coordinated ventures to realize specific aspects of the organization's mission within a specific timeframe and on a specific budget. *Managers* in an organization do more than simply manage the organization's existing resources and abilities. Rather, managers create programs and systems that build new tools to address organizational problems and needs.

Within an organization, there may be several kinds of managers: senior managers (the highest-ranking managers in the organization) guide the organization and establish its long-term mission in broad terms. The task of program managers or project managers is to design and implement programs (or projects within pro-

Chapter 3: Fundamentals of Management for Cybersecurity

grams) that build and sustain capabilities – specific powers or abilities – in response to the needs of their organization's broad mission. The capability-building work of program managers and project managers will be our main focus in this chapter.

Within the massive bureaucratic organization of the U.S. federal government, the president and Congress play the role of senior managers (see Chapter 6 for more on the specific roles of the president and Congress). In a private sector company, the board of directors plays this role and delivers high-level guidance to program and project managers (see Chapter 5 for more on the work of boards of directors).

In either type of organization, senior managers first establish the need for a program by issuing a broad statement of the organization's goals. Fulfilling this high-level mission statement often requires capability-building: developing the ability to perform new tasks (e.g., "protect our networks from intruders") that advance the organization's mission.

Cybersecurity program managers in the public and private sectors face difficulties building and deploying new capabilities on time and within budget. Their jobs involve constant problem-solving and detailed planning for the long-term future. There are nearly infinite ways to turn a high-level vision into an organizational program, but program managers must choose and execute the best way to fulfill a mission given their organization's time and budget limitations.

Example 1: Building the "Warning" Capability

Let's begin our examination of how program managers build new capabilities by considering a specific capability that cybersecurity programs value: the ability to distribute timely and targeted cybersecurity warnings to a diverse group of stakeholders. U.S. presidents, Congress, and DHS all recognize the capability of DHS to "notify" or "warn" users of federal government networks of cyber threats as a fundamental aspect of U.S. cybersecurity. Indeed, the ability to effectively warn actors across the federal government is one of the major priorities identified in CNCI.

There are many difficult decisions that a cybersecurity program manager must make in the process of determining how to best fulfill the attributes of an effective warning system. Developing and implementing a warning system requires the same in-depth planning and managerial skills as any cybersecurity project. There are multiple factors that the program manager must monitor, measure, and evaluate throughout the program's lifetime, and many hurdles during the process that could undermine the project's success.

The first question that the project manager for a warning system faces will arise long before the project gets underway: what does a warning system entail? The actual process of "warning" an organization about cyber threats could take many different forms, and the best type of "warning" capability for an organization depends on the size and nature of the organization and the stakes involved. After considering these factors, a cybersecurity program manager must make choices that make optimal sense for the organization.

Cyber Fact

As previously mentioned in Chapter 2, the **Comprehensive National Cybersecurity Initiative (CNCI)** was the official presidential statement on cybersecurity policy under President George W. Bush, and remains the official policy (with critical updates) of President Barack Obama.

Introduction

> **Cyber Fact**
>
> Cybersecurity experts support the notion that developing a robust warning capability is a crucial aspect of ensuring cybersecurity in any public or private organization. Even if cybersecurity systems are able to accurately gauge vulnerabilities and predict threats, the best risk analysis may be completely futile without a reliable warning system in place. Clear warnings allow key parties to coordinate efforts in preparing for, preventing, and responding to cyber threats.

The program manager must also determine the scope of the organization's target audience for cybersecurity warnings. When a small private company's intrusion detection system picks up on an active threat to the company's computer network, program protocol could be that the company's IT staff warns only the company's senior managers. An alternative plan would be that the system automatically sends email alerts to the company's entire staff. If the risk environment in which the company operates produces threats that could endanger the privacy of customer or external user information, the program manager could build and implement an "automatic alert" warning system that warns customers, users, and other stakeholders of imminent cyber threats.

> **Cyber Fact**
>
> For the U.S. government, the concept of "warning" is much more complicated than it would be for a small business, so determining the target audience for a warning system is an extremely complex process. According to high-level direction from the GAO, adequate preparation and warning capabilities for cyber attacks against the U.S. government include: (1) developing attack and other notifications that are targeted and actionable; (2) providing notifications in a timely manner; and (3) distributing notifications using appropriate communications methods.[1]

In the U.S. federal government, the task of interpreting and taking action pursuant to high-level initiatives falls to program managers working for DHS. In the process of building the warning system mandated by CNCI, DHS has faced significant challenges in fulfilling all the attributes of a successful warning capability. For example, it is difficult for DHS to distribute both timely and accurate notifications. Ideally, DHS would send out warnings of cyber threats as early as possible to provide ample time for appropriate response actions, but DHS must also avoid disseminating incomplete or inaccurate information. Ensuring the accuracy of the notifications necessarily delays them, because the information they contain must be confirmed in a government review process. Therefore, DHS's program manager for federal cybersecurity warning systems must strike a balance by providing relevant notifications of cyber threats that are both timely and accurate.

By requiring cyber threat warnings for the federal government to be both "targeted and actionable," the GAO has prioritized the relevance of cyber threat notifications. The cybersecurity program manager charged with developing the government's "warning" capability must keep this priority in mind. The U.S. government combats cyber attacks against its computer networks every day, so the program manager for the government's warning system must determine the best method for distributing notifications without overwhelming hundreds of federal departments and agencies, incident handlers, the media, and the public at large.

Therefore, the DHS program manager charged with creating a cyber threat warning system for the federal departments and agencies must create a system that can sort warnings for different target audiences depend-

Chapter 3: Fundamentals of Management for Cybersecurity

Cyber Fact

In any organization, the need for effective surveillance and protection must be tempered by the fact that a system that sends out too many warnings may cause recipients to disregard or downplay the seriousness of the warnings. Excessive notifications will become a burden on the recipients, therefore rendering the warnings less effective.

ing on their level of relevance. Creating such a system may involve hiring experts or creating sophisticated computer programs, and could quickly become expensive. Therefore, any small misallocation of resources along the way could cause the whole program to run over budget and fail.

In the next section, we will outline managerial fundamentals necessary for planning and implementing cybersecurity programs.

Managerial Fundamentals

Managing vs. Doing

As discussed in the previous section, **managers** are employees charged with overseeing the "big picture" issues of their organization. Senior managers establish high-level organizational missions. Program managers develop programs that respond to the capability needs identified in these high-level mission statements. Program managers decide which new capabilities (abilities or powers) the organization must build to fulfill the needs of the organization's mission, and how best to build these capabilities, given time and budget constraints. The role of "manager" can take a variety of forms, but all managers are responsible for performing the same basic task: to lead teams from broad missions to measurable results, given constrained resources.

Managing vs. Doing

Managers are planners who think through complicated scenarios from start to finish. Because managerial work involves "big picture" thinking, strategizing, long-term planning, learning, coordinating staff, testing ideas, leading, directing, and measuring, it can be difficult for outsiders to understand exactly what it is that managers "do" on a daily basis. Managers, for the most part, do not perform technical work (e.g., computer programming and IT systems maintenance), but rather, lead groups of people that specialize in various technical fields to complete a coordinated goal or set of initiatives.

Therefore, cybersecurity managers are not the employees writing code or designing software; rather, they organize engineers, programmers, accountants, policy experts, and other technical specialists to work in coordination to complete one unified mission. Managing and "doing" the nuts-and-bolts tasks to fulfill a plan of action are different pursuits, but both are critical to making any project or program successful. Without the direction that managers provide, it would be extremely difficult for any public or private organization to coordinate its "do-ers" to complete a mission.

Managerial Fundamentals

Managerial Work: Translating Broad Goals Into Strategies, Plans, and Coordinated Tasks

Cyber Fact

The essence of managerial work is translating broad goals into specific tasks, in order to fulfill a mission. Fulfilling a broad, long-term mission involves building new capabilities (abilities or powers). One of the most fundamental managerial responsibilities is creating strategies and plans in order to build the capabilities needed to fulfill an organizational mission. The deep and detailed process of building a new organizational capability can take years or decades to complete.

Managers at each level of an organization are tasked with developing and implementing procedures to break down the broad goals of a mission into more specific approaches and tasks. Some organizations have a mission to be a leading technology developer, others to provide top-of-the line cybersecurity consulting. Missions are developed, guided, and advanced through the decisions of an organization's highest-level managers. No matter what specific project the organization plans to do, it is important for all managers and staff to recognize and understand the organization's mission.

Cyber Fact

McAfee, Inc. is an antivirus software and computer security company headquartered in Santa Clara, California. It markets McAfee VirusScan and related security products and services, including the IntruShield, Entercept, and Foundstone brands of anti-virus software.

Program managers break down broad missions into **strategies** and **plans**. *Strategies* refer to the approaches that managers develop with regard to a mission. A strategy is a choice that the manager makes about how best to tackle a mission need. For an anti-virus software company like McAfee, which has a mission to create the most-reliable network security software for personal computers, managers develop strategies to help the company create newer, more reliable anti-virus software. Their strategy might involve hiring new computer programmers or launch-

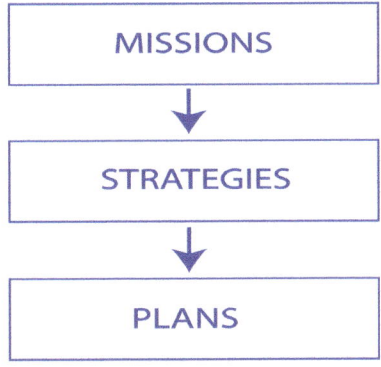

Figure 3-1: Breakdown of missions, strategies, and plans.

Chapter 3: Fundamentals of Management for Cybersecurity

ing new, experimental technology.

Plans are sets of specific tasks necessary to complete previously formulated strategies in the service of goals. Plans are the most-detailed goal breakdowns and are therefore the easiest to measure or quantify. Referring to the previous McAfee example, a plan might consist of the actual tasks necessary to develop and distribute new anti-virus software.

The formal method that a manager uses to turn broad goals and strategies into successful plans may vary from program to program and from organization to organization, but successful managers share the skill of promoting functional integration within the organization. We will discuss the concepts of function and integration in the next section.

Managing as Promoting Coordination Among Functions

Managerial plans and strategies should facilitate the cohesion of an organization's various functions. A **function** is the set of tasks or operations that an employee or department performs for an organization. "Big picture" thinking and guidance is a function of senior managers. Managing projects is a function of program and project managers. Hiring staff is a function of human-resources personnel and other managers. Accounting is a function of accounting departments. IT administration is a function of IT departments. Secretarial work is a function. Janitorial work is a function. Ideally, every employee serves a discrete function that contributes to the overall effectiveness of the organization.

Cyber Fact

Transforming "big picture" ideas into practical activities is the essential task for all managers. The degree to which managers are able to successfully break down broad goals into increasingly specific strategies and plans often indicates how successful their projects will be.

Almost every organization must perform and coordinate at least two types of functions: **line functions** and **staff functions**. Line functions are the departments, staff, and activities that contribute directly to completing the organization's broad mission. In an organization like McAfee, the software engineers or IT architects serve as line functions. These employees contribute directly to the organization's mission goals by building tools and programs. Staff functions are the departments, staff, and activities that help achieve an organization's mission by supporting the line functions. A staff function employee might be an accountant or a policy expert. These particular staff functions support the work of the line functions by securing funding for projects or providing policy guidance, and thus indirectly help the organization achieve its program goals in service of its broad mission.

The roles of staff and line functions are equally important to an organization's mission. The particular staff and line functions that an organization employs will vary depending on the organization's mission, but regardless of the organization's mission and structure, program managers must coordinate functions. Without funding, the software engineer is unable to design new technologies, and without the software engineer's skills, the accountant has no one to finance. Managers must think strategically to properly align and make efficient use of the two kinds of functions within their organization. The figure below offers examples of staff and line functions in a cybersecurity software organization like McAfee:

Managerial Fundamentals

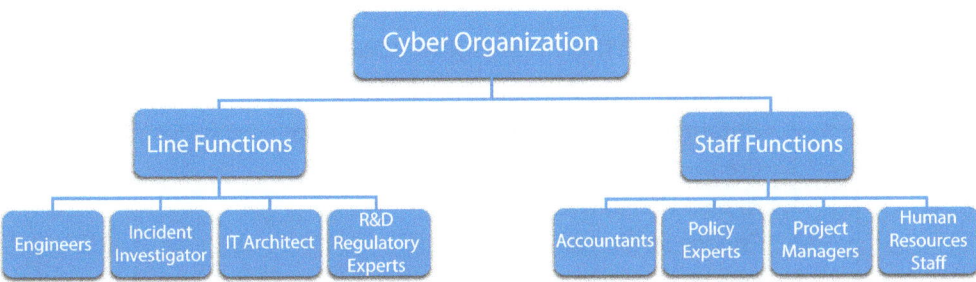

Figure 3-2: Cybersecurity line and staff functions.

Cyber Fact

Using sophisticated metric tools, managers can calculate a program's progress – in terms of time, resources, and outcomes – with mathematical precision. Later in this chapter, we will discuss one such performance measurement technique, earned value management, a requirement for all DHS cybersecurity projects.

Managing as Executing Plans Against Measurable Outcomes

It should come as no surprise that many organizations define success by concrete results and measurable outcomes. It is therefore critical that managers carry out their plans on time and within budget. Keeping programs on schedule and within budget is the fundamental way in which managers give their programs a chance to succeed.

Managers must use the resources they have as efficiently as possible and continuously monitor each step in the program's activities to ensure that the program is on track to produce its intended capabilities and outcomes. A **metric** is a standard for measuring a program's performance. In the long-term, the ability to execute detailed plans that build capabilities in the service of high-level goals is the most significant metric for judging a manager's overall performance. In order to achieve this long-term success, managers often use metrics on each day in a program's lifetime to measure the program in terms of how efficiently it is meeting its goals and using its resources.

A Manager's Decision-Making Process

A manager's primary responsibility is to make decisions. Theorists of management science have formalized the manager's decision-making process into the steps shown in Figure 3-3.

The actual steps that a manager takes in his or her decision-making process will vary when applied to real-world scenarios, but generally, the process of managerial decision making follows the steps of this sequence.

For a deeper understanding of the process of decision making at the managerial level, let's examine each step in the decision-making process, one at a time (for the purposes of the rest of this chapter, we will assume that our hypothetical manager is female).

Chapter 3: Fundamentals of Management for Cybersecurity

> **Decision-Making Process List**
> 1. Establish goals and performance measures
> 2. Obtain internal and external information
> 3. Create alternatives
> 4. Assess alternatives
> 5. Choose an alternative
> 6. Execute the plan
> 7. Assess results

Figure 3-3: Steps in the managerial decision-making process.

1. Establish Goals and Performance Measures

When a manager approaches a project for the first time, she must establish a set of goals and performance metrics by which to judge the outcome of the endeavor. Goal-setting is essential to the success of any operation, but it is a step that is often overlooked by inexperienced managers. In order for any endeavor to be successful, it must have a direction, and in order to determine whether or not the endeavor has been successful, managers must have a means of judging the project's performance against a specific target outcome. There are a number of ways for managers to set internal project goals and performance metrics, but regardless of the method, the key step is to develop a thorough list of goals and metrics that consider the project's target outcome, timeline, and available resources in an unbiased and holistic manner before the project begins.

A manager's goal-setting for a project is closely tied to identifying organizational needs, particularly needed capabilities. When a president issues a new statement on cybersecurity priorities (as President Bush did with CNCI), the secretary of DHS receives and analyzes it. The document states, in broad terms, the cybersecurity capabilities that the president wants to build. After analyzing this document, the secretary of DHS assigns a cybersecurity program manager the task of building one or more of the capabilities that the president has identified as a need – for example, the capability to "warn" in the event of cyber attacks.

The program manager assigned the task of building this capability must now define the scope of her task by thinking about such foundational questions as: (a) what does the capability to "warn" entail? (b) what kind of program will be the best program to build this capability? (c) how much money and time will we need to build this capability? After thinking broadly about these questions, the program manager will set goals based on the answers she develops.

2. Obtain Internal and External Information

After a manager establishes her project's goals, she must obtain relevant information regarding the decisions to be made before the project begins. In order to make effective decisions, managers must gather as much relevant information as possible, but avoid wasting time and mental energy on information overload.

The manager's relevant project information should come from both *internal* (from within the organization) and *external* (from outside of the organization) sources. Internal information might consist of the internal costs associated with the organization's operations, the current organizational structure, or the technological capabilities that the organization currently has in place to devote to the project.

The manager may gather external information from a range of sources. External information might include market statistics, information about the level of risk the organization faces, financial information about rival organizations, or information about users, clients, and customers. All information that informs the manager's decision-making process, whether it comes from internal or external sources, should be as unbiased and relevant to the project's goals as possible.

3. Create Alternatives

Once the manager has gathered and analyzed the relevant information, she may then begin to create a list of potential strategies and plans for building the needed capability. Although some managers may view the process of creating multiple plans as tedious, creating a comprehensive list will ensure that each plan is as thoroughly thought-out as possible.

Creating a range of alternatives also provides an opportunity for a manager to think "outside the box" instead of relying on one particular approach or budget. If the human and financial resources available to the manager change at any point in the project, it will be useful for the manager to have thought through alternative scenarios at this early stage. The alternative plans that the manager develops at this point in the process will not be as detailed as her final plan, but each alternative plan should propose a concrete set of tasks, a timeline, and a budget for completing the project.

4. Assess Alternatives

After the manager has created a strong list of viable alternative plans, the next step is to assess each of these alternatives thoroughly and without bias. The assessment of each proposed plan should point out the potential advantages and drawbacks of each alternative. This process often involves a group of managers discussing and evaluating alternatives based on the goals established during the first step of the manager's decision-making process and the high-level mission that informed those goals. This crucial turning point in the process requires the use of all of the information gathered during the decision-making process, as well as the analytical ability and judgment of highly experienced managers.

5. Choose an Alternative

After this assessment of the alternatives, the manager must use her judgment to choose the best plan, which she will then coordinate, implement, monitor, and evaluate at each step. Sometimes it is unclear to the manager if one alternative is objectively the "best," but a thorough analysis of the alternatives should help her to arrive at a sound decision. After selecting this plan, the manager must be sure to answer any remaining questions and confirm any outstanding details or steps before beginning execution of the plan.

6. Execute the Plan

The way in which the chosen plan is executed, and the results it yields, will define the manager's success. In order for a manager to be successful, she must coordinate and use all resources (time, money, employees, etc.) as efficiently as possible. To perform efficiently, the manager needs to carefully track the performance of her plan as it progresses. We will discuss project monitoring and evaluation techniques in detail later in this chapter.

7. Assess Results

The final step of the manager's decision-making process is to review and analyze the project's final results. This analysis should include the metrics and goals established in the first step of the decision-making process. Analyzing

Chapter 3: Fundamentals of Management for Cybersecurity

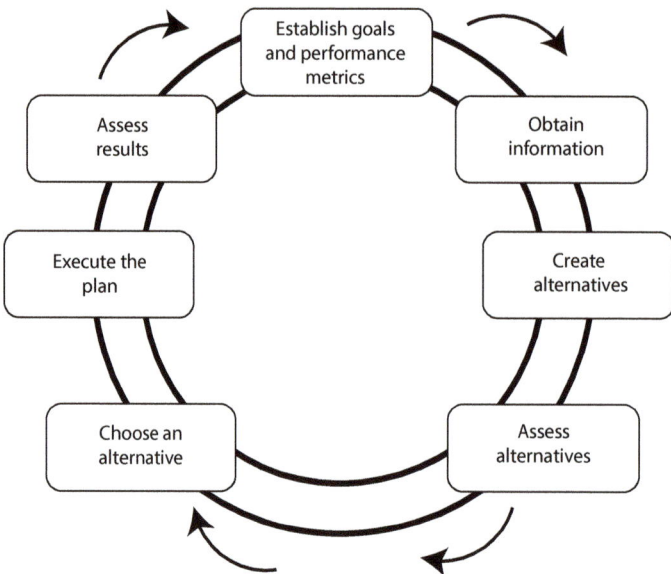

Figure 3-4: The manager's decision-making process

the results of any activity is a learning point for managers; if performed correctly, this analysis allows managers to improve their future performance.

Assessment is also the step in the manager's decision-making process that indicates the cyclical nature of management (see Figure 3-4). Managers never stop making decisions, and successful managers incorporate their analyses of successes and failures into their decision-making process for new projects.

This decision-making process for managers is a standardized guideline – not a concrete set of rules. Managers often find that they don't have the resources (usually time) to follow the decision-making process step-by-step. It is also commonplace for an organization to develop its own formal decision-making process that incorporates the essentials of the process we have outlined here. Often organizations re-arrange or combine steps to fit their particular needs.

In the next section, you will learn about the challenges managers face as they pursue strategic operational activities. These challenges will inform the model cybersecurity management framework that we will explore later in this chapter.

Managerial Challenges for Cybersecurity: Introduction and Case Study (US-CERT)

Managers inevitably face challenges in the course of implementing their plans. In this section, you will learn to identify the specific challenges that cybersecurity program managers should anticipate and address. After learning the questions, challenges and other topics to cover during cybersecurity project planning, you will better understand the impetus behind the decision-making process and possess a solid foundation for a more advanced managerial framework.

Managerial Challenges for Cybersecurity

Case Study: Managerial Failures in US-CERT

The United States federal government comprises hundreds of departments and agencies that control nationally critical cyber assets, from nuclear secrets to Social Security numbers. If the federal government's computer networks were ever compromised by a cyber attack, enormous amounts of highly sensitive information, as well as the country's national security and critical services, could be seriously endangered.

In 2008, President Bush and Congress tasked the **United States Computer Emergency Readiness Team (US-CERT)**, then a division of the now-defunct National Cyber Security Division (NCSD) within DHS, to implement a cyber analysis and warning system. As the first step in this process, US-CERT was charged with creating a **continuous monitoring system (CMS)** for the federal government's computer networks. Continuous monitoring systems detect irregular activities on a computer network, including threats and attacks. The CMS that US-CERT was charged to create was the first of four needed capabilities identified by DHS to form the backbone of the federal government's cyber analysis and warning system.

Cyber Fact

According to its official website, US-CERT "accepts, triages, and collaboratively responds to [cyber] incidents; provides technical assistance to information system operators; and disseminates timely notifications regarding current and potential security threats and vulnerabilities." US-CERT is a branch within the National Cybersecurity and Communications Integration Center (NCCIC), a division of the Office of Cybersecurity and Comunications (CS&C) within DHS's National Protection and Programs Directorate (NPPD).

Later in 2008, the GAO issued a report concluding that US-CERT had failed to implement an effective continuous monitoring system.[2] According to the GAO, the CMS that US-CERT had built: did not effectively monitor the federal government's computer networks; only monitored a limited number of agencies; and could not always generate relevant, real-time information. Moreover, US-CERT did not perform the ongoing risk assessments that would have helped it to develop an effective CMS.

The GAO concluded that the project had failed because of managerial shortcomings. More specifically, the GAO report illustrated that the managers for this US-CERT project failed to establish goals and performance metrics at the outset, failed to coordinate key activities between federal agencies and the private sector, and failed to leverage appropriate technologies. US-CERT's failed attempt to implement a continuous monitoring system is one of many examples of the integral role that managers play in effectively completing cybersecurity operations. This example also sheds light upon a common trend in public and private cybersecurity projects: more often than not, the project's problems stem from failed management.

Overcoming Challenges: Managing Internal and External Constraints

Good management practices address both external and internal environments. Managing the external environment means keeping projects in line with existing laws, regulations, and public duties. Government and private sector projects are increasingly linked through regulation. Therefore, when managers plan a cybersecurity program, they must identify the impact of government agencies, laws, and regulations on the project's operations. Other external environmental factors that may influence or challenge a cybersecurity program

Chapter 3: Fundamentals of Management for Cybersecurity

manager include current and evolving technologies, the progress of competitors in the organization's field, historical events and catastrophes, and the current state of the local and national cultures and economies – all of these factors could affect the program manager, her project, and the organization's ability to fulfill its mission.

Cybersecurity program managers must also identify internal factors that could affect or constrain their project. The primary internal factor that should guide any project is the organization's mission, which sets forth the overall purpose and philosophy of the organization. Statements from high-level managers and organizational leaders articulate the organization's goals in the service of this mission, and should be carefully studied by the program and project managers charged with actualizing these goals. Other internal factors include company policies that govern and direct internal activities, the company's organizational structure, and the resources that may or may not be available to the program's manager.

Addressing Challenges: The Operational Planning Model

The pressure of immediate and emerging issues often causes managers to lose sight of the process of carefully tracking relevant external and internal factors once a project is underway. If a new issue takes precedence due to unplanned circumstances, it is easy for a busy manager to disregard all of the other relevant factors in play. But by losing sight of any one factor, she could miss important opportunities and warning signs that could affect both the success of the project and the entire organization.

Other common problems managers face in the course of implementing a project include a lack of sufficient external and information for planning, a lack of clear thinking and thoughtful planning in generating strategy, insufficient financial control, outdated or ineffective policies and guidelines, and internal issues with staff.

In order to proactively anticipate, address, and prevent such challenges, managers should make sure to monitor the building blocks of the **operational planning model**. The operational planning model is a tool that breaks down an organizational mission into its component parts:

The "programmatic building blocks" (shown in blue) represent the foundational necessities for each program to fulfill its strategic objectives and complete key activities, goals, and initiatives. In the aggregate, the purpose of the model is to highlight the factors managers should recognize, incorporate into programs, and continuously monitor in order to create an organization that is sustainable in both the short-term and long-term. When a manager is constantly attentive to all of these areas, she maximizes her chances for success in a given project.

The "Products and Services" block helps managers determine and recall what outcomes the organization should deliver. The "Inter-/Intra-Agency Requirements" block helps managers gain insight into a diverse set of require-

Figure 3-5: The operational planning model.

ments that their organization must fulfill in its activities. The "Organizational Capital" block expresses an organization's unique strengths that a manager can leverage and build on, including the organizational culture, structure, and processes that can help the company to gain a competitive advantage.[3] The "Human Capital" block expresses the program's ability to hire, train, and retain an effective staff. The "Measurement" block represents the manager's ability to accurately monitor her project's progress and performance against an objective baseline. The "Compliance and Reporting" block establishes standards for employees working on the project to report to managers with project performance information. Lastly, the "Strategic Risk Management" block helps managers determine how to best manage risk.

All of these building blocks require constant managerial attention in order for new capabilities to be delivered on time and on budget. They are the key topics managers should focus on in the process of planning and executing projects in service of an organizational mission. In the remainder of this chapter, you will learn how managers incorporate these building blocks into their planning frameworks.

The Cybersecurity Management Framework: From Day Zero to Execution

Best Practices for Developing Frameworks for Cybersecurity Management

In this section, we will walk through the steps of the model cybersecurity management framework. A *framework* is more than a set of suggestions or guidelines – it is a codified process in which each step in the process is logically integrated with the others. The steps build on and require each other. In a successful program, the steps will add up to a meticulously planned final outcome that takes the form of a new capability.

The framework we will examine in this section is used by cybersecurity program managers in the private sector, the federal civilian government, and the U.S. military. Leading organizations across all three of these sectors share best practices (tested and successful problem-solving solutions) and learn strategies from one another.

The DHS Cybersecurity Program Management Framework

We will now turn to DHS's process and walk through the cybersecurity management framework that DHS uses to plan, execute, and evaluate its cybersecurity programs for the federal civilian government. The DHS framework can serve as a model for program management across diverse fields. The steps of the DHS model are presented in the following figure:

Cyber Fact

The **Clinger-Cohen Act of 1996** explicitly demanded that cybersecurity professionals working in the federal government learn from the best practices of cybersecurity program managers in the private sector. Specifically, the act directly linked the budgeting and execution processes for all federal government IT programs. This connection was drawn from a private sector management framework.

Chapter 3: Fundamentals of Management for Cybersecurity

> 1) MNS development
>
> 2) Capability-based planning
>
> 3) CONOPS
>
> 4) Op model
>
> 5) Execution
>
> 6) Ongoing assessment and evaluation

Figure 3-6: Steps of the DHS model.

We will now examine each step in the framework as a separate entity. The program manager begins by crafting a **mission needs statement (MNS)**, which states what the program manager is required to do by the organization's mission, and the capabilities the program must build in order to fulfill this mission. The MNS frames the program in terms of the needs expressed by Congress and the president, with input from officials within DHS.

Management for the Federal Civilian Government: Developing a Mission Needs Statement (MNS)

In this section, we will discuss the first public step in the cybersecurity program manager's decision-making process: crafting a mission needs statement in response to a high-level mandate from the president, Congress, the secretary of DHS, and other high-level leaders. The MNS is a statement a program manager writes to describe the capabilities that an organization requires, but does not yet possess, in order to fulfill its large-scale mission. The MNS identifies the problem to be solved and the resources the organization will need to solve the problem. An effective MNS identifies the problem that the organization is trying to solve, and the capabilities that the organization will need to solve this problem. The MNS is written in more-specific terms than the high-level directives that inform it, but in much-less-specific terms than the manager's final plan. It addresses the full scale of the problem and outlines the proposed project.

In order for federal programs to secure and retain funding, program managers must clearly demonstrate that their program responds to a need identified at the highest levels of national leadership. In the case of the federal civilian departments and agencies for which DHS oversees cybersecurity projects, these mission re-

Cyber Fact

The cybersecurity management framework we will discuss in this section may go by different names across and within sectors. The steps that make up the framework may also go by different names from organization to organization. For example, the planning stage in the DOD's PPBE (planning, programming, budgeting, and execution) model is analogous to the MNS stage used by DHS in its cybersecurity programs. By extension, the programming stage in the PPBE model for military programs is analogous to the capability-based planning stage in DHS's management framework.

quirements come from executive (presidential) and legislative (congressional) authorities. The president and Congress issue high-level directives in the form of presidential directives and legislation. The secretary of DHS and other high-ranking DHS officials may offer additional direction. Cybersecurity program managers respond explicitly to these high-level statements in their mission needs statements.

For DHS cybersecurity program managers, the task of responding to high-level mission statements in an MNS is rarely a straightforward process. From our previous description of the MNS process, it is easy to appreciate how, in complicated bureaucracies on the scale of the U.S. federal government, several layers of high-level leadership inform the needs and plans that a program manager sets forth in an MNS.

Cyber Fact

DHS is charged by the president and Congress with managing multi-year, multi-billion dollar cybersecurity programs. Every year, the scope and complexity of these programs grows in response to an increasingly dangerous cyber risk environment. As a result, many departments and agencies in the federal government now have their own program managers for cybersecurity. Each of these program managers must create and oversee a unique cybersecurity program to address a specific need and build new capabilities.

Informing the Mission Needs Statement for Cybersecurity: Congress and the President

A program has no basis for operations until the highest level of the federal government identifies an issue that needs to be addressed through policies and programs. The president and Congress formulate a vision for a national policy to address a need. To articulate a national priority, the president may utilize a national security instrument, an often-classified order from the president to his cabinet, ordering them to marshal resources around a policy. A national security instrument lays out the intention and goals behind the priority and establishes a decision-making process involving specific government actors. The president may also articulate a vision through non-classified documents, such as executive office memoranda and executive orders.

Congress is charged with absorbing presidential orders and formulating laws and policies that the president executes through strategies and programs. Nevertheless, the process of policymaking and execution is often messier than this formula would suggest. Congress and the president often go back and forth with policy proposals and struggle to find appropriate compromises (as we witnessed in the battles for control of the nation's computer networks in Chapter 2, and as we will discuss further in Chapter 6). The scope of presidential power expands and contracts based on its ever-changing relationship with Congress and also with the global political climate, which may confer advantages and disadvantages upon certain presidents.

How the President Informs New Federal Programs

President Franklin D. Roosevelt (who expanded federal programs and the volume of the government's information flow during the New Deal), President Harry S. Truman (who founded the NSA in a secret document) and President Ronald Reagan (who tried to confer control of telecommunications security to the NSA) all expanded the scope of presidential power during their terms in office. We discussed all three of these administrations in Chapter 2. All three of these presidents were able to succeed in their policymaking in part because of the perception that they were presiding over moments of national crisis. This perception of national crises may

Chapter 3: Fundamentals of Management for Cybersecurity

make the national security policymaking process run more smoothly than usual because of the perceived need for expedient defense. At these moments, Congress and the president are more likely to agree that new national security measures are a national priority, and to speedily enact said measures.

In more recent history, President George W. Bush played a role in expanding the scope of presidential power to combat physical and cyber attacks against the U.S. After the terrorist attacks of September 11, 2001, Congress issued a series of new laws that empowered the president to take new measures to protect the nation from attacks of all kinds. Among these laws were the HSA and FISMA, both enacted in 2002. The HSA directed the federal government to "[p]revent terrorist attacks within the United States," "[r]educe the vulnerability of the United States to terrorism," and "[m]inimize the damage, and assist in the recovery, from terrorist attacks that do occur within the United States." The language in the HSA did not specifically lay out guidelines or standards for implementation, but rather, stated broad national goals.

The HSA, as discussed in Chapter 2, also created DHS, which assumed many national security responsibilities and services previously assigned to other departments. From its inception, DHS was charged with leading the defense of federal civilian computer networks against cyber threats and coordinating the nation's response to cyber threats and vulnerabilities. Thus, the HSA marked another major turning point in the history of the federal government – it expanded the scope of the federal government on an historic scale.

FISMA mandated the creation of information security programs across all of the federal civilian governments and agencies. In addition, FISMA granted the OMB responsibility for overseeing the budgeting process for these programs. As you will see throughout this chapter, OMB memoranda play an influential role in establishing the parameters within which federal cybersecurity programs are run.

In 2003, just one year after the HSA passed, President Bush signed HSPD-7, which established a national policy for federal departments and agencies to identify and prioritize critical infrastructure protection. From 2004 to 2008, the vast majority of high-level mission requirements flowed from presidential directives like this one.

Cyber Fact

Presidential directives, including both executive orders and national security instruments, express a broad vision of the president's priorities, guide policymaking, and task government agencies to create programs to fulfill high-level missions.

In 2008, President Bush signed NSPD-54/HSPD-23, which formalized CNCI. CNCI, in turn, launched the National Cyber Security Center within DHS, and explicitly stated twelve other cybersecurity-related mission objectives (e.g., "expand cyber education" and "increase the security of classified networks").

Upon assuming office in 2009, President Barack Obama led a Cyberspace Policy Review to expand on President Bush's previous findings. President Obama's twelve priorities to secure cyberspace are consistent with President Bush's, but reflect a greater degree of specificity based on six years of accumulated federal government experience with cybersecurity. Each of the twelve priorities identified and outlined by President Obama became a program area within DHS; as a result, DHS's cybersecurity organizational structure has grown considerably in complexity since 2009.

The priorities identified by the president and Congress are incorporated into the planning of federal cybersecurity programs. This is the step in which the senior leaders within DHS issue their guidance statements.

The Cybersecurity Management Framework

Since 2003, this step has been standardized for all cybersecurity programs for the federal government. DHS program management documents now form the basis for all federal cybersecurity programs.

How DHS Informs Mission Needs Statements for Federal Government Cybersecurity Programs

After President Bush assigned DHS oversight responsibility for critical infrastructure protection in 2003, the Department expanded and refined its role by publishing its own documents pursuant to the HSA and President Bush's presidential directives.

These strategic documents included: the Quadrennial Homeland Security Review (QHSR) report to Congress, which specified key mission priorities, outlined goals for each of these mission areas, and laid out next steps; the Bottom-Up Review (BUR) report, which aligned DHS's programmatic activities and organizational structure with the mission sets and goals identified in the QHSR; and the Blueprint for a Secure Cyber Future, which builds on the QHSR to provide a clear guide for the federal government, the private sector, and international partners to work together towards building the nation's cybersecurity capabilities. DHS's department-specific documents assigned more-precise priorities and responsibilities to DHS agencies and offices, some of which we will discuss in the next section.

The same limited resources (people, money, skills, technologies, time) that restrict any organization's capabilities restrict DHS from addressing all mission areas equally. Still, skilled program managers within DHS can build well-planned cybersecurity programs that yield concrete results.

The Structure of DHS

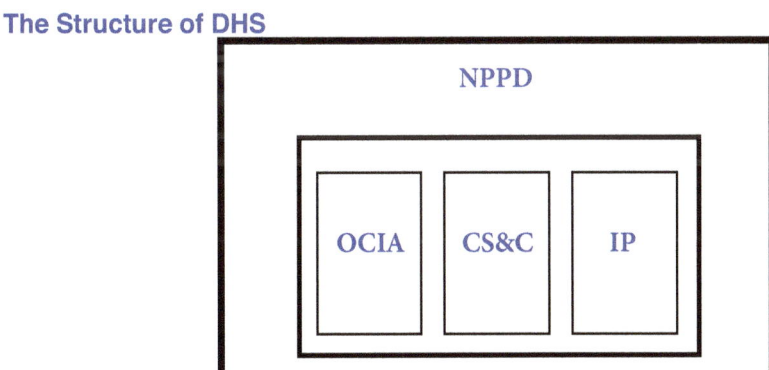

Figure 3-7: DHS's cybersecurity organizational structure.

DHS is a large bureaucracy comprised of many agencies and offices. It may be helpful to think of DHS as a series of boxes within other boxes. Cybersecurity programs within DHS are developed and implemented in the **National Protection and Programs Directorate (NPPD)**, which contains three offices that address cybersecurity issues: the **Office of Cyber and Infrastructure Analysis (OCIA)**, the **Office of Cybersecurity and Communications (CS&C)**, and the **Office of Infrastructure Protection (IP)**. Figure 3-7 illustrates the relationships between these offices.

We have already discussed the ways in which high-level federal government actors inform federal cybersecurity programs. As DHS departments develop their own statements and priorities, these documents become increasingly detailed and department-specific. Therefore, a program manager for any cybersecurity program within the federal government must write an MNS for any new program, based on the high-level input of:

Chapter 3: Fundamentals of Management for Cybersecurity

- Congress
- The president
- The secretary of DHS
- The head of NPPD
- The heads of OCIA, CS&C, and IP
- The heads of of the various branches within OCIA, CS&C and IP

The MNS and High-Level Requirements

As we discussed, cybersecurity program managers for the federal civilian government must research and analyze the high-level mission requirements from leadership and identify the capabilities necessary to fulfill each requirement. They must then synthesize these high-level requirements with the more specific program requirements articulated by leaders of their specific departments. Then, program managers must produce an MNS for their specific program.

Still, the most important information that goes into any program manager's MNS must flow from high-level mission requirements that are set forth by the executive and legislative branch authorities. Briefly defined, **high-level requirements (HLRs)**:

1. Define activities that an organization is authorized to perform
2. Define activities that an organization is required to perform
3. Create an organization or entity
4. Allocate resources to perform activities

In addition to addressing specific needs of the organization's mission, an MNS must justify the creation of new programs and projects in terms of relevant HLRs. HLRs thus form the basis for any given program's programmatic requirements. We will examine how HLRs inform the structure of a program's MNS in the next section.

The Structure of a Mission Needs Statement: Responding Creatively to Need and Vision

After Congress, the president, the secretary of DHS, and the heads of the relevant DHS offices issue their priorities for cybersecurity programs, it is the responsibility of each program's manager to break down these broad top-level directions into actionable plans that will address these priorities and build new and sustainable capabilities over the long-term.

As we discussed earlier, the process of writing the MNS forces the program manager to answer the question of what her organization needs, based on the relevant high-level statements. Surprisingly, this question may be extremely difficult for the program manager to answer at first. When it is time for the program manager to write an MNS for a new program, she has received many different high-level visions, often with subtle and important differences, and she must synthesize and layer the different kinds of needs that have been identified by Congress, the president, the secretary of DHS, and each of the relevant departments within DHS. Thus, the program manager must bring together various statements of priority with different levels of specificity into the program's MNS, and produce a document that addresses them all.

The Cybersecurity Management Framework

> **Cyber Fact**
>
> The program manager's MNS must address the high-level requirements that help to define the activities and scope of the program.

The structure of a cybersecurity program MNS within the DHS framework is:

1. Identify organizational mission and needed capabilities
2. Cite mission authority
3. Identify courses of action to build needed capabilities
4. Establish program lifetime
5. Justify organizational investment

MNS Part 1: Identify organizational mission and needed capabilities ("What do we need to be able to do in order to fulfill our mission?")

Recall that risk management is the practice at the heart of all cybersecurity operations. To begin the MNS, the cybersecurity program manager must first identify the required mission in functional terms and discuss the threats, threat assessment, and threat environment that drive the mission. For a detailed description of the cyber risk management process, see Chapter 1.

Next, the program manager must describe the capabilities the program requires to accomplish the mission, and state whether or not those capabilities currently exist. The MNS thus identifies the **capability gaps** – areas in which specific powers or abilities are needed, but currently lacking. The section on capability gaps should offer an explanation for why existing capabilities and resources are not sufficient to execute the program's mission. The needed capabilities should not be stated in terms of given solutions, such as assets, equipment or staff, but rather, must express the actual capability, power, or ability that the program needs to combat the threat.

For example, a program manager for federal cybersecurity might focus her MNS exclusively on the lack of a capability to "monitor." Rather than propose the monitoring technology or new IT staff that they will need, the MNS simply defines what it means for the federal government to have the capability to "monitor" its computer networks. If the program manager is writing the MNS in response to a change in course or overall mission, the MNS should also discuss how current and required capabilities are changing.

The process of identifying capability gaps links to the program justification section of the MNS. The MNS's justification for federal investment in the program must connect directly with the organization's defined mission statement and provide a clear argument stating how investment in this program will support core mission functions.

MNS Part 2: Cite mission authority ("How are we authorized to do this?")

The MNS should cite the statutory or regulatory authorities for the organization's mission, such as the legislation enacted that granted the program the power to conduct its program activities. See Chapter 6 for more details on how the president and Congress collaborate on the formation of new legislation and regulations. Cit-

Chapter 3: Fundamentals of Management for Cybersecurity

ing mission authority is part of the way in which an MNS fulfills the HLRs we discussed earlier. Specifically, this part of the MNS cites activities that the proposed program is authorized, and sometimes required, to perform, pursuant to presidential and congressional statements and laws.

For example, cybersecurity programs within DHS could argue that their authorities are the HSA and FISMA, because both pieces of legislation provided guidance and direction on a mission need to improve federal cybersecurity operations. An MNS could also derive its authority from a presidential policy statement, an executive order, or a national security instrument. A program manager should take her program's proposed activities into account and cite specific examples from high-level statements, documents, and publications that express the need for her planned program activities.

MNS Part 3: Identify courses of action to build needed capabilities ("How will we build capabilities to fulfill our mission?")

An MNS must identify several specific courses of action that could be taken to implement the program and address the identified need by building the identified capabilities.

MNS Part 4: Establish program lifetime ("How long will it take to build these capabilities?")

In addition to synthesizing high-level directions into a statement of the program's needs and proposing actions to produce new capabilities to fulfill these needs, the MNS must also define a program's lifetime (usually 5-10 years) and establish the program's precise goals for outcomes at each step in this lifetime.

This step in the framework is critical for several reasons. First, establishing the program's lifetime is necessary for determining its budget. A program that takes 10 years to build a capability may be budgeted very differently in comparison to a program that takes 5 years to build the same capability. Second, in an effective program, each step in the life cycle must be planned so that it builds logically on the work done in the previous step. Thus, each year of the program should build on the capabilities established in the previous year.

Establishing the program's life cycle at this point will help to determine important deadlines and milestones in the program at each step in its execution. These deadlines will be important when the program manager is using sophisticated measurement techniques to assess the program's relative success at any given point in its lifetime. We will examine one such assessment techniques, earned value management, later in this chapter.

MNS Part 5: Justify organizational investment in the program ("Why should we pursue this program rather than another?")

To complete the MNS, the program manager needs to justify the organization's investment of time and resources (people, funds, technologies) in the program. If specific investments are required, the program manager must discuss how these specific investments will improve the overall efficiency and effectiveness of the program's work in fulfillment of the organization's mission. For each capability gap the program manager presents, the MNS should clearly state parallel acquisition goals and objectives that will address the stated capability gap.

Lastly, the MNS should discuss the impact on the organization in the case that the program is not approved, including impacts on current and planned missions and capabilities.

The Cybersecurity Management Framework

Management for the Federal Civilian Government: Capability-Based Planning

Capability-based planning is the process of defining a program's activities and charting out a program's lifetime, based on the capability that the program has been charged to build. Capability-based planning is the step in the DHS cybersecurity program management process that informs the MNS, and it continues long after the MNS is written. In order to plan a program based on needed capability, managers must first define –in highly specific terms and through specific programmatic activities – the capabilities that their program must create.

HLRs as Capabilities

The twelve most common HLRs for the federal cybersecurity programs administered by DHS are often expressed in terms of the capabilities to: monitor, protect, detect, alert, warn, analyze, mitigate, respond, assist, coordinate, collaborate, and defend.

As we discussed in the previous section, for each capability need identified by the HLRs, multiple documents will explain the justification, guidance, and general direction for developing the capability. For DHS cybersecurity programs, landmark legislation (e.g., the HSA) and presidential strategy documents (e.g., the National Strategy to Secure Cyberspace of 2003) identify multiple capabilities that must be developed through federal programs.

Program managers for federal cybersecurity must carefully consider the twelve capabilities identified in the above list and determine which specific capabilities their program is charged with building. Different cybersecurity programs within DHS may be responsible for developing and building very different capabilities. Program managers must define the specific meaning and depth of each capability with regard to the parameters and mission of their specific DHS program.

By conducting a periodic gap analysis between the HLRs (desired capabilities) and existing capabilities, a program manager for a DHS cybersecurity program can determine the remaining capabilities, or capability gaps, which in turn become programmatic requirements. Programmatic requirements are the specific capabilities that a specific cybersecurity program within DHS is charged with creating. Programmatic requirements may stem from the president, Congress, the secretary of DHS, or the head of a DHS department.

The program managers for each DHS program compile these programmatic requirements into the MNS that they present to the secretary of DHS. Capability-based planning informs the MNS and continues after the MNS, when the program managers must meticulously plan and execute their programs, with the goal of building and sustaining capabilities. Therefore, the greater the level of specificity and depth that has gone into capability-based planning, the better position a program manager will be in to move on to the next step of the program, which is to develop a concept of operations and operating model for the program.

VIDEO

Watch 'High Level Requirements as Capabilities' at
http://vimeo.com/channels/cybersecurityfoundations

Chapter 3: Fundamentals of Management for Cybersecurity

Management for the Federal Civilian Government: Building a Concept of Operations (CONOPS) and an Operating Model (Op Model)

After a program manager decides which capabilities her program must build in order to address the need identified by the legislative and executive branches, with input from the secretary of DHS and the heads of relevant DHS departments, she must develop an operational plan of action for building those capabilities.

The program manager incorporates these needed capabilities, as well as her perception of organizational limitations to building them, into the next document she must craft before implementing the program: the **concept of operations (CONOPS)**. The CONOPS is a document that describes how a specific capability is to be built and supported within the context of a program's lifetime. The goal of the CONOPS is to realistically depict how the program's proposed solution would work in a real-world scenario, and to outline the systems and functions that the program must build and sustain in order to achieve its objectives and build its target capabilities.

Though CONOPS documents may differ from program to program, they generally include the following topics:

1. goals and objectives of the program;
2. strategies, policies and constraints affecting the program;
3. participants and stakeholders;
4. roles and responsibilities; and
5. specific operational processes for initiating, developing, and maintaining the program over the course of its planned lifetime.

Thus, the CONOPS communicates the overall quantitative and qualitative requirements of the program, and plans out the program's life cycle in highly specific steps. In the process of developing the CONOPS, the program manager should carefully consider the full range of requirements to fulfill the program's mission and describe these factors in the document.

Because the CONOPS is developed before funding has been secured, the program manager must also establish several alternative approaches to building target capabilities, based on different potential funding levels for the program. In the HLRs, capability needs are posed in such broad terms that there may be hundreds of possible approaches, but the program manager must identify the best approaches, taking time and budget limitations into account. The CONOPS is her proposal of the best approach, and her bid to receive a certain amount of funding for that approach.

A crucial aspect of this stage is the program manager's creativity and ability to think innovatively about how high-level vision is turned into concrete action, and how this action will unfold over the program's long-term lifetime. Also critical to this step is the program manager's awareness that her ideal plan for building needed capabilities may not be affordable after she receives her final program budget. Therefore, the program manager must devise several appropriate long-term strategies to achieve the capabilities identified during capability-based planning. Each strategy must present a plan to achieve the same objectives with different budgets.

The Cybersecurity Management Framework

> **VIDEO**
>
> Watch 'CONOPS' at http://vimeo.com/channels/cybersecurityfoundations

CONOPS Case Study: "Manage"

Let's examine an example of CONOPS development. Consider President Obama's first priority from his Twelve Priorities to Secure Cyberspace: "Manage the federal government's connection to the Internet with Trusted Internet Connections". The TIC initiative is a project mandated by OMB Memorandum M-08-05 from 2007. As discussed in Chapter 1, the goal of this initiative is to reduce the number of access points to the computer networks of the federal government, and to maximize the security of these access points.

Because this goal entails raising the level of cybersecurity across 500 different civilian federal departments and agencies, devising an appropriate, comprehensive CONOPS to achieve this goal is a daunting task. The program manager within DHS responsible for building this capability through a cybersecurity program must decide the best course of action to address this need.

Inevitably, challenges will arise in the planning of a program to address the capability gap identified by the president. In addition to budget limitations and time constraints, DHS may not possess the authority to build this capability in a top-down fashion. Indeed, DHS does not have the authority to force other federal government departments and agencies to employ TICs. The program manager must consider all of these different types of limitations in creating her CONOPS.

The program manager must also consider a diverse selection of approaches for actualizing President Obama's priority. One approach could be a plan in which DHS begins, in Year 1 of the program, to send periodic cybersecurity alerts to departments and agencies. The motivation behind this approach is that it would be relatively inexpensive to execute, and would make the departments and agencies aware of their vulnerabilities to cyber threats. As simple as this approach sounds, it would be a challenge to implement for many reasons. For example, in order for this approach to be successful, the alerts program must build trust with every department and agency across the federal network, so that the various other programs are interested, willing, and receptive to the alerts system. It might take five years or more before the program even approaches an agency with the idea of TICs.

The CONOPS as Statement of Methodology

The program manager's approach in a CONOPS will explain her program's specific methodology for realizing its stated goals and objectives. This methodology will inform the specific plans and solutions outlined in the CONOPS. It will also inform the numerous components of the program that the CONOPS defines in detail, such as the program's purpose, output, stakeholders, policies, constraints, potential impact, etc. For example, if the program manager decides to take the "awareness and education" approach, the program's outputs from year to year may take the form of conferences, events, and education tools. If the general concept is developing tools to technically and operationally mitigate risk, then the program's early outputs may be developing requirements and pursuing useful engineering models.

In summary, the CONOPS establishes an approach for addressing the capability gaps identified in the MNS and presents a strategy for building the target capability. It also defines the specific roles and responsibilities of the program's stakeholders. The CONOPS document describes how the program's target capability will be built and supported, but if the target capability is based on a complex system, the CONOPS may require a supple-

Chapter 3: Fundamentals of Management for Cybersecurity

mental operational requirements document to translate the capabilities defined in the MNS into more specific system-level performance requirements.

Managing Systems Capabilities: the Operational Requirements Document (ORD)

Many cybersecurity programs require building and engineering systems. Systems are new combinations of people, processes, and technologies that support the capability that the program is building. Cybersecurity program managers must focus on managing the systems they are building. In order to best manage a system, program managers should determine and articulate the requirements of the system, or "what the system is required to do." This statement of system requirements may be highly specific and technical.

The **operational requirements document (ORD)** is a statement of performance and operational parameters that the proposed system must meet to provide value to the program. The ORD may be prepared and signed by the program manager and a high-level sponsor at each milestone to ensure compliance with its requirements. The ORD, along with the CONOPS, helps translate high-level capability needs into practical requirements.

Management for the Federal Civilian Government: the Operating Model (Op Model)

After the program manager drafts the program's CONOPS, she begins working on the more detailed **operating model (op model)**. While the CONOPS offered program details at the level of program strategy and methodology, the op model gives details at the level of a program plan. Specifically, the op model offers a path for managing the execution of the CONOPS by delineating the manager's approach into outcomes, or measurable objectives and activities, and by accounting for all of the program's costs. While the op model is different and distinct from the CONOPS, it flows naturally from a completed CONOPS.

The op model should reflect a linear trajectory of outcomes, in which each successive year of the program builds on the work completed and capacity built during the preceding years. The program manager needs to lay the initial groundwork for the program in the first several years, so that the program's target capability can be achieved by its final year.

Considering again the example of the program built around raising the overall level of cybersecurity awareness in anticipation of introducing TICs: the first three years of this program might include hiring, training, and

Cyber Fact

A fundamental requirement during the op model-building phase is the manager's ability to plan a process that drives the program from its foundations and preliminary outcomes in Year 1 to achieving the stated goals from the MNS by the end of the program's final year. Thus, the op model articulates the outcomes for the first few years and sets appropriate budgets, milestones, and schedules around these outcomes. It also defines the outcomes in such a way that the program manager is able to define yearly, monthly, or weekly timeframes within the program's lifetime. These smaller timeframes within the program's lifetime will have their own, smaller, target goals and outcomes.

educating the program's staff to create and send the alerts, which will be sent out periodically beginning in Year 4 of the program. With the right staff and an effective training program, the goal of raising overall cybersecurity awareness across federal departments and agencies can be achieved by Year 5. A new program involving TICs may be introduced after Year 5.

The manager's process for writing the op model may proceed backwards, from target outcomes to strategic steps. To return to our example: if the goal is to begin sending out periodic alerts in Year 4, the program manager writing the op model can re-engineer backwards the steps to achieve the goal, and continue re-engineering until she can clearly decipher what tasks need to be completed on any given day of the program. We will discuss the way managers measure their project's progress against the targets of the op model in our discussion of earned value management later in this chapter. In addition to laying out precise timeframes, down to the day and hour, for each step of the program, the op model will provide precise calculations of how much each step of the program will cost.

Objective Values in Program Management

Because cost, schedule, and performance are intrinsically linked, the program manager should articulate the **threshold values** and **objective values** of all program goals with these interlinked relationships in mind.

Objective values refer to the maximum desired operational goal, beyond which additional gains in performance do not warrant additional time and cost. In other words, the objective value is the value the program manager is attempting to obtain through her program. An example of an objective value might be developing the capacity to send targeted cybersecurity alerts across federal civilian departments and agencies whenever they are deemed necessary. Anything developed above this objective value is a "bonus" to the program.

To determine the program's *thresholds*, the program manager must establish the minimum operational value, below which the utility of the program becomes questionable. For example, if an acquisition in the project is meant to hasten the speed of data transmission, the threshold value is the minimum acceptable amount of time required to transfer data. If the amount of time is greater that this value, then the acquisition is useless.

In regards to performance, thresholds refer to a minimum acceptable value, while for schedule and cost parameters, objectives are the maximum allowable values. By determining her program's thresholds and objectives, a program manager can prevent risky delays, and high, untenable costs.

The **acquisition program baseline (APB)** is a document produced by a mathematical algorithm that deconstructs the op model to provide quantified parameters for a program's key performance, cost, and schedule. The APB, signed by an organization's leadership, is essentially a contract between the head of an organization and the program manager, and states that the manager will deliver the objectives within the stated time, performance, and budget parameters.

Taken together, the MNS, capability-based planning documents, CONOPS, op model, and APB form the foundations of the program management framework for cybersecurity.

Management and Acquisition

Once the program manager has analyzed her mission, identified needed capabilities, and planned a strategy taking into account cost, schedule, and milestones, it is time to begin program operations. The program manager may have the op model in place, but not know how to fulfill the outcomes, create measurable objec-

Chapter 3: Fundamentals of Management for Cybersecurity

tives and activities, or determine current industry capabilities. **Management and acquisition** is the process of obtaining and allocating resources to complete the program's activities and achieve outcomes.

The management and acquisition process is meant to help the program manager to execute the op model. Recall that the op model explicitly states the cost and timeline for each step in the program's life cycle. The department or agency in need of products or services pulls language from the milestones identified in the op model to develop the acquisition documents for the program. Then, the GSA, an independent government agency dedicated to assisting federal agencies, identifies potential vendors, awards contracts, and ensures legal contracting requirements are met. Students of cybersecurity may remember our discussion of the GSA in Chapter 2, with regard to the Brooks Act of 1965 and federal standards for computer procurement. The GSA's efforts simplify federal procurement for other agencies and help to negotiate complex, multi-user contracts.

If a program manager or department head is unsure of how to accomplish an objective, she may issue a **request for information (RFI)**. An RFI essentially asks experts in a relevant industry, "If you were to achieve this objective, how would you do it?" This helps to determine whether necessary goods and services are available in the market. For example, DHS may issue an RFI regarding continuous monitoring equipment and technology. This RFI could request information regarding methods for implementing an effective cyber warning and analysis system.

Any company can respond to an RFI and even try to influence future procurements to the company's advantage. For example, if a government agency asks for methods to visualize the security posture of a system, a company (ABC Company) may respond by saying, "We would utilize *x* method, and as it happens, we have a tool that has been tested at different agencies and is proven to be effective." From this response, the agency may favor the approach and issue a future request for a tool that delivers the exact, or similar, capabilities described in the response – clearly giving ABC Company a distinct advantage at being awarded the contract.

From the responses to the RFI, the program manager can refine her objectives, strategy, and planning. After perusing various responses from relevant industries, the program manager has a better idea of potential methods for accomplishing her agency's mission.

Informed by this new information, the program manager develops a **request for proposal (RFP)**, which is a package that invites a company to submit a bid for equipment or services. The **statement of work (SOW)**, **performance work statement (PWS)**, and **statement of objectives (SOO)**, and are a few of the documents that may be included in the RFP. All of these documents are legally binding agreements between a contractor and the U.S. government.

> **Statement of work (SOW):** a document that states the specific expected outcomes of the service or equipment and how to achieve them
>
> **Performance work statement (PWS):** used for performance-based acquisitions; a document that states the specific expected outcomes of the service or equipment and leaves the method open to the contractor
>
> **Statement of objectives (SOO):** a document that states the desired outcomes and leaves the method open to the contractor

Figure 3-8: Definition of terms found in an RFP.

Management and Acquisition

Statement of Work (SOW)

The SOW, as opposed to the SOO or PWS, is typically used when the task is well-defined and relatively familiar. As such, it does not require the levels of flexibility and creativity permitted in the SOO or PWS; instead, it provides explicit direction for the contractor to follow. The SOW defines all non-specification requirements for the goods or services in specific, performance-based, quantitative terms, and acts as the standard for necessary contractor performance. The SOW uses explicit, clear terms. After the contract is awarded, the SOW is used to measure contractor measure and determine rights and obligations. For example, it could include specific language requesting a monthly performance and progress report, a program management plan, a quality assurance plan, as well as a series of additional tasks.

Performance Work Statement (PWS)

The PWS, used for performance-based acquisitions, is similar to the SOW, but slightly different in terms of purpose and scope. The PWS simply identifies the expected capabilities and capacities of the end product or service, and allows the contractor to use its originality and inventiveness to create the process for attaining the end results. The expected results are written in clear, specific, and objective terms with measurable outcomes (e.g., quality, timeliness, quantity). The PWS emphasizes what needs to be done (the results) as opposed to how the results should be achieved (the method). The PWS must be described in specific enough terms to both protect the contracting agency and to encourage competitors to develop innovative and cost-effective approaches. It should also specify procedures for reductions of fees or price when the contractor does not meet contract requirements, as well as incentives for exceeding expectations.

The PWS development process begins with an analytical examination of the agency's requirements and a "bottom-up" assessment. This assessment is the foundation for establishing performance standards, writing the PWS, and developing a quality assurance plan. Though this analytical process may vary from agency to agency, the primary objectives of the PWS remain largely the same. The three end-goals of the analytical process are:

    1. A detailed description of the required outcome of the product or service ("What has to be accomplished to fulfill our requirements?")

    2. Measurable performance standards ("How will I know that the outcome has been satisfactorily achieved? What are the essential standards for reliability, accuracy, quality, cost, etc.?")

    3. **Acceptable quality levels (AQLs)** ("How much deviation from the performance standard is acceptable?")

The AQLs establish the allowable variation from the performance standard. Returning to the earlier example of a project to establish a continuous monitoring system, the performance standard may be to disperse alerts within 15 seconds of recognizing significant abnormalities from the baseline. In this case, the AQL might be no more than a 5-second delay 10% of the time or, alternatively, no more than a 2-second delay 20% of the time.

Using the thought process above, the program manager should be able to draft the PWS, beginning with an identification of the object(s) the contractor will work to change – the object can be a system, an organization, a process, or a person (in the instance of education or training). Then, the program manager must state what type of change the contractor should make to the object, analyze the object to identify parts that need separate prioritization, develop the performance standards, compile the list of service tasks, write the performance requirements summary, determine the scope, list references and deliverables, and publish and present to the contractor.

Chapter 3: Fundamentals of Management for Cybersecurity

Upon publication, to fully assess the PWS, the program manager should closely examine the contractor's requirements and measure them against essential inputs, processes, and outputs. As the program manager parses through the PWS, she must constantly assess and reassess the need for the stated outputs and whether or not the cost and efforts are justified.

Statement of Objectives (SOO)

The SOO is incorporated into the RFP and states overall performance objectives of the contractor, not to be confused with the performance objectives/specifications of the system (which would be in the ORD). It is used in solicitations when the government intends to provide maximum flexibility for potential contractors to propose an innovative approach. As such, the SOO provides an acquisition's basic, high-level objectives, which are broader than those found in the SOW. The SOO should align with the MNS and any preliminary work breakdown structure (we will examine work breakdown structures in greater detail later in this chapter).

Although the SOO approach allows contractors the greatest amount of flexibility in their design approach, there are almost always some conditions and constraints that must be accommodated in the design. These requirements (such as the use of existing equipment that must be incorporated into the alert system, the required availability of the system, etc.) are covered in the various requirements documents and should not be confused with the performance objectives of the operators. The SOO should cover different types of objectives, including the high-level program objectives, contract objectives, and management objectives.

RFP Execution – IGCE and Evaluation Criteria

The RFP includes several other documents, including the **independent government cost estimate (IGCE)** and the **evaluation criteria**. The IGCE lays out exactly how much money the government believes completing the program's objectives will cost. These costs include labor, travel, and materials. The government contracting officer then compares each contractor's proposal to the IGCE to determine its alignment with the SOW, PWS, and SOO requirements and the rationality of its cost elements. The IGCE is not distributed to the potential contractor or any potential task performer.

The evaluation criteria prioritizes the factors that are most crucial in choosing a winning vendor. The evaluation criteria is prepared for the U.S. government contracting officer who will process the procurement (e.g., price, technical approach, qualifications and experience of the assigned workers, completeness of the vendor's response to the specific RFP requirements, etc.). Thus, the evaluation criteria document streamlines the decision process for the contracting officer.

Returning to our continuous monitoring scenario, the evaluation criteria may emphasize, for example, simplicity of design, security, or innovativeness of the approach over the vendor's years of relevant experience in the field. Along with the evaluation criteria document, the RFP should also indicate the relative importance of each factor.. This prioritization can be listed by category, or each factor can be assigned a specific weight or numerical value.

After all documents are carefully crafted, the program manager hands them over to the assigned contracting officer, potentially located in the GSA. The contracting officer then takes the SOW, PWS, and SOO, along with the evaluation criteria, and issues the RFP. The IGCE is not disclosed to the public; if it were, vendors would know the exact amount of money the U.S. government estimates the project will cost, and would thus be able to reduce their cost estimates accordingly. Instead, the U.S. government keeps the IGCE for any given program close at hand for future evaluation.

Measuring Progress Against Projections

Industry Response

After the U.S. government agency or department issues the RFP, relevant industry vendors submit their proposals to the GSA. These proposals include a technical approach for completing the assignment, along with a cost estimate. GSA then evaluates all of the proposals against the evaluation criteria and selects the vendor that will be awarded the contract. After a vendor is selected, the SOW, PWS, SOO, technical approach, and cost estimate are packaged and signed by both parties to signify an agreement. This agreement formalizes the roles, responsibilities, and costs of the vendor. Once the contract is awarded, the vendor usually delivers a **plan of action and milestones (POA&M)**, According to NIST's Special Publication 800-53, a POA&M is "a document that identifies tasks needing to be accomplished" and "details resources required to accomplish the elements of [a] plan, any milestones in meeting [the plan's] tasks, and scheduled completion dates for the milestones." The POA&M is delivered to the program office, and states how the vendor will achieve the activity they are contracted to fulfill in an op model.

The POA&M, which is based on the vendor's technical approach, is then used to create an **integrated master schedule (IMS)**, a graphical representation of the objectives, actions, and milestones in the POA&M. The IMS depicts a network of tasks linked from the start of the activity to the end, including interdependencies between tasks and milestones. It contains all the detailed work packages and planning packages necessary to support the events, accomplishments, and criteria of the larger program plan.

The IMS is primarily developed by the contractor to provide clarity for the government agency as to how the contractor will be fulfilling and managing activities. The IMS feeds into the larger, broader **integrated master plan (IMP)** developed by the agency running the program. The IMP is a visual representation of the work breakdown structure (which we will discuss later in this chapter).

The IMP and IMS together visually verify the program's ability to achieve its objectives within schedule and cost constraints and within an acceptable level of risk. In addition, the documents should help government program office personnel and contractor personnel develop "what-if" exercises and identify and assess problems at any point in the project. Ultimately, the IMP and IMS should focus and strengthen the government-contractor team. The IMP and IMS should be linked to the SOW, PWS, and SOO, and will later provide the foundation for what the earned value management technique will evaluate.

Measuring Progress Against Projections: Earned Value Management (EVM)

Previous sections of this chapter have covered the fundamentals of program management. We will now turn to the process by which program managers assess and evaluate ongoing projects. **Earned value management (EVM)** is the required management accounting system for project managers throughout the federal civilian government, including DHS. EVM helps program managers to effectively manage their program budgets and to evaluate program performance against budget at every step in the program's life cycle.

The federal civilian government requires that all of its program managers use EVM to plan, budget, and track program outcomes against spending at each step in the program. Federal programs use public money, so their activities must therefore be transparent, with every dollar accounted for in a public document. A uniform management accounting system allows the federal government to ensure that all capital assets are being accounted for in the same way.

Furthermore, federal projects and programs require major financial investments and costly acquisitions. EVM embodies the federal government's belief in a uniform system for the budgeting, purchasing, and management of capital assets. According to OMB Circular A-11, the document that mandated the use of EVM for federal

Chapter 3: Fundamentals of Management for Cybersecurity

Cyber Fact

At its most useful, the **IMP** integrates all work efforts into a defined program plan, while the IMS summarizes the detailed schedules for performing those work efforts. The IMP covers the breadth of the entire program, and incorporates multiple IMSs. The events in the IMP are not tied to specific dates, but to the completion, as evidenced by specified criteria, of certain tasks. On the other hand, the **IMS** should be sufficiently detailed for day-to-day execution and tracking of the program.

government programs, a capital asset is any land, equipment, structure, information technology, or intellectual property that has an estimated useful life of two or more years. Useful life in this context means the amount of time that a capital asset will be useful to a program or project. Beyond this useful life, the capital asset is no longer an asset. Because capital assets are never useful forever, any investment in capital assets for a new federal system or a program requires careful pre-purchase planning and post-purchase management. EVM helps program managers measure the effectiveness of their purchase at any point in the program's lifetime.

Even if we disregard its required use within the federal government, EVM is useful for any long-term project with specific goals. EVM uses quantitative equations and charts to track the progress of projects in coordination with budgets. As we continue through this portion of the chapter, we will consider one hypothetical project as a case study that illustrates how EVM works in practice. This project is being undertaken by a website design firm called District Design. This firm has been hired to create a secure website for an entertainment content company. The website will use a payment infrastructure that allows customers to pay with their credit cards on the site, in exchange for access to a collection of movies and TV shows. In order to access the entertainment content site, members must sign in with a user name and password. This company will use EVM to track its progress as it designs the company's website.

Building a Budget: Work Breakdown Structure

Before District Design can use an earned value management system, its project manager must formulate a budget for this project. There are innumerable ways to create a budget. The **work breakdown structure (WBS)** is one of the most highly regarded methods. The WBS was originally developed by the DOD as the military's standard process for project budgeting. Like EVM, the WBS is popular within the federal government, and the DOD still requires all projects to use a standardized form of the WBS (the civilian government has yet to adopt this blanket policy for project budgeting).[4]

The military's WBS regulations give project managers a set of guidelines for listing and graphically representing the various tasks within a project. For program managers, using a WBS to plan budgets provides two significant benefits: (1) guidance on how to plan tasks and sub-tasks according to a budget; and (2) the promotion of the integration of multiple departments in order to work towards the organization's objective. Without a WBS, each department in an organization would complete only its own departmental initiatives. Working with an integrated WBS, departments are forced to combine their skills and work with one another. Having a budget plan that combines the specialties of different departments is critical for managers hoping to complete a unified project.

Budgeting systems such as the WBS are critical in the field of cybersecurity because they turn broad initiatives set by high-level leaders into measurable tasks with a highly detailed budget. Rather than having project managers analyze the daunting question of whether or not information has been secured in cyberspace, a WBS

Measuring Progress Against Projections

Cyber Fact

OMB Circular A-11 comprehensively describes the guidelines for all federal agencies regarding the planning, budgeting, purchasing, and managing of capital assets. The new requirement for EVM on all government projects sparked the necessity for all project managers, even those who only contract with the federal government, to become familiar with EVM.

separates this broad goal into measurable, achievable projects that can be monitored with EVM. It is highly advised for anyone interested in project management to become familiar with WBS legislation.

Budgets at Work

No matter which budgeting system an organization uses, all budgets are built around two elementary factors: time and money. These are often the two most prized resources in any organization. And yet, it is important for managers and organizations to recognize that formulating a perfect budget is nearly impossible. Almost every project will deviate from its original budget, either positively or negatively, due to unforeseeable events that arise during the project's lifetime. Still, this nearly inevitable turn away from the original budget does not mean that budgets are useless; rather, budgets are imperfect yet critically necessary tools.

Our hypothetical company, District Design, decided to use a WBS to plan its website design project. While preparing its budget, the company established five major chronological key phases for developing the site:

The company predicts that the first two phases ("Graphics" and "Security") and the last phase ("Maintenance") will each take two months to complete, while the remaining two phases ("Payment" and "Testing") will each take three months to complete, making the entire project a twelve-month endeavor. Of course, the actual progress of the work could vary (slightly or significantly) from these predictions.

In terms of the cost of each of these phases, the implementation of the payment system is estimated to be the most expensive phase, followed by "Security" and "Testing," while "Graphics" and "Maintenance" are expected to be the least costly phases. The design firm has placed all of its cost estimates for the project into Figure 3-9.B. We will now discuss the three fundamental metrics of EVM: *planned value*, *earned value*, and *actual cost*.

---

1. Designing graphics ("Graphics")

2. Making the site secure ("Security")

3. Creating an online payment system ("Payment")

4. Testing the website (Testing)

5. Maintaining the site (Maintenance)

Figure 3-9.A: Entertainment website development cycle.

Chapter 3: Fundamentals of Management for Cybersecurity

Fundamental Earned Value Management Metrics

EVM is based on three primary metrics for measuring a project's performance. The first of these three metrics is **planned value (PV)**, or **budgeted cost of work scheduled (BCWS)**. As its name makes clear, PV indicates the budgeted cost for the work scheduled to be completed by a specific date. In other words, this is the estimated value of expenditures that the project is budgeted to incur by a specific point in the project. District Design's planned value at 8 months is $540,000, meaning that, when its project manager originally formulated the project's budget, District Design planned to spend $540,000 during the first 8 months (see Figure 3-9.B). This metric uses only estimated values derived from the original project budget.

Months	Planned Value (PV)	Earned Value (EV)	Actual Cost (AC)
1	$10,000	$12,000	$13,000
2	$30,000	$36,000	$39,000
3	$70,000	$84,000	$91,000
4	$130,000	$156,000	$169,000
5	$220,000	$264,000	$286,000
6	$340,000	$408,000	$442,000
7	$450,000	$540,000	$585,000
8	$540,000	$648,000	$702,000
9	$600,000		
10	$640,000		
11	$660,000		
12	$670,000		

Figure 3-9.B: Entertainment website costs: planned value, earned value, and actual cost.

The second fundamental metric of EVM is **actual cost (AC)**, or **actual cost of work performed (ACWP)**. As the name implies, AC measures the actual costs incurred for the work completed at any given point in the project. This metric uses only real values that have actually been incurred during the work process (unlike PV, which is composed of estimated values from the original budget plan). According to the budget chart in our hypothetical case study, District Design has incurred actual costs totaling $702,000 during the first 8 months of this project (see Figure 3-9.B).

The third basic metric of EVM is **earned value (EV)**, or **budgeted cost of work performed (BCWP)**. EV recognizes the budgeted value of the work actually completed. In other words, this metric computes the costs that the company planned to incur for the amount of work actually completed at a given point in the project. EV is different from AC and PV because it accounts for both estimated values from the budget *and* actual values from the project's real-world progress.

Measuring Progress Against Projections

EV is generally the hardest metric to understand and it sometimes is easier, especially for those with experience in managerial accounting, to think of EV as a metric that uses a budgeted cost rate for the actual amount of work that has been completed. This means that EV uses the budgeted cost per unit of work completed multiplied by the actual amount of work completed. In our example of District Design, the firm's EV after 8 months is $648,000 (see Figure 3-9.B).

Due to the complicated nature of this metric, we will consider an additional example. In this example, we will discuss the case of a construction firm called Tim & Son's Construction. Tim & Son's has been contracted to create a large monument in the middle of the city. The company originally estimated that it would complete the monument in 4 months, at a total cost of $1,000,000. The project manager for Tim & Son's will calculate the EV of the project at several points in its life cycle.

As we discussed, EV is the budgeted value of the work that has actually been completed. Thus, the project manager can calculate the progress of her monument at any given time in relation to the total budgeted cost. If the project is 75% completed, the EV will be 75% of the total budgeted cost ($750,000). If the project is 30% completed, the EV will be 30% of the total budgeted cost ($300,000), regardless of actual cost and the budgeted project's lifetime. EV doesn't distinguish between the project being 30% completed in the first week or at the end of the 4-month period. The only factors that determine EV are the actual amount of the project completed and the budgeted total costs.

The ability to understand the difference between PV, AC, and EV is the key to understanding not only the EVM model, but also to understanding why any given project may or may not be on track. The EVM metric breakdown on the following page may help you to further understand the difference between the three primary metrics.

Primary Metric Breakdown

PV: (Budgeted Cost Per Unit of Work Completed) x (Budgeted Amount of Work)

EV: (Budgeted Cost Per Unit of Work Completed) x (Actual Amount of Work)

AC: (Actual Cost Per Unit of Work Completed) x (Actual Amount of Work)

Figure 3-10: Primary metric breakdown.

When Project Targets Miss the Mark: EVM Variances

To understand the next portion of the EVM model, it is vital to have a solid understanding of the three basic metrics for EVM. Before reading this section, it may be wise to review the previous section, noting the subtle, yet significant, differences between each of the metrics.

The greatest use for these metrics lies in their direct application, primarily in their use to calculate **variances**. A variance is any deviation from an original budget or schedule. Variances help project managers understand where they are versus where they had planned to be in a project's life cycle. Variances are always expressed in terms of dollar amounts, though they may represent other factors such as time. For example, in

Chapter 3: Fundamentals of Management for Cybersecurity

order to dictate how far ahead or behind schedule a particular project is, a project manager might use a **schedule variance (SV)**. This variance can be quantified in the following equation:

Schedule Variance (SV) = Earned Value (EV) - Planned Value (PV)

Figure 3-11: Schedule variance equation.

A schedule variance calculates the difference between the earned value of the work actually completed (EV) and the amount budgeted for work planned (PV) at any given time. The calculation for SV can be logically understood by reasoning through the equation. Essentially, the equation states that you subtract the budgeted amount of work estimated to be performed from the earned value of the amount of work actually performed. This equation expresses the differences between the value of the actual work performed and the earned value of the budgeted work performed in terms of dollars.

An SV greater than 0 indicates that the project is ahead of schedule, and therefore represents a favorable variance. A favorable variance is any variance that positively contributes to a project (or operating income). In other words, a favorable variance is a "better than expected" variance from the original budget plan. On the other hand, an SV under 0 will indicate that the project is behind schedule, representing an unfavorable variance. An unfavorable variance is any variance that negatively contributes to a project (or operating income). In other words, an unfavorable variance is a "worse than expected" variance from the original budget plan. The greater the SV is above or below 0, the more significant the variance is.

Although it is unlikely that the project is "right on track" throughout the majority of the **period of performance (POP)** – the amount of time budgeted between the start and end dates of a particular project – the SV will always be equal to 0 at the end of the project's life. This "return to 0" happens because, at the end of the project, the amount of work budgeted to be completed will be equal to the actual amount of work done: the entire budget will be spent on all of the work that was done.

In order for District Design's project manager to judge her project's variation from its budgeted and scheduled performance, she will use the SV equation above (Figure 3-11). Using this equation, she realizes that the project's SV by the end of the 8th month is $108,000 ($648,000 - $540,000). This is great news for the firm because this means that the project is running ahead of schedule (the SV value is $108,000 above 0). Although the project manager originally predicted that District Design would be in the beginning of the testing phase by the end of the eighth month of the POP, the SV indicates that the project is already in the maintenance process.

However, this large schedule variance is only an indicator of how efficiently the project is using its time; although SV is expressed as a dollar amount, it does not measure cost. Rather, it is a measurement of the project's performance in time as expressed by costs incurred up to a given point in the project.

To track the actual costs incurred by a project in comparison with the costs estimated in the budget, EVM uses the equation for **cost variance (CV)**. The CV equation is:

Cost Variance (CV) = Earned Value (EV) – Actual Costs (AC)

Figure 3-12: Cost variance equation.

CV measures the difference between the money budgeted for the work actually performed (EV) and the actual costs incurred by the project (AC) at any given time. Therefore, CV indicates whether and by how much the project is over or under the budget at any given point. Like other EVM equations, the calculation for CV can be reasoned out and expressed in a simple equation. To find the difference between actual and budgeted costs, CV simply subtracts the former from the latter: EV minus AC.

Measuring Progress Against Projections

The answer to this equation then allows the project manager, whether behind or ahead of schedule, to understand whether her costs have been above or below her original estimates for the portion of the project already completed. Like the SV calculation, if the CV is greater than 0, then the project is under budget (favorable variance). If the CV is under 0, this indicates that the project is running over the planned budget (unfavorable variance).

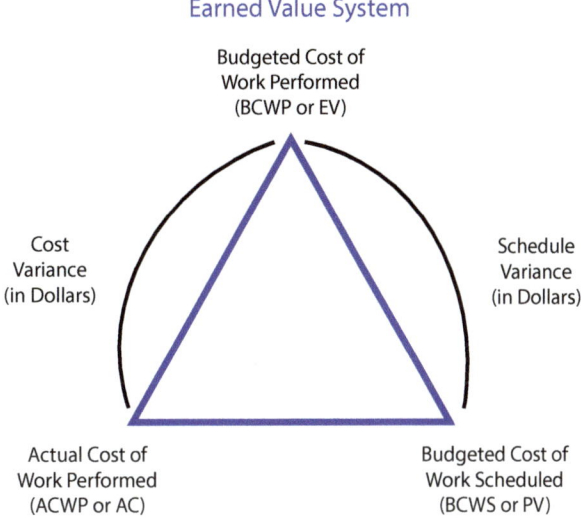

Figure 3-13: Variance triangle.

In the case of District Design, the project manager will use the CV equation noted above (Figure 3-12) to compare the project's actually incurred costs for the work completed with its originally budgeted costs. Doing so, the manager finds she has a CV of -$54,000 ($648,000 - $702,000). This is not ideal for the website designers; their project was budgeted to total $670,000, but three-quarters of the way through the project, costs have already surpassed that number. To an outsider, this variance may seem fairly high, but its true significance can only be determined in comparison to the progress of other projects.

Comparing Projects of Varying Budgets

The fact that all variances are expressed in dollar amounts poses a problem for managers who must compare variances across projects that vary in budget size. All variances are not equally significant: a $2,000 unfavorable CV is much more significant when the total estimated cost of a project is $10,000 than it is when the project is budgeted at $1,000,000. In order to determine how significant a variance is for any given project, project managers can express cost and schedule variances in terms of percentages. The formulas for calculating these percentages are expressed below:

CV% = CV/EV * 100

SV% = SV/PV * 100

Figure 3-14: Cost and schedule variance percentages.

Chapter 3: Fundamentals of Management for Cybersecurity

Expressing variances in terms of percentages neutralizes any discrepancy in budget size between projects and allows managers to make more-informed decisions about how to proceed with projects of varying sizes and budgets. If a CV% or SV% is positive, there is a favorable variance. If a CV% or SV% is negative, there is an unfavorable variance. District Design's manager has calculated a CV% of approximately -8.33% and a SV% of 20%. Figure 3-15 provides a list of data and metrics regarding District Design's entertainment site project, while Figure 3-16 transforms some of this data into the form of a graph.

In brief, EVM allows managers to understand which aspects of each project need to improve their performance and which aspects of each project are on target with projected schedules and budgets. Having a firm

Planned Value	PV=	$540,000
Earned Value	EV=	$648,000
Actual Cost	AC=	$702,000
Cost Variance	CV=EV-AC	-$54,000
Cost Performance Index	CPI=EV/AC	0.92
Schedule Variance	SV=EV-PV	$108,000
Schedule Performance Index	SPI=EV/PV	1.2
Budget at Completion	BAC=	$670,000
Estimate to Complete	ETC=(BAC-EV)/CPI	$23,833
Estimate at Completion	EAC=AC+ETC	$725,833

Figure 3-15: Entertainment site project metrics.

Planned Value	PV=	$540,000
Earned Value	EV=	$648,000
Actual Cost	AC=	$702,000
Cost Variance	CV=EV-AC	-$54,000
Cost Performance Index	CPI=EV/AC	0.92
Schedule Variance	SV=EV-PV	$108,000
Schedule Performance Index	SPI=EV/PV	1.2
Budget at Completion	BAC=	$670,000
Estimate to Complete	ETC=(BAC-EV)/CPI	$23,833
Estimate at Completion	EAC=AC+ETC	$725,833

Figure 3-16: Chart representation of entertainment site project.

grasp on this information helps managers to make sound decisions about how to allocate their remaining time and effort among and within projects, or whether to continue a project at all.

DHS EVM Case Study: Building a Cybersecurity Monitoring System

The case of District Design effectively represents the core concepts of EVM. Nevertheless, for managers of federal government projects, tracking costs and measuring actual results against budgeted figures is a much more complex operation. One of the fundamental differences between the use of EVM in the District Design example and in DHS cybersecurity projects is that, in large federal government projects, the "phases" of each project are usually less defined. Therefore, it is harder to measure a project's progress than it was in our District Design example. In order to get a taste of how EVM is used for cybersecurity projects, we will consider how EVM might be used in a project to implement a network monitoring system within a federal government agency.

As we discussed in an earlier case study, a monitoring system provides an organized structure for detecting potential threats and vulnerabilities that could contribute to a damaging cyber attack. As the capabilities of external threats grow rapidly more complex, it becomes increasingly important for businesses and federal agencies to implement capable monitoring systems. However, implementing such a system is never logistically or financially easy.

In this particular case study, we will be discussing the creation of a network monitoring system within a federal agency that employs about 30,000 people. As we discussed, before the agency can begin its project, it must plan and formulate a budget. This process begins with a list of goals and objectives, shown in Figure 3-17.

VIDEO

Watch 'EVM' at http://vimeo.com/channels/cybersecurityfoundations

1. Monitor the entire federal agency (30,000 people and 1,000 IT assets)
2. Leverage new technology and industry subject matter experts
3. Measurably reduce risk through continuous monitoring
4. Leverage personal relationships to educate and disseminate information

Figure 3-17: Goals and objectives for network monitoring system project.

These are the broad goals that the agency's senior managers have decided to pursue. These goals are expressed in terms of new capabilities to be built, including "Monitor," "Leverage," "Reduce," "Educate," and "Disseminate." As we discussed earlier, large-scale initiatives like these need to be broken down into measurable tasks in order to track the progress and achievements of the project at any given point.

The project managers for the federal agency in our example meet and discuss their capability goals with

Chapter 3: Fundamentals of Management for Cybersecurity

high-level leadership and receive approval and a budget. Through these discussions, the agency establishes six "major phases" required to build a cutting-edge network monitoring system. The project managers then integrate these phases into their WBS, a step which helps to promote the integration of all the agency's departments with regard to the project. The "major phases" are:

1. Establish a baseline understanding of network assets and normal network traffic volume
2. Assess risk to network assets
3. Obtain internal information about network operations
4. Obtain external information about threats and leverage relationships with external sources
5. Conduct analysis to detect anomalous activities
6. Establish a program office to manage the development of a monitoring system

Figure 3-18: Construction phases for networking monitoring system.

The federal agency creates a budget with the estimated time and cost required to complete each of the major phases. The agency uses its discussions with external stakeholders to estimate the schedule and milestones. However, the agency decides to use its own costing system, which takes into account the government and industry averages of various kinds of costs associated with the project. Some of these parameters include the number of federal government **full-time equivalents (FTEs)** (multiple part-time workers could do the work of one FTE), the number of contractor FTEs (accounting for various skill levels), travel costs, IT costs, training costs, and other associated costs.

In order to understand how the agency has budgeted its resources and time, we will briefly describe each of these phases. In a project with such a large scope, the phases are not necessarily sequential, and multiple phases of the project may be underway at any given time. The project manager needs to plan out the implementation of each phase in her detailed Op Model for the project.

The first phase, establishing a baseline, is critical to launching a network monitoring system. Establishing a baseline consists of understanding what IT systems the agency currently has in place. This means that the federal agency will leverage hardware, software, and integration systems in order to understand the operating environment of the agency. The agency will also need to identify all points of ingress and create a map of the network's assets in order to identify what assets the monitoring system will be protecting. The rest of the project hinges on this process. Without a complete picture of the baseline, the project will be operating on a shaky foundation.

Recognizing the fundamental importance of this project phase, the agency has decided to allocate a fairly large amount of money towards this process. The bulk of this process requires the leveraging of hardware and software, so the agency plans to hire a few low and mid-level FTEs to operate the system and gather data, a few high-level government FTEs to manage the process, and a few high level contractor **subject matter experts (SMEs)** to provide guidance. An SME is a similar measurement to an FTE, with the important difference that SMEs generally have higher degrees of specialization, and are therefore much more expensive to employ. Accounting for personnel costs as well as the IT and integration costs, the agency has budgeted this process's cost to be $782,188.

Measuring Progress Against Projections

Process	Budgeted Cost
Establish a baseline	$782,188
Risk assessment	$839,720
Obtain internal information	$1,388,887
Obtain external information	$355,803
Conduct expert analyses	$666,731
Project management	$966,922

Figure 3-19: Budgeted costs for networking monitoring system project.

After the baseline has been established, the federal agency must assess the risk to the network's assets. We discussed the basic process for conducting a risk assessment in Chapter 1. The federal agency's risk assessment will include three sub-components: a threat assessment, vulnerability assessment, and consequence assessment. When these three assessments are considered together, the overall risk assessment will help managers understand all potential threats, the resources at risk, and the specific types of damage that a cyber attack could inflict.

The actual process of risk assessment is extremely complex and requires the costly skills and expertise of specialists. However, risk assessment does not require a large budget for technical resources. Taking these factors into consideration, the agency's algorithm estimated a total cost of $839,720 to complete the risk assessment. The agency calculated 30% of the risk assessment funding to be allocated to the threat and vulnerability assessments combined, 15% of the funding to be allocated to the consequence assessment, and the remaining 25% of the funding to be allocated towards the risk analysis of assessment findings.

Following the risk assessment, the agency will move into its third project phase: obtaining internal information about the network by deploying technical tools. This process is critical in the development of a network monitoring system. During this phase, the agency will use tools such as firewalls, anti-virus software, and IDSs to track and monitor data logs of the entire network. These tools help analysts understand the network flow by detecting anomalies in the system. However, these tools do not always pick up on new attack patterns. Therefore, this process requires analysts to actively sort through the data logs for anything that seems out of place.

Obtaining this internal information doesn't require many high level employees, but deploying all of the tools into the system generally takes a few mid and low-level FTEs. For its purposes, the agency has decided to hire a range of government and contractor FTEs. Since this process requires a fair amount of software, hardware, and integration costs in addition to personnel costs, the federal agency budgeted $1,388,887 towards this phase of the project. Still, there is only so much that the agency can learn from its own findings. To expand the capabilities of their monitoring system, the agency has decided to leverage external sources on potential cyber threats. Obtaining external information can include anything from attending conferences to consulting network security experts. The goal of this process is to obtain new information about potential risks to the network. The more relevant information the agency has, the better the monitoring system will be for detecting cyber attacks.

Fortunately for the agency, this process does not require many resources other than low- to mid-skill level personnel. In fact, this is the only process that does not require at least one high-level FTE from either the federal government or the private sector. This portion of the project is also relatively small in scope, so it was budgeted for only $355,803. Nevertheless, its budget should not detract from our perception of its importance. This process allows the agency to obtain critical information on potential cyber attacks that it may never have learned without external consultation.

Chapter 3: Fundamentals of Management for Cybersecurity

Possibly even more important than obtaining external information about potential threats is the ability to recognize never-before-seen cyber attacks. Cyber attackers are constantly crafting new kinds of attacks that aim to thwart the latest cyber defenses. For this reason, it is necessary for the agency to hire highly skilled analysts to detect anomalies in the data logs that lower-skill personnel, and even technical tools, cannot. These highly skilled personnel have extensive knowledge on a wide range of cyber topics, and generally have at least a decade of experience in the cybersecurity industry. These analysts will identify new forms of attacks, create prototype software for recognizing new attacks, and eventually turn these prototypes into fully functioning tools for the network monitoring system. Therefore, hiring highly skilled analysts for the project will greatly contribute to the strength of the monitoring system as a whole. Predictably, this service is expensive. It requires relatively few physical resources, but does require a number of extremely high-level FTEs from highly specialized private sector companies. Therefore, the agency decided to budget $666,731 towards this process.

Finally, the agency needs to ensure that the project runs smoothly. To this end, the agency has decided that it will dedicate part of its budget to the management of this project. The project management costs include the project manager's salary, all costs associated with retrieving EVM data, the use of non-EVM project monitoring tools, and other tools. The overall management of the project as it unfolds is the only "process" that is not dependent on the others, meaning that project management will take place throughout the project timeline, no matter how far along the other processes are. Managing the project from start to finish requires a range of personnel from various skill levels, both contractor and federal. Because of the wide range of people employed and the importance that the federal agency places on project management, the agency budgeted $966,992 for ongoing project management.

Now that the processes of implementing the network monitoring system and budgeting for the project are understood, the project can begin and the project manager can measure the project's progress at any given point in time. For the purposes of this example, let's posit that the monitoring system project is currently six months underway and is slightly behind schedule and over budget. This delay is directly attributable to early issues that arose during the "establishing a baseline" phase. This phase was the foundation of the entire network monitoring system, so if this process is delayed, the entire project is delayed. The delay in the first phase stemmed from a number of factors, but primarily occurred because the project manager was unaware of a significant amount of paperwork that she needed to complete in order to have access to certain portions of the network's information. Accordingly, while the agency originally budgeted to complete the first phase of the project in two months, it ended up taking three months in total. This one month delay directly resulted in an unfavorable SV of -$125,000. However, because the majority of the process' costs during this phase did not involve hiring FTEs, the project manager escaped with an extremely small unfavorable CV of -$5,000.

Still, this setback during the baseline phase was not the only delay that the project faced during its first six months. Even with the initial delay, the agency had been on track to be in the middle of the third phase (obtaining internal information) by the end of the sixth month. But the agency is just now finishing a second risk assessment. The need for a second risk assessment was the result of a mishap during the first risk assessment. When the project experienced the initial delay during the first phase, the project manager became worried and tried to push the employees to catch up to the budgeted schedule. As a result, when the risk analysts first provided a copy of the risk assessment to the head project manager, they had only assessed 75% of the agency's assets. Because the risk assessment was incomplete, it was useless. Therefore, the project manager required the analysts to repeat the process.

This is all bad news for the project manager. Taking into account the most recent setback, she is now half way through the project's originally budgeted timeline with a -$500,000 SV and a -$100,000 CV.

All good project managers analyze the causes behind cost and schedule variances. In this case, both of these

Measuring Progress Against Projections

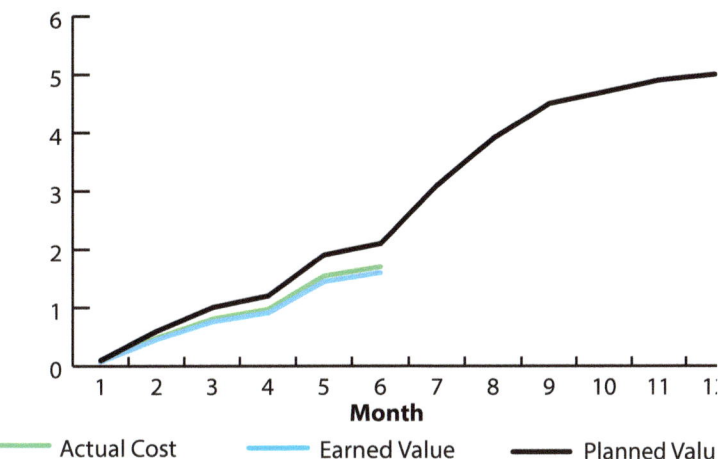

Figure 3-20: Graph of networking monitoring system project progress.

unfavorable variances stemmed from poor project management. It is the project manager's responsibility to plan, budget, and manage the project efficiently. In the case of the network monitoring system, the project manager seems to have failed at those tasks so far. Not only should she have done the research to recognize the need to fill out additional paperwork before the project began, she should have done a better job managing the risk analysts to ensure a thorough and timely assessment. Nevertheless, the project is only six months into the POP. With the proper adjustments and a smart allocation of remaining resources, the project manager has enough time to improve her EVM metrics before the project is completed.

Applied EVM: The Meaning of Red, Yellow, and Green

In the federal government, project managers use a **"red/yellow/green" system** to label the results of their performance metrics. The term "red" indicates that a project is not meeting its expectations. A "yellow" status recognizes that the project is fairly successful, but there are potential issues that the project manager should investigate. A "green" status means that the project is doing well and meeting its targets. This color-coding system is useful when reporting a project's status to someone unfamiliar with all of its specifics. High-level managers may not have time to delve into all of the cost and schedule details of a project, but the color status alerts them to what they should know about a project's performance at any point in its lifetime.

In order to translate all of a project's performance metrics into a color code, project managers must possess a deep understanding of the metrics covered in this chapter, and know exactly how to interpret quantitative evaluations of a specific project's performance. A project manager must understand why her project's CV is favorable or why her SV is unfavorable.

Although a brief understanding of these metrics is helpful in identifying the struggling and over-performing aspects of a project, understanding why the metrics fluctuate is a key aspect of success in project management. Only by knowing the factors that are influencing CV and SV can a manager accurately gauge whether her project's status is "green," "yellow," or "red "at any given point.

In short, project managers must possess the ability to interpret project metrics beyond the numbers. It is important for project managers to realize that extremely small variances and changes to EVM forecasting

Chapter 3: Fundamentals of Management for Cybersecurity

measures are often insignificant. An unfavorable variance in the first month of a multi-year program does not necessarily mean that there is reason for a project manager to be concerned. A good project manager must be able to decipher which variables are potentially significant and which are not. Much of this ability comes from in-depth knowledge of each project, but a solid understanding of EVM is also critical.

EVM performance metrics do not necessarily dictate whether a project is a success or a failure. Rather, they give project managers an idea of what aspects of a project they should pay attention to as the project progresses. It is the job the of the project manager to take the data offered by the EVM model and use these numbers to investigate and discover why a particular project is doing well or not, in order to ensure that the project is completed efficiently and successfully.

Compliance and Reporting

Globalization of the information and communications technology (ICT) marketplace offers tremendous opportunities for efficiency and innovation. As Chapter 4 will discuss, ICT goods also provide increased opportunities for those intent on harming networks and organizations, by providing additional opportunities to penetrate the supply chain to gain unauthorized access to data, alter data, or interrupt the network. Additionally, weaknesses in information security can cause increasingly harmful consequences, such as the compromise of public and private assets including intellectual property, trade secrets and other sensitive information, through acts of espionage, cyber terrorism, and cyber crime. In order to ensure that information is protected from unauthorized access, use, disclosure, disruption, modification, or destruction, organizations must enforce adequate information security to protect the confidentiality, integrity, and availability of their data. Ultimately, information security guarantees that accurate information is available to authorized individuals when it is needed, and inaccessible to unauthorized individuals. Organizations' risk management frameworks should seamlessly integrate information security controls.

As stated earlier in the chapter, the cybersecurity profession can be roughly divided into two categories: doing and managing. The "doing" component includes technical work (e.g., computer programming and IT systems maintenance), while the "managing" component includes reporting, audits, and ensuring compliance with applicable laws and regulations. Reporting, audits, and compliance ensure that proper processes and procedures are followed by the "doing" division, thereby guaranteeing trust in the institution for all stakeholders.

Effective audit and compliance systems are essential to program success, meeting regulatory obligations, and protecting an organization's most critical assets. Audits help in the following ways:

1. Prioritize the application of resources to target areas of greatest risk exposure

2. Preserve the confidentiality, integrity, and availability of information systems

3. Gauge the effectiveness of internal controls, risk management practices, and management's planning and oversight of IT activities

4. Determine the level of program compliance to laws and policies

5. Provide senior leadership with sufficient information to course-correct in deficient areas in a timely manner

In many businesses and organizations, there are two forms of audits: internal and external. The purpose of the internal audit and compliance are linked, as both are crucial in helping management to allocate resources wisely, prevent detrimental outcomes, work towards business or program objectives, and validate ad-

Compliance and Reporting

> **Cyber Fact**
>
> **Compliance** is the action of following established guidelines and specifications, or in the legal system, laws and regulations. Compliance involves documenting adherence to both external laws and regulations (e.g., those created by international standards committees, professional committees, or legislative acts) and internal policies and procedures created by the organization's senior leadership. Compliance is achieved by identifying the applicable requirements, assessing the current state of compliance, assessing the risks and potential costs of non-compliance against the estimated costs of achieving compliance, and initiating corrective actions.

herence to standards and internal policies and procedures. The internal audit must determine the full breadth of risks the program faces, and how these risks relate to each other. In identifying this range of risks, the internal audit relies on clear risk management, control, and governance processes to ensure controls are adequate and operating as designed. Though compliance traditionally helps build and maintain a trusted organizational culture, compliance officers must also play a role in risk identification, management and mitigation.

Independent, third-party firms conduct external audits for companies to validate the accuracy of records, normally financial records. The external auditors also help prepare statements for companies that must fulfill regulatory obligations or file disclosures to the government.

The public and private sectors are subject to various types of auditing. The most commonly-known type of auditing is the financial audit, in which accountants test the accuracy of the numbers a company projects through its financial statements to present past performance and predictions of future growth. Financial audit scandals have become commonplace as large companies have falsely reported profits and manipulated stock value to meet growth targets. However, financial audits are only a single type of audit. **IT audits**, which audit an organization's IT systems, management, operations and related processes, are also essential, since organizations rely so heavily on their IT systems. IT audits provide assurance that IT systems are adequately protected, evaluate the reliability of data from these systems, and avoid waste in their use and management. Just as financial audits identify financial risks to the organization (e.g., Coca-Cola would be concerned about rising sugar prices), IT audits identify risks to IT systems (e.g., counterfeit electronic parts). In general, IT audits are carried out by first establishing IT audit objectives and scope, gathering information about relevant IT controls, and performing audit tests using computer-assisted audit techniques (CAATs), such as the use of analysis software or data extraction.

While the purpose of audits and compliance are fairly similar for the public and private sectors, the artifacts differ. Since federal agencies operate using taxpayer dollars, the U.S. government must ensure that scarce public resources are wisely invested. This includes, for example, contractor compliance to ensure businesses and independent contractors are not in violation of the terms to which they have agreed. In addition to contractor compliance, each federal department or agency must comply with the U.S. government requirement to maximize the value of its investments.

Compliance for the U.S. Government

As discussed throughout this chapter, the federal government works with businesses and independent contractors, who provide specific services to the government in exchange for payment. The documents described earlier in this chapter, such as the SOW, PWS, and SOO clarify the contractors' goals and criteria for success. The

Chapter 3: Fundamentals of Management for Cybersecurity

> **Cyber Fact**
>
> **The Sarbanes-Oxley Act of 2002 (SOX)**: SOX was enacted in response to the high-profile Enron and WorldCom financial scandals, and was an attempt to protect shareholders and the public from fraudulent practices and accounting errors. Administered by the Securities and Exchange Commission (SEC), SOX specified new provisions such as a mandate that required senior management to certify the accuracy of reported financial statements, as well as a requirement that management establish both internal controls and reporting methods to monitor the effectiveness of those controls.

IMP and IMS assist in the planning and scheduling of work efforts. These documents structure and guide the contractors' activities, and provide metrics for the government to gauge contractor performance. To ensure that they are not in violation of the terms to which they have agreed, contractors are subject to specific government regulations and standards. The state or affirmation of meeting rules or standards is referred to as compliance.

In addition to contractor compliance, each federal department or agency must comply with the U.S. government requirement to maximize the value of its investments. Departments and agencies must comply with the requirements of the following:[5]

> The **Clinger-Cohen Act of 1996**, which requires the OMB to oversee major acquisitions and ensure that departments and agencies use the best and most cost-effective technology available. Additionally, it mandates that every federal agency is responsible for its own IT acquisition, and for ensuring the effectiveness of information security policies and procedures. Along with maintaining budgetary oversight, the Clinger-Cohen Act also addresses cybersecurity concerns over potential vulnerabilities within the supply chain for IT products, by requiring departments and agencies to assess and manage the risks of IT investments, and by requiring the OMB and the secretary of DHS to circulate compulsory federal computer standards.
>
> The **Federal Acquisition Streamlining Act of 1994, Title V (FASA V)**, which requires agencies to establish measurable performance goals (related to cost and schedule) for all major acquisition programs, and achieve, on average, 90 percent of those goals.
>
> **Security**, which requires agencies to maintain up-to-date tracking of major information systems.
>
> **Enterprise architecture (EA)**, which requires that the IT investment be included in an agency's enterprise architecture, defined as the 'strategic information base' that defines the mission of an agency and describes the technology and information needed to perform that mission, along with descriptions of how the architecture of the organization should be changed in order to respond to changes in the mission. The business case must explicate the relationship between the IT investment and the EA to guarantee that IT expenditures align with the agency's mission and improve the agency's mission effectiveness.

Exhibit 300 – Planning, Budgeting, Acquisition, and Management of Information Technology Capital Assets

Each department or agency that purchases IT equipment has to submit a "Capital Asset Plan and Business Case," collectively known as the **Exhibit 300**, to the OMB, in order to justify each request for a major IT investment. The intention of an Exhibit 300 is to compel departments and agencies to use effective project management skills and demonstrate defined cost, schedule, and performance goals associated with the IT procurements. The Exhibit 300s cover project planning, cost-benefit analysis, alternative analysis, acquisition planning, risk management planning, human resources planning, enterprise architecture, and security. By reviewing the Exhibit 300s, the OMB is able to identify poorly planned investments for both new and ongoing investments; for new investments, the OMB decides whether or not the procurement should go forward, while for ongoing investments, the OMB evaluates whether the investment has met expectations.[6] The OMB makes quantitative decisions about budgetary resources and qualitative assessments of project resources to determine whether the agency's programming processes align with OMB policy and guidance.

There are two aspects to the Exhibit 300s: 300A and 300B. Exhibit 300A, the "IT Capital Asset Summary," is a brief summary of the investment, with an explanation of benefits and the primary recipient or user of the investment. This section should also clarify dependencies between the investment in question and other investments; for example, if the authorization of one investment requires another to function, this must be spelled out in Exhibit 300A. This section should also specify how the new IT equipment will help close remaining performance gaps, and how new functionality, technological updates, or other enhancements may affect existing assets or systems.

Meanwhile, Exhibit 300B, the "Performance Measurement Report," is used to provide OMB with current fiscal year investment performance data for major investments. This encompasses all ongoing activities and operations from the year prior, as well as activities and operations scheduled to start in the current fiscal year. The Exhibit 300B includes the following sections:

A.1: **General Information**: basic information about the major investment.

B.1: **Projects**: all of the investment's projects that contain activities occurring in the current fiscal year.

B.2: **Activities**: activities that are performed to achieve the outcome of each project.

B.3: **Project Risk**: all significant risks to each project's success.

C.1: **Operational Performance Information**: performance targets for evaluating operations.

C.2: **Operational Risk**: all significant risks to investments achieving operational performance targets.

Therefore, while Exhibit 300A acts as the detailed justification for each IT investment, Exhibit 300B is used for the management of the execution of those investments. Together, Exhibit 300A and 300B combine to serve as a comprehensive audit for departments and agencies.

The Federal Information Security Management Act (FISMA)

As the global supply chain is increasingly interlinked, weaknesses in information security can cause increasingly harmful consequences, such as the compromise of public and private assets including intellectual property, trade secrets, and other sensitive information.

In response, FISMA established information security program evaluation and annual reporting requirements for federal agencies. FISMA compliance helps protect information from unauthorized access, use, disclosure, disruption, modification, and destruction.

Chapter 3: Fundamentals of Management for Cybersecurity

FISMA was passed in 2002 as part of the E-Government Act, Title III, and requires each U.S. federal agency to develop, document, and implement an information security program for all information systems that support the operations and assets of their respective agency, including those managed by other agencies or contractors. The act requires agency program officials, inspectors general, and CIOs to conduct annual reviews of the agency's information security program, and report the results to the OMB, which, in turn, uses the data to prepare an annual report to Congress on agency compliance. The data is aggregated and evaluated against acceptable levels of risk, which vary from agency to agency. Although the agency head (e.g., the secretary of DHS) decides the acceptable level of risk for their agency, system owners, program officials, and CIOs provide input for the decision using OMB policies and NIST standards and guidelines.

One of FISMA's challenges is deciding how to sufficiently measure, aggregate, and evaluate large amounts of information concerning information security. In order to best address this challenge, FISMA has three different sources of questions, each with a different aim. The first category is based on the administration's top priorities, as in the metrics that have the greatest probability of success in mitigating cybersecurity risks to information systems. These priorities are based on input from multiple cybersecurity experts, as well as public, private, and intelligence sources, to select the highest-impact mechanisms or actions. The second category of metrics covers "adequate security," referring to security that ensures "systems and applications used by the agency operate effectively and provide appropriate confidentiality, integrity, and availability, through the use of cost-effective management, personnel, operational, and technical controls."[7] The last set of questions establishes a baseline against which future performance can be measured. By determining the top priorities, the minimum requirements for "adequate security," and a baseline to compare future performance, the FISMA questions cover a range of data about information security practices and the general resilience of a department or agency's system security.

Data from FISMA reporting is a primary criterion in the security certification and accreditation process for an information system. Based on the evaluation of the data, an agency official decides whether or not the information system should be accredited, as defined in NIST SP 800-37 (*"Guide for the Security Certification and Accreditation of Federal Information Systems"*). Through security accreditation, agency officials officially authorize the operation of an information system, and explicitly assume responsibility for the security of the system. Therefore, certification and accreditation are closely linked with accountability – by accepting the risk to agency operations, assets and individuals, the agency official becomes fully accountable for any adverse impacts in the event of a security breach. Security accreditation, required by OMB Circular A-130, Appendix III, establishes a standard level of quality control and compels staff to implement the most effective security controls possible. Although security certification and accreditation strictly focus on specific control implementations, DHS and the OMB continuously improve and update FISMA metrics to better assess the current status and maturity level of departments' and agencies' cybersecurity postures in the face of new vulnerabilities and emerging technologies.

In addition to promoting responsibility and accountability, FISMA also creates clear consequences for non-compliance. Failure to pass a FISMA inspection can result in unfavorable publicity, increased oversight, vulnerable information technology, and a potential reduction of the agency's IT budget.

Compliance in the Private Sector: HIPAA as an example

FISMA is a comprehensive framework for securing the federal government's information technology. The FISMA model can be applied to set specific requirements for planning, budgeting, implementing, and maintaining a secure system for a private business subject to government regulation. These requirements entail: secu-

Compliance and Reporting

rity plans, assurance that appropriate officials are assigned responsibility, and periodic reviews of IT security controls.

Just as U.S. government departments and agencies are subject to IT compliance through FISMA, certain private sector companies must also comply with U.S. federal regulations. All U.S. federal regulations are found in the *Code of Federal Regulation* (CFR).[8]

Since all forms of data in all industries are now stored electronically, there are certain privacy and security controls in place to safeguard this information. One very important type of information that must be safeguarded is patient records. As part of the **Health Insurance Portability and Accountability Act of 1996 (HIPAA)**, the Department of Health and Human Services requires medical offices to "adopt national standards for electronic health care transactions and code sets, unique health identifiers, and security."[9] The following diagram provides a high-level overview of HIPAA, with particular focus on the security element of the act.[10]

The security section is where the IT audit fits—this audit will ensure that the medical office or hospital is compliant with HIPAA standards.

Health plans, health care clearinghouses, and healthcare providers are all subject to HIPAA's Privacy Rule, which attempts to safeguard all "all individually identifiable health information", also known as **protected health information (PHI)**. In other words, any entity that digitally stores, transmits, or processes health information must incorporate HIPAA standards. PHI includes information relating to:

- the individual's past, present, or future physical or mental health or condition
- the provision of health care to the individual, or
- the past, present, or future payment for the provision of health care to the individual, and that identifies the individual or for which there is a reasonable basis to believe can be used to identify the individual.[11]

Now, the question remains: how does a medical office that stores PHI comply with the regulations of HIPAA? The answer is found in the **NIST SP 800-66** (An Introductory Resource Guide for Implementing the Health Insurance Portability and Accountability Act (HIPAA) Security Rule). NIST SP 800-66 outlines the risk management framework suitable for the protection of PHI. In addition, there are specific administrative, physical and technical safeguards. The technical safeguards and controls are compiled from FIPS 200 (Minimum Security Requirements for Federal Information and Information Systems) and NIST SP 800-53 (Recommended Security Controls for Federal Information Systems and Organizations). For example, to maintain HIPAA compliance, a covered entity must ensure that controls are in place for access to systems. One way to ensure the controls are sufficient is to use an automated mechanism. Automated mechanisms "may be used to maintain up-to-date, complete, accurate, and readily available baseline configurations of organizational information systems."[12]

Also briefed in NIST 800-66 are access and audit controls that must be implemented. In addition, there are organizational, policy and procedural requirements of HIPAA-covered entities. An IT audit of a medical office or hospital will determine if the organization is HIPAA-compliant.

HIPAA security criteria and provisions have also been incorporated into other federal departments' and agencies' protection of citizen health information. For example, biometric data is stored by other federal entities for security purposes (e.g., Customs and Border Protection (CBP) in DHS).

Chapter 3: Fundamentals of Management for Cybersecurity

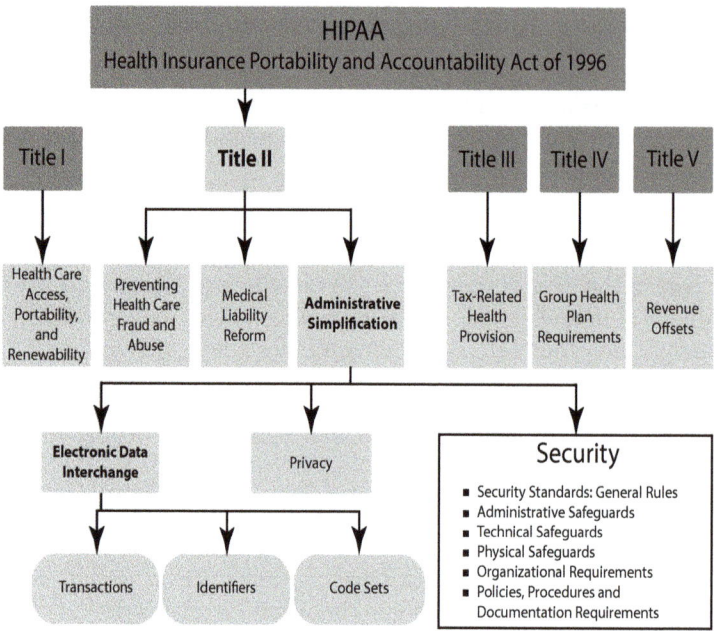

Figure 3-21: Diagram of key HIPAA components.

Conclusion

Program management is a highly complex and technical field. Managers for federal cybersecurity programs must be trained in the art and science of program management and understand the vocabulary, processes, documents, evaluative techniques, and compliance requirements that go into managing a sophisticated federal government program. Although few programs go exactly as planned or stay exactly on budget, the management skills and techniques covered in this chapter can help a program manager to keep his or her project on track and moving towards the objectives established in its earliest phases.

Key Questions

1. Which of the following steps in the program management framework could be described as "a statement of methodology"?

    a) the MNS

    b) the CONOPS

    c) the evaluation criteria

2. What did the Clinger-Cohen Act of 1996 say about U.S. government programs?

    a) It said that all programs must have a program manager

    b) It said that budgeting for all programs would be linked to execution

    c) It said that all U.S. government programs had to be approved by the DOD

Key Questions

3. Cybersecurity programs run by the U.S. federal government are charged with building new_____.

    a) Earned values

    b) Capabilities

    c) Capital assets

4. Which type of statement uses the most specific type of language?

    a) an op model

    b) an organizational mission statement

    c) an MNS

5. What did FISMA do?

    a) Granted budgeting powers for government cybersecurity programs to the OMB

    b) Mandated the use of EVM across the federal departments and agencies

    c) Made cybersecurity programs a national priority, and identified twelve new cybersecutiry capabilities needed by the federal government

Cyber Connections

The requirements for federal civilian cybersecurity programs in the U.S. government flow from high-level requirements issued by the president and Congress. For more details on how the president and Congress issue statements and legislation that give DHS and other departments the authority to create programs, see Chapter 6. For information on this process specific to cybersecurity law and policy, see Chapter 2.

For more on IDSs and other elements of cybersecurity operations, see Chapter 4.

Program management for the private sector shares many similarities with program management for the public sector; indeed, public sector program managers have learned many lessons from the private sector. Cybersecurity programs in the private sector are also informed by the federal government, and its legal requirements for private sector cybersecurity operations. For more information on the legal requirements of the private sector, see Chapter 5.

CHAPTER 4:
Computer Science Fundamentals and Cybersecurity Operations

CHAPTER OUTLINE

- **Overview of Computer Science Fundamentals and Cybersecurity Operations**
- **Technical Fundamentals**
- **An Introduction to the Internet**
- **Cryptologic Methods for Internet Security**
- **Attacks, Exploits, and Vulnerabilities**
- **Cybersecurity Operations**
- **Conclusion**
- **Key Questions**

4 Computer Science Fundamentals and Cybersecurity Operations

Chapter In Focus

- The basic structure of computers at a technical level.
- The structural aspects of computers that make them potentially insecure and vulnerable.
- The structure of the Internet and the components that make it a powerful tool for storing and transferring information.
- Common methods of cyber attacks and the vulnerabilities of the Internet that cyber attackers exploit.
- The basics of cybersecurity operations at a technical level.

Overview of Computer Science Fundamentals and Cybersecurity Operations

The earliest computers and the early Internet were not designed to support millions of users sharing huge amounts of information on a daily basis. In 1970, engineers working on ARPANET established "trust protocols" for computer-to-computer communication that still play a critical role in the technical functions of the Internet. As the Internet has grown in capability and complexity, these tools have revolutionized communication and commerce. It has also become clear that the Internet remains fundamentally insecure.

The inescapability of vulnerabilities in the structure of the Internet makes cyberspace a threat-laden environment, in which attackers and defenders must work constantly to stay ahead of each other. For both cyber attackers and cybersecurity professionals, the discovery of a previously unknown vulnerability in a computer, a piece of software, or the Internet may represent a significant achievement with far-reaching consequences.

Computer engineers and cybersecurity professionals think about computers and the Internet in highly specific ways that may be different from the way the general public understands these modern phenomena. Moreover, computer science and engineering terminology comprises a significant portion of the cybersecurity industry's language. Therefore, in order to understand cyber legislation or carry out cyber-related initiatives, one must first have a basic understanding of the technical language and skills that engineers and computer scientists use, as well as the problems they work constantly to address. This chapter will provide you with a grounding in the fundamentals of computer science and demonstrate how engineers and cybersecurity professionals think about computers, cyber attacks, and cybersecurity operations.

Technical Fundamentals

A **computer** is a device that processes digital (numerical) information, or **data**. A computer receives, processes, stores, and transfers data from a human user or from its internal memory. Computers cannot adapt or think for themselves. At the most basic level, a computer can be understood as a series of "on" and "off" switches, with "on" represented by "1" and "off" represented by "0."

Chapter 4: Computer Science Fundamentals and Cybersecurity Operations

Computers process data encoded as a series of 0's and 1's. These 0's and 1's make up the binary "language" that computers work with. The language of computers is called **binary** (recall that the prefix "bi" means "two," as in "bicycle") because it is a system that only uses two numbers: 0 and 1.

In binary code, the placement of the 0 or 1 determines a value. A series of these values defines and creates data, such as emails, photos, or documents. Even letters on keyboards, such as "D" or "M," have corresponding binary values that the computer processes and responds to in order to display those letters on the monitor.

A computer translates every value, including every letter on the keyboard, into a binary code. Every function performed by a computer is performed in binary. Requiring an everyday user to use binary for entering information into a computer is unrealistic, so there needs to be an interface, or translation, from human language into computer language.

Programming Languages

To answer this problem, computer scientists created **programming languages**. Programming languages allow a human fluent in these languages to use non-binary commands as shorthand for the binary codes a computer can work with.

Early versions of programming languages were much easier than programming in binary, but were still very difficult to learn and understand. These are typically referred to as *lower-order languages*. Examples of lower-order languages include assembly language and machine code.

In recent decades, programmers have developed languages that are much closer to human language and therefore easier for humans to write and understand. These languages, described as *higher-order languages*, include C++ and Java.

Programming languages solve the communication problems that are inherent to the relationship between humans and computers. Today, most computer programmers write programs in a higher-order language. The instructions created by these languages are then translated, by means of a program known as a *compiler*, into a binary form that a computer can process.

How Computers Work: Processors and Program

Now that you understand the binary language in which computers process information, we can discuss the hardware that computers are made up of. A computer is composed of hardware components. **Hardware** is any part of a computer that has a physical form and helps the computer to process information. The keyboard, monitor, and motherboard of your computer are all examples of hardware.

A **processor** is the part of the computer that intakes data that the user inputs into the computer, performs a process upon this data (as instructed by the user through complex sets of digital instructions called *programs*), and outputs a new kind of data. At the most basic level, a processor simply performs mathematical functions on binary numbers. An example of this process occurs when you type something into a Microsoft Word document. Microsoft Word is a software program that instructs the computer to take the letters you type, translate them into binary, and then make letters appear more or less immediately on a digital "page." When you save a Word document, your computer saves it as a complex binary code that you never see.

The most important component in a computer is the **central processing unit (CPU)**. The CPU is the standard processor on most personal computers. The CPU can be thought of as the "brain" of the computer and has

Technical Fundamentals

two basic functions: to perform calculations directed by the user, and to move information from one location to another. The CPU is also the computer's command station: it directs all traffic, processes all incoming information, and sends information to be stored.

The operations a processor conducts may be as simple as adding two numbers, or as complex as moving information from one place in the computer's memory to another. The speed of a processor is measured in terms of calculations per second. One million (1,000,000) calculations per second is equal to one megahertz; one billion (1,000,000,000) calculations per second is equal to one gigahertz. So, if your computer has a 2.4 gigahertz processor, it is capable of performing 2.4 billion calculations per second. In this context, *calculations* refer to commands or instructions, not simply mathematical calculations. Faster processor speeds are generally equated to better overall computer performance.

One way to increase the performance of a computer is to use a *multi-core processor*. The term *multi-core* means that more than one processor exists in the system. The power of the computer's system and its ability to process multiple data requests simultaneously increase as extra processors are added.

Software is a collection of programs, instructions, and processes that the computer uses to perform a limited set of functions. Microsoft Word and Adobe Photoshop are examples of software. Software typically provides an easy-to-use **graphical user interface (GUI)** for the user to interact with and then executes code inside the CPU to perform the actions requested by the user.

How Computer Systems Work

In order to execute programs and run software, a computer needs more than just a CPU. Other components of a computer can include the motherboard (the central board to which all the other components are connected), random-access memory, a hard drive, a CD-ROM drive, and a network card. Each of these components can be broken down into its own basic components. For example, a network card also contains various subcomponents, such as memory, software, and a processor, that enable it to perform the function of communicating with a network.

Components are pieces working together to form a **system**. Independently, components are not necessarily useful to a user, but when combined to perform a specific function or set of functions, they create a system that can be useful. A laptop is a system. A router is a system. A printer is a system. As you can see from these examples, not all systems are useful without being connected to other systems to form a **system of systems**.

A system of systems is a collection of systems working together to produce an effect that is greater than the sum of its parts. A system of systems is created by connecting systems to each other. For example, connecting a laptop to a router with an Ethernet cable, or connecting the same laptop to a printer, creates a system of systems. The laptop, the router, and the printer are all systems, and they can all work together in a synthesized system of systems. A system such as a laptop or desktop computer is useful independently, but a system such as a router is designed to perform a function within a system of systems.

A system of systems could be as basic as a home network connecting a printer, router and desktop computer, or as advanced as the Internet itself, with millions of computers, routers, and networks all working

VIDEO

Watch 'Processors and Program Language' at
http://vimeo.com/channels/cybersecurityfoundations

Chapter 4: Computer Science Fundamentals and Cybersecurity Operations

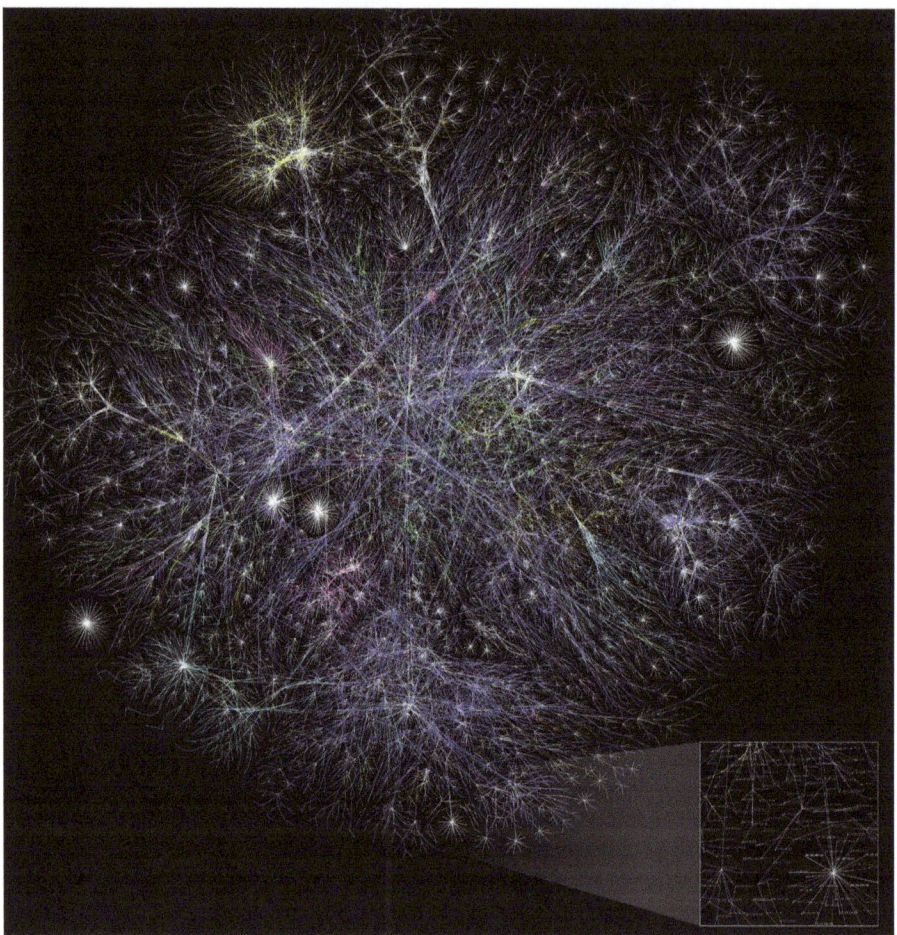

Figure 4-1: The Internet is an example of a system of systems. The above image is a partial map of the Internet based on 2005 data compiled by the Opte Project.[1] Each line represents a connection between two IP addresses. This image represents less than 30% of the networks accessible by Opte's data collection project.

together (see Figure 4-1). In general, the more complex the system is, the greater its chances of having its vulnerabilities exploited. For this reason alone, the Internet is a minefield of vulnerabilities and potential exploits.

Computer Memory

When you are working on a computer, it is convenient to have the computer remember what you have already done, or where you are in a series of steps, so that you don't have to start from the beginning with each new instruction you give the computer. For this reason, computers have **memory**, or **storage**. Early computers had very little storage capacity; if you wanted to run a program, you would have to insert it and then save it on some form of removable storage, like a floppy disk.

Over time, the cost of storage has significantly decreased, so the ability to store large amounts of information on a computer's hard drive has increased. Modern computers can store large amounts of information in the form of documents, photographs, and videos. In addition, programs must store many kinds of information while they are running, much of it information the computer user will never see or be aware of.

At the most basic level, there are two types of computer storage: **volatile** and **non-volatile**. Some information, such as the information that a program needs from moment to moment while it is running, only needs to be stored for a few seconds. Other information, such as a thesis paper in progress, needs to be saved for as long as possible.

The computer stores information that is only needed for a short period of time using volatile storage. Think of volatile storage as a piece of scratch paper that you use to write down a phone number that someone gives you. You transfer that phone number into your computer or phone and then quickly throw away that piece of paper. Any information stored in volatile storage will be lost if the computer loses power.

Examples of volatile storage include the CPU **cache** and **random-access memory (RAM)**. Cache is a high-speed and expensive-to-produce form of volatile memory that a CPU can use as its "scratch paper" while performing calculations. Its high-speed capacity supports billions of calculations per second. However, because cache is a form of volatile memory, if the computer loses power while a user is running a program, anything in the cache will likely be lost. CPUs rely on cache memory to quickly store short-term information.

RAM is another common form of volatile storage. RAM stores short-term information that may not be important enough to keep in cache memory. RAM is made up of small components, called *capacitors*, that briefly store information about 1's and 0's as they pass through a processor. Just as with cache memory, each time a computer is turned off, the computer's RAM is emptied.

For information that is stored for more than a few seconds, computers use non-volatile storage. Non-volatile storage keeps information stored even if the computer is disconnected from a power source. Hard drives, CDs, DVDs, and USB memory sticks are all examples of non-volatile storage. As technology has improved, non-volatile storage has become faster, and can now even be used to replace or enhance traditionally volatile storage. For example, a USB memory stick can increase the RAM available on a computer. Both volatile and non-volatile storage are crucial to the overall functioning of the CPU and the computer as a whole.

An Introduction to the Internet

IT infrastructure provides a critical foundation for the conveniences of the modern world. There are three primary elements of IT infrastructure: the basic technology, such as hardware and software; the communications pathways over which the information travels; and the design and integration of the systems involved. Thus, IT infrastructure is both a technology (a working system, made up of many smaller systems) and a service (a tool that gives users certain capabilities). Banking, e-mail, search engines, and online commerce are all services that depend upon IT infrastructure.

IT infrastructure has evolved from accounting machines (1930-1950), to mainframe and minicomputers (1959-present), to PCs (1981-present). The development of the Internet linked personal computers to large computer networks' centralized servers (1983-present). A *server* is a computer that functions as a "host" to a group of connected computers and provides services to them.

The Internet for public use, linked by **routers** (devices that send data between computer networks linked by large and powerful servers called *enterprise servers*) became widely available in 1992. This was the year of the first "web page" and the introduction of the World Wide Web. Now comprised of more than one million web pages, the web quickly became the Internet's most popular application; however, it does not represent the Internet in its entirety.

Chapter 4: Computer Science Fundamentals and Cybersecurity Operations

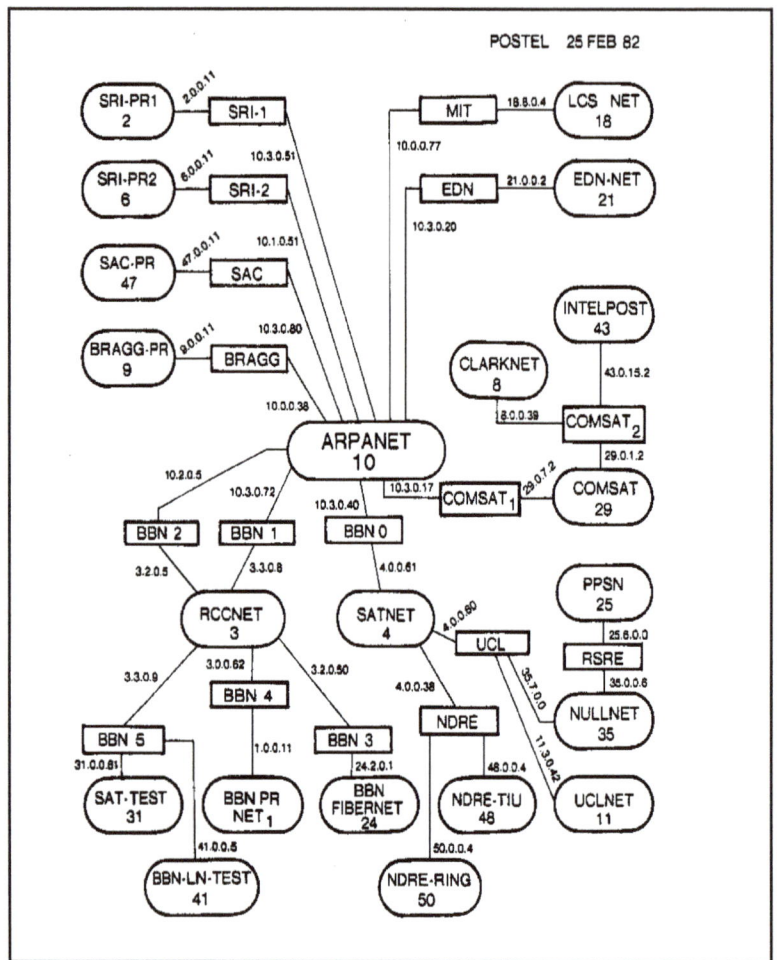

The entire Internet in semi-production phase in February 1982. The ovals are sites/networks, the rectangles are individual routers. (Drawn by Jon Postel of the Information Sciences Institute.)

When the Internet became widely popular in the mid-1990s, many people did not realize that decades of work had gone into creating the deep and fundamental mechanisms that allow this massive global computer network to function reliably. These mechanisms were flexible enough to allow the Internet to grow from a relatively small group of "inter-networks" (located mainly in universities) into the major communications tool (comprising hundreds of thousands of networks) that it is today. These mechanisms, which we will discuss later in this section, allowed the Internet to easily accommodate thousands of new users and established standards and protocols for how the Internet (a tool that has no central authority) would be accessed and experienced.

In order to trust this infrastructure enough to use it for important transactions like banking, data storage, and personal and professional correspondence, computer scientists and engineers had to install and maintain appropriate security mechanisms to prevent violations of data confidentiality (unauthorized access), violations of data integrity (unauthorized data changes), and violations of availability (restricting access to certain data). Every day, hackers and other cyber attackers around the world attempt these types of violations.

An Introduction to the Internet

The Structure of the Internet

The Internet is a massive and extremely complex system of systems. Multiple systems are connected to a single router that communicates with the outside world. Routers communicate with each other and become aware of which systems each router is connected to. In essence, this combination of connected and communicating routers and large servers connected to individual computers forms a system of systems known as the Internet.

In order for the Internet to function, several key principles need to be in place. First, in order to build a system that could withstand disruptions and intermittent connectivity, the Internet must have the capability to break down information into smaller pieces for transit purposes, and then reassemble the pieces when they reach their destination. These pieces are called **packets**, and this mode of transmitting, receiving, and reassembling packets is accomplished primarily through two languages, or protocols: the **Transmission Control Protocol (TCP)** and **Internet Protocol (IP)**. Known together as **TCP/IP**, these protocols dictate how information travels over the Internet. We will discuss TCP/IP in greater detail later in this chapter.

Second, routers must be able to communicate using a common language and methodology that enables information to travel in the most efficient path to its destination. This language is known as **Border Gateway Protocol (BGP)**. BGP is analogous to the "traffic laws" of the Internet. We will also discuss BGP in greater detail later in this chapter.

Finally, while machines are comfortable using complex numbering schemes to communicate, it is very difficult for humans to remember those numbers and use them efficiently. Therefore, the Internet requires a way to translate an IP address (e.g., "74.125.228.70"), into words that a human brain can easily remember (e.g., "google.com"). This translation is accomplished through the **Domain Name System (DNS)**.

TCP/IP, BGP, and DNS are critical to the functioning of the Internet, but they are each vulnerable to attack because they rely on "trust." In other words, TCP/IP, BGP, and DNS depend on the basic trustworthiness of the information they work with; there is no way for an Internet protocol to "doubt" the veracity or motives of a router broadcasting its location. To better understand these vulnerabilities, we must first understand how the Internet became the system of systems that it is today.

How the Internet Works

As discussed earlier, routers are devices that direct the traffic of data packets that are sent from computer to computer. You may have a small router in your home that creates a home network, while your local cable and phone companies also control several larger routers close to your house. The routers controlled by your local cable or phone company are able to send traffic from your local area to routers located all over the world. Among these routers are several Internet *backbones* — large routers that direct traffic from many thousands of computers.

Cable and phone companies are popular **Internet service providers (ISPs)**. ISPs act as an on-ramp to the Internet by connecting customers to an Internet backbone and letting them communicate with other people without having to build their own local or global network. On the ISP side of the connection is a **wide area network (WAN)**, which covers a large area, such as a small town or a portion of a city. The customer side of the network is typically known as a **local area network (LAN)**. A LAN can consist of a laptop and a printer, or an entire business infrastructure. Larger private networks typically include both WANs and LANs, because these networks may connect smaller locations with infrastructure that is potentially spread around the world.

Chapter 4: Computer Science Fundamentals and Cybersecurity Operations

Fundamentally, the Internet was designed to be a highly resilient infrastructure that could transmit information very reliably over unreliable connections. To accomplish this design goal, the Internet follows a protocol (IP) of breaking down information into standard packets that can be read by any system receiving them. These data packets are akin to the envelopes used to send a letter through the mail. Each packet sent over the Internet has a destination address. Due to the nature of the Internet, this information may not necessarily follow a single path; rather, packets that together comprise a single document or photo file may take multiple paths to reach the same destination. A packet's path to its destination may be determined by factors such as the proximity of other routers and the amount of Internet traffic being processed by a router when the package is being sent. Depending on all of these factors, the packets may arrive in any order at the destination computer.

Internet Protocols and Standards: The Rules of the Road

One of the most important elements of Internet communications is how information packets are formed, and how Internet routers must deal with these packets in order to send them along to their final destination. As we discussed earlier, TCP/IP establishes rules for breaking down data packets and then transmitting, receiving, and reassembling those packets. TCP is responsible for the movement of the packets; IP is responsible for breaking-down and reassembling the packets. It is because of TCP/IP that communication across the Internet works. Each router on the Internet "expects" data that passes through to work with TCP/IP standards in order to reach its final destination. TCP/IP ensures that data packets sent through the Internet are reassembled at their destination in their original, unified format. It also ensures that data is not corrupted or lost during transmission from one computer to another.

Every router, computer, or smartphone connected to the Internet must have a unique identifier, or address, in order to send and receive information. This address is commonly referred to as an **IP address**. IP addresses act as the physical address for systems on the Internet and must be publicly known in order to send and receive information.

At this time, there are two numbering systems in existence: *IP version 4 (IPV4)* and *IP version 6 (IPV6)*. IPV4 is the current number system of the Internet. In IPV4, IP addresses are made up of four sets of 8 binary bits—resulting in a 32-bit number. Because the largest number you can create in binary with only 8 bits is 255, each of the four numbers in an IP address can be between 0 and 255. Therefore, theoretically, you can only have 2^{32} addresses on the Internet, or roughly 4.2 billion addresses. While it was once inconceivable that there could ever be a need for this many IP addresses, this notion is not inconceivable anymore.

Rather than only using 32 bits in an address, IPV6 uses 128 bits for an address. This increases the number of unique addresses to 2^{128}, or 340,282,366,920,938,463,463,374,607,431,768,211,456 — a difficult number to conceive of, let alone name! The future of the Internet lies in IPV6, but the process of converting systems and protocols to be able to understand this new addressing system is very complex and will take many years to implement fully.

From a cybersecurity perspective, an IP address represents a way to identify a system on the Internet, whether it is an attacker or a target. When a person sends or receives information on the Internet, or even just visits a website, it is possible to attain information about that person's IP address. The idea of associating an IP address with a specific computer is known as **attribution**. Attribution can be helpful when tracking the source of cyber attacks, but in a limited way. Because the Internet is built on a system of trust, there are countless ways to "trick" systems into believing that a user is operating from a false IP address, or to route all communications through another system. To offer just one example of this kind of trickery, Google cybersecurity experts were able to track the IP address responsible for a massive attack on its system in 2010. The IP address of the attacker corresponded to a university library in China. However, it was unclear whether the IP address and the computer

An Introduction to the Internet

associated with it were directly responsible for the attacks, or whether they had been hijacked by a remote computer and used as a front for the attacks. Therefore, in cybersecurity operations, IP addresses and computers can be identified, but it is still difficult to know who is truly behind a cyber attack.

Connecting Networks: BGP

BGP is a protocol that routers use to communicate with each other and to identify other routers and IP addresses that are in close proximity to one another. Through this communication, routers are able to build lists, or *routing tables*, to help them "understand" what other routers they are connected to and what routers those routers are connected to. Through this process, a router becomes "aware" of a sense of distance, measured in hops, between where they are located in the Internet and where a potential destination is located. Based on this information, routers make decisions to get information to a destination in as few hops as possible and, therefore, as quickly as possible. To illustrate this point, refer to Figure 4-2. In this depiction, Bob and Joe want to send information to each other.

Each of the routers (illustrated by circles) communicates with each other and registers how many routers are between Bob and Joe. For example, Router F knows that Bob is connected to Router A, which is two routers away (through either D or C), while Joe is connected to Router H, which is also two routers away (either through C or G). When Bob sends information to Joe it will take the shortest path—A, C, H, as illustrated by the green lines.

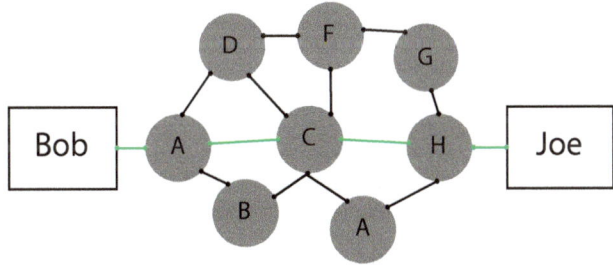

Figure 4-2: Communication between routers, shown here as circles, enables them to calculate the shortest path between Bob and Joe.

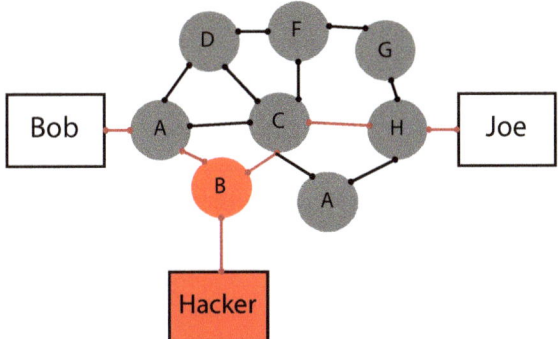

Figure 4-3: The BGP trust protocol can be exploited via falsification of a router's location.

138

Chapter 4: Computer Science Fundamentals and Cybersecurity Operations

As discussed, from a cybersecurity perspective, BGP represents a significant challenge. It is a "trust" protocol, which means that each router trusts what the other routers tell it. For example, if Router B advertised that it was only one router hop from Joe, Router A could send information through Router B, providing the owner of Router B with access to that information. This scenario is depicted in Figure 4-3.

There is no central mechanism for ensuring that routers are close to the systems they indicate, and there is nothing to prevent a router from indicating that it is near a popular IP address when it is not. If a router falsifies the location of its IP address, the Internet traffic directed at that site could potentially pass through that router. Any information that is not encrypted could then be read by the person who controls said router. Therefore, malicious agents with technical expertise can exploit the BGP trust protocol fairly easily.

To offer another example, imagine that Company A is working on a secret product that Company Z wants to learn about. Company Z places a router on the Internet. This router announces that it is one router hop away from Company A's network. Any traffic and router that Company A's router communicates with will then send information through Company Z's router, allowing Company Z to learn about Company A's intellectual property.

Naming the Internet: DNS

The Internet is based on a set of communication protocols, and traffic is routed across the Internet using BGP. However, these systems are not necessarily user-friendly, so a system must exist to translate IP addresses into human-readable names. The solution to this challenge is the DNS. DNS uses a complex network of systems to quickly translate a domain name such as "google.com" into an IP address. Oversight of the DNS system is currently provided by the Internet Corporation for Assigned Names and Numbers (ICANN).

The structure behind DNS is hierarchical. At the highest level, there are **top-level domains (TLDs)**, such as .com and .edu. Each TLD is used to represent a community of associated systems. For example, the .edu TLD is used by educational institutions, while .gov is used for U.S government entities. A TLD is managed by an organization appointed by ICANN. The managing organization acts as the authoritative registry for domain names and operates name servers that translate domain names into IP addresses; this process is also known as DNS translation.

Like other parts of the Internet, the design of the DNS system is based on trust. This trust creates significant vulnerabilities within DNS. For example, if you are connected to a network that tells your system which DNS server to use, you trust that DNS server to provide you with the right IP address for the requested domain. The cybersecurity community is aware of this vulnerability and is instituting **Domain Name System Security Extensions (DNSSEC)** to provide assurance that the information given by the DNS server is accurate. DNSSEC thus protects Internet users from routers that falsify information and gain illicit access to data packets in transit.

DNSSEC is a suite of security-standards tools developed by the Internet Engineering Task Force (IETF). The IETF is a volunteer organization (although it does receive funds from the National Security Agency and private-sector groups) that sets standards for DNS security across IP networks. DNSSEC, when implemented across the Internet, will offer a "digital signature" from routers and IP addresses to verify that they are exactly what they say they are.

Cryptologic Methods for Internet Security

Encryption

As you learned earlier in this chapter, computers process and store information in terms of 1's and 0's; this unique computer language is called binary code. **Encryption** is the process of using mathematical algorithms to

Cryptologic Methods for Internet Security

transform easily read binary information into a form that cannot be easily read. The encryption algorithm must be known by anyone who wants to unlock, or decrypt, the file. The algorithm that is run on the file's binary code uses a secret key as an input to the equation and uses that key to make the information unreadable. To decrypt the file, a user must have access to the encrypted file, the algorithm, and the key.

Still, if a hacker has access to an encrypted file as well as the algorithm that was used to encrypt it, he can attempt to guess the key in order to access the file. The process of using a software program to guess passwords, or decryption keys, is known as a **brute force attack**. The more complex the key and the less that the hacker knows about it, the harder it will be for him to prevail in a brute force attack. Below are three examples of varying complexity for password codes:

Low complexity: Some standard door locks contain push buttons with numbers for a three-digit code. These locks are not digital, and the numbers can't be repeated within the code. A six-button lock would have a total of 120 possible codes (6 x 5 x 4). If you could guess a code once every two seconds, it would take you, at most, four minutes to guess correctly.

Moderate complexity: A bicycle lock has four numbers in a code. Each number could be 0 through 9, and each number can be repeated. The maximum number of possible codes would be 10,000 (10^4, or 10 x 10 x 10 x 10). If you could guess a unique code once every two seconds, it would take, at most, approximately 5.5 hours to successfully execute a brute force attack.

Higher complexity: A file encrypted using a fixed 8-character password field that only uses repeatable lowercase letters has around 208 billion possibilities.

Even with the higher-complexity example above, a modern computer could potentially break the key within seconds or minutes. It is for this reason that modern encryption algorithms typically create at least 256-bit encryption. This means that the key for the algorithm consists of 256 binary numbers. The maximum number of guesses required in a brute force attack of a 256 bit key is 2^{256}, or a number that consists of a 1 followed by 77 0's. Standard user-friendly applications can use 256-bit encryption while still allowing the user to enter a simple password. This is accomplished by creating an algorithm that produces a 256-bit encryption key corresponding to a user-generated password.

Cybersecurity professionals describe encryption methods as being either *in motion* or *at rest*. *In motion* indicates that the file or secured information is not encrypted, but the conceptual Internet "tunnel" through which the information travels is encrypted, preventing someone from capturing that information and viewing it. *At rest* means the information itself is stored in an encrypted form. From a cybersecurity perspective, it is best to employ both encryption methods for sensitive files.

Encrypting Websites: HTTPS

Five to ten years ago, most digital banking and other commercial transactions on the Internet were conducted using the standard **Hypertext Transfer Protocol (HTTP)**. HTTP, the protocol that enables the use of web pages to display information, is not encrypted. This means that any information sent to or from a web page travels "in the clear" and is readable by anyone capable of intercepting the traffic.

Today, growing cyber threats have prompted website operators to use encryption for sensitive communications. Encrypted web communications use a more secure version of HTTP, known as **Hypertext Transfer Protocol Secure (HTTPS)**. HTTPS uses encryption to create a secure connection between the user's browser and the website. The browser and the website share their respective "certificates" to verify the authenticity of each

Chapter 4: Computer Science Fundamentals and Cybersecurity Operations

source and then use a key to encrypt and decrypt communications. HTTPS connections to a website are often represented by a small drawing of a padlock on the browser's navigation bar.

Hashing

Hashing is another tool used to make information difficult for third parties to intercept and use. Like encryption, hashing involves the use of algorithms on files. However, instead of making the file unreadable, hashing generates a unique number, similar to a digital "fingerprint." To create a unique fingerprint, the file is run through a specific algorithm; MD5 and SHA-2 are commonly-employed hashing algorithms. The *Message-digest algorithm (MD5)* generates a 128-bit number. The *Secure Hash Algorithm (SHA-2)*, a more advanced and more secure alternative to MD5, uses a larger-bit number.

The value of hashing is that it gives users the ability to detect even minor changes in files that have been transmitted over the Internet. If you receive a Word document from a friend, you have to trust that the document wasn't changed by someone else before it reached you. To verify that this is the case, the sender can generate an MD5 hash of the file and send the number generated to the receiver. The receiver can then generate an MD5 hash of the received file. If both numbers match, then the file hasn't changed since it was sent.

An organization may use hashing to detect vulnerabilities on its network. For example, it is simple to generate MD5 hashes of known pieces of **malware**—malicious software that attackers plant on victims' computers. Having generated a unique hash for a given piece of malware, the organization can scan files on their network's computers to see if any files match that MD5 hash. Any file that matches the hash contains the malware. The company can also implement systems that scan e-mail attachments for known malware using MD5 hashes.

Attacks, Exploits, and Vulnerabilities

The Internet is a revolutionary communications tool that connects computer networks all over the world. However, as discussed earlier, many critical functions of the Internet are based on trust, rather than security. As a result, any computer, system, or device that is connected to the Internet is vulnerable to attack and exploitation by untrustworthy actors.

A **vulnerability** is a weakness in a system that an attacker could target and exploit. When computer professionals discover a vulnerability for a particular software package, they develop a patch to fix the security "hole" that the vulnerability has created. An **exploit** is a tool or process that is used in an attack to take advantage of a vulnerability and gain access to, or control over, a system. Exploits typically target known, but unpatched, vulnerabilities. An exploit that targets a vulnerability that is not known to anyone but the attacker is called a **zero-day exploit**. The term *zero-day* refers to the fact that the vulnerability is not known until the attack is launched.

A successful attack that provides the attacker with unauthorized access to a system is called a **cyber intrusion**. A system that has been attacked and is under the control of an attacker is known as a **compromised system**. When an attack is detected, there is typically a need to identify who is conducting the attack. The process of identifying the individual and/or system conducting the attack is called *attribution*. In the cybersecurity world, it is exceedingly difficult to gain clarity on who is actually behind the keyboard of an attack, but there are methods and techniques for doing so.

Once an exploit or attack has been successful and the attacker has control of, or access to, the target system, numerous things can happen. Often the purpose of the attack is to remove information from the target system; this is known as *exfiltration*. However, not all attacks are designed for exfiltration; other purposes include, but are not limited, to the following:

Reconnaissance: some attackers gain unauthorized access to networks to learn more about the network, its computers, or its users.

Damage: some attacks are designed to cause damage, prevent access to a system or a network, or reduce the integrity or trustworthiness of a system.

Command and Control: some attacks are conducted to establish the command and control required to conduct larger attacks; by taking over a system and using it to conduct an attack, attribution is made more difficult, as the system conducting the attack may be a compromised system rather than the attacker's own system.

Distribution: many attacks simply take advantage of the target to spread to further systems, thereby creating a large network of compromised systems that can be used for subsequent attacks.

To achieve any of these desired effects, a successful attack must take place. Here are some of the more common types of attack:

Malware

Software or software code that is written to enable an attack or exploit is called *malicious software*; the term is commonly shortened to *malware*. Some examples of malware include computer viruses, worms, and Trojan horses. A *virus* may be written to deliver unwanted advertising to a system, log every key stroke, take pictures with the computer's camera, or even erase all information on a system. A *worm* is a specially crafted version of malware designed to crawl from system to system within a network. A *Trojan horse* is malware that appears to serve a legitimate purpose but actually releases malware on a system. Pirated and freely distributed software sometimes contains Trojan horses. Often the delivery mechanism, like the pirated software, performs as expected and the user has no idea that the computer has been infected.

Phishing Attacks

Phishing is a popular form of cyber attack in which attackers "fish" for a user's personal information. In general, phishing attacks are very broad and not targeted towards specific uses. Attackers use phishing to deceive users into voluntarily entering personal information or giving the attacker access to their system. Many phishing attacks entice users to "Click this link!" or "Open this site." When the user does so, the attacker uses malware to gain entry to the user's computer.

Attackers often send phishing emails to thousands of email addresses at a time, with no particular individual as the targeted victim. Due to the random nature of phishing, most phishing messages get caught by spam filters and are never seen by the user. However, others do make it through to a user's inbox, increasing the likelihood that the user may open the message and launch the attached malware. Beyond email, phishing attackers also use social media sites such as Twitter and Facebook, encouraging users to click on links that contain malicious programs. When an unsuspecting user clicks on of these links, malware can be launched to compromise the user account or computer; the user can also be asked to enter personal information.

Targeted Attacks: Spear Phishing

In contrast to phishing, which is a broad, untargeted form of attack, there are very targeted attacks that employ e-mail, social media, or even compromised websites. Such targeted attacks are known as **spear phishing**. To carry out a spear phishing attack, the attackers often work to gain specific information about the person be-

Chapter 4: Computer Science Fundamentals and Cybersecurity Operations

ing attacked; such information is then used to entice them to "take the bait" and click on a link or open an e-mail. The most sophisticated spear phishing attacks use specific details about the projects a person is involved with, the names of family members, or the names and roles of people they communicate with most often.

Email is the most common method for launching a spear-phishing attack. The spear phisher sends a specially crafted email to the target posing as someone the target knows personally or professionally. The email may include a Word document that claims to be a part of a project the person is involved in. When the target opens the document, malicious code is run to execute an exploit that provides the attacker with access to the user's computer. Now the spear phisher can see everything the target sees and may be able to do such things as log the person's keystrokes, open his documents, and gain access to his company's secrets. Spear phishing attacks aimed at upper management in prominent corporations have garnered publicity in recent years. Examples include the RSA SecurID and Google breaches, both of which occurred in 2011. In both of these incidents, attackers used spear phishing to gain access to the most sensitive information of the target companies.

Once the attacker becomes an "insider" in this manner, standard security measures such as firewalls and "in-motion" encryption no longer protect the target's information. Once attackers are on a trusted system, they have a launching point to begin searching the company network, recording keystrokes, obtaining passwords, posing as trusted users, and sending more highly-targeted spear phishing emails.

Spear phishing is not always this sophisticated. A spear phisher may target a group of disparate people—say, the customers of a given website—rather than a specific individual. One of the great ironies of phishing emails is that phishers often try to trick people into volunteering personal information by warning them (falsely) that the security of one of their accounts (a PayPal, Amazon, eBay, or bank account, for example) has been compromised. These phishing emails prompt users to log into their accounts and enter passwords and other information. When a user clicks on the link of a phishing email, it takes them to a "spoofed" site that looks exactly like the site (Paypal, Amazon, etc.) that the phisher's email had warned was compromised. When a user enters his login information, the phisher captures it.

Botnets

One of the more advanced tools available to a cyber attacker is the command of what is known as a botnet. A **botnet** is a collection of systems that have all been compromised for the purpose of creating a network of zombie computers; the zombie network will, in turn, take commands from whoever commands the botnet. Botnets are spread through many of the methods already discussed, such as malware, and work to build as large of a network as possible. Botnets, which can be employed to conduct large-scale attacks that shut down networks and systems on the Internet, can be controlled by a single, anonymous individual. In an interesting turn of events, cybercriminals have even been known to develop large botnets and then rent them out to paying customers for use in attacks.

In one recent example, a botnet of computers infected by the Coreflood virus affected as many as two million computers. This botnet, dismantled by the FBI in 2011, is only one example of the scale that can be reached by using malware to develop a botnet.[2]

Denial of Service (DoS) Attacks

Some attacks do not even require an attacker to gain access to a system. One example of this type of attack is a **denial of service (DoS)** attack on a network or system. The most basic denial of service attack simply directs such a large volume of network traffic at a target that it overwhelms the target and prevents access to or from the target. DoS attacks are often directed against popular public websites. They often use brute force to overwhelm the computing resources of the target website and don't require a great deal of skill.

A **distributed denial-of-service attack (DDoS)** is carried out by an attacker who works remotely and controls a botnet to use a large number of network systems in the DoS attack. In this way, a DDoS attack is "distributed" among many computers. Perhaps the most famous DDoS attack to date was launched at the Iranian government's computer servers by protesters in 2009.[3] Botnets are essential for DDoS attacks because a remotely controlled team of millions of zombies can quickly flood an IP address with more requests than it can handle. DDoS attacks have targeted major companies, newspapers, governments, and economic institutions around the world.

Man-in-the-Middle Attacks

In its most basic form, a **man-in-the-middle attack** involves an attacker that positions himself between two nodes that are communicating. Such an attack can achieve any number of desired effects. In these kinds of attacks, the intruder may take advantage of protocols that rely on trust, as discussed earlier in this chapter, and pretend to be a trusted party or redirect network traffic through a compromised router to "listen" to all of the traffic crossing the network.

A basic man-in-the-middle attack is perhaps the easiest kind of attack to carry out, because it requires little advanced technical knowledge. In fact, anyone who is able to connect to an unencrypted wireless network may be able to stage a man-in-the-middle attack by intercepting communications as they pass through the wireless network's router. For ease of use, most restaurants and coffee shops offering free Internet don't encrypt the wireless network, making any communication that isn't encrypted "in motion" easily viewable by anyone else on the wireless network.

A more complex man-in-the-middle attack can involve exploiting the BGP protocol to reroute traffic over a compromised router or network. It is theoretically possible that, if you control the network that traffic is crossing, you could save a copy of every piece of information that crosses that network. This concept was presented at the DEFCON hacker convention in 2008 and still represents a real threat on the Internet.[4]

DNS Cache Poisoning

DNS cache poisoning is an attack on a DNS address or a series of DNS addresses. The attacker tampers with the IP address of a specific site, so that all traffic intended for a specific DNS address (e.g., www.amazon.com) travels to a different IP address instead, causing confusion for users and embarrassment for the company that operates the "true" website. DNS cache poisoning can also be used for more-malicious purposes, such as routing users away from trusted websites and toward sites that will download malware onto visiting systems.

Vulnerabilities

The success of any of the attacks discussed above requires the existence of a vulnerability and the tools to exploit that vulnerability. In general, there are three broad classes of vulnerabilities: human, known, and unknown.

Human Vulnerabilities

One of the most significant challenges for any cybersecurity professional is the human component of the network. Systems have users, and users make mistakes—either intentionally or unintentionally. Attacks can be caused by weak user passwords, by a user clicking on a spear-phishing e-mail that exploits a known or unknown

Chapter 4: Computer Science Fundamentals and Cybersecurity Operations

vulnerability, or by users supporting an attack from the inside. This last type of human vulnerability, the "insider threat," is particularly challenging to understand and prevent. A disgruntled user can cause hundreds of thousands, if not millions, of dollars of damage with a few clicks of a mouse. Even well-intentioned users can make mistakes by visiting sites with malicious files, connecting to unsecure networks while on travel, or providing a password over the phone to someone who is pretending to be technical support. Human behavior can be improved, but the potential for mistakes cannot be completely removed from the cybersecurity equation, placing increased importance on patching known vulnerabilities and preventing unknown vulnerabilities from occurring.

Known Vulnerabilities

Today's software is increasingly complex and places increased emphasis on performance and user experience. Unfortunately, this means that there are often features or mistakes in a given program that can be exploited for unintended purposes. Some known vulnerabilities are related to misconfiguration. These can be as simple as a company not changing the default password on its server, allowing anyone to log in to the server and take control. Other vulnerabilities are more difficult to exploit. For instance, *buffer overflow attacks* involve intentionally crashing a program to take advantage of the way a program or system attempts to recover from the crash. Another type of attack is called *code injection* and commonly involves the use of form fields within an application or website to place malicious code for the system to run. Software developers are constantly working to find errors in their software and release patches before those errors can be exploited. Many companies publish patches to their software on a weekly basis to prevent known vulnerabilities from being exploited.

In support of the effort to patch known vulnerabilities, there are systems created by both the private sector and the government to catalog known vulnerabilities and provide information that IT and cybersecurity professionals can use in preventing attacks. One such example is the National Vulnerability Database (NVD), hosted by NIST and DHS. The NVD provides a repository of known vulnerabilities that can be integrated into vulnerability scanning applications. Vulnerability scanning applications look for known vulnerabilities across a network and alert IT managers and cybersecurity specialists of the need to patch or fix those vulnerabilities.

Unknown Vulnerabilities

While software developers are working to find errors in their program code and patch vulnerabilities, attackers are also constantly working to find vulnerabilities that developers are unaware of. This is an arms race of sorts, in which the "defenders" attempt to protect information they have about vulnerabilities and control that information as tightly as possible, while the attackers attempt to find new vulnerabilities by sharing as much information as quickly as possible. Once a vulnerability is discovered by an attacker, an exploit can be developed and an attack can be launched. An attack that exploits a previously unknown vulnerability is known as a *zero-day attack*. Once a vulnerability is publicly known or has been used in an attack, it is described as *in the wild*. The time gap between when the vulnerability is in the wild and when a patch is released is an extremely dangerous period and may require disabling the affected software until it can be appropriately patched.

Cybersecurity Operations

The cybersecurity threat is real. Attackers have proven themselves to be incredibly resourceful in finding new, creative ways to attack systems. Three key factors put defenders at a significant disadvantage:

1. Software, hardware, and the Internet are built for usability and performance and are fundamentally insecure.

Cybersecurity Operations

2. There are countless numbers of target to attack. Defenders have to protect them all, while attackers only need to find one weak target.

3. The most dangerous attacks exploit zero-day vulnerabilities, which means they are unknown until they are exploited.

Given these factors, in order to protect a network, a sophisticated approach is needed for cybersecurity operations, one that is based on an intimate understanding of the risk to the network, the information on the network, and the business performed on the network. Cybersecurity operations involve the portfolio of activities required to protect and defend a network, as well as those activities required to comply with laws and statutes, regulations and policies, standards and guidelines, and best practices.

Effective cybersecurity operations require effective partnerships between an increasing number of parties: users, organizational leadership, ISPs, vendors and suppliers, managed service and cloud providers, regulators (if applicable), and law enforcement.

Applying Capabilities to Cybersecurity Operations

Due to the complexity of cybersecurity operations, it is helpful to think about the specific capabilities required, rather than focusing on technologies or techniques. This section will walk through how a cybersecurity operation monitors data traffic entering and operating in a network, analyzes this data traffic, warns the appropriate authorities, and finally responds in the case where an attack has been successful in causing damage. These four capabilities, as previously discussed in Chapter 3, work together to thwart impending cyber attacks. In this chapter, we will use the same definitions that the GAO uses in its cybersecurity programs. The GAO's review of each capability is provided in full below.[5]

> **Monitoring**: detecting cyber threats, attacks, and vulnerabilities and establishing a baseline of system and communication network assets and normal traffic.
>
> **Analyzing**: using the information or intelligence gathered from monitoring to hypothesize about what the threat might be, investigate it with technical and contextual expertise, and determine possible mitigation steps.
>
> **Warning**: developing and issuing informal and formal notifications that alert recipients in advance of potential or imminent, as well as ongoing, cyber threats or attacks. Warnings are intended to alert entities to the presence of cyber attack, help delineate the relevance and immediacy of cyber attacks, provide information on how to remediate vulnerabilities and mitigate incidents, or make overall statements about the health and welfare of the Internet.
>
> **Response**: taking actions to contain an incident, manage the protection of network operations, and recover from damages when vulnerabilities are revealed or when cyber incidents occur. In addition, response includes lessons learned and cyber threat data being documented and integrated back into the capabiltiies to improve overall cyber analysis and warning.

Cybersecurity Capability 1: Monitoring

The purpose of monitoring is to keep traffic flowing normally and to maintain awareness of anomalous or irregular files entering a computer or network. The monitoring and detecting operations go hand-in-hand. As the cybersecurity analyst is monitoring traffic, it is her job to detect anomalies and patterns in files, routers, and domains. Anomalous network activity may indicate a cyber attack in progress. For example, an unusually

Chapter 4: Computer Science Fundamentals and Cybersecurity Operations

> **Cyber Fact**
>
> **"Black Holes" on the Internet**
>
> A recent cybersecurity trend involves an increasing reliance on ISPs to provide cybersecurity protection for their customers. This is often an effective partnership, as the ISPs typically have a better perspective of what is happening on the larger Internet and how to protect their users.
>
> One example of this partnership is in addressing DoS attacks. ISPs are improving their capability to monitor the networks they operate and can intervene to re-route suspicious traffic at a customer's request. When a DoS attack is detected, the ISP can identify the unique characteristics associated with the traffic involved in the attack and reroute the traffic to a server that is not the intended target – known as a **black hole.**

high amount of traffic heading towards a website may represent a DoS attack in-progress.

Recent years have seen a transition from intermittent human network monitors to automatic and continuous monitoring of networks. In today's advanced threat environment, risk managers recognize that proactive and robust monitoring is essential for preventing malicious activity from entering one's network or system. The emergence of **advanced persistent threats (APTs)**, a category of cyber attacks usually conducted as espionage by highly capable and motivated entities such as adversarial governments or terrorist groups, has led to continuous monitoring. Protective monitoring is also crucial for fulfilling auditing and compliance responsibilities.

Packet analyzers, otherwise known as **sniffers**, are one kind of network monitor. Sniffers are programs that inspect the data packets that pass over a digital network. Sniffers can analyze the raw data that makes up a data packet in transit and can be programmed to spot anomalies or certain types of malicious data.

Another monitoring feature that unites well-designed computer networks is a strategically placed **firewall**. A firewall is a tool that blocks malicious data, files, and viruses from entering a computer. Firewalls are necessary because many attacks are almost impossible to detect. For example, if the malicious file entering a system is encrypted and traveling along an encrypted connection, intrusion detection and intrusion prevention systems will have difficulty identifying the attack. IDS/IPS may be able to ascertain that an encrypted connection is coming into the network from a specific country and alert the appropriate personnel, but that may be all these systems can do.

Beyond IDSs and firewalls, there are many other forms of technology that conduct monitoring and collect information regarding network operations in terms of the threats, vulnerabilities, and potential attacks a network faces. This type of in-house monitoring is known as **internal monitoring**. Internal monitoring gathers both open source and confidential information in order to evaluate and clearly understand the situational environment, analyze the collected data, warn of attacks, and respond to attacks, if necessary. Figure 4-4 presents a table that identifies the main technological tools used in the cybersecurity industry, according to a GAO report.[6] These tools strengthen a network administrator's analytical capabilities, thereby allowing for a more accurate understanding of the system under potential attack.

Identifying Cyber Threats

There are three primary methods for identifying cyber threats: policy monitoring, signature-based detection, and anomaly, or behavioral, detection.

Cybersecurity Operations

Tool	Description
Antivirus software	Provides protection against malicious code, such as viruses, worms, and Trojan horses
Firewalls	Control access to and from a network or computer.
Intrusion detection systems (IDS)	Detect inappropriate, incorrect, or anomalous activity on a network or computer system.
Intrusion prevention systems (IPS)	Build on intrusion detection systems to detect attacks on a network and take actions to prevent them from being successful.
Signature-based tools	Compare files or packets to a list of 'signatures'—patterns of specific files or packets that have been identified as threats. Each signature is the unique arrangement of 0's and 1's that make up the file.
Security event correlation tools	Monitor and document actions on network devices and analyze the actions to determine if an attack is ongoing or has occurred. Enable an organization to determine if ongoing system activities are operating according to its security policy.
Scanners	Analyze computers or networks for security vulnerabilities.

Figure 4-4: Internal monitoring tools.

Policy monitoring, the most basic of the three, involves the definition of a rule and then monitoring to observe if that rule is broken. For example, a company could establish a policy that, due to the insecurity of the **File Transfer Protocol (FTP)** service, FTP servers are not allowed on a network. FTP servers typically operate on port 21, so if FTP activity is detected, or port 21 is open on a system on the network, the policy has been violated. A violation of this policy will raise alarms for the network administrator.

Signature-based detection is a common method for identifying cyber attacks and is used in tools such as IDS and IPS. A *signature*, in effect, is a "fingerprint" for activity on a network that is suspected to be malicious. For example, if a known exploit has a specific pattern of activity on a network, then a signature can be written to detect that activity. The limitation of signature-based identification methods is that they do not detect new (zero-day) attacks for which no signature has been developed. As cyber attackers grow more sophisticated, they develop methods of attack that evade signature-based detection.

For those attacks that can't be detected using signatures or policy, **behavioral or anomaly detection** can be applied. By understanding the typical behavior of users and systems on a network, activity that falls outside of that normal behavior can raise a red flag. For example, if a user typically logs in remotely once a week, but then logs in 10 times in one day from multiple locations, that user could be traveling, but it's also possible that the account is compromised. If a server typically transfers 2,000 files per day and those transfers triple, it could be a sign of exfiltration. Unfortunately, as there are often reasonable explanations for anomalies on a network, this method of detection may not be as reliable as signature-based detection. It is, however, an important element of effective cybersecurity operations.

Cybersecurity Capability 2: Analyzing

In addition to monitoring and identifying potential cyber threats, a network administrator must analyze data traffic in order to determine the severity level of an intrusion or gather specific relevant details of a mali-

Chapter 4: Computer Science Fundamentals and Cybersecurity Operations

cious file or code. The analysis process bears similarities to the risk assessment and risk determination processes discussed in Chapter 1.

Virtual models to simulate real attacks aid the analysis process and fine-tune an analyst's ability to analyze anomalies and potential threats. Analysts must create quantitative evidence to support their determinations that anomalies are either significant or insignificant. For example, comparisons must be drawn to identify false positives, discover potential defects in traffic, and determine the frequency of defects.

Robust and detailed cyber threat analysis can lead to cyber threat extrapolation and estimation methods that can predict future attack trends. Predictive analysis methods can shed light on viable mitigation methods and contribute to the development of new defenses against both known and new attack forms.

Cybersecurity Capability 3: Warning

The purpose of warning is to notify the appropriate personnel of an imminent or current attack so that they may devise a response. Warning directly relates to responsible personnel in the event of an attack. However, the answer to the question of who to warn may change depending on the severity level of an impending or actual attack. Warning tools include, but are not limited to, IDS or IPS, anti-virus software, and human analysis. In many cases, warnings have become automated through continuous automated monitoring.

A warning may not point to an imminent or ongoing attack. Rather, a warning could be a message regarding the possibility of an attack from a specific threat using a specific capability. Therefore, the warning provides guidance for the public or specific audience to alleviate the repercussions or provide reliable protections for a potential attack. A warning yields to an authority that will provide guidance during a turbulent or uncertain time period and provide timely follow-up. Warnings are an important step in awareness campaigns in the event of an attack.

Cybersecurity Capability 4: Response

There are two types of response plans: passive and active. Both types of response are intended to contain or mitigate the cyber attack.

Passive responses include logging, notification, and shunning. *Logging* is the collection of data with the purpose of finally delivering an appropriate device or method to curb an attack. It evaluates data and incorporates lessons-learned to evaluate the best response action. *Notification* is the same as an alert; it provides a message about the attack to the appropriate personnel. *Shunning* ignores the attack.

Active responses include terminating a session by shutting it down and resetting it later; altering the network's configuration to deter an attack or prevent future attacks; and acts of deception, including the creation of **honeypots**— tools that collect reconnaissance by enticing attackers towards locations where they cannot harm the network.

Broader responses may take the form of new internal or external policies, guidance statements, regulation, or legislation.

Conclusion

This chapter serves as an introduction to the basic principles of computer science and provides insight into how cybersecurity professionals approach the challenges of working in a digital world.

Key Questions

Cyber attack methods are constantly evolving in response to more sophisticated cybersecurity operations. The reverse is also true: cybersecurity professionals must stay on top of the latest attack methods in order to engineer new defenses and responses. Keeping ahead of new potential threats is a key part of the work of computer engineers working in cybersecurity, as it is for cyber risk managers. Computer engineers, who may employ ethical hacking skills or perform continuous security audits, must identify the weaknesses in their own systems before an adversary discovers them first.

Because it is a fundamentally insecure network, the Internet requires proactive cybersecurity professionals to address its vulnerabilities and strengthen its ability to store and transfer data securely.

Key Questions

1) Explain three vulnerabilities of the Internet as a system of systems.

2) Explain the differences and similarities between what risk managers do (see Chapter 1) and what computer network administrators do.

3) Explain the three categories of components that make up the IT infrastructure. For each category, give an example and explain the potential vulnerabilities of the component.

Cyber Connections

Chapter 1 discusses the technical aspects and challenges of risk management, a central and recurring aspect of corporate governance and private sector legal obligations. Chapter 2 discusses how policy and laws are made by the federal government, and emphasizes how the federal government is placing greater reliance on the private sector to ensure national cybersecurity through public-private partnerships. Chapter 5 defines and explains some of the tools that are part of the cybersecurity arsenal in the private sector, such as data encryption, firewalls, and two-factor authentication systems. Chapter 6 describes the rule-making processes of the United States government that create cybersecurity laws and regulations for both the public and private sectors.

CHAPTER 5:
Cybersecurity for the Private Sector

CHAPTER OUTLINE

- **Overview of Cybersecurity in the Private Sector**
- **Introduction**
- **The Structure and Legal Obligations of Private Sector Companies**
- **Cybersecurity Law and the Private Sector**
- **The Model Corporate Cybersecurity Program**
- **Internal Controls and Audits**
- **Conclusion**
- **Key Questions**

5 Cybersecurity for the Private Sector

Chapter In Focus

- The unique approaches that private-sector businesses must take with regard to cybersecurity.
- The ways in which private and public-sector cybersecurity interests overlap, and the government laws and regulations that regulate the private sector.
- Specific cases with implications for cybersecurity in the private sector.
- The components of the development of a model cybersecurity program for a private-sector company.
- Ways in which senior management can use internal controls to verify that operations are running efficiently, government laws and regulations are being followed, and corporate reports are accurate.

Overview of Cybersecurity for the Private Sector

Imagine that you've founded a technology company and built it into one of the most-admired young enterprises in Silicon Valley. You were recently crowned the youngest **chief executive officer (CEO)** of a public company with over $100 million in annual revenue, and your picture is on the cover of *Forbes* magazine. In your role as CEO, you are also a key member of your company's board of directors.

A month ago, one of your competitors suffered a devastating cyber attack that crippled the company's business for 72 straight hours. You are concerned that a similar attack could strike your company and profoundly hurt your business.

You've gathered your senior management team, including your chief information officer and the company's general counsel (chief attorney). Your goal for this year is to develop short-term and long-term strategies to strengthen the company's cybersecurity program. Questions you will need to consider include:

- What are your legal duties as a member of the board of directors and as the chief executive officer of the company?
- What federal laws and regulations apply to your company?
- What should your company's cybersecurity program look like?
- How can you ensure that the cybersecurity program is efficient and effective, that government rules are followed, and that required reports are filed?

Chapter 5: Cybersecurity for the Private Sector

Introduction to Cybersecurity for the Private Sector

Today, it is commonplace for business transactions to be conducted online and for business information to be stored in online databases. Across every industry sector, from car insurers and retailers to banks and doctors' offices, corporations are increasingly storing and accessing their customers' information in digital form. As dependence on digital technologies to conduct business operations increases, so too do the risks and threats posed by cyber attacks and security breaches.

Customer information may include personally identifying information (names, addresses, email addresses) or confidential information (Social Security numbers, financial records, health records). Corporations in all industries are responsible for taking steps to safeguard their customers' information and may face legal ramifications for failing to adequately anticipate and protect against threats. In the cases of the financial services and health care industries, Congress has mandated very specific safeguards to protect client information in online databases.

Beyond legal mandates, a business cannot afford to risk the bad publicity and customer dissatisfaction that could result if client information is not properly protected. A successful cyber attack can seriously harm a company's ability to function, the status of its stock, and its public image. Because of the potential business and legal ramifications of an attack on a corporation's cyber database, cybersecurity must be a priority in any corporate risk management strategy.

Cyber attacks on corporate computer networks are increasingly common in the twenty-first century. For example, in March 2011, RSA, a division of the EMC Corporation and a leader in cybersecurity innovation, announced that it had suffered a sophisticated cyber attack. RSA is the maker of SecurID, the popular two-factor authentication security token used by both the federal government and companies in the private sector. The RSA token uses an algorithm to generate a series of numbers that changes throughout the day. A user must enter the series of numbers generated at a given time into a log-in screen for access to be granted to an organization's network. In 2009, the SecurID system was in use by over 40 million customers, according to RSA.[1]

RSA revealed that the 2011 cyber attackers had stolen SecurID authentication technology code, potentially reducing the effectiveness of the security system. However, industry analysts feared that malicious agents could also use stolen data to directly attack government and corporate networks. Indeed, in the months following RSA's announcement, Lockheed Martin and L-3, two major DOD contractors, were hit with cyber attacks in which the attackers may have used cloned SecurID tokens to access the companies' systems. As a result of the breach and the cyber attacks on its clients, RSA offered to replace or monitor all of its SecurID tokens, costing the company millions of dollars.[2]

In light of examples such as the cyber attack on RSA, as well as other large-scale cyber attacks on both public and private-sector entities, companies need to understand the unique threats, vulnerabilities, and criticalities they face in the cyber realm. They also need to understand their legal obligations to their shareholders, customers, and other entities. Companies may incur tremendous liability for carelessness, negligence, or ignorance with regard to accepted cybersecurity standards.

This chapter will focus on the structure and legal duties of corporations, the major laws and regulations relevant to cybersecurity, and the various components of a model corporate cybersecurity program. This chapter will complement the basic principles of Chapter 1 (Risk Management for Cybersecurity) and Chapter 2 (Cybersecurity Law and Policy) by analyzing the different strategies, standards, and laws that apply to cybersecurity for the private sector, and by examining the unique cybersecurity issues that arise in the private-sector context.

The Structure and Legal Obligations of Private-Sector Companies: Corporate Governance and the Duty of Care

To understand cybersecurity in the private sector, it is crucial to understand the basic structure of corporations and their legal obligations. There are two kinds of private-sector companies: **public corporations** and **private corporations**. *Public corporations* sell shares in their ownership, or shares of stock, to public investors who become shareholders, or part-owners of the corporation. A public corporation's stocks may be bought and sold at a stock exchange, such as the New York Stock Exchange. By selling shares of stock to the public, a company can raise capital to fund its business operations. The public corporation's financial mission is to increase the net worth of the shareholders' initial investments.

Corporations may also be private. *Privately owned corporations* are not owned in any part by public shareholders, and shares in the company are not available to the public. Private and public corporations are not always subject to the same legal requirements.

Every corporation has a **charter** and **bylaws**. The *charter* is a document that describes a company's purpose and outlines other basic information about the company. When a corporation is first formed, the corporation's founders file the charter with the relevant state authority, and the corporation is "incorporated," or based for legal purposes, in that state. *Bylaws* are the rules adopted by the corporation for its operations. For example, bylaws would explain how a corporation conducts meetings of its shareholders.

Corporations are governed by directors and officers. The **board of directors** provides leadership for the corporation and formulates corporate business strategy at the highest level. The board of directors' responsibilities include formulating corporate business strategy, selecting top management, and representing and reporting to the shareholders. In a public corporation, board members are elected by the shareholders to represent them as a group and to align the corporation's interests with those of the shareholders. Board members (or directors) create the strategy for running the corporation in both the short term and long term, with an emphasis on making plans that promise a favorable return for the company's shareholders. The board of directors may be composed of corporate officers of the company, or any other respected, influential, or knowledgeable people. The board may even include corporate officers from another company; for example, Eric Schmidt, the CEO of Google for many years, served on the Apple Board of Directors.

In addition to formulating the company's business strategy, the directors are essential players in the development of the company's cybersecurity strategy. A cybersecurity strategy should take into consideration relevant statutes and regulations, as well as industry standards, or recommended ways of doing business that are widely accepted within an industry.

A corporation's day-to-day operations are managed by a team of senior leaders called **corporate officers.** Typically, the board of directors is responsible for choosing the corporate officers, who, in a public corporation, pledge to act in the shareholders' interests. The board gives the corporate officers the task of executing the corporation's business strategy and running important programs, such as the corporation's cybersecurity programs.

The CEO, who acts as the company's lead manager, and the **chief information officer (CIO)** are generally responsible for keeping the board of directors informed about the company's latest cyber risks, cyber vulnerabilities, and cybersecurity operations. Corporate officers are ultimately held accountable for their performance by the board of directors. The board may fire and replace corporate officers if their performance is poor, or if the shareholders demand a shakeup in the corporate leadership to reenergize the company in times of struggle.

Chapter 5: Cybersecurity for the Private Sector

Both the board of directors and the corporate officers play a significant role in corporate governance. **Corporate governance** is the high-level process of setting policies for the corporation, overseeing the corporation's operations, and generally dictating how the corporation is run. One of the directors' major goals for effective corporate governance should be **transparency**—maintaining a full and open record of the corporation's financial status and its governance practices. A public corporation's dissemination of its full corporate records allows public investors to make informed decisions about whether to buy or sell stock in the corporation.

As the day-to-day managers of the company, corporate officers are responsible for ensuring that a corporation's governance policies, such as policies concerning transparency, are followed on a daily basis. Ultimately, corporate officers must uphold the ethical and oversight standards that are established by the board of directors. Directors and officers guide a company, but they do so in accordance with the corporation's own charter and bylaws, legal principles defining their obligations, and state and federal rules and regulations.

Liability for Failures of Oversight

The board of directors and corporate officers have a duty to protect the value of the corporation and, specifically, the value of the shareholders' investments in the corporation. The directors and officers must perform their jobs with the diligence of a reasonable person and must be certain that they are always reasonably informed before making decisions. The sum of these obligations has a technical name with legal implications: the **duty of care**. If directors or corporate officers fail to uphold the obligations that the duty of care demands of them, they may be held personally liable for neglecting their duty to the company. In other words, they will have to pay for any damages out of their own pockets.

Statutes from various states describe the duty of care differently. In the influential Business Corporation Law of New York State (NYBCL), for example, the duty of care means that directors or officers must discharge their duties "in good faith and with that degree of care which an ordinarily prudent person in a like position would use under similar circumstances." State courts, in turn, have applied the statutory language to real-world cases, further articulating what the duty of care requires in any given situation.

What does it mean, in legal terms, for a director to be informed about his company's cybersecurity operations? In general, corporate directors and officers must stay informed about the threats, vulnerabilities, consequences, and criticalities inherent in their company's IT systems, and set up programs and rigorous processes for mitigating cyber and IT risk. As interpreted by courts and cybersecurity professionals, the duty of care generally requires a director to critically assess all information given to him, to question the sufficiency of that information, and to confirm that he has access to all of the relevant information on any given area of the company's operations. With regard to cybersecurity, this requirement means (1) being inquisitive and proactive about investigating cybersecurity threats and vulnerabilities, and (2) considering all aspects of cybersecurity and taking steps to protect the company from the ever-increasing threat of cyber attacks.

Since the late 1990s, there has been an increase in legal activity concerning director and corporate officer responsibilities. *In re Caremark International Inc. Derivative Litigation*, a case decided in Delaware state court in 1996, was one of the most significant developments to emerge from this increase in legal action regarding corporate oversight responsibilities. Specifically, the case dealt with the obligation directors and officers have to develop and implement systems to monitor compliance and risk issues within their companies.

Case Study: *In re Caremark International Inc. Derivative Litigation* (1996)

In re Caremark International Inc. Derivative Litigation (*Caremark*) arose from a lawsuit brought by Caremark's shareholders after actions taken by company employees led to federal indictments and costly settlements with federal and state governments.

Caremark's business was primarily in providing patient care and managed care services, and a portion of its revenues were derived from the Medicare and Medicaid reimbursement programs. Pursuant to the federal Anti-Referral Payments Law (ARPL), Caremark was prohibited from paying hospitals, doctors, or other health care providers as a reward for referring Medicare or Medicaid patients to them. However, the government charged that Caremark employees were making payments to doctors in violation of federal law. Caremark eventually settled with the government for almost $165 million.

Caremark's shareholders sued the company, claiming that the directors had breached the duty of care by failing to adequately supervise the conduct of company employees. Essentially, the shareholders contended that the directors should have been aware of the employees' conduct and stopped it before the company was forced to pay out millions of dollars in penalties to the government.

The shareholders eventually reached a settlement with Caremark that included a stipulation that the company strengthen its corporate oversight practices. In approving the settlement, however, the Delaware Court of Chancery had to consider whether or not the settlement was fair, because it did not involve holding any of the corporate directors personally liable. To this end, Chancellor (Judge) William T. Allen outlined what a plaintiff has to prove to make the case that a corporate director or officer has breached the duty of care. In situations in which employees are violating the law, a plaintiff would have to show that a director either knew about the violations, or should have known about the violations—in other words, that the director was inattentive or "negligent." In addition, a plaintiff would have to show that the knowing or negligent director "took no steps in a good faith effort to prevent or remedy [the] situation."

The court ultimately determined that the settlement was fair because there was no evidence that Caremark's directors did not make a "good faith effort" to prevent employees from breaking the law. However, the court strongly stated the view that directors may, in theory, violate the duty of care if they fail to properly monitor corporate or employee activities:

> "[A] director's obligation includes a duty to attempt in good faith to assure that a corporate information and reporting system, which the Board concludes is adequate, exists, and that failure to do so under some circumstances may ... render a director liable for losses caused by non-compliance with applicable legal standards."

In other words, corporate directors may be legally liable if they fail to create an internal system that will adequately bring problems to the directors' attention before these problems have created financial losses for the company.

Not all instances of director negligence give rise to liability, however. According to the court in *Caremark*, "only a sustained or systematic failure of the Board to exercise oversight—such as an utter failure to attempt to assure that a reasonable information and reporting system exists—will establish the lack of good faith that is a necessary condition to liability."

The ruling in *Caremark* implied that corporate officers have a responsibility to carefully monitor their companies' activities and remedy company problems that others bring to their attention. Carelessness or ignorance is not a defense if preventable events harm the company and its investors. At the same time, however, *Caremark* suggested that the presence of internal systems may serve to shield directors and corporate officers from liability. If internal compliance systems are in place, and if the directors and corporate officers can demonstrate that they paid attention to any red flags raised by these systems, the "sustained or systematic failure" standard for corporate liability under *Caremark* is extremely difficult to prove.

Caremark was a landmark decision because it effectively expanded corporate liability for directors and cor-

Chapter 5: Cybersecurity for the Private Sector

porate officers and also provided a means for them to safeguard themselves in the event that the company suffered a loss beyond the directors' or corporate officers' control.

While *Caremark* was a case in Delaware state court, the decision had a national impact as other courts affirmed and expanded its principles to form the "Caremark standard." Under this standard, directors and corporate officers may be liable if they (1) utterly fail to implement an internal system to monitor compliance and risk; or if they (2) ignore an existing system, voluntarily depriving themselves of information about serious risks or problems needing their attention. The Caremark standard is now a core principle of corporate law that legally requires directors and corporate officers to make sure internal systems are in place within their company to monitor compliance and risk. While the Caremark standard encourages prudent corporate governance, however, it is a difficult standard for plaintiffs to prove in the courtroom. Only in the most egregious cases will courts hold directors or corporate officers liable.

In 2009, for example, Citigroup shareholders sued the company's directors for failing to monitor risk. Citigroup had lost billions of dollars in the subprime mortgage crisis that began in 2008. There had been signs that the subprime mortgage market could collapse, but the Citigroup directors had weighed the risks and decided against taking any significant action. The shareholders blamed management for the losses and cited numerous warning signs of the oncoming crisis, which they claimed should have alerted the directors and corporate officers to the risks and potential consequences they were facing and caused them to take decisive action to prevent financial disaster.

Nevertheless, in the case of *In re Citigroup Inc. Shareholders Derivative Litigation*, the Delaware Court of Chancery refused to hold the directors liable and dismissed the suit because the shareholders couldn't make the necessary showing of director liability. Significantly, there had been an internal committee in place responsible for informing the directors about Citigroup's risk exposure and reviewing internal controls for risk assessment and risk management. Because the directors had been informed of important and reasonably available information through their meetings with this committee, the court determined there wasn't the "sustained or systematic" failure of oversight necessary for liability under the Caremark standard. Though the plaintiffs had presented general evidence about the risks involved with the subprime mortgage market, they had failed to show "particularized facts suggesting that the Board was presented with 'red flags' alerting it to potential misconduct" or to preventable losses.

In addition to the Caremark standard, directors and corporate officers are also protected from liability for losses by the business judgment rule (BJR), another core principle of corporate law that was developed through numerous court decisions. The BJR is the principle that courts will not second-guess a business decision made by a director or corporate officer if it was reasonably well-informed and made with the best interests of the company in mind. Essentially, the BJR is a presumption that directors and corporate officers act within the duty of care. The BJR gives directors and corporate officers the freedom to make good-faith business decisions without being constantly worried about liability. The combination of the Caremark standard and the BJR, however, means that directors and corporate officers will generally only be found liable for the most blatant cases of wrongdoing.

Liability for Data Breaches

Much of a person's day-to-day life is conducted online. People file their taxes electronically, deposit checks and pay bills online, communicate via email or text, and use credit cards to pay for food, clothing, and other necessities. Each of these transactions requires the storage and transmission of electronic data. This data may include a person's name, address, Social Security number, financial information (for example, credit and debit card information

Structure and Legal Obligations of Private-Sector Companies

and bank account numbers), or health records. The data may be stored on a network, owned by a corporation and stored in its database, or stored **"in the cloud"**—a third party's network that serves as a substitute for an in-house network. Of course, much of this personal information is extremely valuable to hackers. Once a hacker gains access to personal data, he has access to a person's credit line, savings, and even identity.

Companies go to great lengths to protect their customers' information from hackers. Securing customers' personal data is critical to maintaining customer trust and avoiding legal liability. In fact, under the duty of care, companies may have a legal duty to proactively safeguard customer information stored on their networks. Proactive steps may include encrypting all company data in transmission, securing all company networks with firewalls, mandating company-wide use of strong passwords, installing anti-virus software on company computers, and physically securing data storage hardware and company servers. A company that neglects to implement these kinds of cybersecurity measures may find itself sued by its customers, shareholders, suppliers, or companies in its supply chain, particularly in the aftermath of a data breach. The following two case studies provide examples of the legal fallout from major data breaches.

Case Study: The TJX Data Breach (2006)

In early 2007, TJX (the parent company of the clothing retailer TJ Maxx) revealed that hackers had gained access to millions of credit and debit card transactions—including card numbers, driver's license information, and other customer data—stored in the company's national database. Investigations revealed that at least 45 million separate customer credit and debit cards had been compromised.[3] Consequently, tens of millions of dollars in fraudulent charges were reported. Credit card companies and credit card-issuing banks incurred millions of dollars in costs to cancel and reissue the cards and, in many cases, to cover the stolen funds. Although intrusions into TJX's system had probably begun in 2005, the company stated that it was not aware of the data breach until the end of 2006.

Customers, state attorneys general, credit card companies, and credit card-issuing banks took TJX to court in multiple lawsuits, contending that TJX had violated the duty of care by failing to adequately safeguard customer information. TJX's mistakes included keeping customer credit and debit card data in company systems for longer than necessary and allowing the central company computer systems to be remotely accessible through the networks of individual stores. In addition, several credit card-issuing banks claimed that TJX had negligently misrepresented its level of data security to the banks when it erroneously claimed that it followed industry best practices for safeguarding and disposing of customer information in its databases.

In the end, TJX settled all the cases out of court. The total cost of the incident to TJX, including legal costs, the cost of the settlements, and the cost of improving its cybersecurity, was estimated at over $256 million.[4] The TJX data breach episode, then, serves as a warning to all companies of the enormous potential liability associated with improperly securing sensitive customer information in company computer systems.

Case Study: The Sony PlayStation Network Data Breach (2011)

In 2011, Sony revealed that its PlayStation Network, an online gaming and digital retail services network, had been compromised. Hackers had gained access to the personal information—including home addresses, telephone numbers, credit card numbers, and computer passwords—of over 77 million of the network's users.[5]

Sony customers quickly sued, claiming that Sony had acted negligently by not adequately securing the network against cyber intrusions. Specifically, plaintiffs claimed that Sony had not followed Payment Card Industry Data Security Standards (industry best practices for companies that receive customer credit and debit card information), such as encrypting customer data. In addition, plaintiffs argued that Sony had not acted to protect

Chapter 5: Cybersecurity for the Private Sector

customer information despite having an understanding of cyber risks. This claim hinged on the fact that Sony had gone to great lengths to secure its own corporate IT systems. It appeared that corporate managers at Sony were conscious of the serious risks posed by cyber intruders but had decided not to act to protect the personal and financial information of their customers from these same risks.

In October 2012, a federal district court judge dismissed the main, customer class-action lawsuit brought against Sony in the U.S. However, the attack cost Sony at least $171 million in lost revenue and the price of programs to respond to the breach and restore customer confidence.[6]

The obligations that directors and corporate officers owe to shareholders and to the corporation are well established. Directors and corporate officers must keep themselves informed of any potential issues with employee conduct, the corporation's compliance with the law, or risks to the company and its bottom line. In order to fulfill this duty, directors and corporate officers must ensure that systems are in place to bring "red flags" to their attention. If these systems are in place, however, it is unlikely that directors and corporate officers will be held liable for violating the duty of care, unless they ignore "red flags" or act in a manner that is intentionally reckless and/or in violation of the law.

In addition to implementing internal risk monitoring and corporate compliance systems, directors and corporate officers should develop policies to protect customer information that is stored on the company's network or transmitted through cyberspace. Companies that neglect cyber threats may face major lawsuits after a data breach, based on their legal duty to safeguard customer information.

If directors or corporate officers fail to uphold the obligations that the duty of care demands of them, they may be held personally liable for neglecting their duties to the company. Consequently, corporate directors and officers must stay informed about the threats, vulnerabilities, consequences, and criticalities inherent in the company's IT systems, and set up programs and rigorous processes for mitigating cyber and IT risk.

Cybersecurity Law and the Private Sector

There is no single law setting corporate cybersecurity standards for every corporation. In many corporate sectors, cybersecurity practices are mainly shaped by the duty of care responsibilities discussed earlier in this chapter. However, in some sectors, specific information security laws do exist to protect sensitive client and company information. In the financial services and health care industries, federal law requires companies to implement specific risk management programs and activities. Consequently, financial institutions and health care companies aggressively protect the information they control, process, access, and store. In addition to rules and regulations relating to the security of financial services and health care information, federal and state laws also promote cybersecurity standards through consumer protection, data breach notification, and financial reporting requirements. Examining these federal and state laws provides a foundational understanding of cybersecurity law for the private sector in the twenty-first century.

The GLB Financial Modernization Act:
Regulating the Information Security Practices of Financial Institutions

Until the late 1990s, it was legal for banks to sell sensitive customer information without notifying the customer or obtaining consent. Unsurprisingly, these sales sometimes resulted in unauthorized credit card charges. In 1997, Charter Pacific Bank, a California bank, sold 3.7 million credit card numbers to Kenneth H. Taves, an operator of X-rated websites and a convicted felon. At the time, nothing was illegal about this sale of financial information. Banks would often sell credit card information databases to merchants so that the merchants could perform "fraud scrubs." A fraud scrub is a process by which an online merchant can compare a credit card number submitted by a customer against a credit card database to determine if the credit card number is associated with prior fraudulent charges or other misuse. However, rather than performing fraud scrubs, Mr. Taves used 900,000 credit card numbers to charge $45.7 million for adult services on his websites.[7]

Two aspects of the case were especially disturbing to analysts. First, there was nothing in the law that would have stopped the bank from selling the credit card numbers to Mr. Taves, even if the bank had known of his criminal record. And second, the credit card numbers were compiled from the accounts of merchants who were clients of the bank—meaning that the bank sold the credit card numbers of people who were not even its customers.

As part of a plea agreement, Mr. Taves was forced to make restitution to the credit card holders. However, consumers demanded action by legislators to tighten privacy and information security standards. In response, Congress passed the **Gramm-Leach-Bliley Financial Modernization Act (GLB Act)** in November 1999. The GLB Act is a landmark because it contained two major rules—the **Financial Privacy Rule** and the **Safeguards Rule**—that completely reshaped information security for financial services companies.

The Financial Privacy Rule requires all financial institutions (including banks and companies that offer financial consulting, loans, or insurance) to disclose their information-sharing and privacy practices to their customers, and allows customers to opt out of having their information shared with third parties. Moreover, each time a financial company's information-sharing policies change, the company must notify its customers and give them the choice to opt out of third-party sharing once again.

The Safeguards Rule requires financial institutions to protect their customers' information in storage and transmission. Under the Safeguards Rule, financial institutions must develop a written information security plan that puts a point person in charge of information security, clearly articulates the company's ongoing risk management strategy, and states what each division of the company is doing to manage its information security risks. Corporate leaders are responsible for the development of the written plan. Additionally, the Safeguards Rule requires that this plan be further tested and modified as new risks surface.

HIPAA: Regulating the Information Security Practices of the Healthcare Industry

During the 1990s, physicians' offices, hospitals, and other healthcare providers dramatically expanded the electronic storage and transmission of patient health records. At the time, there were no applicable, nationwide security standards. Rules and regulations varied from state to state, and healthcare providers could not reach an agreement about the appropriate safeguards to implement.

Congress, however, recognized that national standards were needed to protect electronically stored and transmitted personal health information. In 1996, Congress passed the Health Insurance Portability and Accountability Act (HIPAA). As previously described in Chapter 3, HIPAA was a broad piece of legislation that covered the transferability of employer-based health insurance when workers lose or change jobs. HIPAA also included, however, key provisions governing the way health information is processed, transferred, and protected. The purpose of these provisions was to unify government rules and regulations concerning patient health information and to eliminate inconsistencies between federal and state requirements.

HIPAA's information privacy and security standards are contained in the **Privacy Rule** and the **Security Rule**. The Privacy Rule governs the storage and transmission of protected health information (PHI). A healthcare provider may use and disclose PHI only to facilitate treatment, payment, or healthcare operations. For example, a

Chapter 5: Cybersecurity for the Private Sector

doctor can disclose a patient's PHI to an insurance provider to receive payment for a covered medical procedure. All other disclosures of PHI, such as disclosure for the use of medical research, require a patient's written authorization. In addition, the Privacy Rule requires healthcare providers to keep records of all PHI disclosures and allows patients to ask for an accounting of most types of disclosures.

HIPAA's Security Rule establishes safeguards to ensure the confidentiality, integrity, and availability of electronically stored personal health information. The Security Rule is, in many ways, similar to the Safeguards Rule in the GLB Act. Both rules require that companies demonstrate that they have thorough risk management strategies and policies in place to protect the personal information they store and transmit. The HIPAA Security Rule requires that health care providers:

- certify the security of their electronic networks;
- create a plan to respond to cybersecurity emergencies, including both cyber attacks on the network and physical emergencies;
- create a system to protect sensitive data while it is being processed, transferred or stored;
- control access to certain records and files;
- perform an internal audit of their network security;
- develop a formal cyber risk management policy;
- provide company-wide training and raise awareness about cybersecurity issues;
- contract with third-party associates to ensure that they will protect patient information; and
- require that all vendors (or suppliers) report any security breaches that threaten the privacy of patient information.

In 2009, HIPAA was strengthened by the **Health Information Technology for Economic and Clinical Health Act (HITECH Act)**, which was passed by Congress as part of the American Recovery and Reinvestment Act of 2009. The HITECH Act is a landmark law because it is the first federally mandated data breach notification statute.

The HITECH Act broadened HIPAA's data privacy and security requirements. Specifically, the HITECH Act's requirements apply to health insurance company claims processors, data analysts, accountants, lawyers, and any other person or organization that handles PHI on behalf of a healthcare company. In the event of a data breach involving PHI, the HITECH Act requires these persons and organizations, as well as those entities already covered by HIPAA, to disclose the breach to their customers and to the U.S. Department of Health of Human Services. In certain instances, the entity must also disclose the breach to the public. If companies ignore the obligations set forth in the HITECH Act, they risk the imposition of monetary penalties by the federal government.

Sector-specific laws, such as the GLB Act, HIPAA, and the HITECH Act, mandate the development of corporate cybersecurity risk management programs as essential tools for protecting the privacy and security of sensitive consumer information. Significantly, these laws do not require that financial services companies or healthcare providers guarantee absolute information security. Policymakers and regulators recognize that there is no way of making the cyber environment completely invulnerable. Consequently, companies in these industries must only demonstrate that they have a flexible and thorough risk management approach that can adapt to new threats as they arise.

Cybersecurity Law and the Private Sector

The Federal Trade Commission and the Enforcement of Information Security Laws

The **Federal Trade Commission (FTC)** is the government's consumer protection agency, charged with investigating and stopping "unfair or deceptive acts or practices" by businesses. Part of the FTC's mission is to protect the integrity and confidentiality of consumer information. In instances when a company suffers a data breach, the FTC will investigate the company's business practices and security programs. If the investigation reveals that the company hasn't taken sufficient steps to safeguard consumer information, the FTC will charge the company with violating the **Federal Trade Commission Act (FTCA)**. The FTC was established by, and receives its authority from, the FTCA, which Congress passed in 1914.

VIDEO

Watch 'FTC Consent Agreements' at http://vimeo.com/channels/cybersecurityfoundations

A company charged with violating the FTCA may settle with the FTC through a **consent agreement** A consent agreement is a legally binding document whereby the company agrees to institute a cybersecurity program in exchange for the FTC dismissing its FTCA violation complaint. Generally, a consent agreement requires the company to submit to annual (or more frequent) audits by an independent auditor over a sustained period of time. The audits look at the administrative, technical, and physical safeguards developed, implemented, and maintained by the company, in the context of the company's size and complexity, the nature and scope of the company's work, and the sensitivity of the information the company collects from its clients and consumers. The independent auditor examines and analyzes this information before preparing a report for the FTC. If the auditor reports that the company's security program is inadequate, the company may have to pay civil penalties to the government.

Case Study — FTC Action After the TJX Data Breach (2006)

In the aftermath of TJX's data breach disclosure, discussed earlier in this chapter, TJX was investigated by the FTC and sued based on the alleged inadequacy of its information security practices. Specifically, the FTC accused TJX of not doing enough to protect sensitive customer information that was processed and stored in company-wide computer systems.

The FTC's complaint stated that "[s]ince at least July 2005, [TJX] engaged in a number of practices that, taken together, failed to provide reasonable and appropriate security for personal information on its networks." The complaint described the areas in which TJX could have acted differently to protect its customers' information. Among the security problems noted in the FTC's complaint against TJX were the following:

- TJX stored and transmitted customer information without first encrypting it.

- TJX did not do enough to secure its wireless networks, which transmitted financial information. Because the wireless networks were not protected by a password, a hacker, or any unauthorized person, could easily connect to the network.

- TJX had no protocols in place concerning computer passwords. It did not require that its employees use strong passwords, and it did not require that system users create multiple passwords to access different programs, computers, and networks.

Chapter 5: Cybersecurity for the Private Sector

- TJX did not have tools (such as firewalls) in place specifically to prevent intruders from gaining access to customer information.

- TJX did not move proactively to detect and prevent unauthorized access to its networks. For example, the company did not frequently patch or update its antivirus software or investigate intrusion warnings.

Following the FTC's complaint, TJX entered into a consent agreement with the FTC that required the company to take major steps to improve its cybersecurity practices. In particular, the FTC ordered TJX to "establish and implement, and thereafter maintain, a comprehensive information security program that is reasonably designed to protect the security, confidentiality, and integrity of personal information collected from or about consumers." In addition, TJX was ordered to perform regular risk assessments, to hire independent risk managers to oversee its cybersecurity program, and to submit regular compliance reports to the FTC.

Data Breach Notification Statutes

Almost every state has enacted a **data breach notification law**, or a law that requires companies to notify the public when they experience a data breach. California was the first state to write security breach notification requirements into law. The California statute requires any company that "owns or licenses computerized data that includes personal information [to] disclose any breach of the security of the system following discovery or notification of the breach…to any resident of California whose unencrypted personal data was, or is reasonably believed to have been, acquired by an unauthorized person." Simply put, if unencrypted data is compromised by a hacker or other intruder, a company must take steps to notify its customers about the breach.

In California, the notification takes the form of a letter or other piece of writing, which must include the name and contact information of the reporting person or business, a description of the personal information that was compromised, the date of the breach, a general description of the breach incident, and the toll-free numbers and addresses of credit reporting agencies in the event that the breach exposed a Social Security or driver's license number.

At least 47 states have followed California's lead and enacted data breach notification statutes of their own. Most statutes require that a breach disclosure must be dispatched "in the most expedient time possible and without unreasonable delay" if unencrypted personal information is accessed by an unauthorized person. As in California, most states do not mandate notification procedures if encrypted (as opposed to unencrypted) data are stolen or compromised.

At present, data breach notification is mainly regulated by state law. While many state data breach notification laws are similar, there is no nationwide notification standard. The HITECH Act, discussed earlier in this chapter, deals with data breach notification but is limited to personal health information. Data breach notification legislation has been proposed in Congress. However, as of this book's publication, federal legislators have yet to pass a comprehensive data breach notification statute.

The Securities and Exchange Commission and Cybersecurity Disclosure Guidance

The **Securities and Exchange Commission (SEC)** was established in 1934 in response to calls for banking reform after the 1929 stock market crash. Today, the SEC plays a key role in shaping cybersecurity practices in the private sector. The agency has several responsibilities, including:

Cybersecurity Law and the Private Sector

> **VIDEO**
>
> Watch 'SEC Disclosure Guidance' at http://vimeo.com/channels/cybersecurityfoundations

- interpreting federal securities laws (e.g., the Securities Act of 1933 and the Securities Exchange Act of 1934);
- issuing securities regulations (examples of securities include stocks and bonds);
- overseeing the inspection of brokerage firms (e.g., Scottrade), investment advisors (e.g., Merrill Lynch), and ratings agencies (e.g., Standard and Poor's); and
- overseeing private regulatory organizations (e.g., KPMG, an American accounting firm, which performs financial reviews of companies).

In October 2011, the SEC's Division of Corporation Finance (one of five divisions within the agency) issued a guidance document clarifying how existing corporate disclosure requirements apply to companies' disclosure of material cybersecurity risk and the incidence of cyber attacks ("CF Disclosure Guidance: Topic No. 2"). Disclosure of cyber risk is an issue within the purview of the SEC because part of the agency's job is to ensure that companies disclose any information that may be relevant to investor decision-making.

The SEC recognized that a company may incur substantial losses after a successful cyber attack, affecting the value of an investment in the company. The costs associated with a cyber breach or attack include remediation costs, increased cybersecurity protection costs, lost revenues, litigation costs, and long-term damage to the company's reputation. The Disclosure Guidance gave public companies the responsibility to disclose "material information regarding cybersecurity risks and cyber incidents." Information is "material" if "there is a substantial likelihood that a reasonable investor would consider it important in making an investment decision or if the information would significantly alter the total mix of information made available." According to the Disclosure Guidance, public companies must disclose all "material" information about cyber risks and cyber incidents in their financial disclosures to the SEC.

For no charge, the public can view corporate disclosure filings on the SEC's website, through the **EDGAR (Electronic Data Gathering, Analysis, and Retrieval) system**. As of May 1996 (for domestic companies) and November 2002 (for foreign companies), the SEC required all public corporations to submit financial disclosures and regulatory filings to EDGAR. EDGAR is an excellent tool for locating public company disclosures for a specific company or on a specific topic (e.g., cybersecurity incidents in 2012).

North American Electric Reliability Corporation (NERC) Cybersecurity Standards

The **North American Electric Reliability Corporation (NERC)** also plays a role in shaping cybersecurity in the private sector. NERC is a nongovernmental organization of electrical grid operators that has been delegated the responsibility of creating reliability standards for bulk power systems. Bulk power systems are interconnected electrical systems that include generation (e.g., coal-fired electric power plants) and transmission (e.g., high-voltage transformers) facilities. Bulk power systems are a good example of critical infrastructure, discussed in Chapter 2 (Cybersecurity Law and Policy). Reliability standards created by NERC become law once they are approved by the Federal Energy Regulatory Commission (FERC).

For example, NERC Standard CIP-008-4 ("Cyber Security Incident Reporting and Response Planning") requires that owners and operators of bulk power systems identify, classify, respond to, and report cybersecurity incidents to the Electricity Sector Information Sharing and Analysis Center (ES ISAC). As mentioned in Chapter 2, the idea of the **Information Sharing and Analysis Center (ISAC)** was first proposed by Presidential Decision Directive 63, an important presidential statement discussed in Chapter 2. ISACs are responsible for receiving information regarding threats, vulnerabilities, or cyber incidents, and for facilitating information sharing between the federal government and companies in critical infrastructure sectors, such as the electric power sector. In addition, bulk power system owners and operators must develop and implement a cybersecurity incident response plan for confronting cyber attacks and communicating with the ES ISAC.

The Sarbanes-Oxley Act of 2002

In the early 2000s, several devastating accounting scandals shook the U.S. stock market and caused investors to lose billions of dollars. First, Enron (at one time the nation's seventh-largest company), lied in official statements about its financial health and was eventually forced into bankruptcy. Then, WorldCom (a telecommunications company) and Tyco (a security systems manufacturing company) were revealed to have intentionally misrepresented their finances in accounting statements. In response to these scandals, Congress passed a series of laws intended to prevent corporate accounting fraud.

Congress enacted the **Sarbanes-Oxley Act of 2002** to protect investors by ensuring that corporations report their finances accurately. President George W. Bush characterized the law as "the most far reaching refor[m] of American business practices since the time of Franklin Delano Roosevelt." Perhaps the most well-known (and controversial) aspect of Sarbanes-Oxley is **Section 404**, which requires larger public companies to include a special internal control report in their annual financial reports. This report must certify that the company has internal controls in place to monitor the integrity of its financial accounting. Internal controls may include risk management practices and voluntary financial and technological audits. Internal controls are covered in more detail later in this chapter.

The Model Corporate Cybersecurity Program

Because there is no single cybersecurity standard that all companies must follow, companies base their cybersecurity programs on the standards provided by multiple federal and state rules and regulations. State and federal statutes relating to the financial and healthcare sectors, consumer protection, breach disclosure, and financial reporting all relate to cybersecurity. Shaping a cybersecurity program for a private company involves incorporating many of these diverse standards into a unified program.

Implementing a cybersecurity program for any company is an extremely difficult task. Cybersecurity is a constantly evolving field. Technology and its most savvy users evolve quickly, and what was cutting-edge in computers or hacking one year may be outdated the next. Given the moving-target nature of cyber threats and the vulnerabilities that new technologies create, the best approach that a company can take is to put proactive cybersecurity programs and policies into place and update and revise these programs and policies constantly.

The security risk management rules and regulations discussed earlier present strong cybersecurity standards that corporations in any industry may follow. Based on both these regulations and cross-industry best practices, the following dozen components form the basis of any robust corporate cybersecurity program.

The Model Corporate Cybersecurity Program

1. The Board of Directors

Beginning in the 1990s, and especially after the 9/11 terrorist attacks, corporate leaders increasingly realized that the private sector needed to take more proactive measures to secure corporate assets, including partnering with the federal government to identify and protect against terrorist threats. Corporate leaders understood that private-sector companies, as owners and operators of 80% of the nation's critical infrastructure, from banks to power lines, have a special responsibility to implement security measures that not only serve to protect the integrity of a company's information and assets, but serve national-security purposes as well.

Boardrooms all over the country began prioritizing issues of cybersecurity. At the same time, the new federal laws and regulations that emerged during this time, discussed earlier in this chapter, placed more responsibility than ever before on the shoulders of corporate directors. The main emphasis of these new laws and regulations was that directors must be proactively involved in corporate cybersecurity, from learning about new risks to taking steps to combat these risks before they develop into emergencies with dramatic consequences. As the leading body of a company, a board of directors is ultimately responsible for a company's cybersecurity and must be involved in developing and implementing a comprehensive, company-wide cybersecurity program.

2. The Chief Information Security Officer

The board of directors makes high-level policy decisions with the assistance of the corporate officers. The CEO has the responsibility of communicating and overseeing implementation of the directors' policy decisions. To assist the chief executive officer with this responsibility, a **chief information security officer (CISO)** should be appointed to develop, oversee, monitor, and report back on the company's cybersecurity and corporate liability programs. The role of the CISO can be performed by more than one individual, or even by a committee. The CISO will also usually interact with the CIO, who oversees the company's broader information resource management programs beyond IT security.

3. The Risk Assessment

Risk assessment is discussed in detail in Chapter 1. Risk assessment is the second phase of the risk management process. It is designed to identify the components of a risk, so that the risk can be broken down and analyzed. Using this information, a risk assessor can calculate the potential harm from a risk. Companies that are proactive about managing cyber risk will conduct ongoing cyber risk assessments. While the duty of care does not require that corporate managers themselves perform these risk assessments, it does require them to be informed of the impact from potential threats and to stay apprised of the ongoing risks they face.

A risk assessment typically involves three elements: a threat assessment, a vulnerability assessment, and a consequence assessment. These assessments complement and depend upon one another. As discussed in Chapter 1, careful consideration of these three elements as individual components leads to the most thorough and relevant results for risk assessors.

Threat Assessment

Threats are capabilities linked to a hostile intent. An example of a threat is a hacker or a malicious software program, either of which could harm the integrity of a company's sensitive information, such as personally identifying customer or employee information.

Chapter 5: Cybersecurity for the Private Sector

The threat assessment examines potential threats to information stored on corporate computer systems. As Chapter 1 explained, the assessment quantifies the threat, evaluating, for example, a hacker's ability to gain access to secured systems. A threat assessment might consider:

- What trade secrets or other valuable and sensitive information does the company possess that someone would be motivated to steal?

- Are there any "local" or "insider" threats to the company? These may be employees or other individuals or organizations with access to the company's information or information technology systems.

- How prevalent is espionage in the company's industry?

- What errors or thoughtless actions within the company might cause harm to the company's computer systems?

- What company partners, contractors, or vendors might pose threats to the company's cyber networks?

- What natural or man-made disasters may occur that could affect critical systems?

Vulnerability Assessment

A vulnerability assessment examines weaknesses in IT systems. A vulnerability assessment may analyze the information gathered from the following questions:

- What are the access points to the company's network? Are they secured?

- How strong are passwords and other means of gaining access to the network?

- Are there human behaviors that make a corporate network more susceptible to attack?

Consequence Assessment

Finally, the consequence assessment considers whether or not a given threat will be able to locate and exploit any vulnerability. This assessment considers the following questions:

- Which corporate assets are in danger, and should limited resources be allocated to safeguarding them?

- What would be the separate specific consequence of each vulnerability being exploited by a cyber attacker or a cyber error?

- What would be the significance for the company of each of these consequences?

- How would the company respond in each case?

Refer back to Chapter 1 for an in-depth discussion and examples of threat, vulnerability and consequence assessments.

4. The Written Plan

A company's robust and comprehensive cybersecurity plan should be formalized in writing. This written plan is important for communicating a consistent message to employees regarding the company's policies and internal controls. Additionally, a written cybersecurity plan gives shareholders the assurance that the company is securely storing and transferring sensitive information on company-wide computer systems.

5. Penetration Testing

Once a company develops its cybersecurity program, it should take steps to test and strengthen the safeguards it has put into place. A common method for a company to become aware of gaps in its cybersecurity program is **penetration testing**, or staging a simulated cyber attack on the company.

The purpose of penetration testing is to reveal vulnerabilities in a company's computer systems, such as hardware and software flaws or basic security gaps in the way a system operates. While a penetration test is similar to a vulnerability assessment, it is much riskier, since it involves an actual attack with the potential to disrupt operations and shut down the company's IT systems. In some cases, company employees are not even informed before penetration testing happens.

The benefits of penetration testing are numerous for a company that wants to know more about its security vulnerabilities. The main drawback of penetration testing is that it is very expensive because of the sophisticated labor, potential for disruption, and multiple rounds of testing involved. For this reason, small companies often forgo penetration testing.

Once gaps and vulnerabilities are exposed by the penetration tests, a company may modify and strengthen its cybersecurity program before the next round of penetration testing begins. Penetration testing may continue as long as a company believes that the benefits of further testing outweigh the costs, or until the company is satisfied that its vulnerabilities have been minimized.

6. Employee Education and Training

A company must educate and train all of its employees on how to best comply with company cybersecurity policies. A cybersecurity policy is only as good as the employees who implement and comply with it, and many cybersecurity failures happen because employees carelessly fail to comply with existing company-wide policies. Corporate management has the responsibility not only to train employees, but also to follow up with them to make sure that they are consistently following company-wide policies for cybersecurity.

A comprehensive cybersecurity plan, then, must incorporate policies and training programs that deal with, but are not limited to, onsite email use, offsite email use, downloading, email attachments, social engineering attacks (attacks in which the victim is tricked into voluntarily offering up valuable information), physical information and infrastructure protection, computer screen locks, encryption programs, strong passwords, and how to report suspicious activity. In addition to training, a company's cybersecurity policies may be communicated through handbooks, posters, and company-wide emails.

7. Data Encryption

Even if corporate managers are not technologically savvy, they are still responsible for overseeing the technical aspects of cybersecurity and ensuring that data is secure both in storage and in transit. Encryption is one of the best tools for securing information on computer systems and in cyberspace.

Chapter 5: Cybersecurity for the Private Sector

Companies that use encryption technology to render their data unreadable to unauthorized users gain obvious advantages in keeping their information secure and staying out of legal trouble. As discussed earlier in this chapter, the vast majority of states have laws requiring companies to notify affected customers in the event of a data breach. The cost to notify customers can be several hundred dollars per individual. However, a good portion of these states exempt companies who encrypt their data. Policymakers consider digital information to be much safer if it is encrypted. Therefore, encrypting corporate data helps corporate managers fulfill their legally-mandated duty of care when it comes to protecting customer information.

The strategic process of determining what to encrypt requires a company to first identify its most critical data. The company should use the results of the threat, vulnerability, and consequence assessments to identify critical information assets. The company's technological ability to handle encrypted data should also be taken into account. Based on these assessments, the company may develop its cryptography strategy to match the level of encryption that its assets require in cyberspace.

8. Physical Security

Cybersecurity involves protecting both digital information and the physical sites and hardware devices in which this data is stored, processed, and transferred. Physical sites house hardware devices that may hold terabytes (a terabyte is one trillion bytes, or one thousand gigabytes) of sensitive information.

Companies should install safeguards to protect hardware devices against damage or destruction from physical hazards, such as fire or flooding. This may entail a sprinkler system, or the off-site back-up of company data. Additionally, physical sites housing hardware devices should be secured against unauthorized access. Access may be controlled by assigning identification badges to security personnel, maintaining physical access logs, employing strong door locks, and frequently changing access codes; for example, keychain fobs may be programmed to display the correct access code only to authorized employees. Conspicuous identification badges allow for quick visual confirmation that a person is authorized, and may also contain a magnetic strip or emit a radio signal to open locked doors. Physical access logs record when an identification badge was used to enter and exit a building and may be used to determine what persons are present in the building at any given time.

9. Response Programs

Before a cyber attack or data breach actually occurs, a company should put an emergency response process in place to quickly and systematically notify regulatory and law enforcement entities. Companies create emergency response plans to guide the company's total response to an emergency, assign clear roles during an emergency to employees at every level of the company, and mitigate damages as much as possible following an attack or disruption.

An emergency response plan should outline disclosure protocols, including identifying the individuals who will report an incident and notify the appropriate regulatory and law enforcement contacts. For example, if a cyber attack or data breach significantly affects corporate operations or profits, the directors and corporate officers must be prepared to disclose details of the cyber incident, and the estimated resulting losses, to the SEC. In these instances, directors and corporate officers are responsible for deciding the extent of the information to disclose, based on the materiality standard discussed earlier in this chapter. Typically, corporate counsel, the in-house attorney or legal department of a corporation, is charged with preparing the disclosure statements for the SEC.

Post-incident disclosure to the SEC is an example of a compliance-related response to a cyber emergency. Beyond their duty to comply with the law, however, companies must also have internal policies and procedures for mitigating the damage from a security breach. To this end, companies often establish incident response teams to coordinate and lead the company's response efforts. Response efforts may include identifying the security breach, containing the threat and preventing it from causing further damage, investigating the damage caused by the initial incident, and repairing IT systems so they can return to normal functioning as soon as possible.

10. Intrusion Detection Systems

A response to a cyber attack is most likely to be effective if the attack can be discovered early. **Intrusion detection systems** are technologies that detect cyber attacks by monitoring incoming and outgoing data transmissions for predefined attack signatures and anomalies.

IDSs respond to attacks in two ways: actively and passively. A passive response reports the attack to system administrators, while an active response changes the network settings to prevent the attack from causing damage. For example, an IDS may direct a hacker into a *honeypot*, or a network that is intentionally left vulnerable. The information in the honeypot may appear valuable, but is really public information or other information that, if disclosed, would not harm the company. In this way, the honeypot acts as a decoy, diverting the hacker from the company's sensitive information.

IDSs are becoming more prevalent because they are cost-effective and not susceptible to human error. Moreover, companies and lawyers increasingly regard using these systems as part of the duty of care with regards to corporate cybersecurity.

There are limits to the capabilities of intrusion detection systems, however. While these systems can detect cyber attacks, they cannot truly prevent them. In addition, intrusion detection systems use attack signatures to identify cyber attackers or intruders, and therefore must be updated on a regular basis to stay attuned to new threats. In other words, these systems are only as good as the intelligence used to program and monitor them.

11. Vendor Management

A company's strong cybersecurity plan will be futile if the company is sharing information with vendors and contractors who are not adequately protecting this information. Thus, corporate managers must ensure that any outsourced labor is using secure IT systems. Exercising appropriate care may mean writing strict security measures into contracts with service vendors and providers, as well as ensuring that third parties have security programs that secure a network's sensitive information and physical components. Companies may mandate that third-party vendors disclose any past or ongoing cybersecurity problems and data breaches. In addition, companies must monitor the cybersecurity performance of their vendors and service providers over time.

12. The Business Continuity Plan

A company's specific plan to restore service after a cybersecurity incident is the final component of the model cybersecurity program for the private sector. A **business continuity plan** is essential for maintaining service delivery to customers. A lengthy interruption, even under difficult circumstances, may lead to lower stock prices, decreased customer trust and goodwill, and even disruption to the national economy. Because of these potential costs, many companies purchase business interruption insurance to protect them against

Chapter 5: Cybersecurity for the Private Sector

potential losses in the event of a cyber attack. Directors and corporate officers are responsible for the business continuity plan, but, like most other components of the model cybersecurity program, corporate managers may call in outside experts for assistance in its development and implementation.

Internal Controls and Audits

Directors and corporate officers must design a company cybersecurity program that conforms to a complex mix of judicial precedent, government regulations, and industry standards. At the same time, a cybersecurity program must enable the company to reach its internal goals related to efficiency, customer service, profitability, and long-term growth. Once a company has crafted a cybersecurity program that meets these requirements, however, there is still the challenge of ensuring that the company adheres to the program in its day-to-day operations. To achieve all of these objectives, corporate leaders rely on internal controls and audits.

Internal controls

Internal controls are systematic measures implemented by a company to ensure that (1) company operations are effective and efficient; (2) financial reporting is reliable; (3) the company is following its own internal policies, and (4) the company is in compliance, or obeying applicable rules and regulations. A common example of an internal control is the segregation of duties in accounting. If several employees divide responsibility for keeping a company's financial accounts, no one employee will be in a position to commit and conceal fraud. Internal controls, such as periodic reviews, also help ensure that weaknesses or gaps in corporate systems will be detected in a timely manner. For example, internal controls may prevent corporate IT assets from being compromised; in this case, internal controls may take the form of technologies that detect system vulnerabilities in danger of being exploited by threats, such as computer hackers.

Because creating a comprehensive system of internal controls is a complex process, companies often model their system of internal controls on pre-existing frameworks. For example, comprehensive guidance for internal controls in the private sector is provided by the Committee of Sponsoring Organizations' (COSO) 2004 publication **Enterprise Risk Management—Integrated Framework,** an update of the organization's 1992 publication, *Internal Control—Integrated Framework*. The COSO framework uses an enterprise risk management (ERM) approach to assess risk across an entire company, with the goal of improving company performance.

For guidance specific to IT internal controls, companies turn to the **Control Objectives for Information and Related Technology (COBIT)**, a framework developed by the Information Systems Audit and Control Association (ISACA), a non-profit, global membership association for IT and information systems professionals.

Audits

An **audit** is the professional evaluation of a company's systems and procedures to ensure that they are meeting their core objectives. An audit can be conducted by a company employee (an internal audit) or by an outside professional (an external audit). In either case, the auditor evaluates the company in five areas: control environment, risk assessment, control activities, information and communications, and monitoring.

The first consideration is the *control environment*, or the organizational structure and culture of the corporation. This is the corporate structure that internal controls are built upon. It includes the chain of authority in

Conclusion

the corporation, its ethics and integrity program, and its human resources policies, such as policies concerning employee hiring, training, and discipline.

The second consideration is *risk assessment*. Risk assessment, in this case, is the identification of internal and external risks that may prevent a corporation from meeting its goals. An auditor may identify risks to the corporation by critically examining management's existing techniques for identifying and assessing risks, thereby determining the sufficiency of the company's risk assessment process.

The third consideration for an audit is *control activities*. Control activities make up the corporation's system of internal controls. The auditor seeks to catalog all of the company's controls and judge whether or not these controls are sufficient to accomplish the corporation's overall objectives.

The fourth consideration is *information and communications*. Information and communications encompasses the processes a company uses to communicate relevant and reliable information in a timely fashion. For a corporation, cybersecurity information and communications includes corporate managers communicating information to government oversight agencies and communicating new operational or compliance requirements to employees, as well as employees communicating with IT personnel about critical cyber events, such as attempted cyber attacks. The auditor's task is to understand these processes, whether automated or manual, in order to determine whether or not the system is effective.

The final consideration is *monitoring*. Monitoring is the continuous process by which corporate management evaluates its own internal controls to ensure that these controls are operating as management intended and evolving to meet the company's goals. Proper monitoring includes a corrective process that allows for changes if internal controls are functioning improperly or need to be updated. The auditor will examine the company's processes for monitoring internal controls to determine their effectiveness.

Companies voluntarily hire professional auditors to assess their internal controls. However, mandatory audits are also performed by government agencies at the federal and state levels to ensure that companies are complying with the law. The most famous example of a government audit is the feared audit of tax records performed by the Internal Revenue Service (IRS). However, government audits are also used to assess compliance with laws and regulations concerning cybersecurity and information management.

For example, the U.S. Department of Health and Human Services (HHS) is responsible for auditing certain companies to determine whether or not these companies are in compliance with HIPAA. Pursuant to section 13411 of the American Recovery and Reinvestment Act of 2009, HHS must audit health care providers to determine whether or not they are following the HIPAA Privacy and Security Rules and the HITECH Act's breach notification standards. Just as in other audit processes conducted by government agencies, only a small percentage of medical offices and health care companies are selected to be audited. A government auditor will visit the provider, interview key personnel, and observe the daily functions and processes of the company. In addition, the medical office or health care company will be asked to show documents demonstrating compliance with HIPAA. Subsequently, the auditor submits a report to HHS detailing his findings and describing the actions that the medical office or healthcare company is taking in response to any compliance deficiencies.

Conclusion

Understanding cybersecurity in the private sector is complicated. First, you must understand the structure and governance models of corporations. Second, you must know the legal duties corporations owe to their shareholders and customers and understand that senior management is responsible for fulfilling these obligations. Third, you must be familiar with federal and state laws and regulations concerning cybersecurity and

Chapter 5: Cybersecurity for the Private Sector

how these rules connect and overlap. Furthermore, to fully understand the regulatory framework, you must know how rules are developed and what they look like (see Chapter 6, on Advanced Cybersecurity Studies, for more on this topic).

All of these concepts are in play when a company's management team develops a corporate cybersecurity plan. Creating an effective, comprehensive, and robust cybersecurity plan is a complex task for corporate managers that they must handle on top of their other day-to-day responsibilities. Once a cybersecurity program is implemented, it must be continuously updated as technology evolves and companies make expensive investments in IT personnel and internal controls to keep up with emerging threats in the dangerous cyber environment.

Now that you have a better understanding of cybersecurity for the private sector, do you have a newfound respect for the senior managers and information technology employees across the country who are responsible for securing your information? Think about the scenario at the beginning of this chapter and the way you might have approached the problem of corporate cybersecurity. What would you do differently as the CEO of a young technology company now that you've read this chapter?

Key Questions

1. What does the duty of care require of the board of directors?

    a) To put in place a cybersecurity program in their company.

    b) To be informed before making decisions.

    c) To oversee the day-to-day decisions of corporate officers.

    d) a) and b) only.

    e) a), b), and c).

2. What is the difference between the Gramm-Leach-Bliley Financial Modernization Act and the Health Insurance Portability and Accountability Act?

    a) Only one of the laws contains both a privacy and a security rule

    b) One of the laws is applicable to the financial sector, while the other is applicable to the healthcare sector.

    c) Only one of the laws includes a mandatory data breach notification provision.

    d) a) and b) only.

    e) b) and c) only.

    f) a), b), and c).

3. What are the elements of a risk assessment?

    a) Threat assessment

    b) Vulnerability assessment

Key Questions

    c) Consequence assessment

    d) a) and b) only.

    e) b) and c) only.

    f) a), b), and c).

Cyber Connections

Chapter 1 discusses the technical aspects and challenges of risk management, a central and recurring aspect of corporate governance and private sector legal obligations. Chapter 2 discusses how policy and laws are made by the federal government, and emphasizes how the federal government is placing greater reliance on the private sector to ensure national cybersecurity through public-private partnerships. Chapter 4 defines and explains some of the tools that are part of the cybersecurity arsenal in the private sector, such as data encryption, firewalls, and two-factor authentication systems. Chapter 6 describes the rule-making processes of the United States government that create cybersecurity laws and regulations for both the public and private sectors.

CHAPTER 6:
Advanced Cybersecurity Studies: Research Methods and Sources

CHAPTER OUTLINE

- **Overview of Advanced Cybersecurity Studies: Research Methods and Sources**
- **Introduction to Research Methods**
- **The U.S. Constitution and the Three Branches of Government**
- **The Role of the Executive Branch**
- **The Role of the Legislature**
- **Federal Regulations: The Executive Branch and the Legislative Branch Combined**
- **The Role of the Judiciary**
- **Cybersecurity: A Global Perspective**
- **Conclusion**
- **Key Questions**

6 Advanced Cybersecurity Studies: Research Methods and Sources

Chapter In Focus

- Research methods and how to apply them.
- Researching executive, legislative and judicial sources.
- Federal regulations as sources.
- Research methods and sources on the global scale.
- Cybersecurity in the international community.

Overview of Advanced Cybersecurity Studies: Research Methods and Sources

As this book has demonstrated, cybersecurity is truly an interdisciplinary field. Therefore, delving deeper into cybersecurity problems and proposing new policies and solutions requires a flexible and interdisciplinary approach to academic research. Potential research topics in the field may come from subfields as varied as cyber risk management, cyber law and policy, cybersecurity program management, cybersecurity technology, and cybersecurity for the private sector. Researchers in cybersecurity may pursue new breakthroughs in any of these topics, or create new frameworks, theories, policies, and plans that combine knowledge generated from two or more fields.

Domestic and international events, institutions, and technological developments drive new developments in cybersecurity research. For example, the crippling 2007 cyber attacks against Estonia's banks, media, and government, the Stuxnet worm against Iran's nuclear facilities, and the appearance of the highly complex Flame worm in Middle Eastern critical infrastructure computer systems, are all events that have shaped new cybersecurity methods, policies, and technologies. Thus, the discussions, debates, official policies, new government programs, and technological projects that follow any cybersecurity incident, particularly those that occur on a massive scale, have become rich areas for researchers to investigate and analyze.

National governments and international institutions produce documents of great interest to cybersecurity researchers. In part because the Internet began as a project of the DOD, the U.S. government remains the world's leading institution in the development of cybersecurity law, policy, technology, and research. Moreover, U.S. government documentation of cybersecurity policies, proposals, strategies, debates, legislation, and regulation has served as an invaluable model for other national governments and for the private sector.

A researcher's access to databases and documents is not enough to generate original contributions to the field, however; researchers must begin their investigations by understanding the authorities, processes, histories, and problems that inform these research sources. This chapter will ground you in the practice of researching cybersecurity problems by introducing you to some of the organizations and institutions where these problems are most often discussed, analyzed, and tackled. This chapter will guide you through the structure and policymaking process of the U.S. government as it relates to cybersecurity, and then examine the role of international institutions.

Chapter 6: Advanced Cybersecurity Studies

Finally, it is important to note that academics, intellectuals, and students are not the only people who pose research questions and conduct research. The information in this chapter will benefit both public and private-sector professionals who work on cybersecurity problems in any capacity.

Introduction to Research Methods

As an academic discipline, cybersecurity is a unique fusion of computer science, law and policy, risk management, business, and program management. However a researcher approaches a cybersecurity problem, he will inevitably encounter more than one of these areas of study (in this section, we will assume that our hypothetical researcher is male). But even though cybersecurity is an interdisciplinary field, the researcher's focus must be narrow enough to study, test, and analyze a specific subject.

Besides these potential areas of research, the academic field of cybersecurity has also given rise to a growing collection of theories. **Theories** in this context are statements that have been tested repeatedly and accepted by experts. Rigorous hypothesis testing and research can challenge established theories, propose new theories, and add to the complexity and scope of cybersecurity as an academic discipline.

Therefore, for students contemplating careers in cybersecurity, the challenge is both what to study and how to study it. **Ontology** is the theory of being, or what is being studied or researched. **Epistemology** is the theory of knowledge, or how an event, phenomenon or object is studied, researched, analyzed, and understood. The epistemology of a research project is the project's guiding philosophy about the best way to produce new knowledge.

Once the researcher has determined the epistemological and ontological reference for his work, he can determine the research design that his project will follow. A **research design** is the outline of the research—a complete blueprint for how the researcher will attempt to answer the question posed by his project. There are two kinds of research design: *experimental* (in which the researcher runs an experiment) and *nonexperimental* (in which there is no experiment). Both types of research design may involve a mixture of quantitative and qualitative methods. The type of research design is contingent on the question the researcher posed at the beginning of the project.

Research questions often focus on the main theoretical debates or unanswered questions in a field. Therefore, in cybersecurity, a researcher may examine the debates raised by historical events, judicial precedents, relevant legislation, new policies, and technological advancements. For example, a researcher might ask: "Which U.S. cybersecurity laws and regulations have had the greatest influence on international cybersecurity standards?" Or: "What privacy concerns have been raised by the ability of telecommunications companies to monitor Internet traffic?"

Neither of these cybersecurity research questions would necessarily require the researcher to run an experiment. Experimental research is relatively rare in cybersecurity because it requires the researcher to have total control of the experiment's independent variables. **Independent variables** are the factors that influence outcomes, the **dependent variables**. For example, the growth of a plant is dependent on the plant's exposure to sunlight; thus, growth of the plant is the dependent variable (y), and exposure to the sun is an independent variable (x).

Cybersecurity experiments follow a similar design. For example, researchers may run experiments to test the effectiveness of a new antivirus software or IDS. The researcher's choice to include or omit relevant factors that can influence the outcome will determine whether or not the results are relevant and whether or not the experiment is successful. A successful experiment will be able to show that a meaningful relationship between one or more variables either does or does not exist.

Nonexperimental research is more common in the social sciences. In this type of design, the researcher does not have control over all of the independent variables, and there is only one test group. In most cases, nonexperimental research involves studying a subject "as is," rather than running an experiment upon it. Examples of common nonexperimental research subjects include human behavior, literature, and history.

There are three types of nonexperimental research: exploratory, explanatory, and descriptive. *Exploratory research* provides preliminary concepts and findings about an underdeveloped topic and establishes a baseline for future study. Small focus groups or open-ended interviews with limited participants are examples of exploratory research.

Explanatory research attempts to answer a "why" question. Explanatory researchers may engage in rigorous hypothesis-testing in order to determine a relationship between two or more variables. The case study in Chapter 1 involving an online retailer trying to protect its network from a cyber attack is an example of explanatory research, in which the researcher examined which combination of security controls yielded the most secure website. In this type of research, researchers may manipulate a dataset to test the effect of various independent variables on the dependent variable. Explanatory research cannot prove a causal relationship, but it can prove or disprove a significant relationship between multiple variables.

Descriptive research provides more details than exploratory research, and its results may be more generalizable. Large-sample surveys are examples of descriptive research. Descriptive research does not typically employ hypothesis testing.

Applying Research Methods

This chapter will examine the events, official statements, legislation, publications, international organizations, and other sources that have shaped cybersecurity policy and thought. These sources are all potential **units of analysis**, or research subjects. For new researchers, deciding exactly what question or problem to research, then further refining the research focus, can be a difficult and time-consuming process. Still, the more specific the question a researcher poses at the beginning of an investigation, the easier it will be to choose the most relevant variables, create hypotheses, perform research, analyze the results, and draw conclusions that contribute new knowledge to the field.

As these five steps suggest, even in a nonexperimental research project, the researcher must strive to conduct research with the strict objectivity and step-by-step approach of a scientist. In other words, the basic principles of the **scientific method**—systematic and objective examination of a phenomenon—apply to the work of cybersecurity researchers.

After the researcher selects his unit of analysis, he must decide on the **time dimension** for the research—the precise time period the researcher will investigate. Determining the time dimension establishes a boundary for the scope of the unit of analysis. Once the researcher has narrowed the research question and established the units of analysis and time dimension, he can begin to develop hypotheses, if the project calls for hypothesis testing.

Throughout the research design phase, the researcher should conduct validity and reliability tests. **Validity** means that the researcher is testing precisely the variables and subjects he set out to study; **reliability** means that another researcher could replicate the design and reach the same results. Testing for validity can be difficult in an interdisciplinary field like cybersecurity, as it can sometimes be hard to determine which sources pertain directly to the research question and which do not. In terms of reliability, the success of the researcher's project will depend on how strictly he has adhered to the scientific method throughout the project.

Chapter 6: Advanced Cybersecurity Studies

The researcher must be careful to avoid common mistakes of logic and reasoning when examining, analyzing, and drawing conclusions about his subject. Mistakes of logic and reasoning can undermine a good research question and render an entire research design useless. Common logical mistakes involve logical fallacies. **Logical fallacies** are statements that are based on some kind of misconception. Researchers may unwittingly commit logical fallacies when they make statements that fail to adhere to the rules of logic.

For example, the *ecological fallacy* occurs when the researcher assumes that a fact or relationship that is true for one sample is true for another, typically larger, sample or unit of analysis. The *genetic fallacy* occurs when a researcher rejects an idea based on its origin rather than its merit. The *bandwagon fallacy* occurs when a researcher accepts an idea as true because it is increasing in popularity, and the complex question fallacy occurs at the very beginning of a research project, when a researcher poses a question that depends on a questionable assumption.

Researching Cybersecurity through U.S. Government Documents

The U.S. government is a massive organization that has committed billions of dollars to a long-term cybersecurity effort. The U.S. government's investment in the development of cybersecurity thought, technology, law, and policy is considered a benchmark for the rest of the world. For this reason, this chapter will focus on U.S. government cybersecurity sources, which can inform and strengthen cybersecurity research on any topic.

In any research project, the researcher may need to consult an enormous number of sources related to the U.S. federal government: White House directives and memoranda, federal agency regulations and guidance, legislation and its history, case studies of federally prosecuted cyber crimes, and guidelines for judges to sentence cyber criminals. These sources are only the beginning of a growing list.

Cyber Fact

In Chapter 2 (Cybersecurity Law and Policy), we discussed in detail how catastrophic events can trigger significant policy changes within the highest levels of the U.S. federal government. After the Oklahoma City bombing in 1995 and terrorist attacks of September 11, 2001, national security experts predicted that a massive cyber attack could cripple the domestic economy if the federal government failed to secure its digital infrastructure. As a result, cybersecurity became one of the leading issues in discussions of U.S. national security.

The U.S. Constitution and the Three Branches of Government: Establishing Power to Produce and Enforce Federal Laws

The Constitution of the United States guides the actions of the federal government. In its first three articles, the Constitution created the legislative (U.S. Congress), executive (U.S. president), and judicial (U.S. federal courts) branches of the federal government. The different roles played by the three branches of government in the formation of national cybersecurity policy have produced contrasting types of cybersecurity documents and cybersecurity ideas.

For example, in both appearance and power, a presidential directive is significantly different from a piece of congressional legislation or a Supreme Court decision. In your research on existing and developing cybersecurity issues, you will need to know the difference between the types of documents that each branch of government produces, as well as the different kinds of power that each branch has to create and enforce laws and policies. As you move beyond the U.S. in your cybersecurity research, you will also need to know about the types of cybersecurity work performed by internationally oriented research bodies, such as the IETF, and by global security organizations, such as the United Nations (U.N.) and NATO.

One consistent theme you will encounter in this chapter is that new cyber laws and policies tend to originate in the executive branch of the U.S. federal government. Because the executive branch has the role of "first responder" during national security emergencies, and because national security emergencies often precede new national security policies, new cybersecurity policies naturally flow from the executive branch. These executive policies, issued in executive orders and national security instruments (such as NSDDs, PDDs, NSPDs, etc.), apply to the U.S. government's federal departments and agencies and in this way influence the day-to-day operations of the federal government. In order for presidential policies to take on a broader application, they must be passed into law and funded by the U.S. Congress.

The Role of Congress in Executive Policies

Executive policies need to be formalized and funded by Congress before they can be enacted as national laws with a wide application. After much debate and compromise, Congress enacts legislation committing the resources necessary for the development of new cybersecurity policies, often adopting the executive branch's policies as its own. The executive branch then reinforces and executes Congress's mandate with further regulations and guidance. We will discuss Congress's role in the formation of cybersecurity laws in greater detail later in this chapter.

The Role of the Judiciary in Executive Policies

The judicial branch plays a narrow but critical role in cybersecurity law and policy, as federal courts hear and decide cases against individuals accused of violating the cybersecurity laws that Congress has passed and the president has signed. The courts also draft rules governing the type and length of punishment appropriate for individuals found guilty of violating these laws. We will discuss the judiciary's role in enforcing cybersecurity laws later in this chapter.

The Role of the Executive Branch

Article II of the U.S. Constitution states, "The executive Power shall be vested in a President of the United States of America." The president is the most powerful individual in the government; he is the commander-in-chief of the U.S. armed forces, the nation's chief diplomat, and the head of state. Within the U.S. federal government, only the president possesses the authority to issue executive orders and national security instruments. The president is also responsible for implementing and enforcing the laws created by Congress.

We have already discussed the president's role as "first responder" during national security emergencies. Following such emergencies, the president is the first to respond with policy decisions because, as a policymaker, he is more nimble than Congress; he can create new executive policies at any time. Conversely, congressional processes are more formalized and lengthy. Indeed, final decisions in Congress are usually the result of a long process of debate and compromise between rival parties.

Therefore, for the past 25 years, the executive branch has been the leader in developing U.S. cybersecurity policy. Executive policies identify priorities and direct resources toward particular agencies and programs.

Chapter 6: Advanced Cybersecurity Studies

For executive branch policies to have a wider effect beyond federal departments and agencies, they must be formalized and funded by Congress.

Structure of the Executive Branch

In practice, the executive branch is comprised of the president and the departments and agencies charged with enacting presidential policy. The president appoints the heads of these federal department and agencies. Some of these department and agency heads serve as members of the president's cabinet. Individually and collectively, federal departments and agencies and the cabinet are responsible for implementing, enforcing, and executing federal laws. Their missions, responsibilities, and priorities may evolve and change according to the orders of the president.

In 1939, Congress formed the **Executive Office of the President (EOP)** to assist the president and provide support for the increasingly large bureaucracy of the executive branch. The EOP consists of the following offices:

- The Council of Economic Advisers
- The Council on Environmental Quality
- The Executive Residence
- The National Security Council
- The Office of Administration
- The Office of Management and Budget
- The Office of National Drug Control Policy
- The Office of Science and Technology Policy
- The Office of the United States Trade Representative
- The Office of the Vice President
- The White House Office

The EOP plays an active role in the president's policymaking activities. Indeed, before a president finalizes an executive order or national security instrument, he participates in a deliberative process involving key departments and agencies of the EOP.

Key EOP Players: The National Security Council

The **National Security Council (NSC)** is a key agency in the development of cybersecurity policy in the executive branch. Created during the Truman administration and codified in the National Security Act of 1947, the NSC is the national security and foreign policy arm of the executive branch.

The NSC is comprised of the president, the vice president, the secretary of state, the secretary of defense, and the national security advisor. The president's chief of staff, the White House counsel, and the assistant to the president for economic policy are invited to attend NSC meetings. The chairman of the Joint Chiefs of Staff is the statutory military advisor, and the director of national intelligence serves as the intelligence advisor.

The Role of the Executive Branch

The NSC is instrumental in the creation of national security instruments, a type of presidential directive. These documents directly relate to national defense, foreign affairs, and national security—all areas that directly concern the NSC.

Key EOP Players: The Office of Management and Budget

Congress established the **OMB** (originally named the Bureau of the Budget) in 1921. The Bureau of the Budget became part of the EOP in 1939 and took on significant oversight responsibility for new government programs. Among its duties, the OMB determines and oversees the budget-making process of the federal departments and agencies.

During the administration of President Richard Nixon, the OMB acquired its current mission of managing and evaluating the programs of U.S. federal agencies and helping the president to create a federal budget according to its evaluations. Today, in addition to managing federal agencies and making budget plans for government programs, the OMB houses the federal government's Office of E-Government and Information Technology. This office works to streamline interactions between the government and the public using information technology, and it also works on cybersecurity initiatives.

The OMB's **Office of Information and Regulatory Affairs (OIRA)** works to reduce government paperwork and maintain an efficient flow of information within the government. As previously mentioned in Chapter 2, OIRA was formed after Congress passed the Paperwork Reduction Act of 1980. Because OIRA is charged with overseeing and implementing government-wide information policy, it is often involved in new federal computer-based initiatives. The websites of both the Office of E-Government and OIRA are good sources for policy documents related to federal computer and information security.

Key EOP Players: The Office of Science and Technology Policy

Congress established the **Office of Science and Technology Policy (OSTP)** as part of the EOP in 1976. The OSTP is charged with advising the president and his senior staff on matters related to science and technology. The scientific and technical expertise of the OSTP informs presidential policy and ensures that all new executive branch policies are based on scientifically sound information and analysis. The OSTP Resource Library is available to the public and contains important scientific speeches, documents, reports, testimony, policy guidance, and other potential research sources.

Key Types of EOP Policy Documents

Now that you understand the structure of the EOP, we will examine the most important types of policy documents and memoranda that the EOP produces. The EOP is a rich source of cybersecurity policy documents, many of which are accessible and form the basis of current federal laws, programs, institutions, departments and agencies, government positions, and regulations. Important new policies issued from the EOP may take the form of national security instruments, OMB memoranda, OSTP memoranda, executive orders, and White House strategy guides.

Chapter 6: Advanced Cybersecurity Studies

EOP Policy Document Type 1: National Security Instruments

A **national security instrument** is an often-classified order from the president to his cabinet ordering them to marshal resources around a policy. It lays out the intention and goals behind the policy and establishes a decision-making process involving specific government actors.

National security instruments concern national security policy and are therefore issued with the advice and consent of the NSC. Because of their national security significance, many national security instruments remain classified, even decades after they are issued. The fact that the EOP issued a national security instrument is public, but the content of that instrument may not be. National security instruments maintain their legal effectiveness indefinitely, even after the end of the issuing president's term, until a conflicting action is taken by a successor.

Generally, each administration has created a different name for its national security instruments, and recent presidents have used multiple names. For instance, President George W. Bush issued National Security Presidential Directives (NSPDs), while President Barack Obama issues Presidential Study Directives (PSDs), and Presidential Policy Directives (PPDs).[1]

National Security Instruments and Cybersecurity

Following the 1995 bombing of the Murrah Federal Building in Oklahoma City and the findings of President's Commission on Critical Infrastructure Protection (PCCIP), President Bill Clinton issued Presidential Decision Directive 63. PDD-63 established a structure under White House leadership to coordinate private-public sector sharing of threat and vulnerability information, in order to prevent physical and cyber attacks on critical infrastructure.

This historic directive was the first attempt to organize the government's response to an attack on critical infrastructure and to establish a critical infrastructure plan for cyber systems. PDD-63 formulated policies for national cybersecurity operations that have been reiterated in subsequent directives issued by Presidents Clinton, Bush, and Obama.

EOP Policy Document Type 2: Executive Orders

An **executive order (EO)** is a declaration from the president that is legally binding and does not require the consent of Congress. The president issues executive orders to federal departments and agencies. Many executive orders establish administrative procedures or powers. Like national security instruments, executive orders remain in place until a later president deliberately replaces them. Unlike national security instruments, executive orders are rarely classified.

Many executive orders concern national security and, increasingly, cybersecurity. For instance, in February 2013, President Obama issued **Executive Order 13636**, which called for new measures to enhance the cybersecurity of the nation's critical infrastructure. This EO highlighted cyber attacks as a major national security threat and encouraged the federal government to work with private sector entities to prevent cyber intrusions and enhance the protection of critical infrastructure. Specifically, the order emphasized the improvement of information-sharing as a key priority, calling upon the the federal government to "increase the volume, timeliness, and quality of cyber threat information" shared with the private sector.

Since the Oklahoma City bombing of 1995, presidents have issued many significant executive orders relevant to cybersecurity. As discussed in Chapter 2, President Clinton's Executive Order 13011 established the **Chief Information Officers Council (CIO Council)**. The CIO Council is comprised of CIOs from many federal

The Role of the Executive Branch

> **Video**
>
> Watch 'Executive Order 13636' at http://vimeo.com/channels/cybersecurityfoundations.

agencies. The CIO Council is the principal interagency group tasked with improving agency information resource management practices—including acquisition, design, development, use and sharing of information—in accordance with the Paperwork Reduction Act of 1980, the Government Performance and Results Act of 1993, the Information Technology Management Reform Act of 1996, the Government Paperwork Elimination Act of 1998, and the E-Government Act of 2002. In addition to creating the CIO Council, EO 13011 directed federal agencies to implement the provisions of the Paperwork Reduction Act and the Clinger-Cohen Act in order to improve the federal government's management of information technology.

On October 8, 2001, less than one month after the 9/11 terrorist attacks, President Bush issued Executive Order 13228. This EO created the Office of Homeland Security and the Homeland Security Council as centers of the nation's critical infrastructure protection. These bodies were the predecessors of DHS, which, as we will see in OMB Memorandum M-10-28, shares significant oversight powers for national cybersecurity with the OMB.

Executive Order 13231 created the position of special advisor to the president for cyberspace security. This position is also the head of the Office of Cybersecurity. EO 13231 also gave strategic responsibility for critical infrastructure protection to the executive branch by creating the President's Critical Infrastructure Protection Board (PCIPB). The special advisor to the president for cyberspace security chaired the PCIPB and was responsible for recommending policies and programs to the EOP for protecting U.S. critical infrastructure.

A little more than two years after EO 13231's release, the Bush administration announced another important policy document, referred to as Homeland Security Presidential Directive (HSPD) 7. Isssued in December 2003, HSPD-7 replaced PDD-63. HSPD-7 reiterated the administration's commitment to partnership between lead government agencies and their counterparts in the private sector, and designated DHS as the lead agency for coordinating the nation's overall critical infrastructure protection efforts.

> **Cyber Fact**
>
> Originally, the content of CNCI was classified, but in March 2010, in an effort to increase both the transparency and public awareness of CNCI, the Obama administration released high-level details about CNCI, in addition to publishing a Cyberspace Policy Review outlining the cyber threat environment and the cybersecurity priorities and strategies of the federal government.

> **Cyber Fact**
>
> "Initiative #1" of CNCI ("Manage the Federal Enterprise Network as a single network enterprise with Trusted Internet Connections") reads as follows: "The Trusted Internet Connections (TIC) initiative, headed by [OMB] and [DHS] proposes the consolidation of the Federal Government's external access points (including those to the Internet). This consolidation will result in a common security solution which includes: facilitating the reduction of external access points, establishing baseline security capabilities; and, validating agency adherence to those security capabilities."

Chapter 6: Advanced Cybersecurity Studies

In 2008, the Bush administration issued NSPD-54/HSPD-23, which launched CNCI. With CNCI, President Bush elevated the issue of cybersecurity to a new level of national importance, involving DHS, the OMB, and the NSA. President Bush's CNCI also identified national cybersecurity priorities for the federal government.

Federal departments and agencies are assigned the responsibility of executing initiatives outlined in CNCI and reporting back to the EOP. The goal is for these initiatives to become part of the day-to-day cyber operations of the White House and the federal government.

EOP Policy Document Type 3: OMB Memoranda

OMB memoranda are important policy documents that can shed light on how power over the government's cybersecurity operations can shift at the OMB's discretion. The director of the OMB has issued nationally significant memoranda about cybersecurity, including FISMA reporting requirements for federal departments and agencies. These memoranda clarify the specific responsibilities of departments and agencies with regard to national cybersecurity policy.

An important OMB memorandum for cybersecurity researchers to examine is M-10-28. In this memorandum, the OMB gave DHS "primary responsibility within the executive branch for the operational aspects of Federal agency cybersecurity with respect to the Federal information systems that fall within FISMA [...]" In other words, M-10-28 gave DHS the responsibility to oversee the cybersecurity programs of all federal departments and agencies, with the stipulation that DHS report to the OMB. In turn, the OMB reports directly to the president on the effectiveness and cost-efficiency of these cybersecurity programs. Therefore, this document is the basis for the current federal power structure for enforcing FISMA.

M-10-28 also solidified the role of the cybersecurity coordinator, a position created by President Obama in 2009 (see Chapter 2). The OMB acknowledged the coordinator's lead role in interagency cybersecurity initiatives, and formally tasked the coordinator with working with DHS to oversee FISMA compliance and "[coordinating] interagency cooperation with DHS cybersecurity efforts."

Cyber Fact

The **Federal Information Security Management Act of 2002 (FISMA)** requires all federal departments and agencies to develop and implement robust information security programs on a budget, and to report to the OMB.

EOP Policy Document Type 4: OSTP Memoranda

Another EOP office that issues memoranda related to cybersecurity policy is the OSTP. On December 17, 2010, the OSTP issued a memorandum called **"Scientific Integrity."** This memorandum lays out several principles of importance to the OSTP, including the idea that "[I]t is important that policymakers involve science and technology experts where appropriate and that scientific and technological information and processes relied upon in policymaking be of the highest integrity." OSTP's "Scientific Integrity" memorandum also advocates that government agencies foster open communication between scientific experts, hire spokespeople to articulate scientific work in a nonpartisan fashion, and ensure "[t]he accurate presentation of scientific and technological information" for policymakers and the public.

This memorandum notes that the director of the OMB will issue guidance to OMB staff regarding standards to be upheld in the review of executive branch testimony on scientific issues. It concludes by asking that agencies report back to the OSTP on steps they have taken to improve the scientific integrity of their work and presentations. Although this OSTP memorandum did not create any new rule or reassign power, it is a document that both affects and reflects policymaking at the executive level.

EOP Policy Document Type 5: White House Strategy and Guidance

The White House and federal departments and agencies issue annual reports that inform, guide, and reflect executive policy on cybersecurity. The 2010 Quadrennial Homeland Security Review report and the 2010 Bottom-Up Review report identified cybersecurity as a key mission area for DHS. The 2011 Blueprint for a Secure Cyber Future and the 2012 DHS Strategic Plan set forth a clear strategy for forming private-public partnerships around cybersecurity. These documents, as well as other cybersecurity publications, offer more details than executive orders or PDDs because they deal with specific plans rather than broad policies and executive priorities. Students of cybersecurity should also review the Obama administration's 2009 Cyberspace Policy Review and 2011 International Strategy for Cyberspace. Both of these documents discuss current policy objectives and obstacles for federal cybersecurity.

Executive Branch Research Source: The Federal Register

Certain types of presidential directives are published in the *Federal Register.* The *Federal Register* is a daily publication of the U.S. federal government, created in 1935. According to the official website of the National Archives, each issue of the *Federal Register* is organized around four categories: (1) "Presidential Documents" ("including executive orders and proclamations"); (2) "Rules and Regulations" ("including policy statements and interpretations"); (3) "Proposed Rules" ("including petitions for rulemaking and other advance proposals"); and (4) "Advance Notices" ("including scheduled hearings and meetings open the public, grant applications, and administrative orders"). The simplest way to search for information in the *Federal Register* is online.[2]

The Role of the Legislature

The purpose of this section is to explain how Congress develops and enacts cybersecurity legislation. As previously discussed, when catastrophic events occur, the executive branch is usually the first branch of the federal government to respond, because Congress must go through a formal process of proposing, drafting, debating, and voting on legislation. Executive response may take the form of legally binding executive orders or national security instruments; however, Congress is the only authority that can fund the programs created by executive policies.

Congressional Authorities

Article I of the U.S. Constitution states, "[a]ll legislative Powers herein granted shall be vested in a Congress of the United States, which shall consist of a Senate and House of Representatives." Congress is a bicameral body consisting of the House of Representatives and the Senate. Each state in the U.S. elects two senators. Each state also elects representatives to the House, the number of representatives being proportional to each state's population.

Congress's primary authority is its control of the federal government's ability to fund new and existing programs; that is, it holds the "power of the purse." Congress also has the authority to create new federal departments and agencies, and to reorganize existing ones. For instance, in 2002, Congress created the DHS pursuant to its

Chapter 6: Advanced Cybersecurity Studies

passage of the Homeland Security Act (HSA). The reorganization of federal departments and agencies following the passage the HSA was the largest federal government reorganization since the NSC was established in 1947.

The Homeland Security Act as a Model for Modern National Security Legislation

Congress has typically followed the president's lead on cybersecurity policy. Through Congress, presidential priorities become legal requirements that form the basis of government programs.

As discussed earlier in this chapter and in Chapter 2, President Clinton's PDD-63 is an historic cybersecurity policy document. Indeed, Congress incorporated many of its elements into the HSA. For example, PDD-63 created the **National Infrastructure Protection Center (NIPC)**. This organization is charged with protecting critical infrastructure, with special attention paid to computer systems. The NIPC sends out alerts and warnings regarding new threats and vulnerabilities. Formerly housed within the FBI, the NIPC was codified in the HSA and has been operated by DHS since the latter was formed in 2003.

Thus, the HSA was an important piece of cybersecurity legislation that affected cybersecurity policymaking and operations by creating new offices, programs, and positions dedicated to cybersecurity. It also rearranged and reassigned responsibility among existing departments and agencies. It was a landmark piece of legislation for cybersecurity policymaking at the federal level.

How Congress Passes Bills into Laws

Typically, a legislator (a representative or senator) introduces a bill for consideration. A **bill** is a proposed piece of legislation.

Bills typically originate in the House of Representatives, though they may also originate in the Senate. House members may introduce a bill at any time, and in any way, while Congress is in session. For example, a House member may make a speech about why he is introducing the bill, or he may simply place a written statement in a wooden box called "the hopper," located in the House chamber. A proposed bill is assigned a number (e.g., H.R. 1 for a bill that originates in the House, or S. 1 for a bill that originates in the Senate) and clearly states the name of its sponsor—the member of Congress who wrote it. Bills may also be co-sponsored.

The Speaker of the House passes proposed bills along to the appropriate congressional committees. **Committees** are congressional groups focused on a specific national issue. There are congressional committees on nearly every subject matter, including the budget, finance, and foreign relations. A great deal of congressional work happens in committees, and committees decide which bills will be voted on by the entire House or Senate. Several committees are charged with reviewing each proposed bill.

Discussions of bills begin with closed-door talks between committee members and representatives from the relevant government departments and agencies. These department and agency representatives offer their input before a committee deems the bill to be of sufficient importance to call for public hearings. At public hearings, members of the public may testify before members of Congress on the desirability or importance of passing a given bill and enacting it into law.

Following the public-hearings stage of the legislative process, a congressional committee will consider the bill again in a period known as the mark-up session. During the **mark-up session**, a committee or special subcommittee studies the proposed bill in depth and from both sides of the issue. The members of the committee or subcommittee consider the input and testimony they have received from the departments and agencies, from the public, from advocacy groups and lobbyists, and from experts. They then decide whether or not to recommend the bill and whether or not to amend the bill before recommending it.

At the end of the mark-up session, and after receiving the recommendations of any relevant subcommittee, the full committee votes on whether or not to recommend the bill to the full House of Representatives (or to the Senate, if that is where the bill originated). If the committee does recommend the bill, they must vote on whether or not, and how, to amend the proposed legislation before recommending it. The committee may ultimately decide not to recommend the bill, or to postpone the committee vote indefinitely.

Should the committee vote in favor of recommending the bill to the full House of Representatives (or Senate), it will draft a committee report explaining its reasons for recommendation and, if applicable, explaining any amendments added to the bill. The committee will generally address each section of the bill and explain in detail what each section is meant to accomplish as part of a proposed new law. In order to justify congressional funding, the report must include a proposed budget and a statement of objectives and outcomes. Each committee report must also include a statement that cites the constitutional powers granted to Congress that allow Congress to pass this specific bill into law.

When a bill is recommended by all of the committees in which it was examined, Congress places it on the legislative calendar for floor debates. The **floor** is the term for the conceptual place in which all official activity in Congress happens. During floor debates, the proposed bill is read at least twice on the floor of the House. The second time the bill is read, representatives may propose amendments to each section.

Following floor debates in the House, the representatives take a final vote on whether or not to send the bill to the Senate (or, if the bill originated in the Senate, whether or not to send the bill to the House). Voting in the House may be conducted in several ways: (1) *viva voce*, in which representatives voice their vote aloud; (2) through a method known as *division*, in which representatives vote for or against a bill by standing up; or (3) using an electronic voting system. A majority vote means that the bill has passed the House and will be delivered to the Senate for another vote. The content of the proceedings and debates that take place on the floors of both the House of Representatives and the Senate are published in the *Congressional Record*, a report issued daily when Congress is in session.

A bill that passes in the House of Representatives and is sent to the Senate (or passes in the Senate and is sent to the House) becomes an *act*. An act goes through a similar legislative process in the Senate, with senators debating the its merits on the floor and proposing new amendments. Voting in the Senate is *viva voce* and a majority vote is needed for the act to pass.

If an act passes, but a similar but conflicting piece of proposed legislation has previously been passed in the Senate (for bills originating in the House), a conference committee may be assembled to reconcile differences between the two pieces of legislation before the final legislation is delivered to the president. **Conference committees** are composed of members of both the House and the Senate and are considered especially critical for reconciling legislative differences on bills that are controversial in nature.

A bill that has passed in both the House and the Senate is finally sent to the president for signature. The president has 10 days to publicly approve the bill (by signing it) or to publicly disapprove of it by exercising his **veto power**. The Constitution grants the president this veto power, which allows him to return a proposed bill to the part of Congress (either the House or the Senate) in which it originated. When the president vetoes a bill, he usually adds an explanation of his reasons for vetoing it. The president's veto can be overridden by a two-thirds majority vote in both the House and the Senate. Bills that the president neither signs nor vetoes

Chapter 6: Advanced Cybersecurity Studies

automatically pass into law after 10 days. All bills that pass both the House and Senate and are either signed by the president or not vetoed become public laws that the federal government must enforce.

Where To Find Proposed Bills and Laws

Congress's website offers the complete texts of bills and laws, along with easy access to the *Congressional Record* and other information about Congress

Another fantastic tool for accessing legislation and its history is **THOMAS.gov**, a service provided by the Library of Congress, the federal government's research library. THOMAS, named after Thomas Jefferson, is an exhaustive database of congressional and presidential activity and documents, and allows researchers to search for past and proposed legislation.[3]

Research Source: the Government Accountability Office

The **Government Accountability Office**, previously referred to as the General Accounting Office, is a nonpartisan agency that works for Congress and is charged with making Congress better informed, more efficient, more ethical, and more responsive. The GAO's duties include investigating how taxpayer dollars are spent and auditing the activities and performance of federal departments and agencies. The GAO also assists Congress in conducting audits, investigations, and evaluations. For this reason, the GAO is sometimes referred to as Congress's "watchdog." In addition to these research and investigative activities, the GAO's Office of General Counsel makes legal decisions and submits legal opinions.

The GAO's website is a rich source of cybersecurity research materials. Recent GAO reports and testimonies, as well as legal decisions, are available on this website, and one can search by topic, agency name, or agency type. In addition, the website has a section to help researchers perform more effective searches.[4]

Research Source: Congressional Research Service

The **Congressional Research Service (CRS)** is another legislative branch research and information agency. The CRS is housed in the Library of Congress and works exclusively to perform policy and legal analysis for Congress. The CRS employs over five hundred researchers—policy analysts, attorneys, and experts—and has been nicknamed "Congress's Think Tank."

The mission of the CRS is to provide comprehensive, objective research to members of Congress, and to contribute to informed debate in the national legislature. Therefore, CRS performs research at every step in the legislative process. Its researchers examine all sides of an issue, research specific questions for members of Congress, and provide policy alternatives. CRS research provides members of Congress with analytical information in the topic areas of "American Law," "Domestic Social Policy," "Foreign Affairs, Defense, and Trade," "Government and Finance," and "Resources, Science, and Industry."

Congress controls the distribution of all CRS research, and CRS research remains confidential except in special cases in which Congress authorizes its release. Individual researchers may request access to these specific CRS documents. While these requests are usually declined, individual members of Congress may choose to provide some of the research to researchers who call. Requests for access to CRS research have a better chance of being approved if the researcher can, in turn, assist CRS with its work—for example, if a researcher can contribute an expert opinion to a CRS research project.

Federal Regulations: The Executive Branch and the Legislative Branch Combined

The purpose of this section is to discuss how and why federal regulations are created. A **regulation** is an enforceable law that has been authorized by congressional legislation or an executive order to remedy a specific problem. A regulation may create boundaries or limitations, establish a duty, or assign accountability to an industry, sector, or organization.

Some regulations attempt to exert a degree of control on the economy. Minimum wage laws are an example of this type of regulation. Some regulations focus on public health and safety, such as the regulation that requires all cars to carry seatbelts for passengers. In general, regulations attempt to promote certain kinds of outcomes by imposing restrictions, requirements, or incentives that favor those outcomes. Of course, new federal regulations must be legally justified and authorized by Congress and the president.

Some federal agencies are referred to as **"regulatory agencies"** because issuing regulations is one of their primary activities. The Food and Drug Administration (FDA), a federal agency within the Department of Health and Human Services, is one example of a regulatory agency. The FDA issues specific regulations about food and drugs; for example, the FDA regulates which drugs may be legally manufactured and sold in the United States. The FDA's authority to create these regulations stems directly from a specific piece of congressional legislation: the Food, Drug, and Cosmetic Act of 1938. This act increased the federal government's power to regulate these potentially hazardous products.

Congress (through legislation) or the president (through an executive order) can create an agency and grant it the authority to regulate certain sectors or industries. For a review on the process of how Congress directs a department or agency to fulfill an objective, see Chapter 3. A regulatory agency may decide to issue a new rule on its own. However, this regulation cannot exceed the agency's statutory authority, and the agency must have an open public discussion as required by the **Administrative Procedure Act (APA)** of 1946. As its name implies, this act established the procedures by which federal departments and agencies may propose and enact new regulations.

The Regulation-Making Process: From Advance Notice to Final Rule

At the beginning of the rulemaking process, the regulating agency may publish an **advance notice of proposed rulemaking (ANPR)** in the *Federal Register*. An ANPR is a formal invitation for the public to participate in shaping a proposed regulation. By law, federal agencies are required to keep the public informed about all new proposed regulations, and the *Federal Register* is the forum through which federal agencies communicate proposed regulations to the public.

Following the ANPR, the agency publishes a proposed rule in the *Federal Register*. The **proposed rule** announces and explains the agency's plan to address a problem or accomplish a goal. It begins with a summary section—a brief discussion of the rule and why the agency deems it necessary, along with an explanation of the

VIDEO

Watch 'Regulations Research Tutorial' at http://vimeo.com/channels/cybersecurityfoundations

agency's legal authority to create the rule—followed by an invitation and deadline for public comments. In 1998, an official electronic comment portal was created for the public to participate in the creation of federal regulation.

The **notice and comment period** is the time during which the agency is required to gather input from experts and the general public. Most agencies are legally required to respond to all public comments submitted during the notice and comment period. Agencies may hold public hearings during this period. The notice and comment process allows the agency to evaluate its proposed rule based on the comments, scientific data, and expert opinions it accumulates during this time. Agencies may consider comments submitted after the official close of this process, even though they are not legally bound to do so.

At the end of this process, the agency considering the new rule must conclude that its proposed regulation will help it to accomplish its specified goal or solve its particular problem. The agency must also consider alternative solutions that would be more effective or cost less. Typically, the notice and comment period will be followed by either a new and substantively amended proposed rule or by a **final rule**. The final rule will have an **effective date**. This is the date at which the rule becomes enforceable. The *supplemental information* section that accompanies the final rule sets out the goal or problems that the new rule addresses, describes the facts and data the agency relied on in its rulemaking process, responds to major criticisms made during the notice and comment process, and explains why the agency did not choose alternative rules.

An agency may publish a final rule without a proposed rule in limited cases where the agency has "good cause" to find that the notice and comment process would be impracticable, unnecessary, or contrary to the public interest. These cases may be emergencies in which public health is at risk, cases in which Congress has already directed a specific regulatory outcome by law, or cases of minor technical amendments. An agency gives the label "interim final rule" to a final rule that it has created without first asking for public comment on a proposed rule. An **interm final rule** is effective immediately, and the agency may modify it based on public comments after it goes into effect. After the final rule is published, the regulating agency may publish guidance material, so that individuals and industries will better understand the new regulatory requirements.

Legislative and Judicial Roles in Regulations

By law, agencies must send final rules to Congress and the GAO before these new regulations can take effect. Congress may pass a resolution of disapproval on the regulation, which, if signed by the president, renders the regulation void. A president may also exercise his veto power on a new regulation, though Congress may overrule this veto with a two-thirds majority.

The judicial branch is also involved in the process of enacting new federal regulations. A court may rule that a regulation is unconstitutional, goes beyond the agency's legal authority, was made without following the notice and comment process required by the APA, or was an abuse of the agency's discretion. The rule is then sent back to the agency, and the agency, which can reopen the comment period or correct the legal problems identified by the court.

The Code of Federal Regulations

Federal department and agency rules and regulations are published online in the **Code of Federal Regulations (CFR)**. The CFR provides a complete listing of federal regulations, organized by year and policy title. The CFR is published annually.[5]

The Role of the Judiciary

The purpose of this section is to discuss the role of the judicial branch in cybersecurity law and policy. The **judicial branch** is the federal legal system, or "the courts." Judiciary powers are granted in Article III of the U.S. Constitution. Article III establishes the Supreme Court of the United States and gives Congress the power to establish lower courts. Article III, Section 1, of the Constitution reads, "The judicial power of the United States, shall be vested in one Supreme Court, and in such inferior courts as the Congress may from time to time ordain and establish". **Inferior courts** refer to the district and appeals courts, collectively known as the *federal court system*.

The district courts are the trial courts of the nation. There are a total of 94 federal districts that decide criminal and civil cases. Of the 94 federal district courts, there are 12 regional circuits—known as the Court of Appeals. The Court of Appeals listens to the appeals from the district courts.

Cyber Fact

An **appeal** is a request made after a trial by a party that has lost on one or more issues; a higher court reviews the original decision to determine if it was correct. To make such a request is **"to appeal."** One who appeals is called the **"appellant,"** while the other party is referred to as the **"appellee."**

While the Constitution does not mention laws or measures concerning information security, or even suggest such measures, the broad language of the document gives federal courts the authority to make legal rulings that affect national cybersecurity law and policy. Still, in comparison to the executive and legislative branches, the judiciary's role in cybersecurity policy is limited. Traditionally, the judiciary's role in cybersecurity has been to enforce the federal laws that Congress has enacted to deter cyber crime.

Thus, the judicial branch of the federal government is the venue for the prosecution of accused cyber criminals. The judicial branch also determines sentencing for cyber criminals found guilty in court. Finally, the judicial branch and the federal courts play an important role by adding a voice to the theoretical debates around cybersecurity. As we will see when we examine case studies in depth, court rulings may contribute to philosophical arguments about cybersecurity issues, such as the ongoing struggle between the privacy and security communities, or the question of which entities are ultimately responsible for cybersecurity failures.

To offer just one example, in *United States v. Jones*, the Supreme Court upheld the Court of Appeals' ruling, which reaffirmed privacy rights with regard to new technology. In the case under examination, a man

Cyber Fact

One important aspect of the way the judicial system works is the idea that decisions in important cases are informed by decisions in cases that came before: this is the idea of **judicial precedent**. Because cyber crime is a relatively new field for judicial decisions, the role of the courts will continue to evolve as more cyber crimes are prosecuted in the years and decades to come. Future court decisions, and what these decisions show about the adequacy or inadequacy of existing cyber laws, may influence the development of new laws in Congress.

Chapter 6: Advanced Cybersecurity Studies

was charged with drug trafficking after the police placed a GPS tracking device on his wife's car. The Supreme Court ruled that this action, undertaken without a warrant, infringed upon the man's Fourth Amendment right against unreasonable search and seizure.[6] This case set the current precedent regarding limitations on the use of surveillance technology in law enforcement.

Most cyber crimes are prosecuted as federal crimes rather than state crimes because the jurisdictions (scope of authority) of many state courts do not yet cover cyber crimes. Therefore, individuals accused of committing cyber crimes will likely find themselves tried in the federal criminal court system.

Congress has passed several pieces of legislation regarding cyber crime. This legislation makes it illegal to damage or steal information from computers. Among the laws dealing with cyber crime are the **Computer Fraud and Abuse Act** (1984), the **Electronic Communications Privacy Act** (1986), and the **Identity Theft Penalty Enhancement Act** (2004). Together, these statutes form a comprehensive legal strategy to deter and punish hackers. All three acts escalate sentences and fines based on the severity, sophistication, and magnitude of the offense. A detailed explanation of each act follows.

Cyber Law Example 1: The Computer Fraud and Abuse Act (CFAA)

In order to give the judiciary the authority to both try and convict hackers who commit cyber crimes, Congress passed the Computer Fraud and Abuse Act (CFAA) in 1984. Since its passage, the CFAA has been amended several times to improve its effectiveness and to criminalize new threats.

The first person to be convicted under the Computer Fraud and Abuse Act was Robert Morris, the author of the "Morris worm." The Morris worm was the infamous first computer worm, a malicious software program designed to spread from computer to computer (for more information on computer attacks and exploits, see Chapter 4. For more on the Morris worm specifically, see the Introduction to this book). Robert Morris claimed that, when he created the Morris worm, his intent was not to commit harm but only to determine the size of the Internet. Despite his claim of innocence, the worm caused significant damage to private and public-sector networks. Following multiple appeals, Morris was sentenced to three years of probation, four hundred hours of community service, and a $10,000 fine.

The seven types of criminal activity prohibited by the CFAA are listed below.[7]

Obtaining National Security Information

Disclosing or attempting to disclose classified information, acquired by unauthorized network access, relating to national defense, foreign relations, or atomic energy, with reason to believe the actions could injure the United States or be used to the advantage of foreign nations. The statutory penalty is not more than ten years (not more than twenty years for repeat offenders).

Accessing a Computer and Obtaining Information

Acquiring protected information through gaining unauthorized access to government computers, computers belonging to financial institutions, or computers involved in interstate commerce. Statutory penalties begin at less than one year. For crimes involving more than $5,000, penalties are elevated to five years or less. Repeat offenders may receive ten years or less.

The Role of the Judiciary

Trespassing in a Government Computer

Hacking into federal government computers (computers used exclusively or in part by the federal government). Offenders can be imprisoned for not more than one year, or not more than ten years if they are a repeat offender.

Accessing a Computer to Defraud or Obtain Value

Essentially, hacking into a government computer, financial institution computer, or any computer involved in interstate or foreign commerce (a very broad standard which arguably could apply to the majority of computers), with intent to defraud. Committing computer fraud may include stealing financial information or other confidential information that could be used to perpetrate identity theft. This section carries a statutory penalty that cannot exceed five years, or in the cases of repeat offenders, ten years.

Causing Computer Damage

Unleashing worms or viruses, or other actions that cause damage to government computers, financial institution computers, or computers used in interstate commerce. Statutory penalties range from up to one year for negligent conduct, up to five years for reckless conduct, and up to ten years for intentional conduct. Repeat offenders may receive up to ten years for negligent conduct and up to twenty years for reckless or intentional conduct.

Trafficking Password Information

Trafficking in computer passwords or other computer keys with the intent to defraud. If a person steals a password in order to enter a government system, he or she violates this section. The statutory penalty is up to one year and up to ten years for repeat offenders.

Extortion Involving Computers

Any threat to cause damage to a protected computer (a government computer, financial institution network, or computer involved in interstate commerce) with the intent to extort money. The statutory penalty is not more than five years and not more than ten years for repeat offenders.

Recent amendments of the CFAA significantly broadened the definition of a "protected computer" – that is, a computer protected under terms of the CFAA. Under the CFAA, any computer that affects interstate commerce is considered to be a "protected computer." This inclusive terminology encompasses computers that are connected to the Internet, computers that are not connected to the Internet, and even computers located outside of the United States. The inclusive nature of the CFAA makes this statute the most comprehensive cyber crime law to date, and the statute that courts most often rely upon to convict hackers.

Case Study: Albert Gonzalez and the CFAA

In 2009, one of the country's most infamous hackers was found guilty of violating the CFAA. Albert Gonzalez was charged with orchestrating cyber attacks on TJX and Heartland Payment Systems. These attacks allowed Gonzalez and his team to steal hundreds of millions of credit and debit card numbers and resulted in tens of millions of dollars in fraudulent charges. Gonzalez was indicted and pled guilty to violating the CFAA. He was sentenced to two concurrent twenty-year terms in federal prison for his crimes. For more information on this case, see Chapter 5.

Chapter 6: Advanced Cybersecurity Studies

Cyber Law Example 2: The Electronic Communications Privacy Act and the Wiretap Act

Federal prosecutors may charge hackers with violation of the Electronic Communications Privacy Act (ECPA), in addition to violation of the CFAA. Specifically, the section of the ECPA called the **Wiretap Act** makes it illegal to intercept or disclose illegally intercepted wire, oral, and electronic communications without a search warrant. Spyware, packet sniffers, or any other information collection software that intentionally attempts to intercept electronic communication is prohibited by the Wiretap Act. Penalties under this act include imprisonment for up to five years and fines of up to $250,000 for individuals.

Cyber Law Example 3: The Identity Theft Penalty Enhancement Act

As discussed in Chapter 4, many cyber attacks are motivated by the attacker's desire to obtain personally identifying information—including names, bank account numbers, credit card numbers, and Social Security numbers that can be used to steal a victim's identity. Identity theft is often the result of cyber data breaches.

The Identity Theft Penalty Enhancement Act of 2004 established a new crime: aggravated identity theft against U.S. citizens. The act established two offenses, one that includes general identity theft crimes and another that is a terrorism offense. With regard to the general offense, the act declares that, "Whoever, during and in relation to any felony violation enumerated in subsection (c), knowingly transfers, possesses, or uses, without lawful authority, a means of identification of another person shall, in addition to the punishment provided for such felony, be sentenced to a term of imprisonment of 2 years." Meanwhile, with regard to the terrorism offense, the act declares that "Whoever, during and in relation to any felony violation enumerated in section 2332b(g)(5)(B), knowingly transfers, possesses, or uses, without lawful authority, a means of identification of another person or a false identification document shall, in addition to the punishment provided for such felony, be sentenced to a term of imprisonment of 5 years." Additionally, restitution to the victims may be ordered "equal to the value of the time reasonably spent by the victim in an attempt to remediate the intended or actual harm" caused by the offense.

The Federal Criminal Procedure Process

In a federal criminal case, a **U.S. attorney** is the prosecutor. Each U.S. attorney is a member of the executive branch, and his or her job is to enforce federal law by prosecuting accused federal criminals in U.S. federal courts.

The **grand jury** is a jury, composed of between 12 and 23 citizens, that reviews evidence presented by the U.S. attorney and determines whether or not there is **probable cause** for a criminal charge—known facts leading to a reasonable belief that a crime was committed—that would lead one to believe that an individual has committed a crime. If a majority of the grand jury decides there is sufficient evidence to constitute probable cause, it will issue an **indictment**—a formal accusation. The indictment charges the individual with a violation of the law and gives the FBI and law enforcement officials the authority to arrest the accused individual.

After the individual is charged a violation of a cyber crime statute, he is arrested and a date is set for him to appear before a federal judge. The judge determines whether the defendant should be held in jail until trial or whether he is eligible for bail. If he is eligible for bail, the defendant may deposit funds with the court in exchange for his temporary release, upon the condition that he returns for his trial. At the arraignment, the defendant enters a plea to the charges brought against him. An agreement in which the defendant pleads guilty in return for the U.S. attorney agreeing to drop certain charges or recommend a lenient sentence is called a **plea bargain**. If the defendant pleads not guilty, the judge will proceed to schedule a trial.

In a federal criminal trial, the burden of proof is on the U.S. attorney, who must prove to the jury that the defendant committed the crime **"beyond a reasonable doubt."** This standard means that the evidence against the defendant must be so strong that there remains no reasonable doubt that the defendant committed the crime. The trial jury (composed of 12 citizens, usually selected from the same general pool as the case's grand jury) must vote unanimously that the defendant is guilty in order for him to be found guilty by the court and sentenced.

If the jury returns a verdict of "guilty," the judge will determine the defendant's sentence (statement of punishment) based on: (1) the penalties outlined in the statute and (2) the Federal Sentencing Guidelines. The *Federal Sentencing Guidelines* are issued by the United States Sentencing Commission and determine the length of a convicted criminal's jail time based on a point system.

Cyber Fact

The **United States Sentencing Commission (USSC)** is an independent agency in the judicial branch of government. Its principal purposes are: "(1) to establish sentencing policies and practices for the federal courts, including guidelines to be consulted regarding the appropriate form and severity of punishment for offenders convicted of federal crimes; (2) to advise and assist Congress and the Executive branch in the development of effective and efficient crime policy; and (3) to collect, analyze, research, and distribute a broad array of information on federal crime and sentencing issues, serving as an information resource for Congress, the Executive branch, the courts, criminal justice practitioners, the academic community, and the public."[8] The USSC created a point system that assigns an offense value to crimes. Under this system, a judge assigns a crime an offense value between 1 and 43 points. The more serious the court determines the crime to be, the higher the point value a judge will assign. The point value assigned to a crime helps to determine the criminal's sentence. A crime assigned just 1 point calls for a prison sentence of 0-6 months, while the highest offense level, 43, calls for life imprisonment.

Once the base value is determined for a cyber crime, the judge may add additional points based on a number of factors related to the specific cyber crime, including whether or not it involved a computer used for U.S. national security or defense purposes, and whether or not the conduct disrupted or damaged critical infrastructure. The base offense level for violations against the CFAA ranges between 6 and 35. The base offense level may be increased according to the amount of the victim's monetary loss (which the prosecutor has the burden of proving), the number of victims that suffered a loss as a result of the offense, and where the offense originated. Furthermore, the judge may add additional points if the offense involved "sophisticated means," or tactics that increased the risk of death or serious bodily injury for the victims, or are related to critical infrastructure.

In 2011, the Obama administration called for increased penalties to deter and disrupt the growing number of data breaches and denial of service attacks on the private and public sectors.[9] Administration officials contended the severity of the punishments was not proportional to the seriousness or complexity of the crime and called for increased prison sentences and fines under the CFAA. It is likely that new laws and harsher sentencing guidelines will arise as the number and capabilities of cyber criminals continue to increase.

Cybersecurity: A Global Perspective

The Internet does not belong to any nation or state. This "network of networks" is a global asset involving global management, global risks, and global responsibilities. Cyber crime, cyber espionage, and cyber warfare

Chapter 6: Advanced Cybersecurity Studies

Cyber Fact

A Brief History of International Cyber Attacks

Chechnya, 1990s : Chechen guerilla propaganda and fund-raising websites impact public perception of the Russo-Chechen conflict. The Russian government hacks into these websites and changes their content.

Kosovo, 1999: During the Kosovo war, the pro-Serbian hacker group known as the "Black Hand" targets the U.S. Navy and NATO with virus-infected emails in a DoS attack. The White House website is disrupted, and the NATO Public Affairs website is taken down.

China, 2001: U.S. and Chinese "patriotic hacker" activity flares after the downing of a US Navy EP-3 aircraft. The FBI warns U.S. businesses of "malicious" Chinese hacker activity and investigates a possible compromise of California's electric power grid. In 2002, the Chinese government calls off anniversary attacks, suggesting that Chinese hackers respond to government command and control.

Estonia, 2007: Following Estonian relocation of a Soviet war monument, pro-Russian hackers supplement rioting on the streets by successfully compromising Estonian government, media, and banking websites for three weeks.

Syria, 2007: A cyber attack reportedly deactivates a Syrian air defense system prior to the Israeli Air Force's destruction of an alleged nuclear reactor.

United States, 2010: In January 2010, Google reports that an advanced persistent threat attack originating in China, later dubbed "Operation Aurora," has been carried out against Google and dozens of other organizations for at least six months.

Iran, 2010: The Stuxnet computer worm destroys an estimated 1,000 Iranian nuclear centrifuges, according to *CNN*.[10]

United States, 2011: A computer virus infects networks at the U.S. drone fleet control center in Nevada. Not long after, Iran captures a U.S. military drone, claiming it commandeered the craft's control systems via cyber attack.

are relatively new phenomena, but they are all growing quickly in volume and sophistication. As these threats and tactics evolve, they will present law enforcement, national security planners, and corporate directors across the globe with challenges of increasing magnitude and consequence. Examples of some recent international cyber attacks can be found on the following page.

One area of intense research focus over the last ten years concerns the connection between computer networks and national critical infrastructure. Information systems from telecommunications to banking to power grids are increasingly dependent on the Internet for basic operations. In both the private sector and the public sector, this increased dependence on the Internet implies increased vulnerability to cyber attacks, cyber espionage, and other kinds of cyber crime.

World events, primarily the 2007 attacks in Estonia and the 2010 Stuxnet worm, have defined the formative years of cyberspace warfare. Public testimony before the Senate Homeland Security Committee cites the 2010 Stuxnet worm, which destroyed as many as 1,000 nuclear centrifuges in Iran, as proof that a malicious computer code can inflict physical damage on industrial infrastructure.[11] In 2012, the *New York Times* reported that the United States allegedly continued to use the Stuxnet worm to launch attacks on Iran's nuclear facilities. The report further stated that the U.S. took part in development of the newer and more complex Flame malware to conduct cyber espionage against its adversaries.[12] In April 2012, a Flame cyber attack against Iran forced the country's Oil Ministry to disconnect its computers from the Internet in an attempt to defend itself

Cybersecurity: A Global Perspective

> **Cyber Fact**
>
> Events in the physical world are now mirrored in cyber space. For example, during the 2008 South Ossetia War, concurrent cyber attacks were launched between Russia, Georgia, South Ossetia, and Azerbaijan. These attacks resulted in the defacement of the Georgian parliament's website, as well as the hacking of South Ossetia's primary news website and radio station. Similarly, cyber weapons are prevalent in the ongoing Iran-Israel shadow wars and in the growing military and political tension between the U.S. and China.

from the virus.

While there have been limited verifiable accounts of cyber attacks on critical infrastructure so far, many analysts believe that first-tier militaries and intelligence agencies have sufficient knowledge of both hacking and critical infrastructure functions to conduct such attacks. National risk managers categorize this kind of cyber attacker as an "advanced persistent threat" (APT).

IANA, ICANN, and IETF: Coordinators of the International Internet

In the early days of the Internet, engineers created a global IP address registry, a list of IP addresses, and the details of the organizations that corresponded to these addresses. The **Internet Assigned Numbers Authority (IANA)** was founded by the U.S. government in 1988 to manage global IP address assignments. IANA was quickly overwhelmed as more and more organizations joined the Internet. IANA now operates as a department of the **Internet Corporation for Assigned Names and Numbers (ICANN)**

In 1998, with the encouragement of the U.S. government, ICANN was created both to coordinate the assignment of IP addresses and to keep the Internet running smoothly and securely in the era of its unprecedented and growing popularity. In particular, ICANN would manage the Internet's Domain Name System as it grew with the World Wide Web and became increasingly international. Management and coordination of the DNS ensures that every address is unique and that all valid addresses can be found by all Internet users.

Today, ICANN coordinates the DNS, IP addresses, protocol identifier assignment, and root server system management functions, among other tasks. These tasks were originally performed by the IANA. It is important to note that ICANN has no responsibility for any of the content or activities on the Internet. Its role is simply to organize the Internet according to protocols.

ICANN's core purpose is to preserve and enhance the operational stability, reliability, security, and global interoperability of the Internet. Within the context of its mission related to the Internet's unique identifiers, ICANN plays an active role, contributing to global efforts to address security, stability, and resiliency challenges

> **Cyber Fact**
>
> On a traditional map, we are used to seeing state and town names instead of a technical number, such as a GPS coordinate or measurements of longitude and latitude. The same principle applies on the Internet—instead of complicated IP addresses (e.g., "232.44.12.13"), we use easy-to-remember names (e.g., "www.mydomain.com"). These user-friendly names are automatically translated for Internet users by the DNS, which function as a kind of Internet phone book.

Chapter 6: Advanced Cybersecurity Studies

faced by the Internet.

ICANN functions a non-profit organization that encourages the participation of the public and aims to be transparent in its operations. ICANN views the public sector, the private sector, and technical experts as peers, and seeks input from hundreds of communities of users. ICANN operates under the belief that all users of the Internet deserve a say in how this global resource is managed.

In 2006, ICANN entered into an agreement with the U.S. Department of Commerce. The agreement emphasized the security of the Internet as a primary concern and articulated the joint goal of eventually moving DNS management to the private sector. For cybersecurity researchers, ICANN's website is an excellent source of information and official documents about how the Internet is managed.

In 1992, the **Internet Engineering Task Force (IETF)** recommended the establishment of subsidiary organizations to allocate and manage IP addresses for specific regions of the world. These **Regional Internet Registries (RIRs)** grew over time, and today there are five:

- African Network Information Centre (AfriNIC), covering Africa
- American Registry for Internet Numbers (ARIN), covering the United States, Canada, several parts of the Caribbean region, and Antarctica
- Asia-Pacific Network Information Centre (APNIC), covering Asia, Australia, New Zealand, and neighboring countries
- Latin America and Caribbean Network Information Centre (LACNIC), covering Latin America and parts of the Caribbean region
- Réseaux IP Européens Network Coordination Centre (RIPE NCC), covering Europe, Russia, the Middle East, and Central Asia

Each RIR has the authority within its region to administer and register IP address space and manage services related to IP addresses. The registries are not-for-profit, self-regulatory and self-funded organizations; like ICANN, they have open leadership structures to encourage direct participation by any Internet stakeholder.

Each of the RIRs has been engaged in encouraging and training its members to deploy the newest communications protocol, **Internet Protocol Version 6 (IPv6)**, for global cybersecurity purposes. IPv6 was developed by the IETF in anticipation that the Internet's supply of IP addresses would run short. IPv6 instantly solves the world's urgent shortage of computer addresses, and also supports better security features than IPv4, including mandatory support for **Internet Protocol Security (IPSec)**. IPSec is a tool used not only to encrypt Internet traffic, but also to authenticate it, which, in theory, could help law enforcement and counterintelligence agencies solve the ongoing problem of anonymous cyber attacks.

However, human rights groups fear that governments will use IPv6 to quash political dissent by reducing online anonymity and privacy. In short, next-generation Internet technologies such as IPv6 can redress some of the Internet's current security shortcomings, but the dynamic and rapidly evolving nature of the Internet and the threats against it,

Cyber Fact

Because the Internet is a massively complicated international enterprise, it is important that the information traveling along it follow certain "rules of the road." On the Internet, the rules governing data communications are defined by organizations such as ICANN and IETF.

combined with external political factors, virtually guarantees that no solution will be a silver bullet for cybersecurity.

The Internet Engineering Task Force: Role and Responsibilities

The IETF is a loosely self-organized group of volunteers who contribute to the engineering of Internet technologies. It is the principal body engaged in the development of new Internet standards. The IETF is unusual in that it exists as a collection of activities, new technologies, and events, but is not a corporation and does not have a board of directors, members, or dues. The group hosts meetings and convenes working groups, including a Working Group on Web Security, to fulfill its stated mission: to "make the Internet work better by producing high quality, relevant technical documents that influence the way people design, use, and manage the Internet."

Like other Internet organizations, the IETF encourages anyone from the Internet community to participate in its work. IETF is an "open standards" organization that has no formal membership or membership requirements. This openness and willingness to work through collaboration is truly astonishing, especially given that the Internet was originally created by the DOD, an organization with many confidential aspects to its work.

The IETF's stated mission is "to make the Internet work better by producing high quality, technical documents that influence the way people design, use, and manage the Internet." These documents are also referred to as **Requests for Comments (RFCs)**.[13] RFCs cover a broad range of content and can serve a variety of purposes—some RFCs propose new Internet standards, while others provide summaries of working group meetings. Sometimes, the IETF even has a bit of fun with its RFCs—for instance, RFC 2795, published on April 1, 2000, proposed the creation of an "Infinite Monkey Protocol Suite."

The name "Request for Comments" expresses an important principle behind the IETF's work: the Internet is a constantly changing technical system, and any document published today may need to be updated and improved tomorrow. It also reflects the IETF's philosophy that the best new knowledge is generated through open and collaborative efforts.

Indeed, one way to look at the IETF is as the group of people who work together to improve the technology of the Internet on a daily basis. In addition to producing RFCs, the IETF serves as a forum where network operators, hardware and software creators, and researchers can communicate with each other and ensure that future protocols, standards and products will be better than those that exist today. Therefore, IETF is the forum where the basic technical standards for Internet protocols, including IPv6, are set and maintained.

Issues and Challenges in Global Cybersecurity

The Problem of Attribution

The greatest single advantage a computer hacker has over international protocols, technical breakthroughs, and security standards is anonymity. Hackers hide within the maze-like architecture of the Internet and route attacks through a variety of well-chosen countries. For a hacker, "well-chosen countries" means countries with which the victim's government has poor diplomatic relations or no law enforcement cooperation. This strategy typically allows more than enough time for a hacker to erase any evidence of an attack. According to security experts, the average time between an initial computer intrusion and its discovery is over 400 days.[14]

As a result, positive attribution and identification of an attacker is very difficult in cyberspace. This **"attribution problem"** has a number of implications for cyber attack victims:

Chapter 6: Advanced Cybersecurity Studies

- It reduces the possibility that a government or organization can deter, prosecute, or retaliate against a cyber attacker.

- It increases the odds that attacks will take place during peacetime with little or no warning.

- It encourages "false flagging" operations, where the attacker tries to pin the blame on an innocent third party.

- It creates an environment in which even terrorists can find a home on the Internet.

- It offers the attacker an additional layer of plausible deniability.

- It forces decision makers to respond to cyber incidents based on a preponderance of evidence, rather than clear and convincing evidence.

- It means that positive attribution can often only be determined from non-cyber data points, such as those drawn from traditional law enforcement, counterintelligence and espionage.

Lack of Transnational Authority

There are multiple organizations and sub-organizations across the globe devoted to confronting, tracking, and analyzing cyber crime. Despite this commitment of resources and manpower, the inability of the international community to designate jurisdictions, command authority, and communicate between organizations hinders the security of global cyberspace.

The jurisdiction of any nation-state's law enforcement institutions ends every time a network cable crosses a border. Hackers routinely create enormous headaches for police and counterintelligence personnel by routing attacks through countries with which the victim has few established ties. The transnational nature of cyber crime, such as when a French hacker targets a Chinese company from a U.S.-registered computer, makes it difficult for any single organization to collect sufficient digital evidence against a cyber criminal.

Investigators must be able to articulate the activities of cyber criminals to criminal courts with authority and credibility. In order to do this, there must be clear legal guidelines that allow national agencies to work effectively with international partners. Currently, these guidelines do not exist. This presents a challenge significant enough that it is overcome only in rare cases or when there is an extraordinary international political interest in solving a case.

Amazingly, a common hurdle for international organizations is the simple problem of not knowing whom to call in the event of a cyber attack. This problem is compounded many times over when cultural, linguistic and nationalistic biases get in the way. And because many countries do not have data breach laws, organizations and businesses that suffer cyber attacks may not want to, and may never have to, disclose the attack to any authority figure.

Another challenge for international cybersecurity operations is that governments instinctively fear any perceived loss of national sovereignty. They may worry that cooperation in cybersecurity matters will allow foreign governments to obtain digital evidence through remote and unauthorized search and seizure, even though this would run directly counter to international law.

Yet another challenge mirrors the challenges we discussed in Chapter 2 (Cybersecurity Law and Policy). This challenge is the persistent tension between security and freedom in national security operations. Civilian organizations can have difficulty understanding the reasons for national security requirements. Governments, for their part, may be uncomfortable with the openness of the international Internet. A government that restricts network connectivity or abuses its law enforcement powers runs its own set of unpredictable risks, such as a low-probability but

Cybersecurity: A Global Perspective

high-consequence scenario of a "hacktivist" group threatening the government's network.

The United Nations and Cybersecurity

The U.N., with its 193 member states, represents the highest level of international cooperation and is the largest international organization in the world.

There are two principal U.N. efforts regarding cybersecurity: a politico-military stream focusing on cyber warfare and an economic stream focusing on cyber crime. The U.S., Germany, Canada, and U.K. have been active players in this dialogue, with a vocal Russia playing the role of primary counterweight to U.S. power. One concrete achievement of this dialogue has been the U.N.'s sponsorship of a conference series called the World Summit on the Information Society (WSIS), which has produced several outcome documents. On the U.N.'s official website, the researcher will find many official statements and speeches on international cyber crime and cybersecurity.

The North Atlantic Treaty Organization (NATO) and Cybersecurity

In terms of international peace and security negotiations, no organization can match the experience and legitimacy of NATO. Since its 1949 formation in the turbulent aftermath of World War II, the purpose of NATO has been the collective defense of its member states. NATO links Europe with North America and has a formal dialogue with dozens of additional nations. NATO's Article 4 provides for consultation and coordination in response to any external security threat. Article 5 states that "an armed attack against one ... [is] an attack against all," and supports every member state's right to defend itself.

Before 2010, information technology played no role in NATO's Strategic Concept, and cyber attacks were not recognized as a national security concern. But the 2007 Estonia crisis transformed NATO's thinking. Suleyman Anil, head of cyber defense in NATO's Emerging Security Challenges Division, stated that "Estonia was the first time...[that we saw] possible involvement of state agencies; [and] that [a] cyber attack can bring down a complete national service, banking, media..."[15]

Therefore, in 2008 NATO began to write its first Cyber Defense Policy. In 2010, NATO's new Strategic Concept described cyber attacks as threatening "Euro-Atlantic prosperity, security and stability." Currently, two NATO priorities are to bring every element within the organization under centralized cyber protection and to accelerate the expansion of the NATO Computer Incident Response Capability (NCIRC), a partner organization of US-CERT. Today, NATO policy calls for a crisis-response team of cybersecurity experts to be sent to any member state that is a victimized by a damaging cyber attack.

The Council of Europe and Cybersecurity

The most important international cyber legal agreement to date is the Council of Europe's **Convention on Cybercrime**, issued in 2001 and now signed by 53 nations, including the U.S. This treaty is the only binding international agreement related to cybersecurity and is considered a template for any country wishing to develop comprehensive national legislation on cyber crime. Signatories meet each year for consultations, and the Council of Europe helps governments to ratify, accede, and implement the treaty through cooperative projects. The council's website is an excellent source of documents on cybercrime from an international law perspective.

Chapter 6: Advanced Cybersecurity Studies

Conclusion

The key to conducting effective cybersecurity research is to know the field's most influential research sources. Throughout the late 20th century and early 21st century, the U.S. government has been the world's leading producer of significant cybersecurity statements and legislation. The U.S. continues to cooperate with, coordinate, and partner with leading technological and security organizations to combat the growing threat of cyber crime. Cybersecurity as an academic field may have come to maturity in the United States, but it is quickly transforming itself into a field with an international orientation, as open as the Internet itself.

Key Questions

1. Article I of the U.S. Constitution established which branch of the federal government?

    a) The executive branch

    b) The legislature branch

    c) The judicial branch

2. In the United States, what is the role of a grand jury?

    a) Delivering a verdict of innocence or guilt

    b) Sentencing a convicted criminal

    c) Determining probable cause for a criminal trial

3. Which of the following is NOT part of the Executive Office of the President (EOP)?

    a) The Office of Management and Budget (OMB)

    b) The National Security Council (NSC)

    c) The Department of Defense (DoD)

4. What is the complex question fallacy?

    a) Posing a question that is too difficult to answer

    b) Posing a question based on a questionable assumption

    c) Posing a question that may have multiple answers

Key Questions

5. In the U.S., how do the Federal Sentencing Guidelines work?

    a) Judges assign point values to crimes, and determine the appropriate punishment based on a crime's point value.

    b) Judges determine punishment based on international standards set by the United Nations Security Council.

    c) Judges allow juries to suggest appropriate punishments for convicted criminals, and determine the final sentence according to the jury's unanimous suggestion.

6. Which President made public some aspects of the CNCI?

    a) President Obama

    b) President Bush

    c) President Clinton

7. What event directly preceded Presidential Decision Directive 63?

    a) The terrorist attacks in the U.S. on September 11, 2001

    b) The discovery of the Stuxnet attack on Iran's nuclear facilities in June 2010

    c) The Oklahoma City bombings of 1995

Cyber Connections

Many examples of cyber crime and punishment in this chapter bear significant links with the narratives presented in the Introduction to this book. The U.S. government's role as the world's leading institution on matters relating to the global Internet and its secure operations was also evident in the introductory narratives. Because the Internet was originally a project of the DOD, its security has always been a project of the U.S. government.

The laws and policies discussed in this chapter have roots in the historical events examined in Chapter 2. This chapter may be considered a companion to Chapter 2 and offers the structural backdrop to the events discussed in that chapter.

The technical aspects of the global Internet are a primary concern of organizations such as ICANN and the IETF. The technical concepts and Internet vulnerabilities discussed in Chapter 4 are major concerns of these organizations.

The laws governing the cybersecurity operations of private sector organizations in the United States may prove influential as international cybersecurity efforts increase in the coming years and decades. Understanding the concepts discussed in Chapter 5 will help any student of developing international cyber law and policy. Furthermore, the private sector's roles and responsibilities with regard to U.S. national security will only increase in the years to come, and it is likely that new U.S. cybersecurity laws and policies for the private sector will emerge in the near future.

Appendix A: Risk Management for Cybersecurity

More on Survey Design

Researchers will draft their research questions to suit the type of survey they are conducting. A self-administered survey may require different questions than a personal interview, particularly with regard to closed-ended and open-ended questions. *Closed-ended questions* provide a fixed number of answers, usually in the form of multiple-choice questions. *Open-ended questions* provide space for the responder to provide her own answer.

Clearly-worded questions are essential for any effective survey; there should not be any confusion or ambiguity regarding the meaning, subject, or intent of the question. To refer back to the home invasion example: "Is a house subject to risk?" is an example of an unclear question. This question is unclear because the subject ("the house") is ambiguous —there is no clear context for this question. Since the wording of the question is unclear, the responses will not be relevant. A clearer version of this question would read: "Is a house in a middle-class suburb without a fence and without an alarm system susceptible to burglary?"

The survey designer should also guarantee that questions do not contain assumptions regarding a participant's knowledge or background. Summaries of relevant issues and clarification of specific words should be provided in order to ensure that the participant is able to accurately answer the survey question. The survey designer cannot simply assume that the respondent has the knowledge to accurately respond to a question.

Survey questions should not contain biases, ambiguity, or leading questions. **Biases** may be present in questions that infer an answer or lead the survey participants to choose a certain answer. The presence of bias will skew results and render them invalid and unhelpful to the research. By keeping questions unbiased and providing as much context as possible, the survey designer ensures that as many participants as possible can complete the survey, allowing for the most-accurate results.

Another important guideline when designing a survey is to include a "Not Applicable" or "Other" option for applicable multiple-choice questions. Providing this kind of alternative answer ensures that all participants will be able to complete the survey with total honesty and will not feel pressured to choose an answer that may not apply to their situation. This, in turn, will improve the survey's results and provide the survey designer with the most-accurate possible database of answers to analyze.

Sampling: Deciding Who Takes the Survey

In many research cases, a target population for a survey is too large for the entire group to be surveyed efficiently. For this reason, surveys are administered to a sample of the population. A **sample** is a subset of the population that has been selected for analysis. The sample should reflect the characteristics of the entire population.

Choosing a sample population correctly is an extremely important step in the survey process. If the sample is chosen in a way that permits for inaccuracy, misrepresentation, or bias, then the entire survey and its results become invalid. The sample size that the researchers pursue is directly indicative of the desired accuracy of the survey. Generally, the larger the sample size, the more accurate the findings will be. After

> **Cyber Fact**
>
> **Population**: the unit of analysis from which the researcher is attempting to acquire or extract data.

determining the sample size that makes sense for their survey, researchers must take precautions to prevent sampling biases when selecting participants, in order to avoid invalid results. Among sampling biases, **convenience sampling** and **volunteer sampling** are two of the most common. Researchers commit convenience sampling errors when they select participants based entirely on ease. Convenience sampling could include actions such as choosing the first ten names from a list or the first twenty people that walk by. It is unlikely that a sample selected this way will accurately represent the entire population.

Volunteer sampling also produces skewed results, but for a different reason. Volunteer sampling occurs when all of the sample subjects have volunteered to participate. A classic example of volunteer sampling is when a company asks customers to fill-out an online survey. The issue here is that the entire sample wants to take the survey. This willingness to volunteer for a survey means that the participants are likely to have strong feelings, either positive or negative, about the company. This bias will skew the results of the survey because it will fail to account for the portion of people that do not hold strong feelings about the company and therefore did not volunteer for the survey.

To ensure that the sample represents the survey's target population as accurately as possible, researchers use probability sampling. **Probability sampling** aims to give every member of the population an equal chance of being selected, and is therefore the best method to guarantee that the sample selected represents the characteristics of the population at large. Probability sampling does not mean that the sample selected will be a perfect representation of the population, but it is still the best method for getting a representative sample for a survey.

Multiple sampling designs are possible within the realm of probability sampling. One of the most popular models, especially for small, straightforward surveys, is random sampling. **Random sampling** assigns every subject in the population a number and then, using a number generator, the researchers select numbers that correspond to survey participants.

Once the participants are chosen and the surveys have been completed, the researchers analyze the results. The method chosen to analyze the results of the survey varies according to the question and answer type (e.g., multiple-choice versus open-ended answers). A multiple-choice survey can lend itself to statistical or mathematical analysis. Open-ended answers often lead researchers to analyze the patterns of responses, such as the frequency of certain words.

More on Statistical Modeling

A **test statistic** determines the significance of an individual variable, set of variables, or statistical model that can inform the decision to accept or reject the null hypothesis. We can use multiple test statistics, depending on the type of data. The purpose of a test statistic is to determine: (1) whether or not a relationship exists between variables—if they are statistically significant; and (2) if we can accept or reject the null hypothesis. **Statistically significant** means that the probability of an observed event occurring is extremely unlikely due to chance or random variation. The most common test statistics are explained in the following table:

Appendix A

Test Statistic	Definition
Chi square test (X^2)	Tests the association of a set of variables. It indicates whether the variables of an equation/model are dependent.
z-test	Tests whether an observation is statistically significant if the population standard deviation is known.
t-test	Tests whether an observation is statistically significant if the population standard deviation is unknown.
F-test	Tests how significant a group of independent factors are in determining the output of a regression model.

Figure A-1: Test statistics and their definitions.

For the purpose of our cyber example, we will use a *p*-value to either accept or reject the null hypothesis, based on an established confidence interval. A **confidence interval** calculates an interval of values that estimates the population parameter to some degree of confidence. The ***p*-value** is the probability of observing a test statistic at least as extreme as the one that was actually observed, assuming that the null hypothesis is true. The higher the confidence level, the larger the interval; a larger interval is more likely to contain the true population value. This interval is directly associated with sample size: if the sample size increases, then the interval will decrease, because a larger sample size indicates that the test statistic is more accurate.

$$p \leq \alpha \quad \text{Reject } H_0 \text{ and proceed to test } H_A$$
$$p \geq \alpha \quad \text{Accept } H_0 \text{ (or fail to reject } H_0)$$

Figure A-2: Description of when to reject or accept the null hypothesis using the *p*-value and confidence internal.

If the *p*-value is small enough based on an established confidence interval level (α), which usually is set at 95% or 99%, then the null hypothesis is rejected. For example, if we want to say that, "We are 95% confident that the alternative hypothesis is not due to chance," then our confidence interval level (α) will be at 0.05.

If, after running the test statistic, the *p*-value is less than 0.05, then we can reject the null hypothesis.

Let's assume that we have run our test statistic and we can reject the null hypothesis; we now can proceed to test an alternative hypothesis.

Basics of the Logit Model

A **logit model** calculates a binary dependent variable (y). The word "binary" indicates that there are two possible responses: "yes" or "no." To code a "yes" or "no" answer for statistical purposes, the numbers "1" and "0" are used. In this model, the situation "yes, customer information was leaked" is 1, and "no, customer information was not leaked" is 0.

The logit equation is shown below, where $P(y=1)$ refers to the probability of the dependent variable equaling one; α (alpha) is a constant; β (beta) is the coefficient of its respective independent variable (x).

More on Statistical Modeling

$$logit\ [P(y = 1)] = \alpha + \beta_1 x_1 + ... \beta_K x_K$$

Figure A-3: Logit equation.

In linear regression models, the **R^2**, also known as the **coefficient of determination**, is a valuable tool to determine the "goodness of fit." The coefficient of determination indicates the amount of variation in the dependent variable that is due to a change in the independent variable (regardless of whether the change is positive or negative). In other words, the coefficient of determination indicates the degree to which there is a meaningful relationship between the dependent variable and the independent variable.

The R^2 is helpful in logit models, but is not a hard-fixed determinant of the best model; therefore, risk managers should proceed with caution when interpreting the R^2 value. The goal is to have the R^2 value as close to 1.0 as possible; a value close to 1.0 means the model includes all necessary assumptions, variables, and statistical qualifications.

In the example of an online retailer that faces the risk of customer information being leaked, the company has decided to employ the logit model using a 95% confidence level. Risk managers provide codes for all variables to strengthen the reliability of the research. The two tables below provide the coding for all the variables in this illustrative example.

Building the Model

In this example's dataset, 200 online retailers were randomly selected ($n=200$). The company ran three different models to test the significance of the indicators of critical customer information leakage. These **significance tests** determine whether the various independent variables are good indicators of the outcome generated by the model. The models were built using forward selection. **Forward selection** is the process by which analysts add variables until the model proves to have overall significance and a theoretical purpose, and individual variables prove to be highly significant at various *p*-values.

The first model (Model 1) uses only five dependent variables. In the second model (Model 2), we added another independent variable (Strength of Hackers) to the original five variables. Model 3 included all of the independent variables. Figure A-6 displays the results of the logit analyses of Models 1, 2 and 3. A statistician or risk analyst will interpret these results to determine which variables are the most significant in determining the likelihood of customer information being leaked.

Based on its R^2 value, Model 3, in which we included all variables, proved to be the most complete and appropriate model for identifying significant relationships between independent variables and the dependent variable.

One of the key lessons of this section, and a fundamental aspect of many regression models, is the ability to recognize the most-significant independent variables in a model. An understanding of the most-significant independent variables in a model can guide a theoretical understanding of the factors that strongly influence the dependent variable, or in our case, the risk occurring.

In this example, we want to know which security controls are the most effective in securing customer information. We can examine all of the possibilities in Figure A-6 in order to determine which factors contribute most to overall customer information security.

Appendix A

Coding of Variables	Variable	Possible Values	Description
Dependent Variable (y)	Customer Critical Information leaked?	1 = Yes	Any piece of customer critical information leaked. Critical information can include phone numbers, address, birthdate, SSN, or credit card numbers.
		0 = No	No customer critical information leaked.

Figure A-4: Coding of customer critical information (dependent variable, y).

Coding of Variables	Variable	Possible Values	Description
Independent Variable (IV) (x_1)	Password and Username	1 = Yes	Online retailer requires password and username.
		0 = No	Online retailer does not require password and username.
IV (x_2)	Challenge Questions	0 — ∞	Number of challenge questions online store requires.
IV (x_3)	Strength of Customer Password	1 — 10	1 = Weak; 5 = Moderate; 10 = Strong
IV (x_4)	2-Factor Authentication	1 = Yes	The online retailer uses a 2-Factor Authentication.
		0 = No	The online retailer does not use a 2-Factor Authentication.
IV (x_5)	Number of users per day	0 — ∞	Number of customers per day
IV (x_6)	Time out tries	0 — ∞	Customer must restart after x minutes.
IV (x_7)	Trial out tries	0 — ∞	Customer must restart after x trials.

Figure A-5: Coding of independent variables (x).

Model 3 is the most complete model because it has the greatest R^2 value— the model provides a theoretical understanding and that there were not any obvious variables omitted.

We can determine specific probabilities for customer information being leaked by leveraging Model 3's logit analysis. Model 3 guides the forecasting probability determination because it is the most complete of all the models generated. The coefficients generated from Model 3 were inserted into the logistic regression equation for probabilities (Figure A-7) to produce specific probabilities (probabilities of success) based on various sets of factors, as

More on Statistical Modeling

	Model 1: Only Security Controls	Model 2: All Security Controls and Strength of Hacker	Model 3: Number of Users, Purchases, Strength of Hacker, and Security Controls
Number of Challenge Questions	-0.234524612	-0.241	-0.263
	(0.174)	(0.179)	(0.182)
Strength of Password	-0.206974333	-0.209	-0.225
	(0.100)*	(0.102)*	(0.099)**
2-Factor Authentication	-2.1736115	-2.248	-2.450
	(0.730)**	(0.752)**	(0.777)***
Time-Out Tries	0.019	0.006	0.010
	(0.057)	(0.055)	(0.0553)
Trial-Out Tries	0.043	0.051	0.085
	(0.101)	(0.103)	(0.106)
Strength of Hacker		-0.101	0.104
		(0.058)	(0.0619)*
Number of Users			-1.413E-06
			(6.033E-07)**
Number of Payments			3.134E-06
			(0.001)
Average Purchase Value/Order			0.0001
			(0.001)
Constant	-1.959551302	-2.442	-1.837
	(0.636)	(0.709)	(0.871)
R²	0.388	0.572	0.725
N	200	200	200

Note: standard errors are in parentheses. *p<.05; **p<.01; ***p<.001. Calculations used Stata 11.

Figure A-6: Logit analyses of determinants of critical customer information being leaked.

shown in Figure A-8 (see next page). For the purpose of this illustration, we used the Logistic Regression Equation for Probabilities, which explicitly reveals the probability of success, defined as P(y=1), to determine the probability values for Models A, B, C, and D. The Logistic Regression Equation for Probabilities is defined as:

$$P(y=1) = \frac{e^{a+\beta_1 x_1 + \ldots \beta_K x_K}}{1+e^{a+\beta_1 x_1 + \ldots \beta_K x_K}}$$

Figure A-7: Logistic regression equation for probabilities.

Appendix A

Model	Factor	Value	Probability
Model A	Number of Challenge Questions (0-10)	0	93.136%
	Strength of Password (0-10)	0	
	2-Factor Authentication	0	
	Time Out Tries (minutes)	300	
	Time Out Tries (frequency)	10	
	Strength of Hacker (0-10)	7	
	Number of Users (day)	1,000,000	
	Number of Payments (day)	1,000	
	Average Purchase Value ($)	50	
Model B	Number of Challenge Questions (0-10)	0	44.889%
	Strength of Password (0-10)	5	
	2-Factor Authentication	0	
	Time Out Tries (minutes)	100	
	Time Out Tries (frequency)	10	
	Strength of Hacker (0-10)	10	
	Number of Users (day)	1,000,000	
	Number of Payments (day)	1,000	
	Average Purchase Value ($)	50	
Model C	Number of Challenge Questions (0-10)	1	20.292%
	Strength of Password (0-10)	5	
	2-Factor Authentication	0	
	Time Out Tries (minutes)	10	
	Time Out Tries (frequency)	10	
	Strength of Hacker (0-10)	10	
	Number of Users (day)	1,000,000	
	Number of Payments (day)	1,000	
	Average Purchase Value ($)	50	
Model D	Number of Challenge Questions (0-10)	2	0.641%
	Strength of Password (0-10)	6	
	2-Factor Authentication	1	
	Time Out Tries (minutes)	10	
	Time Out Tries (frequency)	5	
	Strength of Hacker (0-10)	7	
	Number of Users (day)	1,000,000	
	Number of Payments (day)	1,000	
	Average Purchase Value ($)	50	

Where e is an irrational number, a mathematical constant, along with the base of the natural logarithm, the estimated value of e =2.71828; α is a constant; β is the coefficient of x. The following chart provides a break-down of the values for each indicator in all four new models (A, B, C, D).

Figure A-8: Sets of factors for expressing probability of risk.

Appendix B: Fundamentals of Management for Cybersecurity

EVM Indexes

For program managers, an alternative to variance percentages are EVM indexes. Like variance percentages, *EVM indexes* allow managers to compare the progress of several different projects, regardless of project size. The first of these indexes is the **Schedule Performance Index (SPI)**. The SPI equation is shown in Figure B-1, on the following page.

SPI measures the ratio of the budgeted cost of the work actually performed (EV) to the budgeted cost of work planned (PV). Like schedule variance, SPI measures whether a project is behind or ahead of schedule. The difference, however, is that SPI does not measure project performance in terms of currency, but rather, offers a ratio. Instead of the "critical point" of an unfavorable or favorable variance being located at 0, the "critical point" of an SPI is 1. If the ratio is greater than 1, the project is ahead of schedule (favorable variance), but if the ratio is below 1 then the project is behind schedule (unfavorable variance). How far above or below 1 the variance is represents how significantly ahead or behind schedule the project is, regardless of size.

Another way of thinking about this equation is that SPI divides "budget value of actual work performed" by "value for work budgeted." Therefore if "budget value of actual work performed" is greater than "value for work budgeted," the project will be ahead of schedule (more of the project has been completed than was originally estimated) and the SPI ratio will be larger than 1. The same logic can be used to show that if "value for work budgeted" is greater than "budget value of actual work performed," then the ratio will be less than 1, indicating that the project is behind schedule.

Our hypothetical website design company, District Design, is in the process of designing another website for a small coffee shop and would like to compare the progress of this project to the progress of its entertainment content website project. The cost of building the coffee shop's website is much smaller than the entertainment site's cost, primarily because the former does not require a login or payment system, and is therefore much simpler. Thus, in order to compare the progress of the two sites, District Design must use an index such as SPI to neutralize the cost factor in order to compare the progress of the two projects fairly and accurately.

The firm calculates that the entertainment site has an SPI of 1.2 ($648,000/$540,000), which again reinforces the original claim that the entertainment site is experiencing a favorable schedule variance. The firm then calculates the SPI of the coffee shop site to be 1.04. The design firm can now compare the two projects, regardless of each project's total cost. By comparing the two projects, the firm will realize that even with the size discrepancy between the projects, the entertainment site is farther ahead of schedule. At this point, the firm needs to compare the costs of the two projects.

Schedule Performance Index (SPI) = EV/PV

Figure B-1: Schedule Performance Index equation.

Cost Performance Index

Just as schedule variance has a parallel index measurement, so does cost variance. The equation for **Cost Performance Index (CPI)** is shown in Figure B-2.

Measuring Future Progress: EVM Forecasting

Cost Performance Index (CPI) = EV/AC

Figure B-2: Cost Performance Index equation.

As this equation indicates, CPI measures the ratio of the budgeted value of the actual work completed (EV) to the actual costs (AC) incurred. CPI measures whether the costs of a project are above or below the amount budgeted for any given point in a project's lifetime. The interpretation of CPI is similar to that of SPI: a favorable or unfavorable variance depends on whether or not the CPI ratio is above or below 1. If the CPI ratio is above 1, the project is under budget (favorable variance), and if the CPI ratio is below 1, the project is over budget (unfavorable variance). CPI can be thought of as dividing "budgeted value of actual costs" by "actual costs." Therefore, if "budgeted value of actual costs" is higher than "actual costs," the ratio is above 1 and the project is under the budget (actual costs are less than originally budgeted).

In the case of District Design, the firm found the CPI of its entertainment content site to be .92 ($648,000/$702,000). Because the CPI is below 1, the project is shown to be experiencing an unfavorable variance. Even when compared to the CPI of the coffee shop site (which was calculated to be .97), the entertainment site seems to be doing worse in terms of meeting its budgeted cost projection. The comparison of the CPIs and SPIs for each of District Design's projects should help the project manager decide how to allocate remaining resources to each project.

Measuring Future Progress: EVM Forecasting

All of the EVM measurements that we have examined so far have been similar in many regards. The indexes, variances, variance percentages, and basic EVM metrics all are related. Moreover, all of these components have another similarity: they produce measures of performance based on past or current progress in any particular project. All of these metrics can be calculated at any specific point in the project's timeline, or cumulatively until the most recent day in a project's lifetime. With the use of computers, all of this information can be readily calculated and updated daily. But all of these components lack one major characteristic; they offer no way to measure the project's future progress. To quantify the completion of a project, project managers use a method called EVM forecasting. **EVM forecasting** uses data to estimate the final total cost of a project, according to the project's current performance.

Estimate to Complete (ETC) = BAC - EV

Figure B-3: Estimate to complete equation (I).

The first major aspect of EVM forecasting is the **budget at completion (BAC)**. The BAC is the total budgeted cost originally allocated to the project. District Design's entertainment site project has a BAC of $670,000, which is the 12-month total on the costs chart (see Figure 3-9.B on page 152). This metric was set at the beginning of the project, during the budgeting phase. Another significant value in EVM forecasting is **estimate to complete (ETC)**. ETC measures the total estimated costs required to complete the remainder of a project. ETC is expressed in terms of money and relies on other EVM metrics.

ETC has two possible equations. The first equation assumes that past performance is expected to continue. This equation presumes that, in general, the project is incurring fairly typical variances and performance metrics. If the manager believes that the performance metrics will remain relatively constant throughout the remainder of the project's lifetime, then ETC can be calculated using the equation shown in Figure B-3, shown above.

Appendix B

The general reasoning behind the equation is fairly easy to understand. The ETC equation estimates the budgeted dollars until completion and disregards future cost variances. Therefore the equation uses the total budgeted costs originally estimated (BAC) and subtracts the budgeted costs already allocated for the work actually completed so far (EV), leaving a remainder of the budgeted amount until completion.

A second version of the ETC equation can be used if a project manager feels that a project's performance metrics and variances have been atypical. This version of the ETC equation is shown in Figure B-4.

Estimate to Complete (ETC) = [(BAC) - (EV)]/CPI

Figure B-4: Estimate to complete equation (II).

This equation essentially uses the same reasoning as in the previous ETC, except that it divides the estimated difference by CPI.

It is up to firms like District Design to choose which equation to use. District Design's project manager has decided that the variances that they have encountered during the entertainment site project are fairly atypical. The project manager believes that the firm often finishes its projects quickly, but usually controls cost better than it has on this project. Accordingly, the project manager believes that the variances may change during the remaining months of the project. She therefore chooses to use the second ETC equation. With this equation, District Design discovers that its ETC is $23,833. This means that District Design has estimated that it will require another $23,833 to complete the project.

However, the firm now faces a problem. The ETC approximates how far away the project's completion is primarily by using budgeted variables, even though the project has already incurred real costs. Since projects rarely have zero cost variance, it is therefore necessary to calculate **estimate at completion (EAC)**. EAC is another forecasting metric, similar to ETC. The difference is that EAC does not estimate the distance between a point in the project's timeline and the project's completion, but rather, forecasts the final total cost of the project using the project's performance metrics to date. This means that EAC uses actual data incurred by the project rather than data taken only from the original project budget.

Like ETC, EAC has multiple equations. The first equation again assumes that all variances are typical and that they will continue to occur in the future. To calculate EAC, assuming that all variances are typical, project managers will use the equation shown in Figure B-5.

Estimate at Completion (EAC) = (BAC) + (AC) - (EV)

Figure B-5: Estimate at completion equation (I).

This equation adds the difference between actual and budgeted costs already incurred to the estimated final cost. It is therefore important to note the correlation between this equation and other equations, such as the cost variance equation. If EV is greater than AC, then EAC will be lower than BAC, and vice versa. If the actual project costs are less than those predicted for a given point in the project, then the actual cost of completing the project will be less than the original budgeted estimate.

Yet, as with ETC, project managers often encounter atypical variances. If a manager believes that the variances that her firm has incurred up to a certain point in a project will not continue throughout the remainder of that project's lifetime, then she will use either of the two equations shown in Figure B-6.

Measuring Future Progress: EVM Forecasting

Estimate at Complete (EAC) = (BAC)/(CPI)

OR

Estimate at Complete (EAC) = (AC)/(ETC)

Figure B-6: Estimate at Completion equation (II).

Both of the equations shown in Figure B-6 will calculate the same figure for EAC. District Design chooses to use one of these equations, because the project manager believes that the entertainment site project's variances are atypical. Because both equations will calculate the same figure for EAC, District Design can choose to use either equation. The project manager then calculates the EAC of the entertainment site project to be $725,833. This is the project's estimated total cost, incorporating all data up to and including the eighth month of the project.

Appendix C: Advanced Cybersecurity Studies

Types of Policy Documents

Statute/Legislation: A formal written enactment by a legislative authority. Statutes (e.g. FISMA) have been agreed upon by both houses of Congress and the highest executive (the president) and published as part of a code.

Executive Order: A presidential decree carrying the full force of law, issued in pursuance of acts of Congress or based in a power inherently granted to the executive by the Constitution.

Regulation: Rules or regulations are created by federal agencies to execute legislation or executive orders and published in the *Code of Federal Regulations*. Regulations are treated by the courts as being as legally binding as statutory law, provided that the regulations are a reasonable interpretation of the underlying statutes.

Directive: Formal guidance or instructions issued by an organization.

Policy Directive: A directive that is tied to a stated policy goal and establishes the framework for execution of strategy.

Guidance: A statement or publication that provides direction or a course of action aligned with a specific outcome.

Technical Guidance: A statement or publication that provides technical direction aimed at achieving a specific outcome.

Detailed Technical Guidance: Provides detailed technical configuration information or specifications that support a specific outcome.

Standard: A process, procedure or method for accomplishing a specific goal that is agreed upon by a formal body.

Best Practice: A process, technique, or method for accomplishing a specific goal that is either proven or believed to be better than the alternatives.

Appendix D: Case Study Convenience Vs. Security

Case Significance

The security practices of Book Box give significant insight into cybersecurity management because the choices made by the CISO demonstrate the need to balance customer protection with customer satisfaction. Convenience versus security is a typical challenge that CISO's must overcome when protecting the information of online customers.

Summary of Conclusions

- A CISO must make trade-offs and remian within their budget, while still optimizing customer protection.
- Balancing the ability to protect the customer, with the need to retain their business is a necessary challenge for CISO's.
- Simply buying the most expensive security features does not guarentee that customers will remain satisfied

The Cost-Benefit Analysis of the Book Box Website Security Practices

Established in 2003, Book Box is a popular online retailer that sells new and used books. The company exclusively sells their products over the Internet. Book Box operates a secure website and their customers are confident in the company's ability to protect their personal information, including credit card information. However, due to the large volume of transactions done on this online superstore, the Book Box website is still vulnerable to being hacked by cyber criminals. Despite the fact that Book Box has been doing great business for many years, their customers trust them, and they are the largest online book retailer on the web, a data breach could still irreparably harm their reputation. If a hacker were able to successfully steal customer information, the consequences for the company could be devastating. Such an incident could allow Book Box's competition to acquire the customers that no longer trust the site. Moreover, such a data breach could even result in a lawsuit against Book Box. If it could be proven that the company did not take the steps necessary to protect their customers personal information, Book Box could be found liable for losses.

In order to prevent the possible catastrophic consequences of a hacking incident, Book Box decides to redouble their efforts to protect their website. The Chief Information Security Officer (CISO) orders a Risk Assessment to be done immediately.

Company Profile

Established in 2003, Book Box is a popular online retailer that sells new and used books. The company exclusively sells their products over the Internet on their secure website. Within the online book selling market, their customers are confident in the company's ability to protect their personal information, including credit card information. Book Box has never been hacked, nor have they had any other security breach involving sensitive customer data. While not number one in online book sales, the company enjoys healthy profits and high customer satisfaction.

Online Book Seller Environment

Despite the fact that online shopping is as common today as is shopping at brick and mortar stores, customers who shop online are still taking a risk in doing so. Whenever a customer enters their credit card number or bank account number into an online form, she is exposing herself to the potential dangers lurking on the web. Most sites are secure, and all reputable retailers use security controls to ensure that their customers are safe from online predators. However, many well-established and well-intentioned online retailers have been hacked over the past few years, which resulted in financial damages, government inquiries and penalties, and customer distrust.

Just six months ago Read All About It, another online book seller and a close competitor to Book Box, suffered a security breach on their site. The website was hacked and hundreds of customer credit card numbers were stolen. The security of customer names, phone numbers, and billing addresses was also breached. Read All About It is a reputable company with a large customer following. In the wake of the breach, the company faced media scrutiny, customer outrage, lawsuits, and government interventions. While the company had worked for many years to establish themselves as a legitimate online retailer, one security breach might have set them back to square one. It is unlikely that Read All About It will ever fully recover from the cybersecurity breach. Their reputation is now shaky, and they lost both money and their competitive edge in the wake of the breach. Furthermore, the Read All About It incident has led to a far more cautious online consumer base.

Customers of online retailers - and particularly those like Book Box and Read All About It who store sensitive customer information on their sites - are demanding higher security standards from book sellers. Along with this desire for better website security controls, customers still want a convenient and fast shopping experience. This ideal shopping experience fits in with the overall expectations of the online shopping environment. Most people want to have the convenience of a one-button checkout, and the option of having their username and/or password saved in their Internet browser. Customers are put off by strict password strength guidelines and multi-factor authentication procedures.

This means that the average Book Box customer would rather create a password that is personal and easy to remember than one that includes numbers, capitalized letters, symbols, and a minimum length of characters. Similarly, the average Book Box customer does not want to go through an authentication process every time he logs in to buy a book. A customer does not want to answer security questions in addition to inputting his password, nor does he want to go through the process of entering his billing and credit card information as a guest every time he makes a purchase from the site. In an online retail environment in which convenience and security cannot necessarily coexist, and in which marketplace competition makes the alienation of customers disastrous for the bottom line, how does Book Box settle the apparent paradox of keeping their customers both happy and secure?

In the online book store environment, Chief Information Officers (CIO's) and Chief Information Security Officers (CISO's) are often charged with gathering the appropriate information regarding risk, presenting their findings, and working with the Board of Directors and other executive officers to solve the problem of convenience versus security. The problem of satisfying the preferences of online consumers while also effectively managing the risk to sensitive customer information is not an easy task. Managing risk means making trade-offs, and often answering questions that do not actually have a right or wrong answer. Perhaps most importantly, risk management is limited by budgetary constraints.

Appendix D

Case Study

Given the current threat environment, the CISO of Book Box needs an answer to the question, "Which security controls are the best at protecting customer information from being leaked, and within our security budget, and will not inconvenience customers?" On the Book Box website, sensitive information has to be protected through at least three security measures:

Necessary Security Controls

1. Credit card details supplied by the customer, either to the merchant or payment gateway. Handled by the server's SSL and the merchant/server's digital certificates.

2. Credit card details passed to the bank for processing. Handled by the complex security measures of the payment gateway.

3. Order and customer details supplied to the merchant, either directly or from the payment gateway/credit card processing company. Handled by SSL, server security, digital certificates (and payment gateway sometimes).

In order to protect sensitive customer information, Book Box has existing security controls to which any new security measures will be added.

Existing Security Controls

- User ID and Password: Customers login to their Book Box account using an ID and password.
- SSL Certificates: A Secure Sockets Layer (SSL) Certificate encrypts credit card numbers.
- Secure shopping cart software: The shopping cart is secured by third party software.

The question of additional security protections is not merely answered by guessing. A rigorous mathematical process called a Risk Assessment is performed by experts in order to determine how the company ought to improve their cybersecurity posture. Even after the risk assessment is complete, and the CISO has gone over the findings, the Board of Directors must also review the results and finalize any decision made by the CISO. Thus, the CISO has a risk analyst perform a Risk Assessment, the results of which will determine which security features the CISO will choose from.

The Risk Assessment is finished and the risk analyst reports her findings to the CISO (review the Appendix for a detailed example of a Risk Assessment). The risk analyst presents the CISO with a list of security controls, all of which would aptly bolster the security of their website, and further protect their customers. However, the choice of which new security controls to implement is not so simple for several reasons.

First, the CISO has been allotted a budget of $100,000 to purchase additional security features. This means that she may have to sacrifice certain controls, or combinations of controls, that are outside of her budget. Second, each control has been assigned a number score relating to both customer protection and customer inconvenience. The CISO must keep the customer protection score above 8, and keep the customer inconvenience score below 9. The budgetary constraints, coupled with the protection and inconvenience criteria make the CISO's decision quite difficult. Furthermore, the blame for a failure in security or for losing customers due to inconvenience will rest on the CISO's shoulders. The following chart is presented to the CISO for review:

Case Study

Additional Security Options

Security Feature	Cost	Customer Protection (5 being best)	Customer Inconvenience (5 being worst)
Multiple logins: In addition to logging into his account when he enters the site, the customer must confirm his username and password again before he can continue on to his shopping cart.	$20,000	2	2
Enhanced Password Strength: Each customer must include a capital letter, and at least one number or symbol in their password. This password must also be a minimum of eight characters.	$40,000	3	3
Address verification: Book Box must verify a customers address if there are any discrepancies from the address listed on the account from either the shipping or billing address entered in the checkout transaction. If there is a difference between the address that a customer has on file with their bank, or has used to register for their Book Box account, the transaction will be halted and an email notice will be sent to the customer, directing them to contact Book Box customer service.	$60,000	5	4
Card Verification Value: Customers must enter the 3 digit number located on the back of their credit card in order for the transaction to go through.	$80,000	5	2

Security Feature	Cost	Customer Protection (5 being best)	Customer Inconvenience (5 being worst)
Challenge Questions: During log-in, the system requires users to select three challenge questions and responses. If the risk score associated with a particular transaction exceeds 750, the challenge questions are be triggered. If the challenge question responses entered by the user do not match the ones originally provided, the customer receives an error message. If the customer is unable to answer the challenge questions in three attempts, the customer is blocked from his or her account.	$30,000	4	4
Dollar Amount Rule: The system permits Book Box to set a dollar threshold amount above which a transaction automatically triggers the challenge questions even if the user ID, password, and device cookie are all valid. Book Box set this dollar amount threshold at $250 per transaction.	$10,000	3	2

Appendix D

Security Feature	Cost	Customer Protection (5 being best)	Customer Inconvenience (5 being worst)
Invisible Device Authentication: The system places a "device cookie" onto customers' computers to identify particular computers used to access their account. The device cookie is used to help establish a secure communication session with the server. When the cookie is changed, the system asks a security question to verify that the correct user is logging in.	$70,000	4	1
Risk Profiling: The system entailed the building of a risk profile for each customer based on the location from which a user logged in, when and how often a user logged in, what a user did while on the system, and the size, type, and frequency of transactions. The Book Box security system records the IP address that the customer typically uses to log into online banking and adds it to the customer profile. If a user's transaction differs from its normal profile, the security system flags the transaction. Transactions generating risk scores in excess of 750, on a scale from 0 to 1,000, are high-risk transactions. High scores trigger the security questions.	$60,000	4	2

Analysis

The security controls above offer the CISO with many possible combinations, while still keeping her customer protection score above 8 and her customer inconvenience score below 9. The following chart shows two possible combinations that the CISO might choose.

Option 1

Security Feature	Cost	Customer Protection	Customer Inconvenience
Card Verification Value	$80,000	5	2
Multiple Logins	$20,000	2	2
Total	$100,000	7	4

Conclusion

Option 2

Security Feature	Cost	Customer Protection	Customer Inconvenience
Dollar Amount Rule	$10,000	3	2
Challenge Questions	$30,000	4	4
Risk Profiling	$60,000	4	2
Total	$60,000	11	8

If she chooses Option 1, the CISO would spend her entire budget on Card Verification Value and Multiple Logins. While she would have a great customer inconvenience score of 4, well under the threshold of below 9, her customer protection score would not reach the minimum expectation of being over 8. She could still choose to present this option to the Board, however they would likely want more customer protection for the $100,000 price tag.

If the CISO chooses Option 2 she would come in on budget with three new security controls. The customer protection score would be well over the target, thus making the features a good addition to their website. The customer inconvenience score would also remain just at their target. While this Option is good, and perhaps better for the company than Option 1, it is still possible that the Board may not be willing to risk such a high customer inconvenience score.

By analyzing all of the options, some important questions are raised. What are the pros and cons of each additional security measure that she chose? Will enhanced security features like the multiple logins alienate the customers too much? Is it worth allowing for more convenience, yet leaving customers with a less secured shopping experience? Furthermore, what less obvious impacts might new security controls have on the company? For example, will Book Box be able to properly train employees to complete the Risk Profiling? Will they have to hire new employees to complete and/or oversee that task? These questions demonstrate that the job of the CISO is not easy, and that the job of managing risk and securing products and services is complicated.

Conclusion

Many factors go into choosing the best security options for securing an e-commerce website. Customer protection and convenience are important, yet every company has different needs unique to their business model, software, budget, personnel, etc. The challenge of maintaining customer privacy, securing customer data, and ensuring that customers are not alienated by too many security features is daunting. In order balance all of these fragile factors, a CISO of an online retailer must be an excellent manager. This means that she must be able to think through problems, recognize and understand budgetary constraints, be able to look ahead and predict potential problems, understand risks and rewards, answer questions that do not have a right or wrong answer, and have the ability to make trade-offs and compromise when necessary. Perhaps most importantly, the CISO of an online retailer must understand how to balance customer protection with customer convenience.

Appendix D

Appendix

Example Research Model

Book Box wants to find affordable security controls that are appropriate for reducing the risk of customer information being leaked. To evaluate this question, the risk analyst will use a statistical regression model. As described in Chapter 2.6 of Cybersecurity Fundamentals, a regression model uses multiple independent (x) variables to predict or estimate a dependent (y) variable. Presumably, a change to any of the independent variables will affect the outcome(s) of the model. In other words, the y-value is dependent on the x-value(s). In the case of multivariable analysis, each x-value must be mutually exclusive; the x-values cannot be affected by, nor dependent upon, each other.

In order to determine which security controls are the best at protecting information, the risk analyst will survey 200 (n=200) other online retailers. Using 'yes' or 'no' answers, the retailers will respond to the question of whether or not customer information was leaked on one random day (24 hours) in 2011.

Because the risk analyst is dealing with a yes or no question (also called a binary question), she will use a logistic (logit) regression model to evaluate risk. Logit models are used when the dependent variable is a binary response. The model generates a probability value. A logit model reveals (1) the most statistically significant indicators and (2) the type of association the indicators form with the dependent variable - a positive (direct) or a negative (indirect) relationship. A positive relationship indicates that if the independent variable increases, the dependent variable increases; a negative relationship means if the independent variable decreases, the dependent variable acts in the opposite manner, so in this case the dependent variable would increase.

Example Analysis of the Most Significant Factors Influencing Customer Information Leaked

Based on the most complete model generated using the logit equation, Strength of Password and a 2-Factor Authentication are the two most significant security controls. An example of a strong password includes capitalization, a number, a symbol, and at least eight characters, unrelated to any personal information, such as "rh7TL!9". The simplest type of password is a word that is found in a dictionary, such as the word "password". A 2-Factor Authentication is a pair of security controls that requires the user to enter either 1) "something the user knows", such as a password, 2) "something the user has'", such as an account number, and/or 3) "something the user is", such as a biometric data. 2-Factor Authentication is the most significant variable based on its low p-values in all three models.

According to the logit analyses, the independent variable Password is significant in determining the probability of a risk (defined as customer information being leaked), and as the password becomes stronger by gaining in complexity, it becomes less likely that customer critical information will be leaked.

Example of Predicting the Probability of Customer Information Leaked

The strength of multivariate statistical analysis lies in its predictive capabilities. A thorough, valid, and reliable design will allow a risk manager to extrapolate future trends that will help Book Box protect its customer's sensitive information.

Recall that the best security controls for protecting customer information are a strong Password and a 2-Factor Authentication. However, the risk analysis team wants to know the combination of security controls

Appendix

that will best protect customer information from malicious code, based on the resources allocated and constraints placed on Book Box.

Model A is the riskiest scenario: There is a 93.136% likelihood of customer information being leaked under the set of conditions. Model D is the safest and most realistic option, which even takes into consideration a hacker with strength level 7 out of 10, 10 being the strongest.

Model D is the only model that has a 2-Factor Authentication and it has the strongest password. While Model D does contain multiple security controls, it is a realistic option. Consumers may not enjoy having a 2-Factor Authentication; however, on a popular website that is a target for strong and capable hackers, consumers should feel confident that there is only a 0.641% likelihood that their critical information may be leaked.

Example of Findings

The most significant independent variable is the presence or lack of presence of a 2-Factor Authentication. Therefore, if a 2-Factor Authentication is present as a security control on a company's website, then the likelihood of customer information being leaked decreases. According to this analysis, and based on its statistical significance in each model, 2-Factor Authentication is the most significant form of security control that the online retailer can use to reduce the likelihood of customer information being leaked.

Based on these models, the risk manager may suggest to the Book Box CISO that the website requires a strong password and a 2-Factor Authentication in order to secure customer information. Decisions made in these areas should be based on an effective risk management program. However, the CISO has limited resources for the deployment of security controls, so she must choose a combination of controls that securely safeguards customer information, avoids customer inconvenience, and works for the company's budget. At this point, a cost-benefit analysis is necessary to determine which controls should be in place.

Following our risk determination process in this example, the CISO now has four different models to present to the Board of Directors as reasons to promote the security controls of Model D versus Model A. The CISO will emphasize the need for 2-Factor Authentication and a strong Password for customer login.

Appendix E: Case Study
It's Not a Cyber Problem; It's a Management Problem

Case Significance

The case of US-CERT's failed cybersecurity continuous monitoring system is significant because it reveals the essential role of managers in protecting a nation from catastrophic attacks.

Summary of Conclusions

- In order to build the kind of cyber analysis and warning system, US-CERT must have an effective continuous monitoring system in place.
- Hardware and software alone cannot achieve the level of analysis and information sharing needed to effectively monitor critical networks.
- It is up to strong managers to deconstruct the attributes of the monitoring system, find the gaps, and decide how to best fill in those gaps.

Abstract

For the past few decades the United States has consistently met the increasing need to protect critical information and infrastructure from cyber attacks. As modern societies continue to develop new technology and information technology (IT) tools, these societies continue to become more and more reliant on technology and IT tools to complete the most basic of tasks. In order to buy food, access money, or obtain healthcare, citizens rely on IT tools functioning properly. If any organization (including the federal government) were to be compromised by a cyber attack, pure chaos might erupt. Banking systems could crash, plummeting the stock market and prompting traders to sell off the U.S. currency. The power grid could be rendered inoperable, plunging the country back into darkness. People would be unable to access their money due to the inability to complete wire transfers of paychecks, and power loss to ATM's and bank branches. Grocery stores and other essential goods providers would not be able to sell food to hungry customers, and would not be able to store fresh food without refrigeration. Hospitals might experience confusion over electronic medical records and prescription orders. Essentially, a well planned cyber attack (or a series of them) on U.S. cyber-based critical infrastructure and systems could drastically change the safety and quality of daily life in the United States.

US-Cert Profile

Tasked with safeguarding the United States from cyber attacks, the United States Computer Emergency Readiness Team (US-CERT) was formed in 2003 as the 24-hour operational arm of the Department of Homeland Security's (DHS) National Cyber Security Division (NCSD). The mission of US-CERT is to take charge of improving the nation's cybersecurity posture by organizing information sharing, and managing cyber risks to America's cyber-based critical infrastructure. US-CERT is expected to work across sectors in order to keep both public and private critical infrastructure stakeholders apprised of cybersecurity threats.

United States' Cybersecurity Environment

The United States federal government is most vulnerable to IT-related attacks. The US federal government is comprised of hundreds of departments and agencies. These departments and agencies contain thousands of employees and cyber assets. Many of these departments and agencies control extremely important information ranging from nuclear secrets to social security numbers. Moreover, agencies and departments that are in charge of providing vital goods and services to the population use cyber-based technology to do so. If federal government computer systems are infiltrated by a cyber attack, not only could enormous amounts of highly sensitive information be compromised, but the country as a whole could lose many of its essential services (food, water, electricity). In order to ensure that such a catastrophic attack does not occur, the federal government tasked the United States Computer Emergency Readiness Team (US-CERT) to implement a cyber analysis and warning system.

United States' Cybersecurity Environment

The entire world, and in particular the United States, has experienced an unprecedented technological surge over the past two decades. The number of technological assets available to the world's population has sky rocketed since the invention of the personal computer and the Internet. Unfortunately, the rapid increase in technological capabilities has both positive and negative consequences. Although technological tools help millions of people around the world, the increasing number of threats to these technological assets has created massive vulnerabilities to the world's population.

GAO's Investigation into US-CERT's continuous monitoring system, and it's findings

After years of developing and executing their cyber analysis and warning system under the leadership of the Department of Homeland Security (DHS) and the National Cyber Security Division (NCSD), US-CERT was investigated by the General Accountability Office (GAO). This investigation looked deeply at the progress made by US-CERT in order to ensure that they were properly fulfilling their mission to protect the U.S. government computers from cyber attacks. The GAO's findings are detailed in a 2008 report, and concluded that US-CERT failed to implement an effective monitoring system. The failure to create an successful monitoring system in turn led to the failure of the overall warning system because monitoring is one of the four key components to the cyber analysis and warning system. US-CERT's inability to create a viable monitoring system came down to managerial shortcomings.

In its report, the GAO illustrated how the US-CERT failed to establish goals and performance metrics, promote coordination, and leverage technology – all of which are fundamental managerial duties. The US-CERT's failed attempt to implement a monitoring system highlights this trend in failed cybersecurity operations and recognizes the integral role that managers have in effectively completing cybersecurity operations.

In order to prevent critical information and infrastructure from being compromised by cyber attacks, organizations must be able to recognize cyber attacks within their networks. A cyber attack will not likely look the way it does in a movie, with a skull and cross bones appearing on all the computer screens at the White House. In real life, cyber attacks can be subtle and even totally surreptitious. Thus, cybersecurity leadership must continuously watch over critical networks for any and all signs of an attack. Furthermore, cybersecurity leaders must be able to warn the proper authorities if a cyber attack were to be recognized (see "Warning System Case Study" for more details). Appreciating this problem, the federal government tasked the United States Computer Emergency Readiness Team (US-CERT) to develop a cyber analysis and warning program with the intent of creating a system to inform the proper authorities of any cyber attacks against the nation's critical information

Appendix E

and infrastructure. Within this cyber analysis and warning system are four capabilities critical to implementing an effective cyber warning and analysis program, the first of which is a monitoring system. A monitoring system ensures that the organization recognizes any intrusions or irregular activity within their information network.

Unfortunately, establishing an effective continuous monitoring system is highly complex. New technological capabilities allow hackers to access critical information through assets that hold no critical information themselves, but are connected to other assets that hold extremely important tools and information. For example, a hacker might be able to infiltrate a government laptop and steal its information by hacking into a printer connected to the same wifi signal as the laptop. This means that not only must the government monitor critical assets such as the laptop for intrusions, but also the less-critical assets, like the printer. This poses significant difficulties to those hoping to successfully implement a continuous monitoring system. Despite many difficulties, it is possible to track electronic assets because electronic assets each carry a unique Internet Protocol (IP) address.

Unique IP addresses serve as an identification number for each asset. This means that laptops, desktops, printers, and cell phones all have their own individual IP address that identifies them. IP addresses allow analysts to track and monitor cyber assets at all times. While this tracking is relatively easy on an individual level, when done on a large scale tracking individual IP addresses can still be extremely difficult. Individual organizations may have millions of items with IP addresses, and monitoring all of these assets efficiently and effectively creates significant obstacles for cybersecurity managers. Tracking IP addresses is just one piece of a complex puzzle that makes up network monitoring.

The difficulty of successfully implementing a continuous monitoring system illustrates some of the key challenges that cybersecurity managers frequently face. In order to understand how and why the managerial problems occurred it is important to have a basic understanding of what a continuous monitoring system is and what it does.

What is a Continuous Monitoring System?

Continuous monitoring systems are used to detect cyber threats, attacks, and vulnerabilities. A continuous monitoring system is just one of four critical capabilities needed in order to implement an effective cyber warning and analysis system. Monitoring a network as it functions on a normal attack-free day gives analysts a baseline of how a safe network looks and behaves. This baseline is then used to compare future network activities. If analysts notice any deviation from their safe baseline, they can immediately investigate the anomaly. Thus, continuously monitoring networks and systems is critical for organizations to recognize and understand anomalies. These anomalies can take a variety of forms and therefore can be difficult to recognize. However, the successful recognition of a cyber attack can allow analysts to warn the necessary authorities of the potentially harmful intrusion.

Monitoring a network for suspicious activity is very similar to monitoring a home for suspicious activity. Some people do this with in-home security systems, others with a neighborhood watch, and some by themselves. In order to protect a home from robberies or other types of attacks, homeowners will monitor their homes for suspicious activity (odd cars sitting out front, masked men approaching the house, etc.). For the remainder of this section lets consider the case of a neighborhood that has hired a neighborhood security guard in the hope of protecting their individual homes.

Attributes

While analysis and warning systems have four critical capabilities (one of which is a continuous monitoring system), each of these capabilities has a list of necessary attributes that comprise them. Each continuous monitoring system should have the following five attributes:

What is a Continuous Monitoring System?

1. Establish a Baseline

2. Assess Risk to Network Assets

3. Obtain Internal Information

4. Obtain External Information

5. Detect Anomalous Activities

Each of these attributes is crucial for implementing an effective monitoring system. Furthermore, each step is linearly dependent on the previous step(s). Assessing the risk to network assets is dependent on successfully establishing a baseline, and detecting anomalous activities is dependent on obtaining internal and external information. Each attribute plays a key role in implementing a monitoring system.

1. Establish a Baseline

All continuous monitoring systems should first establish a basic understanding of its network assets and normal network traffic. This means that analysts should recognize the normal trends and habits of activities within the network. Every organization will differ in what constitutes "normal activity" and it is therefore crucial that managers establish a proper baseline of each individual network. Establishing a baseline lays the foundation for the rest of the process and creates a standard against which anomalies can be detected, identified, and mitigated.

A variety of techniques can be used to establish a proper baseline of the network. The first of these activities is to create an accurate inventory of the network's assets. This means that analysts will track the IP addresses of all available assets (both physical and cyber). Additionally, this process involves prioritizing assets. Some assets will be inherently more important to monitor than others, and it is crucial that managers recognize what assets are most important to protect. Without a solid understanding of the network's assets and the normal activity within the network, it will be impossible to judge if any future network activity is unusual and therefore potentially a cyber attack.

Referring back to our example of protecting a home with the help of a neighborhood watch, establishing a baseline might consist of the resident on-duty driving around the neighborhood in order to understand the habits of the people living there. While some neighborhoods may have residents that are up late and have friends over during the week, other neighborhoods might have residents that go to bed much earlier in the night and rarely have weekday guests. It is important for the security guard to gain a basic understanding of both the people that live in the neighborhood as well as the habits that those people exhibit in order for the security guard to determine what activities are usual vs. unusual.

2. Assess Risk to Network Assets

After a baseline has been established, analysts must assess the risk to the network assets identified during the establishment of the baseline. This will allow analysts to determine what risks are posed by a combination of threats and vulnerabilities. In other words, this process allows analysts to determine what threats an organization is susceptible to, what resources are at risk, and what potential damage an attack might have. This process is crucial to further prioritizing the network's assets in order to provide to the most effective monitoring of the network.

This process is completed through a formal risk assessment. This means that risk analysts will conduct threat, vulnerability, and consequence assessments for each of the network assets. This is one of the most complicated processes in implementing a monitoring system because no formal procedure has been set to

Appendix E

conduct risk assessments of the variety of assets that are likely to be included even within a smaller organization's network. Furthermore, performing quantitative or qualitative risk assessments for the millions of assets that need protection creates a fairly large obstacle. Nevertheless, performing risk assessments of a network's assets is critical to prioritizing both the cyber and physical assets within any organization's network, as well as for understanding the environment that the assets are in. For the neighborhood example, this process might include formal risk assessments to all of the components within the houses. An effective risk assessment might include threat, vulnerability, and consequence assessments of each of the physical items (couches, fridges, TVs) as well as the homes themselves.

3. Obtain Internal Information

One of the key attributes of any monitoring system is the obtainment of internal information. This includes the continuous tracking of network activity and information flow via technical tools and user reports. If internal information about the network is obtained effectively, cyber analysts can properly identify both known attacks against the network and anomalies within the network.

Cyber analysts obtain information about network activity by leveraging information security-related technology tools. These tools can help to track the flow of data into, out of, and within the organizations network. These technological tools come in a variety of forms. Some of the security-related IT tools include firewalls, antivirus software, and intrusion detection systems. All of these tools serve different functions, but they all inform data analysts about occurrences within the organization's information network.

4. Obtain External Information

In addition to obtaining internal information about the on-going activity within the network, effective monitoring systems also obtain external information about threats, vulnerabilities, and other incidents. This means that the organization looks outside its own network to identify new forms of cyber attacks, identify new types of intrusions, and remain actively aware of the current cyber environment.

In order to obtain new information about potential attacks to the network as well as other information relevant to protecting the organization's critical information and infrastructure, the organization must consult a variety of external sources. This means that the organization should consult public information, alerts issued by the government, vulnerability databases, and other relevant information sources. If external information is properly obtained and utilized, analysts should be able to maintain situational awareness, as well as the ability to detect previously unknown anomalies and attacks.

When considering the protection of a neighborhood, one might consult a variety of sources that range from home security magazines to security specialists. Anywhere that useful information can be gathered outside of the organization should be considered.

5. Detect Anomalous Activities

The detection of anomalous activities is the fifth and final necessary attribute of a continuous monitoring system. This process involves the recognition of significant changes from the baseline operation and is the most fundamental aspect of the entire monitoring system. However, the successful detection of unusual activity is entirely dependent upon the completion of the other attributes. If the monitoring system does not properly establish a baseline, perform risk assessments, and obtain information, it will not be able to detect anomalous activities. With the detection of an anomaly, an analysis of the intrusion can then be completed.

Method

Considering the example of protecting a neighborhood, the detection of anomalous activities is the security guard's primary job. How the security guard detects anomalous activities can take place in a variety of fashions. One such method of detection might occur when the neighborhood security guard recognizes that an unfamiliar van continues to circle the same home during the middle of the night. The security guard might also detect unusual activity when he hears loud noises coming from a usually quite home. No matter how the security guard recognizes these anomalies, she notifies authorities that potentially harmful activity is occurring. This is the essence of a monitoring system.

Continuous Monitoring Attributes Chart

Attribute	Purpose	Method
Establish a Baseline	To create a standard against which anomalies can be detected, identified, and mitigated	1. Create an accurate inventory 2. Prioritize assets
Assess Risk to Network Assets	To determine what risks are posed by a combination of threats and vulnerabilities	Perform a risk assessment to network assets

Attribute	Purpose	Method
Obtain Internal Information	To identify the indicators of anomalies and known attacks	1. Leverage information security-related technology tools 2. Reporting on network activity
Obtain External Information	To obtain new information about potential attacks to the network	1. Consult sources outside of the organization (i.e. conferences, experts, media outlets)
Detect Anomalous Activities	To detect either known attacks or significant changes from the baseline operations	1. Compare changes in the network to the network baseline

Case Study: US-CERT's Continuous Monitoring System

In late 2002, the Department of Homeland Security was established in response to the September 11th attacks with the purpose of coordinating efforts against both cyber and physical attacks to the United States' most critical infrastructure. In response to President George W. Bush's Comprehensive National Cybersecurity Initiative (CNCI) requirements, DHS created the National Cyber Security Division within the Office of Cybersecurity and Communications (CS&C). NCSD works with both public and private entities to secure the nation's critical cyber assets.

The US-CERT is one branch of the NCSD within DHS. The US-CERT is tasked with coordinating the nation's efforts to prepare for, prevent, and respond to cyber threats to systems and communications networks. In or-

Appendix E

der to fulfill its high-level mission, the US-CERT attempted to create a process for detecting potentially harmful cyber intrusions, and then a way of warning the necessary authorities of the intrusions. According to a 2008 GAO study of the US-CERT's cyber analysis and warning system, implementing a continuous monitoring system is the first step needed to establish an effective analysis and warning system.

Goals of US-CERT's cyber warning system

In the 2008 GAO study of the effectiveness of theUS-CERT's cyber analysis and warning system, three goals were adopted:

1. Identify key attributes of cyber analysis and warning capabilities

2. Compare these attributes with the US-CERT's current capabilities to identify gaps in US-CERT's programs

3. Identify US-CERT's challenges to developing and implementing key attributes and successful national cyber analysis

Attributes of US-CERT's cyber monitoring capability

Through this study, the GAO developed a formalized list of capabilities critical to a cyber analysis and warning system, as well as the necessary attributes for these capabilities to be considered fully effective. Developing a continuous monitoring system is the first capability listed in the GAO's report. In addition to formalizing a list of attributes and capabilities critical to implementing an analysis and warning system, the GAO conducted an analysis of how well US-CERT executed the various capabilities and attributes. This included an in-depth investigation of what goals and attributes a continuous monitoring system should have, as well as how US-CERT's performance matched up against these goals and attributes. The US-CERT's cyber analysis and monitoring system must:

1. Establish a Baseline

2. Assess Risk to the Network Assets

3. Obtain Internal Information

4. Obtain External Information

5. Detect Anomalous Activities

The following chart outlines the details of the problems found with the actual performance of those goals.

US-CERT's goals and performance

Goal	Performance
Establish a Baseline	US-CERT has not established a comprehensive baseline across the nation's critical infrastructure networks. They only monitor 16 federal agencies and therefore cannot establish a baseline of the entire federal government.
Assess the Risk to Network Assets	US-CERT does not perform risk assessments. It is impossible to assess the risk to the network's assets without conducting risk assessments.

Analysis

Goal	Performance
Obtain Internal Information	The US-CERT is not always able to obtain real-time internal traffic information. Without real time information, cyber attacks might harm a network without the analysts ever knowing it.
Obtain External Information	The US-CERT monitors all information networks (private, public, etc.), yet there are more information networks that managers need to monitor in order to detect all cyber attacks.
Detect Anomalous Activities	The US-CERT's system does not detect anomalies across all information networks. There are many networks for which the US-CERT's system does not detect anomalous activity.

Analysis

According to the analysis done by the GAO, the US-CERT failed to establish a formal list of measurable goals and performance metrics for their cyber analysis warning system. The GAO was the first organization to break down high-level goals (capabilities) into measurable tasks (attributes). Their findings show the following failures:

- A lack of Coordination and Strategy
- Not all of the federal agencies participated in the US-CERT's analysis and warning program
- No private sector agencies participated in the US-CERT's analysis and warning program

• The US-CERT did not leverage the proper technological tools to obtain real-time information, and therefore they lack the ability to notify the proper authorities when the cyber attack actually is occurring

The US-CERT's ability to continuously monitor critical networks is far too important to national security to contain so many performance gaps. In order to build the kind of cyber analysis and warning system that the United States needs to protect itself from catastrophic harm, the US-CERT must create and maintain an effective monitoring system. This difficult task can only be completed by talented managers. While technology is an essential part of any cybersecurity process, hardware and software alone cannot achieve the level of analysis and information sharing needed to effectively monitor networks for cyber attacks. Strong managers must be able to deconstruct the necessary capabilities of the monitoring system into attributes, find the gaps within the attributes, and decide how to fill those gaps. Once the gaps are filled, managers must maintain a high level of quality control in order to ensure that the continuous monitoring system remains effective in the long run.

Appendix E

Conclusion

The US-CERT's continuous monitoring system did not meet the GAO's standards due to a range of problems. Furthermore, this case sheds light upon a common trend seen in many cybersecurity projects: more often than not the project's issues have more to do with poor management than anything else. Any managers overseeing the mission of the US-CERT continuous monitoring system must have the ability to maintain excellence by employing and overseeing the appropriate people, processes, and technology. Without excellent managers, the US-CERT monitoring system will remain only moderately effective. Because the stakes are too high, this is not acceptable. In order to better protect the United States from catastrophic cyber attacks, solid management must become the central priority at US-CERT.

What kind of managers are capable of carrying out this essential mission? Consider the capabilities and their attributes that make up a continuous monitoring system. In order to establish a national baseline for critical networks, managers must work with more than just 16 federal agencies. What characteristics might a manager need in order to collaborate and coordinate with the entire federal government (not to mention state, local, and tribal governments and the private sector)? What philosophies might a manager need if she were in charge of assessing the risk to critical networks? How would she go about conducting risk assessments of networks on a regular basis across the federal government and relevant private sector entities? What traits might a manager need in order to obtain both internal and external network information? How would he go about obtaining and disseminating this information so that it helped the most people in the most efficient manner? Thinking about the best run system, means thinking about those managers best equipped to run it. Top-tier management is essential for properly running a continuous monitoring system, and for excelling in the cybersecurity field as a whole.

Detailed Monitoring Capabilities

Table 6: US-CERT Capabilities Include Most but Not All Aspects of Monitoring		
Attribute	**Aspects Incorporated**	**Aspects not Incorporated**
Establish a baseline understanding of network assets and normal network traffic volume and flow	The organization has a limited baseline understanding of network assets and normal network traffic volume through the 16 federal participants in its situational awareness tool, US-CERT Einstein. In addition, it receives additional network flow information through contracts with information security vendors.	It does not have a comprehensive national-level baseline across the nation's computer-reliant crucial infrastructure, including the information systems of federal civilian and military entities, state and local governments, the private sector, and other entities. For example, under Einstein, the organization monitors 16 agencies, a practice that does not provide an overall view of federal network traffic. In addition, the tool's current capabilities are manually driven, thereby complicating and slowing the collection and compilation of data.

Conclusion

Table 6: US-CERT Capabilities Include Most but Not All Aspects of Monitoring (cont.)		
Attribute	**Aspects Incorporated**	**Aspects not Incorporated**
Assess risks to network assets		Though US-CERT is involved in cyber-related risk assessment efforts being performed by other DHS organizations and the private sector, it does not perform risk assessments.
Obtain internal information on network operations via technical tools and user reports	The organization obtains internal information using security tools and user reports regarding its presence on the Internet and its internal network operations.	Its ability to obtain real-time internal traffic information is reduced by Einstein's limitation of requiring manually intensive analysis.
Obtain external information on threats, vulnerabilities, and incidents	US-CERT monitors a variety of external information sources, including network traffic data, incident reports, and threat reports from federal, state, local, and foreign governments and the private sector, such as the following: • Federal agencies providing an enhanced view of their networks through participation in Einstein; • Various vendors providing Internet operational data; • The Homeland Infrastructure Threat and Risk Analysis Center (HITRAC), law enforcement, and the intelligence community, providing threat information and other data; • Federal agencies reporting information security incidents to the organization as required by the Federal Information Security Management Act; • Nonfederal entities voluntarily reporting incidents, malware, and other information; • Foreign governments providing information on cyber incidents; • CERT/CC providing vulnerability information; and • Other analysis and warning entities, including the Financial Services-ISAC, Multistate ISAC, the Internet Storm Center, and information security vendors, sharing incident and other situational awareness information.	Its information does not encompass all critical infrastructure information networks. For example, by monitoring only 16 agencies, Einstein does not provide an overall view of federal network traffic. Also, the Department of Energy and DOD use their own similar situational awareness tools, but their data are not currently combined with Einstein's data to provide a more complete view of federal traffic. There are efforts under way to develop automated information exchanges between DOD's system and Einstein, but as of March 2008, this has not been finalized. Regarding nonfederal entities, the organization does not directly monitor any private sector networks, nor are nonfederal entities required to report to it incidents or anomalous activity. Typically nonfederal entities, including the ISACs, that report incident and other data filter sensitive details from the data reported.
Detect anomalous activities	The organization detects anomalies based on its monitoring of network traffic flow. Einstein provides network flow data from 16 agencies with the primary goal of looking for unique activity that may indicate a cyber attack or other undesirable activity. According to the US-CERT officials, Einstein provides the participating agencies a capability to compare their network traffic data with activity at other federal agencies and against law enforcement and intelligence agencies' threat data to determine if they are the victim of serious attacks. In addition, it works with its various partners in the private sector as well as other federal, state, and local governments to determine the extent of abnormal behavior. For example, the organization receives limited information from certain computer security vendors regarding internet traffic flow of their respective customer bases.	The organization does not detect anomalies across the nation's computer-reliant critical infrastructure. For example, it does not directly monitor any private sector networks, nor are nonfederal entities required to report incidents or anomalous activity.

Source: GAO Analysis

Appendix E

Key Attributes of Cyber Analysis Warning Capabilities	
Capability	**Attribute**
Monitoring	• Establish a baseline understanding of network assets and normal network traffic volume and flow • Assess risks to network assets • Obtain internal information on network operations via technical tools and user reports • Obtain external information on threats, vulnerabilities, and incidents through various relationships, alerts, and other sources. • Detect anomalous activities.
Analysis	• Verify that an anomaly is an incident (threat of attack or actual attack) • Investigate the incident to identify the type of cyber attack, estimate impact, and collect evidence • Identify possible actions to mitigate the impact of the incident • Integrate results into predictive analysis of broader implications or potential future attack
Warning	• Develop attack and other notifications that are targeted and actionable • Provide notifications in a timely manner • Distribute notifications using appropriate communications methods
Response	• Contain and mitigate the incident • Recover from damages and remediate vulnerabilities • Evaluate actions and incorporate lessons learned

Source: *GAO Analysis*

Appendix F: Case Study
The Human Element of Risk Management: When Computers Alone Cannot Defend Against e-Banking Fraud

Case Significance

Patco v. Ocean Bank is a significant case for the cybersecurity world, not just because of the court's decision regarding commercially reasonable security procedures under UCC Article 4A. The case is also important because it shows that computers alone cannot protect financial institutions and their clients' money. A fully comprehensive risk monitoring strategy ought to include human management and analysis.

Summary of Conclusions

- Computers alone cannot be relied on to produce effective eBanking security measures
- In order to be able to fully shift risk to customers, banks must go beyond standard security measures by keeping their clients informed of security threats and developing security technologies
- Users of eBanking ought to be more involved in choosing the security processes that protect their money

Abstract

As the practice of electronic banking has become commonplace, financial institutions must prioritize cybersecurity in order to ensure the safety of their customer's money. Increasingly, thieves are using cyberspace to infiltrate online accounts, and to execute fraudulent transactions. This online avenue through which hackers can steal large amounts of money presents a major cybersecurity challenge to banks and their information security officers. Although performing risk assessments and implementing the newest and best security procedures is essential to safeguard e-banking customer information, banks cannot rely solely on automated cybersecurity methods. CIO's, CISO's, and executives of financial institutions must enact robust management strategies that incorporate people and processes into existing technological security measures. Financial institutions that engage in risk monitoring strategies that utilize both the discerning minds of managers and the computational power of computer programs will be far better at protecting their customers money in cyberspace. On the other hand, banks that fail to establish strong managerial strategies to oversee e-banking risk management will not survive in the cyber world. An example of this kind of failure, and the consequences that follow it, can be seen in the 2009 case of Patco Construction v. Ocean Bank.

E-Banking Environment

The use of online banking has become increasingly popular over the years. Since the rise in popularity of online banking, the threats to financial institutions and the money of their clients have been a huge concern. Currently, almost all commercial and personal banking is done online. This means that companies transfer money within and outside of their bank using eBanking platforms, and almost all payments are made and received over the Internet. While eBanking offers a great deal of convenience to customers, it also puts people's money at great risk from cybercriminals.

Patvo V. Ocean Bank

Company Profile

PATCO CONSTRUCTION
Located in Sanford, Maine, Patco is a family-owned property development and contracting company. Since its establishment in the late 1980's, PATCO has constructed hundreds of commercial buildings, municipal buildings, and residential homes throughout New England. Having banked with Ocean Bank since 1985, Patco began banking online (eBanking) with Ocean in September of 2003.

PEOPLE'S UNITED BANK (D/B/A OCEAN BANK)
People's United Bank, founded in 1842, is a subsidiary of People's United Financial, Inc., a financial services company with $29 billion in assets. People's United Bank purchased Ocean Bank in 2008. Ocean Bank is a regional bank in the Northeastern United States, including Maine.

For one week in May 2009 thieves withdrew $588,851.26 from the bank account of Patco Construction Company. The thieves were able to make six fraudulent withdrawals by correctly answering Patco's security questions used on the account. Ocean Bank had a security system in place and the transactions were flagged for several reasons, including the fact that they were irregular and came from an unusual region of the country. However, the Ocean Bank security system did not alert Patco of the transactions. When the bank found out, it was able to recover $243,406.83 of the stolen funds leaving Patco with a total loss of $345,444.43. Patco filed suit against Ocean Bank on September 18, 2009.

Patco v. Ocean Bank is significant to the cybersecurity community for several reasons. First, the details of the fraud committed against Patco highlight the need for robust security measures in eBanking systems. Second, the details of the security procedures put in place at Ocean Bank demonstrate how truly difficult it is to avoid risk. Third, the opinion of the court regarding Ocean Bank's eBanking security procedures offers insight into the cybersecurity expectations placed on financial institutions. Finally, the details of the case show the need for excellent risk managers to complement computer-based security procedures.

In 2005, four years before Patco was victimized by fraudulent eBanking payments (and just two years before Ocean Bank updated their eBanking security system), one of the largest cyber bank heists ever attempted was foiled. In a complex and well-executed operation involving both physical and cyber activities, a gang of cyber thieves almost got away with approximately £220 million from the Sumitomo Mitsui Bank in London, England. Bypassing security cameras, the thieves broke into the bank at night and attached inexpensive keyloggers to the banks computers. While the keyloggers were found and the money was saved, the threat of keylogging to the financial industry became widely known. Cybersecurity experts have been working hard to stay ahead of cyber bank robbers for many years, however this is no easy task. The stakes are high and the threats are real.

Patco v. Ocean Bank Lawsuit

Located in Sanford, Maine, Patco is a small property development and contracting company. Having banked with Ocean Bank since 1985, Patco began internet banking (eBanking) with Ocean Bank in September of 2003. In 2004, Ocean Bank hired Jack Henry & Associates to provide its core online banking platform called NetTeller, which is used by the majority of John Henry's clients.

Patco entered into Ocean Banks' eBanking for Business Agreement, which limited the banks liability if the online banking system became compromised. By agreeing to these terms, the "electronic transmission of confidential business and sensitive personal information" was at Patco's risk. By signing the agreement, Patco was

Appendix F

also responsible for monitoring their own accounts and for alerting the bank of any strange activity on the accounts. Moreover, having reserved their right to change the agreement at any time, Ocean Bank claims that it modified the eBanking agreement before May 2009 to state:

"If you choose to receive ACH debit transactions on your commercial accounts, you assume all liability and responsibility to monitor those commercial accounts on a daily basis. In the event that you object to any ACH debit, you agree to notify us of your objection on the same day the debit occurs."

Patco's Use of E-Banking

Patco used eBanking to make their weekly payroll payments. These weekly payroll payments had a predictable pattern about them. For example, they were always made on Fridays, they always originated from a computer in Patco's Sanford office with a single static Internet Protocol ("IP") address, and the highest payment made was $36,634.74. This predictability established a clear pattern of use.

Ocean Bank's Security Features

In October 2005, the Federal Financial Institutions Examination Council ("FFIEC"), an agency tasked with establishing uniform principles and standards for U.S. financial institutions, issued "Authentication in an Internet Banking Environment." This guidance was meant to help banks evaluate and implement authentication systems to protect eBanking clients. Specifically, the Guidance explains that existing authentication methodologies involve three basic "factors": (1) something the user knows (e.g., password, personal identification number); (2) something the user has (e.g., ATM card, smart card); and (3) something the user is (e.g., biometric characteristic, such as a fingerprint).

In response, Ocean Bank had a risk assessment done in order to comply with the FFIEC guidance. The results of the risk assessment determined that the eBanking system offered by Ocean Bank was at risk and would require more security and multifactor authentication. Ocean Bank worked with Jack Henry and Associates to bolster the security of their eBanking platform. Jack Henry improved the NetTeller platform to meet the FFIEC guidance and offered Ocean Bank two new security options. Ocean Bank chose the better of the two packages. In January of 2007 the bank implemented the six new and improved security features. The security features implemented were later outlined in a July 2012 1st Circuit Court of Appeals document as follows:

1. "User IDs and Passwords: The system required each authorized Patco employee to use both a company ID and password and a user-specific ID and password to access online banking.

2. Invisible Device Authentication: The system placed a "device cookie" onto customers' computers to identify particular computers used to access online banking. The device cookie would be used to help establish a secure communication session with the NetTeller environment and to contribute to the component risk score. Whenever the cookie was changed or was new, that impacted the risk score and potentially triggered challenge questions.

3. Risk Profiling: The system entailed the building of a risk profile for each customer by RSA/Cyota based on a number of different factors, including the location from which a user logged in, when/how often a user logged in, what a user did while on the system, and the size, type, and frequency of payment orders normally issued by the customer to the bank. The Premium Product noted the IP address that the customer typically used to log into online banking and added it to the customer profile. RSA/Cyota's adaptive monitoring provided a risk score to the bank for every log-in attempt and transaction based on a multitude of data, including but not limited to IP address, device cookie ID, Geo location, and transaction activity. If a user's transaction differed from its normal profile, RSA/Cyota reported to the bank an elevated risk score for that transaction. RSA/Cyota considered transactions gener-

ating risk scores in excess of 750, on a scale from 0 to 1,000, to be high-risk transactions. "Challenge questions," described below, were prompted any time the risk score for a transaction exceeded 750.

4. Challenge Questions: The system required users, during initial log-in, to select three challenge questions and responses. The challenge questions might be prompted for various reasons. For example, if the risk score associated with a particular transaction exceeded 750, the challenge questions would be triggered. If the challenge question responses entered by the user did not match the ones originally provided, the customer would receive an error message. If the customer was unable to answer the challenge questions in three attempts, the customer was blocked from online banking and would be required to contact the bank.

5. Dollar Amount Rule: The system permitted financial institutions to set a dollar threshold amount above which a transaction would automatically trigger the challenge questions even if the user ID, password, and device cookie were all valid. In August 2007, Ocean Bank set the dollar amount rule to $100,000. On June 6, 2008, Ocean Bank lowered the dollar amount rule from $100,000 to $1. After the Bank lowered the threshold to $1, Patco was prompted to answer challenge questions every time it initiated a transaction. In May 2009, when the fraud at issue in this case occurred, the dollar amount rule threshold remained at $1.

6. Subscription to the eFraud Network: The Jack Henry Premium Product provided Ocean Bank with a subscription to the eFraud Network, which compared characteristics of the transaction (such as the IP address of the user seeking access to the Bank's system) with those of known instances of fraud. The eFraud Network allowed financial institutions to report IP addresses or other discrete identifying characteristics identified with instances of fraud. An attempt to access a customer's NetTeller account initiated by someone with that characteristic would then be automatically blocked. The individual would not even be prompted for challenge questions."

Security Features NOT Implemented by Ocean Bank

Ocean Bank claims that they implemented the features detailed above on December 1, 2006. (Ocean Bank also began to offer customers the option to receive e-mail's that would alert them of any potentially fraudulent activity on their eBanking accounts. Patco did not sign up for these alert emails, claiming that they were not aware of their availability.) Detailed in the same court document mentioned above, the following is a list of additional security features that Ocean Bank opted NOT to implement:

1. "Out-of-Band Authentication: Jack Henry offered Ocean Bank a version of the NetTeller system that included an out-of-band authentication option. Examples of out-of-band authentication include notification to the customer, callback (voice) verification, e-mail approval from the customer, and cell phone based challenge/response processes.

2. User-Selected Picture: Ocean Bank's security procedures did not include the user-selected picture function that was available through Jack Henry's Premium option. Ocean Bank states that it did not utilize the user-selected picture function because it already utilized other anti-phishing controls.

3. Tokens: Tokens are physical devices (something the person has), such as a USB token device, a smart card, or a password-generating token. Tokens were not available from Jack Henry when Ocean Bank implemented its system in 2007, but were readily available to financial institutions at that time through other sources. Although People's United Bank has used tokens since at least January of 2008, Ocean Bank did not do so until after the fraud in this case occurred.

4. Monitoring of Risk-Scoring Reports: In May 2009, bank personnel did not monitor the risk-scoring reports received as part of the Premium Product package, nor did the bank conduct any other regular review

Appendix F

of transactions that generated high risk scores. In May 2009, the bank had the capability to conduct manual review of high-risk transactions through its transaction-profiling and risk-scoring system, but did not do so. The bank also had the ability to call a customer if it detected fraudulent activity, but did not do so. The bank began conducting manual reviews of high-risk transactions in late 2009, after the fraud in this case occurred. Since then, the bank has instituted a policy of calling the customer in the case of uncharacteristic transactions to inquire if the customer did indeed initiate the transaction."

Of these additional security measures not taken by Ocean Bank, number four - "Monitoring of Risk Scoring Reports" – was important to Patco's case. The failure of Ocean Bank to monitor their risk reports speaks to the importance of the management process. In this case, Ocean Bank relied on their technological processes to generate risk reports for customer accounts, yet did not follow up by having people analyze and monitor those reports.

Fraud and the Monitoring of Risk Scores

The fraudulent withdrawals from Patco's Ocean Bank accounts started on May 7, 2009, and continued over several days. The first withdrawal on May 7 in the amount of $56,594 was made using the online ID, password, and challenge question answers of an actual Patco employee. However, the money was sent to a number of separate accounts that had never been paid by Patco before. Moreover, the thieves used a computer and IP address that were not recognized by the banking system as belonging to Patco. Thus, the first fraudulent transaction triggered a risk score of 790. According to a court case document, Patco's risk scores for transaction were usually between 10 and 214. The unusually high score of 790 came from several criteria, among them that the transaction had a "Very high risk non-authenticated device", a "High risk transaction amount," and an "IP anomaly." not notified. The success of their first withdrawal prompted the thieves to continue taking money over the next few days. Each subsequent transaction prompted high risk scores, and Patco was not notified. Finally, on May 13 an employee got a notice in the mail that some of Patco's transferred funds had been returned to their account because of some invalid recipient account numbers. Patco alerted Ocean Bank about the fraudulent activities, prompting, the bank to block an additional transaction that had been processed that very morning.

The failure of the Ocean Bank security system to monitor high risk transactions allowed Patco to argue that Ocean Bank's security system was not "commercially reasonable." On the other hand, Ocean Bank argued that they could shift the risk of the transactions to Patco because the bank's security system and procedures were indeed commercially reasonable Under the Uniform Commercial Code § 4A.

Security Procedures & Commercially Reasonable Security

Under the Uniform Commercial Code § 4A, banks must accept the risk for unauthorized transfers and payments unless they are able to prove that either the payment order was authorized, or that they followed their commercially reasonable security procedures. The July 2012 court decision on the case explains two ways that Ocean Bank could have proved that the risk of the unauthorized payment transactions belonged to Patco. Ocean Bank would have been absolved of responsibility (and have proven that their security procedures were commercially reasonable) if they had taken into account:

1. "[T]he wishes of the customer expressed to the bank, the circumstances of the customer known to the bank, including the size, type and frequency of payment orders normally issued by the customer to the bank, alternative security procedures offered to the customer and security procedures in general use by customers and receiving banks similarly situated."

Patco V. Ocean Bank

This means that in order to be commercially reasonable, the bank must also be familiar with the specifics of the banking practices of their client. In this case, Patco argued that the security procedures implemented by Ocean Bank were not appropriate for their use of the banking system.

2. "If a bank and its customer have agreed that the authenticity of payment orders issued to the bank in the name of the customer as sender will be verified pursuant to a security procedure, a payment order received by the receiving bank is effective as the order of the customer, whether or not authorized, if:

(a) The security procedure is a commercially reasonable method of providing security against unauthorized payment orders; and

(b) The bank proves that it accepted the payment order in good faith and in compliance with the security procedure and any written agreement or instruction of the customer restricting acceptance of payment orders issued in the name of the customer. The bank is not required to follow an instruction that violates a written agreement with the customer or notice of which is not received at a time and in a manner affording the bank a reasonable opportunity to act on it before the payment order is accepted."

Patco argued that Ocean Bank could not transfer the risk onto them because the bank's security procedures were not commercially reasonable. In the Uniform Commercial Code § 4A-201, a "security procedure" regarding a payment is:

"a procedure established by agreement of a customer and a receiving bank for the purpose of (i) verifying that a payment order or communication amending or cancelling a payment order is that of the customer, or (ii) detecting error in the transmission or the content of the payment order or communication."

According to the court decision, a security procedure is considered to be commercially reasonable if:

"(a) The security procedure was chosen by the customer after the bank offered and the customer refused, a security procedure that was commercially reasonable for that customer; and

(b) The customer expressly agreed in writing to be bound by any payment order, whether or not authorized, issued in its name and accepted by the bank in compliance with the security procedure chosen by the customer."

Regarding letter (a) above, Patco argued that the security procedures implemented for all of their customers by Ocean Bank were not commercially reasonable for Patco. This points again to the breakdown in Ocean Bank's management. Implementing a "one-size-fits-all" security plan without considering the differing needs of their e-banking clients was not an ideal cybersecurity posture for the bank.

A Closer Look Ocean Bank's eBanking Security Procedures

After the risk analysis of their banking system, Ocean Bank opted to improve their security procedures. They purchased the best security package presented to them by John Henry and Associates, but opted not to implement additional security procedures. The security procedures that they chose were User IDs and Passwords, Invisible Device Authentication, Risk Profiling, Challenge Questions, Dollar Amount Rule, and a Subscription to the eFraud Network. Of these procedures, the two that Patco (and the court) believed were least commercially reasonable are Risk Profiling and the Dollar Amount Rule.

The Risk Profiling mechanism would use several factors of each transaction in order to give the trans-

Appendix F

action a risk score. The scores range from 0 to 1000, with 750 considered high risk. Each of the fraudulent transactions taken from Patco's account by cyber criminals scored as high risk. Despite generating these scores, the bank did not appear to monitor them. So while the security procedure was working on a computing level, the lack of monitoring by bank personnel rendered the risk reports useless in and of themselves.

The Dollar Amount Rule was deemed commercially unreasonable by the court because it did not take into account the banking practices of Patco, or the threat environment. The procedure worked by allowing the bank to select a minimum dollar amount that would activate a set of security challenge questions for the user to answer in addition to entering their user ID and password. When Ocean Bank implemented the dollar amount rule, they set the minimum amount to $100,000. This initial amount was appropriate for the transactions made by Patco, however a year later in 2008 the bank lowered the dollar amount to $1. This meant that instead of answering the security questions only when making the occasional large transaction, Patco had to answer the questions for every transaction they completed. This drastically increased the risk of every transaction and left Patco vulnerable to theft by keystrokers, who could eventually figure out the answers to the challenge questions.

In court, Patco argued that these security procedures were not commercially reasonable. The court agreed that these procedures led to the processing of unauthorized transactions, thus ruling them to be commercially unreasonable.This means that in order to be commercially reasonable, the bank must also be familiar with the specifics of the banking practices of their client. In this case, Patco argued that the security procedures implemented by Ocean Bank were not appropriate for their use of the banking system.

Case Analysis: The Opinion of Chief Judge Sandra Lynch

What did the court conclude about the argument over whether or not the security procedures implemented by Ocean Bank were commercially reasonable? The following opinion was written by Chief Judge Sandra Lynch on July 3, 2012:

"In our view, Ocean Bank did substantially increase the risk of fraud by asking for security answers for every $1 transaction, particularly for customers like Patco which had frequent, regular, and high dollar transfers. Then, when it had warning that such fraud was likely occurring in a given transaction, Ocean Bank neither monitored that transaction nor provided notice to customers before allowing the transaction to be completed. Because it had the capacity to do all of those things, yet failed to do so, we cannot conclude that its security system was commercially reasonable. We emphasize that it was these collective failures taken as a whole, rather than any single failure, which rendered Ocean Bank's security system commercially unreasonable.

The Jack Henry Premium Product was designed to harness the power of the risk-scoring system and included a device identification system to trigger an additional layer of authentication -- challenge questions -- whenever the bank's system detected unusual or suspicious transactions. In May of 2009, bank personnel did not monitor the risk-scoring reports, nor did the bank conduct any other regular review of transactions that generated high risk scores. Thus, the only result of a high risk score or an unidentified device was that a customer would be prompted to answer his or her challenge questions.

When Ocean Bank lowered the dollar amount rule from $100,000 to $1, it essentially deprived the complex Jack Henry risk-scoring system of its core functionality. The $1 dollar amount rule guaranteed that challenge questions would be triggered on every transaction unless caught by a separate eFraud network which depended on the use of known fraudulent IP addresses. The eFraud network was of no use if the address and like information were not already known to law enforcement. Accordingly, cyber criminals equipped with keyloggers had the much more frequent opportunity to capture all information necessary to compromise an account every time the customer initiated an ACH transaction. In Patco's case, ACH transactions were initiated at least weekly, and often several times per week. In the event a customer's computer became infected with a keylogger, it was likely that the customer would be prompted to answer its challenge questions before the malware was discovered and removed from the customer's computer.

Ocean Bank's decision to set the dollar amount rule at $1 for all of its customers also ignored Article 4A's mandate that security procedures take into account "the circumstances of the customer" known to the bank. Article 4A directs banks to consider such circumstances as "the size, type and frequency of payment orders normally issued by the customer to the bank." Id. In Patco's case, these characteristics were regular and predictable. Patco used eBanking primarily to make payroll payments to employees. These payments were made weekly, generally on Fridays; they originated from a single static IP address; and they were always made from the same set of computers at Patco's offices in Sanford, Maine. The highest such payment Patco ever made was $36,634.74, well below the former $100,000 threshold. The bank does not assert that it ever offered to adjust the threshold amount for particular customers. Instead, the bank adopted a "one- size-fits-all" dollar amount rule of $1 for its customers."

Conclusion

Patco v. Ocean Bank is a significant case for the cybersecurity world, not just because of the court's decision regarding commercially reasonable security procedures under UCC Article 4A. The case is important because it shows that computers alone cannot protect financial institutions and their client's money. A fully comprehensive risk monitoring strategy ought to include human management and analysis.

Ocean Bank implemented a risk reporting system that worked to generate accurate risk scores. Along with other controls, they implemented multifactor authentication, which is a standard for mitigating risk. Despite these efforts to implement effective automated security procedures, the court still ruled that their security procedures were not commercially reasonable. In the opinion of the court, there were many management oversights that led to nearly a half a million dollars in losses to Patco.

Perhaps it is not enough to rely solely on automation in the cyber realm. As cybersecurity software evolves to prevent new cyber crime tactics, cyber criminals also design new ways to outsmart those security controls. While this battle will likely never end, better cybersecurity management can help to reduce risk by complimenting technological security procedures. Both financial institutions and cyber criminals are armed with computers, so it is up to the human element to tilt the scales to one side or the other. Thus, innovations in risk management must come not only from software upgrades and computer programs, but also from the ideas and processes implemented by risk managers.

Appendix: From the Opinion of Judge Lynch

"… The activities of May 7 having successfully resulted in payment, on Friday, May 8, 2009, unknown third parties again successfully initiated an ACH payment order from Patco's account, this time for $115,620.26. As before, the perpetrators wired money to multiple individual accounts to which Patco had never before sent funds. The perpetrators again used a device that was not recognized by Ocean Bank's system. The payment order originated from the same IP address as the day before. The transaction was larger by several magni-

Appendix F

tudes than any ACH transfer Patco had ever made to third parties. Despite these unusual characteristics, the bank again took no steps to notify Patco and batched and processed the transaction as usual, which was paid by the bank on Monday, May 11, 2009.

On May 11, 12, and 13, unknown third parties initiated further withdrawals from Patco's account in the amounts of $99,068, $91,959, and $113,647, respectively. Like the prior fraudulent transactions, these transactions were uncharacteristic in that they sent money to numerous individuals to whom Patco had never before sent funds, were for greater amounts than Patco's ordinary third-party transactions, were sent from computers that were not recognized by Ocean Bank's system, and originated from IP addresses that were not recognized as valid IP addresses of Patco. As a result of these unusual characteristics, the transactions continued to generate higher than normal risk scores. The May 11 transaction generated a risk score of 720, the May 12 transaction triggered a risk score of score of 785. The Bank did not manually review any of these transactions to determine their legitimacy or notify Patco.

Portions of the transfers, beginning with the first transfer initiated on May 7, 2009, were automatically returned to the bank because certain of the account numbers to which the money was slated to be transferred were invalid. As a result, the bank sent limited "return" notices to the home of Mark Patterson, one of Patco's principals, via U.S. mail. Patterson received the first such notice after work on the evening of May 13, six days after the allegedly fraudulent withdrawals began.

The next morning, on May 14, 2009, Patco called the bank to inform it that Patco had not authorized the transactions. Also on the morning of May 14, another alleged fraudulent transaction was initiated from Patco's account in the amount of $111,963. Despite the information from Patco, the bank initially processed this payment order on May 15, 2009. However, because of the alert from Patco of the ongoing fraud, the bank then took steps to block completion of a portion of this transaction and recovered a portion of the transferred funds shortly thereafter.

At the end of the string of thefts, the amount of money fraudulently withdrawn from Patco's account totaled $588,851.26, of which $243,406.83 was automatically returned or blocked and recovered."

"According to Ocean Bank, on May 14, 2009, immediately after the allegedly fraudulent withdrawals occurred, the bank gave instructions to Patco. It instructed Patco to disconnect the computers it used for electronic banking from its network; to stop using these computers for work purposes; to leave the computers turned on; and to bring in a third-party forensic professional or law enforcement to create a forensic image of the computers to determine whether a security breach had occurred. Ocean Bank claims, and Patco disputes, that Patco did not isolate its computers or forensically preserve the hard drives; and that Patco employees continued to use their computers during the week following the alleged fraud. In another dispute of fact, Patco states that Ocean Bank recommended only that Patco check its system for a security breach using a third-party forensic professional, which Patco did.

Shortly after the fraudulent transfers, Patco hired an IT consultant, who ran anti-malware scans on the computers. A remnant of a Zeus/Zbot malware was found. However, the Zeus/Zbot malware, which contained the encryption key for the Zeus/Zbot configuration file, was quarantined and then deleted by the anti-malware scan. Without the encryption key, it is impossible to decrypt the configuration file and identify what information, if any, the Zeus/Zbot malware would have captured, if in fact it was of a type that would have intercepted authentication credentials."

Appendix G: Case Study
Technology Needs Management: US-CERT's Cybersecurity Analysis and Warning System

Case Significance

The US-CERT's failed attempt at creating a cyber analysis and warning system demonstrates that while technology is an essential part of a warning system, hardware and software alone cannot achieve the level of analysis and information sharing needed to effectively warn of cyber attacks.

Summary of Conclusions

- It is up to strong managers to deconstruct the four capabilities of the system, find the gaps, and decide how to best fill in those gaps.
- Once capability gaps are filled, managers must maintain a high level of quality control in order to ensure that the warning system remains effective in the long run.
- Without excellent managers, the US-CERT warning system will remain only moderately effective.

Abstract

The public and private sectors rely on advance cyber warnings to protect computer-based critical infrastructure, and national security systems from devastating cyber attacks. Computers, software, and the computer programmers that develop them are the critical foundations of a successful cyber warning system. However, the creation of such a cyber warning system cannot be achieved using technology and technological experts alone. The difficult and complex capability to warn of cyber attacks requires excellent managers to properly plan, budget, and oversee the execution of the system. Managers must identify their High Level Requirements, define the necessary capabilities, implement the attributes of those capabilities, oversee the execution of the system, and manage its daily operations. When they were tasked with creating a national cyber analysis and warning system, the United State's Computer Emergency Readiness Team (US-CERT) failed to apply the management techniques needed to realize their assignment. US-CERT's failure of management resulted in a national cyber analysis and warning system with capability gaps, thus leaving critical cyber-based infrastructure vulnerable to attack.

US-Cert Profile

Tasked with safeguarding the United States from cyber attacks, the United States Computer Emergency Readiness Team (US-CERT) was formed in 2003 as the 24-hour operational arm of the Department of Homeland Security's (DHS) National Cyber Security Division (NCSD). The mission of the US-CERT is to take charge of improving the nation's cybersecurity posture by organizing information sharing, and managing cyber risks to America's cyber-based critical infrastructure. The US-CERT is expected to work across sectors in order to keep both public and private critical infrastructure stakeholders apprised of cybersecurity threats.

United States' Cybersecurity Environment

One essential component in protecting vulnerable cyber-based critical infrastructure from attacks is a strong warning system. Cyber technology has been and continues to be developed and used as weaponry by nation states, thus making it essential that governments invest heavily in cybersecurity. Failing to protect critical systems can result in devastating consequences to an unprotected country. The United States government is well aware of the potential harm that can be caused by cyber war. This knowledge comes from first hand experience. By 2012, in the details of a Congressional research report, the public learned about a massive cyber attack on an Iranian uranium enrichment facility. The report indicates that, through a series of cyber attacks likely spread over several years, a powerful worm called Stuxnet infected and shut down centrifuges at the Natanz nuclear facility. The worm damaged computers, expensive manufacturing equipment, and delayed Iran's ability to enrich uranium. Stuxnet also demonstrates the potentially devastating results of a cyber attack on the critical infrastructure of any given country.[1]

Having allegedly perpetrated a major cyber attack on a foreign power, the U.S. intelligence and defense communities do not merely have the theoretical basis for an attack; they know what the exploitation of a vulnerability can look like. Moreover, having made the first move, the U.S. must be prepared for cyber retaliation. Therefore, the success of Stuxnet reinforces the need for the United States government to implement a comprehensive cyber warning system.

A cybersecurity warning system is essential to America's national security and defense. United States critical infrastructure relies heavily on interconnected computer systems. The power grid, air traffic controls, banks and markets, health records, and criminal databases are all entrenched within cyberspace. National security secrets and defense department plans are also vulnerable to the battleground that has materialized in cyberspace. Both the government and the private sector are locked into the high-stakes effort to prevent critical infrastructure assets from being disturbed and/or destroyed by cyber threats.

Rogue nations, terrorist groups, organized crime groups, and hacktivists are some of the actors that have much to gain by launching cyber attacks against the United States. If, for example, the terrorist group Al-Qaeda wanted to perpetrate another attack on the United States using airplanes, theoretically they could hack into and disrupt air traffic control systems. What might happen if the real-time data being received by air traffic controllers was manipulated by a malicious cyber attack? How would the FAA know whether or not there is an immediate threat lurking in its air traffic control systems?

While the hypothetical above has yet to happen, there have been several real cybersecurity breaches of United States computers within the past several years. Companies like Google have been hacked, a water filtration plant in Pennsylvania was compromised, and attempts at intrusion into critical government systems occur every day. Because many nations and individual actors around the world continue to build and strengthen their presence and capabilities within cyberspace, the United States government created the United States Computer Emergency Readiness Team (US-CERT). It is the US-CERT that has been given the responsibility of operating a cyber warning system.

DHS, NCSD, and US-CERT's Roles and Responsibilities

Operating under the Department of Homeland Security's (DHS) National Cyber Security Division (NCSD), the US-CERT runs a twenty-four hour cybersecurity operations center that, "accepts, triages, and collaboratively responds to incidents; provides technical assistance to information system operators; and disseminates timely notifications regarding current and potential security threats and vulnerabilities."[3] The many responsibilities overseen by the US-CERT are also meant to help critical infrastructure stakeholders in the public and private sectors. The US-CERT therefore acts as a hub for the public-private relationship integral to protecting critical cyber assets. Specifically, and most relevant to this

---

1. Paul K. Kerr, John Rollins & Catherine A. Theohary, Congressional Research Service, R41524, *The Stuxnet Computer Worm: Harbinger of an Emerging Warfare Capability* (2010).

2. *http://www.us-cert.gov/about-us/*

Appendix G

case study, the US-CERT is responsible for analyzing cyber threats, and warning of cyber attacks. It is important to note that the capabilities to analyze and warn go hand in hand. This is because an established baseline of acceptable cyber activity must be analyzed in order to discover an anomaly. If an anomaly is detected, analysts can investigate whether or not a threat is present. Once US-CERT analysts discover a threat, they can issue the appropriate warning.

As mentioned above, one of the most important capabilities of US-CERT is to notify appropriate stakeholders of current and potential cyber threats in a timely manner. As is common for an undertaking of such importance and magnitude, the Government Accountability Office (GAO) did an investigation into US-CERT's ability to effectively execute their cybersecurity capabilities. GAO wanted to "(1) identify key attributes of cyber analysis and warning capabilities, (2) compare these attributes with US-CERT's current capabilities to identify whether there are gaps, and (3) identify US-CERT's challenges to developing and implementing key attributes and a successful national cyber analysis and warning capability."[2]

2008 GAO Report

In July of 2008, the GAO released a detailed report to a subcommittee of the House of Representatives Committee on Homeland Security entitled, Cyber Analysis and Warning: DHS Faces Challenges in Establishing a Comprehensive National Capability. The GAO found that US-CERT failed to implement many key attributes of the capability to warn of cyber incidents. The GAO findings made it clear that US-CERT would not be effectively executing their critical role to analyze and warn in the cybersecurity community until corrective actions were taken. The necessary corrective actions were outlined in great detail within the report.

What is a Cyber Analysis and Warning System?

A cyber warning system is essential in the battle to protect U.S. cyber infrastructure from cyber attacks. When fully realized, a national cyber warning system will allow experts to analyze data from past attacks in order to warn public and private sector stakeholders of impending attacks on their critical assets. A cyber analysis and warning system ought to provide officials with the information needed to foresee an attack before it occurs, thereby increasing the chances of preventing the attack. This is accomplished through timely cross-sector information sharing and resource allocation. Operating such an important and complicated system is no easy task. Managers of a national cybersecurity warning system must draw from an impeccable set of managerial skills in order to provide the appropriate level of planning and coordination needed to protect the nation from harm.

First, those running a cyber warning system must know exactly what they are issuing warnings about. This means that a cyber analysis and warning system must be able to analyze information and then decide how to issue a warning, who the warning should go to, why the warning is critical, and offer guidance about how such warnings ought to be responded to. In this way, the ability to analyze and warn are closely joined together. The cornerstone of a good cyber analysis and warning system is having a baseline that establishes normal network activities. Understanding the baseline of a network allows analysts to detect anomalies when they occur. Once an anomaly is detected, the appropriate response can be made. With knowledge of the baseline as the barometer, a warning system can be developed that keeps tabs on cyber activities and notifies relevant parties of an incident. Having a clear mission and process, along with technical abilities is one part of executing an effective warning system. The other part is having an outstanding organization planning, overseeing, and running the system.

---

2. *GAO. Cyber Analysis and Warning: DHS Faces Challenges in Establishing a Comprehensive National Capability. 2008*

Case Study: The US-CERT's Cybersecurity Analysis and Warning System

Second, in the age of global cyber terrorism, a cyber analysis and warning system must be working twenty-four hours a day, all year long. A fully functional warning system will be staffed with a team of experts with technological and managerial skills. The staff of the warning system will be able to analyze the past, and present, in order to attempt to predict future cyber incidents. Proper analysis leads to legitimate and timely warnings to both public and private sector stakeholders. A strong attention to process and detail must be paid in order to realize a comprehensive 24/7 cybersecurity warning system. Such a focus can only be achieved through strong planning, budgeting, management, and execution. Thus, a successful cyber warning system must have talented personnel with the technical abilities to execute the mission, as well as strong managerial skills to oversee the mission.

Challenges of Operating a Successful Cyber Warning System

One key function of an effective cyber analysis and warning system is the ability to predict an attack before it happens. The ability to defend against future attacks and to identify emerging threats is a necessary preventative measure of a national cyber analysis and warning system. Because of the potentially devastating consequences of a cyber attack on U.S. critical infrastructure or on the intelligence community, the ability to predict such an attack is imperative. The capability to predict who might attack, when the attack may occur, what their capabilities are, and the potential consequences of the attack are just a few examples of pieces of information that might make it easier to predict cyber attacks. When shared across the public and private sectors, this sort of valuable information can act as the basis for a coordinated cybersecurity effort.

For example, one of the lessons learned after the attacks on the Pentagon and the World Trade Center on September 11, 2001 was that the U.S. government did not have a satisfactory and unified system in place to prevent the events. Hijackers were able to carry weapons onto airplanes, the cockpit doors on the planes were penetrable, no armed security personnel were on any of the flights, and the U.S. intelligence community did not warn airport authorities of the malevolent intentions of the men boarding the planes. In short, there were a number of breakdowns in communication, as well as technological and physical failures on the part of government and law enforcement community.

Case Study: The US-CERT Cyber Analysis and Warning System

GAO's Expectations & Gap Analysis

As determined by the above-mentioned law and policies, the formation of DHS was, among other reasons, a way to protect America from various attacks. In order to protect America from cyber attacks, DHS created the US-CERT and placed them in charge of the national warning system. The task of US-CERT and the cyber warning system is critical to national security because of their contribution to preparing for, preventing, and responding to potentially devastating cyber attacks on U.S. critical infrastructure. Thus, the importance of the role given to US-CERT to head the warning system meant that their efforts would be scrutinized. The need for US-CERT to succeed led the GAO to complete a gap analysis of their existing capabilities in order to determine the needs of the warning system. The gap analysis looked at the capabilities that US-CERT would need in order to implement a successful warning system, and then subtracted their current capabilities to warn. This left the GAO with the gaps in the warning system. The GAO wrote a report describing the 10 gaps that they identified in the warning system.

In their 2008 report, the GAO identified the attributes needed by US-CERT in order to fulfill the capability to analyze cyber incidents and to create a warning system. The GAO found that the capabilities to analyze and warn consist of:

Appendix G

1. monitoring network activity to detect anomalies;

2. analyzing information and investigating anomalies to determine whether they are threats;

3. warning appropriate officials with timely and actionable threat and mitigation information; and

4. responding to the threat.

If in place, these four specific capabilities constitute an effective cyber threat warning system. The GAO defined the attributes that make up each capability. The attributes in the chart below reveal how the warning system is meant to work. The capability to Monitor, Analyze, Warn, and Respond are each made up of several attributes. A capability is effective if each one of the attribute identified for it is implemented.

In the chart below, almost like an addition problem, the attributes of "contain and mitigate the incident," plus "recover from damages and remediate vulnerabilities," plus "evaluate actions and incorporate lessons learned" equals the capability of Response. The capabilities of Monitoring, plus Analysis, plus Warning, plus Response equals a cyber analysis and warning system. Thus, in the opinion of the GAO, an effective cyber analysis and warning system would accomplish all four capabilities by fulfilling each of the 15 associated attributes. However, if the US-CERT failed to properly execute each of the attributes and capabilities, the cyber analysis and warning system would not be functioning to the level necessary to protect the nation from cyber attacks.

Key Attributes of Cyber Analysis Warning Capabilities	
Capability	**Attribute**
Monitoring	• Establish a baseline understanding of network assets and normal network traffic volume and flow • Assess risks to network assets • Obtain internal information on network operations via technical tools and user reports • Obtain external information on threats, vulnerabilities, and incidents through various relationships, alerts, and other sources. • Detect anomalous activities.
Analysis	• Verify that an anomaly is an incident (threat of attack or actual attack) • Investigate the incident to identify the type of cyber attack, estimate impact, and collect evidence • Identify possible actions to mitigate the impact of the incident • Integrate results into predictive analysis of broader implications or potential future attack
Warning	• Develop attack and other notifications that are targeted and actionable • Provide notifications in a timely manner • Distribute notifications using appropriate communications methods
Response	• Develop attack and other notifications that are targeted and actionable • Provide notifications in a timely manner • Distribute notifications using appropriate communications methods

Source: *GAO Analysis*

Case Study: The US-CERT's Cybersecurity Analysis and Warning System

Gaps Identified in US-CERT's Warning System

In the 2008 report entitled Cyber Analysis and Warning: DHS Faces Challenges in Establishing a Comprehensive National Capability, GAO released findings concluding that DHS had not incorporated all of the attributes necessary to achieve the capabilities essential to a comprehensive cyber analysis and warning system. The aforementioned capabilities and attributes that comprise the capabilities were identified as non-negotiable by the GAO. Meaning, the GAO would not acknowledge that the warning system was fully capable of performing the way it ought to until the capability gaps were filled. Through their investigation, the GAO identified and explained the attributes that comprise an optimally functioning monitoring capability, and then broke down the attributes that the US-CERT failed to implement.

Monitoring

The first attribute of the capability of monitoring is to understand a networks baseline. US-CERT established a limited baseline to understand normal network traffic for sixteen participating federal entities. However, they have not established a baseline for national-level network traffic for critical infrastructure information systems. This gap exists in federal, state, and local government, as well as private sector information systems. The second attribute is to perform network risk assessments. US-CERT does not perform network risk assessments for network assets. The third attribute is to obtain network information using technical tools. US-CERT uses technical tools to gain information about network operations, however their ability is reduced because of the need for manual analysis. The fourth attribute is to gather and share information about threat, vulnerabilities, and incidents. The US-CERT obtains information on threats, vulnerabilities, and incidents from the private sector and federal, state, local, and foreign governments. Despite this, private sector networks are not monitored and are not required to report information or incidents to US-CERT. The fifth attribute is to detect network anomalies. In order to detect network anomalies, the US-CERT monitors network traffic but does not monitor private sector and other non-federal networks.

Analyzing

The first attribute of the capability to analyze is to confirm that a network anomaly is an incident. While US-CERT works to confirm incidents within its public-private partnership, the overall weakness of the monitoring capability impedes their ability to scrutinize anomalies and verify threats. The second attribute is to identify the kind of cyber attack and determine the consequences of it. Although US-CERT is able to investigate incidents, there capacity to consider multiple incidents at once is inadequate. The third attribute is to find options to mitigate incident impact. US-CERT's network analysts cooperate within US-CERT in order to find appropriate forms of mitigation. However, due to the sensitive nature of the information that they handle, analysts are only able to seek limited help from the outside. The fourth attribute of the capability of analyzing is to engage in predictive analysis. Although US-CERT leadership is attempting to evolve their tactical views of cyber infrastructure, they do not have the capacity to predict future cyber attacks.

Warning

The first attribute of the capability of warning is to develop helpful and specific attack notifications. US-CERT does develop and share various notifications, however many government entities that receive them complain that the notifications do not contain novel information. The second attribute is to provide prompt notifications. US-CERT has not been consistent in providing timely notifications because of the need to screen classified information, and the

Appendix G

need for a assessment process to ensure precise information. The third attribute of the capability of warning is to disseminate notifications using the most useful channels of communication, an attribute which US-CERT is not realizing.

Responding

The first attribute of the capability of responding is to isolate and lessen the damages of cyber incidents, but US-CERT does not have the authority to make any federal agencies act during an incident. The second attribute is to recover from an attack. US-CERT has two teams of experts that respond to serious attacks on federal agencies, however officials there claim that they would need an additional three teams in order to properly recover from a national incident. The third attribute of the capability of responding is to be able to assess actions and integrate lessons learned. US-CERT uses training exercises that mimic national cybersecurity incidents and then use the lessons learned to gauge their performance. Despite this effort, US-CERT has yet to establish performance measures in order to determine the effectiveness of their training exercises.

The aspects of the attributes that US-CERT failed to incorporate into their capabilities rendered the capabilities incomplete, which is unacceptable within the cyber threat environment. The US-CERT cyber analysis and warning system is far too important to national security to be underdeveloped. As executed at the time of the GAO investigation, the warning system did not reflect the overall mission of DHS, NCSD, and US-CERT to continually maintain the highest level of cybersecurity possible. US-CERT's failure to meet their high level mission requirements by not properly executing the attributes and capabilities of a national cyber warning system stemmed from problems with management. (See the Appendix for more detailed GAO findings from their investigation of US-CERT.)

Analysis

A good approach to managing a mission like that of the US-CERT national cyber warning system is formulaic. First, managers must identify their high level mission requirements. For US-CERT, one of the mission requirements received from Congress and the president was to maintain and work to improve the cybersecurity posture of the United States. Second, managers must define their capabilities. This is done by evaluating existing capabilities, comparing them to needed capabilities, and then identifying the capability gaps. Third, managers must deconstruct the capabilities that they need down to attributes. Essentially, the attributes of a capability answer the question, 'How do I build the system that I need to build?'. In order to build a complex and critical cyber analysis and warning system, manager must be exceptional.

Deconstructing the attributes of the four capabilities needed for a cyber warning system, and analyzing the capability gaps identified by GAO can provide insight into the managerial qualities needed to oversee them. For example, within the capability of Monitoring is the attribute to detect anomalous activities. According to GAO, while US-CERT "detects anomalies based on its monitoring of network traffic flow," it "does not detect anomalies across the nation's computer-reliant critical infrastructure." What is the managerial deficit in this example? What kind of manager would be able to solve the problem of widening the capacity to detect anomalies to more networks across the country? What qualities, philosophies, and strengths must a manager possess in order to improve on this attribute? Essentially, the needs of the mission dictate the qualities needed by those managers that would offer the best potential for success.

Conclusion

The following is a review of the gaps identified by GAO in the US-CERT cyber analysis and warning system:

Monitoring:

- US-CERT has not established a baseline for national-level network traffic for critical infrastructure information systems on the federal, state, and local government levels, as well as in private sector information systems.
- US-CERT does not perform network risk assessments for network assets.
- US-CERT uses technical tools to gain information about network operations, however their ability is reduced because of the need for manual analysis.
- Private sector networks are not monitored and are not required to report information or incidents to US-CERT.
- US-CERT monitors network traffic but does not monitor private sector and other non-federal networks.

Analyzing:

- The overall weakness of their monitoring capability impedes US-CERT's ability to scrutinize anomalies and verify threats.
- US-CERT's capacity to consider multiple incidents at once is inadequate.
- Due to the sensitive nature of the information that they handle, analysts are only able to seek limited help from the outside.
- US-CERT does not have the capacity to predict future cyber attacks.

Warning:

- Many government entities that receive US-CERT notifications complain that the notifications do not contain novel information.
- US-CERT has not been consistent in providing timely notifications because of the need to screen classified information, and the need for a assessment process to ensure precise information.
- US-CERT does not disseminate notifications using the most suitable channels of communication.

Responding:

- US-CERT does not have the authority to make any federal agencies act during an incident.
- US-CERT would need an additional three teams in order to properly recover from a national incident.
- US-CERT has yet to establish performance measures in order to determine the effectiveness of their training exercises.

The US-CERT cyber analysis and warning system is far too important to national security to contain gaps that render it a failure. In order to build the kind of cyber analysis and warning system that the United States

Appendix G

needs to protect itself from catastrophic harm, the US-CERT must look to strong managers. While technology is an essential part of a warning system, hardware and software alone cannot achieve the level of analysis and information sharing needed to effectively warn of cyber attacks. It is up to strong managers to deconstruct the four capabilities of the system, find the gaps, and decide how to best fill in those gaps. Once the gaps are filled, managers must maintain a high level of quality control in order to ensure that the warning system remains effective in the long run.

Any managers overseeing the mission of the US-CERT cyber analysis and warning system must have the ability to maintain excellence by employing and overseeing the appropriate people, processes, and technology. Without excellent managers, the US-CERT warning system will remain only moderately effective. This is not acceptable. The stakes are too high and the United States government cannot gamble with cybersecurity preparedness.

Appendix

Policy Establishing US-CERT and a National Cyber Analysis and Warning System

Five primary federal law and policy documents established the need for the United States government to create a cyber analysis and warning system. Those documents are the Homeland Security Act of 2002, the National Strategy to Secure Cyberspace (2003), Homeland Security Presidential Directive 7 (2003), and the National Response Framework (2008), and Homeland Security Presidential Directive 23 (2008). The following table contains detailed information from GAO report 08-588 explains how each document contributes to the expectations of the US-CERT cyber analysis and warning system currently in place.

Document	Implications for a Cyber Analysis and Warning System
Homeland Security Act of 2002	"The Homeland Security Act of 2002 established the Department of Homeland Security and gave it lead responsibility for preventing terrorist attacks in the United States, reducing the vulnerability of the United States to terrorist attacks, and minimizing the damage and assisting in recovery from attacks that do occur. The act assigned the department, among other things, a number of critical infrastructure protection responsibilities, including gathering of threat information, including cyber-related, from law enforcement, intelligence sources, and other agencies of the federal, state, and local governments and private sector entities to identify, assess, and understand threats; carrying out assessments of the vulnerabilities of key resources to determine the risks posed by attacks; and integrating information, analyses, and vulnerability assessments in order to identify priorities for protection. In addition, the department is responsible for disseminating, as appropriate, information that it analyzes—both within the department and to other federal, state, and local government agencies and private sector entities—to assist in the deterrence, prevention, preemption of, or response to terrorist acts."

Appendix

Document	Implications for a Cyber Analysis and Warning System
National Strategy to Secure Cyberspace	"The National Strategy to Secure Cyberspace proposes that a public/private architecture be provided for analyzing, warning, and managing incidents of national significance. The strategy states that cyber analysis includes both (1) tactical analytical support during a cyber incident and (2) strategic analyses of threats. Tactical support involves providing current information on specific factors associated with incidents under investigation or specific identified vulnerabilities. Examples of tactical support include analysis of (1) a computer virus delivery mechanism to issue immediate guidance on ways to prevent or mitigate damage related to an imminent threat or (2) a specific computer intrusion or set of intrusions to determine the perpetrator, motive, and method of attack. Strategic analysis is predictive in that it looks beyond one specific incident to consider a broader set of incidents or implications that may indicate a potential future threat of national importance. For example, strategic analyses may identify long-term vulnerability and threat trends that provide advance warnings of increased risk, such as emerging attack methods. Strategic analyses are intended to provide policymakers with information that they can use to anticipate and prepare for attacks, thereby diminishing the damage from such attacks."
Homeland Security Presidential Directive 7 (HSPD 7)	"HSPD 7 directs DHS to, among other things, serve as the focal point for securing cyberspace. This includes analysis, warning, information sharing, vulnerability reduction, mitigation, and recovery efforts for critical infrastructure information systems. It also directs DHS to develop a national indications and warnings architecture for infrastructure protection and capabilities, including cyber, that will facilitate an understanding of baseline infrastructure operations, the identification of indicators and precursors to an attack, and create a surge capacity for detecting and analyzing patterns of potential attacks."

Appendix G

Document	Implications for a Cyber Analysis and Warning System
National Response Framework	"The National Response Framework, issued by DHS in January 2008, provides guidance to coordinate cyber incident response among federal entities and, upon request, state and local governments and private sector entities. Specifically, the Cyber Incident Annex describes the framework for federal cyber incident response in the event of a cyber-related incident of national significance affecting the critical national processes. Further, the annex formalizes the National Cyber Response Coordination Group (NCRCG). As established under the preceding National Response Plan, the NCRCG continues to be cochaired by DHS's National Cyber Security Division (NCSD), the Department of Justice's Computer Crime and Intellectual Property Section, and the DOD. It is to bring together officials from all agencies that have responsibility for cybersecurity and the sector-specific agencies identified in HSPD 7. The group coordinates intergovernmental and public/private preparedness and response to and recovery from national-level cyber incidents and physical attacks that have significant cyber-related consequences. During and in anticipation of such an incident, the NCRCG's senior-level membership is responsible for providing subject matter expertise, recommendations, and strategic policy support and ensuring that the full range of federal capabilities is deployed in a coordinated and effective fashion."
Homeland Security Presidential Directive 23 (HSPD 23)	"In January 2008, the President issued HSPD 23—also referred to as National Security Presidential Directive 54 and the President's "Cyber Initiative"—to improve the federal government's cybersecurity efforts, including protecting against intrusion attempts and better anticipating future threats. While the directive is a classified document, US-CERT officials stated that it includes steps to enhance cyber analysis related efforts, such as requirements that federal agencies implement a centralized monitoring tool and that the federal government reduce the number of connections to the Internet, referred to as Trusted Internet Connections."

Glossary

Acceptable quality levels (AQL): a metric that establishes a project's allowable variation from its performance standard.

Acquisition program baseline (APB): a document, produced by a mathematical algorithm, that deconstructs an operational model to provide quantified parameters for a program's performance, cost, and schedule.

Active response: a type of response to a cyber attack that may include terminating a session by shutting it down and resetting it later; altering a network's configuration to deter an attack or prevent future attacks; and acts of deception, such as the creation of a honeypot.

Actual cost (AC): the actual costs incurred by a project for the work completed at any given point in the project's timeline; also known as actual cost of work performed (ACWP).

Actual cost of work performed (ACWP): see *actual cost (AC)*.

Administrative Procedure Act (APA): a 1946 law that established the procedures by which federal departments and agencies may propose and enact new regulations.

Advance notice of proposed rulemaking (ANPR): a formal invitation published in the *Federal Register* that encourages the public to participate in shaping a proposed regulation.

Advanced persistent threats (APT): a category of sophisticated cyber attacks usually conducted as espionage by highly capable and motivated entities, such as adversarial governments or terrorist groups.

Advanced Research Project Agency Network (ARPANET): a system of interconnected research computers, initially launched in 1969, that served as a predecessor to the modern Internet

Alternative hypothesis: represents the relationship between the variables being tested. The goal of research is to reject the null hypothesis in favor of the alternative hypothesis.

Assumptions: the reasonable expectations of actions, tools, and policies that may already be in place to protect critical assets, or reasonable expectations of the risk faced.

Attribution: the act of associating an IP address with a specific computer.

Attribution problem: a problem resulting from the fact that the positive attribution and identification of a cyber attacker is very difficult.

Audit: the professional evaluation of a company's systems and procedures to ensure that they are meeting their core objectives.

Automatic Data Processing Act: See *Brooks Act*.

Behavior/anomaly detection: a method for detecting cyber attacks that monitors for network activity falling outside of the typical behavior of users and systems on a network.

Beyond a reasonable doubt: a legal standard asserting that the evidence against a defendant must be so strong that there remains no reasonable doubt that he or she committed a crime.

Glossary (A-C)

Bias: a prejudice that infers an answer or leads a survey participant to choose a certain answer.

Bill: a proposed piece of legislation.

Binary: the "language," consisting of a series of 0s and 1s, that a computer works with.

Board of directors: a body that provides leadership for a corporation and formulates corporate business strategy at the highest level.

Border Gateway Protocol (BGP): a protocol that provides a common language and methodology to facilitate the efficient travel of information over the Internet; can be understood as the "traffic laws of the Internet."

Botnet: a collection of systems that have been compromised for the purpose of creating a network of "zombie" computers that can be used in a cyber attack. Botnets are typically employed to conduct large-scale attacks that shut down networks and systems on the Internet.

Brooks Act: a 1965 law that attempted to make federal computer procurement a more coordinated effort. The Brooks Act gave the General Services Administration broad responsibility for overseeing how computer equipment would be procured and used by federal departments and agencies, and also charged the Department of Commerce with creating security standards for computer systems. Officially referred to as the *Automatic Data Processing Act*.

Brute force attack: the process of using a software program to guess passwords; the greater the complexity of a password, the lower the effectiveness of a brute force attack.

Budget at completion (BAC): the total budgeted cost originally allocated for a project.

Budgeted cost of work performed (BCWP): see *earned value (EV)*.

Budgeted cost of work scheduled (BCWS): see *planned value (PV)*.

Business continuity plan: a company's specific plan to restore service after a cybersecurity incident.

Business judgment rule (BJR): a core principle of corporate law asserting that courts will not second-guess a business decision made by a director or corporate officer if it was reasonably well-informed and made with the best interests of the company in mind.

Bylaws: the rules adopted by a corporation for its operations.

Cache: a high-speed and expensive-to-produce form of volatile memory that a CPU can use as a type of "scratch paper" while performing calculations.

Capability gaps: areas in which specific powers or abilities are needed.

Capability-based planning: the process of defining a program's activities and charting out a program's life cycle, based on the capability that the program has been charged to build.

Caremark standard: a legal standard asserting that directors and corporate officers may be held liable for damages if they (1) fail to implement an internal system to monitor compliance and risk, or if they (2) voluntarily deprive themselves of information about serious risks or problems requiring their attention.

Central processing unit (CPU): the "brain" or "command station" of a computer. The CPU has two basic functions: performing calculations directed by a user, and moving information from one location to another.

Charter: a document that describes a company's purpose and outlines other basic information about the company.

Glossary

Chief executive officer (CEO): the individual who acts as a company's lead manager.

Chief information officer (CIO): an individual who, along with the CEO, is responsible for keeping the board of directors informed about a company's latest cyber risks, vulnerabilities, and operations.

Chief Information Officers Council (CIO Council): a body created by President Clinton with Executive Order 13011; the CIO Council is comprised of CIOs from various federal agencies and serves as the principal interagency group tasked with improving federal information resource management practices.

Chief information security officer (CISO): a corporate officer who takes the lead in developing, overseeing, monitoring, and reporting on a company's cybersecurity and corporate liability programs.

Clinger-Cohen Act: a 1996 law that replaced the Brooks Act and made each federal agency responsible for purchasing its own information technology systems subject to OMB policies and oversight. Thus, Clinger-Cohen stripped the General Services Administration of the information technology oversight role that it had been granted under the Brooks Act.

Code of Federal Regulations: a government publication that is published annually and provides a complete listing of federal regulations, organized by year and policy title.

Coefficient of determination (R^2): a number that indicates the amount of variation in the dependent variable that is due to a change in the independent variable.

Committees: congressional groups focused on a specific national issue.

Components: pieces that work together to form a system.

Comprehensive National Cybersecurity Initiative: a program created by NSPD-54/HSPD-23 that focuses on establishing a frontline defense for reducing current vulnerabilities in U.S. federal networks and preventing cyber intrusions into these networks.

Compromised system: a system that has been attacked and is under the control of an attacker.

Computer Fraud and Abuse Act (CFAA): a 1984 law that provides the judiciary with the authority to both try and convict hackers who commit cyber crimes. The CFAA has been amended several times in order to improve its effectiveness and criminalize new threats.

Computer Security Act (CSA): a 1987 law that empowered the National Institute of Standards and Technology to create minimum acceptable information security practices for all federal departments and agencies. In doing so, the CSA shifted the cybersecurity balance of power away from the military-centered focus of NSDD-145, and back to the civilian-centered focus of the Brooks Act.

Computer: a device that processes digital information; at its most basic level, a computer can be understood as a series of "on" and "off" switches.

Concept of operations (CONOPS): a document that describes how a specific capability is to be built and supported over the course of a program's lifetime.

Conditional probability: the probability of one event occurring with the knowledge of the outcome(s) of another event(s) (i.e., "the probability of A given B").

Conference committees: congressional committees composed of members of both the House and Senate. Conference committees are formed when two similar but conflicting pieces of legislation are passed by the House and Senate, and are tasked with reconciling the differences between the two bills.

Glossary (C)

Confidence interval: an interval of values that estimates a population parameter to some degree of confidence

Congressional Record: a report, issued daily when Congress is in session, that includes the contents of proceedings and debates that take place on the floors of both the House of Representatives and Senate.

Congressional Research Service (CRS): an agency that provides policy and legal analysis for Congress; the CRS is often referred to as "Congress's think tank."

Consent agreement: a legally binding document whereby a company charged with violating the FTCA agrees to institute a cybersecurity program in exchange for the FTC dismissing said violation.

Consequence assessment: a product or process that evaluates the potential impact on an organization in the event that a critical asset is exploited by a threat.

Consequence: the effect or impact of an occurrence. Consequence is also defined as the product of *criticality* and *impact*.

Continuous monitoring system (CMS): a system that provides uninterrupted monitoring of irregular activities on a computer network.

Control Objectives for Information and Related Technology (COBIT): a framework, developed by the Information Systems Audit and Control Association, that provides guidance specific to IT-related internal controls.

Convenience sampling: a sampling bias that occurs when researchers select participants based entirely on ease (e.g., choosing a sample by selecting the first ten names on a list).

Convention on Cybercrime: an international cyber legal agreement drafted by the Council of Europe in 2001. The convention currently has 53 signatories, and is the only binding international agreement on cybersecurity.

Corporate governance: the high-level process of setting policies for a corporation, overseeing its operations, and generally dictating how it is run.

Corporate officers: a team of senior leaders that manages a corporation's day-to-day operations.

Cost Performance Index (CPI): an index that measures the ratio of earned value to actual costs; CPI measures whether the costs of a project are above or below the amount budgeted for any given in a project's life.

Cost variance (CV): a metric that measures the difference between the money budgeted for the work actually performed in a project and the actual costs that the project has incurred; used to determine the degree to which a project is over or under its original budget.

Critical Infrastructure Working Group (CIWG): a working group formed by Attorney General Janet Reno in the aftermath of the 1995 Oklahoma City bombing. The group recommended that President Clinton form the President's Commission on Critical Infrastructure Protection.

Criticality: the importance of an asset.

Cyber intrusion: a successful attack that provides an attacker with unauthorized access to a system.

Cybersecurity Act of 2012: a major piece of proposed cybersecurity legislation, ultimately defeated in the Senate in 2012, that would have shifted responsibility for cybersecurity oversight within the federal government from the OMB to DHS and created a National Cybersecurity Council to develop and encourage the

Glossary

adoption of sector-specific cybersecurity best practices.

Data: digital information that is processed by a computer.

Data breach notification law: a law that requires companies to notify the public when they experience a data breach.

Denial of service (DoS): a relatively unsophisticated type of cyber attack that often uses brute force to shut down a target website by overwhelming its computing resources.

Department of Defense (DOD): a federal department responsible for most of the activities of U.S. military and intelligence agencies. Historically, the DOD has battled with civilian agencies for control over U.S. cybersecurity policy.

Department of Homeland Security (DHS): a federal department created by the Homeland Security Act of 2002; upon its creation, DHS absorbed many existing cybersecurity programs and functions from other departments and agencies.

Dependent variables: the variables being observed for a causal relationship in an experiment. The significance of a relationship is shown by how much a specific independent variable influences the dependent variable's value.

Distributed denial of service (DDoS): a type of cyber attack in which an attacker uses a remotely-controlled botnet to execute a denial of service (DoS) attack.

DNS cache poisoning: a type of attack in which an attacker tampers with the IP address of a specific site, so that all traffic intended for a specific IP address travels to a different address.

Domain Name System (DNS): a system that facilitates the translation of IP addresses (e.g., "74.125.228.70") to words that a human being can easily understand ("www.google.com").

Domain Name System Security Extension (DNSSEC): a series of Internet specifications that aims to ensure the accuracy of information given by DNS servers to protect Internet users from routers that falsify information and gain illicit access to data packets in transit.

Duty of care: a legal principle referring to the idea that corporate directors and officers have a duty to be reasonably informed before making decisions and to perform their jobs with the diligence of a reasonable person. Corporate officers who fail to uphold these obligations may be held personally liable for any damages that occur because of their actions.

Earned value (EV): the costs that an organization planned to incur for the amount of work actually completed at a given point in the project; also known as budgeted cost of work performed (BCWP).

Earned value management (EVM): a management accounting system that helps program managers to effectively manage their program budgets and evaluate program performance. The use of EVM is required throughout the federal civilian government.

Effective date: the date at which a final rule becomes enforceable.

Einstein 3: the federal government's primary intrusion prevention system, developed from NSA threat signature technology.

Electronic Communications Privacy Act (ECPA): a 1986 law that is often invoked in federal cases against hackers. Specifically, the ECPA includes the Wiretap Act, which makes it illegal to intercept or disclose illegally intercepted wire, oral, and electronic communications without a search warrant.

Electronic Data Gathering, Analysis, and Retrieval System (EDGAR): an online database that allows the public to view corporate disclosure filings.

Encryption: the process of using mathematical algorithms to transform easily-read binary information into a form that cannot be easily read.

Enterprise architecture (EA): the "strategic information base" that defines the mission of an agency and describes the technology and information needed to perform that mission.

Enterprise Risk Management – Integrated Framework: a framework, published by the Committee of Sponsoring Organizations, that provides comprehensive guidance for internal controls in the private sector.

Epistemology: the theory of knowledge; how an event, phenomenon, or object is studied, researched, analyzed, and understood.

Estimate at completion (EAC): a metric that forecasts that estimate the final total cost of a project using the project's performance metrics to date.

Estimate to complete (ETC): the total estimated costs required to complete the remainder of a project.

Evaluation criteria: an RFP document that prioritizes the factors that are most crucial in an agency's selection of a vendor. The criteria could include factors such as price, technical approach, and the completeness of a vendor's response to specific request for proposal requirements.

Event tree analysis: an analytic method that begins with an initiating event, and then traces the possible outcomes after this event, indicating the probability of each event. Ultimately, the probability of each final outcome is calculated by multiplying the probabilities of the incidents that preceded it.

EVM forecasting: a method that uses data to estimate the final total cost of a project, according to its current performance.

Exclusive (probability): when used in reference to probability, indicates that two events can never occur at the same time; also known as *disjoint*.

Executive Office of the President (EOP): a group of offices created to provide support for the bureaucracy of the executive branch. The EOP plays a key role in the president's policymaking activities, including those related to cybersecurity.

Executive Order (EO): a declaration from the president that is legally binding and does not require the consent of Congress. Like national security instruments, executive orders remain in place until they are deliberately replaced by a subsequent administration. Unlike national security instruments, executive orders are rarely classified.

Executive Order 13228: an executive order issued by President Bush in October 2001 that created the Office of Homeland Security and the Homeland Security Council.

Executive Order 13231: an executive order issued by President Bush in October 2001, shortly after the release of Executive Order 13228. Executive Order 13231 reiterated many of the principles of President Clinton's Presidential Decision Directive 63 and created the President's Critical Infrastructure Protection Board (PCIPB) to help develop voluntary standards and best practices for protecting critical infrastructure.

Executive Order 13636: an executive order, issued by President Obama in February 2013, that outlined

Glossary

several new measures to enhance the cybersecurity of the United States' critical infrastructure, specifically emphasizing the improvement of information-sharing as a key priority.

Exhibit 300: a document that federal departments and agencies are required to submit to the OMB in order to justify a request for a major IT investment. Exhibit 300s are intended to compel departments and agencies to use effective project management skills and demonstrate defined cost, schedule and performance goals associated with the IT procurements.

Exploit: a tool or process that is used in a cyber attack to take advantage of a vulnerability and gain access to, or control over, a system.

Fault tree analysis: a deductive methodology that examines an entire system from a top-down perspective and identifies the combination of failures that may contribute to its failure.

Federal Acquisition Streamlining Act, Title V (FASA V): a 1994 law that requires federal agencies to establish measurable cost, schedule performance goals for all major acquisition programs, and achieve 90% of those goals.

Federal Information Security Management Act (FISMA): a 2002 law that aimed to protect the integrity of the federal government's information systems by requiring every federal agency to develop and implement an agency-wide information security program.

Federal Register: a daily publication of the federal government that is organized around four categories: (1) "Presidential Documents;" (2) "Rules and Regulations;" (3) "Proposed Rules;" and (4) "Advanced Notices."

Federal Sentencing Guidelines: a set of guidelines that are issued by the United States Sentencing Commission and determine the length of a convicted criminal's jail time based on a point system.

Federal Trade Commission (FTC): the federal government's consumer protection agency. Part of the FTC's mission is to protect the integrity and confidentiality of consumer information.

Federal Trade Commission Act (FTCA): the 1914 law from which the FTC derives its regulatory authority. Companies charged with violating the FTCA may settle with the FTC through a consent agreement.

File Transfer Protocol (FTP): a type of network protocol used to transfer files between two hosts; FTP traffic is not encrypted, and so this protocol is considered to be insecure by cybersecurity specialists.

Final rule: a rule submitted by an agency after a notice and comment period. Final rules typically include an effective date and a supplemental information section, the latter of which includes information about the problems that the new rule addresses, the facts and data that the agency relied upon in its rulemaking process, and responses to major criticism levied against the rule during the notice and comment period.

Financial Privacy Rule: a component of the GLB Act that requires all financial institutions to disclose their information-sharing and privacy practices to their customers, and allows customers to opt out of having their information shared with third parties.

Firewall: a tool that blocks malicious data, files, and viruses from entering a computer.

Flame: a computer worm used by the U.S. military to turn on cameras and microphones within Iranian nuclear facilities, thus providing the U.S. with intelligence needed to plan the subsequent Stuxnet attack.

Floor: the conceptual place in which all official activity in Congress occurs.

Forward selection: the process by which analysts add variables until the model proves to have overall signif-

Glossary (E-H)

icance and individual variables prove to be highly significant at various *p*-values.

Full-time equivalent (FTE): a measure used to determine the manpower that will be needed for a given project; multiple part-time workers can do the work of one FTE.

Function: the set of tasks or operations that an employee or department performs for an organization.

General Services Administration (GSA): an agency established in 1949 to improve the efficiency of the federal government's administrative work. The GSA's responsibilities include maintaining and constructing federal buildings, as well as procuring goods and services for the federal government. The GSA plays a key role in federal information security.

Government Accountability Office (GAO): a federal agency charged with making Congress better informed, more efficient, more ethical, and more responsive; the GAO is often referred to as Congress's "watchdog."

Gramm-Leach-Bliley Financial Modernization Act (GLB Act): a 1999 law that contained two major rules – the Financial Privacy Rule and the Safeguards Rule – that reshaped information security for financial services companies.

Grand jury: a jury, composed of between 12-23 citizens, that reviews evidence presented by a U.S. attorney and determines whether or not there is probable cause for a criminal charge.

Graphical user interface (GUI): a type of interface that an individual can interact with to request that a computer take certain actions.

Hardware: any part of a computer that has a physical form and helps the computer to process information.

Hashing: a tool used to make information difficult for third parties to intercept and use. Hashing generates a unique number for a given file by running the file through a specific algorithm, such as the Message-digest algorithm (MD5) and Secure Hash Algorithm (SHA).

Health Information Technology for Economic and Clinical Health Act (HITECH Act): a 2009 law notable for being the first federally-mandated data breach notification statute.

Health Insurance Portability and Accountability Act (HIPAA): a 1996 law that requires medical offices to adopt standards for the protection of electronic health care data and protected health information.

High-level requirements (HLRs): requirements that help to guide a program manager's mission needs statement by creating an organization or entity, defining activities that an organization is authorized or required to perform, and/or allocating resources to perform activities.

Homeland Security Act (HSA): a 2002 law that created the Department of Homeland Security and placed many existing cybersecurity programs and functions under the new department's control.

Homeland Security Presidential Directive 7 (HSPD-7): a presidential directive issued by President Bush in 2003 that, most notably, gave the Department of Homeland Security a lead role in coordinating national critical infrastructure protection efforts. HSPD-7 also tasked the secretary of DHS with creating what would ultimately become the National Infrastructure Protection Plan.

Honeypots: a type of active response that collects reconnaissance by enticing attackers towards locations where they cannot harm the network.

Human reliability analysis (HRA): a type of analysis that calculates the human errors that may affect a risk-induced incident.

Glossary

Hypertext Transfer Protocol (HTTP): the unencrypted protocol that enables the use of web pages to display information.

Hypertext Transfer Protocol Secure (HTTPS): a more secure version of the Hypertext Transfer Protocol that uses encryption to create a secure connection between a browser and website.

Identity Theft Penalty Enhancement Act (ITPEA): a 2004 law that established the crime of aggravated identify theft against US citizens.

Impact: the result of damage to a critical asset.

In the cloud: refers to information stored in a third party's network, which serves as a substitute for an in-house network.

Independent (probability): when used in reference to probability, indicates that the knowledge of one event occurring does not affect the probability of another event occurring. For instance, rolling a "4" on one roll of dice does not impact the probability of the subsequent roll also being a "4."

Independent government cost estimate (IGCE): an RFP document that lays out exactly how much money the government believes completing a given program's objectives will cost.

Independent variables: the factors that measurably influence an experiment's outcome (the dependent variable).

Indictment: a formal accusation; an indictment charges an individual with a violation of the law and gives law enforcement officials the authority to arrest the accused individual.

Inferior courts: refers to the district and appeals courts, collectively known as the "federal court system."

Information Sharing and Analysis Center (ISAC): a type of entity, initially proposed in Presidential Decision Directive 63, that is responsible for receiving information regarding threats, vulnerabilities or cyber incidents, and for facilitating information sharing between the federal government and companies in critical infrastructure sectors.

Insider threat: a type of cybersecurity vulnerability involving the possibility of a disgruntled individual within an organization deliberately undermining the organization's cybersecurity.

Integrated master plan (IMP): a visual representation of a work breakdown structure. The IMP covers the entire breadth of a program and incorporates multiple integrated master schedules.

Integrated master schedule (IMS): a graphical representation of the objectives, actions, and milestones identified in a plan of action and milestones. An IMS is developed by a contractor to provide clarity for a government agency as to how the contractor will be fulfilling and managing project activities.

Interim final rule: a final rule that becomes effective immediately, without the submitting agency asking for public comment.

Internal controls: systematic measures implemented by a company to ensure that (1) company operations are effective and efficient; (2) financial reporting is reliable; (3) the company is following its own internal policies; and (4) the company is in compliance with applicable rules and regulations.

Internal monitoring: a type of in-house cyber monitoring that gathers both open source and confidential information in order to evaluate and clearly understand the situational environment, analyze collected data, warn of attacks, and respond to attacks.

Glossary (H-L)

Internet Assigned Numbers Authority (IANA): an organization founded by the U.S. government in 1988 to manage global IP address assignments. IANA now operates as a department of the Internet Corporation for Assigned Names and Numbers (ICANN).

Internet Corporation for Assigned Names and Numbers (ICANN): a nonprofit organization created in 1998 to coordinate the assignment of IP addresses and maintain the security and smooth operation of the Internet.

Internet Engineering Task Force (IETF): a loosely-organized group of volunteers that serves as the principal body engaged in the development of new Internet standards. The IETF outlines these standards in high-quality technical documents called Requests for Comments.

Internet Protocol (IP): a protocol that, along with the Transmission Control Protocol (TCP), dictates how information travels over the Internet.

Internet service provider (ISP): companies that act as an "on-ramp" to the Internet by connecting customers to an Internet backbone and letting them communicate with other people without having to build their own local or global network. Cable and phone companies are popular examples of ISPs.

Intrusion detection system (IDS): a system that detects cyber attacks by monitoring incoming and outgoing data transmissions for predefined attack signatures and anomalies.

Intrusion prevention system (IPS): a type of network defense that automates inspection of Internet traffic entering or leaving a network, in order to allow for a response to malicious software threats before the network is harmed.

IP address: a series of numbers that serves as a unique identifier allowing a router, computer, or other device to connect to the Internet and send and receive information.

IPSec: a tool used to encrypt and authenticate Internet traffic. In theory, this tool could be used to help law enforcement and counterintelligence agencies solve the problem of anonymous cyber attacks; however, human rights groups have expressed fears that IPSec will make it easier for governments to quash political dissent by reducing online anonymity and privacy.

IPV6: an Internet communications protocol developed by the IETF to increase the global supply of computer addresses and provide support for security features such as Internet Protocol Security (IPSec).

IT audit: an in-depth examination and evaluation of an organization's IT systems, management, operations, and related processes.

IT infrastructure: the technology, communications pathways, and system design and integration that provides a critical foundation for the conveniences of the modern world.

John Poindexter: a Reagan administration official and chief architect of National Security Decision Directive 145, which was most notable for giving the defense community control over securing private sector computers.

Judicial branch: the federal legal system, or "the courts."

Kevin Mitnick: one of the first "boy-genius hackers"; notable for hacking into the computer systems of the Digital Equipment Corporation and Pacific Bell, and for his subsequent arrest by the FBI in 1995.

Line functions: the departments, staff, and activities that contribute directly to completing an organization's broad mission.

Glossary

Local area network (LAN): a network that covers a variety of relatively small areas, ranging from a home network to an entire business infrastructure.

Logical fallacies: statements that are based on some kind of misconception (e.g., the ecological fallacy, the genetic fallacy, and the bandwagon fallacy).

Logistic regression model: a specific type of regression model used when the dependent (y) variable is a binary response; reveals the most statistically significant indicators and the type of association the indicators form with the dependent variable, the latter of which is expressed as *positive* (direct) or *negative* (indirect).

Logit model: a statistical model that calculates a binary dependent variable.

Malware: malicious software that attackers plant on victims' computers.

Man in the middle attack: a type of a cyber attack in which an attacker positions himself between two nodes that are communicating and tampers with traffic crossing the network.

Management and acquisition: the process of obtaining and allocating resources to complete a program's activities and achieve outcomes.

Manager: an employee charged with overseeing the "big picture" issues of his/her organization.

Mark-up session: a period in which a congressional committee or special subcommittee studies a proposed bill in depth and considers whether or not to recommend, reject, or amend the bill.

Memorandum 97-02 (M-97-02): a 1996 OMB memorandum ("Funding Information Systems Investments") containing "decision criteria" that would guide agency procurement of IT systems and be enforced through the budget process. This memorandum required agencies to take risk management principles into account when procuring computer systems.

Memorandum M-10-28: a 2010 OMB memorandum that designated DHS as the lead agency in overseeing agencies' cybersecurity activities, thus shifting some of those responsibilities away from the OMB.

Memory: also known as *storage*, allows a computer to store information. The two primary types of memory are *volatile* and *non-volatile*.

Metric: a standard for measuring a program's performance.

Mission needs statement (MNS): a document that states what a program manager is required to do by an organization's mission and the capabilities that the program must build in order to fulfill this mission.

Monte Carlo model: a form of multivariate statistical analysis for computing mathematical risk; considers possible variations in each individual factor of the analysis and examines the many possible ways in which the factors may interact.

National Cybersecurity and Communications Integration Center (NCCIC): a division of the Office of Cybersecurity and Communications that, according to its website, "serves a central location where a diverse set of partners involved in cybersecurity and communications protection coordinate and synchronize their efforts."

National Infrastructure Protection Center (NIPC): a body, created by Presidential Decision Directive 63 and currently operated by DHS, that is charged with protecting critical infrastructure by sending out alerts and warnings about new threats and vulnerabilities.

Glossary (L-N)

National Infrastructure Protection Plan (NIPP): a document, mandated by Homeland Security Presidential Directive 7, in which DHS sets out goals, objectives, and governmental roles and responsibilities for a national strategy for the protection of critical infrastructure and key resources.

National Institute of Standards and Technology (NIST): a federal agency that works with technology companies to craft information technology standards and procedures.

National Protection and Programs Directorate (NPPD): the central directorate within the Department Homeland Security tasked with protecting U.S. physical and cyber infrastructure. NPPD houses three primary offices that deal directly with cybersecurity issues: the Office of Cybersecurity and Communications (CS&C), the Office of Cyber and Infrastructure Analysis (OCIA), and the Office of Infrastructure Protection (IP).

National Science Foundation Network (NSFNET): a three-tiered network consisting of a "backbone," three regional networks, and five supercomputing centers; created in 1985, this network formed the basis for the modern Internet.

National Security Agency (NSA): an intelligence agency, housed within the Department of Defense, that is responsible for the United States' signals intelligence, as well as for preserving the integrity of the U.S. government's information systems. The NSA is also in charge of the U.S. Cyber Command, which oversees the DOD's cyber operations.

National Security Council (NSC): a body within the EOP that plays a key role in the development of executive branch cybersecurity policy. The NSC is particularly instrumental in the creation of national security instruments.

National Security Decision Directive 145 (NSDD-145): a 1984 Reagan administration policy document most notable for its assertion that the defense community, rather than the civilian government, should be responsible for the nation's computer security, including computers in the private sector.

National security instrument: a legally binding, often classified, order from the president ordering his cabinet officials to marshal resources around a certain policy. National security instruments issued with the advice and consent of the National Security Council. Each presidential administration typically creates a different name for its national security instruments.

National Security Policy Directive 54/Homeland Security Presidential Directive 23 (NSPD-54/HSPD-23): a presidential directive issued by President Bush in January 2008, most notable for launching the Comprehensive National Cybersecurity Initiative.

National Strategy to Secure Cyberspace: a 2003 DHS document that outlined a framework for prioritizing and implementing cybersecurity programs, in the hopes of preventing cyber attacks against American critical infrastructure, reducing national vulnerability to cyber attacks, and minimizing damage and recovery time from attacks that did occur.

National Vulnerability Database (NVD): a database hosted by NIST and DHS that provides a repository of known cyber vulnerabilities.

NIST 800-66: a NIST publication ("An Introductory Resource Guide for Implementing the Health Insurance Portability and Accountability Act") that provides medical offices with guidance on how to comply with HIPAA's regulations on protected health information.

Non-volatile memory: a type of computer memory that stores information needed for more than a few seconds (e.g., hard drives, CDs, DVDs, and USB memory sticks).

Glossary

North American Electric Reliability Corporation (NERC): a nongovernmental organization tasked with creating reliability standards for bulk power systems. One such standard requires that owners and operators of bulk power systems identify, classify, respond to, and report cybersecurity incidents to the Electricity Sector Information Sharing and Analysis Center (ES ISAC).

Notice and comment period: a period in which an agency is required to gather input from experts and the general public about a proposed rule. Most agencies are legally required to respond to all public comments submitted during the notice and comment period.

Null hypothesis: describes the lack of a relationship between variables. The goal of research is to reject the null hypothesis in favor of the alternative hypothesis.

Objective values: the maximum desired operational goal of a program, beyond which additional gains in performance do not warrant additional time and cost; in other words, the value that a program manager is attempting to obtain through the execution of a program.

Office of Cyber and Infrastructure Analysis (OCIA): an office within DHS's National Protection and Programs Directorate, tasked with providing analysis of various threats to cyber and physical infrastructure, and of the potential consequences of disruptions to this infrastructure.

Office of Cybersecurity and Communications (CS&C): an office within DHS's National Protection and Programs Directorate, tasked with protecting the nation's cyber and communication infrastructure.

Office of Information and Regulatory Affairs (OIRA): an office within the OMB that works to reduce government paperwork and maintain an efficient flow of information within the federal government.

Office of Infrastructure Protection (IP): an office within DHS's National Protection and Programs Directorate, tasked with overseeing the nation's critical infrastructure protection programs, including the programs outlined in the National Infrastructure Protection Plan, such as the public-private partnerships across critical infrastructure sectors.

Office of Management and Budget (OMB): an office within the Executive Office of the President, tasked with implementing and enforcing presidential policy across the federal government through budget development and execution, oversight and review of all federal agencies and regulations, and coordination of legislative agendas with presidential policy. The OMB plays a key role in federal information security.

Office of Science and Technology Policy (OSTP): an office within the EOP that is responsible for advising the president and his senior staff on matters relating to science and technology.

Olympic Games: a cyber warfare program initiated under President Bush and continued under President Obama; this program gave birth to the Flame and Stuxnet worms.

OMB memoranda: official OMB policy documents that clarify the specific responsibilities of departments and agencies with regard to national cybersecurity policy.

Ontology: the theory of being; what is being studied or researched.

Operating model (op model): a document that offers a path for managing the execution of a concept of operations by delineating a manager's approach into measurable objectives and activities, and by accounting for all of a program's costs.

Operational planning model: a tool that breaks down an organizational mission into its components parts, such as products and services, organizational capital, human capital, and strategic risk management.

Glossary (N-P)

Operational requirements document (ORD): a statement of performance and operational parameters that a proposed system must meet to provide value to a program.

Packet analyzers: a type of network monitoring tool that inspects data packets as they pass through a digital network. Packet analyzers can be programmed to detect anomalies or specific types of malicious data. Packet analyzers are also known as "sniffers."

Packets: the pieces of information that are broken down during transit through the Internet and reassembled upon reaching their destination. This process of transmitting, receiving, and reassembling packets is accomplished primarily through the Transmission Control Protocol (TCP) and the Internet Protocol (IP).

Paperwork Reduction Act (PRA): a 1980 law that aimed to improve the "productivity, efficiency, and effectiveness" of government programs through the creation of government-wide information resource management policies. The PRA charged the OMB with overseeing this initiative across the federal government.

Passive response: a type of response to a cyber attack that may include logging (the collection of data with the purpose of delivering an appropriate device or method to curb an attack), notification (providing a message about the attack to appropriate personnel), and shunning (ignoring) the attack.

Penetration testing: a test of network security in which a company stages a simulated cyber attack on its own network in order to reveal vulnerabilities in its computer systems.

Performance work statement (PWS): a document that states the specific expected outcomes of a project (written in clear, specific, and objective terms with measurable outcomes) and leaves the method of achieving these outcomes open to a given contractor. A PWS is used for performance-based acquisitions, and is often included as part of an RFP.

Period of performance (POP): the amount of time budgeted between the start and end dates of a particular project.

Phishing: a broad, generally untargeted form of cyber attack in which attackers "fish" for an individual's personal information, using deceptive tactics to trick users into voluntarily revealing personal information or giving the attacker access to their system.

Plan of action and milestones (POA&M): from NIST Special Publication 800-53—a POA&M "identifies tasks needing to be accomplished" and "details resources required to accomplish the elements of [a] plan, any milestones in meeting [the plan's] tasks, and scheduled completion dates for the milestones."

Planned value (PV): the estimated value of expenditures that a project is budgeted to incur by a specific point in its timeline; also known as the budgeted cost of work scheduled (BCWS).

Plans: a set of specific tasks necessary to complete previously formulated strategies in the service of goals.

Plea bargain: an agreement in which a defendant pleads guilty in return for a U.S. attorney agreeing to drop certain charges or recommend a lenient sentence.

Policy monitoring: a type of cyber monitoring that involves the definition of a rule and subsequent monitoring to observe if that rule is broken.

President's Commission on Critical Infrastructure Protection (PCCIP): a commission formed in the aftermath of the 1995 Oklahoma City bombing. The commission's 1997 report, *Critical Foundations: Protecting America's Infrastructure*, argued that the federal government should work with other key stakeholders to create a national cybersecurity policy.

Glossary

Presidential Decision Directive 63 (PDD-63): a national security instrument issued by President Clinton in 1998, which incorporated many of the recommendations that had been made by the President's Commission on Critical Infrastructure Protection and reiterated the commission's views on the necessity of public-private partnerships in the cybersecurity realm.

Presidential directives: executive branch documents that set policy or require an agency to take a certain action; along with congressional legislation, presidential directives have played a major role in shaping U.S. cybersecurity policy. Presidential directives include both executive orders and national security instruments.

Presidential Policy Directive 21 (PPD-21): a national security instrument issued by President Obama in February 2013 that emphasized the need for the federal government to approach infrastructure protection in an "integrated, holistic manner" and identified DHS as the primary coordinating agency for national infrastructure protection.

Priorities and trade-offs: decisions that stakeholders in a scenario must make about the relative importance of various goals and objectives.

Privacy Rule: a component of HIPAA that governs the storage and transmission of protected health information.

Private corporation: a corporation that is not owned in any part by public shareholders; public and private corporations are not always subject to the same legal requirements.

Probabilistic risk assessment (PRA): a quantitative risk assessment strategy specifically concerned with (1) the magnitude or severity of the consequence; and (2) the probability of an event occurring.

Probability: a value between 0 and 1, representing 0% and 100% probabilities that an event will occur. The sum of all of the probabilities for a given scenario must equal 1, or 100%.

Probability sampling: a type of sampling that aims to give every member of a given population an equal chance of being selected. Probability sampling is the best method to guarantee that a given sample represents the characteristic of the population under study.

Probable cause: known facts leading to a reasonable belief that a crime was committed.

Processor: the part of a computer that intakes data that the user inputs, performs a process on this data, and outputs a new kind of data.

Programming languages: "languages" that allow a human to use non-binary commands as shorthand for the binary codes that a computer can work with.

Proposed rule: an item published in the *Federal Register* that announces and explains an agency's plan to address a problem or accomplish a goal through a new regulation.

Protected health information (PHI): sensitive health care information that may include information relating to an individual's various health conditions and the provision of health care to that individual.

Public corporation: a corporation that sells shares in its ownership to public investors, or shareholders; public and private corporations are not always subject to the same legal requirements.

p-value: the probability of observing a test statistic at least as extreme as the one that was actually observed, assuming the null hypothesis is true.

Qualitative risk determination: a process that approaches risk determination using non-numerical data,

Glossary (P-R)

such as past records and data, patterns of data, behavior of technology and/or personnel, and interviews with personnel.

Quantitative risk determination: a process that approaches risk determination using numerical data and assigns numerical values to qualitative statements.

Random sampling: a type of probability sampling that assigns every subject in a given population a number and uses a number generator to select a random sample.

Random-access memory (RAM): a type of volatile memory that stores short-term information that may not be important enough to keep in cache memory. RAM is made up of small components, called *capacitors*, that briefly store information as they pass through a processor.

Red/yellow/green system: a system used by project managers in the federal government to label the results of their performance metric. "Red" indicates that a project is not meeting expectations, "yellow" indicates that a project is fairly successful, but still experiencing some challenges, and "green" indicates that a project is doing well and meeting its objectives.

Regional Internet Registries (RIRs): a series of registries promoted by the IETF that administer and register IP address space and manage services related to IP addresses.

Regression model: a statistical model that uses multiple independent (x) variables to predict or estimate a dependent (y) variable.

Regulation: an enforceable law that has been authorized by congressional legislation or an executive order to remedy a specific problem.

Regulatory agency: an agency that counts issuing regulations as one of its primary activities (e.g., the Food and Drug Administration).

Reliability: indicates the consistency of the research design – in other words, if others were to conduct the same test through the same process, they would reach the same conclusion.

Request for Comments (RFC): high-quality technical documents produced by the IETF. The content of RFCs ranges from new Internet standards to summaries of working group meeting to humorous reports.

Request for information (RFI): a document that allows a program manager or department head to solicit feedback from experts in a relevant industry regarding how they would achieve a certain objective. This feedback allows a program manager to refine his or her objectives, strategy, and planning.

Request for proposal (RFP): a set of documents that invites a company to submit a bid for equipment or services. Examples of documents that may be included in an RFP include a statement of work, statement of objectives, and performance work statement.

Research design: a research project's general outline, serving as a complete blueprint for how a researcher will attempt to answer a given research question. The two primary kinds of research design are *experimental* and *non-experimental*.

Research question: a central question that guides the risk determination process. Research questions should be clear and concise, and should also accurately test the research subject.

Risk acceptance: a type of risk response that recognizes the reality of a certain degree of risk being unavoidable(e.g., using an email service, even though there is a possibility that a received email may contain harmful malware).

Glossary

Risk assessment: from the DHS Risk Lexicon – "a product or process which collects information and assigns values to risks for the purpose of informing priorities, developing or comparing courses of action, and informing decision making."

Risk avoidance: evading or circumventing a threat by removing a critical asset from potential harm (e.g., protecting against cyber threats by eliminating the use of computers within a company). Risk avoidance is rarely a practical strategy for an individual or organization operating in a risk-filled world.

Risk constraints: the factors that inhibit the execution of a fully secure risk management plan. In most scenarios, the primary risk constraint is the finite nature of financial resources.

Risk determination: the step in the risk management process following the risk assessment; provides a complete overview of the possible levels of risk and provides a guide to the appropriate risk response at each particular level.

Risk framing: the process of examining and evaluating the "big picture" risk environment in which a company or organization operates. Risk framing establishes the context for making risk-based decisions, and ultimately helps to produce a risk management strategy.

Risk Lexicon: an official publication of the Department Homeland Security that defines various terms with relevance to the fields of risk assessment and management.

Risk management: the process by which risk specialists develop and implement a continuous and systematic plan for containing risk; this practice is at the heart of the cybersecurity field.

Risk mitigation: a strategy to contain an imminent or current risk-related incident (e.g., taking steps to limit the damage of a cyber intrusion after it occurs).

Risk monitoring: an ongoing process that takes place after the response plan has been implemented and involves developing a strategy for constantly observing changes in threats, vulnerabilities, and criticalities. The three key elements of risk monitoring are compliance, effectiveness, and identifying changes.

Risk response: the most appropriate reaction to a determined risk; should prevent harm to an individual or organization, while also staying within various resource constraints.

Risk tolerance: the degree to which an organization can handle or incur a specific harm.

Risk transfer: from the DHS Risk Lexicon – an "action taken to manage risk that shifts some or all of the risk to another entity, asset, system, network, or geographic area" (e.g., purchasing insurance).

Risk-based decisions: from the DHS Risk Lexicon – "determination[s] of a course of action predicated primarily on the assessment of risk and the expected impact of that course of action on that risk."

Routers: devices that send data between computers or networks.

Safeguards Rule: a component of the GLB Act that requires financial institutions to protect their customers' information in storage and transmission by developing a written information security plan that puts a point person in charge of information security, clearly articulates the company's ongoing risk management strategy, and states what each division of the company is doing to manage its information security risks.

Sample: a subset of a population that has been selected for analysis in an experiment.

Sarbanes-Oxley Act (SOX): a 2002 law that aimed to protect investors by ensuring that corporations correctly report their finances. SOX is perhaps most notable for including Section 404, which requires larger

Glossary (R-S)

public companies to include a special internal control report in their annual financial reports.

Schedule Performance Index (SPI): an index that measures the ratio of earned value to planned value; like schedule variance, SPI measures whether a project is behind or ahead of schedule.

Schedule variance (SV): a metric that measures the difference between a project's earned value and planned value; used to determine how far ahead of or behind schedule a particular project is.

Scientific Integrity: an OSTP memorandum issued in 2010 that laid out several principles of importance to the OSTP, including the idea that science and technology experts should play key roles in policymaking, where appropriate, and that the scientific processes incorporated into policymaking should be of high quality and integrity.

Scientific method: the systematic and objective examination of a phenomenon.

Section 404: a component of the 2002 Sarbanes-Oxley Act that requires larger public companies to include a special internal control report in their annual financial reports.

Securities and Exchange Commission (SEC): a federal agency that is tasked with interpreting federal securities laws; issuing securities regulations; overseeing the inspection of brokerage firms, investment advisors, and ratings agencies; and overseeing private regulatory organizations. In the course of carrying out this mission, the SEC plays a key role in shaping cybersecurity practices in the private sector.

Security Rule: a component of HIPAA that establishes safeguards to ensure the confidentiality, integrity, and availability of electronically stored personal health information; very similar in content to the GLB Act's Safeguards Rule.

Sensitive but unclassified: a term used in NSDD-145 to refer to information and information systems that, while unclassified, could still pose a threat to U.S. national security if leaked or compromised.

Signature-based detection: a method for identifying cyber attacks that involves the creation of a signature, or fingerprint, for activity on a network that is suspected to be malicious, and a subsequent monitoring for that signature.

Significance tests: statistical tests that determine whether a given set of independent variables are good indicators of the outcome generated by a model.

Software: a collection of programs, instructions, and processes that a computer uses to perform a limited set of functions.

Spear phishing: a targeted form of phishing in which attackers use specific information about a target to convince him or her to click on a malicious link or open a malicious email attachment.

Staff functions: the departments, staff, and activities that help achieve an organization's mission by supporting line functions.

Statement of objectives (SOO): a document that states the desired outcome of a project and leaves the method of achieving this outcome open to a given contractor. SOOs are often included as part of a request for proposal, and are intended to provide potential contractors with maximum flexibility to propose an innovative approach.

Statement of work (SOW): a document that states the specific expected outcomes of a project's intended service or equipment, and an outline of how to achieve these outcomes. SOWs are often included as part of a request for proposal and are typically used when the task in question is well-defined and familiar.

Glossary

Statistically significant: a term meaning that the probability of an observed event occurring is extremely unlikely to be due to chance or random variation.

Strategy: an approach that a manager develops with regard to a mission.

Stuxnet: a computer worm introduced to Iranian nuclear facilities sometime before 2010, allegedly used to infect Iran's industrial computer systems; led to the damaging of more than 1,000 Iranian centrifuges.

Subject matter experts (SME): a measure similar to a full-time equivalent, but with the important caveat that SMEs generally have higher degrees of expertise and specialization, and are therefore more expensive to employ.

Survey: a series of questions created in order to gather information about a particular research question.

System: an entity made up of interactions between various components (e.g., a laptop, printer, router, etc.).

System of systems: an entity made up of interactions between various systems (e.g., a network connecting a printer, router, and computer; the Internet).

TCP/IP: a term used to refer to the Transmission Control Protocol (TCP) and Internet Protocol (IP), which dictate how information travels over the Internet.

Test statistic: a statistic that determines the significance of an individual variable, set of variables, or statistical model that can inform the decision to accept or reject a null hypothesis.

The 414s: a group of teenage hackers, based in Wisconsin, who infiltrated several high-profile computer systems in 1983, including that of the Los Alamos National Laboratory.

The Morris Worm: a computer worm created by Cornell University student Robert Morris in 1988. The worm was programmed in such a way as to allow it to infect every computer it encountered, which allowed it to cause widespread chaos and up to $100 million in total damages.

Theories: statements that have been tested repeatedly and are accepted by experts.

THOMAS.gov: an online service provided by the Library of Congress that grants users access to an exhaustive database of congressional and presidential activity and documents.

Threat: an agent that exploits a vulnerability and causes harm to an organization's processes, systems, personnel, hardware, software, or physical location. Threats can be either *intentional* or *unintentional*.

Threat assessment: from the DHS Risk Lexicon – "a product or process of identifying or evaluating entities, actions, or occurrences…that have or indicate the potential to harm life, information, operations, and/or property." The purpose of a threat assessment is to identify the intention, capability, and lethality of a threat.

Threat shifting: occurs when an intentional threat actor alters its strategy or tactics after becoming aware that mitigations or controls are in place to thwart its activities.

Threshold values: the minimum operational value of a program, below which its utility becomes questionable.

Time dimension: the precise time period that a researcher investigates; determining the time dimension helps to establish a boundary for the scope of a research project.

Top-level domain (TLD): the highest level of the Internet's domain name hierarchy (e.g., .com and .edu).

Transmission Control Protocol (TCP): a protocol that, along with the Internet Protocol (IP), dictates how information travels over the Internet.

Glossary (S-Z)

Transparency: the process of maintaining a full and open record of a corporation's financial status and its governance practices.

Trusted Internet Connection (TIC): a program initiated by the Office and Management and Budget that aims to decrease Internet access points in government networks and verify that all access to these networks is routed through designated providers.

U.S. attorney: the prosecutor in a federal criminal case. A U.S. attorney is a member of the executive branch, and his or her job is to enforce federal law by prosecuting accused federal criminals in U.S. federal courts.

Unit of analysis: a project's research subjects.

United States Computer Emergency Readiness Team (US-CERT): from its official website—a component of DHS's National Cybersecurity and Communications Integration Center that "accepts, triages, and collaboratively responds to [cyber] incidents; provides technical assistance to information system operators; and disseminates timely notifications regarding current and potential security threats and vulnerabilities."

Validity: indicates that a given set of research answers the research question – in other words, validity ensures that a researcher is measuring and/or testing exactly what he or she is interested in studying.

Variables: the various factors that influence the likelihood of a risk occurring; also known as *indicators*.

Variances: any deviation from a program's original budget or schedule.

Veto power: the president's constitutional power to return a proposed bill to the part of Congress in which it originated; a presidential veto can be overridden by a two-thirds majority vote in both the House and Senate.

Volatile memory: a type of computer memory that stores information only needed for a short period of time (e.g., CPU cache and random-access memory).

Volunteer sampling: a sampling bias that occurs when all of a survey's sample subjects volunteered to participate; this willingness to volunteer means that the participants are likely to have strong feelings about the survey topic.

Vulnerability: a weakness in a system that an attacker could target and exploit. From the DHS Risk Lexicon – a "feature or operational attribute that renders an entity, asset, system, network, or geographic area open to exploitation or susceptible to a given hazard."

Vulnerability assessment: from the DHS Risk Lexicon – a "product or process of identifying physical features or operational attributes that render an entity, asset, system, network, or geographic area susceptible or exposed to hazards."

Warner Amendment to the Brooks Act: a 1988 amendment to the 1965 Brooks Act which effectively gave the NSA a limited sphere of control over specific types of "sensitive but unclassified" information technology. In doing so, the Warner Amendment restored some cybersecurity power to the military and intelligence sectors that had previously been taken away by the Computer Security Act.

Wide area network (WAN): a network that covers a relatively large area, such as a small town or a portion of a city.

Wiretap Act: a component of the ECPA that makes it illegal to intercept or disclose illegally intercepted wire, oral, and electronic communications without a search warrant.

Work breakdown structure (WBS): a project budgeting method, popular within the federal government, that provides program managers with guidance on how to plan tasks and sub-tasks according to a budget and promotes the integration of multiple departments in order to work towards an organization's ultimate objective.

Zero-day exploit: an exploit that targets a vulnerability that is not known to anyone but the attacker.

Notes

Introduction

1. *DARPA: Bridging the Gap, Powered By Ideas*, DARPA, February 2005, <http://oai.dtic.mil/oai/oai?verb=getRecord&metadataPrefix=html&identifier=ADA510795>, p. 1.

2. TJ O'Connor, *Violent Python: A Cookbook for Hackers, Forensic Analysts, Penetration Testers, and Security Engineers*, (Boston, MA: Newnes, 2012), p. 31.

3. *See generally* David Sanger, *Obama Order Sped Up Wave of Cyberattacks Against Iran*, N.Y. Times (June 1, 2012), http://www.nytimes.com/2012/06/01/world/middleeast/obama-ordered-wave-of-cyberattacks-against-iran.html?_r=2.

4. *Iranian Cyber Threat to the U.S. Homeland: Hearing Before the Subcomm. on Cybersecurity, Infrastructure Prot., & Sec. Tech. and the Subcomm. on Counterterrorism & Intelligence of the H. Comm. on Homeland Sec.*, 112th Cong. (2012) (statement of Ilan Berman, Vice President, American Foreign Policy Council).

5. *See Id. See also* Sanger, *supra* note 3.

6. *Id. See also* Advisory ICSA-10-272-01, *Primary Stuxnet Advisory*, ICS-CERT, September 29, 2010, https://ics-cert.us-cert.gov/advisories/ICSA-10-272-01.

7. Paul K. Kerr, John Rollins & Catherine A. Theohary, Congressional Research Service, R41524, *The Stuxnet Computer Worm: Harbinger of an Emerging Warfare Capability* (2010).

8. *See Id. See also, e.g., Securing Critical Infrastructure in the Age of Stuxnet: Hearing Before the S. Comm. on Homeland Sec. & Gov't Affairs*, 111 Cong. (2010) (statement of Michael Assante, President and Chief Executive Officer, National Board of Information Security Examiners of the United States Inc.).

9. *See Examining the Cyber Threat to Critical Infrastructure and the American Economy: Hearing Before the Subcomm. on Cybersecurity, Infrastructure Protection, & Sec. Tech. of the H. Comm. on Homeland Sec.*, 111th Cong. 5-13 (2010) (statement of Philip Reitinger, Deputy Undersecretary, National Protection and Programs Directorate, Dep't of Homeland Sec.).

Chapter 1

1. Figure 1-1, as well as subsequent explanations of this figure's concepts, is drawn from the following source: *Managing Information Risk: Organization, Mission, and Information System View*, NIST Special Publication 800-39, March 2011, <http://csrc.nist.gov/publications/nistpubs/800-39/SP800-39-final.pdf>.

2. The *DHS Risk Lexicon* can be accessed at the following link: <http://www.dhs.gov/xlibrary/assets/dhs-risk-lexicon-2010.pdf >.

3. "Trusted Internet Connections," Department of Homeland Security, <https://www.dhs.gov/trusted-inter-

Notes

net-connections>

4. Chart content drawn from the following source: "Critical Foundations: Protecting America's Infrastructures," report by the President's Commission on Critical Infrastructure Protection, October 1997, < https://www.fas.org/sgp/library/pccip.pdf>, p. 20.

5. Database available at the following link: <http://nvd.nist.gov/>.

6. *Homeland Security: Key Elements of a Risk Management Approach: Hearing Before the Subcomm. on Nat'l Sec., Veterans Affairs, and Int'l Affairs of the H. Comm. on Gov't Reform,* 112 Cong. (2011) (statement of Raymond J. Decker, Director, Defense Capabilities and Management, G.A.O.).

7. *See generally Iranian Cyber Threat to U.S. Homeland: Hearing Before the Subcomm. on Cybersecurity, Infrastructure Prot., & Sec. Tech. and the Subcomm. on Counterterrorism & Intelligence of the H. Comm. on Homeland Sec.*, 112th Cong. (2012) (statement of Frank Cilluffo, Director, Homeland Sec. Policy Institute, The George Washington University).

8. This "PRA" is not be confused with the Paperwork Reduction Act, examined in Chapter 2.

9. Strength of Password has a p-value of 0.038 in Model 1, 0.040 in Model 2, and 0.023 in Model 3.

10. In Model 3, Number of Users had a p-value of 0.01.

11. Figure 1-26 draws upon content from the following source: *Managing Information Risk*, p.7.

Chapter 2

1. "The Mission and Structure of the Office of Management and Budget," The Office of Management and Budget, < http://www.whitehouse.gov/omb/organization_mission>.

2. "Summary Report on Scientific Integrity," Office of the Director, National Institute of Standards and Technology, 26 May 2011, <http://www.nist.gov/director/scientific_integrity_summary.cfm>

3. The distinction between presidential directives, executive orders, and national security instruments can be a confusing one. The Congressional Research Service has published an excellent breakdown of the difference between various types of executive policy instruments. See *Presidential Directives: Background and Overview* (April 2007), available at <www.fas.org/irp/crs/98-611.pdf>. This textbook utilizes the framework articulated by the aforementioned report, which characterizes "presidential directives" as a catch-all term, encompassing both executive orders and national security instruments, the latter of which, in turn, includes documents (such as the Reagan administration's National Security Decision Directives, the Clinton administration's Presidential Decision Directives, and the Bush administration's National Security Presidential Directives) that are given different names by each administration, but largely serve the same legal function.

4. *Critical Infrastructure Protection: Challenges for Selected Agencies and Industry Sectors*, report for the House Committee on Energy and Commerce, February 2003, <http://www.gao.gov/assets/240/237449.pdf>, p. 1.

5. *See generally* U.S. Dep't of Homeland Sec., DHS/PIA/NPPD-027, Privacy Impact Assessment for EINSTEIN 3 Accelerated, at 2 (2013).

6. *Id.* at 4.

282

Notes

7. *Id.* at 3.

8. *Id.*

9. Toomas Hendrik Ilves, "Rebooting Trust? Freedom vs. Security in Cyberspace," opening address at Munich Security Conference Cyber, 31 January 2014, < http://www.president.ee/en/official-duties/speeches/9796-qrebooting-trust-freedom-vs-security-in-cyberspaceq/index.html>.

10. Frank Gardner, "Nato's cyber defence warriors," *BBC News*, 3 February 2009, <http://news.bbc.co.uk/2/mobile/europe/7851292.stm>.

11. The Comprehensive National Cybersecurity Initiative: Initative #3 (2010), *available at* https://www.whitehouse.gov/issues/foreign-policy/cybersecurity/national-initiative.

12. *See* Sanger, *supra* Introduction note 3.

Chapter 3

1. *Cyber Analysis and Warning: DHS Faces Challenges in Establishing a Comprehensive National Capability,* report by the United States Government Accountability Office for the House Subcommittee on Emerging Threats, Cybersecurity, and Science and Technology, July 2008, <http://www.gao.gov/new.items/d08588.pdf>, p. 3.

2. Ibid., pp. 28-50.

3. Jose Emilio Navas Lopez, Elsa Alama Salazar, Gregorio Martin de Castro, Pedro Lopez Saez, *Organizational Capital as Competitive Advantage of the Firm*, paper presented at the Fifth European Conference on Organizational Knowledge, Learning, and Capabilities, 2-3 April 2004, <www2.warwick.ac.uk/fac/soc/wbs/conf/olkc/archive/oklc5/papers/k-3_navas.pdf>

4. The memo calling for a standardization of a WBS within the DOD can be viewed here: <http://www.dsp.dla.mil/app_uil/content/documents/MIL-HDBK-881_USD%28AT%26L%29memo.pdf>.

5. Text in the blue box is drawn from the following source: "Guidance on Exhibit 300 – Planning, Budgeting Acquisition, and Management of Information Technology Capital Assets, " Office of Management and Budget, 2011, <http://www.whitehouse.gov/sites/default/files/omb/assets/egov_docs/fy13_guidance_for_exhibit_300_a-b_20110715.pdf>, p. 2.

6. *Information Technology: Agencies Need to Improve the Accuracy and Reliability of Investment Information,* report by the United States General Accountability Office for congressional requesters, January 2006, <http://www.gao.gov/new.items/d06250.pdf>.

7. "Management of Federal Information Resources," memorandum for heads of executive departments and agencies, Office of Management and Budget, 28 November 2000, <http://www.whitehouse.gov/omb/circulars_a130_a130trans4>, Appendix III.

8. The CFR can be accessed at the following link: <http://www.gpo.gov/fdsys/browse/collectionCfr.action?collectionCode=CFR>.

9. "HIPAA Administrative Simplification Statute and Rules," US Department of Health and Human Services,

Notes

<http://www.hhs.gov/ocr/privacy/hipaa/administrative/index.html>.

10. This diagram is a re-creation of a graphic found in the following publication: Matthew Scholl, Kevin Stine, Joan Hash, et al., *An Introductory Resource Guide for Implementing the Health Insurance Portability and Accountability Act (HIPAA) Security Rule*, NIST Special Publication 800-66 Revision 1, October 2008, <http://csrc.nist.gov/publications/nistpubs/800-66-Rev1/SP-800-66-Revision1.pdf>, p. 2.

11. This PHI criteria is drawn from the following source: "OCR Privacy Brief: Summary of the HIPAA Privacy Rule," US Department of Health and Human Services, <http://www.hhs.gov/ocr/privacy/hipaa/understanding/summary/privacysummary.pdf>, p. 4.

12. *Recommended Security Controls for Federal Information Systems and Organizations*, NIST Special Publication 800-53 Revision 3, August 2009, <http://csrc.nist.gov/publications/nistpubs/800-53-Rev3/sp800-53-rev3-final_updated-errata_05-01-2010.pdf>, p. 21.

Chapter 4

1. "Internet map 4096," by Matt Britt, licensed under Creative Commons Attribution 2.5 Generic (CC BY 2.5). Original image can be found at the following link: <http://commons.wikimedia.org/wiki/File:Internet_map_4096.png>.

2. "Botnet Operation Disabled," Federal Bureau of Investigation, 14 April 2011, <http://www.fbi.gov/news/stories/2011/april/botnet_041411>.

3. Evgeny Morozov, "Iran Elections: A Twitter Revolution?" online discussion hosted by the *Washington Post*, 17 June 2009, < http://www.washingtonpost.com/wp-dyn/content/discussion/2009/06/17/DI2009061702232.html>.

4. Alex Pilosov and Tony Kapela, "Stealing the Internet: An Internet-Scale Man In The Middle Attack," presentation for Defcon 16, 10 August 2008, < http://www.defcon.org/images/defcon-16/dc16-presentations/defcon-16-pilosov-kapela.pdf>.

5. This capability review is drawn from the following source: *Cyber Analysis and Warning: DHS Faces Challenges in Establishing a Comprehensive National Capability,* report by the United States Government Accountability Office for the House Subcommittee on Emerging Threats, Cybersecurity, and Science and Technology, July 2008, <http://www.gao.gov/new.items/d08588.pdf>, pp. 16-17.

6. The content of Figure 4-4 is drawn from the following source: *Cyber Analysis and Warning*, p. 20.

Chapter 5

1. John Markoff, "SecurID Company Suffers a Breach of Data Security," *The New York Times*, 17 March 2011, < http://www.nytimes.com/2011/03/18/technology/18secure.html?src=busln&_r=0>.

2. Matthew J. Schwartz, "RSA SecurID Breach Cost $66 Million," *Information Week*, 28 July 2011, < http://www.darkreading.com/attacks-and-breaches/rsa-securid-breach-cost-$66-million/d/d-id/1099232?>.

3. Jaikumar Vijayan, "TJX data breach: At 45.6M card numbers, it's the biggest ever," *ComputerWorld*, 29 March 2007, <http://www.computerworld.com/s/article/9014782/TJX_data_breach_At_45.6M_card_numbers_it_s_the_biggest_ever>.

Notes

4. Ross Kerber, "Cost of data breach at TJX soars to $256m," *Boston.com*, 15 August 2007, <http://www.boston.com/business/articles/2007/08/15/cost_of_data_breach_at_tjx_soars_to_256m/?page=full>

5. Liana B. Baker and Jim Finkle, "Sony PlayStation suffers massive data breach," *Reuters*, 26 August 2011, <http://www.reuters.com/article/2011/04/26/us-sony-stoldendata-idUSTRE73P6WB20110426>.

6. Matthew J. Schwartz, "Sony Data Breach Cleanup To Cost $171 Million," *Information Week*, 23 May 2011, <http://www.darkreading.com/attacks-and-breaches/sony-data-breach-cleanup-to-cost-$171-million/d/d-id/1097898?>.

7. "Web gumshoe runs credit card scam to ground," *NBCNews.com*, 23 September 1999, <http://www.nbcnews.com/id/3078814/ns/news-internet_underground/t/web-gumshoe-runs-credit-card-scam-ground/#.U2pZwvldVuM>.

Chapter 6

1. President Bush also issued Homeland Security Presidential Directives (HSPDs) with relevance to federal cybersecurity policy. These directives are categorized separately from national security instruments, according to a 2007 report from the Congressional Research Service. See *Presidential Directives: Background and Overview* (April 2007), available at <www.fas.org/irp/crs/98-611.pdf>. However, the Bush administration often issued HSPDs in tandem with national security instruments (as in the example of NSPD-54/HSPD-23).

2. The *Federal Register* can be found online at the following link: <http://www.gpo.gov/fdsys/browse/collection.action?collectionCode=FR>.

3. THOMAS will be available at the following link (<http://thomas.loc.gov/home/thomas.php>) until the end of 2014, at which point it will be replaced by Congress.gov.

4. The GAO's "Resources for Researchers" can be found at the following link: <http://www.gao.gov/researchers.html>.

5. The CFR can be accessed at the following link: <http://www.gpo.gov/fdsys/browse/collectionCfr.action?collectionCode=CFR>.

6. The opinion of the Supreme Court, written by Justice Antonin Scalia and delivered in October 2011, can be found at the following link: <http://www.law.cornell.edu/supct/pdf/10-1259.pdf>.

7. This breakdown of the seven types of criminal activity prohibited by the CFAA paraphrases the act's actual text, which can be found at the following link: <http://www.law.cornell.edu/uscode/text/18/1030>.

8. "Overview of the United States Sentencing Commission," United States Sentencing Commission, <http://www.ussc.gov/about>.

9. Gautham Nagesh, "Obama administration seeking tougher penalties for cybercrimes like hacking," *The Hill*, 7 September 2011, <http://thehill.com/policy/technology/179897-obama-administration-wants-tougher-penalties-for-cyber-crimes>.

10. Atika Shubert, "Cyber warfare: A different way to attack Iran's reactors," *CNN*, 8 November 2011, <http://www.cnn.com/2011/11/08/tech/iran-stuxnet/>.

11. *See, e.g.,* Iranian Cyber Threat to the U.S. Homeland Statements, *supra* Introduction note 4, 6.

12. *See* Sanger, *supra* Introduction note 3.

13. The IETF's mission statement can be viewed at the following link: <http://www.ietf.org/about/mission.html>. The RFC page can be viewed at the following link: <https://www.ietf.org/rfc.html>.

14. *Connect to Everyone, Trust No One: Data Integration for Cyber Attack and Threat Mitigation Solutions,* whitepaper by Data Integration, 2014, < http://www.dataintegration.com/assets/lib/documents/DataIntegrationWhitepaper_UK_final.pdf>, p. 6.

15. Frank Gardner, "Nato's cyber defence warriors," *BBC News*, 3 February 2009, < http://news.bbc.co.uk/2/mobile/europe/7851292.stm>.

References

Active Engagement, Modern Defence: Strategic Concept for the Defence and Security of the Members of the North Atlantic Treaty Organization, November 2010, <http://www.nato.int/nato_static/assets/pdf/pdf_publications/20120214_strategic-concept-2010-eng.pdf>.

Administrative Procedure Act (APA), 1946, <http://www.justice.gov/jmd/ls/legislative_histories/pl79-404/act-pl79-404.pdf>.

Blueprint for a Secure Cyber Future: The Cybersecurity Strategy for the Homeland Security Enterprise, Department of Homeland Security, November 2011, <http://www.dhs.gov/xlibrary/assets/nppd/blueprint-for-a-secure-cyber-future.pdf>.

Bottom-Up Review Report, Department of Homeland Security, July 2010, <https://www.dhs.gov/xlibrary/assets/bur_bottom_up_review.pdf>.

Brooks Automatic Data Processing Act, 1965, <http://www.itl.nist.gov/History%20Documents/Brooks%20Act.pdf>.

"Bucharest Summit Declaration," North Atlantic Council, 3 April 2008, <http://www.nato.int/cps/en/natolive/official_texts_8443.htm>.

California Security Breach Notification Act, 2002, <http://www.leginfo.ca.gov/pub/01-02/bill/sen/sb_1351-1400/sb_1386_bill_20020926_chaptered.html>.

"CF Disclosure Guidance: Topic No. 2," Securities and Exchange Commission, 13 October 2011, <http://www.sec.gov/divisions/corpfin/guidance/cfguidance-topic2.htm>.

Clinger-Cohen Act of 1996, <http://www.fismacenter.com/Clinger%20Cohen.pdf>.

COBIT 5 (Preview Version): A Business Framework for the Governance and Management of Enterprise IT, ISACA, 2012, <http://www.isaca.org/cobit/Documents/COBIT-5-Introduction.pdf>.

"Complaint," In re TJX Companies, Inc., FTC File No. 072-3055, 27 March 2008, <http://www.ftc.gov/sites/default/files/documents/cases/2008/08/080801tjxcomplaint.pdf>.

"The Comprehensive National Cybersecurity Initiative," WhiteHouse.gov, <http://www.whitehouse.gov/issues/foreign-policy/cybersecurity/national-initiative>.

Computer Fraud and Abuse Act (CFAA), 1986, <http://www.law.cornell.edu/uscode/text/18/1030>.

Computer Security Act of 1987, <http://csrc.nist.gov/groups/SMA/ispab/documents/csa_87.txt>.

Convention on Cybercrime, Council of Europe, 23 November 2001, <http://conventions.coe.int/Treaty/en/Treaties/Html/185.htm>.

Critical Foundations: Protecting America's Infrastructures, report by the President's Commission on Critical Infrastructure Protection, October 1997, <https://www.fas.org/sgp/library/pccip.pdf>.

Cybersecurity Act of 2012, <http://www.gpo.gov/fdsys/pkg/BILLS-112s2105pcs/pdf/BILLS-112s2105pcs.pdf>.

References

Cyberspace Policy Review: Assuring a Trusted and Resilient Information and Communications Infrastructure, May 2009, <http://www.whitehouse.gov/assets/documents/Cyberspace_Policy_Review_final.pdf>.

Department of Homeland Security Strategic Plan: Fiscal Years 2012-2016, Department of Homeland Security, February 2012, <http://www.dhs.gov/xlibrary/assets/dhs-strategic-plan-fy-2012-2016.pdf>.

DHS Risk Lexicon: 2010 Edition, Department of Homeland Security Risk Steering Committee, September 2010, <http://www.dhs.gov/xlibrary/assets/dhs-risk-lexicon-2010.pdf>.

E-Government Act of 2002, <http://www.gpo.gov/fdsys/pkg/PLAW-107publ347/pdf/PLAW-107publ347.pdf>.

Electronic Communications Privacy Act of 1986, <http://www.justice.gov/jmd/ls/legislative_histories/pl99-508/act-pl99-508.pdf>.

Enterprise Risk Management – Integrated Framework (Executive Summary), Committee of Sponsoring Organizations of the Treadway Commission (COSO), September 2004, <http://www.coso.org/documents/COSO_ERM_ExecutiveSummary.pdf>.

Executive Order 13228, "Establishing the Office of Homeland Security and the Homeland Security Council," 8 October 2001, <https://www.fas.org/irp/offdocs/eo/eo-13228.htm>.

Executive Order 13231, "Critical Infrastructure Protection in the Information Age," 16 October 2001, <http://www.dhs.gov/xlibrary/assets/executive-order-13231-dated-2001-10-16-initial.pdf>.

Executive Order 13636, "Improving Critical Infrastructure Cybersecurity," 12 February 2013, <http://www.gpo.gov/fdsys/pkg/FR-2013-02-19/pdf/2013-03915.pdf>.

Federal Acquisition Streamlining Act of 1994, <http://www.gpo.gov/fdsys/pkg/BILLS-103s1587enr/pdf/BILLS-103s1587enr.pdf>.

Federal Information Security Management Act of 2002 (FISMA), <http://csrc.nist.gov/drivers/documents/FISMA-final.pdf>.

Federal Trade Commission Act of 1914, <http://www.law.cornell.edu/uscode/text/15/chapter-2/subchapter-I>.

FIPS Publication 200, *Minimum Security Requirements for Federal Information and Information Systems*, March 2006, <http://csrc.nist.gov/publications/fips/fips200/FIPS-200-final-march.pdf>.

Government Paperwork Elimination Act of 1998, <http://www.gpo.gov/fdsys/pkg/PLAW-105publ277/html/PLAW-105publ277.htm>.

Government Performance and Results Act of 1993, <http://www.gpo.gov/fdsys/pkg/BILLS-103s20enr/pdf/BILLS-103s20enr.pdf>.

Gramm-Leach-Bliley Financial Services Modernization Act (GLB Act), 1999, <http://www.law.cornell.edu/uscode/text/15/chapter-94/subchapter-I>."Guidance on Exhibits 53 and 300 – Information Technology and E-Government," Office of Management and Budget, 2012, <http://www.whitehouse.gov/sites/default/files/omb/assets/egov_docs/fy14_guidance_on_exhibits_53_and_300.pdf>.

Guidelines Manual, United States Sentencing Commission, November 2013, <http://www.ussc.gov/sites/default/files/pdf/guidelines-manual/2013/manual-pdf/2013_Guidelines_Manual_Full.pdf>.

References

Health Information Technology for Economic and Clinical Health (HITECH) Act, 2009, <http://www.hhs.gov/ocr/privacy/hipaa/understanding/coveredentities/hitechact.pdf>.

Health Insurance Portability and Accountability Act of 1996 (HIPAA), <http://www.gpo.gov/fdsys/pkg/PLAW-104publ191/html/PLAW-104publ191.htm>.

Homeland Security Act of 2002, <http://www.dhs.gov/xlibrary/assets/hr_5005_enr.pdf>.

Homeland Security Presidential Directive 7, "Critical Infrastructure Identification, Prioritization, and Protection," 17 December 2003, <https://www.dhs.gov/homeland-security-presidential-directive-7#1>.

Identity Theft Penalty Enhancement Act, 2004, <http://www.gpo.gov/fdsys/pkg/PLAW-108publ275/pdf/PLAW-108publ275.pdf>.

In Re Caremark International Inc. Derivative Legislation, 1996, <http://www.wlrk.com/docs/INRECAREMARKINTERNATIONALINCDERIVATIVELITIGATION.pdf>.

In Re Citigroup Inc. Shareholder Derivative Litigation, 2009, <http://courts.delaware.gov/opinions/download.aspx?ID=118110>.

I*nternal Control – Integrated Framework (Executive Summary)*, Committee of Sponsoring Organizations of the Treadway Commission (COSO), 1992, <http://www.coso.org/documents/Internal%20Control-Integrated%20Framework.pdf>.

International Strategy for Cyberspace: Prosperity, Security, and Openness in a Networked World, May 2011, <http://www.whitehouse.gov/sites/default/files/rss_viewer/international_strategy_for_cyberspace.pdf>.

National Infrastructure Protection Plan: Partnering to enhance protection and resiliency, 2009, <http://www.dhs.gov/xlibrary/assets/NIPP_Plan.pdf>.

National Security Decision Directive Number 145, "National Policy on Telecommunications and Automated Information Systems Security," 17 September 1984, < https://www.fas.org/irp/offdocs/nsdd145.htm>.

NERC Standard CIP-008-04, "Cybersecurity – Incident Reporting and Response Planning," 24 January 2011, <http://www.nerc.com/files/CIP-008-4.pdf>.

New York Business Corporation Law, <http://codes.lp.findlaw.com/nycode/BSC>.

NIST Special Publication 800-30, *Risk Management Guide for Information Technology Systems*, July 2002, <http://csrc.nist.gov/publications/nistpubs/800-30/sp800-30.pdf>.

NIST Special Publication 800-53 Revision 4, *Security and Privacy Controls for Federal Information Systems and Organizations,* February 2014, <http://nvlpubs.nist.gov/nistpubs/SpecialPublications/NIST.SP.800-53r4.pdf>.NIST Special Publication 800-66 Revision 1, *An Introductory Resource Guide for Implementing the Health Insurance Portability and Accountability Act (HIPAA) Security Rule*, October 2008, <http://csrc.nist.gov/publications/nistpubs/800-66-Rev1/SP-800-66-Revision1.pdf>.

"The North Atlantic Treaty," 4 April 1949, <http://www.nato.int/cps/en/natolive/official_texts_17120.htm>.

OMB Circular No. A-11, "Preparation, Submission, and Execution of the Budget," July 2013, <http://www.whitehouse.gov/sites/default/files/omb/assets/a11_current_year/a11_2013.pdf>.

OMB Circular No. A-130 Revised, "Management of Federal Information Resources," 28 November 2000, <http://www.whitehouse.gov/omb/circulars_a130_a130trans4>.

References

OMB Memorandum M-10-28, "Clarifying Cybersecurity Responsibilities and Activities of the Executive Office of the President and the Department of Homeland Security (DHS)," 6 July 2010, <http://www.whitehouse.gov/sites/default/files/omb/assets/memoranda_2010/m10-28.pdf>.

OMB Memorandum M-97-02, "Funding Information Systems Investments," 25 October 1996, <http://www.whitehouse.gov/omb/memoranda_m97-02>.

Paperwork Reduction Act of 1980, <http://www.gpo.gov/fdsys/pkg/STATUTE-94/pdf/STATUTE-94-Pg2812.pdf>

Presidential Decision Directive 63, "Critical Infrastructure Protection," 22 May 1998, <https://www.fas.org/irp/offdocs/pdd/pdd-63.htm>.

Presidential Policy Directive 21, "Critical Infrastructure Security and Resilience," 12 February 2013, <http://www.whitehouse.gov/the-press-office/2013/02/12/presidential-policy-directive-critical-infrastructure-security-and-resil>.

Quadrennial Homeland Security Review Report: A Strategic Framework for a Secure Homeland, Department of Homeland Security, February 2010, <https://www.dhs.gov/xlibrary/assets/qhsr_report.pdf>.

RFC 2795, "The Infinite Monkey Protocol Suite (IMPS)," Internet Engineering Task Force, 1 April 2000, <http://tools.ietf.org/html/rfc2795>.

Sarbanes-Oxley Act of 2002, <http://www.gpo.gov/fdsys/pkg/PLAW-107publ204/pdf/PLAW-107publ204.pdf>.

"Scientific Integrity," Office of Science and Technology Policy, 17 December 2010, <http://www.whitehouse.gov/sites/default/files/microsites/ostp/scientific-integrity-memo-12172010.pdf>.

The National Strategy to Secure Cyberspace, February 2003, <https://www.us-cert.gov/sites/default/files/publications/cyberspace_strategy.pdf>.

Warner Amendment, 1988, <http://www.law.cornell.edu/uscode/text/10/2315>.

Extended Reading

Lesson 1: Introduction to Cybersecurity

1. Basulto, Dominic. "Stuxnet, Flame and Fulfilling the Dream of Sun Tzu." *Washington Post (Washington, D.C.)*, June 1, 2012, sec. National. http://www.washingtonpost.com/blogs/innovations/post/stuxnet-flame-and-fulfilling-the-dream-of-sun-tzu/2012/06/01/gJQA6lJv6U_blog.html (accessed September 11, 2012).

2. Clarke, Richard A., and Robert K. Knake. *Cyber War: The Next Threat To National Security and What To Do About It*. New York: Ecco, 2010.

3. Lachow, Irving. "The Stuxnet Enigma: Implications for the Future of Cybersecurity." *Georgetown Journal of International Affairs* International Engagement on Cyber, no. Establishing International Norms and Improved Cybersecurity (2011): 118-126.

4. EPIC - Electronic Privacy Information Center. "EPIC - Computer Security Act of 1987." N.p., n.d. Web. 19 Sept. 2012. http://epic.org/crypto/csa/.

5. Mitnick, Kevin D., and William L. Simon. *Ghost In The Wires: My Adventures as the World's Most Wanted Hacker*. New York: Little, Brown and Company, 2011.

6. Mitnick, Kevin D., and William L. Simon. *The art of deception: controlling the human element of security*. Indianapolis, Ind.: Wiley Pub., 2002.

7. Reed, Warren G. "Statement on the Potential Impact of National Security Decision Directive (NSDD) 145 On Civil Agencies." Washington: Government Printing Office, June 27, 1985. http://archive.gao.gov/d40t12/127279.pdf

8. Sanger, David E.. "Chapter 10: The Dark Side of the Light Footprint." In *Confront and Conceal: Obama's Secret Wars and Surprising Use of American Power*. New York: Crown Publishers, 2012. 243-273.

9. Stoll, Clifford. *The Cuckoo's Egg: Tracking a Spy Through the Maze of Computer Espionage*. New York: Doubleday, 1989.

10. Sudduth, Andy. "The What, Why, and How of the 1988 Internet Worm." www.snowplow.org. http://snowplow.org/tom/worm/worm.html (accessed September 20, 2012).

Lesson 2: Risk Management

1. Committee on National Security Systems. 2007/2008 Committee on National Security Systems (CNSS) Report: *An Agenda for Safeguarding National Security Systems*. 2008. http://niatec.info/GetFile.aspx?pid=621

2. Committee on National Security Systems. *Information Assurance (IA) Education, Training, and Awareness*. 2006. http://niatec.info/GetFile.aspx?pid=622

3. Committee on National Security Systems. *National Directive On Security of National Security Systems*. 2004.

Extended Reading

http://niatec.info/GetFile.aspx?pid=595

4. Department of Homeland Security. *National Infrastructure Protection Plan (NIPP) Risk Management Framework*. 2009.

5. Department of Homeland Security. *Risk Lexicon*. September 2010.

6. National Institute of Standards and Technology. NIST SP 800-39, *Managing Information Security Risk*. March 2011.

7. National Institute of Standards and Technology. NIST SP 800-53, *Recommended Security Controls for Federal Information Systems*. August 2009.

Lesson 3: Law and Policy

1. Brooks Automatic Data Processing Act of 1949. Public Law 89-306.

2. Clinger Cohen Act of 1996. Public Law 104-106.

3. Computer Security Act of 1987. Public Law 100-325.

4. Dycus, Stephen. "Congress's Role In Cyber Warfare." *Journal of National Security Law & Policy* vol. 4, no. 1 (2010): 155-171.

5. Executive Order 13011, *Federal Information Technology*. 1996.

6. Executive Order 13228, Establishing the Office of Homeland Security and the Homeland Security Council. 2001.

7. Executive Order 13231, Critical Infrastructure Structure in the Information Age. 2001.

8. Homeland Security Act of 2002. Public Law 107-296.

9. Homeland Security Presidential Directive 7, Critical Infrastructure Identification, Prioritization, and Protection. 2003.

10. National Security Decision Directive 145. National Policy on Telecommunications and Automated Information Systems Security. 1984.

11. National Security Presidential Directive 54/Homeland Security Presidential Directive 23 (NSPD-54/HSPD-23). Comprehensive National Cybersecurity Initiative, Cybersecurity & Monitoring. 2010.

12. Nunn-Warner (Warner) Amendment. 10 U.S.C. 2315. 1988.

13. Office of Management and Budget. Memoranda 97-02, Funding Information Systems Investments. 1996.

14. Office of Management and Budget. OMB Circular No. A-130, Management of Federal Information Resources. 1996.

15. Paperwork Reduction Act of 1995. Public Law 104-13.

16. Presidential Decision Directive 63, Critical Infrastructure Protection. 1998.

17. Public Law 107-347, Federal Information Management Security Act. 2002.

Extended Reading

18. Sharp Sr., Walter G. "The Past, Present, and Future of Cybersecurity." Journal of National Security Law & Policy vol. 4, no. 1 (2010): 13-26.

19. White House. *Cyberspace Policy Review.* 2009

Lesson 4: Project Mangement

1. Department of Homeland Security. *Appendix C - Mission Need Statement.* 2011.

2. Office of Management and Budget. Circular A-11, Section 300, P*lanning, Budgeting, Acquisition, and Management of Capital Assets.* 2008.

Lesson 5: Computer Science and Engineering Fundamentals

1. United States Government Accountability Office. *GAO-08-588, Cyber Analysis and Warnings* (p 5-9). 2008.

Lesson 6: The Private Sector

1. Federal Trade Commission. *FTC Consent Decree, Twitter, Inc.* 2010.

2. TJX. "TJX Value: The TJX Companies, Inc. 2007 Annual Report." (p 13, 19). 2007. http://www.sec.gov/Archives/edgar/vprr/08/9999999997-08-022833

Lesson 7: Research and Methods

1. Brunner, Elgin M. and Manuel Suter. *International CIIP Handbook 2008/2009.* pp 463-521 http://www.css.ethz.ch/publications/pdfs/CIIP-HB-08-09.pdf

2. Computer Fraud and Abuse Act. CRS Summary. 1986. http://thomas.loc.gov/cgi-bin/bdquery/z?d099:HR04718:@@@D&summ2=m&

3. Davis, Joshua. "Hackers Take Down the Most Wired Network in Europe." Wired Magazine. 2007.

4. Department of Homeland Security. *The Comprehensive Cybersecurity Initiative.* http://www.whitehouse.gov/sites/default/files/cybersecurity.pdf

5. Dove, Robert B. "Enactment of a Law." Library of Congress. http://thomas.loc.gov/home/enactment/enactlaw.pdf

6. Jacobs, Andrew and Miguel Helft. "Google, Citing Attack, Threatens to Exit China." New York Times. World. January 12, 2010.

7. Maurer, Tim. *Cyber Norm Emergence at the United Nations.* Harvard. September 2011.

8. Sullivan, John V. "*How our Laws Are Made.*" Government Printing Office. 2007. http://www.gpo.gov/fdsys/pkg/CDOC-110hdoc49/pdf/CDOC-110hdoc49.pdf

Cybersecurity Foundations:
Syllabus

I. Course Overview

Cybersecurity is a dynamic and growing industry. As an academic discipline, cybersecurity has never been deeper or more important, having evolved from a relatively obscure concentration into a highly complex, interdisciplinary field rich in both research possibilities and real-world applications.

As the world enters an age increasingly defined by information technology systems, we find ourselves increasingly reliant upon computer-based technologies. As this reliance on computers grows stronger in all aspects of modern life, so too do attacks on computers and networks. It therefore becomes increasingly necessary – and increasingly challenging – to secure the technological tools that play a critical role in our personal and professional lives.

Cyber threats against individuals, governments, and businesses are continually taking on newer, more complex, and more dangerous forms. At this moment, highly skilled cyber attackers around the world are in the process of crafting revolutionary attack methods to thwart the latest cybersecurity innovations. As a consequence, cybersecurity professionals today must possess a range of academic and technical skills to secure information and infrastructure and combat new attacks.

The purpose of this course is to provide an introduction to the range of disciplines that are fundamental to protecting cyber assets in the modern world. Students will learn what cybersecurity is, how it has evolved since the 1940s, and how cybersecurity frameworks can be applied across a wide range of contexts and industries. This course will also provide an introduction to the various technical and non-technical skills that are foundational in any cybersecurity career. During this course, students will gain the professional and academic foundations to pursue further study and concentration in any aspect of cybersecurity.

II. Prerequisites

There are no prerequisites for this course

III. Course Topics

- Introduction to Cybersecurity
- Risk Management
- Cybersecurity Law, Policy, and Analysis
- Management Theory and Practice
- Fundamentals of Computer Science
- Private Sector Applications of Cybersecurity
- Cybersecurity Research and Methods

Syllabus

IV. Learning Objectives

1. Gain an appreciation and basic understanding of the key disciplines that support cybersecurity capabilities, including computer science, risk management, program management, and federal law and policy
2. Understand the depth and breadth of cyber-based threats in the modern world
3. Become familiar with key national and global institutions and their influence on international cybersecurity policies and standards
4. Understand the structure and functions of the U.S. federal government with regard to national cybersecurity
5. Learn the obligations of private sector companies with regard to information security
6. Recognize the government-mandated initiative to leverage both public and private sector cybersecurity capabilities in order to respond to growing physical and computer-based threats against U.S. critical infrastucture
7. Gain basic fluency in the quantitative disciplines that support advanced cyber security practice, including risk quantification, management sciences, Earned Value Management, and cost-benefit analyses
8. Understand the theory and practice of risk management, as well as ways to assess and mitigate risk
9. Become familiar with key computer science and engineering concepts that inform cybersecurity capabilities, including programming, hardware and software, and IT architecture
10. Learn common methods of cyber attacks and exploits, and some of the ways that organizations have learned to anticipate and protect themselves from these threats
11. Understand how to plan and execute cybersecurity programs, and how this process is conducted at the federal level
12. Gain a deep appreciation for cybersecurity research, including ways to research the evolving cybersecurity laws and policies of the U.S. federal government

V. Required Text

Lee Zeichner, <u>Cybersecurity Foundations: An Interdisciplinary Introduction</u>, ZRA ©2012

VI. Course Requirements

<u>Homework:</u> Each week, students will receive a set of practice problems. These problems will be due at the beginning of class each Tuesday and will be graded for completion. Late assignments will receive 25% credit.

<u>Quizzes:</u> There will be a weekly quiz. These quizzes will cover any material mentioned in class or within the textbook chapter assigned for the week.

<u>Team Project</u>: During the middle of the semester, students be required to complete a case study project. Each group of five students will have three project topics to choose from. Each group will be required to complete ONE 7-page paper, create a slide show, and give a 20-minute presentation. This project will be DUE AT THE BEGINNING OF CLASS **OCTOBER 11TH**.

<u>Term Paper:</u> One 8-page term paper will be DUE AT THE BEGINNING OF CLASS **NOVEMBER 27TH**. A list

Cybersecurity Foundations: An Interdisciplinary Introduction

of topics and additional information about the term paper will be available in-class on the date listed within the course schedule below. NO LATE PAPERS WILL BE ACCEPTED.

<u>Final Exam:</u> At the end of the semester, each student will be responsible for completing a 2-hour final exam. The exam will be comprehensive, including all of the information covered throughout the semester.

VII. Grading System

Course Item	Percent of Final Grade
Homework	5%
Quizzes	10%
Team Project	20%
Term Paper	25%
Final Exam	40%
Total	**100%**

VIII. Office Hours

Virtual office hours will take place each Wednesday from 13:00 – 15:00. I will also be available TR from 14:00 – 16:00 for in-person office hours in my office, Mumford Hall – 208C.

IX. Course Schedule

Week 1: Introduction to Cybersecurity

This week, we will define cybersecurity as a field and explore how cybersecurity challenges have unfolded in the past seventy years. We will learn the fundamental areas of knowledge that professionals need to master in order to solve modern cybersecurity problems.		
Read Before Class	Day 2	• National Security Decision Directive-145 • Sanger, David E. "Chapter 10: The Dark Side of the Light Footprint." In *Confront and Conceal: Obama's Secret Wars and Surprising Use of American Power*. New York: Crown Publishers, 2012. 243-273. • Zeichner, Lee. "Introduction: From ARPANET to Stuxnet." In *Cybersecurity Foundations: An Interdisciplinary Introduction*.
Cover In Class	Day 1	• Syllabus overview • Interdisciplinary nature and importance of cybersecurity
	Day 2	• Cybersecurity principles and challenges

Syllabus

Week 2: Risk Management for Cybersecurity: Overview

This week, we will discuss Risk Management for cybersecurity, and learn about Threat and Vulnerability Assessments.		
Read Before Class	Day 2	• National Energy Regulatory Commission (NERC). "Cyber Attack Task Force: Final Report." May 9, 2012. pp. 1-10. http://www.nerc.com/docs/cip/catf/12-CATF_Final_Report_BOT_-clean_Mar_26_2012-Board%20Accepted%200521.pdf • U.S. Department of Energy. "Electricity Subsector Cybersecurity Risk Management Process 2012." http://energy.gov/sites/prod/files/Cybersecurty%20Risk%20Management%20Process%20Guideline%20-%20Final%20-%20May%202012.pdf • Zeichner, Lee. "Chapter 1: Risk Management for Cybersecurity." In *Cybersecurity Foundations: An Interdisciplinary Introduction*.
		• Department of Homeland Security, National Infrastructure Protection Plan (NIPP) Risk Management Framework (2009) • Department of Homeland Security, Risk Lexicon (September 2010) • National Institute of Standards and Technology (NIST), NIST SP 800-53, Recommended Security Controls for Federal Information Systems (August 2009) • National Institute of Standards and Technology (NIST), NIST SP 800-39, Managing Information Security Risk (March 2011)
Cover In Class	Day 1	• Introduction to risk management for cybersecurity • Interactive case study, protecting a home
	Day 2	• Threat assessments and vulnerability assessments

Week 3: Risk Management for Cybersecurity: Consequence and Risk Determination

This week, we will cover Consequence Assessments and Risk Determination, and quantitative and graphical risk determination models.		
Read Before Class	Day 1	• Department of Homeland Security, National Infrastructure Protection Plan (NIPP) Risk Management Framework (2009) • Department of Homeland Security, Risk Lexicon (September 2010)
	Day 2	• U.S. Department of Energy. "Electricity Subsector Cybersecurity Risk Management Process 2012." http://energy.gov/sites/prod/files/Cybersecurity%20Risk%20Management%20Process%20Guideline%20-%20Final%20-%20May%202012.pdf
Cover In Class	Day 1	• Consequence assessment and risk determination
	Day 2	• Quantitative and graphical risk determination models

Cybersecurity Foundations: An Interdisciplinary Introduction

Week 4: Risk Management for Cybersecurity: Risk Response and Monitoring

This week, we will cover Risk Response and Monitoring techniques.		
Read Before Class	Day 1	• Zeichner, Lee. "Chapter 1: Risk Management for Cybersecurity." In Cybersecurity Foundations: An Interdisciplinary Introduction.
	Day 2	• Risk management Tabletop Worksheet
Cover In Class	Day 1	• Risk response and monitoring techniques
	Day 2	• Risk management Tabletop exercise

Week 5: Cybersecurity Law and Policy: Introduction to Cybersecurity and the Federal Government

This week, we will introduce fundamental cybersecurity concepts regarding law and policy. We will learn the history of cybersecurity and its development as a national and global policy challenge. We will study the roles and responsibilities of the President and Congress in producing cybersecurity laws and policies, and critically examine the information security laws and policies of the United States government since 1965.		
Read Before Class	Day 1	• Brooks Act CRS Summary • Computer Security Act CRS Summary • NSDD 145 • Sharp Sr., Walter Gary. "The Past, Present, and Future of Cybersecurity." Journal of National Security Law & Policy vol. 4, no. 1 (2010): 13-26. http://jnslp.com/wp-content/uploads/2010/08/03_Sharp.pdf • Warner Amendment • Zeichner, Lee. "Chapter 2: Cybersecurity Law and Policy." In Cybersecurity Foundations: An Interdisciplinary Introduction.
	Day 2	• Clinger-Cohen Act CRS Summary • Executive Order 13011 • Memoranda 97-02 • OMB Circular No. A-130 • Paperwork Reduction Act CRS Summary
Cover In Class	Day 1	• Cybersecurity and the federal government
	Day 2	• Civilian versus military control of federal information systems

Syllabus

Week 6: Cybersecurity Law and Policy: Development of Modern Cybersecurity Policy

This week, we will discuss the development of modern cybersecurity policy and the state of contemporary cybersecurity policy.		
Read Before Class	Day 1	• Executive Order 13228 • Executive Order 13231 • Federal Information Security Management Act (FISMA) CRS Summary • Homeland Security Act (HSA) of 2002 CRS Summary • Homeland Security Presidential Directive 7 (HSPD-7) • NSPD-54/HSPD-23 • Presidential Decision Directive 63 (PDD-63)
	Day 2	• Cyberspace Policy Review, White House, 2009 http://www.whitehouse.gov/assets/documents/Cyberspace_Policy_Review_final.pdf • Department of Homeland Security. "Blueprint for a Secure Cyber Future." November 2011. http://www.dhs.gov/xlibrary/assets/nppd/blueprint-for-a-secure-cyber-future.pdf • Dycus, Stephen. "Congress's Role In Cyber Warfare." Journal of National Security Law & Policy vol. 4, no. 1 (2010): 155-171. http://jnslp.com/wp-content/uploads/2010/08/11_Dycus.pdf
Cover In Class	Day 1	• Modern cybersecurity policy
	Day 2	• Contemporary and future cybersecurity policy

Week 7: Fundamentals of Management for Cybersecurity: Introduction

This week, we will establish a clear distinction between managerial and technical work. We will see how management skills apply to cyber problems, and we will study and critically examine the formal managerial framework used in federal government cybersecurity programs.		
Read Before Class	Day 1	• Schwalbe, Kathy. "Chapter 1: Introduction to Project Management" and "Chapter 2: The Project Management and Information Technology Context." In Information Technology Project Management. • Zeichner, Lee. "Chapter 3: Fundamentals of Management for Cybersecurity." In Cybersecurity Foundations: An Interdisciplinary Introduction.
	Day 2	• National Response Framework Summary • National Strategy to Secure Cyberspace Summary • NIST. "Frequently Asked Questions: Continuous Monitoring." June 2010. http://csrc.nist.gov/groups/SMA/fisma/documents/faq-continuous-monitoring.pdf
Cover In Class	Day 1	• What do managers do?
	Day 2	• US-CERT case study

Cybersecurity Foundations: An Interdisciplinary Introduction

Week 9: Fundamentals of Management for Cybersecurity: Government Tools and Frameworks

This week, students will be introduced to the many complexities and challenges of program management. Students will learn how the Department of Homeland Security (DHS) plans and manages its cybersecurity programs. Students will read real-world examples of project management processes in order to connect theory and practice.

Read Before Class	Day 1	• "Chapter 1.2: Planning, Programming, Budgeting and Execution (PPBE) Process" in Defense Acquisition Guidebook https://acc.dau.mil/CommunityBrowser.aspx?id=488289#1.2 • (Sample CONOPS) Federal Interagency Geospatial Concept of Operations. http://www.nsgic.org/public_resources/DHS_Geospatial_CONOPS_v30_85x11.pdf • (Sample DHS CONOPS) DHS Interaction With State and Local Fusion Centers Concept of Operations http://www.fas.org/irp/agency/dhs/conops.pdf • (Sample DHS MNS Template) TSA Mission Need Statement Guide http://www.tsa.gov/video/pdfs/mds/TSAMNSGuide%28042607%29.pdf • (Sample DHS MNS) Integrated Deepwater System Mission Needs Statement http://www.uscg.mil/history/docs/2004_USCG_revisedmns.pdf • DoD PPBE An Executive Primer https://www.documentcloud.org/documents/293931-dodarmyppbeprimernov-2011.html
Cover In Class	Day 1	• Managerial challenges & the DHS Managerial Framework
	Day 2	• The DHS Managerial Framework: Theory and Practice

Week 10: Computer Science Fundamentals and Cybersecurity Operations

Students will learn the basic structure of computers and IT tools, as well as the various languages and processes that are fundamental to the efficient transfer of information via the Internet. Students will be introduced to the various attack methods that threaten information in cyberspace, as well as the processes and tools organizations use to protect themselves and their information from cyber attacks.

Read Before Class	Day 1	• Zeichner, Lee. "Chapter 4: Computer Science Fundamentals and Cybersecurity Operations." In Cybersecurity Foundations: An Interdisciplinary Introduction.
		• Maps, diagrams, and illustrated facts about the Internet: http://mountpeaks.wordpress.com/2012/03/06/what-has-the-internet-evolved-into-nowadays/ • Commercial Communications Satellite map http://comsoft-sat.com/app/download/5782687752/Commercial+Communications+Satellites.png • Internet History Timeline: http://www.computerhistory.org/internet_history/
Cover In Class	Day 1	• Computing and information technology fundamentals
	Day 2	• The Internet

Syllabus

Week 11: Computer Science Fundamentals and Cybersecurity Operations: Cyber Attacks and Cybersecurity Operations

Students will be able to identify the characteristics of cyber attacks and exploits, and learn technical ways to anticipate and defend against them.		
Read Before Class	Day 1	• Frontline: Cyberwar Interactive Website http://www.pbs.org/wgbh/pages/frontline/shows/cyberwar/ • ICS-CERT. "Incident Response Summary Report 2009-2011." https://ics-cert.us-cert.gov/sites/default/files/documents/ICS-CERT%20 Incident%20Response%20Summary%20Report%20%282009-2011%29_accessible.pdf • NIAC Prioritizing Cyber Vulnerabilities 2004. http://www.dhs.gov/xlibrary/assets/niac/NIAC_CyberVulnerabilitiesPaper_Feb05.pdf • Zeichner, Lee. "Chapter 4: Computer Science Fundamentals and Cybersecurity Operations." In *Cybersecurity Foundations: An Interdisciplinary Introduction*.
	Day 2	• An Annex to the NIPP: Communications Sector-Specific Plan 2010. http://www.dhs.gov/xlibrary/assets/nipp-ssp-communications-2010.pdf • FERC Example Security Plan http://www.ferc.gov/industries/hydropower/safety/guidelines/security/security-plan-example.pdf • NIST SP 800-64 http://csrc.nist.gov/publications/nistpubs/800-64-Rev2/SP800-64-Revision2.pdf • The DHS Cybersecurity Mission: Promoting Innovation and Securing Critical Infrastructure. http://www.gpo.gov/fdsys/pkg/CHRG-112hhrg72229/pdf/CHRG-112hhrg72229.pdf
Cover In Class	Day 1	• Cyber attacks and exploits
	Day 2	• Cybersecurity operations

Cybersecurity Foundations: An Interdisciplinary Introduction

Week 12: Cybersecurity for the Private Sector

We will introduce fundamental private sector concepts and principles. Students will learn basic legal and regulatory challenges facing the private sector, including legal liability. Students will be able to identify, explain, and analyze major legal and regulatory rules that the private sector must address as a routine part of cybersecurity planning. We will outline models for robust cybersecurity plans and programs for the private sector.

Read Before Class	Day 1	• Zeichner, Lee. "Chapter 5:Cybersecurity for the Private Sector." In *Cybersecurity Foundations: An Interdisciplinary Introduction*. • Management's Role in Information Security in a Cyber Economy http://irps.ucsd.edu/assets/001/501280.pdf.
	Day 2	• Cyber Security Incident Reporting and Response Planning 008-04 (CIP-008-04) • FTCA violation against TJX • Gramm-Leach-Bliley Financial Modernization Act CRS Summary http://thomas.loc.gov/cgi-bin/bdquery/z?d106:SN00900:@@@D&summ2=m& • Health Information Technology for Economic and Clinical Health Act (HITECH) CRS Summary (American Recovery and Reinvestment Act of 2009, Title XIII) http://thomas.loc.gov/cgi-bin/bdquery/z?d111:HR00001:@@@D&summ2=m& • Health Insurance Portability and Accountability Act (HIPAA) CRS Summary http://thomas.loc.gov/cgi-bin/bdquery/z?d104:HR03103:@@@D&summ2=m& • Sarbanes-Oxley Act (SOX) CRS Summary http://thomas.loc.gov/cgi-bin/bdquery/z?d107:HR03763:@@@D&summ2=m&
Cover In Class	Day 1	• What is a corporation? • The legal obligations of corporations
	Day 2	• Cybersecurity operations

Week 13: Cybersecurity for the Private Sector: Methods of Protecting Private Sector Networks

Students will learn the many ways in which leaders of private sector companies think, plan, and act in order to protect their IT systems.

Read Before Class	Day 1	• Allen, Julia H. Governing for Enterprise Security Implementation Guide. "Article 1: Characteristics of Effective Security Governance." Carnegie Mellon University, Software Engineering Institute. http://www.cert.org/governance/ges.html • Dunn, Catherine. Boards of Directors Largely Ignoring Corporate Cyber-Risk Management http://www.law.com/jsp/cc/PubArticleCC.jsp?id=1202544750336&Boards_of_Directors_Largely_Ignoring_Corporate_CyberRisk_Management • FEMA Business Continuity Plan website http://www.ready.gov/business/implementation/continuity
	Day 2	• Jain, Raj. Intrusion Detection Systems http://www1.cse.wustl.edu/~jain/cse571-07/ftp/l_23ids.pdf • Kundra, Vivek. "25 Point Implementation Plan to Reform Federal Information Technology Management," Dec. 9, 2010. http://www.dhs.gov/sites/default/files/publications/digital-strategy/25-point-implementation-plan-to-reform-federal-it.pdf • Sample Business Continuity Plan (worksheet) http://www.ready.gov/sites/default/files/documents/files/BusinessContinuityPlan.pdf
Cover In Class	Day 1	• The model cybersecurity plan for the private sector

Syllabus

Week 14: Cybersecurity for the Private Sector: Methods of Protecting Private Sector Networks

Students will learn some of the "big picture" complications associated with implementing cybersecurity measures in the private sector. Students will gain insight into the connections between cybersecurity and sound business practices. Students will understand the legal and financial consequences of neglecting cybersecurity. Moving into Chapter 6.0, students will learn how federal rules and regulations are created and how cyber crimes are prosecuted, and gain a foundation of knowledge for performing research in the field.

Read Before Class	Day 1	• FTC Complaint Against TJX http://www.ftc.gov/sites/default/files/documents/cases/2008/08/080801tjxcomplaint.pdf • FTC Agreement with TJX http://www.ftc.gov/sites/default/files/documents/cases/2008/03/080327agreement_0.pdf • FTC Complaint Against Twitter http://www.ftc.gov/sites/default/files/documents/cases/2011/03/110311twittercmpt.pdf • FTC Agreement with Twitter http://www.ftc.gov/sites/default/files/documents/cases/2010/06/100624twitteragree.pdf • FTC Complaint Against Sony http://www.ftc.gov/sites/default/files/documents/cases/2008/12/081211cmp0823071.pdf • FTC Agreement with Sony http://www.ftc.gov/os/caselist/0823071/081211consentp0823071.pdf
	Day 2	• (Video) "Legislative Research" • Albert Gonzalez Case Study • Computer Fraud and Abuse Act (CFAA) CRS Summary http://thomas.loc.gov/cgi-bin/bdquery/z?d099:HR04718:@@@D&summ2=m& • Dove, Robert B. "Enactment of a Law." http://thomas.loc.gov/home/enactment/enactlaw.pdf • Sullivan, John V. "How Our Laws Are Made." 2007. http://www.gpo.gov/fdsys/pkg/CDOC-110hdoc49/pdf/CDOC-110hdoc49.pdf • Zeichner, Lee. "Chapter 6: Advanced Cybersecurity Studies." *Cybersecurity Foundations: An Interdisciplinary Introduction*.
Cover In Class	Day 1	• TJX, Twitter, and Sony Case Studies
	Day 2	• The roles of the President, Congress, and the courts in cybersecurity legislation, regulation, crime, and punishment

Cybersecurity Foundations: An Interdisciplinary Introduction

Week 15: Advanced Cybersecurity Studies

Students will be able to identify major executive branch policy documents on cybersecurity and understand the role of the President in shaping cybersecurity policy. Students will further understand the interplay between the three branches of government regarding cybersecurity laws and policies. Students will understand the federal regulations process and be able to use and analyze the Federal Register.		
Read Before Class	Day 1	• (Video) "Executive Policy" • (Video) House Committee on Homeland Security. "Subcommittee Hearing: Preventing Nuclear Terrorism: Does DHS have an Effective and Efficient Nuclear Detection Strategy?" http://homeland.house.gov/hearing/subcommittee-hearing-preveting-nuclear-terrorism-does-dhs-have-effective-and-efficient • Clinton, William J. PDD-63. 1998 • DHS strategy and business model • Organization of the National Security Council Packet (PDD-1, NSPD-1, PPD-1, HSPD-1 clips)
	Day 2	• "The Reg Map" http://www.reginfo.gov/public/reginfo/Regmap/regmap.pdf • (Video) "Federal Regulations" • DHS. The Comprehensive Cybersecurity Initiative. http://www.whitehouse.gov/sites/default/files/cybersecurity.pdf
Cover In Class	Day 1	• TJX, Twitter, and Sony Case Studies
	Day 2	• The roles of the President, Congress, and the courts in cybersecurity legislation, regulation, crime, and punishment

Week 16: Advanced Cybersecurity Studies: Federal Cybersecurity Regulations & Global Cybersecurity Policy

This week we will discuss how the interactions between Congress and the President shape cybersecurity regulations.		
Read Before Class	Day 1	• Brunner, Elgin M. and Manuel Suter. International CIIP Handbook 2008/2009. pp 463-521 http://www.css.ethz.ch/publications/pdfs/CI-IP-HB-08-09.pdf • Davis, Joshua. Hackers Take Down the Most Wired Network in Europe. Wired Magazine, 2007. http://archive.wired.com/politics/security/magazine/15-09/ff_estonia?currentPage=all • Jacobs, Andrew and Miguel Helft. "Google, Citing Attack, Threatens to Exit China." New York Times. January 12, 2010 http://www.nytimes.com/2010/01/13/world/asia/13beijing.html • Maurer, Tim. Cyber Norm Emergence at the United Nations. September 2011. http://belfercenter.ksg.harvard.edu/files/maurer-cyber-norm-dp-2011-11-final.pdf
	Day 2	• Review of Chapter 6 readings.
Cover In Class	Day 1	• Global cybersecurity institutions and policies
	Day 2	• Exam review

Syllabus

Wk	Month	Tues	Thurs	Relevant Reading	Material Covered in Tuesday Lecture	Material Covered in Thursday Lecture
1	Aug.	28	30	Intro	Importance of Cybersecurity	Cybersecurity Principles and Challenges
2	Sept.	4	6	Ch. 1	Introduction to Risk Management	Threats and Vulnerabilities
3		11	13	Ch. 1	Consequences and Risk Determination	Quantitative Risk Determination Models
4		18	20	Ch. 1	Risk Response and Monitoring	Risk Management Tabletop Exercise
5		25	27	Ch. 2	Cybersecurity and the Federal Government	Civilian vs. military control of federal information systems
6	Oct.	2	4	Ch. 2	Development of Modern Cybersecurity Policy	Contemporary & Future Cybersecurity Policy
7		9	11	Ch. 3	Introduction to Management ("What do managers do?")	Continuous Monitoring Systems, US-CERT Case Study **(Team Project Due)**
8		**16**	**18**		**Fall Break**	**Fall Break**
9		23	25	Ch. 3	Managerial Challenges & the DHS Managerial Framework	The DHS Managerial Framework: Theory & Practice
10	Oct./Nov.	30	1	Ch. 4	Computing and IT Fundamentals	The Internet
11		6	8	Ch. 4	Cyber Attacks & Exploits	Cybersecurity Operations
12		13	15	Ch. 5	What is a corporation?	Cybersecurity Legislation and the Private Sector
13		20	22	Ch. 5	The Model Cybersecurity Plan for the Private Sector	**Thanksgiving**
14		27	29	Ch. 6	Table Top Exercise – TJX, Twitter, Sony (Term Paper Due)	Congress and the Courts – Cyber Crime and Punishment
15	Dec.	4	6	Ch. 6	Executive Branch - Policy	Federal Cybersecurity Regulations
16		11	13	Ch. 6	Global Cybersecurity Institutions and Policies	Exam Review

Final Exam – Thursday December 20th @ 19:00-21:00 (7:00pm-9:00pm) Rooms TBA

Lesson Plan

Lesson 1: Introduction to Cybersecurity

Lesson 1: Teaching Objectives-

In this lesson, students will be introduced to the field of cybersecurity and its origins. The class will explore case studies involving core cybersecurity concepts, key terms, and principles, and learn the cybersecurity challenges that face both the public and private sectors. Students will learn how cybersecurity challenges have unfolded over the last five decades. Finally, students will be introduced to the fundamental areas of knowledge that are necessary for understanding and approaching modern cybersecurity problems.

Day 1: Introduction to Cybersecurity

Syllabus Review (15min)

The class will walk through each section of the course syllabus so that all students understand the course requirements, objectives, and schedule.

Lecture: Importance of Cybersecurity (1h)

Materials:

- Class Syllabus
- "Introduction: From ARPANET to Stuxnet." in Zeichner, Lee. Cybersecurity Foundations: *An Interdisciplinary Introduction.*
- NSDD-145 handout

Lecture Objectives:

- Students will be introduced to cybersecurity as a multi-disciplinary, research-based academic field.
- Students will understand the major actors, events, and technologies that have influenced the study and practice of cybersecurity since the early 1980s
- Students will gain a foundation of knowledge to better understand the critical importance of cybersecurity, as well as the interdisciplinary nature of the field.

Activities and Procedures:

1) Students will learn about Admiral John Poindexter, his role in the implementation of National Security Decision Directive-145, and how NSDD-145 marked the beginning of cybersecurity as a field for

Lesson 1: Introduction to Cybersecurity

academic research and heated policy debate. Students will learn about the origin and significance of personal computers (PCs) and Poindexter's vision for how to protect United States information stored on government computers.

2) Students will learn about the "Morris Worm", the implications of experiments with computer viruses, and how this attack set the precedence for the denial of services (DoS) attacks launched by today's more sophisticated cyber attackers.

3) Students will learn about the Stuxnet virus as a prime example of the development of global cyber warfare.

Assessment:

Throughout the lesson, the instructor will repeatedly expose students to the following key concepts and terms: Cybersecurity, Cold War espionage, Department of Defense, federal civilian government, asymmetrical warfare, hacking, virus, worm, Denial of Service (DoS) attack, cyber warfare, and Critical Infrastructure.

Day 2: Introduction to Cybersecurity

Lecture: Cybersecurity Principles and Challenges (1h15min)

Materials:

- Reagan, Ronald. *National Security Decision Directive-145*.
- Sanger, David E. "Chapter 10: The Dark Side of the Light Footprint." In *Confront and Conceal: Obama's Secret Wars and Surprising Use of American Power*. New York: Crown Publishers, 2012. 243-273.
- Halpern, Sue. "Are Hackers Heroes?" in *The New York Review of Books, Sept. 27*, 2012. http://www.nybooks.com/articles/archives/2012/sep/27/are-hackers-heroes/
- Zeichner, Lee. "Introduction: From ARPANET to Stuxnet." In Cybersecurity Foundations: An Interdisciplinary Introduction.

Lecture Objectives:

Students will discuss the definition of cybersecurity and situate this interdisciplinary field within the fundamental frameworks of Risk Management, Law and Policy, Program Management, Computer Science and Engineering, The Private Sector, and Research and Methods.

Activities and Procedures:

1) Review the main points from the previous lecture about Admiral Poindexter and NSDD-145, and discuss the case studies from the Introductory Narratives.

2) Discuss the fundamentals of cybersecurity that the book and the course will cover. Discuss the scope and key concepts encompassed by each fundamental, as well as each fundamental's significance to the practice of cybersecurity.

3) Discuss ways in which the fundamental areas might overlap and intersect with each other.

Lesson Plan

4) Discuss Risk Management, the foundation of cybersecurity, as the formalized and highly sophisticated process by which organizations assess and respond to risks that threaten critical assets, information, and infrastructure.

5) Discuss the development and application of Law and Policy for cybersecurity. Emphasize the connection between historical events, technological developments, and federal government cybersecurity laws and policies.

6) Explain that Program Management encompasses the efficient management of projects and initiatives with the goal of building new capacities over the long term. Students will explore the highly complex nature of DHS cyber initiatives, which flow from high-level government policy decisions.

7) Explain the role of Computer Science and Engineering within the field. Explain the work of computer science and engineering professionals in designing and producing the tools necessary to protect critical information and infrastructure. These professionals are essential in the maintenance of network and system security. Computer Science and Engineering terminology dictates the language of the cybersecurity industry.

8) Discuss the critical role that private sector actors play in cybersecurity. The private sector helps the federal government to protect public infrastructure. Private companies also have legal responsibilities to protect their customers' sensitive information from cyber criminals and data breaches.

9) Explain how Research and Methods give cybersecurity professionals the ability to research government and non-government legislation. This skill is a crucial advantage in a rapidly expanding field.

Assessment:

At the end of the lecture, students may ask questions in order to clarify their understanding of the fundamentals of cybersecurity, or to review any new terminology.

Lesson 2: Risk Management

Lesson 2: Teaching Objectives-

Students will learn that in the cyber realm, as in the physical world, risk can never be eliminated. Students will learn the formal process of risk management, and be able to explain both the steps involved and the cyclical nature of the risk management process. The class will discuss Threat Assessment, Vulnerability, Assessment, and Consequence Assessment, as the three separate elements of Risk Assessment. Analyzed together, these three assessments offer a detailed view of the level and/or probability of risk. Students will be able to draw conclusions from quantitative and graphic models, and the outputs of probabilistic risk assessments (PRAs). Students will be able to explain the importance of cost-benefit analyses and the establishment of priorities in the practice of cyber risk management.

Lesson 2: Risk Management

Day 1: Introduction to Risk Management

Interactive Case Study: Protecting a Home (30min)

Materials:

- Home Blueprint Worksheet

- U.S. Department of Energy. "Electricity Subsector Cybersecurity Risk Management Process 2012." http://energy.gov/sites/prod/files/Cybersecurity%20Risk%20Management%20Process%20Guideline%20-%20Final%20-%20May%202012.pdf

Case Study Objectives:

At the end of the lecture, students may ask questions in order to clarify their understanding of the fundamentals of cybersecurity, or to review any new terminology.

Activities and Procedures:

1) The class will begin by contemplating the scenario of a family that needs to protect its home. Using the Protecting a Home Worksheet, the students will break up into small groups in which they will work together to come up with a plan to secure the family's home from intruders.

2) Each group of students will present the answers to their assigned question for class discussion. Given the family's constrained resources and recognizing the Threats, Consequences, and Vulnerabilities discussed, what are the options available to the family? What are the most effective mitigations? What are the most expensive mitigations? Which protection options are the most challenging to implement? The least challenging? What other externalities should the family consider? Are there activities that are of no cost or relatively low cost that might mitigate the risk to the home?

Interactive Case Study: Protecting a Home (30min)

Lecture Materials:

- National Energy Regulatory Commission (NERC). "Cyber Attack Task Force: Final Report." May 9, 2012. pp. 1-10. http://www.nerc.com/docs/cip/catf/12-CATF_Final_Report_BOT_clean_Mar_26_2012-Board%20Accepted%200521.pdf

- U.S. Department of Energy. "Electricity Subsector Cybersecurity Risk Management Process 2012." http://energy.gov/sites/prod/files/Cybersecurity%20Risk%20Management%20Process%20Guideline%20-%20Final%20-%20May%202012.pdf

- Zeichner, Lee. "Chapter 1: Risk Management for Cybersecurity." In *Cybersecurity Foundations: An Interdisciplinary Introduction*.

Lecture Objectives:

Students will gain a deeper understanding of Risk Management fundamentals, the technical meanings of Risk Management terms, and the relationship between Risk Management and the practice of cybersecurity. Students will learn the Risk Management Process and the Risk Management Formula. Students will be introduced to the concept of Risk Framing.

Lesson Plan

Activities and Procedures:

1) Having completed the home protection exercise, use the class findings to introduce the concept of Risk Management. Risk Management is the formalized process used to determine one's most critical assets and how best to protect those assets given limited resources. Risk management is employed across many industries—most commonly in engineering, nuclear, or chemical related industries and financial industries. There are different types of risk management processes depending on the industry and the scope of the risk.

2) Discuss how Risk Management and cybersecurity are intertwined. Securing cyberspace means examining a threat to a system or a network, and the vulnerabilities associated with that system or network. The terms of cybersecurity and the terms of risk management are the same. Cybersecurity in practice is an exercise in risk management.

3) Identify the key concepts and terms of Risk Management. Define critical assets. Explain the cyclical process of risk management beginning with Framing Risk, then Risk Assessment (T x V x C), followed by Risk Determination, Risk Response, and Risk Monitoring. What are the threats and vulnerabilities inherent in every situation? Discuss examples from both the physical and cyber realms. Introduce the National Institute for Standards and Technology (NIST) and the formal Risk Assessment process NIST created. Explain how professional risk managers, including risk managers employed by DHS, use this formula to protect the cyber assets of the U.S. government.

4) The class will discuss Risk Framing, with an emphasis on the idea that risk framing evaluates the "big picture" of a situation and its key components: Assumptions, Constraints, Risk Tolerance, Priorities, and Trade-offs. Each of these components of Risk Framing changes a risk manager's picture of the risk and what can be done to effectively contain it.

Assessment:

Short Paper: In writing, the students will frame the risk to their most valuable possession in their home. Have them state what the critical asset is (laptop, credit card, SS card, etc.), and then outline the Assumptions, Constraints, Tolerance, and Priorities & Trade-offs that inform their picture of the risk they face.

Day 2: Threats and Vulnerabilities

Lecture: Threat and Vulnerability Assessment (45min)

Materials:

- Department of Homeland Security, *National Infrastructure Protection Plan (NIPP) Risk Management Framework* (2009)

- Department of Homeland Security, *Risk* Lexicon (September 2010)

- National Institute of Standards and Technology (NIST), NIST SP 800-53, *Recommended Security Controls* for *Federal Information Systems* (August 2009)

- National Institute of Standards and Technology (NIST), NIST SP 800-39, *Managing Information Security Risk* (March 2011)

Lesson 2: Risk Management

- U.S. Department of Energy. "Electricity Subsector Cybersecurity Risk Management Process 2012." http://energy.gov/sites/prod/files/Cybersecurity%20Risk%20Management%20Process%20Guideline%20-%20Final%20-%20May%202012.pdf

Lecture Objectives:

Students will learn the Risk formula and its component parts: Threat Assessments, Vulnerability Assessments, and Consequence Assessments.

Activities and Procedures:

1) What is a Risk assessment? A risk assessment is a multi-part process that defines and reveals the nuances of risk. Risk is any action or inaction that could cause harm to a critical asset. The Risk equation is Threat times Vulnerability times Consequence. Professional risk managers use complex quantitative methods to quantify and calculate risk using this formula.

2) Introduce the components of a Threat Assessment. A threat is an agent that has the ability to cause harm to a critical asset by exploiting a weakness. Threats can be internal or external actors. The DHS Risk Lexicon defines a Threat as a "natural or man-made occurrence, individual, entity, or action that has or indicates the potential to harm life, information, operations, the environment, and/or property." Threat assessments reveal the actions and entities that indicate potential harm to critical information and infrastructure. Because threats can be either intentional or unintentional, it is important to evaluate the intentions, motivations, capabilities, tools and resources, access, and lethality of all potential Threats.

3) Discuss Vulnerability Assessments and vulnerability, including the subtle but critical difference between a threat and a vulnerability. A vulnerability is a weakness in the design, function, or process of a subject (i.e. family, organization, company, or government entity). Nearly every system, process, organization, and technology has vulnerabilities than can be exploited by Threats.

Discussion Session (25min): Threat and Vulnerability Assessment

Materials:

- Threat and Vulnerability Chart

Activities and Procedures:

1) As a class, conduct both a Threat and Vulnerability assessment for the student ID card system at your university. Using the Threat and Vulnerability Chart to guide the discussion, have the students call out the answers and write them on a vulnerability chart on the board. What are the Threats to the ID card system? What are the Vulnerabilities of the ID card system?

Assessment:

Short Paper: Using the U.S. Department of Energy's Electricity Subsector Cybersecurity Risk Management Process 2012 and the discussion questions, have students write a short paper that frames the threat environment of the computer operated elements of the electric power grid. Remind the students that Threats to the power grid are a common debate topic in Congress. Students should conduct a Threat and Vulnerability assessment, positing some of the potential threats and vulnerabilities to the system. Students should carefully distinguish between intentional and unintentional threats, as well as between threats and vulnerabilities, in this paper.

Lesson Plan

Day 3: Consequence and Risk Determination

Lecture: Consequence Assessment and Risk Determination (50min)

Materials:

- Consequence and Risk Determination Chart
- Department of Homeland Security, *National Infrastructure Protection Plan (NIPP) Risk Management Framework* (2009)
- Department of Homeland Security, Risk Lexicon (September 2010)
- National Institute of Standards and Technology (NIST), NIST SP 800-53, *Recommended Security Controls for Federal Information Systems* (August 2009)
- National Institute of Standards and Technology (NIST), NIST SP 800-39, *Managing Information Security Risk* (March 2011)
- U.S. Department of Energy. "Electricity Subsector Cybersecurity Risk Management Process 2012." http://energy.gov/sites/prod/files/Cybersecurity%20Risk%20Management%20Process%20Guideline%20-%20Final%20-%20May%202012.pdf

Lecture Objectives:

Students will learn the Consequence formula and its two key components: Criticality and Impact. Students will be introduced to the concept of Risk Determination and quantitative approaches to determining risk.

Activities and Procedures:

1) Discuss Consequence as the impact in the event that a critical asset is exploited, and the Consequence Assessment formula. Consequence equals Criticality multiplied by Impact. Criticality is the importance of an asset and Impact is the result of damage to an asset. The Consequence Assessment is the final step in the Risk Assessment.

2) Introduce Risk Determination as the process that follows risk assessment. In many models, risk determination is part of the consequence assessment and determines the severity and likelihood of risk. Define Severity and Likelihood. Explain different degrees of risk, and show the quadrant system. Give examples of risk at each level of the quadrant and review the various "quadrant graphs." Explain the relationship between Threat/Vulnerability versus Consequence and discuss both Qualitative and Quantitative approaches to determining risk. What are the pros and cons of using the Qualitative versus Quantitative approaches to risk determination?

Discussion Session (25min)

Discussion Materials:

- Consequence and Risk Determination Worksheet

Discussion Objectives:

Students will learn how to perform a Consequence Assessment and Risk Determination.

Lesson 2: Risk Management

Activities and Procedures:

1) Conduct both Consequence Assessment and Risk Determination analyses of the student ID case discussed the previous day. Use the Consequence and Risk Determination chart to guide the students in a discussion.

2) What are the Consequences if a student's identification card is stolen, tampered with, or copied?

3) Apply what students have learned about Risk Determination. What is the relationship between Risk and Consequence in the student ID system? Create graphs for Threat, Vulnerability, and Consequence.

Assessment:

Students will make a Consequence chart showing the relative Consequences of four catastrophic events. Students will show the Criticality and Impact, as well as the Severity and Likelihood, of different hypothetical events and chart these different levels of Consequence in an attractive visual.

Day 4: Quantitative Risk Determination Models

Lecture: Quantitative and Graphical Risk Determination Models (50min)

Materials:

- Zeichner, Lee. "Chapter 1: Risk Management for Cybersecurity." In *Cybersecurity Foundations: An Interdisciplinary Introduction*.

- DSMC Risk Management Guide for DoD Acquisition: http://www.mitre.org/work/sepo/toolkits/risk/references/files/DSMC_RiskMgmt_Guide.pdf

Lecture Objectives:

Students will be introduced to the basics of probability, and learn how concept related to probability are used in cybersecurity Risk Assessments.

Activities and Procedures:

1) Discuss the basic characteristics of different Risk Determination methodologies.

2) Define Independent (x) and Dependent (y) variables. Independent variables are factors that influence the dependent variable; the dependent variable is the outcome.

3) Mitigations can also be independent variables, based on the situation. For instance, a firewall may represent mitigation against an attack, but the lack of a firewall is also an independent variable in the determination of risk.

4) Cover basics of probability, such as the 0%-100% probability of an event occurring, conditional probability (given A, then B), and hypotheses. Examine "if- then" statements and how they do not explain causality of an event, but rather establish an association or relationship between the independent (indicators) and dependent variables.

5) Explain that a qualitative assessment, past records and data, patterns of data, behavior of technology, behavior of personnel, and interviews may all be sources that play into the determination of a risk's level and/or likelihood. A qualitative assessment will produce a "high" "medium" or "low" rating. When is it useful to use qualitative design?

Lesson Plan

6) Quantitative risk assessments assign technical and mathematical values to qualitative statements.

7) What is an Event Tree and when is it used? What is a Fault Tree and when is it used?

8) Introduce multivariable statistical models. Explain that these models help determine which variables contribute the most to any outcome and allow analysts to identify the most significant factors within an equation or system.

9) Provide examples of likelihood of risk graphs and explain that they are used in conjunction with consequence graphs to determine the severity and probability of risk.

Assessment:

Students will design either an Event Tree or a Fault Tree to illustrate a risk situation.

Day 5: Risk Response and Monitoring

Lecture: Response and Monitoring Techniques (50min)

Materials:

- Response and Monitoring Chart
- Zeichner, Lee. "Chapter 1: Risk Management for *Cybersecurity*." In *Cybersecurity Foundations: An Interdisciplinary Introduction*.

Lecture Objectives:

Students will learn the choices available to risk managers after they have determined risk: Accept, Avoid, Mitigate, and Transfer. Students will understand the Risk Monitoring process and its components: Compliance, Effectiveness, and Continuous Monitoring. By the end of the lecture, students will be able to apply the concepts of Risk Determination and Risk Monitoring to a real-world scenario.

Activities and Procedures:

1) Discuss Risk Response, the process that takes places after Risk Determination, and the actions that organizations must take once they have reached an understanding of the risk they face.

2) What are the components of Risk Response? Acceptance is the amount of risk that an organization is willing to accept. Is Avoidance ever practical? Mitigation means managing and containing the level of risk. Transfer displaces or shifts the risk. What is the cost/benefit analysis method? How do managers use constrained resources to guide their selection of the best response method?

3) Monitor, the final stage in the Risk Management process, is the process of continually observing an organization's system in Risk Management terms. Risk Monitoring may involve beginning the Risk Management process again.

4) What is Compliance? What does it measure? What is the Effectiveness of the system?

Lesson 3: Law and Policy

Discussion Session (25min)

Discuss the response and monitoring alternatives available to the company found in the example in the textbook: a popular online company facing the risk of critical customer information being leaked. Use the Response and Monitoring Worksheet to guide the discussion.

Assessment:

During the class discussion, students should learn the concepts of Risk Response and Risk Monitoring and how these processes fit into the bigger picture of Risk Management. They should understand that the Risk Management process is cyclical, and that Risk Managers often begin the process again at Risk Framing in response to anticipated or actual new threats and vulnerabilities.

Day 6: Risk Management Tabletop Exercise

Tabletop Exercise: Risk Management (1h15min)

Materials:

- Risk Management Tabletop Exercise Worksheet

Tabletop Exercise Objectives:

Students will apply the Risk Management process to a real-world scenario.

Activities and Procedures:

1) Create a flow chart illustrating timeline and risk management goals, then chart out the individual points in the risk management process. Establish the perspective of a small business trying to protect itself from cyber attacks and run through the cost-benefit analysis.

2) Students will break into small groups and complete a tabletop exercise using the Risk Management Tabletop Exercise Worksheet.

Assessment:

Evaluate and critique the students' performance and presentations of the Risk Management Tabletop Exercise Worksheet.

Lesson 3: Law and Policy

Lesson 3: Teaching Objectives-

Students will be introduced to the history of cybersecurity and its development as a national policy challenge. Students will learn the laws and policies underpinning cybersecurity at the federal level. Students will be able to understand current policy decision-making trends, and gain the skills to predict future legal and political debates. Students will learn the roles that the President and Congress play in the creation of new federal cybersecurity laws and policies. Students will learn to research original source materials relating to cybersecurity, and to analyze core principles and concepts in these materials.

Lesson Plan

Day 1: Introduction to Cybersecurity and the Federal Government (1945-1995)

Lecture: An introduction to the Relationship between Cybersecurity and the Federal Government (1h15min)

Materials:

- Brooks Act CRS Summary
- Computer Security Act CRS Summary
- Reagan, Ronald. *National Security Decision Directive-145*.
- Sharp Sr., Walter Gary. "The Past, Present, and Future of Cybersecurity." Journal of National Security Law & Policy vol. 4, no. 1 (2010): 13-26. http://jnslp.com/wp-content/uploads/2010/08/03_Sharp.pdf
- Warner Amendment
- Zeichner, Lee. "Chapter 2: Cybersecurity Law and Policy." In *Cybersecurity Foundations: An Interdisciplinary Introduction.*

Lecture Objectives:

Students will recognize the connections between the development and evolution of computer technology and the legislation and policies created to secure information stored and transferred on that technology. Students will be introduced to the historical actors who rose to prominence as securing computers emerged as a pressing national security concern. Students will be able to identify and distinguish between the positions of these historical figures, and understand the terms of the federal cybersecurity debates they provoked.

Activities and Procedures:

1) What are the three branches of the U.S. federal government, and what does each branch do?

2) What role do the Executive and Legislative branches play in shaping national cybersecurity policy?

3) Discuss the development of the mainframe computer, which first appeared in the 1940s. How and why did the government use mainframes? What security concerns did these computers raise?

4) The Brooks Act, passed by Congress in 1965, responded to a lack of federal security standards and purchasing guidelines for government computers. The Brooks Act gave responsibility for creating IT standards to the General Services Agency (GSA). This responsibility meant that any government computer needed to meet basic security standards set by the GSA. What is the GSA and what is its function in the federal government?

5) Discuss the development of personal computers (PCs) in the 1980s. These computers offered more advanced capabilities and presented fewer glaring vulnerabilities than mainframes. What were the security drawbacks of PCs?

6) National Security Decision Directive-145 (NSDD-145) was developed by Admiral John Poindexter and issued by President Reagan in 1984. It was created in response to the Cold War nuclear struggle

Lesson 3: Law and Policy

between the US and USSR, and the fear that the USSR would infiltrate U.S. information systems. NSDD-145 gave the National Security Agency (NSA) full responsibility for establishing and implementing federal IT standards, stripping power from the GSA. NSDD-145 instigated an immediate controversy over whether or not Reagan and Poindexter had given the military government (represented by the NSA) too much power.

7) The Computer Security Act (CSA), passed by Congress in 1987, served as a direct response to NSDD-145 and gave power to the National Institute of Standards and Technology (NIST) to create minimum computer security standards for federal agencies. The CSA allowed the NSA to maintain control over classified computer systems.

8) The Warner Amendment, passed by Congress in 1988, clarified the division of responsibility between the NSA and NIST, and gave the NSA control over Sensitive-But-Classified IT (SBU IT), as well as IT used for military or intelligence missions.

Assessment:

Students should possess a firm grasp of the roles of members of the three branches of government. An understanding of how the federal government produces and enforces federal laws must precede any discussion of cybersecurity law and policy. After the class, students should understand where the laws and policies discussed fit into the government structure and the lawmaking process.

Day 2: The INTERNET ERA (1996-2008)

Lecture: The Modern Legal and Policy Foundations for National Cybersecurity (1h15min)

Materials:

- Clinger-Cohen Act CRS Summary
- Clinton, William J. *Executive Order 13011*
- Memoranda 97-02
- OMB Circular No. A-130
- Paperwork Reduction Act CRS Summary

Lecture Objectives:

Students will recognize how the development of the Internet, particularly the growth and popularity of the World Wide Web, caused changes in the ways that the public and private sectors protect information. Students will be introduced to the types of government statements and documents that dictate cybersecurity law and policy. Students will learn to analyze government documents that inform ongoing national discussions of cybersecurity law and policy.

Activities and Procedures:

1) Explain the development of the Internet between the 1970s and the 1990s. How did the growth of the Internet drastically change the approaches of both the federal government and the private sector to the problem of cybersecurity? What new critical assets emerged during this time?

Lesson Plan

2) Review the legislative documents assigned for this class and discuss the significance of each, as well as the historical and technological shifts that influenced each new piece of legislation.

Assessment:

Short Paper: Students will write a short paper in which they will choose one of the documents discussed in class and analyze its impact for federal cybersecurity policy in its historical context. What kind of language is used and why? What are the expectations created for public and private sectors in relation to information assurance? Students should highlight and interpret specific lines and passages from their chosen document.

Day 3: The Development of Modern Cybersecurity Policy (1996-2008)

Lecture: Modern Cybersecurity Policy (1h15min)

Materials:

- Bush, George W. *Executive Order 13228*
- Bush, George W. *Executive Order 13231*
- Bush, George W. *Homeland Security Presidential Directive 7 (HSPD-7)*
- Bush, George W. *NSPD-54/HSPD-23*
- Clinton, William J. *Presidential Decision Directive 63 (PDD-63)*
- Federal Information Security Management Act (FISMA) CRS Summary
- Homeland Security Act (HSA) of 2002 CRS Summary

Lecture Objectives:

Students will learn the connection between physical and cyber critical infrastructure. They will understand how catastrophic events influence policymaking at the federal level. Students will be able to explain the origins of modern cybersecurity policy and the historical events that have informed ongoing debates about federal cybersecurity policy. Students will become familiar with public-private partnerships and their importance for securing cyber infrastructure.

Activities and Procedures:

1) Discuss the Oklahoma City bombing in 1996, and its significance for discussions of national security.

2) President Clinton created the Critical Infrastructure Working Group (CIWG) in response to the Oklahoma City bombing. The President tasked the CIWG with reviewing all legislation regarding resource management, terrorism, law enforcement, and national security. In addition, the CIWG was charged to analyze threats to critical infrastructure from three perspectives: the federal government, the private sector, and state and local governments. The activities of the CIWG represented the first time that the federal government explicitly recognized a need to partner with the private sector to protect critical infrastructure.

Lesson 3: Law and Policy

3) Presidential Decision Directive 63 (PDD-63), issued by President Clinton in 1998, recognized that civilian and military organizations rely upon the security of critical infrastructure and cyber assets. It emphasized the need for the federal government to create security policies in coordination with the private sector, and proposed that private organizations agree to voluntary risk assessments and disclose more security information to the federal government. It placed federal agencies in charge of formulating mitigation strategies in coordination with private sector companies in related fields (i.e. energy, defense, etc.), and hinted that public-private partnerships were the best way to protect critical infrastructure.

4) Executive Order 13228, issued by President Bush in 2001 in response to the September 11th attacks, created the Office of Homeland Security (OHS) within the federal civilian government. OHS became the Department of Homeland Security (DHS), which is tasked with coordinating all of the federal agencies involved in homeland security. EO 13228 also created the Homeland Security Council (the Council), to represent the military sector of the government. The Council was tasked with advising and assisting the President with homeland security issues.

5) Executive Order 13231, issued by President Bush in 2001 just weeks after Executive Order 13228, created the Special Advisor to the President for Cyberspace Security. This position is tasked with coordinating the private and public sectors to protect infrastructure and report directly to the director of OHS. This position is also in charge of recommending policies to the Executive branch. EO 13231 recognized the importance of the private sector in regard to protecting information system connected to critical infrastructure, and re-emphasized the need for a voluntary, public-private partnership for national cybersecurity.

6) The Homeland Security Act (HSA) of 2002, passed by Congress in 2002, created the Department of Homeland Security (DHS). DHS is tasked with overseeing national security risk management. DHS published the "National Strategy to Secure Cyberspace" and the "National Strategy for Homeland Security" in 2003. What is the significance of these documents?

7) Homeland Security Presidential Directive 7 (HSPD-7), established by President Bush in 2003, updated President Clinton's PDD-63. The policy recognized DHS as the federal government's lead coordinator for protecting the nation's critical infrastructure, and required specific agencies to implement their own risk assessment programs and report back to DHS.

8) The Federal Information Security Management Act (FISMA), passed by Congress in 2002, was created to fix information security gaps by giving the civilian government the power of formulating cybersecurity legislation and establishing OMB as the chief agency for cybersecurity. It authorized NIST to develop a new information security framework.

9) NSPD-54/HSPD-23, issued in 2008 by President Bush, created the Comprehensive National Cybersecurity Initiative (CNCI) which recognized that as threats and government information systems evolve and develop into more complex forms, government capabilities to combat cyber threats must evolve as well. Additionally, CNCI increased the role of the military intelligence sector in securing government information in cyberspace.

Assessment:

Short Paper: Students will write a short paper on an Executive Order or Presidential Decision Directive of their choosing. Students should summarize the chosen document in their own words. What does the document say? What king of language is used? What is the purpose and reasoning behind the policy? What historical events and technological advancements does it respond to? What other policies does it replace or supplement? What are the cybersecurity expectations set forth in the document for the public and private sectors?

Lesson Plan

Day 4: Contemporary AND FUTURE Cybersecurity Policy

Lecture: Contemporary Cyber Security Policy (15min)

Materials:

- *Cyberspace Policy Review*, White House, 2009. http://www.whitehouse.gov/assets/documents/Cyberspace_Policy_Review_final.pdf

- Department of Homeland Security. "Blueprint for a Secure Cyber Future." November 2011. http://www.dhs.gov/xlibrary/assets/nppd/blueprint-for-a-secure-cyber-future.pdf

- Dycus, Stephen. "Congress's Role In Cyber Warfare." *Journal of National Security Law & Policy* vol. 4, no. 1 (2010): 155-171. (http://jnslp.com/wp-content/uploads/2010/08/11_Dycus.pdf)

- The Comprehensive National Cybersecurity Initiative (CNCI), White House, 2012. http://www.whitehouse.gov/cybersecurity/comprehensive-national-cybersecurity-initiative

Lecture Objectives

Students will learn about the U.S. federal government's new offensive cyber weapons and its current cybersecurity policies and debates.

Activities and Procedures:

1) Discuss the rapid growth in cyber attacks against U.S. federal networks since 2005.

2) Discuss the worm attacks on Iran's nuclear weapons production facility. Flame was first launched in 2010. This worm took control of Iran's nuclear facilities' controls. It also mapped out Iran's nuclear facilities' computer infrastructure. Stuxnet, first known to launch in 2012, was a joint US-Israeli attack on the Iranian nuclear facility.[1]

3) What has been the cybersecurity policy of the Obama Administration?

4) Does President Obama's cybersecurity policy signal a return to the philosophies of Admiral Poindexter and NSDD-145? Will the role of DHS in cybersecurity continue to expand or will the Department of Defense take on a more significant role in the age of cyber warfare and sophisticated attacks against U.S. networks? What policy debates will characterize the future of cybersecurity lawmaking?

Discussion Session (1h)

Students will break into groups and discuss one question from the Contemporary Cybersecurity Policy Questions Worksheet. The class will come back together to discuss the answers. Discuss the questions as a class in reference to the legal landscape of cybersecurity from 1945 until the present day.

Students are encouraged to find and share newspaper articles that characterize the contemporary cybersecurity law and policy debates in Congress and the White House.

Assessment:

Students will write short papers offering their perspectives on the future of national cybersecurity law and policy. Students must offer concrete and convincing evidence for their predictions.

---

[1]. Paul K. Kerr, John Rollins & Catherine A. Theohary, Congressional Research Service, R41524, *The Stuxnet Computer Worm: Harbinger of an Emerging Warfare Capability* (2010).

Lesson 4: Management for Cybersecurity

Lesson 4: Teaching Objectives-

Student will be introduced to the theory of management and how these concepts apply to cyber problems. Students will establish a clear distinction between managerial and technical work. Students will learn about the formal managerial frameworks applied to federal cybersecurity programs. Students will appreciate the importance of managers' abilities to coordinate and lead groups of employees toward goals and initiatives. Students' critical reasoning and decision making skills will be developed through exercises.

Day 1: Introduction to Management

Discussion: Protecting a Neighborhood – Monitoring System (30min)

Materials:

- Protecting a Neighborhood Worksheet

- Schwalbe, Kathy. "Chapter 1: Introduction to Project Management." In *Information Technology Project Management.*

- Schwalbe, Kathy. "Chapter 2: The Project Management and Information Technology Context." In *Information Technology Project Management.*

- Zeichner, Lee. "Chapter 3: Fundamentals of Management for *Cybersecurity.*" In *Cybersecurity Foundations: An Interdisciplinary Introduction.*

Discussion Objectives:

Students will apply their understanding of Risk Management from Chapter 2.0. Students will begin thinking like program managers. Students will be able to explain the three central components that program managers must coordinate: people, processes, and technologies.

Activities and Procedures:

1) Begin the class with a discussion of protecting a neighborhood. This discussion should consider the various methods of and complications monitoring the safety of a gated community. Assume that the gated community has a budget of $200,000 to protect a neighborhood of 500 homes. What are the technological tools that might be used to protect the neighborhood? How might these tools detect intrusions into individual homes? How much will this system cost? How will the neighbors ensure that all areas of the neighborhood are protected equally? How will they ensure that areas not owned by any individual (i.e. playgrounds, parks, etc.) are protected? How will the neighborhood deter potential threats from entering the neighborhood? Who will protect the neighborhood? Should the neighborhood hire a full-time security team? Part-time? Where will they hire this team? How many people will they hire? Should the residents assume any duty in personally monitoring the neighborhood? What personal responsibility should each individual take in protecting their home? Who will coordinate this effort? What kinds of communication systems must be built?

2) What are the various processes associated with monitoring the safety of the neighborhood? (Processes are the various standardized procedures and policies used to focus on and check behavior). If security guards are hired, how should they inform residents of potential intrusions? Who will they manage the

Lesson Plan

guards and ensure that that they are doing their jobs correctly? What processes should the individual residents undertake to ensure that their homes are as safe as possible?

3) What should be done in the event of a technological or personnel failure? What if the technology is not quick enough to detect intruders? What if communication technologies and processes break down? What is the back-up plan in an emergency?

4) Discuss the ways in which the successful completion of projects requires more than technology. In order for cybersecurity operations to be successful they must consider the "people" and "processes" necessary to complete the cyber initiatives. Furthermore, successful cybersecurity operations require managers to promote oversee and promote the success of these operations. Technology only enhances "people" and "processes," and managers promote the coordination of all three of these project components.

Lecture: Why do we need Managers? (45min)

Materials:

- Schwalbe, Kathy. *Information Technology Project Management*.
- Zeichner, Lee. "Chapter 3: Fundamentals of Management for Cybersecurity." In *Cybersecurity Foundations: An Interdisciplinary Introduction*.

Lecture Objectives-

Students will learn why project managers are necessary in the IT security field. Students will understand the specific roles and responsibilities of IT program managers. Students will be able to identify the goals of project managers for cybersecurity and the many challenges cybersecurity program managers face.

Activities and Procedures:

1) Establish an understanding that cybersecurity problems often have nothing to do with cyber or security issues. Managers oversee "big picture" issues, promote teams of people, and coordinate and organize resources (people, processes, money, technology etc.) according to a timeline and a budget.

2) Discuss the Managerial Fundamentals: Managing vs. Doing; Breaking Down Goals into Missions, Strategies, and Plans, Coordinating Functions (line and staff); Executing Plans and Strategies, and the steps in the manager's decision-making process.

Assessment:

Have students write up their management plans for securing the gated community. Students must justify and explain the decisions they have made and explain how they will monitor their program's successes and failures.

Day 2: US-CERT CASE STUDY

Lecture: Continuous Monitoring Systems (30min)

Materials:

- Continuous Monitoring System Chart

Lesson 4: Management for Cybersecurity

- *National Strategy to Secure Cyberspace Summary*
- Homeland Security Act of 2002 CRS Summary
- Bush, George W. *Homeland Security Presidential Directive 7*
- *National Response Framework Summary*
- Bush, George W. *Homeland Security Presidential Directive 23*
- NIST. *"Frequently Asked Questions: Continuous Monitoring."* June 2010. http://csrc.nist.gov/groups/SMA/fisma/documents/faq-continuous-monitoring.pdf

Lecture Objectives:

Students will grasp the components and purpose of continuous monitoring systems. Students will be able to explain the US-CERT continuous monitoring system case study in evaluative management terms.

Activities and Procedures:

1) Why is a Continuous Monitoring Systems (CMS) needed? What are the challenges and environment? Due to the increasing capabilities of cyber threats, we need to monitor all potential access points to critical information and infrastructure.

2) A Continuous Monitoring Systems (CMS) is a process that leverages various technologies and skills to continuously detect threats to an organization's networks. The steps to establishing a CMS are: 1) Establish a baseline understanding of the network, which gives analysts an idea of what the "normal activity" of information flow and network activity looks like; 2) Assess risk to network assets by performing risk assessments which allow analysts to prioritize both cyber and physical assets; 3) Obtain internal information within the network, which includes leveraging IT tools and reporting network activity used to identify both known attacks and irregular activity; 4) Obtain external information in order to gain new information about potential attacks to the network by consulting sources outside of the organization, including security experts, white-papers, and Government Notifications, and 5) Detect anomalous activity with the help of IT tools and/or the monitoring of network activity by analysts.

3) The Homeland Security Act of 2002 expressed the need for a Federal Monitoring System. It gave the Department of Homeland Security (DHS) primary responsibility for protecting the United States from terrorist attacks, including cyber attacks, and assigned DHS a lead role in protecting critical US infrastructure. Other legislation and policy documents that support the need for a Federal Monitoring System are the National Strategy to Secure Cyberspace, Homeland Security Presidential Directive 7, the National Response Framework, and Homeland Security Presidential Directive 23.

Discussion Session (45min) – US-CERT

Materials:

- NIST. *"Frequently Asked Questions: Continuous Monitoring."* June 2010. http://csrc.nist.gov/groups/SMA/fisma/documents/faq-continuous-monitoring.pdf
- US-CERT Case Study Worksheet

Lesson Plan

Discussion Objectives:

Students will be able to explain the importance of continuous monitoring systems. Students will be able to analyze the consequences of failing to implement a continuous monitoring system, and identify the steps involved in creating a program to build a CMS.

Activities and Procedures:

1) After discussing why continuous monitoring systems are essential, as well as the various attributes associated with implementing an effective continuous monitoring system, the class should discuss the United States Computer Emergency Readiness Team's (US-CERT) failed attempt to implement a successful monitoring system. The students should be prepared for this discussion by reading the US-CERT case study.

2) How did the US-CERT fail to implement technology? What technology could US-CERT have used? What capabilities should this technology have? How would US-CERT implement this technology? How would US-CERT educate the various employees of the federal agencies and private sector organizations of how to use this technology? Who would develop/pay for this technology?

3) How did the US-CERT fail to coordinate key actors? Who else should the US-CERT have included in their monitoring system? Is it plausible for the US-CERT to assume that they will be able to coordinate with the majority of private sector organizations? How would US-CERT organize the incoming information from these organizations?

4) How might the US-CERT go about improving their coordination with other federal agencies? Should/could the US-CERT ask another federal or private organization to help them implement and sustain an effective monitoring system? How did the US-CERT fail to establish goals and performance metrics? Did the US-CERT breakdown their high-level goals into measureable tasks?

5) What were some ways that US-CERT could have broken down the goals of the monitoring system? How did the US-CERT measure its performance? How would you measure the performance of a monitoring system (technology, people, and processes)? How would you compare the actual results of monitoring system to the established results (technology, people, and processes)?

Assessment:

Students will create the program plan for a federal government CMS. Taking the mistakes of US-CERT into account, students will create an improved plan for this program.

Day 3: Government Tools and Frameworks

Lecture: Methods of Solving Managerial Problems – Government Tools and Frameworks (1h15min)

Materials:

- Sample DHS MNS Template) TSA Mission Need Statement Guide http://www.tsa.gov/video/pdfs/mds/TSAMNSGuide%28042607%29.pdf

- (Sample DHS MNS) Integrated Deepwater System Mission Needs Statement http://www.uscg.

Lesson 4: Management for Cybersecurity

mil/history/docs/2004_USCG_revisedmns.pdf

- (Sample CONOPS) Federal Interagency Geospatial Concept of Operations. http://www.nsgic.org/public_resources/DHS_Geospatial_CONOPS_v30_85x11.pdf
- (Sample DHS CONOPS) DHS Interaction With State and Local Fusion Centers Concept of Operations http://www.fas.org/irp/agency/dhs/conops.pdf

Lecture Objectives:

Students will be introduced to the complexities of DHS cybersecurity program management. Students will learn the framework for planning a cybersecurity project for DHS. Students will read real-world documents from DHS projects in order to connect theory and practice.

Activities and Procedures:

1) Introduce student to the Civilian Government Project Management Framework used by DHS in all of its cybersecurity projects

2) What is a Mission Needs Statement (MNS)? The MNS identifies the problem to be solved as well as the resources the organization will need to solve the problem. It is written in broad terms and identifies the need for the project. To develop a MNS, a manager must first identify Organization Mission and Needed Capabilities, define and give examples of capability gaps, cite Mission Authority, identify Courses of Action, establish a Program Life Cycle, and finally justify Organizational Investment in the Project.

3) What is a Concept of Operations (CONOPS)? A CONOPS describes the quantitative and qualitative requirements of the project as well as plans the specific steps necessary to complete the plan proposed in the MNS. It explains how the project's plan stated within the MNS will be applied in practice, and covers goals and objectives of the system, strategies, policies and constraints affecting the system, participants and stakeholders, roles and responsibilities, and specific operational processes for initiating, developing, and maintaining the system. CONOPS are developed before budgets are approved and therefore must present multiple alternative approaches to completing the project and building new capabilities.

4) The Operating Model (Op Model) documents the measurable tasks and activities required to complete the project and establish the program's costs. Good Op Models predict the costs at every stage of the project, and identify project milestones along a highly detailed timeline. An Op Model should reflect a linear set of outcomes and tasks that build upon each other from year to year.

5) Earned Value Management (EVM) is a sophisticated accounting system DHS uses to ensure that projects currently underway are completed on-time and within budget.

Day 4: Table Top Exercise – Government: Warning System, Private: E-Commerce

Table Top Exercise – Government: Warning System, Private: E-Commerce (1h15min)

Lesson Plan

	Pros	Cons
Model A	• Lowest cost • Easy to implement • Least hassle to customers	• Highest probability of being hacked • Potential loss of customers if security measures are viewed as weak • No use of two-factor authentication or strong passwords
Model B	• Relatively low cost • Moderate hassle to customers • Requires the use of relatively strong passwords • Accounts for attacks from the strongest possible hacker (10/10)	• Relatively high probability of being hacked • No use of two-factor authentication
Model C	• Relatively low probability of being hacked • Requires the use of relatively strong passwords • Accounts for attacks from the strongest possible hacker (10/10)	• Moderately high cost of implementation • No use of two-factor authentication
Model D	• Extremely low probability of being hacked • Only model to use both two-factor authentication and require strong passwords • Greatest customer protection	• Hardest model to implement • Most expensive model to implement • Only accounts for a relatively strong hacked (7/10) • Large hassle to customers

Materials:

- E-Commerce Site Security Case Study
- Government Warning Case Study

Exercise Objectives:

Students will apply their knowledge of the various managerial frameworks to a real world scenario. Students will gain a better understanding of how to apply management concepts. Simulating an actual business environment, the exercise will allow students to work as a team to make decisions and compromises.

Activities and Procedures:

1) During this class period, the students should discuss a hypothetical case study. Throughout the discussion, the students will apply their knowledge of the DHS managerial framework to the scenario. A suggested case study is the development of a federal government warning system: What would you include in the Mission Needs Statement (MNS) for the implementation of a warning system? Why does the federal government need a warning system? What are the most significant goals of a warning system? What capabilities should the warning system have? How would you justify the implementation of a warning system? What authority does the federal government have to implement a warning system? How would you include in the Concept of Operations (CONOPS) for the implementation of a warning system? What might the measureable requirements of a warning system be? What monetary constraints might the federal government face? Policy constraints? Who would be responsible for implementing a warning system? Who would benefit if the federal government instituted a warning system? Who would lose? What would the Operating Model (Op Model) for the implementation of a warning system look like? How will the federal government budget the cost of a warning system? How will the federal government develop a detailed project life estimate? What measurable tasks should the Op Model include? How

will the project manager use EVM?

2) Below is a list of pros and cons for hypothetical plans that an e-business might implement to protect customer information. Discuss the program manager's decision-making process when faced with these four plans.

Assessment:

The assessment will be based on the students' understanding of cybersecurity program management as reflected in these exercises.

Lesson 5: Computer Science and Engineering Fundamentals

Lesson 5: Teaching Objectives-

Students will learn the basic structure of computers and IT tools that allow digital information to stored and transferred. Students will learn the languages, hardware, software, and processes that are fundamental to the efficient transfer of information via computers connected to the Internet. Students will understand the various attack methods that threaten critical infrastructure and information. Students will learn the processes and tools that organizations use to protect their critical assets from cyber attacks.

Day 1: Computing and IT Fundamentals

Lecture: Computing and Information Technology Fundamentals (1h15min)

Materials:

- Zeichner, Lee. "Chapter 4: Computer Science Fundamentals and Cybersecurity Operations." In *Cybersecurity Foundations: An Interdisciplinary Introduction*.

Lecture Objectives:

Students will receive a technical introduction to computers and their components. Students will understand the idea of computer components, systems, and systems of systems.

Activities and Procedures:

1) What is a computer? The primary function of computers is to store digital data. Computers receive, process, store, and transfer data. The basic "language" of computers is binary.

2) Discuss Central Processing Units (CPU), which serve as the brain of the computer, perform calculations, move data from one are to another, direct processes and send information. Discuss the benefits of multi-core processors, which allow for increased computer speed.

3) Discuss computer languages, explaining the need to create computer languages so that humans don't have to write in binary. Explain the difference between lower and higher order computer languages. Discuss compilers, which translate computer languages into a language that the computer can understand.

Lesson Plan

4) What is software? Software consists of collections of programs, instructions, and processes.

5) Discuss the development of computer memory from its basic beginnings of floppy disks and punch cards, to large internal memory boards.

6) What is storage? What is the difference between volatile and non volatile storage?

7) Discuss other computer components including motherboards, random access memory (RAM), hard drives, CD-ROM drives, and network cards. What functions do these computer components play in the overall system?

8) Talk about computer systems, which are a collection of all of the components of a computer that work together towards one task or set of tasks. Discuss specific systems, as well as system of systems, which include groups of systems that work together within one greater system.

9) Discuss the inherent vulnerabilities of computers, which increase as systems expand.

Assessment:

Students should be thinking about computers in the larger context of the Internet and cybersecurity. After learning this material, students should see each part of the whole of IT systems as having the potential to be harmed by malicious actors or technical failures.

Day 2: The Internet

Lecture: The Internet (1h15min)

Materials:

- "What is the Internet?" Tutorial: http://www.centerspan.org/tutorial/net.htm
- Commercial Communications Satellite map http://comsoft-sat.com/app/download/5782687752/Commercial+Communications+Satellites.png
- How The Internet Works diagram http://mountpeaks.files.wordpress.com/2012/03/internet_infographic.jpg
- Internet Components Worksheet
- Maps and other Illustrated facts about the Internet http://mountpeaks.wordpress.com/2012/03/06/what-has-the-internet-evolved-into-nowadays/

Lecture Objectives:

Students will learn the history of the Internet. Students will be introduced to the technical components of the Internet.

Lesson 5: Computer Science and Engineering Fundamentals

Activities and Procedures:

1) Discuss the history of the Internet, emphasizing its technical progression. The Internet was first conceived during the 1950s in academic papers discussing the theory of packet-switching. The Eisenhower administration commissioned ARPA to develop new technologies that would help the United States achieve technological and scientific superiority over the Soviet Union. The Department of Defense (DoD) tasked the Defense Advanced Research Project Agency (DARPA) to create the first Internet prototype in 1968. Seminal moments in Internet history included the creation of email in 1971, the establishment of America Online (AOL) in 1985, the release of the World Wide Web (www) in 1991, and the creation of the dial-up internet in 1995.

2) What is the Internet? The Internet is a series of connected routers that facilitate the transfer of information between computers. The Internet is a system of systems.

3) Discuss the components of the Internet: Internet Service Providers (ISPs), Local Area Networks (LANs), routers, data packets.

4) Internet Protocol (IP) is the collection of procedures that dictate the transportation of data across the Internet, and break down data packages for transfer. Transmission Control Protocol (TCP) is the collection of procedures that reassemble data packets at their destination. What are IP Addresses and how do they function?

5) Border Gateway Protocol (BGP) routers use other routers to detect the relative locations of IP addresses and routers.

6) What is Domain Name System Security Extension (DNSSEC)? What is the Internet Engineering Task Force (IETF)?

Assessment:

Internet Component Worksheet: Students will complete a take-home worksheet covering all of the components and mechanisms of the Internet covered in class.

Day 3: Cyber Attacks

Lecture: Cyber Attacks (1h15min)

Materials:

- Cyber Attacks Worksheet

- Frontline: Cyberwar Interactive Website http://www.pbs.org/wgbh/pages/frontline/shows/cyberwar/

- ICS-CERT. "Incident Response Summary Report 2009-2011." https://ics-cert.us-cert.gov/sites/default/files/documents/ICS-CERT%20Incident%20Response%20Summary%20Report%20%282009-2011%29_accessible.pdf

- NIAC *Prioritizing Cyber Vulnerabilities* 2004. http://www.dhs.gov/xlibrary/assets/niac/NIAC_CyberVulnerabilitiesPaper_Feb05.pdf

- Zeichner, Lee. "Chapter 4: Computer Science Fundamentals and *Cybersecurity Operations.*" In *Cybersecurity Foundations: An Interdisciplinary Introduction.*

Lesson Plan

Lecture Objectives:

Students will learn the characteristics of different types of cyber attacks.

Activities and Procedures:

1) What is Malware?

2) What is a virus?

3) Review the technical and superficial features of the cyber attacks covered in the textbook, including Man in the Middle, DNS Cache Poisoning, and Denial of Service (DoS) (including Spoofing, Distributed Denial of Service (DDoS), and Zombies).

4) What are Bots, Botnet, and Worms?

5) Discuss email attacks such as Phishing, drive-by-download, and Spear Phishing.

Assessment:

Cyber Attack Worksheet: Students will complete a take-home worksheet in which they will write detailed definitions for the types of cyber attacks and attack mechanisms covered in class.

Day 4: Cybersecurity Operations

Lecture: Cybersecurity Operations (1h15min)

Materials:

- An Annex to the NIPP: Communications Sector-Specific Plan 2010. http://www.dhs.gov/xlibrary/assets/nipp-ssp-communications-2010.pdf
- FERC Example Security Plan http://www.ferc.gov/industries/hydropower/safety/guidelines/security/security-plan-example.pdf
- NIST SP 800-64 http://csrc.nist.gov/publications/nistpubs/800-64-Rev2/SP800-64-Revision2.pdf
- The DHS Cybersecurity Mission: Promoting Innovation and Securing Critical Infrastructure. http://www.gpo.gov/fdsys/pkg/CHRG-112hhrg72229/pdf/CHRG-112hhrg72229.pdf

Lecture Objectives:

Students will learn how cybersecurity professionals protect networks and computers from attacks.

Activities and Procedures:

1) The class will discuss the NIST life cycle and the Network Security System Process: Monitor, Analyze, Warn, and Respond.

2) What does it mean to monitor? Monitoring methods include using internal monitoring tools such as Sniffers, Firewalls, Intrusion Detection Systems (IDS), and Intrusion Protection Systems (IPS).

3) Warnings notify personnel about intrusions and attacks. What constitutes a proficient warning system? Discuss the variety of forms a cyber attack warning system could take.

4) A Response attempts to mitigate attacks and intrusions through passive and active response methods. Passive response methods include Logging, Notification, and Shunning. Active response methods include terminating a session, altering the networks configuration, and deception.

Assessment:

Students will choose one method of cyber attack and write how a hypothetical organization could best protect its crucial assets against this type of attack. Students should use the Network Security System Process: Monitor, Analyze, Warn, and Respond.

Lesson 6: The Private Sector

Assessment:

Students will be introduced to the fundamental principles of private sector cybersecurity. Students will be able to define basic legal and regulatory challenges facing the private sector, including legal liability. Students will be able to identify the major legal and regulatory rules that private businesses must address in their cybersecurity planning. Students will outline models for robust cybersecurity programs for private sector organizations.

Day 1: Laying a Foundation

Lecture: Corporate Structure (50min)

Materials:

- Management's Role in Information Security in a Cyber Economy http://irps.ucsd.edu/assets/001/501280.pdf
- Zeichner, Lee. "Chapter 5: Cybersecurity for the Private Sector." In *Cybersecurity Foundations: An Interdisciplinary Introduction.*

Lecture Objectives:

Students will learn how private corporations are structured, and the cybersecurity roles and responsibilities within the corporate structure.

Activities and Procedures:

1) What is the purpose of a corporation? Corporations are designed to earn profits and deliver value to share holders through the production of a product or service. In other words, the existential goal of corporations is to earn profits, not to provide services. The profit motivation of corporations is thought by many economists to spur economic growth and innovation beyond the corporation.

2) Discuss the governing structure of corporations: the Board of Directors, the Shareholders, and the Managers.

Lesson Plan

3) What Roles, Responsibilities, and Duties do the three governing groups within a corporation have with regard to cybersecurity?

4) Discuss the ramifications of some key corporate requirements:

    Caremark vs. Derivative Litigation required "duty of care" to oversee the companies cybersecurity practices. The Business Judgment Rule created the notion that the board of directors is not liable to be sued in regards to cybersecurity practices as long as the board has acted in "good faith."

5) What is the role of management in ensuring that these requirements are met? Who is in charge of compliance?

Discussion: E-Commerce (25min)

Discussion Objectives:

Students will analyze the roles and responsibilities that pertain to the practice of corporate cybersecurity

Activities and Procedures:

Students should discuss two issues:

1) Imagine you are an upper-level manager for a corporation. What role do you play in implementing and monitoring the corporation's cybersecurity measures? How would you fulfill your "duty of care" clause? What questions do you ask the CEO during your cybersecurity briefing? What strategy would you suggest to your Board of Directors? What legal precedents would you cite? How would you ensure that your plan is followed? Who is responsible if your plan fails and the corporation suffers a cybersecurity breach? What might the consequences of a breach be? What are the best and worst case scenarios in the event of a breach?

2) What roles does your board of directors have in implementing cybersecurity measures?

Assessment:

Students should have an understanding of corporate structure, particularly the roles and responsibilities of corporate leaders with regard to corporation-wide cybersecurity.

Day 2: Legislation and the Private Sector

Lecture: Cybersecurity Legislation and the Private Sector (1h15min)

Materials:

- Cyber Security Incident Reporting and Response Planning 008-04 (CIP-008-04)
- FTCA violation against TJX
- Gramm-Leach-Bliley Financial Modernization Act CRS Summary http://thomas.loc.gov/cgi-bin/bdquery/z?d106:SN00900:@@@D&summ2=m&
- Health Information Technology for Economic and Clinical Health Act (HITECH) CRS Summary (American Recovery and Reinvestment Act of 2009, Title XIII) http://thomas.loc.gov/cgi-bin/bdquery/z?d111:HR00001:@@@D&summ2=m&

Lesson 6: The Private Sector

- Health Insurance Portability and Accountability Act (HIPAA) CRS Summary http://thomas.loc.gov/cgi-bin/bdquery/z?d104:HR03103:@@@D&summ2=m&
- North American Electric Reliability Committee. Cyber Security Incident Reporting and Response Planning 008-04 (CIP-008-04)
- Sarbanes-Oxley Act (SOX) CRS Summary http://thomas.loc.gov/cgi-bin/bdquery/z?d107:HR03763:@@@D&summ2=m&

Lecture Objectives:

Students will learn the laws that require private sector companies to be accountable to their customers in the case of cyber breaches.

Activities and Procedures:

1) There is no comprehensive private sector cybersecurity law that applies to all private sector businesses. However, there are industry-specific laws that may serve as models for future cybersecurity legislation.

2) The Gramm-Leach-Bliley Financial Modernization Act of 1996 contains the Financial Privacy Rule. The Financial Privacy Rule requires all financial institutions to disclose their information-sharing and privacy practices to their customers, and allows customers to opt-out of these practices. It states that financial institutions must also inform customers when their privacy or information-sharing policies change.

4) A Response attempts to mitigate attacks and intrusions through passive and active response methods. Passive response methods include Logging, Notification, and Shunning. Active response methods include terminating a session, altering the networks configuration, and deception.

3) Gramm-Leach-Bliley also created the Safeguards Rule that requires financial institutions to protect their customers' information in transmission and storage, and requires financial institutions to develop a written plan to protect customer information.

4) The Health Insurance Portability and Accountability Act (HIPAA) of 1996 is intended to unify government regulation regarding healthcare information, and eliminate inconsistencies between federal and state requirements. HIPAA created the Security Rule, which requires that companies demonstrate that they have thorough risk management strategies in place to protect customer information. HIPAA also created the Privacy Rule, which established rules for storing and transmitting Protected Health Information (PHI).

5) The Health Information Technology for Economic and Clinical Health Act (HITECH) of 2009 strengthened HIPAA by broadening the HIPAA Privacy and Security requirements. HITECH was the first federally mandated data breach notification statute.

6) The Federal Trade Commission (FTC) plays a major role enforcing the laws that protect of customers in the case of private sector data breaches. The FTC is commissioned to investigate and stop unfair or deceptive actions regarding private sector business practices towards consumers. The FTC charges companies that fail to protect consumer information with Federal Trade Commission Act (FTCA) violations.

7) The Securities and Exchange Committee (SEC) oversees companies' disclosure and accuracy of financial reporting. The SEC was organized in the early 20th century to regulate securities related industries. The SEC created the "Disclosure Guidance" that requires public companies to disclose any cyber risks that may potentially be important to investors. The SEC also created the Electronic Data Gath-

Lesson Plan

ering, Analysis, and Retrieval (EDGAR) system, which is a tool that anyone can use to find companies' financial statements and disclosures. Since 2002, all companies are required to post their financial statements to EDGAR.

8) Sarbanes-Oxley Act (SOX), passed by Congress in 2002, is intended to ensure that private corporations filed their financial statements accurately. SOX requires private sector companies to implement internal control systems to monitor financial accounting.

9) North American Electric Reliability Committee (NERC) is responsible for creating reliability standards for "Bulk Power Systems". NERC created Cyber Security Incident Reporting and Response Planning 008-04 (CIP-008-04), which requires Bulk Power Systems to identify, respond to, and report cybersecurity incidents.

Assessment:

Short Paper: Using the readings and information learned about private sector cybersecurity requirements, students will research and write about legislation and regulation regarding cybersecurity in a critical infrastructure sector. Students may choose to write about the telecommunications sector, the chemical sector, or any other major sector. What authorities are in charge of overseeing sector-specific cybersecurity requirements? What are the specific rules?

Day 3: Methods of Protecting Private Sector Networks

Lecture: Methods of Protecting Private Sector Networks (1h15min)

Materials:

- Allen, Julia H. *Governing for Enterprise Security Implementation Guide*. "Article 1: Characteristics of Effective Security Governance." Carnegie Mellon University, Software Engineering Institute. http://www.cert.org/governance/ges.html
- Business Continuity Plan Worksheet http://www.ready.gov/sites/default/files/documents/files/BusinessContinuityPlan.pdf
- Dunn, Catherine. Boards of Directors Largely Ignoring Corporate Cyber-Risk Management http://www.law.com/jsp/cc/PubArticleCC.jsp?id=1202544750336&Boards_of_Directors_Largely_Ignoring_Corporate_CyberRisk_Management
- FEMA Business Continuity Plan website http://www.ready.gov/business/implementation/continuity
- Jain, Raj. *Intrusion Detection Systems* http://www1.cse.wustl.edu/~jain/cse571-07/ftp/l_23ids.pdf
- Kundra, Vivek. "25 Point Implementation Plan to Reform Federal Information Technology Management," Dec. 9, 2010. https://www.dhs.gov/sites/default/files/publications/digital-strategy/25-point-implementation-plan-to-reform-federal-it.pdf

Lecture Objectives:

Students will understand the many ways in which private sector companies strategize and act in order to protect their IT systems.

Lesson 6: The Private Sector

Activities and Procedures:

1) Discuss model methods of protecting private sector infrastructure and information. How do these methods help corporate managers to fulfill their "Duty of Care"?

2) New cybersecurity legislation pushes corporate leaders to prioritize cybersecurity issues. Boards of Directors are the highest authority in any company and therefore most responsible for their company's cybersecurity policies. Boards designate Chief Information Security Officers to oversee the protection of resource management systems, a position which can take a variety of forms. The CISO position can be filled by one person, two people, or an entire committee. Boards should create a written plan to formally outline the company's cybersecurity policies and the internal controls in place to ensure that these policies are implemented and followed.

3) Discuss cybersecurity Risk Assessments in a corporate setting.

4) Response Programs should contain mechanisms to notify regulatory and law enforcement of unauthorized entries. All response plans should provide detailed protocols of what employees should do in case of an unauthorized intrusion into a corporate network. Many companies employ incident response teams that identify security breaches, mitigate damage, and investigate the extent and type of damage caused by the breach.

5) Discuss how employee education promotes cybersecurity best practices. Companies use training programs and classes to ensure that all employees are aware of the organization's cybersecurity policies and responsibilities. Business Continuity Plans are an organization's plan to recover from a cyber attack or disaster. Vendor Management ensures that outsourced labor has sufficient cybersecurity systems in place.

Assessment:

Business Continuity Plan Worksheet: Using the readings and their notes from the lecture, students should fill in the Business Continuity Plan Worksheet for a hypothetical company of their own creation.

Day 4: Table Top Exercise – TJX, Twitter, Sony

Table Top Exercise – TJX, Twitter, Sony (45min)

Materials:

- FTC Complaint Against TJX
  http://www.ftc.gov/sites/default/files/documents/cases/2008/08/080801tjxcomplaint.pdf
- FTC Agreement with TJX
  http://www.ftc.gov/sites/default/files/documents/cases/2008/03/080327agreement_0.pdf
- FTC Complaint Against Twitter
  http://www.ftc.gov/sites/default/files/documents/cases/2011/03/110311twittercmpt.pdf
- FTC Agreement with Twitter
  http://www.ftc.gov/sites/default/files/documents/cases/2010/06/100624twitteragree.pdf

Lesson Plan

- FTC Complaint Against Sony
  http://www.ftc.gov/sites/default/files/documents/cases/2008/12/081211cmp0823071.pdf
- FTC Agreement with Sony
  http://www.ftc.gov/os/caselist/0823071/081211consentp0823071.pdf

Exercise Objectives:

At the end of this exercise, students will understand some of the "big picture" complications associated with choosing the correct level of cybersecurity measures for a private sector company. Students will understand that although cybersecurity is critically important, it would be unwise for any business to spend all of its money of cybersecurity measures. Students will appreciate that the pressure on both the managers and board of directors to earn profits in order to satisfy shareholders as well as the company's overall business strategy often dictate the level of cybersecurity measures that the company undertakes.

Activities and Procedures:

Create six small groups in which students will discuss the implications of the lawsuits levied against TJX, Inc., Twitter, Inc., and Sony Computer Entertainment, LLC. Each group will be assigned one case to analyze. Each case offers a unique perspective as to the potential for cyber attacks to seize critical information as well as the repercussions that private corporations face if they do not effectively institute cybersecurity practices. Each group will present its case to the class.

Discussion: TJX, Twitter, Sony (30min)

Materials:

- Sony Worksheet
- TJX Worksheet
- Twitter Worksheet

Discussion Objectives:

Students will gain insight into the connections between cybersecurity and sound business practices. Students will understand the legal and financial consequences of ignoring cybersecurity in the private sector.

Activities and Procedures:

1) Each group will report its findings to the class. Use the following questions to guide the discussion session.

2) TJX: What are TJX's business goals? What types of products do they sell? Who do they sell to? Do they produce high-end or low-end goods? How does cybersecurity enhance TJX's business goals? Do TJX's cybersecurity practices increase or decrease how many people are willing to shop a TJX stores? How often do you believe managers assessed TJX's ability to protect customer information? In what ways were TJX's cybersecurity practices inadequate? What could TJX have done better? What do you believe that the TJX managers and board of directors discussed when they originally decided not to implement more security measures? What were the repercussions for the inadequacy of their cybersecurity programs?

Lesson 7: Cybersecurity Research Methods

3) Sony: What are Sony's business goals? What did the FTC require of Sony? How did this requirement affect customer satisfaction? How did this affect Sony's market share? How did this requirement inhibit Sony's ability to achieve its business goals? To whom does Sony sell its online gaming system? What did Sony market as its biggest feature of its online gaming system? What were the pros and cons of Sony's online gaming system? How does increased cybersecurity enhance Sony's business goals? Does an increased level of cybersecurity increase or decrease how many people are willing to join the gaming network? How often do you believe people assessed Sony's ability to protect customer information? In what ways were Sony's cybersecurity practices inadequate? What could Sony have done better? What do you believe that the Sony managers and board of directors discussed when they originally decided not to implement more security measures? What were the repercussions for the inadequacy of their cybersecurity programs?

4) Twitter: What are Twitter's business goals? Who do they try to sell their product to? What is Twitter's main attraction for customers? What are Twitter's business goals? How does an increased level of cybersecurity enhance Twitter's business goals? Does is increase or decrease how many people are willing to join Twitter? How often do you believe people assessed Twitter's ability to protect customer information? In what ways were Twitter's cybersecurity practices inadequate? What could Twitter have done better? What do you believe that the Twitter employees discussed when they originally decided not to implement more security measures? What role do you believe the relative newness of the company had in its security issues? What were the repercussions for the inadequacy of their cybersecurity programs? What did the FTC require of Twitter? How did this affect their customer satisfactions? How did this affect their market share? How did this inhibit Twitter's ability to achieve their business goals?

Assessment:

Student presentations.

Lesson 7: Cybersecurity Research and Methods

Lesson 7: Teaching Objectives-

Students will be introduced to formal processes and foundational knowledge for researching a wide range of cybersecurity problems. Students will recognize the leading role of the U.S. federal government on cybersecutiry issues. Students will be able to differentiate roles and responsibilities for cybersecurity across the three branches of government, and identify cybersecurity research trends for public and private sector issues. Students will understand how cyber events around the world shape the legal and political environment in which important cybersecurity documents are produced. Students will gain tools to research the essential question: What is the United States federal government's national policy on cybersecurity?

Day 1: Congress and the Courts – Cyber Crime and Punishment

Lecture: Congress and the Courts (1h15min)

Materials:

- Computer Fraud and Abuse Act (CFAA) CRS Summary http://thomas.loc.gov/cgi-bin/bdque-

Lesson Plan

ry/z?d099:HR04718:@@@D&summ2=m&

Dove, Robert B. "Enactment of a Law." http://thomas.loc.gov/home/enactment/enactlaw.pdf

Sullivan, John V. "HOW OUR LAWS ARE MADE." 2007. http://www.gpo.gov/fdsys/pkg/CDOC-110hdoc49/pdf/CDOC-110hdoc49.pdf

Video "Legislative Research"

Zeichner, Lee. "Chapter 6: Research Methods." *Cybersecurity Foundtions: An Interdisciplinary Introduction*.

Lecture Objectives:

Students will understand how rules and regulations are created, and how cyber crimes are prosecuted in the United States, and gain a foundation of knowledge for conducting original research in the field.

Activities and Procedures:

1) How does the federal government create the rules and regulations that govern global computer crime? Where does this authority come from?

2) What is Congress? What is Congress's role in creating cybersecurity legislation? What is the process of cybersecurity legislation from bill to law?

3) What are the U.S. Courts? What role do courts play in cybersecurity rules and regulations? Discuss the sentencing of cyber criminals based on the criteria established by Congress. Due to the lack of judicial precedent in cybersecurity issues, the role of the courts in regulating cybersecurity laws is constantly evolving.

4) Discuss the Morris Worm as a case study for the roles and responsibilities of Congress and the Courts to create, implement, and enforce cybersecurity laws.

Assessment:

Legislative Research Worksheet: After watching the video about how to find legislation on Thomas, students will search for a piece of cybersecurity legislation of their choosing, and then fill out the worksheet.

Day 2: The Executive Branch - Policy

Lecture: The Executive Branch (45min)

Materials:

- Bush, George W. HSPD-7
- Clinton, William J. PDD-63
- DHS strategy and business model
- Organization of the National Security Council Packet (PDD-1, NSPD-1, PPD-1, HSPD-1 clips)
- Video "Executive Policy"

Lesson 7: Cybersecurity Research Methods

Lecture Objectives:

Students will be able to identify major Executive Branch policy documents on cybersecurity. Students will understand the role of the Executive branch in shaping policy. Students will understand the interplay between the three branches of government in shaping cybersecurity policy. Students will become familiar with the National Security Council's role in national cybersecurity policy.

Activities and Procedures:

1) What is the Executive Branch and who comprises it? What is the Executive Branch's cybersecurity policy? Discuss Executive statements on cybersecurity policy. To whom are these statements directed?

2) What is the National Security Council? Who sits on the NSC? Why does the NSC have so much authority regarding cybersecurity policy?

3) What is the Department of Homeland Security (DHS)? What role do DHS and its associated groups play in national cybersecurity policy?

Discussion: Warning Systems (30min)

Materials:

- Video: House Committee on Homeland Security. "Subcommittee Hearing: Preventing Nuclear Terrorism: Does DHS have an Effective and Efficient Nuclear Detection Strategy?" http://homeland.house.gov/hearing/subcommittee-hearing-preventing-nuclear-terrorism-does-dhs-have-effective-and-efficient

Discussion Objectives:

Students will learn about Federal cybersecurity warning systems, and examples of their use in the Federal government.

Activities and Procedures:

1) What is the Executive Branch's responsibility to warn people of cyber attacks? Who in the Executive Branch is in charge of issuing cybersecurity warnings? What is the relationship between federal, state, local, and tribal governments in the cybersecurity warning system process?

Assessment:

Short Paper: Students will write a short research-based paper based about cybersecurity warning systems. What are the current procedures for government warnings in the event of a cyber attack? What department or agency is in charge of creating and operating these systems? What is the chain of command? How does the government ensure that the systems will function during a real cyber attack?

Lesson Plan

Day 3: Federal Cybersecurity Regulations

Lecture: Regulations, Congress, and the Executive Branch (1h15min)

Materials:

- "The Reg Map" http://www.reginfo.gov/public/reginfo/Regmap/regmap.pdf
- Department of Homeland Security. The Comprehensive Cybersecurity Initiative. http://www.whitehouse.gov/sites/default/files/cybersecurity.pdf
- Video "Federal Regulations"

Lecture Objectives:

Students will understand the federal regulations process. Students will be able to search for federal regulations and analyze the Federal Register.

Activities and Procedures:

1) What is the federal government's role in establishing cybersecurity regulations for the private sector? Where do regulations come from, who creates them, and what gives them the authority to create them?

2) Discuss the steps of creating federal regulations. Explain how to research Federal regulations online, and how to effectively read and understand regulations in the Federal Register.

Assessment:

Research Assignment: Students will use their understanding of Federal regulations to locate the HIPAA Security Rule in the Federal Register. Using the regulations research tutorial, students will find the regulatory requirements within HIPAA, and then locate the actual Security Rule within the pages of the Federal Register. Students will print out and highlight the appropriate pages of both HIPAA and the Federal Register.

Day 4: Global Cybersecurity Policy

Lecture: Global Cybersecurity Policy (1h15min)

Materials:

- Brunner, Elgin M. and Manuel Suter. *International CIIP Handbook 2008/2009.* pp 463-521 http://www.css.ethz.ch/publications/pdfs/CIIP-HB-08-09.pdf
- Davis, Joshua. *Hackers Take Down the Most Wired Network in Europe*. Wired Magazine, http://archive.wired.com/politics/security/magazine/15-09/ff_estonia?currentPage=all
- Jacobs, Andrew and Miguel Helft. "Google, Citing Attack, Threatens to Exit China." New York Times. January 12, 2010 http://www.nytimes.com/2010/01/13/world/asia/13beijing.html
- Maurer, Tim. *Cyber Norm Emergence at the United Nations.* September 2011. http://belfercenter.ksg.harvard.edu/files/maurer-cyber-norm-dp-2011-11-final.pdf

Lesson 7: Cybersecurity Research Methods

Lecture Objectives:

Students will learn about global institutions dedicated to cybersecurity issues. Students will learn about cyber attacks throughout the world and the ramifications of these attacks on the global cybersecurity discourse. Students will understand the ways in which U.S. cybersecurity policy drives the global conversation.

Activities and Procedures:

1) Discuss famous cyber attacks throughout the globe. How did local, national, and global communities respond to these attacks? What cybersecurity measures were in place when each of these attacks happened?

Assessment:

Students should apply their knowledge of risk management, U.S. law and policy, systems of systems, cyber attack methods, and cybersecurity operations to analyze these events and the responses to them. What could the countries and entities attacked have done to prevent them? How did they recover from the attacks? What new laws and policies were developed after these attacks? How did the global community respond?

Index

Symbols

2-factor authentication 42, 210, 211, 225, 226
9/11/2001. *See* September 11, 2001
60-Day Cyberspace Policy Review 73–74, 95, 186
256-bit encryption 140
300A and 300B reports 124
414s (hackers) 4, 279
1930s IT infrastructure 134
1940s IT infrastructure 56
1950s IT infrastructure 56–57, 134
1960s cybersecurity issues 2, 57–58, 69
1970s cybersecurity issues 2, 130
1980s cybersecurity issues 3–8, 58–62, 60, 134
1990s cybersecurity issues 6, 60–69, 160–162, 197
2000s cybersecurity issues 6, 65, 66–77, 158, 197
2010s cybersecurity issues 6, 74–77, 158–159, 197

A

A circulars. *See* under OMB
AC (Actual Cost) xvi, 111–113, 214–215, 216, 261
acceptable levels of risk 28, 276
Acceptable Quality Level (AQL) xvi, 106, 261
accepting risks 13, 16, 18, 45–46
access codes 169
accessibility of systems
  corporate systems 167
  health care systems 161
  mainframe computers 57
  network access points 167, 184
  physical sites 169
access points 167, 184
account number access 195
accounting 108–109, 165
accounting machines 134
accounts, banking 239–247
accreditation (IT systems) 125–126
accuracy of warnings 82
ACH debit transactions 241
Acquisition Program Baseline (APB) xvi, 104, 261
acquisitions and procurement
  acquisition documents 104–109
  acquisition phase 104–109
  Brooks Act 57–58
  CIOs and 62–63
  compliance 123–124
  GSA and 57
  OMB and 61, 61–62
  Paperwork Reduction Act 61
  supply chain security 121, 124
active responses to threats 149–150, 170–171, 261
acts of law 188
Actual Cost (AC) xvi, 111–113, 214–215, 216, 261
ACWP (Actual Cost of Work Performed) xvi, 111, 261
adaptive monitoring 241
address verification 222
"adequate security" 125
Administrative Procedure Act (APA) xvi, 190, 261
Advanced Notices of Proposed Rulemaking (ANPR) xvi, 186, 190, 261
Advanced Persistent Threats (APTs) xvi, 147–148, 197, 198, 261
Advanced Research Projects Agency (ARPA) xvi, 2
Advanced Research Projects Agency Network (ARPANET) xvi, 2, 130, 261
African Network Information Centre (AfriNIC) 199
agencies
  audits 172
  budgets 186
  civilian. *See* civilian agencies
  classified/unclassified protective markings 59
  creation of 190
  cybersecurity policy role 52–53
  FISMA requirements 71–72, 125
  impact on projects 90
  intelligence. *See* intelligence agencies
  inter-agency cooperation 66
  military. *See* Defense Department
  operational planning model 91
  procurement responsibilities 61
  public hearings 190–191
  public-private partnerships. *See* private-public partnerships
  regulations, role in 190–193
  regulatory agencies 190–191
  supervision of 55
  top-down analysis 38–40
aggravated identity theft 195
agriculture as critical infrastructure 70
"ahead of schedule" variances 113, 213–214
Air Force 54
alerts
  as cybersecurity capability 146, 149
  as high-level requirement 100
  bank emails 242
  external information 231
  trusted Internet connections example 102

Index (A)

warning systems 81–84, 90–91, 100, 146, 149
alternative hypotheses (Ha) 30, 37, 207, 261
alternative scenarios 88–89, 101
ambiguity in survey design 205
amendments, bills 188
American Recovery and Reinvestment Act 161, 172
American Registry for Internet Numbers (ARIN) 199
analyzing threats 100, 146, 148–149
Anil, Suleyman 73, 202
anomalies 254
  corporate detection 170–171
  DHS monitoring case study 118–119
  network detection 146, 148, 231, 232, 233, 234, 254, 261
  simulating 149–150
anonymity 199, 200
Anonymous 15
ANPR (Advance Notice of Proposed Rulemaking) xvi, 186, 190, 261
Antarctica 199
anti-phishing methods 242
Anti-Referral Payments Law 156
antivirus software
  as warning system 149
  corporate obligations and 158
  informing internal information 118, 231
  in internal monitoring 148
  McAfee 84
  TJX data breach and 163
APA (Administrative Procedure Act) xvi, 190, 261
APB (Acquisition Program Baseline) xvi, 104, 261
APNIC (Asia-Pacific Network Information Centre) 199
appeals and appeals courts 192
APT (Advanced Persistent Threat) xvi, 147–148, 197, 198, 261
AQL (Acceptable Quality Level) xvi, 106, 261
ARIN (American Registry for Internet Numbers) 199
Army 54
ARPA (Advanced Research Projects Agency) xvi, 2
ARPANET (Advanced Research Projects Agency Network) xvi, 2, 130, 261
arraignments 195
Asia 199
Asia-Pacific Network Information Centre (APNIC) 199
assembly language 131–132
assessing plans 88
assessing results 88–89
assessing risks. *See* risk assessments
assessing threats. *See* threat assessment
assets
  capital 108, 109, 123–124
  corporate 167
  critical 24–26, 45
  FISMA compliance 124–126
  GAO labeling system 24–26
  identifying 117–118
assistance as high-level requirement 100
Assistant for Homeland Security and Counterterrorism 73
assumptions 261
  in risk management framework 15, 16

in survey design 205
risk determination and 26
spear phishing survey 32
asymmetrical warfare 4
atomic bombs/nuclear arms 4
atomic energy. *See* nuclear facilities
"at rest" encryption 140
attachments (email) 141, 168
attacks and exploits 141–142
  active/passive responses 149–150, 170–171
  alerts. *See* alerts
  anomalies and 118–119, 146, 148–149, 170–171
  BGP 138–139
  botnets 143
  brute force 140
  buffer overflow 145
  code injection 145
  crashing and recovery 145
  data breaches. *See* data breaches
  denial of service 143, 146, 147, 196
  DHS monitoring case study 118–119
  DNS cache poisoning 144
  exploits, defined 267
  factors aiding in 145
  growth in 2000s 72
  history of 197–198
  identifying 254
  insider threats 144, 167
  malware 141, 142, 194
  man in the middle 144–145
  phishing/spear phishing 31–36, 142–143
  private sector breaches 153
  private sector plans 152–153
  SEC disclosures 164
  simulating 149–150, 168–169
  threat signature technology 73–74
  time before discovery 200
  types of 135
  unknown vulnerabilities 145–146
  warnings. *See* warning systems
  zero-day exploits 145–146
attributes
  CMS systems 229–232, 233
  warning systems 252–257
attribution for attacks 137, 141, 200, 261
attribution problems 261
audits 171, 261
  agencies 172
  corporate policies 171–173
  financial 122
  FTC Consent Agreements 162
  health care systems 126, 161
  internal/external 121–123, 171–173
  IT 122, 126
  monitoring functions and 147
  risk assessment 172
  Sarbanes-Oxley Act 165
  technical 122

Index

types of 121–123
Australia 199
authentication cookies 223, 241
Authentication in an Internet Banking Environment 241
authority, transnational 201–202
authorization 98, 98–99
automatic alert systems 82
Automatic Data Processing Act (Brooks Act) 57–58, 60, 61, 262
availability, threats to 135
avoiding risks 13, 16, 45, 277
awareness campaigns 149, 161
Azerbaijan 198

B

BAC (Budget at Completion) xvi, 114, 214, 215, 216, 262
backbones 3, 136
back-ups, off-site 169
backwards engineering (Op Models) 104
badges 169
bail 195
bandwagon fallacy 179
banking and finance systems
   as critical infrastructure 63, 64
   criminal information access 194, 195
   cyber threats 64
   Estonian attacks 73
   fraud case study 239–247
   GLB Financial Modernization Act 159–160
   merchant security 221
   Sarbanes-Oxley Act 123, 165
   TJX breach losses 158, 194
   written security plans 160
baselines, establishing 117–118, 125, 229, 230, 232, 233, 235, 251, 254
BCWP (Budgeted Cost of Work Performed) xvi, 111, 262. *See also* EV (Earned Value)
BCWS (Budgeted Cost of Work Scheduled) xvi, 111, 262. *See also* PV (Planned Value)
behavioral detection 148, 167, 261
"behind schedule" status 119, 213–214
best practices 75, 217
"beyond a reasonable doubt" 261
BGP (Border Gateway Protocol) xvi, 136, 138–140, 144–145, 262
biases 205, 262
big picture, senior managers and 85
bills, legislative 187–189, 262
binary code 131, 139, 262
binary dependent variables 207
BJR (Business Judgment Rule) xvi, 157, 262
Black Hand 197
black hole servers 147
blackouts 68
"Blueprint for a Secure Cyber Future" 96, 186
Boards of Directors 262
   as senior managers 81
   Business Judgment Rule 157
   Duty of Care 155–159
   liability 157
   obligations 159–160
   role in company 154
   role in cybersecurity 152–153, 154, 166–167
bookseller case study 219–226
Border Gateway Protocol (BGP) xvi, 136, 138–140, 144–145, 262
botnets 143, 262
bottom-up assessments (PWS) 106
Bottom-Up Review Report (BUR) xvi, 96, 186
boy genius hackers 3–4, 21
brokerage firms 164
Brooks Act 57–58, 60, 61, 262
Brooks, Jack 57
brute force attacks 262
Budget at Completion (BAC) xvi, 114, 214, 215, 216, 262
Budgeted Cost of Work Performed (BCWP) xvi, 111, 262. *See also* EV (Earned Value)
Budgeted Cost of Work Scheduled (BCWS) xvi, 111, 262. *See also* PV (Planned Value)
budgets
   APBs 104
   as constraints 17
   comparing projects 114–115, 213–217
   Congressional control 55
   CONOPS and 101
   developing 88, 109–112
   EVM development of 109–112
   EVM indexes 213–217
   EVM management 108
   in proposed legislation 188
   manager's role 86
   OMB control 62
   online bookstore case study 220–226
   over or under status 114
   trade-offs in risk management 18
   understanding 109–111
buffer overflow attacks 145
bulk power systems 164–165
BUR (Bottom-Up Review Report) xvi, 96, 186
Bureau of the Budget. *See* OMB (Office of Management and Budget)
Bush administration
   CNCI founding 72–74
   critical infrastructure directives 70–72
   E-Government Act 71–72
   Executive Orders 184
   FISMA act 71–72
   Homeland Security history 66–75
   PDDs 70–72, 183
   Presidential power expansion 95–96
   Sarbanes-Oxley Act 123, 165
business continuity plans 170, 262
Business Corporation Law of New York State (NY BCL) 155

Index (A-C)

business interruption insurance 170
Business Judgment Rule (BJR) xvi, 157, 262
businesses. *See* private sector
bylaws, corporate 154, 262

C

C++ 131
CAATs (Computer-Assisted Audit Techniques) 122
cable companies 136
cache 134, 262
cache poisoning 144
California
   data breach laws 163–164
   electrical grid attacks 197
callbacks (bank alerts) 242
cameras, activating 74
Canada 199
capabilities
   capability-based planning 100–101, 262
   capability gaps 98–99, 99, 100, 102, 255, 262
   CONOPS 101–104
   defining for monitoring systems 116
   examples 20–21, 146–150
   identifying for threat assessment 20
   identifying in PWSs 106
   mission needs statements 97–98
   Op Models 103
   organizational needs 87–88
   translating goals into 84
   US-CERT monitoring systems 229–232
   US-CERT warning systems 252–257
capability-based planning 100–101, 262
capability gaps 98–99, 99, 100, 102, 233, 262
capacitors 134
capital 80
Capital Asset Plan and Business Case (Exhibit 300) 123–124
capital assets 108, 109, 123–124
Caremark International lawsuit 155–158
Caremark standard 262
Caribbean region 199
case studies
   Book Box 219–226
   US-CERT monitoring system 227–237
   US-CERT warning system 249–259
catastrophes. *See* disasters
"catastrophic" label (GAO) 24–26
CDs 134
Central Asia 199
Central Intelligence Agency. *See* CIA
central processing units (CPUs) xvii, 131, 262
CEOs (Chief Executive Officers) xvi, 263
   Business Judgment Rule 157
   cybersecurity role 152–153, 154, 166
   Duty of Care 155–159
   liability 157
certificates (HTTPS) 140

certification (IT systems) 125–126
CFAA (Computer Fraud and Abuse Act) xvi, 6–7, 193–195, 263
CFR (Code of Federal Regulations) xvi, 126, 191, 263
challenge questions 210, 211, 222, 224, 242, 244, 245
changes, identifying
   evolution of threats 76
   in file data 141
   monitoring risks 46–47, 48
   risk management framework 16
charging criminals 195
Charter Pacific Bank 159
charters, corporate 154, 262
Chechnya 197
checklists, going beyond 49
Chief Executive Officers (CEOs) xvi, 152–153, 154–158, 166, 263
Chief Information Officers. *See* CIOs (Chief Information Officers)
Chief Information Officers Council (CIO Council) 62, 183
Chief Information Security Officers (CISOs) xvi, 166, 219–226, 263
Chief Infrastructure Assurance Officers (CIAOs) 66
child prodigy hackers 3–4, 21
China 28, 197
Chi square test 207
CIA (Central Intelligence Agency) xvi, 54, 55, 57, 66
CIAO (Critical Infrastructure Assurance Office) xvi, 66, 69–70
CIAOs (Chief Infrastructure Assurance Officers) 66
CICG (Critical Infrastructure Coordination Group) xvi, 65
CIKR (critical infrastructure and key resources) xvi, 71. *See also* critical infrastructure
CIO Council 62, 183
CIOs (Chief Information Officers) xvi, 43, 263
   Business Judgment Rule 157
   cybersecurity role 62–63, 152–153, 154, 166
   Duty of Care 155–159
   FISMA compliance 125
   liability 157
CISOs (Chief Information Security Officers) xvi, 166, 219–226, 263
Citigroup 157–158
citizen concerns, military information control 59
civilian agencies
   Brooks Act responsibilities 57
   capability-based planning 100–101
   CONOPS 101–104
   cybersecurity role 52–54, 55
   DHS as 69
   Einstein 3 monitoring 73
   EVM accounting and 108
   FISMA requirements and 72
   Mission Needs Statements 93–94
   national cybersecurity threats management 5
   Op Models 103–105
   tensions with military 52, 53, 59–62, 76–77
CIWG (Critical Infrastructure Working Group) xvi, 63, 264
claims processors 161

346

Index

classified information
  CNCI declassification 74
  criminal information access to 193
  document markings 59
  early cybersecurity policies 5
  notifications and 254–255
  NSA classified computer systems 60
  NSA SBU IT 60
  personal computer security 58
classified technology 60
Clinger-Cohen Act of 1996 61–62, 92, 123–124, 263
Clinton administration
  CIO Council 62
  cybersecurity and terrorism 63–68
  Executive Orders 183
  Presidential Decision Directives 56, 64–68, 183, 187
  Y2K preparations 65
closed-ended questions 205
cloud providers 158–161
CMS (continuous monitoring system) xvii, 90–91, 227–237, 264
CNCI (Comprehensive National Cybersecurity Initiative) xvii, 81, 232, 263
  history of 72–75
  mission requirements in 95
  partial declassification 74, 184
  TIC initiative 184
  warnings capability 81
Coast Guard 54
Coast Guard Intelligence 54
COBIT (Control Objectives for Information and Related Technology) 171–172, 264
code breaking agencies. *See* NSA
code injection 145
Code of Federal Regulations (CFR) xvi, 126, 191, 263
coefficient of determination 208, 263
Cold War 2–3, 57, 58
collaboration, as high-level requirement 100
color-coding project status 120
.com domains 139
command and control attacks 142
commenting on Proposed Rules 191
Commerce Department 57, 66, 71, 199
"commercially reasonable" security 243–244
Committee of Sponsoring Organizations (COSO) 171
committees, Congressional 187, 263
communication pathways 134, 172–173. *See also* networks
communications, intercepting 195. *See also* attacks; data breaches
communication systems 63, 64, 70
companies. *See* private sector
completion dates (POA&M documents) 108–109
compliance 122
  audits 121–123
  compliance officers 121
  corporate employees 168
  Exhibit 300 123–124
  Federal CIOs' role 62
  Federal practices 122–123
  FISMA requirements 124–126
  HIPAA example 125–127
  internal controls 171–172
  monitoring risks 46–47, 48, 147
  noncompliance consequences 125
  operational planning model 92
  Operational Requirements Documents 103
  post-breach reports 169
  risk management framework 16
Compliance and Reporting block 92
compliance officers 121
components (hardware) 131, 132–133, 263
Comprehensive National Cybersecurity Initiative. *See* CNCI
compromised systems 141, 263
Computer-Assisted Audit Techniques (CAATs) 122
Computer Crime and Intellectual Property (DOJ) 259
Computer Fraud and Abuse Act (CFAA) xvi, 6–7, 193–195, 263
Computer Readiness Team (US-CERT) 90–91
computer science 130–131
Computer Security Act of 1987 xvii, 59, 60–61, 263
computers 130, 263
  as systems 132–134
  attacks and exploits. *See* attacks
  cryptographic technologies 139–141
  cybersecurity operation capabilities 146–150
  Federal standards for 123
  history of 130
  mainframes 56–57
  memory 133–134
  multiple processors 132
  personal computers. *See* PCs
  processors 131–132
  procurement. *See* acquisitions and procurement
  programs 131–132
  protected 194
  research systems 2
  vulnerabilities 144–146
Concept of Operations (CONOPS) xvii, 101–104, 263
conditional events (probability) 37–38, 263
conference committees 188
confidence intervals (statistics) 207, 264
confidential information. *See* classified information; customer information; personal information
confidentiality breaches 135
configuration, network 145, 170
Congress
  agency creation 190
  agency supervision 55
  as senior managers 81
  authority 186
  Congressional Research Service xvii, 189–190, 264
  cybersecurity policy role 52–53
  federal regulations 190–193
  GAO information 189
  legislation process 187–189
  military/civilian security control policies 53

Index (C)

mission requirements 93, 94
power of the purse 186
proposed bills and law research 189
research sources 179–180, 189
response to NSDD-145 60–61
Congressional Record 189, 264
Congressional Research Service (CRS) xvii, 189–190, 264
CONOPS (Concept of Operations) xvii, 101–104, 263
Consent Agreements 162, 163, 264
consequence assessments 24–27, 254, 264
  conducting 230–231
  DHS monitoring case study 118–119
  in consequence equation 24
  metrics 25
  model corporate cyber program 166, 167
consequences 18, 24, 264
  analyzing threats/vulnerabilities 26–30
  assessing. *See* consequence assessments
  assigning values to 27–29
  corporate governance and 155
  direct/indirect 24
  identifying 29
  illustrated 29
  in consequence equation 24
  in PRA risk management 36
  in risk assessment 19, 29
  in risk determination 28
  in risk equation 19
  in risk management framework 13, 16
  increases in 27
  metrics 25
Constitution 179, 188, 192
constraints
  identifying 102
  in CONOPS 101–104
  in risk management framework 13, 16, 17–18
  internal/external 90
  user-friendly websites and 43, 44
containing threats
  as capability 146
  "contain" task in risk management 12
  corporate policies 170
  risk responses 45
continuity plans 170
continuous monitoring system (CMS) xvii, 90–91, 227–237, 264
contracting officers 107–108
contractors. *See* vendors/contractors
contracts 170
control activities (businesses) 172
control environments (businesses) 171
Control Objectives for Information and Related Technology (COBIT) 171–172, 264
convenience sampling 206, 264
Convention on Cybercrime 202, 264
cookies 223, 241
coordination role (management)
  as high-level requirement 100

failures of 90
functions 85–87
managing vs. doing 83–84
Corporate Finance Division (SEC) 164
corporate governance 264
corporate officers 264
corporations. *See* private sector
COSO (Committee of Sponsoring Organizations) 171
cost-benefit analysis 219–226
Cost Performance Index (CPI) xvii, 114, 213–214, 215, 216, 264
costs
  attack simulations 168
  Cost Variances 113–115, 119–120
  data breaches 6, 158, 159, 164, 169
  DHS monitoring case study 117–118
  District Design case study 110–113
  IGCE estimates 107–108
  in budgets 110–112
  objective and threshold values 104–105
  Op Models 103–105
  Sony PlayStation breach 159
  TJX data breach 158
  worm damage estimates 6
Cost Variances (CVs) xvii, 113–116, 119–120, 264
Council of Europe 202
counterintelligence 73–76, 201. *See also* espionage; intelligence agencies
counterterrorism review of policies 73–74
course lesson plans 307–342
courses of action 99. *See also* plans; strategies
course syllabus 295–306
Court of Appeals 192
courts
  international 201
  U.S.. *See* judicial branch of government
CPI (Cost Performance Index) xvii, 114, 213–214, 215, 216, 264
CPU (central processing unit) xvii, 131, 262
credit and debit cards
  criminal information access 195
  liability for breaches 157–160
  online bookstore case study 221
  personal information sales 159
  prosecutions for breaches 194
  Sony PlayStation Network breach 158–159
  TJX data breach 158, 162–163, 194
  verification 222, 223
credit reporting agencies 164
criminal acts. *See also* attacks; data breaches
  Computer Fraud and Abuse Act 193–195
  Federal crimes 193–194
  federal prosecution process 195–197
  fraudulent money transfers 239–247
  identity theft 158, 193, 194, 195
  international issues 201
  Wiretap act 195
criminals. *See* hackers; nation-state hackers; organized crime groups

348

Index

crisis management, DHS role in 70
critical assets
   consequence assessments 24
   GAO labeling system 24–26
   removing 45
"Critical Foundations: Protecting America's Infrastructures" 64–65
Critical Infrastructure Assurance Office (CIAO) xvi, 66, 69–70
critical infrastructure components 63. *See also* critical infrastructure protection
   agriculture 70
   banking and finance systems 63, 64
   blackouts 68
   CIKR (critical infrastructure and key resources) xvi, 71
   communication systems 63, 64, 70
   electrical grid 63, 64
   emergency services 64
   Energy Department management 70
   food systems 70
   identifying critical infrastructure 70–72
   in policy formation 56
   Internet 197
   power plants 164–165
   private sector ownership 63
   sectors of 70
   transportation systems 63, 64, 70
   water systems 64, 70
   Y2K preparations 65
Critical Infrastructure Coordination Group (CICG) xvi, 65
"Critical Infrastructure Identification, Prioritization, and Protection" 70–72
critical infrastructure protection. *See also* critical infrastructure components
   Board of Directors role 166–167
   CIWG review 63
   corporate policies 168
   Critical Infrastructure Assurance Office 66
   Critical Infrastructure Protection Board 68–69, 184
   Critical Infrastructure Working Group 63
   Cybersecurity Act of 2012 74
   DHS responsibilities 14, 66–67, 68–70, 70, 71
   Executive Orders. *See* EOs
   National Coordinator for Security, Infrastructure Protection and Counter-Terrorism 65
   National Infrastructure Advisory Council 68
   National Infrastructure Assurance Council 66
   National Infrastructure Protection Center 69–70, 187
   National Infrastructure Protection Council 68–69
   National Infrastructure Protection Plan 14, 66, 70
   National Policy for Infrastructure Protection 64
   NSC (National Security Council) 64, 68
   Office of National Infrastructure Assurance 64
   PDDs. *See* PDDs
   policies 56, 64–67
   President's Commission on Critical Infrastructure Protection 64–65, 183
   private sector ownership 63, 76
   public-private partnerships 53, 63, 65–66, 76
   sentencing and 196
   Y2K preparations 65
Critical Infrastructure Protection Board 68–69
"Critical Infrastructure Security and Resilience" 75–76
Critical Infrastructure Working Group (CIWG) xvi, 63, 264
"critical" label (GAO) 24–26
criticality, defined 24, 264
CRS (Congressional Research Service) xvii, 189–190, 264
cryptographic technologies 139–141
cryptological agencies. *See* NSA
CSA (Computer Security Act of 1987) xvii, 59, 60–61, 263
CS&C (Office of Cybersecurity and Communications) xvii, 69, 96, 184, 232, 273
customer inconvenience scores 221–223, 224
customer information
   banks selling 159
   business's duty towards 153–154
   criminal access to 194, 195
   FTC and 162–165
   leak example 41–46
   protecting 221–223
   Sony PlayStation Network 158–159
   statistical models for risk 208–212
   TJX data breach 158, 162–163, 194
customer protection scores 221–223
CVs (Cost Variances) xvii, 113–116, 119–120, 264
Cyber Analysis and Warning: DHS Faces Challenges in Establishing a Comprehensive National Capability 251, 254
Cyber Defense Policy (NATO) 202
Cyber Incident Annex 259
"Cyber Initiative" 259
Cyber Intelligence Sharing and Protection Act 75
cyber intrusions, defined 141, 264
cyber retaliation 250
cybersecurity. *See also* computer science; Federal government; legislation; policies; private sector; research
   capabilities 146–150
   facets of 7–9
   global issues in 196–204
   history of issues 3–10
   model corporate framework 165–172
   risks in cyberspace 12–14
Cybersecurity Act of 2012 74–75, 264
Cybersecurity Coordinator (White House) 73, 75, 185
"Cyber Security Incident Reporting and Response Planning" 164
Cyber Security Incident Response Plans 164
cybersecurity insurance 46–47
cybersecurity management framework
   best practices 92
   capability-based planning 100–101
   civilian agencies 100–106
   Congressional/Presidential input 94–97
   CONOPS and Op Models 101–106
   DHS framework 92–93
   high-level requirements 97–101
   mission needs statements 93–94, 97–101

Index (C-D)

objective values 104–105
sector differences 93
cybersecurity managers. *See* program/project managers
cybersecurity operation capabilities 146–150
Cyberspace Policy Review 73–74, 95, 186
cyber warfare
  Estonia 73
  history of 197–198
  Olympic Games program 74
  UN and 202
cyclical nature of management 89

D

damages
  attacks 141
  business data breaches 153
  examples 20–21
  identifying in threat assessment 20
  lethality 20, 21–22
  mitigating 170
  model corporate cyber program 166
  risk tolerances 18
data 130, 265
  analyzing traffic 148–149
  backing up 169
  business transactions 153–154
  cryptographic technologies 139–141
  encryption 168–169
  monitoring 146–148
  packet analyzers 147
  removal/exfiltration 141
databases 153–154
data breaches
  business implications 153–154
  costs of 6, 158, 159, 164, 169
  Federal Trade Commission and 162–165
  HIPAA 160–162
  international issues 201
  liability for 157–160
  notification laws 265
  notifications 169–170
  sentencing penalties 196
  Sony PlayStation Network 158–159
  TJX case study 158, 162–163, 194
  types of violations 135
data breach notification laws 265
DCA (Defense Communications Agency) 2
DDoS attacks (distributed denial-of-service) xvii, 6, 144, 265
deadlines, project 99
DEA (Drug Enforcement Administration) 54
debit cards. *See* credit and debit cards
debit transactions 241
decision-making process 86–90
declassification of CNCI 74
decryption 139
defense, as high-level requirement 100
Defense Communications Agency (DCA) 2

Defense Department xvii, 265
  agencies and commands 53–55
  ARPANET 2
  CNCI directives 73
  computer procurement 57
  FISMA and 72
  ISAC participation 66
  managing national cybersecurity threats 5
  NCRCG role 259
  on Homeland Security Council 67
  Planning, Programming, Budgeting and Execution 93
  situational analysis tools 236
  WBS budgeting 109
Defense Information Systems Agency 3
Defense Intelligence Agency (DIA) xvii, 54
Delaware Court of Chancery 156, 157
Denial of Service (DoS) attacks xvii, 143, 146, 147, 196, 265
departments of government. *See* names of specific departments (Defense Department, DHS, EPA, etc.)
dependent variables (modeling) 42, 207, 208, 209, 265
dependent variables (research) 177
descriptive research 178
detailed technical guidance 217
detection, as high-level requirement 100
device authentication 223, 241, 244
DHS (Department of Homeland Security) xvii, 265
  agencies collected under 68–70, 96, 227, 232
  capability-based planning 100–101
  Critical Infrastructure Protection Board 68
  cybersecurity agencies in 68
  cybersecurity management framework 92–93
  cybersecurity policies 71
  cybersecurity reports 96–97
  DHS Risk Lexicon. *See* DHS Risk Lexicon
  EVM systems 108, 116–122
  expanded scope of government and 95
  FISMA and 74–75, 185
  founding of 66–67
  guidance statements 95
  infrastructure protection 68
  military and intelligence agencies 54–56
  mission needs statements 96–97, 98
  monitoring system case study 116–122
  National Infrastructure Protection Plan 14, 71
  National Response Framework 259
  "National Strategy to Secure Cyberspace" 69
  National Vulnerability Database 145
  program managers 94
  Security Strategic Plan 186
  structure of 96
  TIC mandate 184
  warning systems challenges 81, 250–251
DHS Risk Lexicon 277
  consequences 24
  game theory 42
  likelihood 29
  risk assessment 19
  risk transfer 46

Index

threats 20
threat shifting 21
vulnerabilities/vulnerability assessments 22
DIA (Defense Intelligence Agency) xvii, 54
Digital Equipment Corporation 3
digital signatures (domains) 139
direct consequences, defined 24
direct relationships (logit models) 42
directives
 defined 217
 Presidential. *See* PDDs (Presidential Decision Directives)
disasters
 as unintentional threats 20
 "catastrophic" label 24–26
 risk management models and 13
 threats resulting from 167
disclosures 164–165, 169
disjoint events (exclusive events) 37–38
disseminating information, as capability 116
distributed denial-of-service attacks (DDOS) xvii, 6, 144, 265
distribution attacks 142
district courts 192
District Design case study
 budgeting 109–114
 cost variances 114–115
 EVM indexes 213–217
 introduction 109
 schedule variances 113, 115
Division (voting) 188
DNS cache poisoning 144, 265
DNS (Domain Name System) xvii, 136, 139, 198, 265
DNSSEC (Domain Name System Security Extensions) xvii, 139, 265
document classification 59
DOD. *See* Defense Department
"doing," vs. managing 83–84
dollar amount rules 222, 224, 242, 244–245
domain name registries 139
Domain Name System (DNS) xvii, 136, 139, 198, 265
Domain Name System Security Extensions (DNSSEC) xvii, 139, 265
DoS (Denial of Service) xvii, 143, 146, 147, 196, 265
downloading files 168
drones 197
Drug Enforcement Administration 54
Duty of Care 155–162, 170, 265
DVDs 134

E

E-Government Act of 2002 71, 125
EAC (Estimate at Completion) xvii, 114, 216–217, 266
EA (Enterprise Architecture) xvii, 123, 266
Earned Value. *See* EV (Earned Value)
Earned Value Management. *See* EVM (Earned Value Management)
eBanking agreements 240–241
eBanking and fraud 239–247

ecological fallacy 179
eCommerce case study 219–226
economic incentives 65, 75, 106
ECPA (Electronic Communications Privacy Act) xvii, 195, 265
EDGAR (Electronic Data Gathering, Analysis, and Retrieval) xvii, 164, 266
educating users. *See* training
.edu domains 139
Effective Dates (regulations) 191, 265
effectiveness
 monitoring risks 46–47, 48
 risk management framework 13, 16
 warning systems 83
eFraud Network 242, 244
Einstein 3 program 73–74, 74, 235, 236, 265
Eisenhower administration 2–3
electrical grid
 as critical infrastructure 63, 64
 California attacks 197
 damage and consequences 25
 Northeast Blackout, 2003 68
 power plants 164–165
Electricity Sector Information Sharing and Analysis Center (ES ISAC) xvii
Electronic Communications Privacy Act xvii, 193, 195, 265
Electronic Data Gathering, Analysis, and Retrieval (EDGAR) xvii, 164, 266
electronic voting systems 188
email
 as vulnerability 144
 attachments 141, 168
 bank alerts 242
 corporate policies 168
 phishing attacks 31–36, 142–143
 testing vulnerability to 31–36
 threats to 64
EMC Corporation 153–154
emergency corporate policies 169
emergency services 64, 161
Emerging Security Challenges Division (NATO) 202
employees 145, 167, 168. *See also* users
encryption 266
 corporate data 158, 168–169
 methods 139–140
 NSA responsibilities 54
 Sony PlayStation breach 158
 TJX data breach 162
 websites 140
Energy Department 54, 65, 70, 236
energy systems 64, 70, 164–165. *See also* electrical grid
enforcement of law and regulations 192
enhanced password strength 222
Enron 123, 165
Enterprise Architecture (EA) xvii, 123, 266
Enterprise Risk Management (ERM) xvii
"Enterprise Risk Management-Integrated Framework" 171, 266
enterprise servers 134

Index (D-E)

Environmental Protection Agency (EPA) 36
EO. *See* EOs (Executive Orders)
EOP (Executive Office of the President) xvii, 266
  information management functions 61
  National Security Council 181
  OMB role 182–183
  OSTP technical advice 182, 185
  research sources 182
    Executive Orders 183–185
    Federal Register 186
    OMB Memoranda 185–186
    OSTP Memoranda 185
    PDDs 183
    White House strategy/guidance 186
  structure of 181–182
EOs (Executive Orders) xvii, 183–184, 217, 266
  as authorization 99
  Bush post-9/11 orders 66–69, 184
  Clinton's infrastructure protection 64–65, 183
  EO 13011 (CIO Council) 183
  EO 13228 (Homeland Security) 66–67, 184, 266
  EO 13231 (Cyberspace Security) 67–68, 184, 266
  EO 13636 (Critical Infrastructure Cybersecurity) 183, 266
  EO 13636 (Infrastructure Cybersecurity) 75–76
  Federal Register listing 186
  functions of 55, 183–184
  mission requirements and 94–97
EPA (Environmental Protection Agency) 36
epistemology 177, 266
equations
  consequence equation 24
  Cost Performance Index 213–214
  cost variances 113–115
  Estimate at Completion 114, 215–216
  Estimate to Complete 214, 215
  Logistic Regression Equation 210
  logit model 207
  risk equation 19–21, 27–28
  Schedule Performance Index 213
  schedule variances 113–114
  total risk equation 27
  variance percentages 114–115
ERM (Enterprise Risk Management) xvii
errors
  of omission 20
  survey design 205–207
ES ISAC (Electricity Sector Information Sharing and Analysis Center) xvii, 165
espionage
  attribution 201
  corporate 167
  early network threats 3
  Flame worm 74, 197
  in threat spectrum 22
  monitoring for 147
Estimate at Completion (EAC) xvii, 114, 215–216, 266
Estimate to Complete (ETC) xvii, 114, 214, 216, 266
Estonia 73, 197, 202

ETC (Estimate to Complete) xvii, 114, 214, 216, 266
ethical hackers 150
Europe 199, 202
European Network and Information Agency 28
Evaluation Criteria (RFPs) 107–108, 266
EV (Earned Value) xvii, 265
  as percentages 114–115
  cost variances 113
  CPI equations 213–214
  District Design case study 111–113
  EAC equations 215
  ETC equations 214, 215
  schedule variances 113–114
  SPI equations 213–214, 214
event tree analysis 37–40, 266
events in probability analysis 36–40
evidence 201
EVM (Earned Value Management) xvii, 108–109, 265
  budgets 109–112
  comparing projects 114–115
  DHS monitoring system case study 116–122
  forecasting 214–216, 266
  indexes 213–217
  Primary Metric Breakdown 112–113
  red, yellow, and green status 120
  tracking projects (variances) 112–115
  variances as percentages 114–115
  Work Breakdown Structure 107, 108, 116
EVM forecasting 214–216, 266
EVM indexes 213–217
EVM Primary Metric Breakdown 112–113
exclusive events (probability) 37–38, 266
executive branch of government 180–181. *See also* Presidents
  Cybersecurity Coordinator 73
  Executive Office of the President 61, 181–189
  Federal Register 186
  federal regulations 190–193
  mission requirements 94, 94–97
  policy documents 182
    Executive Orders 183–185
    OMB Memoranda 185–186
    OSTP Memoranda 185
    PDDs 183
    White House strategy and guidance 186
  research sources 179–180
  role in cybersecurity law 52–53
  structure 181–182
    National Security Council 181
    Office of Science and Technology Policy 182
    OMB 182–183
Executive Office Memoranda 94
Executive Office of the President xvii, 61, 181–189, 266
Executive Orders. *See* EOs (Executive Orders)
exfiltration 141
Exhibit 300 reports 123–124, 267
experimental research 177
experts, RFIs and 105–106
explanatory research 178

Index

exploits. *See* attacks and exploits
exploratory research 178
Explorer 1 2
extended readings 291–293
external audits 122–124, 171
external constraints 90
external information gathering 118, 231, 232, 234
external project information 87
external risks 172
external threats 21
extortion 194
extrapolation in research 30

F

Facebook phishing attacks 142
failed projects 90–91
false flagging operations 201
familiarity with customer patterns 243–244, 245
FASA V (Federal Acquisition Streamlining Act) xvii, 123, 267
fault tree analysis 38–40, 41, 267
Favorable Variances 113, 114, 115, 213, 214–215
FBI (Federal Bureau of Investigation) xviii, 54, 66
FDA (Food and Drug Administration) xviii, 190–191
FedCIRC (Federal Computer Incident Response Center) xviii, 69–70
Federal Acquisition Streamlining Act (FASA V) xvii, 123, 267
Federal Bureau of Investigation xviii, 54, 66
Federal Computer Incident Response Center (FedCIRC) xviii, 69–70
Federal courts. *See* judicial branch of government
Federal Emergency Management Agency (FEMA) 68
Federal Energy Regulatory Commission (FERC) 164
Federal Financial Institutions Examination Council (FFIEC) 241
Federal government
 agencies. *See* names of specific agencies (CIA, FBI, etc.)
 Cold War and technology development 2–3
 compliance 122–123
 criminal computer access penalties 194
 cyber attack capabilities 28
 cybersecurity research documents. *See* research sources
 departments. *See* names of specific departments (Defense Department, DHS, etc.)
 early hackers' threats 3–4
 executive branch. *See* executive branch of government
 expanded scope of 95
 growth and information needs 56
 judiciary. *See* judicial branch of government
 legislation, history of. *See* legislation
 legislative branch. *See* Congress
 managerial roles 81
 military, intelligence, and civilian agencies 52–56
 personal computer security 58–62
 policies. *See* policies (Federal)
 regulations. *See* regulations
 tensions related to cybersecurity 52, 53, 59, 59–62, 76–77
Federal Information Security Management Act. *See* FISMA

Federal legal system. *See* judicial branch of government
Federal Network Resilience division (FNR) 69
Federal Register 186, 190, 267
Federal regulations. *See* regulations
Federal Sentencing Guidelines 196–197, 267
Federal Trade Commission Act (FTCA) xviii, 162, 267
Federal Trade Commission (FTC) xviii, 162–165, 267
FEMA (Federal Emergency Management Agency) 68
FERC (Federal Energy Regulatory Commission) 164
FFIEC (Federal Financial Institutions Examination Council) 241
file transfer protocol (FTP) xviii, 267
final events (probability analysis) 39
Final Rules (regulations) 186, 191, 267
final total costs 214–216
finance systems. *See* banking and finance systems
financial audits 122
Financial Privacy Rule 160, 267
Financial Services ISAC 236
"FIPS 200 Minimum Security Requirements for Federal Information and Information Systems" 126
fire hazards 169
firewalls 24, 267
 as vulnerabilities 23
 corporate networks 158
 DHS monitoring case study 118
 informing internal information 231
 internal monitoring 148
 phishing attacks and 143
 role in cybersecurity 147
 TJX data breach 163
FISMA (Federal Information Security Management Act) xviii, 267
 as authorization 99
 compliance and reporting 124–126
 establishment of 185
 focus on government resources 71–72
 OMB's oversight 74–75, 95
 scope of 95
 System Security Plan 125–126
 US-CERT and 236
Flame worm 74, 197, 267
flood hazards 169
floor, Congressional 188, 267
floor debates 188
FNR (Federal Network Resilience) 69
focus groups in research 30
FOIA (Freedom of Information Act) 59
Food and Drug Administration (FDA) xviii, 190–191
food systems 70
forecasting (EVM) 214–216
foreign hackers. *See* nation-state hackers
foreign relations 193. *See also* global cybersecurity issues
forensic professionals 247
formulas. *See* equations
forward selection (modeling) 208, 267
frameworks 92. *See also* cybersecurity management framework; Information Exchange Framework; risk manage-

ment frameworks
framing risks 15, 277
  assumptions 15
  constraints 15, 17–18
  illustrated 13
  priorities 15, 18
  risk management and 16
  risk management framework 14, 14–18, 15
  risk management frameworks 14
  risk tolerance 15, 18
  trade-offs 15, 18
France's cyber defenses 28
fraud 194, 239–247, 242
fraud scrubs 160
freedom issues 201
Freedom of Information Act (FOIA) 59
FTC Consent Agreements 162
FTC (Federal Trade Commission) xviii, 162–165, 267
FTCA (Federal Trade Commission Act) xviii, 162, 267
FTE (Full-Time Equivalent) xviii, 117, 268
F-test 207
FTP (file transfer protocol) xviii, 267
Full-Time Equivalent. See FTE (Full-Time Equivalent)
functions (line and staff) 85–87, 268
"Funding Information Systems Investments" 62
funds. See budgets; resources
further readings 291–293

G

game theory 42
GAO (Government Accountability Office) xviii, 25, 268
  asset criticality labeling system 24–26
  capability definitions 146
  functions 189
  internal monitoring tools 147
  proposed federal regulations 191
  US-CERT failure 90–91, 228–229, 233–235, 251, 252–257
  warning notification 82
gap analysis 98–99, 99, 100, 102, 252–257
GB (gigahertz) 132
General Accounting Office. See GAO
General Councils (corporate) 152–153
General Services Administration. See GSA
genetic fallacy 179
Geo locations 241
Georgia 198
German cyber defenses 28
gigahertz (GB) 132
GLB Financial Modernization Act xviii, 159–160, 268
global cybersecurity issues 196–198
  attribution problems 200
  Council of Europe 202
  foreign relations 193
  IETF 139, 198, 200–201
  Internet coordination 198–200
  lack of transnational authority 201–202
  NATO and 202–203
  United Nations efforts 202
globalized supply chains 121, 124
goals
  CONOPS 101
  establishing 87–88
  failure to establish 90
  missions 84
  operational planning model 91
  reviewing plans against 88–89
Gonzalez, Albert 194
"good faith efforts" 156–157
"goodness of fit" 208
Google 143, 197, 250
.gov domains 139
Government Accountability Office. See GAO
GPS tracking devices 193
Gramm-Leach-Bliley Financial Modernization Act (GLB) xviii, 159–160, 268
grand juries 195, 268
graphical user interface (GUI) xviii, 132, 268
Great Worm (Morris) 5–6, 193
green project status 120, 276
GSA (General Services Administration) xviii, 268
  Brooks Act procurement 57
  functions of 55
  procurement role 61
  project management/acquisition phase 105
  responses to RFPs 108–109
guidance, defined 217
guidance statements (DHS) 95–96
"Guide for the Security Certification and Accreditation of Federal Information Systems" (NIST SP 800-37) 125
GUI (graphical user interface) xviii, 132, 268
guilty pleas 195

H

Ha (alternative hypotheses) 30, 37, 207
hackers
  attribution 137, 141, 200
  boy genius 3–4, 21
  Computer Fraud and Abuse Act 193–195
  criminal prosecution 193–195
  ethical hackers 150
  Federal crimes 193–194
  federal prosecution process 195–197
  fraudulent money transfers 239–247
  history of 3–10, 197–198
  identity theft 158, 193, 194, 195
  international issues 200–201
  in threat spectrum 22
  keyloggers 240
  monitoring for 146, 250
  nation-state. See nation-state hackers
  organized crime. See organized crime groups
  personal information breaches 158–161
  prosecution of 4, 6, 193–200
  strength of 43, 210, 211

Index

types of attacks 135
    Wiretap act 195
hard drives 134
hardware 131, 268
    insecurity of 145
    IT systems 134
    physical security 169
    procurement. *See* acquisitions and procurement
    securing 158
harms. *See* damages
hashing 141–142, 268
Health and Human Services Department (HHS) xviii, 126, 161, 172
healthcare fraud 156
healthcare provider security 160–162
healthcare records 125–127, 157–160, 160–162
Health Information Technology for Economic and Clinical Health Act (HITECH) xviii, 161, 172, 268
health insurance companies 161
Health Insurance Portability and Accountability Act (HIPAA) xviii, 125–127, 160–162, 172, 268
Heartland Payment Systems 194
HHS. *See* Health and Human Services Department
high-level directives 94, 94–97, 97–101
high-level requirements (HLRs) xviii, 97–102, 268
higher courts 192
higher-order languages 131
HIPAA (Health Insurance Portability and Accountability Act) xviii, 125–127, 160–162, 172, 268
HITECH (Health Information Technology for Economic and Clinical Health Act) xviii, 161, 172, 268
HLRs (High-Level Requirements) xviii, 97–102, 268
Ho (null hypotheses) 30, 37, 206, 207
"holes," patching 141
Homeland Infrastructure Threat and Risk Analysis Center (HTRAC) 236
Homeland Security. *See* DHS
Homeland Security Act of 2002 xviii, 68–70, 95, 99, 187, 257, 268
Homeland Security Council 67
Homeland Security Presidential Directives. *See* HSPDs
honeypots 149, 170, 268
"the hopper" 187
hops 138
hosts 134
House of Representatives 186–188. *See also* Congress
HRA (Human Reliability Analysis) xviii, 39, 268
HSA (Homeland Security Act of 2002) xviii, 68–70, 95, 99, 187, 268
HSPDs (Homeland Security Presidential Directives) xviii
    Bush administration 184
    HSPD-7 (Homeland Security Presidential Directive 7) 70–72, 95, 184, 257, 268
    HSPD-23 (Homeland Security Policy Directive 23) 72–75, 185, 259
HTRAC (Homeland Infrastructure Threat and Risk Analysis Center) 236
HTTP protocol xviii, 140, 269
HTTPS protocol xviii, 140, 269
Human Capital block 92
human error 31–36, 39, 144, 167
human reliability analysis (HRA) xviii, 39, 268
human rights groups 199
hypotheses
    creating 178
    cybersecurity research 177
    designing 30
    examples 30
    null and alternative 30, 37, 206, 207
    quantitative testing 37

I

IANA (Internet Assigned Numbers Authority) xviii, 198, 270
IBM personal computers 3–4
IC (intelligence community) xviii
ICANN (Internet Corporation for Assigned Names and Numbers) xviii, 139, 198–199, 270
ICT (information and communications technology) xviii, 121
ideal levels of risk 28
identifying
    attackers (attribution) 137, 141, 200
    critical infrastructure 70–72
    threats 147–150
identity theft 158, 193, 194, 195
Identity Theft Penalty Enhancement Act 193, 195, 269
IDS (Intrusion Detection System) xviii, 24, 270
    corporate implementation 170–171
    DHS monitoring case study 118
    informing internal information 231
    internal monitoring 148
    role in cybersecurity operations 147
    signatures and 148
    vulnerabilities 23
    warning systems 82, 149
IETF (Internet Engineering Task Force) xviii, 139, 198–199, 200, 270
IGCE (Independent Government Cost Estimate) xviii, 107–108, 269
ignoring attacks 149
IGs (inspectors general) 125
illegal wiretaps 195
impact 24, 269
    identifying for projects 90
    identifying in CONOPS 102
    identifying in MNS 99
IMP (Integrated Master Plan) xix, 108, 109, 122, 269
"improbable" events 12–13
"Improving Critical Infrastructure Cybersecurity" 75–76
IMS (Integrated Master Schedule) xix, 108, 109, 122, 269
in-house monitoring 147–148
"in motion" encryption 140, 143
"in the cloud" 269
"in the wild" vulnerabilities 145–146
incentives 65, 75, 106
inconvenience scores 221–223, 224

Index (G-I)

independent events (probability) 37–38, 269
Independent Government Cost Estimate (IGCE) xviii, 107–108, 269
independent variables (modeling) 42, 208, 209, 269
independent variables (research) 177
indicators (variables) 36, 39
indictments 195, 269
indirect consequences 24
indirect relationships (logit models) 42
industrial espionage 22. *See also* espionage
industries. *See* private sector
inferior courts 192, 269
information and communications technology (ICT) xviii, 121
information assurance 54
information auditing 171–172
information resources
  CIWG review 63
  cybersecurity and 52, 53
  data. *See* data
  government's growth in 60–61
  internal and external 87
  researching. *See* research methods; research sources
information security 71, 121, 124–126
information sharing 66–67, 75, 160, 165
Information Sharing and Analysis Center (ISAC) xix, 66–67, 165, 269
information sharing policies 160
Information Systems Audit and Control Association (ISACA) 171
information technology. *See* IT systems
Information Technology audits 122
Information Technology Management Reform Act (Clinger-Cohen) 61–62, 92, 123–124
information warriors 22
infrastructure. *See* critical infrastructure
initiating events (probability analysis) 37
Initiative #3 (CNCI) 73
insider threats 144, 167, 269
inspectors general (IGs) 125
insurance 46–47, 170
Integrated Master Plan (IMP) xix, 108, 109, 122, 269
Integrated Master Schedule (IMS) xix, 108, 109, 122
integrity of data 135
intelligence agencies
  CNCI directives 73–76
  FISMA requirements and 72
  ISAC participation 66
  military and civilian 53–55
  monitoring civilian networks 73
intelligence community (IC) xviii
intention (threat assessment) 20–21
intercepting communications 195
interdependencies (IMS) 108
Interim Final Rules 191, 269
Inter-Intra-Agency Requirements block 91
internal audits 121–123, 171–173
internal constraints 90
"Internal Control-Integrated Framework" 171

internal controls 165, 171–173, 269
internal information gathering 118
internal monitoring 147–148, 269
internal network information 231, 232, 234, 236
internal project information 87
internal systems (corporate) 156
internal threats 21
international issues. *See* global cybersecurity issues
International Strategy to Secure Cyberspace 186
Internet
  attacks and exploits 141–148
  BGP connections 138–140
  dependency 197
  diagrammed 135
  DNS system 139
  encryption methods 139–141
  global management of 196
  growth of 135–136
  history of 130, 134–136
  IANA/ICANN/IETF 198–201
  insecurity of 145
  operations of 136–137
  origins of 3
  protocols 137–138
  structure of 136–137
Internet Assigned Numbers Authority (IANA) xviii, 198, 270
Internet banking 239–247
Internet Corporation for Assigned Names and Numbers xviii, 139, 198–199, 270
Internet Engineering Task Force (IETF) xviii, 139, 198–199, 200, 270
Internet Protocol. *See* IP; IPv4; IPv6: TCP/IP
Internet Protocol Security (IPSec) xix, 199
Internet Service Providers (ISPs) xix, 136, 146, 147, 270
internet shopping. *See* online retailer examples
Internet Storm Center 236
interstate commerce crimes 193
interviews 31, 205
"An Introductory Resource Guide for Implementing the HIPAA Security Rule" (NIST 800-66) 126, 272
Intrusion Detection Systems. *See* IDS (Intrusion Detection System)
Intrusion Prevention Systems. *See* IPS (Intrusion Prevention System)
inventories, network 230
investment
  Duty of Care 155–159
  justifying 98, 99–100
  SEC disclosures and 164
investment advisors 164
IP (Internet Protocol)(TCP/IP) xix, 136, 137, 270
IP (Office of Infrastructure Protection) xix, 69, 273
IP addresses 137–138, 270
  BGP functions 138–140
  DDoS attacks 144
  DNS and 139, 198
  DNS cache poisoning 144
  faking 139–140

Index

global Internet management 198–200
human-readable 139
risk profiling and 241
translating 136
unique, and attacks 229
vulnerabilities 137
IPS (Intrusion Prevention System) xix, 270
  as warning system 149
  cybersecurity operations role 147
  Einstein 3 73–74
  internal monitoring 148
  signatures and 148
IPSec (Internet Protocol Security) xix, 199, 270
IPv4 (Internet Protocol version 4) xix, 137, 199
IPv6 (Internet Protocol version 6) xix, 137, 199, 270
Iran
  Cyber Army 28
  DDoS attacks 6, 144
  drones 197
  Flame virus 74, 197
  Stuxnet virus 6, 74, 197–198, 250
ISAC (Information Sharing and Analysis Center) xix, 66–67, 165, 236, 269
ISACA (Information Systems Audit and Control Association) 171
isolating attacks 255
ISPs (Internet Service Providers) xix, 136, 146, 147, 270
Israel 6, 28, 74, 198, 250
IT audits 122, 270
"IT Capital Asset Summary" 124
IT infrastructure 270
IT systems xix, 14
  attacks on federal systems 227–228
  audits 122, 126
  best practices 92
  Clinger-Cohen Act 92
  communication pathways 134
  corporate assessments 167
  corporate governance and 155
  costs 117
  Exhibit 300 reports 123–124
  hardware in 134
  health care providers 161
  internal controls 171–172
  procurement 61
  repairing 170
  software in 134
  Sony PlayStation breach 158
  standards for 123
  US-CERT and 227
  vulnerabilities 23
ITPEA (Identity Theft Penalty Enhancement Act) 195, 269

J

Jack Henry & Associates 240, 241, 242, 244, 245
Java 131
judicial branch of government 192–194, 270
CFAA rulings 193–195
cybersecurity role 180–181, 192–193
federal criminal process 195–197
federal regulations and 191–192
identity theft rulings 195
Justice Department 54
structure of 192–193
Wiretap Act rulings 195
judicial precedent 192
jurisdiction 193–194, 201–202
Justice Department 54, 259
justification section (MNS) 98, 99–100

K

Kennedy administration 69
keyboards 131
keyloggers (keystrokers) 240, 245, 246
keys (encryption) 139, 194
kiddy hackers 3–4, 21
known exploit signatures 148
known vulnerabilities 145
Kosovo 197

L

labor 80, 92, 107
LACNIC (Latin America and Caribbean Network Information Centre) 199
LANs (local area networks) xix, 136, 271
laptops 132
Latin America and Caribbean Network Information Centre (LACNIC) 199
law enforcement agencies 66–67, 146, 169–170, 200
laws 52. *See also* legislation
lawsuits 155–158, 158, 158–159, 239–247
leading questions (surveys) 205
legal system. *See* judicial branch of government
legislation 217. *See also* specific acts of law (Brooks Act, Computer Security Act, etc.)
  CIWG review 63
  compliance 122
  Congressional process 187–189
  Congress's mandates 180, 186
  crafting 55
  cybersecurity and 52–53, 187
  federal regulations and 190–193
  government agencies/branches 53–57
  history of cyber law
    CNCI/cyber warfare (2008-present) 72–75
    control conflict (1984-1995) 58–62
    cyber developments (1995-2001) 60–69
    Homeland Security (2001-2008) 66–74
    origins (1945-1984) 56–59
    recent developments 74–76
  impact on projects 90
  law, defined 52
  mission requirements and 94

Index (I-L)

passing bills into law 187–189
private sector regulations 159–167
protecting personal information 152
state laws 163–164
legislative branch of government. *See* Congress
lesson plans 307–342
lessons learned 253, 255
lethality 20, 21–22
leveraging technologies 116
liabilities
   banks' 240
   data breaches 157–160
   Duty of Care 156–157
Library of Congress 189–190
Lieberman, Joseph 74–75
lifetimes (programs) 98, 99, 100
likelihood 28, 29, 44. *See* also probability
linear regression models 208
line functions 85, 270
local area networks (LANs) xix, 136, 271
local governments 254
local threats 167
logging attacks 149
logic decision processes 41
logical fallacies 179, 271
logins, multiple 222
Logistic Regression Equation for Probabilities 210
logistic regression (logit) 42–43, 271
logit models 42–43, 207–208, 225, 271
logs 169
Los Alamos National Laboratory 4
lower-order programming languages 131–132
Lulz Security (LulzSec) 15
Lynch, Sandra 245–247

M

M memoranda. *See* under OMB
machine code 131–132
magnetic badges 169
magnitude of risk 28, 36
mainframe computers 56–57, 134
malware 141, 142, 194, 247, 271
man in the middle attacks 144–145, 271
"manage" task (risk management) 12
management and acquisition phase (Op Model) 104–109, 271
"Management of Information Resources" 62
managers 80, 83–84, 271. *See* also program/project managers; senior managers
   compliance and reporting 121–128
   constraints 90–91
   coordinating functions 85–87
   corporations 154–155
   cybersecurity framework. *See* cybersecurity management framework
   cyclical nature of management 89
   decision-making processes 86–90
   "doing," vs. managing 83–84
   Earned Value Management 108–125
   functions of 80–81
   goals/missions and 84–85
   in cybersecurity operations 146
   management and acquisition 104–109
   measurable outcomes 86
   operational planning model 91–92
   strategies and plans 84–85
   types of 80–81
   US-CERT failure case studies 90–93, 227–237, 255
managing risks. *See* risk management
manual analysis 254
"marginal" label (GAO) 24–26
Marine Corps 54
Marine Corps Intelligence 54
mark-up sessions 187, 271
material costs 107
"material information" disclosures 164
mathematical risks 40–42
MB (megahertz) 132
McVeigh, Timothy 63
MD5 (message digest hash) xix, 141–142
Measurement block 92
measurements. *See* metrics and measurements
medical records 126–128, 157–163. *See* also HIPAA
megahertz (MB) 132
memory 132, 133–134, 271
message digest hash (MD5) xix, 141–142
metrics and measurements 271
   DHS monitoring case study 119
   establishing 87–88, 90
   EVM accounting 108
   EVM measurements 110–113
   failure to establish 90
   FISMA requirements 125
   identifying in MNS 99
   in PWSs 106
   metrics, defined 86
   operational planning models 92
   Op Models 103–105
   plan outcomes 86
   qualitative research 30
   red, yellow, and green status 120
   reviewing plans against 88–89
   risk research questions 30
   WBS tasks 109
microphone activation 74
Middle East 199
milestones
   DHS monitoring case study 117
   identifying 99
   IMS depiction 108
   Operational Requirements Documents 103
   POA&M documents 108–109
military. *See* also Defense Department
   agencies and commands 53–55
   CNCI directives 73
   FISMA requirements and 72

Index

role in cybersecurity 52–54
tensions over control 52, 53, 59–62, 76–77
Military Network (MILNET) xix
minicomputers 134
minimum operational values 104
misconfiguration 145
Mission Needs Statement. *See* MNS
missions 80
   driving projects 91
   operational planning model 91–92
   strategies and plans 84
mistakes of logic 179
mitigating damages 170, 254
mitigating risks 277
   as high-level requirement 100
   Federal CIOs' role 62
   in risk management framework 13, 16
   risk levels and 28
   risk responses 45, 46
Mitnick, Kevin 3–4, 270
MNS (Mission Needs Statement) xix, 271
   authorization section 98–99
   capabilities in 98–99
   capability gaps 98–99
   courses of action 99
   developing 93–94
   high-level input sources 96, 96–100
   high-level requirements 97–102
   justification section 98, 99–100
   lifetimes 99
   outcomes 99
   translating into capabilities 97–98
model corporate cybersecurity program 165
   Board of Directors 166–167
   business continuity plans 170
   CEO and CIO roles 166
   education and training 168
   encryption 168–169
   intrusion detection systems 170–171
   penetration testing 168–169
   physical security 169
   response program 169–170
   risk assessment 166–168
   vendor management 170
   written plans 167
monitoring internal controls 172
monitoring risks 277
   as high-level requirement 100
   attributes 237, 253
   Citigroup lawsuit 157–158
   compliance 46–47, 48
   corporate implementation 170–171
   corporate responsibilities 156
   cybersecurity operations 146–148
   DHS case study 116–122
   effectiveness 46–47, 48
   identifying changes in environment 46–47, 48
   internal monitoring 147–148

   obligations 159–160
   policy monitoring 148–149
   risk management framework 13, 16
   risk management frameworks 14
   risk scores 242–243
   tool list 148
   US-CERT case studies 227–237, 253–257
Monte Carlo analysis 40–42, 271
Morris, Robert Tappan 5–6, 193
Morris worm 5–6, 193, 279
mortgage crisis 157–158
motherboards 131
multi-core processors 132
multiple-choice questions 205–206, 206
multiple logins 222
multiple processors 132
Multistate ISAC 236
multivariate statistical analysis 40–42, 43–45, 225–226
mutually-exclusive events (probability) 37–38

N

NASA (National Aeronautics and Space Administration) 36
Natanz nuclear facility 6, 250
nation-state hackers
   early cyber spying 4
   international cyber defense capabilities 28
   international law enforcement 201–202
   levels of risk and 27
   monitoring for 147, 250
   threat assessments 21
National Aeronautics and Space Administration (NASA) 36
National Bureau of Standards. *See* NIST
National Communications System 69
National Coordinator for Security, Infrastructure Protection and Counter-Terrorism 65
National Cyber Response Coordination Group 259
National Cybersecurity and Communications Integration Center (NCCIC) 69, 271
National Cyber Security Center 95
National Cybersecurity Council 75
National Cyber Security Division (NCSD) 90–91, 96, 227, 232, 250–251, 259
National Geospatial Intelligence Agency 54
National Infrastructure Advisory Council 68
National Infrastructure Assurance Council 66
National Infrastructure Protection Council (NIPC) xix, 66–67, 69–70, 187, 271
National Infrastructure Protection Plan. *See* NIPP (National Infrastructure Protection Plan)
National Institute for Standards and Technology. *See* NIST
national intelligence workers 22
National Nuclear Security Agency (NNSA) xix, 31–36
"National Plan to Secure Cyberspace" 69
National Policy for Infrastructure Protection 64
National Policy on Telecommunications and Automated Information Systems Security (NSDD-145) 5–6, 58–60, 272

Index (L-N)

National Protection and Programs Directorate (NPPD) xix, 69, 96, 272
National Reconnaissance Office 54
National Response Framework 259
National Science Foundation 3
National Science Foundation Network (NSFNET) xix, 3, 272
national security
   Board of Directors role in 166–167
   criminal information access 193
   personal computers and 3
   procurement function and 57
   sentencing and 196
   threat spectrum 22
National Security Act 181
National Security Agency. *See* NSA
National Security Council (NSC) xix, 55, 64, 68, 181, 272
National Security Decision Directives (NSDDs) xix, 5–6, 58–60
national security instruments 55, 183, 272. *See also* NSPDs; PPDs; PSDs
National Security Policy Directives. *See* NSPDs
"National Strategy to Secure Cyberspace" 258, 272
National Vulnerability Database (NVD) xix, 145, 272
NATO (North Atlantic Treaty Organization) xix, 73, 197, 202–203
NATO Computer Incident Response Capability (NCIRC) 202–203
Navy
   attacks on 197
   Office of Naval Intelligence 54
NCCIC (National Cybersecurity and Communications Integration Center) 69, 271
NCIRC (NATO Computer Incident Response Capability) 202–203
NCRCG (National Cyber Response Coordination Group) 259
NCSD (National Cyber Security Division) 90–91, 96, 227, 232, 249, 250–251, 259
negative relationships (logit models) 42
"negligible" label (GAO) 24–26
NERC (North American Electric Reliability Corporation) xix, 164–165, 273
NERC Standard CIP-008-4 164
Netherlands' cyber defenses 28
NetTeller 240, 241
network cards 132
networks
   altering configuration during attacks 149, 170
   anomalies 118–119, 146, 148–149, 170–171
   baselines 229, 230, 232, 233, 251
   BGP connections 138–140
   civilian network monitoring 73
   CNCI protections 72
   continuous monitoring systems 90–91
   cybersecurity operation capabilities 146–150
   denial of service attacks 143, 146, 147, 196
   early policy decisions 5–6
   firewalls. *See* firewalls
   FISMA protection 71
   honeypots 149, 170
   inventories 230
   ISP access to 136
   liability for data breaches 158–161
   monitoring case study 116–122
   types of 136
   vulnerabilities 144–146
   zombie networks 143
Network Security Deployment division (NSD) 69
New Deal agencies 56
New York state law 155
New Zealand 199
Nichols, Terry 63
NIPC (National Infrastructure Protection Center) xix, 66–67, 69–70, 187, 271
NIPP (National Infrastructure Protection Plan) xix, 71, 272
   DHS goals in 71
   DHS risk management 14
NIST (National Institute for Standards and Technology) xix, 272
   compliance 125
   functions of 55
   "Guide for the Security Certification and Accreditation of Federal Information Systems" 125–126
   IT vulnerabilities list 23
   NIST 800-53 (Recommended Security Controls for Federal Information Systems and Organizations) 272
   NIST 800-66 (An Introductory Resource Guide for Implementing the HIPAA Security Rule) 126
   NVD (National Vulnerability Database) 145
   "Recommended Security Controls for Federal Information Systems and Organizations" 126
   risk management frameworks 14, 71
   security practices role 60
Nixon administration 182–183
NNSA (National Nuclear Security Agency) xix, 31–36
non-compliance consequences 125
non-experimental research 178–179
non-volatile memory 134, 272
normal network activity 230
North American Electric Reliability Corporation (NERC) xix, 164–165, 273
North Atlantic Treaty Organization (NATO) xix, 73, 197, 202–203
Northeast Blackout, 2003 68
Norway 2
"Not Applicable" answers 205
not-mutually exclusive events (probability) 37–38
Notice and Comment period 191–192, 273
notifications. *See also* alerts; warning systems
   as capability 146
   as passive response 149
   bank alerts 242, 247
   best channels for 255
   costs of 169
   lack of novel information in 254
   prompt 254
   state laws 163–164

Index

US-CERT role in 250–251
NPPD (National Protection and Programs Directorate) xix, 69, 96, 272
NRC (US Nuclear Regulatory Commission) 36
NSA (National Security Agency) xix, 272
  civilian/military control tensions 59–62
  classified computer systems and 60
  Einstein 3 program 73–74
  founding of 94
  role in cybersecurity 54–56
NSC (National Security Council) xix, 55, 64, 68, 181, 272
NSD (Network Security Deployment division) 69
NSDD-145 (National Policy on Telecommunications and Automated Information Systems Security) 5–6, 58–60, 272
NSDDs (National Security Decision Directives) xix, 5–6, 58–60
NSFNET (National Science Foundation Network) xix, 3, 272
NSPDs (National Security Policy Directives) xix
  Bush administration 183
  CNCI 72
  NSPD-54 (National Security Policy Directive) 72–75, 95, 185, 259, 272
nuclear arms 4
nuclear facilities
  criminal information access 193
  PRA risk management 36
  virus attacks 74, 197
Nuclear Regulatory Commission (USNRC) 36
null hypotheses (Ho) 30, 37, 206, 207, 273
NVD (National Vulnerability Database) xix, 145, 272
NY BCL (Business Corporation Law of New York State) 155

O

Obama administration
  cybersecurity directives 75–76
  cybersecurity initiatives and policies 73–78
  Cyberspace Policy Review 95
  presidential decision directives 183
objective values (management) 104–105, 273
objectives 101, 107
Ocean Bank case study 239–247
OCIA (Office of Cyber and Infrastructure Analysis) xx, 69, 273
ODNI (Office of the Director of National Intelligence) 54
OEC (Office of Emergency Communications) 69
Office of Cyber and Infrastructure Analysis (OCIA) xx, 69, 273
Office of Cybersecurity and Communications (CS&C) xvii, 69, 96, 184, 232, 273
Office of E-Government and Information Technology 182
Office of Emergency Communications (OEC) 69
Office of Homeland Security. See DHS
Office of Information and Regulatory Affairs xx, 61, 182, 273
Office of Infrastructure Protection (IP) 69, 273
Office of Management and Budget. See OMB
Office of National Infrastructure Assurance 64
Office of Science and Technology Policy (OSTP) xx, 182, 185, 273
Office of the Director of National Intelligence (ODNI) 54
Office of the National Counterintelligence Executive (ONCIX) 54
off-site back-ups 169
OHS (Office of Homeland Security). See DHS
OIRA (Office of Information and Regulatory Affairs) xx, 61, 182, 273
Oklahoma City bomb 63–64, 183
Olympic Games cyberwar program 74, 273
OMB (Office of Management and Budget) xx, 273
  circulars
    A-11 (capital assets) 110
    A-130 (information resource management) 62, 125
  Exhibit 300 reports 123–124
  FISMA compliance 71, 125
  FISMA oversight 74–75, 95
  functions of 55
  information management 61–63
  IT system requirements 123–124
  memoranda 185–186
    M-08-05 (trusted Internet connections) 102–103
    M-10-28 (DHS responsibilities) 75, 184, 185–186, 271
    M-97-02 (funding information systems) 62, 271
  role of 182–183
  TIC mandate 17, 102–103, 184
ONCIX (Office of the National Counterintelligence Executive) 54
"one size fits all" security plans 244, 246
online banking case study 239–247
online retailer examples 41–46, 208–212, 219–226
online surveys 206–207
ontology 177–178, 273
Op Models (Operating Models) 103, 103–108, 117, 273
open-ended questions 205, 206
open standards organizations 200
Operating Models (Op Models) 103, 103–108, 117, 273
Operation Aurora 197
Operation Olympic Games 250
operational planning models 91–92, 273
operational processes (CONOPS) 101
Operational Requirements Document (ORD) xx, 103, 274
opting out (financial information) 160
oral communications 195
ORD (Operational Requirements Document) xx, 103, 274
Organizational Capital block 92–93
organizational structure 91
organizations 80
  impacts of structures 91
  top-down analysis 38–40
organized crime groups 15
  in threat spectrum 22
  levels of risk and 27
  monitoring threats by 250
  prosecution 193–200
  risk determination example 28

risk management outline 16
threat assessment 20, 20–21
OSTP (Office of Science and Technology Policy) xx, 182, 185, 273
OSTP Resource Library 182
"Other" answers 205
outcomes
  defining 99
  in CONOPS 102
  in Op Models 103–105
  in PWSs 106
  measurable 86
  operational planning model 91
  regression modeling 42
  success and 88
over budget status 114, 119
overriding vetoes 188
oversight
  Congressional 55
  corporate failure 155–159
  Duty of Care 156

P

p-values 207, 275
Pacific Bell 3
packet analyzers (sniffers) 147, 195, 274
packets 137, 274
Paperwork Reduction Act (PRA) xx, 61, 182, 274
participants in CONOPS 101
passive responses to threats 149–150, 170–171, 274
passwords
  as vulnerabilities 144
  banking systems 241, 244
  brute force attacks 140
  corporate data 158
  corporate policies 168
  corporate systems 167
  logit analysis 210, 211
  online retailer case study 220–226
  selling 194
  strong passwords 42, 158, 168, 225
  token-generated 242
  wireless systems 162
patches 141, 145, 163
Patriotic Hacker attacks 197
Payment Card Industry Data Security Standards 158
payments, fraudulent 239–247
payroll payments 241
PCCIP (President's Commission on Critical Infrastructure Protection) xx, 64–65, 183, 274
PCIPB (President's Critical Infrastructure Protection Board) xx
PCs (personal computers) xx
  attacks and exploits 141–148
  changes in national security and 58–62
  criminal information access 194
  cybersecurity operation capabilities 146–150

early Federal policies 5–6
early years of 3–4
FISMA protection 71
in IT infrastructure 134
protected computers 194
systems 132–134
virus attacks 74
vulnerabilities 144–146
worms 5–6
PDDs (Presidential Decision Directives) xx, 56, 95, 183, 275. *See also* EOs (Executive Orders); HSPDs (Homeland Security Presidential Directives)
  as authorization 99
  Clinton administration 56, 183
  Federal Register 186
  mission requirements and 94, 94–96
  Obama administration 183
  PDD-63 275
    critical infrastructure protection 64–67
    energy information sharing 165
    HSA elements of 187
    Oklahoma City response 183
    replacement of 184
pedagogy x–xv
penetration testing 168–169, 274
People's United Bank 240
percentages (comparing projects) 114–115
performance
  APBs 104
  objective and threshold values 104–105
  red, yellow, and green status 120
performance-based acquisitions 106–107
"Performance Measurement Report" 124
Performance Work Statements (PWS) xx, 105, 106–107, 274
Period of Performance (POP) xx, 113, 120, 274
personal computers. *See* PCs
personal information
  bank sales of 159
  business's duty towards 158
  business's duty towards 153–154
  criminal computer access 194
  criminal information access 195
  customer information leak example 41–46
  liability for breaches 157–160
  phishing attacks 142–143
  protected health information 126
  Sony PlayStation Network breach 158–159
  spear phishing attacks 31–36
  TJX data breach 158, 162–163, 194
personal interviews 31, 205
PHI (protected health information) xx, 126, 161, 275
phishing attacks 31–36, 142–143, 274
phone companies 136
phone surveys 31
physical security 169
pictures, user-selected 242
Plan of Action and Milestones (POA&M) xx, 108–109, 274
Planned Value. *See* PV (Planned Value)

Index

Planning, Programming, Budgeting and Execution (PPBE) xx, 93
plans 84–85, 85–86, 274
   alternative scenarios 88–89
   assessing 88
   capability-based planning 100–101
   choosing 88
   CONOPS 101–104
   executing 88
   measurable outcomes 86
   operational planning model 91–92
   POA&M documents 108–109
plausible deniability 201
plea bargains 195, 274
POA&M (Plan of Action and Milestones) xx, 108–109, 274
Poindexter, John 4–5, 58–61, 71, 270
point system (sentencing) 196–197
policies
   as authorization 99
   compliance 122
   Federal. *See* policies (Federal)
   impact on projects 91
   in CONOPS 101, 102
   internal controls 171–172
   Mission Needs Statements and 94–96
   policy directives 217
   policy monitoring 148–149
policies (Federal) 52
   agencies involved in 53–57
   crafting 55
   cybersecurity and 52–53
   Cyberspace Policy Review 73–74
   DHS frameworks 69
   FISMA requirements 71
   history of cybersecurity 53–57
      CNCI/cyber warfare (2008-present) 72–75
      control conflict (1984-1995) 58–62
      cyber development (1995-2001) 60–69
      Homeland Security (2001-2008) 66–74
      origins (1945-1984) 2–4, 56–63
      recent developments 74–76
   sentencing 196
policy directives 217
policy monitoring 148–149, 274
POP (Period of Performance) xx, 113, 120, 274
population 32, 205–206
positive relationships (logit models) 42
power grid. *See* electrical grid
power plants 164–165
PPBE (Planning, Programming, Budgeting and Execution) xx, 93
PPDs (Presidential Policy Directives) xx, 75–76, 275
PRA (Paperwork Reduction Act) xx, 61, 182, 274
PRA (probabilistic risk assessment) xx, 275
   event tree analysis 37–40
   fault tree analysis 38–40, 41
   human reliability analysis 39
   logistic regression equation 210

Monte Carlo analysis 40–42
   quantitative risk determination 36–37
precedents, judicial 192
predicting leaks 43–45
predicting threats 149–150
predictive analysis 149–150, 225–226, 251, 252, 254
preponderance of evidence 201
Presidential Decision Directives. *See* PDDs
Presidential Policy Directives (PPDs) xx, 275
Presidential Study Directives (PSDs) xx, 183
Presidents
   agency creation 190
   agency supervision 55
   as first responders 180
   as senior managers 81
   bill signing or vetoing 188
   cybersecurity policy role 52–53
   Executive Office of. *See* EOP
   Executive Orders. *See* EOs
   military or civilian security control policies 53
   mission requirements 94, 94–97
   National Security Instruments 55
   Presidential Directives 56. *See also* HSPDs; PDDs
   scope of power 94–96
President's Commission on Critical Infrastructure Protection (PCCIP) xx, 64–65, 183, 274
President's Critical Infrastructure Protection Board (PCIPB) xx
primary consequences, defined 24
printers 132
priorities 275
   FISMA requirements 125
   risk management framewoek 18
   risk management framework 13, 16, 17, 18
privacy issues
   bank sales of personal information 159
   court cases 192
   IPv6 and 199
   policy formation 56
Privacy Rule (HIPAA) 160, 275
private corporation governance 154–156, 275
private-public partnerships
   Board of Directors role 166–167
   critical infrastructure protection 53, 63, 65–66, 76
   DHS agencies charged with 70
   DHS strategies 186
   incentives for 65, 75
   National Infrastructure Assurance Council 66
   outlining shared threats 64, 65
   policy formation 56
   post 9/11 67–68
   threats to critical infrastructure 65
   US-CERT role in 250–251
private sector
   business interruption insurance 170
   corporate governance 154–163
   critical infrastructure owned by 63
   cyber incident reports 75

Index (O-P)

cybersecurity overview 152–154
Duty of Care 155–164
electrical grid 164–165
HIPAA compliance 125–127
incentives for partnerships 65, 75
internal audits and controls 171–173
lack of reports to US-CERT 254
legislative requirements 159–167
model cybersecurity programs 165–172
NSDD-145 computer security issues 5
partnerships. *See* private-public partnerships
policy formation 56
protecting critical infrastructure 53, 63–66, 76
risk management strategies 153
Sarbanes-Oxley Act and 165
SEC disclosures 164
security roles 165–166
strategy questions 152–154
US-CERT failures and 234
proactive safeguards 158, 165
probabilistic risk assessment. *See* PRA (probabilistic risk assessment)
probability 275
  calculating 27–29
  illustrated 29
  logistic regression equation 210–211
  PRA risk management 36. *See also* PRA
  predicting leaks with statistical analysis 43–45
  probability distribution 36
  probability sampling 206, 275
  probability theory 36–37
  quantitative risk determination 36–37
  values 41
probable cause 195, 275
procedures 84, 122
processors 131–132, 275
procurement. *See* acquisitions and procurement
Products and Services block 91
professional auditors 172
program/project managers 80, 82, 83–84
  comparing projects 114–115
  compliance and reporting 121–128
  CONOPS 101–104
  defining capabilities 100
  DHS cybersecurity programs 94
  Earned Value Management 108–125, 213–217
  forecasting 214–216
  function coordination 85–86
  high-level requirement analysis 97
  management and acquisition 104–109
  Mission Needs Statements 93–94
  objective and threshold values 104–105
  Op Models 103–105
  tracking projects 112–116
  warning system example 81–84
programming languages 131–132, 275
programs. *See* software
project managers. *See* program/project managers

proposed bills 187–190
Proposed Rules 186, 190, 275
prosecution of cybercriminals 4, 6, 192–199
prosecutors 195
protected computers 194
protected health information (PHI) xx, 126, 160, 275
protection
  as capability 146
  as high-level requirement 100
  infrastructure. *See* critical infrastructure protection
  networks 71, 72–75
  PCs 71
  personal information 126
  protected computers 194
protective markings 59
protocol identifier assignments 198
protocols 136, 137–138, 198
PSDs (Presidential Study Directives) xx, 183
public corporation governance 154–156, 275
public hearings 186, 187, 191
public image 153
public-private partnerships. *See* private-public partnerships
PV (Planned Value) xx, 274
  District Design case study 111–113
  percentages 114–115
  schedule variances 113–114
  SPI equations 213
PWS (Performance Work Statement) xx, 105, 106–107, 274

Q

Quadrennial Homeland Security Review Report to Congress (QHSR) xx, 96, 186
qualitative risk determination 28–37, 231, 275
quantitative risk determination 28–30, 36, 231, 276
  event tree analysis 37–40
  fault tree analysis 38–40, 40, 41
  human reliability analysis 39
  Monte Carlo analysis 40–42
  online retailer example 41–46
  probabilistic risk assessment 36–37
  probability basics 36–37
  statistical modeling 41
questionnaires. *See* survey designs
questions
  advanced research methods/sources 203–204
  challenge. *See* challenge questions
  computer technical fundamentals review 150
  cybersecurity law and policy review 76–78
  cybersecurity management review 127–128
  private sector cybersecurity review 173–174
  qualitative research questions 30–32
  research questions 177
  risk determination review 48–49
  risk research questions 29–30

Index

R

radio signal badges 169
RAM (random access memory) xx, 132, 134–135, 276
random sampling 206, 276
ratings agencies 164
readings 291–293
Reagan administration 4–5, 56, 58–60, 94
reason, mistakes of 179
reasonable doubt 196
reckless behavior 194
"Recommended Security Controls for Federal Information Systems and Organizations" (NIST SP 800-53) 126
reconciliation 188
reconnaissance attacks 142
recovery from attacks
  as capability 146
  business continuity plans 170
  corporate policies 170
  "National Strategy to Secure Cyberspace" 69
  strategies 255
red project status 120, 276
reducing risk (capability) 116
re-engineering backwards 104
regional Courts of Appeals 192
Regional Internet Registries (RIRs) xx, 199–200, 276
registries (Internet addresses) 199–200
regression modeling 42, 207, 208, 208–209, 225, 276
regulations 190–191, 217, 276
  Code of Federal Regulations 191
  compliance 122
  Congressional and Judicial roles in 191–192
  creating 190–191
  Federal Register publication 186
  impact on projects 90
regulatory agencies 169–170, 276
reliability 30, 276
reliability standards (NERC) 164
reliability tests 178
Reno, Janet 63
rental botnets 143
repairing systems 170
reports
  audits 121–123
  corporate policies 168, 169
  DHS cybersecurity reports 96–97
  energy grid cybersecurity 164
  Exhibit 300 123–124
  Federal government practices 122–123
  FISMA requirements 124–126
  health care system breaches 161
  internal controls 171–172
  lack of, to US-CERT 254
  operational planning model 92
  Sarbanes-Oxley Act 165
Requests for Comments (RFCs) xx, 200, 276
Requests for Information (RFIs) xx, 105–106, 276
Requests for Proposals (RFPs) xx, 105–109, 276

research design 177, 276
research methods 176–180
research questions 276
  creating 177
  dependency on Internet 197
  risk research 29–30
  spear phishing attack vulnerabilities 31–36
  statistical modeling 42
  survey design 205–213
research sources
  Code of Federal Regulations (CFR) 191
  Council of Europe 202
  executive branch 181–190, 182
    Executive Orders 183–185
    Federal Register 186
    OMB Memoranda 185–186
    OSTP Memoranda 185
    PDDs 183
    White House strategy and guidance 186
  GAO website 189
  government documents 179–181
  Internet Engineering Task Force 200
  legislative 189–190
    Congressional Record 189
    Congressional Research Service 189–190
    proposed bills and law 189
  NATO 202–203
  THOMAS.gov 189
  United Nations 202
research subjects 178
Réseaux IP Européens Network Coordination Centre (RIPE NCC) 199
resources
  as constraints 17
  decision-making process 89
  identifying in MNS 99
  impact on projects 91
  management and acquisition phase 104–109
  POA&M documents 108–109
  risk monitoring and 47
  time and money 110–112
  trade-offs in risk management 18
responding to attacks
  active responses 149–150, 170–171
  attributes 237, 253–258
  containing threats 46
  corporate plans 167, 169–170
  isolation 255
  NATO teams 202
  passive responses 149–150, 170–171
  Presidents as first responders 180
  types of responses 149–150
responding to risks 277
  acceptance 16, 18, 28, 45–46
  as capability 146
  as high-level requirement 100
  avoidance 45
  cybersecurity insurance 46–47

mitigation 45, 46
risk management framework 13, 16
risk responses, defined 45
transfer 13, 16, 45, 46–47
unacceptable risks 18
response rates (surveys) 32
responsibilities in CONOPS 101, 102
restitution to victims 195
results, assessing 88–89
retail case study 219–226
retaliation 250
reviewing warnings 82
RFCs (Requests for Comments) xx, 200, 276
RFIs (Requests for Information) xx, 105–106, 276
RFPs (Requests for Proposals) xx, 105–109, 276
Ridge, Tom 66
RIPE NCC (Réseaux IP Européens Network Coordination Centre) 199
RIRs (Regional Internet Registries) xx, 199–200, 276
risk 13
  assessing. See risk assessments
  benefits of 47
  determination. See risk determination
  framing. See framing risks
  graphing 28
  internal audits 121
  levels of 27–31
  management. See risk management; risk management frameworks
  responding to. See responding to risks
  risk equation 19
  risk formula 19–29
  risk profiling 223, 224
  severity 28, 36
  tolerances 13, 16, 17, 18
  unacceptable 18
risk acceptance 276
risk assessments 19–20, 277
  audits 172
  Book Box case study 219, 221
  conducting 230–231, 232
  Cybersecurity Act 75
  DHS monitoring case study 118–119, 119
  FISMA requirements 71–72
  model corporate cyber program 166–168
  risk analysis attributes 237
  risk determination and. See risk determination
  risk equation 19–20, 27–28
  risk management framework 13, 14, 16
  US-CERT failures 233, 236, 253, 254
risk avoidance. See avoiding risks
risk-based decisions 15, 71, 277
risk constraints 277
risk determination 26–30, 277
  methodologies 28–30
  quadrant diagram 28
  qualitative methods 28–37
  quantitative methods 28–30, 36–49

review questions 48–49
risk assessment in 26
risk equation 19–21, 27–28
risk framing. See framing risks
Risk Lexicon. See DHS Risk Lexicon
risk management 12–14, 277
  consequence assessment 24–27
  Federal agency roles in 62–63
  frameworks 14
  health care systems 161
  operational planning model 92
  organized crime example 16
  plans 12
  presidential directives for 70
  private sector strategies 152
  process 14–15
  risk, defined 13
  risk assessment 19–29
  risk determination 26–50
  risk formula 19–29
  risk framing 15–19
  risk managers 20
  SEC guidelines 163–164
  strategies, not checklists 49
  threat assessment 20–23
  threat shifting 21
  vulnerability assessment 22–23
risk management frameworks 14, 16
risk management plans 12
risk mitigation. See mitigating risks
risk monitoring. See monitoring risks
risk profiling 223, 224, 241–242, 244–245
risk reports 243
risk research questions 29–30
risk responses. See responding to risks
risk scores 241–242, 247
risk tolerances 13, 16, 17, 18, 277
roles (CONOPS) 101, 102
Roosevelt administration 56, 94
root server management 198
routers 132, 134, 136, 138–140, 144–145, 277
routing attacks through other countries 201
routing tables 138
RSA/Cyota 241–242
RSA SecurID breach 143, 153
rules 148–149, 190
Russian-Chechen conflict 197
Russian Federation 199
Russian-Georgian conflict 198

S

Safeguards Rule 160, 277
sample populations 32, 205–206, 277
Sarbanes-Oxley Act (SOX) xxi, 123, 165, 277
satellites 2
SBU IT (Sensitive-But-Unclassified Information Technology) xx, 60

Index

scanning systems 145, 148
schedule variances (SVs) xxi, 112–116, 119–120, 278
Schedule Performance Index (SPI) xxi, 114, 213–214, 278
schedules
   Acquisition Performance Baselines 104
   delays in 119–120
   DHS monitoring case study 117
   Integrated Master Schedules 108, 109
   manager's role 86
   objective and threshold values 104–105
   variances 112–113
"Scientific Integrity" 185, 278
scientific issues 185
scientific methods 178, 278
screen locks 168
search warrants 195
SEC (Securities and Exchange Commission) xx, 163–164, 169, 278
SECIR (Stakeholder Engagement and Cyber Infrastructure Resilience division) 69
Secret Service 66, 68
Section 404 278
Sector-Specific Agencies (SSAs) xxi, 70
sectors in management framework 93
secure hash algorithm (SHA-2) xxi, 141–142
SecurID data breach 143, 153
Securities and Exchange Commission (SEC) xx, 163–164, 169, 278
security
   certification and accreditation 125–126
   OMB role in 61
security even correlation tools 148
"security procedures" 244
Security Rules (HIPAA) 160, 278
self-administered surveys 31, 31–36, 205
Senate 186–188
senior managers 80, 83, 85
sensitive, but unclassified information 5, 58, 59, 278
Sensitive-But-Unclassified Information Technology (SBU IT) xx, 60
sensitive information 167
sentencing 192, 193–195, 196–197
September 11, 2001
   Executive Orders after 184
   lessons learned 252
   reorganizations after 66
   risk planning after 12–13
   scope of Presidential power and 95
sequences of events 37
servers 134, 147, 158
service providers (ISPs) 136, 146, 147
severity of attacks 149
severity of risk 36
SHA-2 (secure hash algorithm) xxi, 141–142
shared threats 22, 64, 65
shareholders 154, 159–163
shopping cart software 221
shunning attacks 149

signal intelligence 54
signature-based tools 73–74, 148, 170–171, 278
signatures
   digital, for DNS 139
   IDS/IPS tools 148
   internal monitoring 148
   known exploits 148
   threat signature technology 73–74, 170–171
significance tests 278
simulating attacks 149–150, 168–169
smart cards 242
SME (Subject Matter Experts) xxi, 117, 279
sniffers (packet analyzers) 147, 195
social engineering attacks 168
social media phishing attacks 142
Social Security numbers 195
software 132, 278
   antivirus. *See* antivirus software
   exploits 141
   IDS/IPS tools 148
   in IT systems 134
   insecurity of 145
   malware 141, 142, 194
   programs, defined 131
   signature-based tools 73–74, 148, 170–171
   vulnerabilities 144–146
Sony PlayStation Network 158–159
SOOs (Statements of Objectives) xxi, 105, 107, 278
South Ossetia 198
sovereignty 201
Soviet Union. *See also* Russian Federation
   Cold War 2, 57, 58
   computer security and 58
   Sputnik 2
SOWs (Statements of Work) xxi, 105, 278
SOX (Sarbanes-Oxley Act) xxi, 123, 165, 277
SP 800-37 (Guide for the Security Certification and Accreditation of Federal Information Systems) 125
space allocation (ICANN) 198
Space Race 2
spam filters 142
Speaker of the House 187
spear phishing attacks 31–36, 142–143, 278
Special Advisor for Cyberspace Security 68, 184, 185
speed of processors 132
SPI (Schedule Performance Index) xxi, 114, 213–214, 278
spies. *See* espionage
sponsors, bills 187
spoofed websites 143
Sputnik 2
SSAs (Sector-Specific Agencies) xxi, 70
SSL certificates 221
staff functions 85, 278
staffing in models 92
Stakeholder Engagement and Cyber Infrastructure Resilience division (SECIR) 69
stakeholders 101, 102, 117
standard deviations 207

standards 217
state attorneys general 158
state court jurisdictions 193–194
State Department 54
state governments 254
Statements of Objectives (SOOs) xxi, 105, 107, 278
Statements of Work (SOWs) xxi, 105, 278
statistical modeling 206–208
   Monte Carlo analysis 40–42
   online retailer probability example 41–46
   predicting leaks 43–45
   quantitative risk determination 41
   regression modeling 42, 225
"statistically significant" 206, 207, 279
statutes 217. *See also* legislation
steps (Op Models) 104
stock 154–155, 163–164, 170
stock values 153
stockholders 154
storage 133–134
strategic analysis 258
strategic objectives in models 91
Strategic Risk Management block 92
strategies 84, 279
   alternative scenarios 88–89
   capability-based planning 100–101
   choosing 88
   CONOPS 101
   executing 88
   failures in 234
   mission needs statement 98
   operational planning model 91–92
strengths in models 92–93
strong passwords 42, 158, 168, 225
Stuxnet 6, 28, 197–198, 250, 279
Subject Matter Experts (SMEs) xxi, 117, 279
subprime mortgage crisis 157–158
Sumitomo Mitsui Bank 240
supercomputing centers 3
supply chains 121, 124
Supreme Court 192. *See also* judicial branch of government
survey designs 30, 205–216, 279
   building models 208–211
   logit models 207–208
   NNSA example 31–36
   online retailer security 225
   qualitative risk determination 30–32
   response rates 32
   sample populations 205–206
   statistical models 206–208
SVs (schedule variances) xxi, 112–116, 119–120, 278
syllabus 295–306
symbols, fault tree 40
Syria 197
System Security Plan (FISMA) 125–126
systems, computer 103, 132–134, 134, 141, 279
systems of systems 132–134, 136, 279

T

t-test 207
tactical analysis 258
target audiences 82
"targeted and actionable" warnings 82–83
targets 20, 21, 137, 146
tasks 88, 108, 109
Taves, Kenneth H. 159
TCP/IP (Transmission Control Protocol/Internet Protocol) xxi, 136, 137, 279
technical audits 122
technical guidance 217
telephone surveys 31
tensions
   between military and civilian control 52, 53, 59–62, 76–77
   between security and freedom 201
terminating sessions 149
terrorism
   aggravated identity theft 195
   Board of Directors role in prevention 166–167
   counterterrorism reviews 73–74
   international issues 201
   in threat spectrum 22
   monitoring for 147, 250
   Oklahoma City, 1995 63–64
   September 11th, 2001 12–13, 95
   World Trade Center, 1993 63
test groups 178
test statistics 206, 279
testing
   FISMA requirements 71
   hypotheses 177–178
   penetration testing 168–169
   risk research questions 30
theories (cybersecurity research) 177, 279
THOMAS.gov 189, 279
threat assessment 279
   components 20–23
   conducting 230–231
   DHS monitoring case study 118–119
   mission needs statements 98
   model corporate program 166–167
   US-CERT role in 250–251
threat environments 98
threat shifting 21, 279
threat signature technology 73–74
threats 19, 20, 279
   analyzing consequences/vulnerabilities 26–30
   assessing. *See* threat assessment
   attacks. *See* attacks and exploits
   corporate governance and 155
   critical infrastructure focus 64
   espionage 3
   evolution in 76
   external 21
   factors aiding in 145
   growth in 72

Index

identifying 29, 98, 147–150
increases in 27
in risk determination 28
in risk equation 19
in risk management framework 13, 16
insider 144, 167
internal 21
malware 141, 142, 194
researching external 231
risk assessment and 19
shared 3, 65
signature technology 73–74, 148, 170–171
simulating 149–150
spectrum, illustrated 22
threat environments 98
threat shifting 21
worms. *See* worms
threshold values 104–105, 279
TIC (Trusted Internet Connection) xxi, 17, 102–103, 103, 184, 259, 280
TIC Access Providers 17
time dimensions 279
time in budgets 110–112
time-out tries 210, 211
timelines 88
TJ Maxx 158
TJX data breach xxi, 158, 162–163, 194
TLDs (top level domains) xxi, 139, 279
tokens, security 153, 242
tolerances, risk 13, 16, 17, 18
top-down analysis 38–40
top level domains (TLDs) xxi, 139, 279
total risk equation 27
tracking projects
  atypical variances 215
  comparing projects 114–115
  EVM budgeting 112–117
  EVM indexes 213–215
  over budget status 119
  red, yellow, and green status 120
  variances, significance of 120
trade secrets 167
trade-offs
  risk management framework 13, 16, 17, 18
  secure websites 44
training
  corporate programs 168
  costs 117
  education as capability 116
  FISMA requirements 71
  health care systems 161
transactions, normal (banking) 241, 243
transferring money 239–247
transferring risks 13, 16, 45, 46–47
Transmission Control Protocol (TCP/IP) xxi, 136, 137, 279
transnational issues. *See* global cybersecurity issues
transparency in corporate governance 155, 280
transportation systems 63, 64, 70

travel costs 107, 117
Treasury Department 54
treaties 202
trial courts 192
trial-out tries 210, 211
trials 195
Trojan horses 142
Truman administration 94
trust, customers 158, 170
Trusted Internet Connections Initiative 102–103, 184
Trusted Internet Connection (TIC) xxi, 17, 102–103, 103, 184, 259, 280
trust protocols 130, 136, 139, 139–140, 144–145
Twitter phishing attacks 142
two-factor authentication. *See* 2-factor authentication
Tyco 165

U

UCC Article 4A 239, 243–244, 246
unacceptable risks 18
unauthorized access 6
unclassified information 59
unconstitutional regulations 191–192
under budget status 114
undesired events (probability analysis) 39
Unfavorable Variances 113, 114, 115, 213, 214–215
Uniform Commercial Code Article 4A 239, 243–244, 246
unintentional threats 20–21
unique IP addresses 229
United Kingdom cyber defenses 28
United Nations cybersecurity efforts 202
United States
  government. *See* Federal government
  government agencies. *See* under agency names (i.e., Defense Department, EPA)
  Internet number registry 199
  Stuxnet virus 6, 74, 197–198, 250
United States Sentencing Commission (USSC) xxi, 196
units of analysis 178, 280
unknown vulnerabilities 145–146
updating tools 170
U.S. Attorneys 195, 280
US-CERT (U.S. Computer Readiness Team)
  cyber monitoring functions 232–234
  cybersecurity analysis and warning functions 249–259
  monitoring system failure 227–237
  profile 227
USB memory sticks 134
USB tokens 242
"useful life," defined 109
user IDs
  banking systems 241, 244
  online retailers 221
user-selected pictures 242
users
  as vulnerabilities 144
  behavioral detection 148

Index (S-T)

in cybersecurity operations 146
numbers of, in modeling 43, 210, 211
user-friendly websites 43, 44
USNRC (Nuclear Regulatory Commission) 36
USSC (United States Sentencing Commission) xxi, 196

V

validity tests 178, 280
values (binary code) 131
variables 280
  logit models 207
  PRA risk management 36
  regression modeling 42
  research 178
  test statistics 207
variances (EVM) 280
  atypical 215
  comparing projects 114–115
  favorable/unfavorable 113, 114, 115, 213, 214–215
  percentages 114–115
  significance of 120
  understanding 112–116
  Variance Triangle 114
vendors/contractors
  compliance 122
  cybersecurity operations 146
  health care systems 161
  IMS documents 108
  POA&M documents 108–109
  policies for managing 170
  PWS documents 106
  RFIs and 105–106
  RFP responses 108–109
  selection 108–109
  SOO documents 107
  threats resulting from 167
vetoing
  bills 188, 280
  regulations 191
victims 195, 196
virus software. *See* antivirus software
viruses
  capabilities 142
  criminal prosecution 194
  Flame 74, 197
  government efforts to focus on 64
  Stuxnet 6, 74, 197–198, 250
viva voce 188
voicemail hacking 3
volatile memory 134–135, 280
volunteer sampling 206–207, 280
voting 188
vulnerabilities 19, 141–142, 280
  analyzing threats/consequences 27–31
  assessing 19, 22–23, 118–119, 166, 167, 230–231
  BGP 139–140
  complexity of systems and 132

corporate governance and 155
databases of 145
DHS monitoring case study 118–119
hash detection methods 141
human, known, and unknown 144–146
identifying 29
increases in 27
Internet 130
IP addresses 137
mainframes 57
"National Strategy to Secure Cyberspace" 69
personal computers 58–60
public-private shared research 64
researching externally 231
risk determination 28
risk equation 19
risk management framework 16
trust protocols and 136
vulnerability assessments 19, 22–23, 118–119, 166, 167, 280
vulnerability databases 231

W

WANs (wide area networks) xxi, 136, 280
War Games 4
Warner Amendment 60, 280
warning systems 81–84
  as capability 146, 149
  as high-level requirement 100
  attributes 237, 252–257
  defined 251–252
  effectiveness 83
  importance of warnings 81
  management 81–84
  too many warnings 83
  US-CERT failure 90–91, 228, 249–259
water systems 64, 70, 250
WBS (work breakdown structure) xxi, 107, 108, 116, 280
weaknesses. *See* vulnerabilities
websites
  cyber attacks 197
  District Design. *See* District Design case study
  DNS cache poisoning 144
  encrypting 140
  fraudulent credit card usage 160
  history of 134–135
  phishing attacks 142–143
White House 186. *See also* EOP; Presidents
wide area networks (WANs) xxi, 136, 280
WiFi networks (wireless systems) 144, 162
Wiretap Act 195, 280
work breakdown structure (WBS) xxi, 107, 108, 116, 280
Working Group on Web Security 200
WorldCom 123, 165
World Summit on the Information Society (WSIS) 202
World Trade Center attacks
  1993 63
  2001 12–13, 66–75, 95, 184

Index

World Wide Web 6, 134–135
worms
  capabilities 142
  criminal prosecution 194
  Flame 74, 197
  Morris 5–6, 193
  Stuxnet 6, 74, 197–198, 250
written cybersecurity plans 167
WSIS (World Summit on the Information Society) 202

Y

Y2K preparations 65
yellow project status 120, 276

Z

z-test 207
zero-day exploits 141, 145–146, 148, 280
Zeus/Zbot malware 247
zombie networks 143

Index (T-Z)

Afterword

By now, this book should demonstrate the many academic and professional backgrounds that comprise the interdisciplinary nature of cybersecurity. This book should also illustrate the enormity of the subject and the enduring issues that have thus far proven to be intrinsic elements of the industry. Even after decades of existence, the Internet remains in a nascent stage. Creative minds have repeatedly broken down and redefined this powerful tool in order to improve our lives, and the worldwide web now behaves with more complexity than ever before. But this complex nature consequently presents the challenge of ensuring that these operations remain uncorrupted. The cybersecurity industry has grown in ways that experts are still trying to discover, while still others are left to determine how best to secure it. The industry evolves so rapidly that experts now observe a divide between those who have the awareness and resources to keep up, and those who don't. This divide demonstrates that the Internet is a major part of our lives, and underscores the need for educated individuals with an interdisciplinary understanding who can work in unison to protect this powerful asset.

Cyber risk is one of the most complex enduring issues that challenges cybersecurity experts. Risk management in cyberspace is confounded by the complex operations and an environment whose risk elements are unique from the physical world. As this book has demonstrated, risk modeling requires one to frame, assess, respond to, and monitor risk in order to properly execute, analyze, and standardize an effective strategy. Risks abound in cyberspace and are difficult to gauge, measure, assess, understand, or even identify. This knowledge gap complicates the process of developing responses and monitoring their effectiveness. This knowledge gap also leaves cybersecurity professionals without standards for cyber risk management. Developing best-practices and standards for cyber risk management requires more data analysis and collaboration among multiple disciplines in order to properly frame cyber risks and establish contextual awareness of the threat environment. Risk management is a long-term process, and in the near-term, cybersecurity professionals must come up with solutions based on the limited knowledge in reach.

Cybersecurity policy has become one of the U.S. government's top concerns since the advent of the commercial Internet in 1995. More recent efforts to put forth cybersecurity legislation have been conflated by a lack of consensus on the best legal approach to cyberspace. The federal government has a role in cybersecurity to protect federal systems while offering guidance and leadership in protecting nonfederal systems. Many statutes address aspects of cybersecurity, and Congress has debated on new cybersecurity legislation. Additionally, successive administrations have issued executive orders to incentivize private sector collaboration. However, government and cybersecurity professionals have taken note of cybersecurity laws that age poorly as technology progresses. Moreover, political constraints leave Congress and the White House without consensus on an enduring solution to cybersecurity issues. However, the greatest challenge lawmakers face involves producing laws that address near-term conflicts without becoming defunct in the long-term with another change in the digital environment. These laws must protect physical and digital assets, individuals and companies, and they must not clog user access or stifle innovation. The U.S. government continues to spearhead cybersecurity law and policy in lieu of an existing structure, but federal officials must reach a consensus before they can produce enduring legislation.

The business world struggles with cybersecurity because they have no enduring cyber risk management strategy. Business models must now be designed with cybersecurity in mind in order to remain operational. Managers have to consider cybersecurity training and awareness programs for employees, proper network and device security, proper network and device usage, proper authentication, and other factors that were considered specific to the IT department. Cybersecurity issues now affect a company's ability to go global, to go online, or even remain in business. Major cyber attacks on a company impact consumer trust, and some even result in bankruptcy. Businesses now face serious real-world consequences that culminate from digital events, and their decisions affect the national economy as well as their own company.

Engineering and security professionals face the most rigorous issue of developing enduring technical solutions for cybersecurity. The Internet has become fundamental to business and federal operations, but technology is the kinetic force that drives the web. While innovations over time have made the Internet accessible and has improved our lives, but no software is without its flaws, and code is subject to manipulation by program-savvy users. The foundation of the web was built without proper security in mind, and traditional security measures do not operate at the speed and accuracy necessary to catch adversaries in the act. Technical thinkers are now challenged to take a step back in order to retroactively secure existing cyber infrastructure. At the same time, these same individuals must continue to develop new security operations that keep pace with the daily and rapid growth of the Internet's capabilities. A breakthrough in technology that could concretely put an end to the cybersecurity issue may facilitate its transition to the backburner, or perhaps one day render the industry obsolete in its entirety. However, technical experts seem no closer to a permanent solution than their cybersecurity colleagues in business and policy.

Regardless of where the solutions to these enduring issues come from, there will be a need for cybersecurity academics as long as there is a need for cybersecurity. The fundamental principles presented in this book may one day be part of a tradecraft, and securing networks will be as much a general practice of public safety as installing locks on the doors of an office building. Cybersecurity could also become obsolete as a result of a major breakthrough in technology that comprehensively halts cybercrime in one fluid deployment. Indeed, the materials of this book may become a mere subset of other educational disciplines. Regardless, while policymakers, engineers, and business leaders labor to develop the means to resolve the enduring issues of cybersecurity, we will need to educate more individuals on the subject through an interdisciplinary approach. In lieu of a permanent solution, the cybersecurity community must have more contributors with a fundamental understanding of what is at stake for our country's infrastructure. By raising the baseline of standard cybersecurity awareness and education, we can produce more policy, computer science, and business professionals who focus on cybersecurity. There is no guarantee that cybersecurity will carve its own niche as an academic discipline, but with no permanent solution to the enduring issues of cybersecurity in sight, the best solution before us is to educate our nation's people.

About the Author

Lee Zeichner is the author of *Cybersecurity Foundations: An Interdisciplinary Introduction*, as well as the Founder and President of Zeichner Risk Analytics LLC. Since his service as senior counsel to the President's Commission on Critical Infrastructure Protection from 1996-1998, he has led development of cybersecurity policy and operations for both leading public and private sector clients. Mr. Zeichner has published extensively on multiple aspects of cybersecurity law and is the author of *Cyber Security & Corporate Liability*, a guide for corporate counsel on cybersecurity and risk management, published by LexisNexis Publishing in 2001.

Mr. Zeichner currently consults on cybersecurity issues for the Department of Homeland Security, and has performed multiple risk assessments, including a review of the Executive Office of the President and other Federal Departments. He has served as Security Counsel for the Business Roundtable's Information and Technology Committee since 2001 and promotes cybersecurity as a member of the American Bar Association's Standing Committee on Law and National Security, where he has served since 1998.

Mr. Zeichner is a graduate of Georgetown University Law Center. He graduated from the University of Florida (Phi Beta Kappa) and received his M.A. in East Asian Studies from Stanford University. Mr. Zeichner is a member of multiple bar associations, including the Florida and District of Columbia Bars, the Court of International Trade, and the Court of Appeals for the Federal Circuit. Mr. Zeichner speaks Mandarin Chinese.

Milton Keynes UK
Ingram Content Group UK Ltd.
UKHW050413050424
440543UK00004B/69

9 781939 798091